STUDIES IN
CONTEMPORARY
JEWRY

The publication
of *Studies in Contemporary Jewry*
has been made possible through the generous assistance
of the Samuel and Althea Stroum Philanthropic Fund,
Seattle, Washington

INSTITUTE OF CONTEMPORARY JEWRY
THE HEBREW UNIVERSITY
OF JERUSALEM

A NEW JEWRY?

America Since
the Second World War

STUDIES IN
CONTEMPORARY
JEWRY
AN ANNUAL

VIII

1992

Edited by Peter Y. Medding

Published for the Institute by
OXFORD UNIVERSITY PRESS
New York • Oxford

To the memory of
Marshall Sklare (1921–1992)
whose sociological studies of American Jewry
have established a new field of academic enquiry.
His publications and research serve as a model of scholarship,
combining scientific analysis of the highest order with deep
personal and communal commitments.

Oxford University Press

Oxford   New York   Toronto
Delhi   Bombay   Calcutta   Madras   Karachi
Petaling Jaya   Singapore   Hong Kong   Tokyo
Nairobi   Dar es Salaam   Cape Town
Melbourne   Auckland

and associated companies in
Berlin   Ibadan

Copyright © 1992 by Oxford University Press, Inc.

Published by Oxford University Press, Inc.,
200 Madison Avenue, New York, New York 10016

Oxford is a registered trademark of Oxford University Press

All rights reserved. No part of this publication may be reproduced,
stored in a retrieval system, or transmitted, in any form or by any means,
electronic, mechanical, photocopying, recording, or otherwise,
without the prior permission of Oxford University Press.

ISBN 0-19-507449-1
ISSN 0740-8625
Library of Congress Catalog Card Number: 84-649196

1 3 5 7 9 8 6 4 2

Printed in the United States of America
on acid-free paper

STUDIES IN CONTEMPORARY JEWRY

Editors
Jonathan Frankel
Peter Y. Medding
Ezra Mendelsohn

Institute Editorial Board
Michel Abitbol, Mordecai Altshuler, Haim Avni, David Bankier, Yehuda Bauer, Moshe Davis, Sergio DellaPergola, Sidra Ezrahi, Allon Gal, Moshe Goodman, Yisrael Gutman, Menahem Kaufman, Israel Kolatt, Hagit Lavsky, Eli Lederhendler, Pnina Morag-Talmon, Dalia Ofer, U. O. Schmelz, Gideon Shimoni, Geoffrey Wigoder

Managing Editors
Laurie E. Fialkoff
Hannah Levinsky-Koevary

Book Review Editor
David Rechter

International Advisory and Review Board
Chimen Abramsky (University College, London); Abraham Ascher (City University of New York); Arnold Band (University of California, Los Angeles); Doris Bensimon (Université de la Sorbonne Nouvelle); Bernard Blumenkrantz (Centre National de la Recherche Scientifique); Lucjan Dobroszycki (YIVO Institute for Jewish Research); Solomon Encel (University of New South Wales); Henry Feingold (City University of New York); Martin Gilbert (Oxford University); Zvi Gitelman (University of Michigan); S. Julius Gould (University of Nottingham); Irving Howe (City University of New York); Paula Hyman (Yale University); Lionel Kochan (University of Warwick); David Landes (Harvard University); Seymour Martin Lipset (George Mason University); Heinz-Dietrich Löwe (Albert-Ludwigs-Universität, Freiburg); Michael Meyer (Hebrew Union College—Jewish Institute of Religion, Cincinnati); Alan Mintz (University of Maryland); George Mosse (University of Wisconsin); Gerard Nahon (Centre Universitaire d'Études Juives, Paris); F. Raphaël (Université des Sciences Humaines de Strasbourg); Jehuda Reinharz (Brandeis University); Monika Richarz (Germania Judaica, Kölner Bibliothek zur Geschichte des deutschen Judentums); Joseph Rothschild (Columbia University); Ismar Schorsch (Jewish Theological Seminary of America); Marshall Sklare (Brandeis University); Michael Walzer (Institute of Advanced Study, Princeton); Bernard Wasserstein (Brandeis University); Ruth Wisse (McGill University).

Preface

The end of the Second World War proved to be a major turning-point for American Jews. Their position in American society, their role in American culture, the basis of community, their relation to a far-off homeland, the way in which those themes entered their literary imagination—and indeed, what they conceived to be the very meaning of Judaism—all changed significantly after 1945, as the authors in the symposium make clear.

A common set of themes and ideas pervades these essays, and certain words and concepts that express them recur frequently. Terms such as autonomy, self-definition, self-understanding, pluralism, personal choice, self-selection, voluntary affiliation, participation, creation of community, group pride, appear often in these essays in a variety of contexts and connotations. As such, they suggest that the underlying ethos of American Jewry since 1945 has been one of choice, freedom and autonomy rather than one of coercion, inhibition and heteronomy.

American Jews now make residential, educational, occupational, professional, and employment choices, unimpeded by external pressures of prejudice and discrimination, or the fear of them, and exhibit strong personal and communal identification with and political support for a Jewish state, uninhibited by apprehensions of being accused of dual loyalty. Such extensive structural integration of Jews in American society, epitomized by the high level of representation of Jews in most of America's major elites, is indicative of a major historical shift that has resulted in a fundamentally changed status for Jews in America, as compared with their situation before the Second World War. It also attests to the strength of a prevailing liberal pluralism in American society that underpins and permits, indeed, encourages, such freedom of choice.

Nevertheless, many American Jews are unsure about the extent and permanence of the conditions providing such freedom and choice, and harbor feelings of insecurity and vulnerability arising from the belief that the change in Jewish status might be more apparent than real, or the fear that it might be reversed. Others are ambivalent about freedom and choice, and point to the negative consequences and outcomes for American Jewry of some of the actual choices made by individual Jews, that are not only facilitated by pluralism but are its quintessential expression.

The symposium has amply documented and illustrated that American Jews are able to choose what sort of Americans they wish to be and what type of American society they would like to see, and to act upon these choices. But the freedom of choice afforded by the prevailing liberal pluralism also permits them to determine what kind of Jews they wish to be, and to define the nature and content of the Judaism that they choose to believe in, practise and transmit to their children.

Indeed, it goes even further than that and enables them to choose not only not to believe in, practice or transmit any definition of Judaism, but also to choose whether to be Jewish at all.

The thrust of these essays is that after the Second World War, overwhelmingly American Jews actively chose to express their Jewishness in new and varied ways, some of which related only to Jews, while others became part of the shared literary, cultural, social and political consciousness and heritage of American society as a whole. Individual and group Jewish identity and pride developed to such an extent that very few exercised the choice not to be Jewish.

It may well be, however, that the symposium presents a historical snapshot of an era that may be passing, and captures a unique response to a particular set of conditions in the American Jewish community that may no longer obtain today. Although their full impact has not yet been felt with regard to the aforementioned issues, ongoing social processes may be changing the American Jewish community immeasurably.

The individual and group Jewish identity and pride that underlay the choice to be Jewish (even more than the specific content of the Jewishness chosen) used to develop in a community consisting in the main of families in which both spouses were Jewish, either by birth or conversion. Under such circumstances, irrespective of its precise content, the Jewish identity that was transmitted in the household was *unambiguously* Jewish, even when it was very weak and attenuated. Children were raised knowing that they were Jewish and nothing else.

Over the past twenty years there has been a marked and accelerating increase in the rate of mixed marriages, which create households where one spouse continues to choose to be Jewish and the other continues to choose to be non-Jewish. By the middle of the 1980s, about half of the new households involving a Jewish spouse resulted from mixed marriages, and by the end of the 1980s the proportion was about two thirds. Such marriage patterns are likely to have far-reaching implications for the very possibility of Jewish identity transmission and marked impact upon its character. Children of parents with mixed religious heritages are extremely unlikely to receive an *unambiguous* Jewish identity, or even to receive one at all, and even more unlikely to develop Jewish group pride.[1]

Thus, if present trends continue, an American Jewish community in which a large proportion, if not a majority, of households are mixed marriages, will militate toward and legitimate choice by children not to be Jewish, and as such will prove to be terminal for Jewish identity and group pride. Clearly, such a community will be fundamentally different from the American Jewish community as it was constituted after the Second World War, which forms the subject of our symposium.

Indeed, it may be very different from any Jewish community known to Jewish history. It may not be alone, however, as there are indications that marriage patterns in other diaspora Jewish communities currently follow suit.

This volume could not have been produced without the devoted and expert editorial work of Dr. Eli Lederhendler, Laurie Fialkoff and Hannah Levinsky-Koevary, who at various times occupied the role of Managing Editor, and of David Rechter, who was Book Review Editor throughout: their contribution is gratefully acknowledged. Likewise, as ever, I am indebted to my fellow editors Jonathan Frankel and Ezra Mendelsohn for their friendship, individual and collective wisdom, scholarly judgment, and collegial support.

Jerusalem
April, 1992

P. Y. M.

Notes

[1] I have presented the empirical evidence upon which these arguments are based, and the theory underlying the relationship between Jewish identity and marriage types, in Peter Y. Medding, Gary A. Tobin, Sylvia Barack Fishman and Mordecai Rimor, "Jewish Identity in Conversionary and Mixed Marriages," *American Jewish Yearbook,* vol. 92 (American Jewish Committee, and Jewish Publication Society, New York and Philadelphia, 1992), pp. 3–76.

Contents

Symposium

A New Jewry?
America Since the Second World War

Essays

Review Essays

Book Reviews
(*arranged by subject*)
Antisemitism, Holocaust and Genocide

Jewish Communal and Social History

Language, Art and Literature

Religion, Thought and Education

Social Sciences and Politics

Zionism, Israel and the Middle East

Symposium

A New Jewry? America Since the Second World War

A "Golden Decade" for American Jews: 1945–1955

Arthur A. Goren

(COLUMBIA UNIVERSITY
THE HEBREW UNIVERSITY)

Few would deny the proposition that American Jewish life has undergone a radical transformation in the half century since the end of the Second World War. Lucy Dawidowicz, in a synoptic review of American Jewish history, recently captured this sense of major change in two chapter titles. She designated the years 1920 to 1939, "Decades of Anxiety," and the years 1945 to 1967, "The Golden Age in America." "Recovery and Renewal" is how Dawidowicz conceived of the postwar period as a whole.[1]

Remarkably, the essential features of that transformation—the suburbanization of the Jews, the fashioning of a new communal order and the emergence of a collective self-confidence and sense of well-being—were already in place by the mid-1950s. At that point, American Jewry seemed to pause to take stock. The occasion was the yearlong celebration, beginning in the fall of 1954, of three hundred years since the first group of Jews settled on the shores of North America. The flood of tercentenary events intensified group consciousness and pride. The celebrations also encouraged the search for self-definition and self-understanding. Alongside the official and dominant theme of achievement and thanksgiving, a contrapuntal note of disquiet and discontent with the state of American Jewish life was sounded. In this respect, too, the culminating event of the decade set the terms for the years to come. Important publicists and ideologues recognized and debated what Charles Liebman would later pose as the tensions between "two sets of values." In Liebman's formulation, the "ambivalent American Jew" is torn between "integration and acceptance into American society" and "Jewish group survival."[2] Precisely because Jews were fulfilling, at last, their aspiration to integrate into the society at large, identifying with the group and maintaining it were becoming increasingly matters of personal choice. For the most part, Jews responded to their new condition by instinctively adopting a dual construct of identity that aided them in locating and relocating themselves in the volatile pluralism that characterized the nation as well as the Jewish community. This essay seeks to place the first decade of our times, with its new conditions and new perceptions, in historical perspective. It also

3

examines the Jewish community's endeavors to fix its place on the map of the new era and set its future course.

Surely, the subject most discussed among observers of the American Jewish scene in the late 1940s and early 1950s was the exodus of Jews from city to suburb. This was the most concrete expression of the new affluence of the rising Jewish middle class. Entering the professions and the higher levels of entrepreneurship on the wave of postwar prosperity, benefiting from the decline in occupational and social discrimination, integrating culturally both in the workplace and in the classroom and pursuing leisure-time activities similar to those of their social class, the new Jewish suburbanites embraced the tolerant, cosmopolitan image of the suburbs. For the majority of Jews, the creation of an amiable and lenient communal order, religious by definition, went hand in hand with the suburban ethos.[3]

The suburban setting was a far cry from the compact, big-city, middle- and working-class neighborhoods where they had grown up and where some had started their own families during the interwar decades. The Jewish group life in those urban neighborhoods as recalled by the newly arrived suburbanites had contained a multiplicity of synagogues, Jewish secular societies, informal social street settings and "neutral" public institutions that possessed a Jewish ethnic coloration merely by virtue of the high ratio of Jews attending. Less by design than geography, the Jewish neighborhoods had served the broad spectrum of interests, convictions and degrees of Jewish identification both of second-generation Jews and of acculturated immigrant Jews.[4]

The communal order reconstructed during the 1945–1955 decade reflected the new affluence and the rapid pace of social and cultural integration. The synagogue, now including educational and recreational facilities, became the primary guardian of ethnic identity and continuity. The social and educational services of the suburban synagogue expanded enormously when compared with the synagogues of the urban neighborhoods, at the same time as its ritual functions contracted. The years from 1945 through the 1950s witnessed the construction of some six hundred synagogues and temples. In their imposing size and sumptuous architectural design, they reflected their preeminent place in the suburban landscape as the accepted presence of a Jewish community. At the same time, the secular ideologies and particularistic interests that had existed in the urban neighborhoods faded away or were absorbed by the synagogue-centers or by the broad-based federations of philanthropies.

This blurring of differences during the early postwar years enabled the national coordinating agencies of American Jewry to flourish, particularly those agencies that guided fund-raising campaigns and the policy-making implicit in allocating the funds. The local communities channeled vast sums of money and political influence to these bodies through their federations. They, in turn, dispersed overseas relief, aid to Israel, support for the community relations organizations and help for the national denominational and cultural institutions. There is a striking correlation between the enormous increase in the sums raised to aid Jewish displaced persons in Europe and their resettlement in Israel, which peaked between 1946 and 1948, and the decline in such revenue in the 1950s when the overseas crises seemed to have abated and synagogue-building and domestic concerns were high on the community's agenda. Nevertheless, American Jewry was sufficiently affluent and committed enough to Israel to give more aid to the young state than to any other nonlocal cause.[5]

Two compelling experiences during the first few years following the end of the Second World War gave coherence to these developments and provided the basis for the collective behavior of American Jews that has persisted ever since. The first, the establishment of Israel, has defined the one arena of greatest concern to the Jews. The second, the emergence of an aggressive liberalism, has directed the political energies of the Jewish community into the general American domain. This parity of interests and commitments, which has been at the heart of the Jewish communal consensus for nearly half a century, was firmly in place by the mid-1950s.

In the first instance, at the war's end, American Jews confronted the enormity of the destruction of European Jewry and the urgent need to resettle and rehabilitate the one-third that had survived. This task merged almost immediately with the struggle for Jewish sovereignty in Palestine. Linking the solution of the problem of the survivors with the attainment of statehood created a unity of purpose on a scale unprecedented in the modern history of the Jews.

The American Jewish community mobilized its communal, financial and political resources in a massive outpouring of support. One gauge of this response was the dramatic rise in the contributions to the central communal campaigns. These soared from $57.3 million in 1945 to $131.7 million in 1946 and to $205 million in 1948, when 80 percent of the monies raised went for settling immigrants in Israel. There were other indications of momentous change. Eminent Jews who had taken little part in Jewish affairs now assumed crucial leadership roles, while others who until then had rejected all affirmations of Jewish nationalism rallied their organizations to the common endeavor. Henry Morgenthau, Jr.'s acceptance of the general chairmanship of the United Jewish Appeal in 1946 is one striking case; the collaboration of Joseph Proskauer, president of the American Jewish Committee, with the Jewish Agency in the final diplomatic push for statehood is another. Political figures and presidential advisers such as Herbert Lehman, Felix Frankfurter, David Niles, Samuel Rosenman and Bernard Baruch overtly or covertly aided the Zionist cause, which they now considered to be the sole means of saving Jews.[6]

The three years between the surrender of the German armies and the declaration of Israel's independence also saw many rank-and-file American Jews take part in European rescue work at considerable personal risk. Soldiers, chaplains and merchant mariners participated in the clandestine operations directed by the Jewish Agency and the Yishuv to transport refugees from the Allied-occupied zones in Germany to Mediterranean ports and from there in ships (purchased in the United States) to Palestine. Arms, too, were acquired surreptitiously in the United States with funds given by wealthy American Jews and shipped illegally to the Jewish underground in Palestine. At the same time, Jewish war veterans were recruited for the fledgling Israeli army.[7]

Pockets of animosity or indifference remained. The small but vocal American Council for Judaism opposed the widespread support for a Jewish state with singular passion. Denouncing Jewish nationalism as an aberration of Judaism and support of a Jewish state as a violation of American loyalty, the council was soon swept to the fringes of the community. Some left-wing circles remained outside the consensus. Pro-Soviet, Jewish radicals, except for the brief period when the Soviet Union supported the partitioning of Palestine, opposed the Jewish state; and a number of ex-socialist writers, the children of Jewish immigrants who were beginning to make their mark in intellectual circles, simply took no notice. However, mainstream Jewish America from the very beginning accepted the state of Israel as haven and protector of the Jews. Sovereignty was recognized as the guarantee of security for the dispossessed.[8]

The alacrity with which statehood was embraced was in fact quite extraordinary. The specter of charges of divided loyalties, and the fear of providing grist for the mills of antisemites, had long haunted the Zionist movement in America. Even after the Biltmore Conference in May 1942 declared a Jewish commonwealth to be the immediate postwar goal of Zionism, the American Jewish leadership (including some Zionists) viewed the demand for a sovereign state as being at best an opening gambit for later bargaining and compromise, or at worst an unrealistic if not perilous political program. Yet four years later, nearly the entire American Jewish community joined in the political battle for a Jewish state. To take one symbolic act, in May 1947, in the absence of David Ben-Gurion, Rabbi Abba Hillel Silver of Cleveland, representing the Jewish Agency (then the shadow government of the state-to-be), presented the case for a Jewish state before the United Nations General Assembly.[9]

Today it is a truism that the security and welfare of Israel have literally become articles of faith in the belief system of American Jews. Nurtured by the writings of publicists and theologians, encapsulated in the slogans of communal leaders and celebrated in commemorative and fund-raising events, Israel, as nearly every observer of Jewish life has suggested, has become "*the* religion for American Jews." One must stress, however, that *the conjunction of circumstances*—the crying need, on the one hand, to resettle the surviving remnant somewhere, and the growing recognition, on the other hand, that establishment of a Jewish state in Palestine was the only feasible means of saving the remnant—was the nexus at the heart of the overwhelming support for statehood between 1945 and 1948.[10]

This coupling of circumstances molded the sentiments and attitudes of American Jews. At its birth, Israel's survival became inextricably bound to that other primal remembrance of our times, the destruction of European Jewry. Later events, such as the alarm for Israel's survival in the weeks preceding the Six-Day War in 1967, demonstrated the depth of American Jewry's concern. True, in the 1950s and early 1960s, other concerns appeared to diminish the emotional identity with Israel that marked the years 1945 to 1948 and the years following 1967. Nevertheless, the transcendent place of the "destruction and renewal" theme in the group consciousness of American Jews was actually set in the formative decade beginning in 1945.

At the same time, American Jews were deepening and intensifying their identity as Americans. America's role in the defeat of Nazism and its emergence as leader of the free world—the one effective force blocking Soviet expansion—induced American Jews not only to participate in the civic and political life of postwar America but to do so with unprecedented vigor and effectiveness. The high percentage of

Jewish participation in elections compared with the voting public as a whole, the prominence of Jewish contributors as financial backers for political candidates and the increase in the number of Jewish elected officials are some of the outward indications. No less notable is the ease with which political figures of Jewish background began to move out from Jewish organizational life into the larger political world and then, with their enhanced stature, back again to the Jewish. Philip Klutznik is perhaps the most striking example. His Jewish leadership track took him through the ranks of B'nai B'rith to the presidency of the organization in 1953. In a parallel career in government, Klutznik moved from commissioner of Federal Public Housing under Franklin D. Roosevelt and Harry Truman to U.S. representative to the United Nations at various times during the Eisenhower, Kennedy and Johnson administrations and then to a cabinet post during Jimmy Carter's presidency. [11]

Most significant of all was the new departure of Jewish communal institutions in assuming an active role in American civic affairs. Community relations agencies, formerly almost exclusively concerned with discrimination against Jews, now entered the realm of social action in its broadest sense. They lobbied for legislation directed against racial discrimination, in favor of social welfare programs, against weakening trade unionism and for a foreign policy that stressed internationalism, aid to democratic governments and a tempering of superpower confrontations. So, too, they joined in litigation against racial discrimination and for the strict interpretation of the constitutional principle of separation of church and state. In 1945, the American Jewish Congress created its Commission on Law and Social Action and committed itself to "working for a better world . . . whether or not the individual issues touch directly upon so-called Jewish interests." Soon after, the American Jewish Committee, in a more circumspect manner, moved beyond its original purpose (as expressed in its charter) "to prevent the infringement of the civil and religious rights of Jews and to alleviate the consequences of persecution." It now declared its intention to "join with other groups in the protection of the civil rights of the members of all groups irrespective of race, religion, color or national origin." [12]

The religious wings of Judaism followed suit. By the end of the Second World War, both the Reform and Conservative rabbinic associations had longstanding commitments to pursue the goals of social justice, and the Orthodox Rabbinical Council of America began taking a similar stand. In the 1930s, for example, Reform's Central Conference of American Rabbis had declared that the "individualistic, profit-oriented economy is in direct conflict with the ideals of religion." At the same time, the Conservative Rabbinical Assembly of America announced a program for world peace, declared for a thirty-hour workweek and proclaimed a goal of "a social order . . . based on human cooperation rather than competition inspired by greed." These resolutions, which undoubtedly reflected the social sensibilities of the rabbis, did not go beyond the ritual of affirmation by the annual conferences. But beginning in the mid-1940s, the Reform and Conservative movements as a whole, and not merely the rabbinate, placed both specific domestic issues and international policy matters on their lay agendas. They established commissions, organized local action groups, and collaborated with parallel Protestant and Catholic agencies on behalf of social justice issues. (In contrast, although the Orthodox Rabbinical Council began adopting annual resolutions on a number of welfare state issues such as price and rent controls and continuation of federal housing programs, social activism did not become an integral part of the Orthodox lay associations.) Thus, the militancy demonstrated by rabbinic leaders and Jewish organizations during the 1960s over civil rights, school integration and the Vietnam War stemmed from the Jewish community's active stand on political issues that began in the 1940s.[13]

In a broad sense, American Jewry's two public commitments—assuring Israel's security and striving for a liberal America (and, by extension, a liberal world order)—have constituted the basis for a "functional consensus" ever since the linkage between the two was forged in the aftermath of the defeat of Nazism and the establishment of the Jewish state. On the whole, the two elements have meshed well, and in fact have reinforced each other. American Jewish leaders have presented Israel as both a haven for the persecuted and a doughty democracy surrounded and threatened with destruction by totalitarian Arab regimes allied, until recently, with an expansive Soviet Union. This has been a theme repeated often when U.S. presidents address American Jews and when party platforms are formulated. As a consequence, the dual identity of American Jews has resulted in less anxiety than some would have anticipated. The fear that vigorous support of Israel would give rise to charges of divided allegiance and fan the fires of antisemitism has not been borne out. The patriotic fulminations of right-wing extremists, bearers of a fundamentalist antisemitism, and the revolutionary rhetoric of the radical Left that has equated Zionism with racism have of course been causes for concern, but they have not infected mainstream America. This is not to say that a latent disquiet has never been present, rising on occasion to the surface. For example, Jacob Blaustein, president of the American Jewish Committee, intervened with the government of Israel on a number of occasions until he obtained formal assurances from Prime Minister David Ben-Gurion in 1950 that the Jewish state held no claim on the political loyalties of American Jews, whose sole allegiance, it was stressed, was to the United States.[14]

Nevertheless, American Jews intuitively sensed that the functional consensus based on supporting Israel and defending a liberal America was not sufficient. What was needed was a doctrinal or ideological core that, while identifying the group, would also justify the operative elements of the consensus. During the first postwar decade, American Jews almost unanimously viewed religion as that doctrinal core. It was the way Jews identified themselves. Sociologists studying the new Jewish communities documented its currency. They also noted the paradox of Jews defining themselves overwhelmingly by religion while at the same time showing indifference and apathy for actual religious practice. Contemporary observers explained this incongruity as a form of adjustment to an American society that recognized religious activity alone as justifying self-segregation. These were the years when Jewish communal leaders found so congenial the notion that a trifaith America— Protestant, Catholic and Jewish, "the religions of democracy"—formed the underpinning of the "American Way of Life." This interpretation of American society placed Judaism and its bearers in the mainstream of the nation's cultural and spiritual tradition.[15]

Since Judaism as interpreted by the American rabbi taught its followers to seek social justice, being Jewish in America meant fighting for open housing and fair employment practices, for social welfare and prounion legislation—in short, for the New Deal, the Fair Deal and their successors. Judaism also demanded fulfillment of the religious commandment that "all Israel are responsible for one another," hence the duty to rescue Jews and strengthen the Jewish state. As individuals, Jews identified themselves as belonging to a religious community. As a group, they acted like an ethnic minority.

It is important to remember that, for American Jews, Judaism and Jewishness became identical only during the decade beginning in 1945. Although such a religious self-definition long preceded the postwar years (it was the cornerstone of American Reform Judaism), the East European immigrants had earlier created an ethnic and secular reality that overran without obliterating the purely religious formulation of Jewishness of the older, established community. One need merely mention the variegated Jewish associational life the immigrants created and the flowering of Yiddish literature—the most impressive cultural creation in a foreign language by an American immigrant group—to indicate the range and depth of this Jewish ethnic world. In acculturated form, significant elements of this world carried over into the second generation. Obviously, Zionism and an aggressively secular Jewish radical tradition stand out. Yet the considerable numbers who were brought up in this milieu in the urban neighborhoods of the years before 1945 failed to seriously challenge or to qualify the religious identification of American Jewry that so quickly became so universal in the post-1945 decade. Surely, the prevailing drive for conformity, which was in part a by-product of the Cold War and the accompanying fear of Communist influence at home, saw religion (*any* religion, to paraphrase Eisenhower) as the cornerstone of democratic society and an antitoxin against the Communist heresy. And quite possibly the political and financial aid being so prominently extended to the Jewish state was best explained to the nation as religiously motivated. Separation for religious purposes did conform, after all, with patriotic norms. In part, these factors hastened the trends toward consensus within the Jewish community.

On occasion Jewish secular thinkers gave explicit and anguished expression to this change. In 1951, the Labor Zionist Organization published an essay by C. Bezalel Sherman, "Israel and the American Jewish Community." The Labor Zionist movement, an amalgamation of socialist Zionist parties transplanted to the United States with the mass migration, was staunchly secularist. It had favored the formation of democratically elected Jewish communal polities and bilingual education in a manner similar to its European sister parties. Sherman himself was an ideologue of the organization's left wing. Nevertheless, in reappraising the future of the American Jewish community in the new era ushered in by the establishment of the Jewish state, he abandoned the position that American Jews should strive for the status of nationality. Now he wrote, "America, insensible to the existence of a Jewish nation, insisted on classing them [American Jews] with the religious communities," the only type of ethnic group recognized by "American constitutional life." Sherman continued:

> Jews thus have no other alternative but to constitute themselves as a community operating in a religious framework. . . . The irreligious Jew . . . will have to accept a religious designation for the group of which he wishes to be a member without sharing the tenets of its faith. This is the price a secularist Jew will have to pay for his voluntary sharing in a minority status.[16]

Ten years later, in his study *The Jew Within American Society,* Sherman used this redefinition of Jewish identity to explain Jewish group survival in America. It was the key to understanding Jewish "ethnic individuality." On a note evoking Mordecai Kaplan's analysis of Jewish identity, Sherman concluded: "American Jews can no more conceive of the Jewish faith severed from the framework of Jewish peoplehood than they can conceive of a Jewish community removed from its religious base." Since Jewish peoplehood embraced Jews everywhere, concern for persecuted brethren abroad and the well-being of the state of Israel had increased the sense of "belongingness" among American Jews. "For this reason, they may be expected to continue as a distinct ethnic group—on the level of spiritual uniqueness, religious separateness, ethnic consolidation and communal solidarity, but not in a political sense."[17]

In terms of the Jewish establishment (the synagogue movements, federations, defense agencies and the Zionist organizations), American Jews had created by the early 1950s a consensus and a degree of equanimity they had not known before. They were meeting their dual responsibilities as Americans and Jews admirably. On domestic issues, they aligned with the liberal-centrist position and upheld America's role as defender of the free world. Within the Jewish community, the divisive issues of the interwar years—class differences, the intergenerational tensions between immigrant and native-born, conflicting notions of Jewish identity, the assimilationist-radical deprecation of Jewish life and the strident polemics over Zionism—were vanishing or were gone altogether. Not surprisingly, then, the tercentenary planners proposed stressing not only communal harmony and achievement but also the beliefs and values Jews held in common with all Americans.

In December 1951, Ralph E. Samuel, the vice-president of the American Jewish Committee, announced the formation of a committee to plan the three-hundredth anniversary of the establishment of the first permanent Jewish community in North America. Samuel emphasized the opportunity such celebrations would provide to pay homage to the "American heritage of religious and civil liberty." American Jews had built a "flourishing American Judaism," he declared, and at the same time they had taken part "in building the American democratic civilization that we have today." In his single reference to contemporary affairs, Samuel concluded his remarks with the note that the tercentenary celebration would demonstrate to the world "the strength of the American people's commitment to the principles of democracy in our struggle against communism and other forms of totalitarianism of our day."[18]

This collective undertaking to popularize an American Jewish ideology proved to be an extraordinary enterprise in itself. It also raised a number of questions. Who indeed did the tercentenary organizers represent? How meaningful and tenable could a least-common-denominator ideology be? What were the constraints the planners faced in relating to the American-political and Jewish-political context? Were the provisional tenets Samuel set forth adequate for setting a course for postwar American Jewry?

In January 1952, when the committee on organization met to launch the tercentenary project, Samuel stressed that the American Jewish Committee saw its role as initiator rather than sponsor of the enterprise. In fact, it had been the American Jewish Historical Society that had first proposed the tercentenary celebration. Eager for the broadest communal participation, it had turned to the American Jewish Committee for organizational assistance; the success of the project depended on leaders whose eminence and integrity assured the nonpartisanship of the endeavor.

In addition to Samuel, who was chosen general chairman, two eminent members of the American Jewish Committee were appointed to key committees. Simon Rifkind, who had distinguished himself as a federal judge and special adviser on Jewish affairs to General Dwight D. Eisenhower in 1945 and 1946, headed the "Committee of 300," the policy-making body of the organization. Samuel Rosenman, also a judge, who had served as a principal adviser to Presidents Franklin D. Roosevelt and Harry Truman, chaired the program committee. Another important committee, that of research and publication, was headed by Salo W. Baron, professor of Jewish history at Columbia University.

The composition of the committee reflected nearly the entire spectrum of Jewish religious and communal life. Among the members of the steering committee were Samuel Belkin, president of Yeshiva University; Louis Finkelstein, president of the Jewish Theological Seminary; Israel Goldstein, president of the American Jewish Congress; Samuel Niger, the Yiddish journalist and critic, and Jacob S. Potofsky, president of the Amalgamated Clothing Workers Union.

In April 1953, after nearly a year of deliberations, the program committee, which, in addition to Rosenman, included Benjamin V. Cohen, Adolph Held, William S. Paley and David Sarnoff, submitted its report on the "meaning of the anniversary" to a national meeting of the Committee of 300. Obviously the presence of Paley, the head of CBS, and Sarnoff, the head of NBC, indicated the direction and scale of the celebrations. The proposed theme of the celebration— "Man's Opportunities and Responsibilities Under Freedom"—was in fact suggested by Sarnoff and was approved at this meeting.[19]

The major opening event, the National Tercentenary Dinner with President Eisenhower as guest of honor and keynote speaker, took place on October 20, 1954, at the Hotel Astor in New York. It was preceded and followed by forums, exhibitions, pageants, musical festivals and public dinners organized by local committees in at least four hundred cities and towns. New York, for instance, was the venue of a coast-to-coast radio broadcast of the reconsecration of Congregation Shearith Israel (founded by the original settlers of New Amsterdam) in the presence of representatives of the Jewish and Christian congregations that had either aided or functioned alongside it in the eighteenth century. A special national committee supervised the preparation of a national historical exhibit on the theme "Under Freedom," which was shown at the Jewish Museum in New York and the Smithsonian Institution in Washington, D.C. The Chicago committee commissioned Ernst Toch to compose a symphonic suite for the occasion, while the national committee commissioned David Diamond to compose the tercentenary symphony *Ahavah,* which was given its premiere by the National Symphony on November 17, 1954, in Washington. (The other works on the program were Ernest Bloch's *Israel Symphony* and Leonard Bernstein's *The Age of Anxiety,* a thematically balanced program by Jewish composers.) In Atlanta, Georgia, the local committee presented the city with a portrait of Judah P. Benjamin, secretary of state of the Confederacy.[20]

Television played a major role. The main events, such as Eisenhower's address, received national coverage. Leading commercial programs offered commemoration salutes. CBS broadcast a four-part teledrama, "A Precious Heritage," while NBC followed suit with a four-part series entitled "Frontiers of Faith." The tercentenary also generated a plethora of educational material—filmstrips, curricula and guidebooks on American Jewish history—for use in schools and adult education circles that were sponsored and published by the national organizations. B'nai B'rith organized a nationwide search for historical source materials and provided programs and speakers for its lodges and Hillel foundations. The American Jewish Committee commissioned a series of studies that it published in the *American Jewish Year Book* and an *Inventory of American Jewish History* to further historical research. A volume of studies subsidized by the Workmen's Circle and other Jewish labor organizations gave special attention to the era of the East European Jewish migration.[21]

This history-mindedness anteceded the tercentenary "revival." It was one expression of a self-assertiveness that stemmed from the new position of centrality that had been thrust upon the American Jewish community. And it paralleled the notion of the "American Century," the conviction that became popular during the war years that America had at last taken its "rightful" place as the leader of the free world and the guardian of world order. This national temper stimulated a reexamination of the American past. Historians and political scientists elaborated the idea of an "American exceptionalism." Typical of their writing was Daniel Boorstein's book *The Genius of American Politics.* "I argue, in a word," Boorstein wrote, "that American democracy is unique. It possesses a 'genius' all of its own."[22]

The new era that began in 1945 was, in a sense, also perceived as "the American Jewish Century." The conviction that American Jews were at last "making history" required recovering a "usable past" showing that Jews had indeed been "making history" for some time. One important expression of this sentiment was the Hebrew Union College's announcement, in the fall of 1947, of the establishment of the American Jewish Archives to document the historical record of American Jewry. The need for such an institution was explained in these words:

American Jewry has become the "center" of world Jewish spiritual life. When the Jewish historian of the next generation reaches the year 1939, he will begin a new chapter in the history of his people, a chapter which must be called, "The American Jewish Center." This Jewish community has now become the pivotal and controlling factor in that historic development which began in the thirteenth pre-Christian century in Palestine.[23]

There were more manifestations of a search for "American Jewish exceptionalism." In 1953, the Jewish Theological Seminary established the American Jewish History Center. Soon after, the center commissioned a series of communal studies and organized regional conferences to generate interest in the projects. The tercentenary accelerated this newfound interest in an American Jewish past. Jewish communities—Buffalo, Rochester, Milwaukee, Cleveland and Los Angeles—allocated money for writing their communal histories. In September 1954, a revitalized American Jewish Historical Society convened the most impressive conference of historians ever held on the writing of American Jewish history. Thus the new self-consciousness American Jewry displayed after the conclusion of the war swelled under the impetus of the tercentenary. Pride and awareness of its preeminence in the Jewish world reverberated in the public and institutional interest in recording and interpreting the Jewish experience in America.[24]

One interpretive history of Jewish life in America that appeared during the tercentenary year captured the tercentenary ideology faithfully. Oscar Handlin's *Adventure in Freedom* (1954) stressed the process of Jewish integration into a society that was distinguished by its "diversity, voluntarism, equality, freedom, and democracy." Handlin, who taught American social history at Harvard and who had won a Pulitzer Prize for his 1951 study on immigration in American life, *The Uprooted,* was perhaps the most influential writer on the American pluralist tradition. Handlin insisted that American Jews be viewed as one ethnic group among many in a pluralist America that neither impeded nor encouraged ethnic group maintenance. This was the open-ended, wholesome "adventure in freedom." Yet Handlin also struck an ominous note. Although the Jews of America were celebrating the year 1654, they could not forget "the stark facts of our present situation." Jews had not recovered "from the shock of the six million victims of the European catastrophe;" at the same time they shared in the "enormous burden upon American society," which was "locked in unremitting struggle" with "the forces of totalitarianism."[25]

It was the tercentenary theme, "Man's Opportunities and Responsibilities Under Freedom," that required explication. When the program committee presented its recommendations after months of deliberations and after soliciting the opinions of scores of leaders from all fields and walks of life, it explained the criteria it had used in these words:

> The theme should express the outstanding fact of the past 300 years of our participation in America; that it should describe the significance of the present day for American Jews, and that it should express the hopes and aspirations and objectives of the future for ourselves and for all Americans—indeed, for all human beings throughout the world.

When the recommendations were published as a brochure—thirty thousand copies were distributed—no explicit reference was made to the Jewish community itself, or to the American Jew's "responsibility under freedom" to help other Jews, although the members of the committees in their other communal capacities were deeply involved in Jewish affairs. In a section entitled "All-Embracing Nature of

Celebration," the committee warned that the tercentenary should not be made "a vehicle for propagation of any particular ideology in American Jewish life. . . . It should be neither Zionist, non-Zionist, nor anti-Zionist. It should not try to formulate or advance any particular definition of Jewishness."[26]

The tercentenary committee defined the principal goal of the observance as a celebration of America's democratic ideals. Thus the American Jewish experience was significant in that it bore witness to the success of this free society. No less important was the emphasis placed on the congruence between Judaism and American democratic ideals. Indeed, the authors of the report declared, "The teachings of the Hebrew prophets have vitally affected the growth of freedom and the development of human dignity in America and throughout the world." In a summing-up statement at the conclusion of the year of festivities, David Bernstein, the tercentenary committee's executive director, justified the choice of the theme in these words:

> At a time when the Jewish community and its leaders felt that they were on display before the world, they chose to speak, first, in religious terms and, next, in terms of such political ideas as civic responsibility, strengthening democracy, protecting individual liberty, and expanding civil rights.[27]

Was there perhaps, in the midst of the deserved self-congratulations, also a measure of anxiety and insecurity? What seemed implicit in Bernstein's statement and had been alluded to in Samuel's first announcement of a tercentennial committee four years earlier was stated explicitly in Handlin's measured words. Praising democracy and liberty at a time when the nation was locked in what it perceived to be a global struggle with an aggressive and ruthless totalitarianism was understandable enough. The "golden decade" for American Jews was also the decade of the Cold War, McCarthyism, and fear of Communist subversion.

Abroad, postwar America confronted an expansive Communist power that now possessed nuclear weapons. Not only had an "iron curtain descended across the continent," in Winston Churchill's words in his March 1946 address, but it was followed by the fall of China to the Communists and the invasion of South Korea by the North in 1950. At home, an alarmed government responded with drastic measures to curb and root out real and perceived instances of Communist infiltration. It began in 1947, when Harry Truman put into effect his loyalty program, and it ended, at least symbolically, in December 1954 when the United States Senate censured its member Joseph McCarthy—a time span nearly identical with the first years in the new American Jewish postwar era. Thus the years of optimism were also the years of the "Attorney General's list" of subversive organizations, the Alger Hiss case, the loyalty oaths and security clearances, the high-handed investigations of Senator Joseph McCarthy and the congressional committees who went hunting for Communists and who blacklisted those they termed "Fifth Amendment Communists."

Here was the snake in the garden: the agony and trepidation caused by the conspicuous presence of Jews among those accused of disloyalty and even espionage, and the presence of a marginal but vocal radical Left within the organized Jewish community. Thus the arrest in 1950 of Julius and Ethel Rosenberg for handing atomic secrets to the Soviet Union, and their trial, conviction and execution in 1953, jarred the self-confidence of American Jews. (The trial judge, prosecuting attorney, defense attorneys and the principle witnesses who turned state's evidence were all Jewish.) Arnold Forster, general counsel of the Anti-Defamation League (ADL), recalled the period as a time when American Jewish leaders "came to fear the establishment of a link between being a Jew and being a 'communist traitor' in the popular mind." A bitter fight ensued within the Jewish community over aiding Jewish victims of the anti-Communist crusade. The most prominent instance was the campaign for clemency for the Rosenbergs in which Communist and left-wing groups were active.

The American Jewish Committee created a special committee to combat the "Jewish/Communist stereotype." It launched an educational program exposing the techniques and strategies used by the Communists to infiltrate Jewish organizations and called on the community to expel Jewish "Communist-front" organizations. During the height of the hysteria, the American Jewish Committee was less than forthright in its commitment to civil liberties. On this last score, in contrast, both the ADL and the American Jewish Congress maintained their aggressive stand in defense of civil liberties. In 1952, at the height of McCarthy's influence, the ADL chose to honor Senator Herbert Lehman at its annual convention because of his opposition to McCarthy. The American Jewish Congress, for its own part, waged an incessant battle against congressional and state legislation that required loyalty oaths, providing legal aid in appealing cases where there appeared to have been infringements of constitutional rights. To a considerable degree, the Red Scare hastened the political integration of American Jews. It greatly weakened Jewish radicalism, fortified the liberalism of "the vital center" and drew American Jews, as never before, into a whirl of "American" issues. In dealing with these issues, both civil libertarians and anti-Communist activists operated through Jewish agencies.[28]

The official tercentenary ideology, orchestrated by a group of conservative and cautious leaders, aroused a spirited debate over the direction of American Jewish life. Jewish journals of opinion provided the platforms for a more reflective consideration of the issues. Robert Gordis, editor of *Judaism,* devoted an entire issue to the tercentenary in which contributors evaluated Jewish philosophy, culture and communal life in America. Eugene Kohn gathered a dozen articles from *The Reconstructionist* on the communal and cultural life of American Jews and published them in a volume commemorating the tercentenary. The score of mass-circulation house organs published by B'nai B'rith, Hadassah, the American Jewish Congress and others devoted whole issues to critical essays that examined American Jewish life. For the most part, the conclusions were laudatory and the prognosis for the future optimistic. Typical was Gordis's introduction to the tercentenary issue of *Judaism.* American Jewry, Gordis wrote, had not been "altogether without influence or creativity within the confines of Judaism." It had been innovative in the fields of religion, philanthropy, education and group defense. Indeed, "the instruments for a renaissance of Judaism, in the days to come, are at hand."[29]

There were also dissenting voices. Horace Kallen, the philosopher and ideologue of cultural pluralism, published a blistering piece in the *Congress Weekly* entitled "The Tercentenary, Yomtov or Yahrzeit." He accused the organizers of violating the essence of the "American Idea," that is, of his well-known notion of cultural pluralism. Kallen had interpreted American freedom as granting the right to any ethnic, religious or racial group to preserve and diversify its communal culture. Nothing in the rhetoric of the tercentenary encouraged American Jews to do this, he argued; even the tercentenary emblem was assimilationist. Not a Hebrew word was on it, and above the menorah that dominated the face of the emblem was a star—but it was a five-pointed, American star rather than the six-pointed Magen David. For Kallen, the challenge of American freedom for the American Jewish community meant creating, first of all, a democratic communal polity. A community so organized would then be able to nurture—and here Kallen employed his famous metaphor of the orchestra—the specifically Jewish part in the total orchestrated production that was the pluralistic culture of the American people.[30]

Mordecai Kaplan, the philosopher of Reconstructionism, criticized the planners for failing to confront one of the crucial questions in American Jewish life. "Why is no reference made in all the literature, speeches and lectures concerning the tercentenary to what it means from the standpoint of our survival as a people in dispersion? . . . This is the first time in the history of the Jewish people that it is jubilant over its sojourn in any land outside of Eretz Yisrael." What was the Jewish context of the celebration? What signposts for the future course of American Jewry had the tercentenary offered? The establishment of the state of Israel had raised the question of "the ultimate destiny of the Jewish People." Was Eretz Israel to be the ingathering of the exiles or merely the creative nucleus of the Jewish people? Building on his formulation of living in two civilizations (American and Jewish), Kaplan emphasized the permanence of diaspora and rejected the Israel-Zionist claim that American Jews were in *galut* (exile). For Kaplan, the influence of the American democratic tradition on the Jews *and* "the inexhaustible reservoir of Jewish creativity in Israel" promised a creative future for "the American sector of the Jewish people [that had] at last found a resting place for its feet." But these matters had to be debated, clarified and decided upon.[31]

Ben Halpern, the secularist Zionist thinker, began his study of the American Jewish community, *The American Jew, A Zionist Analysis,* by considering the conviction underlying the tercentenery that "America is different." Indeed it was different, Halpern agreed. In the shadow of Hitler's destruction of Europe's Jews and in the presence of Soviet totalitarianism and Stalin's antisemitism, Jews had special reasons for celebrating America's democratic tradition. However, American Jews had missed one crucial way in which America was different *for them.* As a historic entity, American Jews constituted one of the youngest Jewish centers of the diaspora. In terms of "real history"—of grappling with the specific problems of their existence as a group—American Jewish history began at most with the rise of the first, authentic American Jewish creation, Reform Judaism, and the formation of native American Jewish institutions. Unlike European Jewry, Halpern argued, American Jews had never had to wrestle with the question of emancipation and self-emancipation; American Jewish history began long after the questions of equality and political rights were resolved. His analysis led him to conclude that the indigenous ideologies of American Jews, as programs intended to foster a creative Jewish group life, were failing. Neither the secular ideologies such as cultural pluralism and neo-Zionism nor an innovative religious movement such as Reconstructionism could prevent the erosion of Jewish life. Assimilation? Survival? Was America different than Europe? His answer was: "In Europe, the stick; in America, the carrot." Indeed, Halpern, the fundamentalist Zionist, was utterly pessimistic about American Jewish group survival.[32]

Surely by the final years of the 1950s one could confidently point to a baseline that demarcated American Jewry from what had existed prior to 1945 and that would hold, for the most part, during the decades ahead. The searing recollections of the poverty of immigrant parents or the crushing collapse into destitution of the Great Depression years had been replaced with an affluence that opened new social opportunities. This affluence enabled the postwar generation to devote some of its time and wealth to societal needs. Establishing entirely new communities in the suburbs demanded an enormous collaborative effort. Building communities, expanding the institutions and agencies serving American Jewry as a whole and meeting the needs of world Jewry also required politically sophisticated leaders, trained professionals and efficient organization. An organizational ideology developed "of acts and tasks, of belonging and conforming," of *na'aseh venishma'*. "To be a Jew," one perceptive observer wrote, "is to belong to an organization. To manifest Jewish culture is to carry out . . . the program of an organization."[33] Support for Israel as refuge and home—which more than it swept aside its opponents, co-opted them—became the overarching endeavor, the one that transcended the local and the particular. Hence it came to define the active community.

Purely *Jewish* concerns could also be linked to liberal politics through the argument that to support American liberal causes was in the "Jewish interest," or else group interests could be denied in favor of appealing to the universal teachings of Judaism. Whatever the justification, Jewish *communal* participation in American politics in the decade beginning in 1945 became widespread and was found acceptable. For postwar America commended communal ties that encouraged spiritual self-preservation and self-fulfillment. In the state of fluid pluralism then prevailing—of changing self-images and expectations of religious, ethnic and racial groupings—any number of ways were possible for identifying oneself. Understandably, the Jews, eager to take their place in the more tolerant postwar society, defined their group identity to fit the reigning mood. Judaism as ethnic religion and Judaism as "peoplehood," as "religious civilization" and as one of the three "religions of democracy" were some of the terms that came into use. In the case of the tercentenary platform, Judaism became American democracy, reflecting a strand of insecurity that was present during the golden decade.

A number of ideologues were distressed by the assimilationist thrust of this formulation. They called on American Jews to instead confront the complexity of their dual identity, indeed to view it as the source of an American Jewish distinctiveness. Rabbis and theologians challenged the cult of organization and the emptiness of "religion as the American way." Yet ideologues and rabbis were also committed to a pluralist America. They collaborated in ways that were inconceivable during the prewar years, not only accepting but applauding the internal pluralism of Jewish group life. Precisely the give-and-take of contending movements and ideas within a communal consensus indicated a commitment to group survival. One could understand, for example, the much-criticized slogan, "Man's Opportunities and Responsibilities Under Freedom," as a shrewd strategy to maintain the community. (Rabbis used the phrase as the text for their sermons on the need for better Jewish education, support for Israel and a richer synagogal life.)[34] Unmistakably, whatever ideological issues were placed on the Jewish public agenda during the decade beginning in 1945—which have remained there to this day—no longer called into question the worth or desirability of Jewish survival. The issue henceforth would be the quality and character of Jewish group survival.

Notes

I would like to thank William B. Goldfarb of Goldfarb, Levy, Giniger, and Company, Tel-Aviv, for his close reading of the manuscript and his insightful suggestions. All unpublished letters, reports and minutes are in the tercentennial files of the American Jewish Committee Papers on deposit in the YIVO Institute, New York. I also want to thank Oscar Handlin for allowing me use of his files of the tercentennial committee.

1. Lucy Dawidowicz, *On Equal Terms: Jews in America, 1881–1981* (New York: 1982). Murray Friedman in his *The Utopian Dilemma: New Political Directions for American Jews* (Washington, D.C.: 1985) entitles one of his chapers "The Golden Age of American Jewry (1945–1965)."

2. Charles Liebman, *The Ambivalent American Jew: Politics, Religion and Family in American Jewish Life* (Philadelphia: 1973), vii.

3. In order of their appearance, some of the key studies of the suburbanization of American Jews are Herbert J. Gans, "Park Forest: Birth of a Jewish Community," *Commentary* 11, no. 4 (April 1951), 330–339; *idem,* "Progress of a Suburban Jewish Community, Park Forest Revisited," *Commentary* 23, no. 2 (Feb. 1957), 113–122; Marshall Sklare and Marc Vosk, *The Riverton Study: How Jews Look at Themselves and Their Neighbors* (New York: 1957); Judith Kramer and Seymour Leventman, *Children of the Gilded Ghetto: Conflict Resolution of Three Generations of American Jews* (New Haven: 1961); Marshall Sklare and Joseph Greenbaum, *Jewish Identity on the Suburban Frontier: A Study of Group Survival in an Open Society* (New York: 1967).

4. Deborah Dash Moore, *At Home in America: Second Generation New York Jews* (New York: 1981), 19-149, 201–242.

5. Marc Lee Raphael, *Profiles in Judaism: The Reform, Conservative, Orthodox and Reconstructionist Traditions in Historical Perspective* (New York: 1984), 119; *idem, A History of the United Jewish Appeal, 1939–1982* (New York: 1982), 136–137.

6. Daniel Elazar, *Community and Polity: The Organizational Dynamics of American Jewry* (Philadelphia: 1976), 297; Melvin I. Urofsky, *We Are One: American Jewry and Israel* (Garden City, N.Y.: 1978), 144–145; Peter Grosse, *Israel in the Mind of America* (New York: 1982), 265–268.

7. Alex Grobman, "The American Jewish Chaplains and the Remnants of European Jewry: 1944–1948" (Ph.D. diss., The Hebrew University, 1981), 100–111, 233–244, 270–280, 308–334; Yehuda Bauer, *Flight and Rescue: Bricha* (New York: 1970), 241–255; Leonard Slater, *The Pledge* (New York: 1970), 92–97, 120–124, 209–218; Doron Almog, *Harekhesh bearzot-haberit* (Tel-Aviv: 1987), 31–34, 43–52.

8. Elmer Berger, *Judaism or Jewish Nationalism: The Alternative to Zionism* (New York: 1957), 15–44; 92–107; Thomas H. Kolsky, "Jews Against Zionism: The American Council for Judaism, 1942–1948" (Ph.D. diss., George Washington University, 1986), 405–479; Arthur Liebman, *Jews on the Left* (New York: 1979), 511–515; Sidney Hook, *Out of Step: An Unquiet Life in the 20th Century* (New York: 1987), 5, 33; Nathan Glazer, "Jewish Intellectuals," *Partisan Review* 51 (1984), 674–679.

9. Emanuel Neumann, *In the Arena: An Autobiographical Memoir* (New York: 1976), 243–245, 349–355; see also Aaron Berman, *Nazism, the Jews and American Zionism* (Detroit: 1990), 178–179.

10. Marshall Sklare, *America's Jews* (New York: 1971), 211–222; Nathan Glazer, *"American Judaism* Thirty Years Later," *American Jewish History* 77 (1987), 284; Jacob Neusner, *Stranger at Home: The "Holocaust," Zionism, and American Judaism* (Chicago: 1981), 66–67; Chaim Waxman, *America's Jews in Transition* (Philadelphia: 1983), 114–115, 119–123.

11. Lawrence H. Fuchs, *The Political Behavior of American Jews* (Glencoe, Ill.: 1956), 79–120, 171–177; Liebman, *Ambivalent American Jew*, 136–139, 148–159; Deborah Dash Moore, *B'nai B'rith and the Challenge of Ethnic Leadership* (Albany, N.Y.: 1981), 213–221; Waxman, *America's Jews in Transition*, 98–103.

12. For this and the following paragraph, see Friedman, *Utopian Dilemma*, 1–35; Naomi W. Cohen, *Not Free to Desist* (Philadelphia: 1972), 384–404. For a political scientist's highly suggestive analysis of these developments, see Peter Y. Medding, "Segmented Ethnicity and the New Jewish Politics," in *Studies in Contemporary Jewry*, vol. 3, *Jews and Other Ethnic Groups in a Multi-Ethnic World*, ed. Ezra Mendelsohn (New York: 1987), 26–48.

13. Albert Vorspan and Eugene J. Lipman, *Justice and Judaism: The Work of Social Action* (New York: 1956), passim.

14. For the exchange of statements between Jacob Blaustein and David Ben-Gurion, see *American Jewish Year Book* 53 (New York: 1952), 564–565. See also Charles S. Liebman's discussion in *Pressure Without Sanctions: The Influence of World Jewry on Israel Policy* (Rutherford, N.J.: 1977), 118–131. For a more recent indication of a continued sensitivity to the question of dual loyalties, see Arthur J. Goldberg, "The Canard of Dual Loyalty," *Hadassah Magazine* (March 1983), 16–17.

15. Will Herberg, *Protestant-Catholic-Jew: An Essay in American Religious Sociology* (Garden City, N.Y.: 1955); for a review of the literature on religious identification, see Waxman, *America's Jews in Transition*, 81–95.

16. C. Bezalel Sherman, *Israel and the American Jewish Community* (New York: 1951), 12. This caveat appeared on the inside of the title page of the pamphlet: "The particular views expressed by the author do not necessarily constitute the official policy of the Labor Zionist Organization of America."

17. C. Bezalel Sherman, *The Jew Within American Society: A Study in Ethnic Individuality* (Detroit: 1961), 223, 226. For an early statement of this thesis, see *idem*, "Secularism in a Religious Framework," *Judaism* 1, no. 1 (Jan. 1952), 36–43.

18. Quoted by Nina Warnke, "The American Jewish Tercentenary" (unpublished ms.), 1. I am grateful to the author for allowing me to examine this illuminating paper on the ideological meaning of the tercentenary.

19. *American Jewish Tercentenary: 1654–1954, Scope and Theme* (report of the Steering Committee to the Tercentenary Committee of 300, National Planning Conference, 12 April 1953); Minutes, Committee on Organization, Tercentenary Celebration of Jewish Settlement in the United States, 15 January and 24 March 1952; Minutes, Steering Committee, American Jewish Tercentenary Committee, 3 June and 18 November 1952; Minutes, National Planning Conference, American Jewish Committee, 12 April 1953; Ralph E. Samuel to the Tercentenary Committee of 300, final report, 14 July 1955.

20. See David Bernstein, "The American Jewish Tercentenary," *American Jewish Year Book* 57 (New York: 1956), 101–118; see also n. 19.

21. *National Jewish Monthly* 69 (Sept. 1954), 8–12. Beginning with the October issue, the *Monthly* ran feature stories depicting episodes in American Jewish history. Nathan Glazer, Oscar and Mary F. Handlin, and Joseph C. Blau in *American Jewish Year Book* 56 (New York: 1955), 3–170; Moses Rischin, *An Inventory of American Jewish History* (Cambridge, Mass.: 1954); *The Jewish People: Past and Present, 300 Years of Jewish Life in the United States* (New York: 1955) (no ed. named).

22. Daniel Bell, "The End of American Exceptionalism," *The Public Interest*, no. 41 (Fall 1975), 203–205; Daniel Boorstein, *The Genius of American Politics* (Chicago: 1953), 1.

23. *American Jewish Archives* 1, no. 1 (June 1948), 2–3.

24. Moshe Davis and Isidor S. Meyer (eds.), *The Writing of American Jewish History* (New York: 1957); American Jewish History Center *Newsletter*, no. 1 (Spring 1961).

25. Oscar Handlin, *Adventure in Freedom: Three Hundred Years of Jewish Life in America* (New York: 1954), vii–viii, 260.

26. Memorandum, Judge Samuel I. Rosenman to David Bernstein, 7 October 1952; "American Jewish Tercentenary, Scope and Theme (for Steering Committee use only)," n.d.

27. *American Jewish Year Book* 56: 103, 107.

28. Deborah Dash Moore, "Reconsidering the Rosenbergs: Symbol and Substance in Second Generation American Jewish Consciousness," *Journal of American Ethnic History* 8, no. 1 (Fall 1988), 21–37; *idem, B'nai B'rith and the Challenge of Ethnic Leadership,* 226–229; Arnold Forster, *Square One: A Memoir* (New York: 1988), 126–129; *Congress Weekly,* 12 March 1951, 1–3, *ibid.,* 16 Nov. 1953, 3–10, and 23 Nov. 1953, 10–12.

29. Robert Gordis, "American Jewry Faces Its Fourth Century," *Judaism* 3, no. 4 (Fall 1954), 298.

30. Horace Kallen, "The Tercentenary: Yomtov or Yahrzeit?" *Congress Weekly,* 22 Nov. 1954, 8–11; "The Tercentenary Symbol and Slogan: An Exchange of Letters," *ibid.,* 20 Dec. 1954, 14–15.

31. Mordecai M. Kaplan, "The Meaning of the Tercentenary for Diaspora Judaism," *The Reconstructionist* 20, no. 12 (15 Oct. 1954), 10, 16–18.

32. Ben Halpern, *The American Jew: A Zionist Analysis* (New York: 1956), 11–14.

33. Harold Weisberg, "Ideologies of American Jews," in *The American Jews: A Reappraisal,* ed. Oscar I. Janowsky (Philadelphia: 1964), 347–356.

34. See, for example, Israel Goldstein, *American Jewry Comes of Age: Tercentenary Addresses* (New York: 1955). In an address entitled "Facing the Fourth Century," he notes that interpretations of the tercentennial theme "can be as varied as the viewpoints of those who interpret it. The theme itself is more Jewish than would appear" (p. 120).

American Judaism:
Changing Patterns in
Denominational Self-Definition

Arnold Eisen
(STANFORD UNIVERSITY)

American Judaism has been significantly transformed in the past two decades. All four of the principal religious movements—Reform, Conservatism, Reconstructionism and Modern Orthodoxy—have adopted new prayer books for use in their congregations. All but the Orthodox have issued new statements of principles; all, including the Orthodox, have engaged in an unprecedented degree of public self-scrutiny and self-explanation. Thus, although we still know next to nothing about the religious beliefs and experiences of the average American Jew—survey data about synagogue attendance and ritual performance being of little help in this regard—we can document the transformation in the religious options among which American Jews may choose. Such a transformation will be examined here via a careful reading of prayer books, statements of principles, and essays by representative figures of the major denominations. Such an analysis can shed light on the changed self-presentation of the movements and the changed self-understanding of their elites and can also—albeit indirectly—serve as a basis for evaluation of the altered religious landscape of American Jews and Judaism as a whole.[1]

Before turning to the four movements' new presentations of self, we should note that the language of "elite" and "folk," so crucial to Charles Liebman's study of *The Ambivalent American Jew* a generation ago,[2] will be crucial to the present analysis as well in two respects. First, the research methods needed to get at folk beliefs and experiences have been employed only rarely in the study of American Jews. We therefore do well to eschew unwarranted generalizations about them. "Quantitative data," as one historian observed recently, "shed little light on the quality of religious experience."[3] Moreover, as Liebman demonstrated convincingly, one cannot make inferences about the average congregant from the testimony of religious professionals whose demands upon faith are in the nature of the case very different. Thus, the analysis presented here will not attempt to glean "the self-image of American Jews . . . from the prayer books of their respective movements,"[4] as one recent study would have it. The object of scrutiny is neither theology strictly understood—which is the exclusive province of the elite—nor the religion of the folk, but rather the point at which the two come together: the self-image of American Jewish elites (rabbis, theologians, and seminary faculty), and of the movements that they above all others shape.

Second, however, we should remember that the "shaping" goes in both directions. Efforts of the elites to redefine their respective movements are of course influenced by their perceptions of what congregants want or are prepared to tolerate, what they believe or wish to believe. It is precisely the continuing gap between "elite" and "folk" religion as perceived by the elite, and the continuing attempt to overcome it, that accounts for the significant changes in style and substance to be examined here. The attempt to narrow the distinction between elite and folk generally takes the form of a call for increased observance among the latter. However, it is often the laity that exercises decisive influence—whether by refusing to meet elite demands or, as will be shown here, by encouraging the elite both to avoid theological issues in which the "folk" are not interested and to recast existing commitments in language more suited to popular taste. If, as the survey data reveal, "this has been an era of perceptible change in patterns of behavior among American Jews, particularly in the religious sphere,"[5] that change has been both cause and effect of no less perceptible changes in the thinking of the men and women who define the limited range of intellectual and institutional options that constitute American Judaism. Reform, Reconstructionism, Conservatism and Modern Orthodoxy are not what they were twenty years ago, even if the dilemmas these movements face have not altered in the interim but only intensified.

Reform and the Language of Mitzvah

Transformation is most apparent in the Reform movement. Reform has always been more prolific than its rivals in the publication of its principles,[6] and the change in Reform discourse of late has also been most graphic. A movement that as recently as 1972 could not agree to issue a "guide" to the religious practice of its members lest it infringe upon their autonomy[7] was able by 1979 to publish *Gates of Mitzvah: A Guide to the Jewish Life Cycle,* which from its title onward speaks of "mitzvah"—commandment. Rabbi Gunther Plaut is careful to note in his foreword that Judaism "was never meant to be merely an institutional religion. Its ultimate focus remains the individual. . . ." But he now turns that focus on the individual to a new emphasis on "personal observance and personal deed, at home and at work . . . [giving] continual expression to our belief in God and . . . the significance of our membership in the historic people"[8]—hardly staples of past Reform discourse. The volume's editor, Rabbi Simeon Maslin, similarly follows the unequivocal assertion that "mitzvah is the key to authentic Jewish existence and the sanctification of life" with a footnote referring readers to four essays included in the guide that set forth "different points of view on why, how, and to what extent a modern Jew may feel required to perform mitzvot." The individual Reform Jew— still the final arbiter of observance, according to the movement—would then be in a position to "develop a personal rationale through which the performance of a mitzvah *may* become meaningful."[9]

The movement had cleared the way for this strategy of combining the language of commandment with a renewed commitment to autonomy in its 1976 Statement of Principles, the first to be issued since the Columbus Platform of 1937. In almost all respects there is no substantive difference between the statements. Only one paragraph breaks new ground: "Our Obligations: Religious Practice." It goes well beyond the 1937 affirmation of "such customs, symbols and ceremonies as possess inspirational value," paired there with "distinctive forms of religious art and music and the use of Hebrew." The aesthetic emphasis of 1937—ceremony, like art, enriches one; it does not obligate—gives way in 1976 to talk of obligation: "claims made upon us" that extend beyond ethical obligations to "many other aspects of Jewish living." The paragraph's concluding sentence seeks to balance newly affirmed obligation and still-regnant autonomy. "Within each area of Jewish observance Reform Jews are called upon to confront the claims of Jewish tradition, however differently perceived, and to exercise their individual autonomy, choosing and creating on the basis of commitment and knowledge."[10]

One could of course regard this formulation as trivial, on two counts. In the modern West, all religious observance is voluntarily assumed. No communal coercion is possible. Likewise, when Maslin points out in *Gates of Mitzvah* that "all Jews who acknowledge themselves to be members of their people and its tradition thereby limit their freedom to some extent,"[11] he is perhaps calling attention to the obvious. What adult is not aware that freedom is never absolute? What Jew does not know that Hitler counted even the "unaffiliated" among his victims? Nonetheless, it can be argued, the two assertions in context are highly significant. What Maslin and Plaut have done—following the 1976 statement—is contain the hallowed Reform commitment to autonomy within an ambitious new project of providing specificity to Reform observance. The movement is now prepared to do more than guide. It even lends its authority to the traditional notion that God actually *commands,* and is willing to say *what* God commands.

At times, it is true, that command is rather equivocal. The pregnant woman considering abortion is advised to "determine" the proper course "in accordance with the principles of Jewish morality," which are then left undefined.[12] On kashruth, *Gates of Mitzvah* can only recognize the various attitudes and degrees of observance among Reform Jews and recommend that such "an essential feature of Jewish life for so many centuries" bears study by each family.[13] At the same time, however, "it is a mitzvah" for a couple to be tested for genetic disease before marriage, to bring children into the world and thank God after doing so, and to bring children into the covenant; "it is a mitzvah" to pray on a daily basis, to affix a mezuzah to the doorpost and to celebrate Shabbat with candles, kiddush, challah and the appropriate blessings; "it is a mitzvah" to write an ethical will, to attend a funeral service, to prepare a first meal for mourners and to recite kaddish.[14]

The source of authority for these commandments—certainly not the Shulhan Arukh—seems to vary considerably. At times it is the application by Reform rabbis of "fundamental principles" such as "the sanctity of life" (as in the cases of abortion and genetic testing). At other points (as with circumcision or the Sabbath) it seems to be the weight of "Jewish tradition," again as defined by Reform rabbinic interpreters. Understanding of the "ultimate authority" varies still more, as the essays on the nature and extent of mitzvah included in *Gates of Mitzvah* reveal.

Herman Schaalman, in his interpretive essay,[15] argues that the source of commandment must be a Commander, though the precise character of revelation— "for that is what we are talking about"—remains a mystery. Moses heard "the impact and meaning of God's Presence" in this way, experiencing himself as "commanded, summoned, directed." Jews have reexperienced this commandedness ever since. "Thus the Divine Presence waits for us, and we for It. Thus the commandment comes to us in our time, asking to be heard, understood, and done." The guiding theological presence here, clearly, is Franz Rosenzweig. Schaalman has also adapted Rosenzweig's notion that some mitzvot performed by the ancestors will not be adequate or possible for us, while we may feel obligated by new mitzvot unknown to our tradition.

In a somewhat different formulation,[16] David Polish traces the commandments' authority to Jewish history. Mitzvot "mark points of encounter by the Jewish people with God." They are signs of a continuing covenant. "The self-imposed discipline of observance, to which the Jew submits as a sacred mitzvah, thus becomes a symbol of the commitment of his faith and of his people to the unending struggle to enthrone God in the world within the bounds of human history." Here the presiding presence seems to be Martin Buber: Mitzvot stem from the Jewish people's "encounter" with God. Jews have promised in their covenant to enact God's will in history. That covenant obligates every Jew—but it is one to which the individual Jew must decide to "submit."

Roland Gittelsohn[17] offers a naturalistic variant of Polish's interpretation derived from Mordecai Kaplan, defining the "something [that] happened between God and Israel" to be an "historic encounter between the Jewish people and the highest Spiritual Reality human beings have ever known." Just as the construction of the universe mandates that we breathe, nature commands us to be ethical, and ritual mitzvot serve those moral imperatives by "visually and kinetically remind[ing] us of our noblest values and stimulat[ing us] to pursue them." Mitzvot, finally, bind the religious naturalist "to his people and his tradition. They speak to him imperatively because he is Jewish and wants to remain so."

If so much attention has been paid here to these brief statements, it is because they exhaust the possible inventory of current Reform rationales for observance. One cannot hold to a more literal understanding of "Torah from Sinai" or "Torah from Heaven" and either safeguard individual autonomy or legitimate Reform's departures from halakhah. Nor is the current temper of Reform thinking content with Hermann Cohen's equation of revelation with reason's instruction concerning our ethical duty. Rosenzweig thus represents the most "Orthodox" theological position available, one that maintains belief in the divine origin of the commandments while allowing great room for human initiative, wrapping the relation between "divine and human" in ultimate mystery. Buber, with his emphasis upon individual encounter with the Eternal Thou and the ethical obligations that emerge from such an encounter, is the ideal source for contemporary Reform language of mitzvah, particularly when his individualism is tempered (as in Polish) with the ideal of loyalty to the Jewish people. The Reform thinker who has best articulated a synthesis of all three tendencies, Eugene Borowitz, was also the principal author of the "Centenary Perspective" of 1976 and his "covenant theology," via *Gates of Mitzvah*, has now stamped the entire movement in his image.

Three problems with such covenant theology are apparent. First, Reform has accounted for Jewish obligation while adroitly avoiding the theological issues that have plagued such attempts throughout the modern period. According to Reform, one can opt for Rosenzweig's approach to revelation, or Buber's, or Kaplan's, or none at all; the point of the *Gates* series,[18] despite views such as those presented above, is not so much to clarify the authority behind the commandments as to set forth a new standard of expectation for Reform Jews. The rabbis are taking advantage of a new willingness among the laity to study texts and perform traditional rituals without worrying overmuch about the theological basis of that observance. This strategy, by no means unique to Reform, may well work—or else the laity, less committed to observance than the elite, may well decide that, if God has not directly commanded action A or B, their time can be better spent on other things.

Second, in the absence of clear theological rationales, Reform rabbis have effectively assumed authority for the direction of their congregants' Jewish life—a role they may have played for some time but were prevented, because of considerations of "autonomy," from assuming formally. A telling footnote in *Gates of the Seasons* (a companion volume to *Gates of Mitzvah*) reports that "the following list of mitzvot is a revision of the earlier 'Catalogue of Shabbat Opportunities.' "[19] When does an "opportunity" become a mitzvah? When a movement's rabbis decide to make it such. Why is it "a mitzvah for every Jew to mark Yom Ha'atzmaut" publicly and "a mitzvah to remember the six million" on Yom Hashoah, but not a mitzvah to observe Tisha B'av? Again, particularly if no other reason is given, because the Central Conference of American Rabbis (CCAR), Reform's rabbinic association, has so ruled. The movement's rabbis have reasserted the legislative role first assumed in the rabbinic conferences of the 1840s but often limited, in the interim, out of deference to the principle (and the fact) of the layperson's individual autonomy. Again, only time will tell whether the "folk" embrace, reject or acquiesce in this attempt to guide them. Elements of the elite more committed to autonomy than the majority that voted in the new policy have already expressed their discomfort.[20]

The folk may simply go on doing more or less what they have been doing for some time. To the degree that the Reform movement employs a fictitious present tense in its official pronouncements—as in "Unlike on Shabbat and the other festivals, Yom Kippur candles are lit after the meal"[21]—it will open up the same sort of gap between official pronouncements and lay reality that for decades has bedeviled Conservatism. The rabbis have now gone on record with commands to their congregants to behave more as they, the rabbis, behave. Congregants may enjoy having greater demands made upon them; they may even respond to those demands. It is unlikely, however, that they will meet them. Reform may then sacrifice the appeal that it had gained by validating low levels of observance— telling Jews, as Conservatism could not, that despite minimal practice "you are a good Jew, your people can be proud of you, you are carrying on a precious tradition. God bless you!" The movement may lose in numbers of affiliated members what its elite gains in its own greater sense of authenticity.

The movement's new prayer book *Gates of Prayer* (1975) has run precisely the same risk, in the same manner, for the same reasons. No "objective" reading is possible of any prayer book; no "ideal reader" exists to undertake it.[22] However, a number of general features are immediately apparent and have been singled out for notice by critics of the prayer book from inside and outside the movement. First, they note that deference has been paid to autonomy. The individual congregant (and individual rabbi!) is presented with four evening or morning services for weekdays, ten services for Friday evenings and six for Sabbath mornings. Length, style, theme and even theology vary considerably. Every principal current of thought within the movement finds representation, from Alvin Reines's "polydoxy" and partisans of classical Reform to Borowitz's covenant theology and advocates of a more traditional liturgy. Pluralism rules.

However, even congregants less well-versed in the distinctions among services cannot escape the impression that overall their movement has moved to the "right." They in fact now hold a siddur that opens from right to left instead of the reverse; that contains a great deal more Hebrew than its predecessor (with the Hebrew placed on the same page as the English, thereby stressing its centrality in the service); and that not only restores reference to Zion but contains a special service for Yom Ha'atzmaut. Tisha B'av is back; there are prayers for tallit and tefillin. *Gates of Prayer* seems utterly comfortable in using traditional language that cannot in any way be justified in a rational, literal reading. In short, there has been a "return to tradition."[23] The combination of pluralism and tradition in *Gates of Prayer* directly parallels the coexistence of autonomy and commandment found in *Gates of Mitzvah*.

Reform rabbis evaluating the prayer book in a 1985 symposium in the *Journal of Reform Judaism*[24] could and did complain about its excessive length, the flatness of its prose, the inconsistencies and evasions of its theological premises. But they could not deny the immense transformation the movement had wrought—to what effect upon their congregants no one seemed sure. Several aspects of their discussion are particularly pertinent. As the rabbis responsible for it have observed, *Gates of Prayer* represented an attempt to bring Jewish prayer into line with "contemporary" trends in American society and culture; as a result, it has already been rendered somewhat anachronistic. The late 1960s and early 1970s saw a proliferation of "creative services" reflected both in the array of choices that *Gates of Prayer* offers worshipers and in its seventy-odd pages of suggested material for meditation and reflection. Participants in the evaluative symposium found both excessive. The period likewise saw the rise (but not yet the impact) of feminism; in *Gates of Prayer, avot* is translated as "ancestors" (or "all generations"), and there is mention of Reform's commitment to "the equality of the sexes," although God is still referred to exclusively in male pronouns. Disenchantment with high rhetoric and a desire for intimacy led the book's authors to include far more congregational participation and to avoid eloquence that might have seemed to ring hollow. The result, as many Reform critics charged, is all too often "pedestrian." Poetry is in short supply.

The issue here seems to be more than stylistic. *Gates of Prayer* is attractive in its honesty. It may exceed the level of faith attained by most Reform congregants, but it is always true to the doubts and disbelief of the movement's elite. At times, however, this honesty proves problematic. Entire services are devoted to "the struggle to believe" and "the confrontation with estrangement." The congregant opens the prayer book and finds directed reflection upon how difficult it is to relate to prayer altogether. "For our ancestors, Shabbat was a sign of God's covenant. . . . Our ways are not theirs. . . . We speak many words, but few prayers. . . . But here, now, we can begin again." This meditation precedes *Lekha Dodi.* Immediately after it, we read that "the words do not always speak for us, nor can we always understand them. Yet once we understood: to speak the ancient words returns us to that simpler time when as children we felt the world was one, and it was ours."[25] The "gates" metaphor now pervasive in Reform publications takes on new meaning in this connection. The prayer book seems an entry for those on the outside of prayer to walk through, rather than the thing itself. As one rabbi put it, "It is a way in to prayer. It may not yet enable us to pray, that is, to daven (by which I mean the traditional Jewish sense of devoting all one's faculties, thoughts, words, melodies, limbs, and soul to the encounter with God)."[26] Another commented that "we often are faced with the double task of providing our people with religious experience while simultaneously revealing the meaning of the experience itself. However, this should be done in a non-discursive and non-distancing manner." He cited a note introducing *Lekha Dodi* in terms of how "the mystics of Israel conceived the Sabbath," what they saw and did, instead of emphasizing that "*we* welcome Shabbat with joy. *We* sing Lecha Dodi."[27]

A book with such an array of options, arranged explicitly by theme and composed largely of readings and meditations that hammer home specific lessons or work on specific emotions, seems aimed at the worshiper as much as at God. Put another way: It aims less at providing language for the soul's outpouring before God than at opening the worshiper to the possibility of such encounter. This, however, is less the case where the traditional liturgy is more predominant—leaving the clear implication that the more comfortable with *davening* a person is, the more likely he or she is to prefer the traditional service. The CCAR may not be happy with such an implication, but it is there, and it testifies to the movement's current state. Reform stands at the gate: at the beginning of a tentative and widely contested turn back to a more traditional liturgical style and message.

Gates of Prayer, finally, marks a return in another sense: to the pattern of German liberalism from which Isaac Mayer Wise and David Einhorn departed so radically more than a century ago. As Jakob Petuchowski's *History of Prayerbook Reform in Europe* makes eminently clear (and his critiques of *Gates of Prayer* reiterate),[28] the German prayer books by and large were quite hesitant in introducing changes and often took care when they did so to justify them with venerable Jewish precedent. *Gates of Prayer,* like the previous Union Prayer Books, has no room for sacrifice or the restoration of the Davidic monarchy; it takes pains to stress the ethical character of Jewish monotheism; and it is committed to the legitimacy of liturgical innovation. However, unlike its immediate predecessors, *Gates of Prayer* has restored Hebrew to prominence and has assumed the metaphoric character of the liturgy, thereby allowing it to sing in traditional voice with renewed sincerity. It thereby revives the tradition of German liberals from whose theology the current Reform repositioning draws inspiration.

In the American case, as noted, there has been no comparable theological innovation. "Despite initial position papers and discussion, those actually engaged in the process of producing *Gates of Prayer* never finally came to terms with fundamental questions," writes Herbert Bronstein, the head of the CCAR's liturgy committee.[29] Richard Levy, who served on that committee when *Gates of Prayer* was produced, makes a similar complaint: The prayer book reintroduced the kaddish and several other traditional texts, but

> has persisted in denying Reform worshipers the necessity of struggling with the relation
> between nature and our own deeds. . . . Having been present at the meeting of the
> CCAR Executive Board when it voted against the inclusion of [the issue of] *techiyat
> hametim* [resurrection of the dead], I remain saddened that such a profound, troubling,
> complex, ecstatic idea could have been dispensed with in so trivial a fashion. Re-
> form . . . should not mean the censoring of certain texts, ideas, and commands by the
> extremely unspiritual mechanism of majority vote.[30]

The effects of the committee process are evident throughout *Gates of Prayer*. One does not find articulation of a coherent, carefully thought-out theological consensus. Nor does one see the guiding hand of an authoritative figure in the mainstream of the movement who has so internalized its ethos and worldview that he or she can confidently lend its pronouncements the vitality of a personal voice.

All the more reason, then, to attend to the writings of Eugene Borowitz, the Reform thinker who comes closest to this stature and who, more than any other, has influenced the movement's recent course. Borowitz holds the senior position in theology at the Hebrew Union College, and several years back he published a definitive statement of Reform beliefs intended for laypeople.[31] This is not the place for a comprehensive treatment of Borowitz's substantial oeuvre, but several elements of this particular work bear scrutiny.

First, from its title onward—*Liberal Judaism* rather than Reform Judaism—the volume harks back to Borowitz's German masters (Cohen, Rosenzweig, Buber, Leo Baeck) and through them to the tradition as a whole. The book is organized according to the popular threefold division of Israel, God and Torah (the last divided into two parts titled "the Bible and the Tradition" and "living as a Jew.") Borowitz is uncompromising in his assertion of God's reality and involvement with the world and the binding force of the age-old Jewish covenant with God. He defines "a good Jew" as one "who has a living relationship with God as part of the people of Israel and therefore liv[es] a life of Torah." Covenant and divine encounter, then, are central.[32] Thus far, Conservative and Modern Orthodox thinkers no less indebted to Buber and Rosenzweig than the Reform elite could agree wholeheartedly.

But there are several elements in Borowitz's writings that place him squarely in the Reform movement and no other, perhaps because he has played such a significant role in defining that movement's ideological boundaries. One is the emphasis upon faith and covenant rather than peoplehood and history. Conservatives and Reconstructionists would shift the balance. A second distinctively Reform element is the embrace of Israel, but only from a distance. It is doubtful that any non-Reform thinker would have felt the need in 1984 to stress that

American Jews owe political allegiance only to the country of their citizenship. . . . The "Star-Spangled Banner" or "Hail Canada" is our national anthem; "Hatikvah," for all that an effort was once made to have it become the chief song of the Jewish people, is the anthem of a foreign country. It, like the Israeli flag, must be treated with the protocol established by our country's laws.[33]

Reform remains the movement most devoted to America. It also, if Borowitz is representative, remains the movement that most emphasizes the primacy of ethical commandment. "Of all the lessons the liberals derived from the prophets, none affected them more profoundly than the principle that ethics are more important than worship in Judaism."[34]

Finally, Borowitz's thrust is profoundly individualist. He does not address himself to the Jewish people but to the individual Jew, and he will never seek to direct that Jew but only to present him or her with options. The book makes "no special claims to 'authority'" but only hopes "to persuade." No "creed" is intended.[35]

This reluctance to direct others seems to stem from a commitment to individual freedom so deep that neither Borowitz's personal authority nor the weight of Jewish tradition can be permitted to infringe upon it. The rabbis' role, he feels, is to suggest options. Autonomy must not be compromised—even if, as Borowitz well knows, the philosophical grounding for moral autonomy is precarious indeed. Perhaps because his intended audience is the laity, Borowitz avoids this dilemma by taking refuge in romanticism. Assuming, he writes, that a decision is made out of the depth of knowledge and out of a sense of deepest commitment, "whatever we choose from the past or create for the present should rest upon us with the full force of commandment. For only by being false to ourselves and to what we believe will we be able to ignore or transgress it." Borowitz, however, cannot and does not satisfactorily explain why the commitment to Judaism and the Jewish people is or should be of ultimate importance.[36]

Herein lies perhaps the most significant step taken by the movement in the past generation, a step to which the language of mitzvah, the return to more traditional liturgy, the commitment to pluralism and the reformulation of Reform principles all give expression—namely, the sidestepping of the issue of revelation, which has vexed Jewish theology for two hundred years, in favor of renewed deference to the weight of the past and the new appeal that ritual observance has for American Jews. The authority for Reform, as for Conservatism, Reconstructionism and (in a different sense) Orthodoxy, is no longer God or faith but rather tradition. Gunther Plaut, like Borowitz an heir to German liberal Judaism, captured the point well when he formulated the current Reform preoccupation as: What will my life say? How can I give meaning to life?[37] Ritual observance and study are time-tested means for providing such meaning. Hence, perhaps, the renewed Reform attention to Shabbat, study, and ritual—as well as the popular formation within synagogues of small *havurot* for study and celebration—all with no attempt at justification beyond appeal to "tradition" and the palpable sense of meaning that such activity confers. By doing the mitzvot, Reform says in effect, Jews have traditionally felt themselves partners to the covenant and witnesses to the presence of God. If one asks (as Reform did in the past) why we should not actively search out *other* means to the same end, discarding those that do not work for us, the answer is, as Rabbi William Braude put it, "we may not play fast and loose with the tradition."[38]

Reform Jews, then, continue to value autonomy. Pluralism is the order of the day. Their movement will continue to feel the impact of rabbis such as the one who confessed to feeling indignant when he was told that if he did not put on a *kipah* he would not be admitted to a Reform temple: "I was sorely tempted to absent myself, because I believe that a rule which permits no freedom of choice really violates a basic principle of Reform."[39] The movement will probably continue to get around such concerns with Borowitz's language of gentle persuasion rather than authority. Yet it will also probably continue to invoke the language of mitzvah because, for contemporary Reform congregants, there *does* seem to be commandment in Judaism: above all, the command not to sever the link that binds the Jewish generations. Convincing theologies of revelation may be unavailable and the commitment to autonomy may be unassailable, but the current generation of Reform's leadership seems convinced as well that "one cannot play fast and loose with tradition." American Reform Judaism, as a result, is very different than it was only a generation ago.

Conservatism and the Appropriation of "Tradition"

The Reform movement's "return to tradition" heightened the sense within Conservative ranks that the movement could no longer avoid clarification of where precisely it stood. Lack of such a guiding ideology had long been a sore point within the movement and the object of criticism from without.[40] Now, with Reform tearing down the easy markers by which laypeople had been able to distinguish the two denominations—adding Hebrew to Reform services, embracing Israel, introducing head covering and tallit for men, speaking freely of "mitzvot" and positively of ritual—the need for clarity gained in urgency. In 1988, the movement finally did what it had debated and even attempted without issue in the past. It published a "Statement of Principles of Conservative Judaism" entitled *Emet Ve-Emunah*— "Truth and Faith." The statement commission was chaired by Robert Gordis, who had long provided a centrist, de facto definition of the movement. His introduction to *Emet Ve-Emunah* confirmed the path that he had laid out half a century before, thereby confirming as well that those dilemmas plaguing the movement since the 1930s were still far from resolution.

Gordis began, as one would expect, by positioning his movement at the center of the spectrum of Jewish possibility and rejecting the alternatives on either side as unacceptable. Reform had "denied the authority of Jewish law . . . in the name of 'individual autonomy.' " Orthodoxy was divided into many factions but "theoretically united under the dogma that both the Written and the Oral Law were given by God to Moses at Sinai, and have remained unchanged and unchangeable through the ages."[41] Clearly, then, Conservatism had halakhah, while Reform did not, but it also had freedom, intellectual integrity and flexibility—all of which Orthodoxy lacked. Hence, "it is Conservative Judaism that most directly confronts the challenge to integrate tradition with modernity. By retaining most of the tradition while yet being hospitable to the valuable aspects of modernity, it articulates a vital, meaningful vision of Judaism for our day."[42]

Just what is "the tradition," and how might one measure its presence or absence in a given modern Jewish life? One clue—perhaps the most important—is provided by Gordis at once. He cites "the Sages." Gordis's movement has in effect conceded the Prophets to Reform and the Shulhan Arukh to Orthodoxy, while claiming for itself the much broader canvas of history and belief bequeathed to us by the Sages and known, in the parlance common to the elites of all four movements, as "the tradition."

The appropriation of "tradition" (and thereby the center) as Conservatism's own has generated an enormous ideological self-confidence that belies the self-doubt often attributed to the movement's elite, even by members of the elite themselves. Gerson Cohen, then chancellor of the Jewish Theological Seminary (JTS) wrote in a 1977 symposium that the future of Judaism as a whole would largely be determined by the "present state of things" within the central institutions of Conservative Judaism.[43] David Gordis (son of Robert, and a guiding force of the Seminary's West Coast affiliate, the University of Judaism in Los Angeles) wrote the same year that "Conservatism remains the only authentic approach to Jewish tradition today," the "only acceptable orientation for the Jew who wishes to maintain an attachment to the creative existence of his people while not detaching himself from the adventure of discovery of self and of society which characterizes modern man at his best." His polemic against the alternatives to Right and Left is unrelenting.[44] Elliot Dorff, another leading figure at the University of Judaism, accomplished much the same purpose in his 1978 attempt at a comprehensive explanation of the movement, primarily directed at young people. Dorff's historical survey has the movement developing in response to Reform extremism (the "trefe banquet" figures prominently) and Orthodox inflexibility. "Positive-historical" Judaism, he argues, offered a middle path, one distinguished by its balance of tradition and change.[45]

In the eyes of most of its spokesmen, the movement could make that claim credibly only if it made central what the Rabbis had made central: halakhah. "The first thing that you must understand about the Conservative approach to Jewish law," Dorff counsels his readers, "is that Conservative Judaism requires observance of the laws of classical Judaism."[46] The first substantive chapter of his book (and by far the longest) is concerned with "Jewish Law Within the Conservative Movement." Similarly, *Emet Ve-Emunah* arrives quickly at those points that both unite and distinguish the Conservative movement: "The Indispensability of Halakhah" and "Tradition and Development of Halakhah." The statement explicitly identifies this twin commitment to halakhah and its alteration with "our ancestors" and "the thrust of Jewish tradition."[47] Dorff cites "tradition and change" as "virtually . . . the motto of our movement," noting later that for "the Rabbis," it was not true that "anything goes."[48]

This identification of Conservative Judaism with flexible halakhah above all else has not always been accepted by all factions of the movement, but of late it seems virtually unopposed. When Mordecai Kaplan formulated his understanding of the Conservative consensus in 1947, he offered four principles: the centrality of Israel, the primacy of religion in Jewish life, the commitment to a maximal amount of

Jewish content in public and private observance, and a commitment to *Wissenschaft,* the scientific study of Judaism. He noted two areas of divergence rather than consensus: attitudes toward God and halakhah.[49] As late as 1975, Rabbi Edward Feld objected in the pages of *Conservative Judaism* to a definition of the movement as "halakhic," conceding that "even the most 'Leftist' [Conservative] Rabbis" seemed to include themselves "within the halakhic fold," but only through "a serious misconception of what the halakhic process is." Feld emphasized instead that one could be traditional while not halakhic; that Jewish law to the Rabbis of old had been meaningful because of their belief that God commanded it; that most current practice, even if "traditionalist" was nonhalakhic. (His own path was to look at traditional ritual—say, Sabbath observance—seek to find "the spiritual meaning in its essence," and then fashion "the details of the religious action out of this aggadah.") Feld's Kaplanian position was a minority view when published. Today, in Conservative writings, it is virtually absent.[50]

For Kaplan's Reconstructionist approach is now outside the Conservative movement rather than within. Gerson Cohen had not been alone in celebrating the fact that, with Reconstructionism a separate movement, Conservatism was free to shift back to its classical position at the center.[51] In fact, it seems to have done so decisively in the past two decades; the key words in its rhetorical lexicon of late have been *halakhah, tradition* and *pluralism.*

The invocation of pluralism is necessary for Conservatives on two counts. First, while Conservative thinkers can criticize the Orthodox for insufficient flexibility, they cannot deny that Orthodoxy as well represents an authentic voice of Jewish tradition. Their object is rather to make room *alongside* Orthodoxy for the Conservative approach. Halakhically, this is accomplished by arguing that human interpretation is the only means for learning about God's will and that such interpretation can never be monolithic. Conservative thinkers are fond of citing the talmudic "Tanur shel Akhnai" story in which a voice from heaven that cites the correct halakhah is rebuffed by Rabbi Joshua, "It [the Law] is not [determined] in heaven" (Baba Meẓiyah: 59b). As Dorff puts it, "The Rabbis clearly and consciously shifted the operation of the law from the Prophets to the Judges, from revelation to interpretation."[52] Authentic interpreters can and will disagree; "these and these are the words of the living God" (Eruvin: 13b).

By this reasoning, Conservative jurists are in fact *more* like the Rabbis of old than their Orthodox colleagues because the Conservatives are more willing to disagree with the Rabbis. Where the medievals, and now the Orthodox, regard themselves as "immensely inferior to the Rabbis of the Mishnah," Dorff writes, "we do not see ourselves bound by the specific decisions of the Rabbis of any generation." The Conservative method rather "reflects tradition" in the way its rabbis determine Jewish law. "I firmly believe," he concludes, "that we are doing exactly what the tradition would have us do, if only we master the personal qualities necessary to carry out our program wisely." Dorff follows this statement with a footnote referring to the Rabbis' comments on the same "It is not in heaven" prooftext found in the "Tanur shel Akhnai" story.[53] The message, in short, is that it ill befits any movement that claims adherence to the tradition to break with halakhah—and equally ill befits any movement to claim that it alone can determine halakhah, let alone claim to speak for God.

The second locus for pluralism in the movement, not coincidentally the second ground of its divergence from Orthodoxy, concerns the meaning of "Torah from Heaven." Neil Gillman, the Seminary faculty member who perhaps best articulates the "left wing" inside the new halakhic consensus, insists in his 1983 effort to define "a theology for Conservative Judaism" that "it is beyond question that throughout its history, Judaism recognized the legitimacy of theological pluralism." Abraham Heschel's *Torah min hashamayim* (1962) had proven "that the contemporary traditionalist view" of revelation "far from exhausts the range of options reflected in that literature." Buber's dispute with Rosenzweig about revelation and law had demonstrated "how a shared theology of revelation can yield vividly contrasting conclusions on the status and authority of halakhah." Pluralism, in short, Gillman argues, had been the rule rather than the exception in the realm of belief. The Rabbis had tolerated a wide diversity of views on so basic a question as the meaning of revelation. Just as it was wrong to speak of "the halakhah" rather "a halakhah" (for "what becomes halakhah on any one issue is whatever a community and its authorities in fact decide it is"), it was an error to pretend that theological unity had ever been achieved.[54] Dorff, for his part, lists an array of respectable Conservative positions on revelation (some of them held in common with Reform thinkers such as Petuchowski).[55] The very lack of agreement is held by Dorff to make a twofold authenticity in Conservatism that is lacking in Orthodoxy—it is authentic in that the Rabbis, too, had held conflicting views and in that not all Orthodox Jews believe in the "dogma of verbal revelation" proclaimed as essential by the movement's leaders. In short, Dorff implies, Conservatives are more honest.

One sees the same general thrust of combining a heavy dose of "tradition" with evidence of flexibility in the movement's new prayer book *Sim Shalom* (1985) and *Mahzor for Rosh Hashanah and Yom Kippur* (1972). Two voices of the Jewish elite are most helpful in providing a perspective on these two works: Rabbi Jules Harlow, the editor of both, and Jakob Petuchowski, the foremost expert on modern liturgical reform and a strident critic of his own movement's *Gates of Prayer*.

"*Siddur Sim Shalom,*" Petuchowski writes trenchantly, "presupposes that the worshiper wants to participate in the kind of worship which, for the last two thousand years or so, the historical faith-community of Israel has offered to the God of Israel." It does not provide "radical variety"; it is "unashamedly traditional." Yet it is also enlightened and knowledgable, he continues, particularly with regard to what counts as obligatory prayer in rabbinic Judaism as opposed to the "free outpourings of the heart with which later generations have enriched the liturgy." Petuchowski then points to Harlow's principal method of achieving this balance: a Hebrew text substantially identical with the one in use among Orthodox congregations (and amended with great erudition when it is not), combined with an English translation that avails itself of paraphrase, "poetic metaphor," to express "sincerely held belief" at variance with the Hebrew as literally understood. In addition, Harlow has assembled more than seventy pages of readings and meditations from a variety of sources spanning all denominational affiliations. In a gesture toward feminist critics of existing liturgy, *Sim Shalom* avoids male pronouns where possible and adds feminine versions of the prayers said when one puts on tallit and tefillin. In short, "*Sim Shalom* is a liberal, modernist affirmation of traditional Jewish teaching."[56]

Harlow's own preface to the siddur makes it clear that this was precisely his intent. Every Jewish worship service has a formal structure and a prescribed text, he begins. His rationale for prayer, however, is stated in very contemporary language—for example, "prayer, which begins with the self, can move us away from self-centeredness and an unreflective routinization of life."[57] The English readings make it clear, he continues, that doubts or even alienation are not unexpected as the worshiper approaches the prayer to be offered in its more or less traditional Hebrew form.[58]

Indeed, the siddur "works" for the worshiper only if he or she, like Petuchowski, stands more or less where Harlow does on the line of balance between tradition and modernity. If one is more "Orthodox" the meditations will be superfluous, even jarring; if one is more "Reform" (or more a feminist) the Hebrew text may be unprayable, the English meditations insufficient. Harlow has drawn his line to the right of the one expressed by *Gates of Prayer*. Where pluralism is shouted from the rooftops in *Gates of Prayer,* for example, its voice is heard in but a muted form in *Sim Shalom:* The *davener* who uses only Hebrew and never turns to the alternative weekday Amidah may never encounter Rabbi Andre Ungar's meditation, "Help me, O God, to pray."[59]

One cannot know whether *Sim Shalom,* true to the religious situation of its editor and probably of the Conservative elite, accurately reflects the belief and practice of the movement's laity. (Dorff, for one, is driven to concede that with respect to observance of Shabbat and kashruth—two staples of prescribed Conservative practice—the rabbis had generally failed to sway their folk.[60]) *Emet Ve-Emunah,* the Conservative movement's statement of principles, is generally unspecific with regard to belief and observance. Part I of the statement, "God in the World," is devoted largely to explaining Conservatism's stance as a halakhic movement that maintains the legitimacy of competing viewpoints concerning God and revelation and which is committed to halakhic flexibility. Part II, "The Jewish People," contains an inexplicably lengthy section in which the commission members call for an end to the Orthodox monopoly on official religious authority in the state of Israel. While affirming "the central role of Israel," the authors (like their Reform counterparts) argue as well for the vitality and legitimacy of "various centers of Jewish life" and make lengthy reference to the legitimacy of other faiths and Judaism's commitment to social justice. Only in Part III, "Living a Life of Torah," is there a discussion of how Conservative Jews are meant to live, and even here the question is never really answered. The first section is devoted to the status of women (surprisingly so, given that the statement must confess to serious disagreement within the movement on this point) and the second to general pieties concerning "the Jewish home," prayer and study—generalities that could equally well have found their place in the Reform statement. Only at the very end is there included what critics of the movement from within and without have urged for decades: a description of "the ideal Conservative Jew."[61] But instead of finding that such a Jew should strive above all to do A, B, and C for reasons X, Y and Z, we learn instead that "three characteristics mark the ideal Conservative Jew." First, he or she is a "willing Jew," for whom "nothing human or Jewish is alien." Kashruth, Shabbat and holidays are mentioned specifically here, but beyond that there are only generalities—for example, "the Jewish home must be sustained and guided by the ethical insights of our heritage." Second, the ideal Conservative Jew is a "learning Jew." Hebrew literacy is essential. So is acquaintance with contemporary Jewish thought. Finally, he or she is a "striving Jew," open to "those observances one has yet to perform" and "those issues and texts one has yet to confront." One wonders if the statement is not more specific because its authors did not want to read out most of their readers from the movement.

The current chancellor of the seminary, Ismar Schorsch, remarks in his preface to *Emet Ve-Emunah* that what makes the entire statement so intriguing is "the tension that lies beneath the surface." The principal tension seems to relate to the question of how much the elite can or should demand of the folk. Put another way: Should the movement seek to keep the mass base that it attracted in the 1950s and 1960s and struggle for the allegiance of that base against a newly tradition-minded Reform movement? Or, as David Gordis seems to advise in his polemic, should Conservatism rather look to the right and put its efforts into explaining to those Jews affiliated with Orthodoxy (but who dissent from its "rigidity and fundamentalism") that the Conservative way of being halakhic is really more in keeping with their commitments?[62] One wonders whether lay support is to be found on either side. Shorn of its Reconstructionist wing and firmly committed to halakhah, the movement may not appeal to those Reform congregants who are quite content with their movement's renewed traditionalism. But having ordained women rabbis, embraced biblical criticism and propounded a theory of halakhic flexibility, Conservatism may also not have allowed itself any room to attract adherents from the right, who may not actually believe or do all that their elite would want but who prefer to affiliate with an elite that *wants* them to believe and do those things.

In the end, it may be that Shlomo Riskin (then the rabbi of a leading Modern Orthodox congregation in New York City) was right in 1977 when he defined Conservatism's main problem as the lack of a community that actually and visibly lives according to the movement's ideals.[63] Although there are small elite communities of this sort around the Conservative seminaries, the perceived problem of the movement all along has been the inherent elitism of its approach.[64] Dorff's book, which delves into the complexities of various approaches to revelation, only makes implicitly the point that *Emet Ve-Emunah* makes explicit. Namely: Conservative Judaism is distinguished by its method of adjusting halakhah to contemporary conditions, but that process "requires thorough knowledge of both Halakhah and the contemporary scene as well as carefully honed skills of judgment."[65] It requires, in other words, an elite that really understands what the movement is about, and a laity willing to accede to that elite's authority. This is not a recipe for success in egalitarian, antiauthoritarian America. "Tradition" is valued (and obeyed) only up to a point. The only way to win a laity's allegiance under such conditions is to provide them with a tangible, attractive reality shaped by Conservative commit-ments. But this is impossible, for reasons explored above, and so the circle is not broken.

Conservatism, in sum, has staked its claim to the center in the last two decades more forcefully than ever before, arguing its middle position on grounds of halakhic flexibility and aggadic pluralism. It may well find, however, that these grounds are beyond the understanding of the laity—that the center as the Conservative elite understands it is not where most American Jews now want to stand.

Reconstructionism: Language, Myth and Community

For Reconstructionism, which claims the allegiance of perhaps one percent of American Jewry, minority status is a given, not a problem. It is therefore free to strike out in new directions, mandated by its elite, that will be followed by those few among the folk (primarily in the cohort that reached maturity in the 1960s and 1970s) who find these directions meaningful. Even in Reconstructionism, however, there is a striking disparity between elite and folk. For one thing, the intention of the current elite is to shape the movement in a way quite different from the one first envisioned by its founder, Mordecai Kaplan. In addition, there is a clear paradox between the stated aim of the movement—that of "maximalist Judaism," demand-ing a significant degree of knowledge and commitment—and the nature of the following to which the movement today largely appeals, which in the main is new to Judaism, unversed in its ways and unwilling to involve itself in the serious commu-nal obligation demanded by Reconstructionism's elite.

The contrast between the former Kaplanian tenor of the movement and the new approach being formulated by the current president of the Reconstructionist Rab-binical College, Arthur Green, is evident when one compares recent essays by Green with a statement of the movement's aims that appeared as recently as 1988 but was composed before Green's innovations had taken root. The statement of aims, *Exploring Judaism: A Reconstructionist Approach,* begins with a historical survey of Kaplan's efforts to create a new kind of Judaism in America, continues with a summary of his understanding of Judaism as an "evolving religious civiliza-tion" and then examines in detail Kaplan's reconception of divinity. "Many Recon-structionists have difficulty accepting Kaplan's approach to God in all of its facets," the authors state, "and it is not necessary to do so to identify with the Reconstruc-tionist movement." Even the "experience of God as a Person" can find a place inside the movement "as long as it does not include affirmation of Torah-from-Sinai and direct supernatural intervention in our individual lives."[66]

The contrast with Reform and Conservatism here is quite apparent. While the latter two movements stress the multiple possible interpretations of "Torah from Sinai," Reconstructionism rather implies that its meaning is apparent—and un-acceptable. It has no hesitation in unequivocally excluding possible affiliates on the basis of their (traditional!) beliefs about God. Those Reconstructionists who do speak of God in personal terms or even address God in prayer are not in fact subscribing to beliefs that they, like Kaplan, reject. Rather, they are using "traditional formulations because of their mythic and poetic power to move us."[67]

The remainder of this volume is strictly Kaplanian in tone. Chapter 4 is even titled with one of Kaplan's more memorable formulations of Reconstructionist policy, "The Past Has a Vote, Not a Veto." In this chapter, the authors lament the definition of halakhah as a "rigid body of law, changeable only under rarefied circumstances," rather than as "the Jewish process of transmitting tradition"—in which case Reconstructionism, too, could be defined as a halakhic movement. Chapter 5, "Living in Two Civilizations," is likewise devoted to a faithful explication of the master's teaching, while Chapter 6, "Zion as a Spiritual Center," sets forth the Kaplanian formulation of dual centers now standard in all four movements. "Suggestions for Further Reading" refer readers by and large to the writings of Mordecai Kaplan.

One gets a somewhat different picture of the movement if one reads the essays published recently by Green, whose approach was adumbrated in a 1976 address before Conservative rabbis in which he urged them to join him in the "seeking out of contemporary theological meaning in the sources of Jewish mystical experience." Green's suggestion was twofold. First, where neither rationalism nor the rabbinic effort to discern God's involvement in history has been of use in confronting the Holocaust, Jewish mysticism—particularly that of Rabbi Nahman of Bratslav—has offered valuable assistance. If *zimzum* (divine self-contraction) is taken seriously, there is a substantial portion of reality from which God is absent, "a level of truth on which God does not exist." On this level, the one we moderns know from experience, one cannot find God because God is not there: "Only by confronting the void and transcending it do we find God." Second, Green argued, there is a need to recognize that, even without the Holocaust, many traditional beliefs, such as covenant, would have proven alien. Here, too, he said, Rabbi Nahman can be our guide in reminding us that knowledge of God comes first and foremost from inner experience. Thus, while God cannot be claimed as the "direct author of our traditions," we can "let ourselves be guided by the great depths of faith" that Judaism has fostered.[68]

More recent essays enlarge upon these themes. In fact, Green argues, one source of contemporary difficulties with faith is the lack of authentic language in which to talk about God—this despite the presence, in our mystical-Hasidic tradition, of a rich vocabulary "for discussion of religious states." Green sets out to provide such a language, always stressing that contemporary Jews must remain both "insiders" and "outsiders" in relation to Jewish tradition. The task here is "spiritual wakefulness and awareness," "cultivation of the inner life," a higher level of insight. "Not faith, but vision is what such a religion demands."[69] The language is strictly contemporary, born of the counterculture and authentically fused, in Green's own religiosity, with elements of Hasidic theology.

That fusion enables him to describe a viewpoint that is "that of mystic and naturalist at once"—in other words, appropriate both to the new Reconstructionism and to the old. God, YHWH, is all of being, "the universe so utterly transformed by integration and unity as to appear to us as indeed 'other,' a mirror of the universe's self that becomes Universal Self." We picture God in personal terms and then pray to God because we must; more precisely, the need to pray generates the pictures necessary to our praying. "'God' is in that sense a symbol, a human creation that we need to use in order to illuminate for ourselves, however inadequately, some tiny portion of the infinite mystery."[70] Green and Kaplan can agree, then, on what in rational terms cannot be true. They disagree on whether those terms should predominate in our religious lives—most particularly, in our religious language.

A second important shift in the new Reconstructionism is the way in which it places religion (the dimension of spirituality, the search for higher awareness) squarely at the center, building outward from it. The religious life makes demands upon our behavior that we express in the mitzvot; we choose Jewish tradition rather than some other because it is "our spiritual home"; we choose as much of Jewish tradition as we possibly can because "traditions work best when they are least diluted."[71] Green is correct in pointing to agreement with Kaplan on the latter points, but his thrust is radically at variance with Kaplan's. The master, seeking to win back Jews by convincing them that Judaism encompassed far more than "religion," put the emphasis upon other aspects of Jewish life. Green, seeking to win back Jews in search of transcendent meaning, reemphasizes the essentially spiritual character of Jewish commitment. "Inner life" is primary, "civilization" is taken for granted.

Hence the importance of the movement's projected series of new prayer books, which are intended at once to give a sense of what "inner life" is and to direct its cultivation. The problems with this attempt are apparent in the recently issued draft of the first prayer book, *Kol Haneshamah,* consisting of prayers for Shabbat eve.[72] This siddur presumes a serious and functioning community in which experiments with liturgy can be confidently undertaken and new liturgy actually created. It also presumes a laity sufficiently at home with the act of prayer and the traditional content of prayer to know just how to experiment without destroying all connection to the Jewish past. ("While experimentation is certainly called for," Green has written, "a sense of authenticity and deep-rootedness in tradition . . . should not be sacrificed.")[73] *Kol Haneshamah,* by far the most creative prayer book to emerge from any movement in decades, is explicitly a group effort and yet informed by a single sensibility. It may prove to be an effort by and for an elite; the focus here, however, will be on what that elite has apparently sought to articulate.

First, despite the avowal that the siddur's readings "are not didactic; they are meant to help us discover what is ready to be revealed within ourselves" (a degree of 1960s jargon that no other movement would permit itself), it is also noted in the introduction that "a large number of those who will use the new prayer book have little knowledge of the structure or history of the siddur."[74] The siddur thus includes many quite elementary notes of explanation, and (like *Gates of Prayer*) often seems to be addressed to the person who prays rather than to God. (This of course is appropriate if, as Kaplan maintained, we ourselves are the true intended audience for prayer, not the God whom we purport to address.) On occasion this turn to the worshiper comes in the form of notes that explain why a traditional prayer has been altered or retained. A series of meditations offered as an alternative to the Amidah, for example, directs us to "allow yourself to feel gratitude and joy," or "allow yourself to feel the holiness of all life," and so on—thereby rendering explicit the engendering of particular moods that all prayer implicitly attempts.[75] At other points, despite their avowed shunning of didacticism, the authors have inserted notes that use prayer to drive home an ideological point (e.g., we are told that the tetragrammaton "hints at the absurdity of assigning a name to an ineffable divinity").[76]

Ideology is most evident in the book's most experimental feature, an alternative and feminist Amidah composed by the contemporary poet and scholar Marcia Falk. Theologically, Falk breaks new ground by creating Hebrew and English prayers that do not mention, let alone address, any deity. "Let us bless" replaces "Blessed are you, O Lord," and "Let us hallow the Sabbath day in remembrance of creation" replaces a blessing of God "who hallows the Sabbath."[77] The nature of creation is left unspecified. The liturgy also goes much further than any other siddur of the four movements in articulating "an inclusive feminist approach to the themes of the service." The "avot" section of the Amidah becomes "re-calling our ancestors, re-membering our lives," the re-callers and the re-called being Jewish women. Leah Goldberg's poem "From My Mother's House" begins this section, and it is soon followed by Malka Heifetz Tussman's "I Am a Woman." Feminist themes are less evident in the remainder of the Amidah, but the imagery and language rigorously avoid the masculine.

Falk guides the worshiper's reflection with a strong hand, and not only in her new blessings and her selection of poetry. For example, she explains at the start of the "avot" section that "Re-calling our past, we re-member our selves, making the branches part of the whole again."[78] Every liturgy seeks to shape the mood and reflection of the worshiper. In *Kol Haneshamah*, the authors do so openly and unreservedly, to the point where prayer sometimes seems advocacy for one position rather than another. Falk's Amidah, precisely because of its "inclusive language," drives home the *exclusion* of traditional theists that was encountered in *Exploring Reconstructionism*. If you seek encounter with a personal God here rather than introspective meditation, says this Amidah, look elsewhere—much as (it might add) Jews put off by sexist or hierarchical language are still excluded by more traditional prayer books, including those recently issued by Conservatism and Reform. As noted, however, *Kol Haneshamah* also contains an alternative liturgy that is quite traditional. This alternative is deft in its integration of contemporary concerns such as the Holocaust into received liturgical texts.[79]

In sum: With the Reform movement having embraced Zionism, Hebrew, ritual and *havurot*, and with Reconstructionism having joined Reform in opting for "patrilineal descent," the Reconstructionist elite has rendered itself distinctive by proving more venturesome than Reform in the realm of liturgy and more creative in the realm of theology. It has apparently targeted two groups as potential adherents: disaffected members on the "Left" of the Reform and Conservative movements; and those among the unaffiliated who are drawn to the new Reconstructionist spirituality. The main obstacle to Reconstructionism's growth is that it in fact demands *more* from its adherents than any other movement, stressing the need for constant "revitalization, reevaluation [and] repair" of Judaism on the part of all Jews and demanding a true community in which "no one's duty may be done vicariously by others."[80] It is also not clear that those whom Reconstructionism now seeks to attract are interested in a Judaism focused once again on an element that Kaplan had displaced from the center—religion. If Nathan Glazer's classic analysis still holds, most American Jews prefer Jewishness (an ethnic identity conferring a sense of transcendence) to Judaism (faith more strictly understood).[81] The quintessential movement of American "Jewishness" now seeks to move American Jews back to a creative and demanding Judaism—and may well find that only the elite is capable of that transformation, or even concerned that it occur.

Modern Orthodoxy: The Triumphant Under Siege

When *Tradition* magazine polled a group of leading Modern Orthodox rabbis and intellectuals in 1982 about "the state of Orthodoxy today,"[82] three concerns seemed paramount in the mind of the editor and his respondents. First, to combat the smugness and triumphalism that they perceived among Orthodox Jews following the movement's resurgence in the past two decades—a resurgence that, to the journal's delight, had confounded widespread predictions of Orthodoxy's imminent decline. Second, to shore up the defenses of Modern Orthodoxy against the continuing assault upon its legitimacy emanating from more traditionalist Orthodox circles.[83] Third, despite repeated calls for more intellectual openness—in other words, for palpable distance from the Orthodox Right—many of the participants seemed concerned to establish that Orthodoxy, whether modern or traditionalist, constituted a single movement, albeit not a "monolithic" one. The mark of that unity, more often than not, was held to be commitment to halakhah as codified in the Shulhan Arukh.

Limits of space and competence preclude detailed treatment of Modern Orthodoxy in the compass of this essay, and the same limits—plus the fact that the elite of traditionalist Orthodoxy does not interact intellectually with the other three movements—place the latter outside our purview altogether. Nonetheless, the movement of Modern Orthodoxy's elite in the past two decades can be gauged by an examination of the *Tradition* symposium, the decision of the Modern Orthodox rabbinic association to adopt a new siddur for use in its synagogues, and a recent (and representative) essay in *Tradition* magazine by the president of Yeshiva University, Orthodoxy's principal institution. To say that the elite has "moved right" would be simplistic and perhaps even wrong. One should rather note its refusal, in the wake of challenge from the right, either to move left (thereby making room for Conservative Jews disgruntled by their movement's embrace of egalitarianism) or to articulate its own long-stated commitments (personified in the leadership of Rabbi Joseph Soloveitchik) more forcefully.

For all its complaints about the Right, Modern Orthodoxy has benefited from the latter's perceived success. If the *Tradition* symposium is an accurate indication, Modern Orthodoxy also seeks to claim the Jewish center as its own. (It may be recalled that Reform positions itself rhetorically between assimilators and fundamentalists, Conservatism between Reform and Orthodoxy.) *Tradition*'s respondents spoke of two tendencies in Jewish life—insulation from the world and too much being in it—with Orthodoxy as the "party of the middle";[84] and of the mainstream and extremes present in every period of Jewish history, with Modern Orthodoxy currently constituting the "most legitimate expression of authentic Judaism."[85] Philosopher and theologian Michael Wyschogrod called Orthodoxy (presumably in its modern form) "most clearly continuous with classical Jewish self-understanding," and the "self-conscious heart of the people of Israel.[86] The presence of the Right is indispensable to the definition of the center.

Without that presence, moreover, the definition of the Orthodox center might have taken a form less conducive to distinction from Conservatism. Aharon Lichtenstein's description of Orthodoxy as "consistent halakhic living"[87] is rather ambiguous, "consistency" existing primarily in the eye of the beholder. His intent is self-evident only because his category includes traditionalist Orthodox Jews whose notion of "consistency" is not open to confusion with Conservatism. Marc Angel's suggestion that Orthodoxy is united by belief in the divine authority of Torah[88] leaves open the question of what precisely that means—and must leave this matter open if Yeshiva University graduates and Borough Park hasidim are to be counted in the same grouping. Indeed, as seen previously, the Conservative elite generally distinguishes itself from Orthodoxy and Reform on precisely this theological ground, arguing that the latter rejects belief in the Torah's divine authority while the former understands it too narrowly. The Modern Orthodox elite might have been tempted to stress the matter more were it not for this counterclaim by Conservatism and the recognition that, if put to the test, it would have to confess that traditionalist Orthodoxy is, as Conservatism charges, far too fundamentalist. Hence the preferred differentiation put forward by Immanuel Jakobovits: commitment to the Shulhan Arukh.[89] This marker highlights Conservative deviation (in the name of the Sages of the Mishnah and the Talmud) from halakhah as codified by the medievals. Conservative Jews call themselves halakhic, reads the subtext, but just look at what they do. For example, they ordain women as rabbis.

A comparison of *Tradition* with the organs of other movements—*Journal of Reform Judaism, Conservative Judaism* and *The Reconstructionist*—reveals far more concern with halakhic applications in contemporary life, a more reverent (even apologetic) stress on classical and medieval sources and less engagement with recent intellectual approaches such as anthropology and literary criticism. Sustained attention is also given (in a variety of ways) to the issue of Jewish faith, science and the lack of conflict between them—a matter that for the elites of other movements is apparently no longer a live issue. It is perhaps worthwhile to take a brief look here at a representative essay from *Tradition*—one that, like many others, approaches a matter of considerable contemporary interest through an historical and philosophical investigation of halakhah: Norman Lamm's "Loving and Hating Jews as Halakhic Categories" (1989).[90]

Lamm accepts the question as defined in halakhic sources, assuming that the biblical injunction to "love your neighbor as yourself" applies only to Jews and that it is a problematic injunction because Jews are also commanded to combat evil and injustice. In more concrete terms, what happens if certain Jews reject the fundamentals of their faith and its practice? Must one love them or hate them? Lamm carefully examines an array of halakhic authorities, the focus being Maimonides (who, as both philosopher and halakhist, personifies the synthesis for which Modern

Orthodoxy strives). Lamm concludes, on four grounds, that one must love fellow Jews even if they do not accept the fundamentals of Judaism. Two grounds originate in opinions from previous authorities: that the modern zeitgeist represents a sort of "coercion" that frees heterodox Jews from full responsibility for their behavior; moreover, the lack of "proper rebuke"—a warning that leads to full understanding of what their heterodoxy involves—precludes invoking all the punitive sanctions for which the law provides. To these Lamm adds two further considerations: Doubt of fundamental beliefs does not constitute actual rejection; and the fact that, in his view of the halakhah, removal of apostates from Jewry's midst makes sense only when the great majority of Jews are observant and God-fearing, such that heresy constitutes a demonstrable denial of Jewish identity. This, Lamm concludes, is not so in our time.

This article simply could not have appeared in the journal of any other movement; any article written on the same subject (and many may have been, over the years) would have to have had very different contents. Would the elites of other movements have accepted the classical rabbinic position that "love of neighbor" applies only to Jews—or insisted on a change in light of present circumstances? Would they have arrogated to themselves the right to judge who stands inside and outside the borders of true faith—or argued on historical grounds that those borders were never fixed precisely, were not always fixed in the same way and, furthermore, there was also a principle of pluralism to consider that urged respect for those whose Jewish self-understanding was at variance with their own? Would they have taken the tradition on its own terms, or invoked, say, the anthropologist Mary Douglas's insight in *Purity and Danger* (1966) on how groups maintain boundaries, or that of her colleague, Clifford Geertz, on the functioning of religious ideology? These questions are of course rhetorical, pointing to the distinctive character of Lamm's essay and, by extension, of his movement. A more traditionalist Orthodox figure would likely have approached the subject in somewhat different fashion, perhaps denying Maimonides pride of place and paying more attention to codes such as the Shulhan Arukh as well as specifying (as Lamm does not) precisely what the fundamentals of faith are and who, even among the Orthodox, currently violate them.

One can only speculate on what, if any, influence the viewpoint of traditionalists has had on an article such as Lamm's. In at least one important instance, however, traditionalist influence has been clear. The Rabbinical Council of America recently replaced its authorized siddur (edited by David De Sola Pool in 1960 and accepted as the movement's official prayer book, after much hesitation, a decade later) with the *Complete Artscroll Siddur,* edited by Nosson Scherman and originally published in 1984.[91] Where the De Sola Pool siddur, in the words of one (Reform) scholar, conveyed a message of modernity and science that led to its rejection by Orthodox Jews opposed to liturgical renewal, the *Artscroll* siddur, in the words of a (Conservative) scholar, "traces its inspiration to rabbis associated with the rightist yeshivah world." Transliterations from the Hebrew are in "Ashkenazis" rather than the Sephardic form; down-to-earth idiom ("A mind-boggling investment of time and resources was required to make this Siddur a reality") replaces the dignity and decorum of the previous siddur; the latter's minimal notation, generally providing historical information, has given way in the *Artscroll* siddur to voluminous commentary from rabbinic and kabbalistic sources. We are told, without even a bow to *Wissenschaft,* that the Shemoneh Esrei was authored by "one of the most august bodies in history, the Men of the Great Assembly," that the "entire leadership of the nation" took the task of composing the liturgy upon itself, and that as a result "every word and syllable has a thousand effects in ways we cannot imagine."[92]

Sophistication as defined in the university world is not a value; in Brooklyn's yeshivah world one need not fear the reverberations of the claim that "women, on the other hand, both historically and because of their nature, are the guardians of tradition, the molders of character, children, and family." Almost every prayer comes with a preface and/or commentary on its meaning. Mystical interpretation is unabashed. "The twenty-two sacred letters [of the Hebrew alphabet] are profound, primal, spiritual forces. They are, in effect, the raw material of Creation."[93]

One cannot say with certainty, no survey having been undertaken, how Modern Orthodox congregants have received the *Artscroll* siddur. Nor can one say how the Modern Orthodox elite has received it less than a decade after *Tradition* published a blistering and even nasty critique of the *Artscroll* Bible series that emphasized (in boldface type), "Artscroll is not modern," "Artscroll is not scientific," "Artscroll is not scholarly," and so on[94]—in other words, that the Artscroll series does not live up to norms that *we,* as Modern Orthodox Jews accept, and *they,* more traditionalist Jews, do not. Adoption of the siddur, however, does seem to support the frequent depiction of Orthodoxy's "shift to the right," this despite the inclination of many intellectuals (witness the *Tradition* symposium and the thrust of many of its articles) to define and hold to the center, thereby taking up the challenge of Conservatism. Once again, a movement is seen to be standing at a crossroads. Time alone will tell whether the Orthodox center holds—or whether it moves, with demography and the prevailing winds, to the right.

Conclusion

What, then, is it possible to learn from this brief overview? Principally, that several oft-heard characterizations of American Judaism seem to be at best premature, and probably wrong.

To begin with, whatever its merits in the Orthodox case, the generalization of a "shift to the right" is simply not applicable to the other movements. Reform, as has been seen, has reinstated the language of mitzvah, the use of Hebrew and the importance of ritual. But it has done so in a context of pluralism and has not renounced the principle of individual or congregational autonomy. What is more, it has accomplished its "return to ritual" in the absence of any theological transformation, thereby conveying the message that the laity should not regard theological issues as paramount but rather set aside their problems with faith in favor of study and observances that, if they prove meaningful, need no further justification. Mitzvot are to be undertaken piecemeal rather than as a whole, just as one can pick and choose from the lengthy and varied menu of the *Gates of Prayer* services. Reconstructionism, too, has returned to a more traditional language, replacing Kaplan's borrowings from Emile Durkheim and John Dewey with the Zohar and

Rabbi Nahman. Yet it has bracketed this language in another one, the modern understanding of myth and symbol, in the hope that Jews freed of the requirement to think literally will be able, paradoxically, to think more traditionally. As the authors put it in their preface to the new Reconstructionist siddur, "Fears that more traditional worship styles inevitably carry with them more traditional theology have been put to rest."[95]

Conservatism, too, has not moved right, despite its freedom (thanks to the exodus of Reconstructionists from its ranks) to define itself more strictly in terms of halahkah and "Torah from Heaven." True, the current tendency of the elite is to demand more observance from the laity, to appeal to Modern Orthodox disquiet with its movement's move to the right, and to concede the Left to Reform. But the elite has also increasingly proclaimed its readiness for significant halakhic innovation—witness the decisive break with Orthodoxy represented by the ordination of women rabbis. All four movements have altered their self-presentation in the past two decades, then, but only Orthodoxy has moved to the right. Even there, as has been seen, there is much disquiet among the Modern Orthodox elite, and growing doubts (expressed by several participants in the *Tradition* symposium) that Orthodoxy can be described anymore as a single, unified movement.

Second, while there is ample support for Petuchowski's observation that "American Conservative Judaism, rather than American Reform Judaism, is carrying on the tradition of German Liberal Judaism,"[96] there seems no evidence to support the comment that denominational lines in the United States are no longer relevant. The Reform Right, it is true, often shares a great deal with the Conservative Left (or even center) and some Reconstructionists; the Conservative center, and of course those who have opposed women's ordination, share much with Modern Orthodoxy. But although individual members of the various elites may pray together, members of the various congregations are certainly united with affiliates of other movements by ties of marriage and friendship, and the rabbis of various movements frequently cooperate on communal matters, the ideological lines dividing the movements do in fact remain.

Reform still lays claim to the mantle of the Prophets, Conservatism to the Sages, and Orthodoxy to a combination of Maimonides and the Shulhan Arukh. (Reconstructionism, the "wild card" in this respect, has apparently abandoned the Jewish rationalist tradition in favor of the mystical.) Reform thinkers cite Abraham Geiger and stress Martin Buber and Franz Rosenzweig, while Conservative thinkers tend to draw on Rosenzweig and Heschel, and the Orthodox on halakhic authorities and "the Rav," Joseph Soloveitchik. Reform Jews still carry the marks of their history, evident for example in Borowitz's presentation of Liberal Judaism, just as Reconstructionists will never entirely discharge the legacy of Kaplan and Conservative Jews will continue to emphasize the fragile union between halakhah and *Wissenschaft*. Orthodox Jews perhaps invoke the shibboleth of "tradition" so much less than the other movements because they are so thoroughly identified with it— the Modern Orthodox in fact being burdened by identification with more right-wing Orthodox "traditionalists." In short, the existing markers remain in place, and what is more, all four movements have moved of late to sharpen the lines when they have been in danger of becoming blurred. Gunther Plaut's prediction of a merger between the Rabbinical Assembly and the Central Conference of American Rabbis[97] seems to be wishful thinking by a member of the Reform Right more at home with like-minded Conservative colleagues than with the Left of his own movement. More than organizational inertia will prevent such a merger if the analysis offered here is correct; the competing ideological thrusts are too powerful to permit it.

Finally, it seems that recent reevaluations of Nathan Glazer's classic analysis of American Judaism are correct in faulting him for overemphasizing the ethnic concerns that he called "Jewishness" and underestimating the vitality of more strictly religious concerns, which he called "Judaism."[98] Unlike Glazer and his critics, this essay makes reference only to the elites of American Judaism. But in their case, at least, there can be no doubt that religion—in the sense of concern with transcendent meaning and encounter with God—is of paramount importance, even if theology in the sense of rigorous, systematic articulation of belief continues to be fragmentary or even absent. It will not do, at least for the elite, to attribute Orthodoxy's revival exclusively to sociological factors such as the growing preference for parochial rather than public schools, the growing strength of Orthodoxy in Israel or the ability of American manufacturers to accommodate small interest groups such as those who demand kosher products.[99] Such factors are not irrelevant, of course, but neither are they predominant. The elites examined here are engaged in the exercise that has preoccupied religious Jewish intellectuals throughout the modern period: the search for intellectually credible and traditionally authentic syntheses between the Jewish past as they understand that past and those aspects of modernity they have come to value.

Survey data and sociological analysis of the laity will of course find less evidence of that search, while examination of American Jewish theology more strictly understood (a decidedly elitist enterprise) will find the concern with synthesis to be predominant. The present essay, looking at "ideological" materials in which the elite presents itself both to itself and to the folk, has in the nature of the case focused both on organizational needs for distinctive self-definition and on the quest by elites of the various movements to shape those movements in a way that satisfied their own needs and desires. Glazer is still inclined to believe that in Orthodoxy and Conservatism concern with Judaism is predominant, whereas in Reform and Reconstructionism Jewishness holds sway.[100] However, no such generalization is possible on empirical grounds. Indeed, the distinction between Jewishness and Judaism will become increasingly impossible if the elites succeed in making observance of sacred ritual and the study of sacred texts key components of Jewishness, irrespective of theological belief, and if they describe Jewish existence itself after the Holocaust—whether religious or secular, in Israel or in the United States—as a demonstration of the ultimate mystery underlying Jewish destiny. A certain skepticism has been expressed here concerning the elite's chances of remaking the folk in its image, but the effort is not foolish or hopeless, and such evidence as we have about the laity indicates that it finds Judaism most satisfactory when it emphasizes the transcendent meaning of Jewish history to which Holocaust and Israeli statehood bear witness.[101] Jewishness and Judaism are increasingly interrelated, and in a time of immense transformations in American Judaism, this may prove the most significant transformation of all.

Notes

1. This present essay builds upon the survey by Jack Wertheimer, "Recent Trends in American Judaism," *American Jewish Yearbook* 89 (Philadelphia: 1989), 63–162. Its methodology follows the one employed in Arnold Eisen, *The Chosen People in America: A Study in Jewish Religious Ideology* (Bloomington: 1983).
2. Charles Liebman, *The Ambivalent American Jew* (Philadelphia: 1973), ch. 1.
3. Wertheimer, "Recent Trends in American Judaism," 86.
4. Lawrence Hoffman, *Beyond the Test: A Holistic Approach to Liturgy* (Bloomington: 1987), 67. I agree wholeheartedly with Hoffman's argument that the study of liturgy must involve far more than texts; among other things, it must also deal with the authors, worshipers and social context.
5. Wertheimer, "Recent Trends in American Judaism," 63.
6. See Eisen, *Chosen People in America*, ch. 3.
7. W. Gunther Plaut, "Reform Judaism—Past, Present and Future," *Journal of Reform Judaism* (Summer 1980), 8. Plaut was referring to the CCAR's *A Shabbat Manual* (New York: 1972).
8. Gunther Plaut, "Foreword" to *Gates of Mitzvah*, ed. Simeon J. Maslin (New York: 1979), ix.
9. Maslin (ed.), *Gates of Mitzvah*, 3, emphasis added.
10. The 1976 statement is conveniently available in Eugene Borowitz, *Reform Judaism Today*, vol. 1 (New York: 1978), xix–xxv.
11. Maslin (ed.), *Gates of Mitzvah*, 4.
12. *Ibid.*, 11.
13. *Ibid.*, 40.
14. *Ibid.*, 11–16, 30, 37–38, 41, 51, 54–62.
15. *Ibid.*, 100–103.
16. *Ibid.*, 104–107.
17. *Ibid.*, 108–110.
18. See the bibliography in Wertheimer, "Recent Trends in American Judaism," 102n. The comments made in the present essay about *Gates of Mitzvah* apply equally well to the companion volume, *Gates of the Seasons*, ed. Peter S. Knobel (New York: 1983).
19. Knobel (ed.), *Gates of the Seasons*, 21.
20. See, e.g., Leon I. Feuer, "Some Reflections on the State of Reform Judaism," *Journal of Reform Judaism* (Summer 1980), 22–31. Debates on the merits of "Reform halakhah" fill the pages of the CCAR's *Yearbook* and journals in the past two decades.
21. Knobel (ed.), *Gates of the Seasons*, 52.
22. On this point, see Hoffman, *Beyond the Text*, particularly chs. 1 and 4, to which my own analysis is greatly indebted. I have also benefited from a fine analysis of *Gates of Prayer* by David Ellenson, "Reform Judaism in Present-Day America: The Evidence of the Gates of Prayer," forthcoming in a volume honoring Rabbi Seymour J. Cohen. The views of the Reform elite concerning its new prayer book—before, during and after its publication—have been gleaned from the following: Jakob J. Petuchowski, "New Directions in Reform Liturgy," *Journal of the CCAR*, no. 2 (1969), 26–34; "Gates of Prayer" [a symposium], *Journal of the CCAR* (Spring 1973), 73–91; "Report of the Liturgy Committee," *Yearbook of the CCAR* (1976), 47–51; "A Critique of *Gates of Prayer*," in *ibid.*, 115–126; "*Gates of Prayer:* Ten Years Later—A Symposium," *Journal of Reform Judaism* (Fall 1985), 13–61. See also, of course, the siddur itself, *Gates of Prayer: The New Union Prayerbook*, ed. Chaim Stern (New York: 1975), and the explanatory volume, *Gates of Understanding*, ed. Lawrence Hoffman (New York: 1977), which contains historical and theological essays on Reform worship as well as "Notes to Shaarei Tefillah" [Gates of Prayer] by Chaim Stern and A. Stanley Dreyfus. Finally, a comparable analysis could be written of the Reform mahzor, *Gates of Repentance*, ed. Chaim Stern (New York: 1977), and its explanatory volume, *Gates of Understanding 2*, ed. Chaim Stern (New York: 1984). The output of prayer books, guides and explanatory volumes is truly prodigious.

23. Sefton Temkin, "The Reform Liturgy," *Conservative Judaism* (Fall 1975), 17.

24. "*Gates of Prayer:* Ten Years Later."

25. Stern (ed.), *Gates of Prayer*, 246–247. On the rationale for this service, see *idem, Gates of Understanding*, 175.

26. Richard N. Levy in "*Gates of Prayer:* Ten Years Later," 26–28.

27. Herbert Bronstein in *ibid.*, 18.

28. See Jakob J. Petuchowski, *History of Prayer Book Reform in Europe* (New York: 1968), and the perceptive review by Yosef Heinemann in *Tarbiẓ* 39 (1969), 218–221. Petuchowski's comments on *Gates of Prayer* appear in "*Gates of Prayer:* Ten Years Later," 33–34, and (implicitly) in his review of the new Conservative prayer book, "*Siddur Sim Shalom,*" *Conservative Judaism* (Winter 1985/1986), 82–87.

29. Bronstein in "*Gates of Prayer:* Ten Years Later," 17.

30. Levy in *ibid.*, 27.

31. Eugene Borowitz, *Liberal Judaism* (New York: 1984). Hoffman calls Borowitz the theological presence behind *Gates of Prayer* in *Gates of Understanding*, 6.

32. Borowitz, *Liberal Judaism*, 129–136.

33. *Ibid.*, 95, 125.

34. *Ibid.*, 296.

35. *Ibid.*, 125.

36. *Ibid.*, 331.

37. Plaut, "Reform Judaism," 7.

38. William G. Braude, "Recollections and an Attempt to Project," *Journal of Reform Judaism* (Summer 1980), 14.

39. Feuer, "Reflections on the State of Reform Judaism," 27.

40. For the "outside" critique, see Marshall Sklare, *Conservative Judaism: An American Religious Movement* (New York: 1972). See also the evaluation of Sklare's book, with a rejoinder by Sklare, in *American Jewish History* 74, no. 2 (Dec. 1984), 102–168. For the critique within the movement, see Robert Gordis, "The Struggle for Self-Definition in Conservative Judaism," *Conservative Judaism* (Spring 1987), 7–19, and Gordis's introduction to *Emet Ve-Emunah: Statement of Principles of Conservative Judaism* (New York: 1988), 7–16, as well as the foreword to the statement by Kassel Abelson, 1–4.

41. Gordis, *Emet Ve-Emunah*, 8–9.

42. *Ibid.*, 10.

43. Gerson Cohen in "Conservative Judaism on its Ninetieth Birthday: An Evaluation," *Judaism* (symposium issue, Summer 1977), 268.

44. David M. Gordis, "Communicating Conservative Judaism," *Conservative Judaism* (Spring 1978), 16–22.

45. Elliot Dorff, *Conservative Judaism: Our Ancestors to Our Descendants* (New York: 1977), 11–29.

46. *Ibid.*, 60.

47. *Emet Ve-Emunah*, 17–24, esp. 23.

48. Dorff, *Our Ancestors to Our Descendants*, 59, 103. See also his revealing comment on the identification of Conservative Rabbis with the Sages as a function of JTS rabbinic training, which stresses Mishnah and Talmud but not Codes. Elliot Dorff, "Towards a Legal Theory of the Conservative Movement," *Conservative Judaism* (Summer 1973), 76–77.

49. Cited in Sidney H. Schwarz, "Conservative Judaism's 'Ideology Problem,' " *American Jewish History* 74, no. 2 (Dec. 1984), 150.

50. Edward Feld, "Towards an Aggadic Judaism," *Conservative Judaism* (Spring 1975), 79–84.

51. Cohen, "Conservative Judaism on its Ninetieth Birthday," 269.

52. Cf. Dorff, *Our Ancestors to Our Descendants*, 82–83.

53. Dorff, "Towards a Legal Theory," esp. 74–77.

54. Neil Gillman, "Towards a Theology for Conservative Judaism," *Conservative Judaism* (Fall 1983), 4–22. I have argued elsewhere, as does Gillman, that this was precisely

Abraham Heschel's intent. See my "Re-reading Heschel on the Commandments," *Modern Judaism* 9, no. 1 (1989), 1–33.

55. Dorff, *Our Ancestors to Our Descendants*, 118–157.

56. Petuchowski, *"Siddur Sim Shalom,"* 82–87.

57. Jules Harlow (ed.), *Siddur Sim Shalom* (New York: 1985), xi–xii.

58. *Ibid.*, 800, 812, 844ff.

59. *Ibid.*, 232.

60. Elliot Dorff, "The Ideology of Conservative Judaism: Sklare After Thirty Years," *American Jewish History* 74, no. 2 (Dec. 1984), 113. For the closest thing to a Conservative Shulhan Arukh, see the extensive and demanding vision of halakhic life set forth in Isaac Klein, *A Guide to Jewish Religious Practice* (New York: 1979). Klein served for many years as head of the law committee of the (Conservative) Rabbinical Assembly.

61. *Emet Ve-Emunah*, 17–57. For the "ideal Conservative Jew" see 56–57.

62. Gordis, "Communicating Conservative Judaism," esp. 17–18.

63. Shlomo Riskin in "Conservative Judaism on its Ninetieth Birthday," 330ff.

64. Cf. Daniel Gordis, "The Elusive Conservative Third Generation: A Reaction to Elitism," *Conservative Judaism* (Fall 1983), 29–39.

65. *Emet Ve-Emunah*, 23. This perhaps explains why the original composition of the commission charged with drawing up the statement included only rabbis and seminary faculty, and no laity.

66. Rebecca T. Alpert and Jacob J. Staub, *Exploring Judaism: A Reconstructionist Approach* (Wyncote, Pa.: 1988), 1–28, esp. 24–25.

67. *Ibid.*, 25.

68. Arthur Green, "The Role of Jewish Mysticism in a Contemporary Theology of Judaism," *Conservative Judaism* (Summer 1976), 10–23. Green is also the author of an acclaimed biography of Nahman of Bratslaw entitled *Tormented Master* (University, Ala.: 1979).

69. Arthur Green, "Rethinking Theology: Language, Experience, and Reality," *The Reconstructionist* (Sept. 1988), 8–11.

70. *Ibid.*, 11–12.

71. *Ibid.*, 10, 13.

72. *Kol Haneshamah: Shabbat Eve* (Wyncote, Pa.: 1989).

73. Arthur Green, "Imagining the Jewish Future: Prayer, Liturgy, Religious Language." Typescript of address at a conference sponsored by the Reconstructionist Rabbinical College, 25 December 1988, Philadelphia.

74. *Kol Haneshamah*, xvii.

75. *Ibid.* For notes, see e.g., 67, 71, 74, 77, 83, 112. I am assuming these notes are not intended for the draft edition only. For the meditations, see 179–183.

76. *Ibid.*, 10.

77. *Ibid.*, 150–178. Compare the similar effort in Service VI for Friday evening in *Gates of Prayer*, the so-called equivocal service inspired by Alvin Reines. But in this service belief in a personal God, while not stated, is not excluded by the language, and some Hebrew blessings remain quite traditional. See *Gates of Prayer*, 204–218, and *Gates of Understanding*, 173–174.

78. *Kol Haneshamah*, 151.

79. *Ibid.*, 82–83.

80. Alpert and Staub, *Exploring Judaism*, vi–vii.

81. Nathan Glazer, *American Judaism* (Chicago: 1957, rpt. 1972), and the recent symposium, "Revisiting a Classic: Nathan Glazer's *American Judaism*," *American Jewish History* 77, no. 2 (Dec. 1987), 211–282.

82. "Symposium—The State of Orthodoxy," *Tradition* (Spring 1982), 3–81. See in particular the foreword by Walter Wurzburger and contributions by Marc Angel, David Berger, Louis Bernstein and Shubert Spero.

83. On the categorization of Orthodox Jews, see Wertheimer, "Recent Trends in American Judaism," 110.

84. Thus Joseph Grunblatt in "Symposium," 32.

85. Thus Louis Bernstein in *ibid.*, 14.

86. Michael Wyschogrod in *ibid.*, 81.

87. Aharon Lichtenstein in *ibid.*, 47.

88. Marc Angel, in *ibid.*, 6.

89. Emanuel Jakobovits in *ibid.*, 40.

90. Norman Lamm, "Loving and Hating Jews as Halakhic Categories," *Tradition* (Winter 1989), 98–123.

91. On the original adoption of the de Sola Pool siddur, see Hoffman (the "Reform scholar" mentioned in the text), *Beyond the Text,* 68–70. On its replacement with the *Artscroll* siddur, see Wertheimer (the "Conservative scholar"), "Recent Trends in American Judaism," 119. See also the *Complete Artscroll Siddur,* ed. Nosson Scherman (Brooklyn: 1984). Comments made about the de Sola Pool apply even more forcefully to another Orthodox siddur that has been used by modern Orthodox congregations, Philip Birnbaum's *Daily Prayer Book* (New York: 1949).

92. *Artscroll,* x, xv.

93. *Ibid.,* xvi, 19.

94. Barry Levy, "Judge Not a Book by Its Cover," *Tradition* 19, no. 1 (Spring 1981), 89–95. I am indebted to David Ellenson for bringing the review to my attention.

95. *Kol Haneshamah,* xvi.

96. Petuchowski, *"Siddur Sim Shalom,"* 84.

97. Plaut, "Reform Judaism," 11.

98. Glazer, *American Judaism,* ch. 6.

99. Thus Glazer in "Revisiting a Classic," 280.

100. *Ibid.,* 282.

101. See Jonathan Woocher, *Sacred Survival: The Civil Religion of American Jews* (Bloomington: 1986).

State and Real Estate: Territoriality and the Modern Jewish Imagination

Sidra DeKoven Ezrahi

(THE HEBREW UNIVERSITY)

I like a golem believed everyone. In the first place, everything is possible, as it is written in the Wisdom of the Fathers, I've forgotten just how. . . .

Forgetting, like remembering, can be a collaborative effort, and may even be compounded rather than alleviated by the recuperative effort of translation. The above passage is from Saul Bellow's famous translation of Isaac Bashevis Singer's short story "Gimpel the Fool."[1] It is in this text, which has become something of a classic in modern Jewish literature, that Gimpel and his bride, the "virgin" Elka, stand under the canopy while the "master of revels makes a 'God 'a mercy' in memory of the bride's parents."[2] The distance between "God 'a mercy" and *El maleh raḥamim* is, it seems, the terrain that Gimpel *tam* must cross in order to enter the pages of *Partisan Review* and become naturalized on American soil. The year is 1953. Can it be said now, nearly forty years later, that the deterritorialized "God 'a mercy"—Gimpel in a Baptist church, as it were—served as a marker or way station until readers would be ready once again to hear *El maleh raḥamim* under the *ḥuppah?* Or is this displacement, like Gimpel's forgetting the prooftext from Pirkei Avot, symptomatic of a more endemic condition—a kind of collective Alzheimer's—in relation to which there could be dramatic acts of compensation but no recovery?

There was, in any case, as much cover-up as exposure in Bellow's "Gimpel." The translation that launched Bashevis Singer's American career made the text available without making it transparent, so obscuring many of the original signs as to render them all but irretrievable.[3] The mass migration of Jews from Eastern Europe to the United States had been followed, within one generation, by a cultural amnesia that is manifested in the displacement of Jewish territories and texts.

There are in effect two levels of effacement here. When Gimpel forgets the passage from Scriptures, the presumption is that his primary, intratextual audience will "remember"; but Bashevis Singer, writing the original Yiddish story in America in 1945, when already faded memories of canonic Jewish texts are being undermined altogether by the annihilation of the world that housed those texts, could be invoking the signs of a more radical loss.[4] Every act of literary appropriation becomes from now on an act of rescue, measured not within the normal parameters of interlinguistic discourse but as one more outpost against oblivion. With the appearance of Bellow's Gimpel and Irving Howe and Eliezer Greenberg's "treasury" of Yiddish stories, 1953 becomes the year that inaugurates the American attempt to reclaim a lost Jewish place and a severed Jewish story.

"I am Gimpel the fool. I don't think myself a fool," the American Gimpel announces. Eleven years later, in 1964, Gimpel's translator published a novel that begins, "If I am out of my mind, it's all right with me, thought Moses Herzog."[5] As privileged readers we come to the text expecting that Herzog is no more out of his mind than Gimpel is a fool.[6] Bellow in his translation has provided not only cultural mediation but also the subtext for his own writing; I. B. Singer becomes, perhaps more than any other East European Jewish writer in America, the most authentic and authenticating Jewish reference, as his shtetl becomes authentic Jewish geography.[7] We can also recognize in this little intertextual transaction a cultural type who managed to survive the war and the rocky voyage between Jewish spaces and languages. Ruth Wisse defined the type in her illuminating book on the shlemiel as modern hero.[8] The transmigration of the fool, with his clearly defined social role in the European imagination, into the neurotic academic in his American isolation suggests something about the cultural contexts and their respective definition of the critical outsider.

Moving east and translated into Hebrew, the shlemiel never made it past the port authorities in Israel. Natan Alterman even wrote his epitaph in the wartime poem, "Mikhtav shel Menahem Mendel" ("Menahem Mendel's Letter"). Published in *Hatur hashevi'i* on March 9, 1945, Menahem Mendel's "letter"to his wife, Shaineh Shendel, contains a graphic report on the deaths of the characters in Sholem Aleichem's house of fiction. But these lines are more than a memorial to the Yiddish spirit; they also serve as a compassionate barrier of exclusion of certain nonviable figures from Eretz Israel:

> . . .'ad nizavnu betokh hagolah,
> abirei hehalom,
> geonei ha'oni,
> giborei hasifrut hayehudit hagedolah
> hanofelet basheleg kamoni . . .[9]

Tevye, Mottl, Pinyi, Stempenyu and Menahem Mendel himself—the quixotic "knights of the dream," "geniuses of penury," "heroes of the great Jewish literature that falls in the snow" in the very midst of (*betokh*) a place called *golah*—are by definition unsuited for the topography and climate of Palestine. The viability of the shlemiel in America and his near-extinction in Israel may be a function of such atmospheric forces exercised on Jewish characters in different spaces. Following Dov Sadan, Ruth Wisse suggests an affinity, at least in popular European culture, between the Wandering Jew and the shlemiel; Peter Schlemihl's "lack of a shadow . . . is the closest metaphorical equivalent for the lack of a homeland."[10] And Paul Celan, survivor of labor camps in Transnistria, living in France and writing in German—perhaps the most unmoored Jewish poet in the post-Holocaust world— wrote, in his prose parable, "Gespräch im Gebirg," of the Jew who left his house and set out through the mountains, "went under clouds, went in the shadow, his own and not his own—because the Jew, you know, what does he have that is really his own, that is not borrowed, taken and not returned."[11]

It goes without saying that even if they make it to the "homeland," not all of the ingathered are content to stay put. The dialectics of a culture predicated on the teleology of territory as *homeland* and travel as *homecoming* almost requires the adversarial presence of dislocated and unpatriated souls. In no smaller measure after the Second World War than in the early decades of the century, what seems to distinguish the Hebrew *helekh* or *talush* or *mehager* (the wanderer, the misfit)[12] from his American Jewish counterpart is precisely the dark and heavy shadow he must drag with him over consecrated ground, the burden of territoriality and the elusiveness of homecoming. His subversive presence within Hebrew culture reflects a normative intolerance for the gap in which the shlemiel thrives elsewhere—the gap between inner and outer reality or between ideal and real worlds. Gimpel is, ultimately, the shlemiel as storyteller, the wandering bard whose gullibility is a kind of negative capability generative of an infinity of possible worlds: "There were really no lies. Whatever doesn't really happen is dreamed at night. It happens to one if it doesn't happen to another, tomorrow if not today, or a century hence if not next year."[13] The Israeli struggle with reality as an unrealized utopia may encourage the imagination to remain confined within more rigid binary structures.[14]

Tested by such liminal figures as the shlemiel, the wanderer and the storyteller, the Zionist cultural alternatives are meant to reify and stabilize collective visions of redeemed spaces and stories; not only grounded in this soil but coterminous with it, the sacred texts and language are repatriated and once again become autochthonous. Territory and text are as public and overdetermined in Israel as they are private and underdetermined in America; the borders become, over time, as confining and claustrophobic, as defining of the nonnegotiable line between self and not-self in the Holy Land as the American frontiers are the elastic signposts of the infinitely expandable self.[15]

If until the middle of this century the most widespread orientation toward Jewish space was as protean and permeable, bounded at its outer limits only by the extremes of exilic time—as, above all, nonterritorial—the Second World War foreclosed this option. "Kasrilevke on wheels"[16] becomes an anachronism beside the redrawn Jewish map with its specific physical coordinates: New York, Montreal, Chicago, Buenos Aires, Tel-Aviv, Jerusalem. America in the twentieth century afforded the Jew a unique opportunity to begin over—while marking the place of the discarded culture through reference, through *partial* translation and through transmutation of an inherited vocabulary into indigenous terms. There develops, then, a strange dialectic of simultaneous reference to and effacement of the Jewish literary and linguistic canons. The journey motif, coded in modern Jewish literature as either an exercise in immobility (S. Y. Abramovitch's [Mendele's] *Travels of Benjamin III*) or as a voyage of redemption (S. Y. Agnon's *In the Heart of the Seas*), was redefined almost from the moment Jewish writers found their voice in the American chorus; the sortie into American spaces was a voyage of discovery and of naturalization, an adaptive strategy that took the lay of the land and then staked out a personal claim.

Once the children of the immigrant Jews had left the urban ghetto with its intermediate linguistic and geographical spaces, the search for constitutive texts would take on greater urgency as part of the larger search for cultural territory. These native Americans were in fact engaged in aggressive and dazzling acts of appropriation that parallel and, in certain respects, faintly echo the monumental dramas of repatriation being enacted in the Holy Land.

The repression of or very selective access to Jewish memory is supported, on the one hand, by the image of the American Adam who embodies new beginnings in life and language ("the origin of words is lost like the origin of individuals," comments Alexis de Tocqueville on nineteenth-century America)[17] and, on the other, by the association with vestiges of Puritan rhetoric that link the early American conquests with the reclamation of sacred territory by the ancient Hebrews.[18] Both images were so empowering that even immigrants writing in Yiddish believed, for a moment anyway, that they might succeed in inscribing their lives on the American landscape. H. Leyvick envisioned the words "Here lives the Jewish people" emblazoned on the New York skyline.[19] (That these writers remained, ultimately, alien on such hospitable soil—and that their chapter in American letters proved to be written in invisible ink that would become partially legible only through the recuperative efforts of translators and scholars some sixty years later—is one of the profound ironies of this enterprise; it is, nevertheless, consistent with the larger cultural patterns of repression, substitution and partial recovery that we are exploring.)[20]

The poetry and prose of the immigrant generation were largely an exercise in spatial reorientation and a search for literary correlatives of the drama of acculturation. The iconography of the *goldene medinah* embraced, in the first instance, the Statue of Liberty and the vertical architecture of the urban landscape.[21] The democratic tropes of mobility were captured in the infinitely expanding frontiers of Whitman's verse and in the city cadences and cacophonies available in contemporary modernist forms. But the mimetic impulse is present even among the most avant garde of the Yiddish poets; and it is the predominant force among the immigrant writers who venture into English prose. The evolution of Jewish approaches to inner and outer spaces can be measured in the changing state of the *real* in the literary imagination. The realism in the fiction of the first generation was a mapping out, the realism of the second an appropriation and a realignment. The precise naturalism of writers such as Abraham Cahan, Anzia Yezierska, Mary Antin, Daniel Fuchs and later, in modified form, the realism of Alfred Kazin mirror the keen, object-focused eye of the surveyor and the language of democracy.[22] Henry Roth's *Call It Sleep* (1934), in which the myriad forces of the immigrant experience and forms of expression culminate and are refashioned, is the full realization of the shift from the language of the naturalist or observer to that of the actor who participates in the very definition of the environment. The odyssey of David Shearl proceeds by carefully constructed, concentric geographical circles, from the inner sanctum of the home through the circumscribed arena of the neighborhood into the vast undefined regions beyond. The claustrophobia and semiotic boundaries of the known world vie with the dangers and seductions of unexplored space. The linguistic correlative of this dynamic diminishes the strict ontological status and confinement of the palpable, mundane world, introducing new possibilities for mobility; the lyrical prose of the narrating self[23] is a redemptive poetic repatriation of the displaced syntax of the child locked in a universe of misunderstanding and incomprehension.

One cannot overstate the centrality of *Call It Sleep* as a site of magical transformation in the process of displacement and relocation in the modern Jewish imagination. That it represents or anticipates in certain key respects a postwar consciousness may be supported by the fact that, although it first appeared in 1934, it gained a significant audience only thirty years later. When Irving Howe or Murray Baumgarten argues that Yiddish is the subtext of much of the fiction of the postwar decades[24] he refers to a gesture or an inflection, but rarely to the practice of literary allusion that would indicate that a culture is engaged in an ongoing renegotiation of its past. Such continuity would be measured of course as much in the discontinuities, the misreadings, as in the innocent allusions. But the second generation of American Jewish writers had so succeeded in suppressing or camouflaging the culture of origin that *Call It Sleep* appears to be nearly the only text demonstrating a true interlinguistic dialogue. Yet even here, despite explicit allusions to the Hebrew scriptures as repository of the language of revelation and the presumption of Yiddish as the normative language, the Jewish languages and texts are in fact salient by their *absence*. The warm dyadic speech that flows between Genya Shearl and her son David is a "Yiddish" translated for purposes of the narrative into a lyrical English. That is, the Yiddish is presumed but not really enacted as a linguistic layer, except for occasional aphoristic or inflected phrases. And that is the true achievement of Henry Roth: rather than being content as some of his predecessors were with transcribing Yiddish into a limping English dialect—the street language of the immigrant—he transposes it in the mother's discourse so that it receives a poetic cadence of its own. The culture or language of origin is thus marked off and engaged through the most radical act of translation, of carrying over, into the highest register of the host language.[25] The Hebrew, on the other hand, is present as an untranslated, indecipherable medium: Hebrew is a

> strange and secret tongue. . . . If you knew it, then you could talk to God. (Furtively [in *heder*], while the rabbi still spoke David leaned over and stole a glance at the number of the page.) On sixty-eight. After, maybe, can ask. On page sixty-eight. That blue book—Gee! it's God.[26]

Here place, in the sense of *makom* and **hamakom,** human and divine, is not only marked or embedded in the text; it *is* the text. But it is the text as seen through a glass darkly, the text as effaced, as absence, as loss. For the moment, both the Hebrew and the Yiddish as canonic languages and texts are as present as those dark squares in the family photo album where the pictures of the patriarchs are missing.[27]

The Hebrew literature in Palestine of these same years reveals an (at times oppressive) sense of presence that parallels the absences salient in immigrant cultures elsewhere. S. Y. Agnon, a writer who straddles several cultural universes, dramatizes the intricacies of placement and displacement, the role of metaphysical yearnings in the reclamation of physical places in the Holy Land, in his story "Tehila," set in the Mandate period: *"misha'ar yafo ulema'alah 'ad lakotel hama'aravi nimshakhim veholkhim anashim venashim mikol ha'edot shebirushalayim 'im 'olim ḥadashim sheheviam haMakom lemekomam va'adayin lo maẓu et mekomam."*

("From Jaffa Gate as far as the Western Wall, men and women from all the communities of Jerusalem moved in a steady stream, together with those newcomers whom The Place had restored to their place, albeit their place had not yet been found.")[28] While the English concept of "home" as a private, inviolable yet widely encompassing arena[29] hardly finds its correlative in the Hebrew lexicon, the correspondence (and distance) between the human plane and the divine, translated here as "place" and "Place," are embedded in the renewed contact between the Jews and their sacred center.

Such a center is inaccessible to nine-year-old David Shearl on two counts: It has been deterritorialized and it has become indecipherable. If we can project him into an extratextual future, we can envision him as a young adult rediscovering the Bible in all its majesty—through the King James Version. The loss of what Harold Bloom calls an "ancestry of voice"[30] will find compensation in monumental cultural acts of appropriation that again involve the mediation of translated texts.[31] Simultaneously, however, a direct and unmediated relationship is being established with the American physical and literary terrain. It has been argued that, in the competition over the "usable past" between the native-born and the "barbarians" that filled many of the literary pages in the early and middle decades of this century, the immigrants or their children, "having no culture in which to be home," fabricated one. "The children of the Mayflower tended to invent Western culture," claims Marcus Klein, and "children of the immigrants . . . tended to invent America."[32] In 1942—the ironies of synchronic Jewish-American time are as old as 1492— Alfred Kazin published a book enunciating a critical vocabulary that might be seen as the hallmark of the postwar group broadly associated with *Partisan Review.*[33] Kazin demonstrates the connection between territory and text in the very title of this book, *On Native Grounds;* in the five-page introduction to his study of modern American writers, Kazin uses the possessive pronoun *our* twenty-seven times; the repeated invocation of "our national civilization," "our modern American literature," "our society," "our culture,"[34] is a catechism by which the son of immigrants appropriates the American canon as surely as he appropriates the American landscape by walking the length and breadth of Brownsville in his autobiographical *A Walker in the City.* As Mark Shechner observes, the library has replaced the synagogue as sacred center;[35] it is, however, differentiated from religious space by the sense that, as reader, "Alfred" both receives and constructs a tradition out of the plurality of texts on its "public" shelves.[36] Reflecting but also fixing the terms of the enterprise, Kazin in 1942 invokes a vocabulary of alienation or marginality meant to signal both a Jewish and an American sensibility. "The greatest single fact about our modern American writing," he writes in that same preface, is

> our writers' absorption in every last detail of their American world together with their deep and subtle alienation from it. There is a terrible estrangement in this writing, a nameless yearning for a world no one ever really possessed. . . . What interested me here was our alienation *on* native grounds—the interwoven story of our need to take up our life on our own grounds and the irony of our possession.[37]

The endemic American quest for a lost—and irrecoverable—community will dovetail eventually, as I have suggested, with a nostalgia for Jewish spaces in the poetry and prose of some of these writers and their successors. Whether through acts of translation or imaginative appropriation, both the shtetl and the Lower East Side will become mythic Jewish fields of reference.[38] Delmore Schwartz's story "America, America" becomes the locus classicus of this complex pilgrimage for writers who, as Irving Howe put it, may have

> left behind the immigrant world but [still carried] its stigmata . . . stamped on their souls. . . . If they were uncertain . . . as to who they were, they knew what they had been. . . . The immigrant world gave its literary offspring . . . memories, it gave them evocative place names and dubious relatives, it gave them thickness of milieu.

It gave them "just enough material to see them through a handful of novels and stories."[39]

For some time, though, the "usable past" will continue to consist primarily in a posture and the fragments of a language. What a number of critics and writers, including Kazin, Schwartz and Isaac Rosenfeld, were offering as cultural currency was the critical function of alienation or estrangement in American democratic tradition. Although already articulated as a theme of modernist literature, the alienated sensibility became so fully identified with a specific circle of New York Jewish intellectuals in the 1940s that the *New Yorker* is reported as inquiring whether there were "special typewriters in the *Partisan Review* office with entire words like 'alienation' stamped on each key."[40]

In symposia held in 1944 and 1946 and in subsequent essays, poetry and fiction, the theme of Jewish marginality is explored from every possible angle but one. During the very years that Europe has turned all its Jews into aliens and is proceeding to exterminate them, second-generation Jewish writers in America are adopting alienation as a voluntary moral stance—a perception anchored neither in the current events in Europe nor in the theodicy of exile and redemption that had structured Jewish itinerancy for two millennia and the Jewish homecoming of the twentieth century.[41] The rhetoric of displacement is the same, but the tenor is entirely different, suggesting the longevity of rhetoric beyond the viability of other forces of cultural consciousness. When these writers affirm, paradoxically, both the marginality and the centrality of the Jews in America (or of what is defined as "Jewish" in America), alienation represents not only or primarily a historical or a collective condition but an existential and a moral choice. It may also have provided, for a time, a conceptual bridge facilitating and to some extent camouflaging the shift in intellectual loyalties from Marx to Freud, from communal or social reform to self-absorption, or from what Mark Shechner calls the politics of "social redemption" to the "politics of self-renewal . . . from Socialism to Therapy."[42] The spirit of the 1940s is manifest in dramatic reinterpretations or "revisions" of such patently proletarian texts from the previous decade as Clifford Odets's *Awake and Sing*. In 1946, Daniel Bell explored the sociology of alienation in an article in the *Jewish Frontier;* claiming that "the quality of being lost" was the "most pervasive symptom of the alienation of our times," he assigned to the "footsore" Jew a synecdochical function as the "image of the world's destiny." "As long as moral corruption exists, alienation is the only possible response," he continued, and went on to indict Odets for "delineating the frustration of Jewish life, not its alienation, the effect, not the source." Bell would turn Odets's social reformer, Ralph Berger, into an *alienated intellectual,* and substitute contemplation ("understanding") for action ("muddled aggression") as the truly Jewish moral imperative.[43]

In the quarter century beginning in the mid-1940s, Saul Bellow's fiction becomes a crossroads of these themes. His territorialism originates, like that of his predecessors, in the realism of the immigrant son's primary bid for a foothold: "I am an American, Chicago-born," proclaims Augie March in the 1953 novel that bears his name[44]—and if his claims to localism appear to be at war with his dazzling antics as a picaro, as a kind of secularized, camouflaged wandering Jew, it may be because we have not yet taken the full, continental, measure of acculturation in the American landscape.[45] Augie's preoccupation with the minutest details of his environment is an urban recapitulation of the voyages of discovery that are also self-conscious acts of possession:

> Look at me going everywhere! Why, I am a sort of Columbus of those near-at-hand and believe you can come to them in this immediate *terra incognita* that spreads out in every gaze. I may well be a flop at this line of endeavor. Columbus too thought he was a flop, probably, when they sent him back in chains. Which didn't prove there was no America.[46]

By the time Moses Elkana Herzog appears on the horizon of Bellow's fictional landscape (1964), a process has been completed whereby *wandering* as a Jewish condition and curse has been largely supplanted by *mobility* as an American opportunity. As Herzog rides through the city's bowels by subway, drives along its main arteries by car, races along the surrounding countryside and waterways by train and ferry—and hovers, finally airborne in a westbound jet, over the entire continent— his reach expands infinitely ("as heaven is my witness")[47]. He has scattered his life over the entire continent, carrying keys to his home in Ludeyville, to his mistress's and his own New York apartments, to the faculty lounge at the University of Chicago and sundry other places. (The key as metonymy of the real estate of the American Jew invites comparison with the key as metonymy of sacred—and collective—space in Agnon's interbellum novel, *A Guest for the Night*.)[48] Herzog in the city, Herzog as a walker in the city—Montreal, New York or Chicago—like Kazin's "Alfred" before him, is alternately assaulted and caressed by its sights, sounds and smells and embraced in powerful rituals of consecration; he is as organically connected to it as he professes to be estranged from it.[49] "He was perhaps as midwestern and unfocused as these same streets. . . . Out of [the city's] elements, by this peculiar art of his own organs, he created his version of it."[50]

The urban setting that challenges the imagination to transform Jewish into American tropes of itinerancy and community yields ultimately to a powerful myth of homecoming. The vacation house in the Berkshires, which Herzog himself defines as a "symbol of this Jewish struggle for a solid footing in White Anglo-Saxon Protestant America"[51]—a clear claim for private property as the *real estate* of the Jew—reflects a profound form of patriation.[52] As the final station in his frenetic wandering over the North American continent, it represents both the urban American sanctification of the pastoral realm and a remythification of the Jewish fantasy of return to a prelapsarian, pre- (or post-) exilic state. The home in the Berkshires comes close enough to being reclaimed as wilderness to qualify as primary American space. Sitting or lying in the disrepair of his home or in the overgrown tangle of his garden, Herzog suspends the search for an historical or interpersonal resolution of his urban estrangement and supplants it with a biblical acquiescence that suggests an entirely different order of being-at-home: "Here I am. Hineni," he says, echoing what is a profoundly *spatial* response to the divine summons. "I am pretty well satisfied to be, to be just as it is willed, for as long as I may remain in occupancy."[53] The presence of the original Hebrew text—with its translation—reinstates an explicit intertextuality into this discourse. Herzog has repossessed both text and territory *and* the matrix that unifies them. (Perhaps now *El maleh raḥamim* can again be heard under the *ḥuppah?*)

If Gimpel and Herzog begin their "autobiographical" tales with a very similar presentation of self vis-à-vis society ("I am Gimpel the fool. I don't think myself a fool." . . . "I'm out of my mind, it's all right with me, thought Moses Herzog"), it is in the closure of each narrative that we can measure the real distance between them. Gimpel takes up his staff and goes out into the world, invoking in his wandering both the theodicy of exile and his designated cultural role as storyteller. Herzog at the end of his narrative is lying perfectly still. Having recapitulated inherited categories of exile within the expanse of a long interior monologue, he now realizes the profound possibilities for their resolution within the confines of his own—private—property as mythic American space and the recaptured rhetoric of the Hebrew scriptures.

When the cultural boundaries of the group have become so permeable that migrant types find their way easily into the surrounding culture, when fragments of historical and textual memory have been recalled and subjected to a new syntax, the parameters and the nature of the literary discourse have undergone radical revision. It is precisely here, in this intersection of cultural exchange, that we may begin to discern a new paradigm informing the literature of American Jews. There has been much critical discussion about whether the Jews over the last century, and especially since the Second World War, have developed a "regional" literature in America comparable to southern literature or black literature, and if so, what is the longevity—or "shelf life," as it were—of such a phenomenon.[54] Since whatever else that literature may be, it has only partially recaptured the bilingual or polylingual quality that characterized all the Jewish literatures of the diaspora, it is tempting to look for analogues in the German Jewish literature in the first half of this century. The German literature of the Jews of Prague, particularly that of Kafka, is defined by Gilles Deleuze and Felix Guattari as a *"litterature mineure"* constructed by a minority within a major language. The "first characteristic of minor literature . . . is that in it language is affected with a high coefficient of deterritorialization." And if the "writer is located in the margins or completely outside his or her fragile community, this situation allows the writer all the more possibility to express another possible community." "Minor" literature manifests the profound restlessness of "living in a language not one's own." What is a problem for immigrants becomes, in this view, an *opportunity* for their children: "How to become a nomad and an immigrant and a gypsy in relation to one's own language?"[55]

What appears to be a tailor-made definition of the Jewish presence in American letters is reinforced, of course, by the growing influence in postwar America of

Kafka and the existentialist philosophers, mediated and authenticated by the presence of such Jewish refugees as T. W. Adorno and Hannah Arendt. For the New York intellectuals loosely identified with *Partisan Review,* Arendt herself becomes a figure of the compounded exile of the Jewish "pariah" and the European émigré;[56] yet it is precisely in the ensuing discourse on exile that one can measure the real distance between the identity of German Jewish writers in America and the reflected rhetoric of their American-born colleagues.[57]

The unharnessed generation that came of age in the late 1930s and 1940s, that inherited a repressed tradition, a cultural amnesia, succeeded in encoding in the language of alienation what had already become in fact a profound claim to being-at-home. These writers do not so much articulate a subversive or revolutionary alternative to the major or dominant culture as seek a place in it; it is in this sense that they fail ultimately to inscribe on the American landscape a truly deterritorialized, "minor" literature.

All newcomers have had to "forget" in order to become Americans, and acts of partial retrieval by successive generations may involve only so much memory as is needed to retain the license to hold American society at some distance. The alienation of the immigrants and their descendants becomes in America a means for the democratization of individualism, a part of the larger American epic of the negotiations between self and society; alienation and marginality are subsumed, then, under the very American concept of community as a structure that rests on individual autonomy, dissent and the radical option. Although for the Jewish children of immigrants the act of self-alienation is dialectically related to the Jewish theme of wandering, it only highlights the enormous distance between the condition and the gestures of exile. While writers such as Isaac Bashevis Singer and philosophers such as Hannah Arendt provided a vocabulary, a reference and an authenticating presence, it was precisely by adopting or co-opting "alienation" as a voluntary condition and a central moral position—by becoming the outsider as insider—that the first generation of native American Jews superseded their inherited status as strangers, as "aliens," as the unshadowed other. Irving Howe locates the crisis in late twentieth-century American Jewish fiction in the loss of the immigrant milieu, that is, as a "crisis of subject matter";[58] Shechner locates it in the loss of a critical stance.[59] Whether it is to be celebrated or lamented, the extent to which the writers who came of age in the 1940s managed to exchange mobility for wandering, Herzog for Gimpel, is the extent of their reterritorialization on American soil.

Notes

This essay is an expansion of a talk given at the Truman Institute of the Hebrew University on 26 December 1989.

1. Isaac Bashevis Singer, "Gimpel the Fool," trans. Saul Bellow, *Partisan Review* 20 (May 1953), reprinted in Bashevis Singer, *Gimpel the Fool and Other Stories* (New York: 1957), 10, emphasis added. "Gimpl tam" was first published in *Yidisher kemfer,* 30 March 1945.

2. *Ibid.,* 12.

3. There are a few words from the original text that are left untranslated in Bellow's

"Gimpel"—words from the culinary lexicon ("kreplach"), the sacramental lexicon ("mezzuzah") and the rogues' gallery ("golem," "schnorrer") that had already established their own place in the American conversation.

4. That the relations between Gimpel's "amnesia" and the vagaries of the English text go deeper than the changing decorums of translation can be seen in the relative function of internal knowledge. The correctives for "amnesia" embedded in the internal knowledge shared by a storytelling circle are a locus of much of the humor in Yiddish fiction; the malapropisms and misquotes of Sholem Aleichem's semiliterate characters, for example, are a function of group memory and can help us delineate the boundary between collective knowing and collective forgetting: "When the wise men of Kasrilevke quote the passage from the Holy Book, 'Tov shem meshemen tov,' they know what they're doing. I'll translate it for you: We were better off without the train." Sholem Aleichem, "On Account of a Hat," in *A Treasury of Yiddish Stories*, ed. Irving Howe and Eliezer Greenberg, trans. Isaac Rosenfeld (New York: 1954), 113. In this case, in which translation is of the essence, the English version is a fair equivalent of the original ("Iber a hitel," in *Fun Pesakh biz Pesakh: Ale verk fun Sholem Aleichem* [New York: 1927], 246).

5. Bashevis Singer, "Gimpel the Fool," 9; Saul Bellow, *Herzog* (Harmondsworth: 1964), 7.

6. There is, however, a great distance between Gimpel as "tam"—a spiritual category that connotes integrity and fullness as well as gullibility and receptivity—and Herzog's psychic imbalance as possible moral response to the world's inadequacies. Of the many discussions of insanity or madness as a mid-twentieth-century cultural stance, the conclusion to Lionel Trilling's *Sincerity and Authenticity* (Cambridge, Mass.: 1972) is still one of the most provocative. See also Janet Hadda, "Gimpel the Full," *Prooftexts* 10, no. 2 (May 1990), 283–295.

7. Compare, in this regard, the trajectory of Bashevis Singer's career with that of his brother, I. J. Singer. See Anita Norich, *The Homeless Imagination in the Fiction of Israel Joshua Singer* (Bloomington: 1991). Most of Bashevis Singer's critics, like most of his readers, are familiar only with the translated texts; the mediating function of the translator in recovering a lost cultural memory is explored in Cynthia Ozick's programmatic story "Envy: or Yiddish in America" in her *The Pagan Rabbi and Other Stories* (New York: 1971). The main character, patterned after the Yiddish poet Jacob Glatstein, writes to his would-be translator:

whoever forgets Yiddish courts amnesia of history. Mourn—the forgetting has already happened. A thousand years of our travail forgotten. Here and there a word left for vaudeville jokes. Yiddish, I call on you to choose! Yiddish! Choose death or death. Which is to say death through forgetting or death through translation. Who will redeem you? . . . All you can hope for, you tattered, you withered, is translation in America! (74–75).

8. Ruth R. Wisse, *The Schlemiel as Modern Hero* (Chicago: 1971).

9. Natan Alterman: "Mikhtav shel Menahem-Mendel," from "Mikol ha'amim," in *Hatur hashevi'i* 1 (Tel-Aviv: 1977), 12–14.

10. Wisse, *Schlemiel as Modern Hero*, 125–126.

11. Paul Celan, "Conversation in the Mountains," in *Paul Celan: Collected Prose*, ed. and trans. Rosmarie Waldrop (New York: 1986), 17.

12. In an interview, Aharon Appelfeld referred to his own characters, Holocaust survivors in Israel, as "mehagrim" (emigrants). See Shulamith Gingold-Gilboa, "Aharon Appelfeld: Bein traumah lemuda'ut," *Iton 77* 46 (Oct. 1983), 28–29. Much has been written on the figure of the "misfit" in Hebrew literature; most recently, a renewed interest in the work of Y. H. Brenner and his displaced characters may reflect the general malaise in Israeli culture and the renegotiation of certain fundamental assumptions. See Menahem Brinker, *'Ad hasimtah hateveriyanit* (Tel-Aviv: 1990).

13. Bashevis Singer, "Gimpel the Fool," 22–23.

14. An alternative to the utopia/dystopia dichotomy is offered in Ernst Bloch's Marxist

theory of the utopian function of art as a theory of desire and "anticipatory illumination" that does not deny the connection between landscapes and "wish-landscapes." "The concrete utopia stands at the horizon of every reality; the real possibility encloses the open dialectic tendency-latency until the very last moment," he writes in his essay on "The Artistic Illusion as the Visible Anticipatory Illumination" (in Ernst Bloch, *The Utopian Function of Art and Literature: Selected Essays*, trans. Jack Zipes and Frank Mecklenburg [Cambridge, Mass.: 1988], 155). "The unconcluded movement of the unconcluded matter," a gloss on Aristotle's "unfinished entelechy" (*ibid.*) allows one to translate despair over the absence of utopian fulfillment, which can generate binary artistic structures, into the hope of the not-yet-realized that can generate an infinitude of fictive possibilities.

15. The phenomenon of Harold Bloom's *Book of J* (1990) and the controversy it has stirred are an extreme example of the ludic, open-ended nature of American Jewish approaches to sacred texts. For a discussion of the ideological implications of myths of the American frontier, see Sacvan Bercovitch and Myra Jehlen (eds.), *Ideology and Classic American Literature* (Cambridge: 1986).

16. Quoted from I. I. Trunk's 1937 essay on Sholem Aleichem in Dan Miron, "Mas'a beezor hadimdumim" (afterword to *Sipurei rakevet*, trans. Dan Miron [Tel-Aviv: 1989]), 243. A comparative overview of changing Jewish concepts of exile and territoriality from the perspective of the end of our millennium might begin by acknowledging that monotheism as it developed in rabbinic and postrabbinic Judaism actually allowed the Jews to be in "God's country" anywhere in the premessianic world, providing a normative framework for being (provisionally) at home in the remotest corners of "*golus.*" As such, the territorial embrace of the religious Jewish imagination is far broader than the confines of a nationalism conceived within specific boundaries. This broad sense of entitlement, underscored by Enlightenment ideas, facilitates early Jewish mobility and acculturation in America. The impact of Israel as a territorial option on the imagination of American Jews in the latter half of the century is a subject onto itself. For a wide-ranging analysis of "exile" in ancient and modern Jewish thought, see Arnold Eisen, *Galut: Modern Jewish Reflection on Homelessness and Homecoming* (Bloomington: 1986).

17. Alexis de Tocqueville, *Democracy in America*, vol. 2 (New York: 1945 [Paris: 1835]), 72. See also R. W. B. Lewis, *The American Adam: Innocence, Tragedy and Tradition in the Nineteenth Century* (Chicago: 1955).

18. See Sacvan Bercovitch, quoting Melville on the rejection of the past and the Americans as the new Hebrews conquering sacred land, in *The American Jeremiad* (Madison: 1978), 177.

19. H. Leyvick, "Here Lives the Jewish People," in *Yiddish Poetry in America*, trans. and ed. Benjamin and Barbara Harshav (Berkeley: 1986), 697.

20. See Ruth Wisse, "*Di Yunge:* Immigrants or Exiles?" *Prooftexts* 1, no. 1 (Jan. 1981), 43–61 and *idem, A Little Love in Big Manhattan* (Cambridge, Mass: 1988). It would take a few more decades and the mediating presence of such diverse critics, translators and anthologizers as Irving Howe and Ruth Wisse and a host of scholars demonstrating new hermeneutic approaches to Jewish texts before the vast realms of Yiddish and Hebrew literature, Jewish mysticism and Hasidism as well as biblical, midrashic and medieval texts would become available to the fully acculturated children and grandchildren of the immigrants. "How can we sing our songs in a foreign land?" asks Geoffrey Hartman in 1986; "the Jewish imagination, like any other, must exert itself and risk profanation, or fall silent and risk atrophy" ("On the Jewish Imagination," *Prooftexts* 5, no. 3, [Sept. 1985], 201–220). His own later work is a mighty attempt to recapture the text as a scholarly and personal resource from the silence that was also the deafness of his generation.

21. "When the New York skyline burst upon him, the Jewish immigrant immediately perceived of America's greatness in vertical terms," writes Judd Teller, who, as Y. Y. Teller, was an important voice in Yiddish poetry before the Second World War (see his *Strangers and Natives: The Evolution of the American Jew from 1921 to the Present* [New York: 1968], 38). For a fascinating exploration of the presence of Miss Liberty in the immigrant imagination, as well as a comparative analysis of immigrant cultures and their place in the American mind,

see John Higham, *Send These to Me: Jews and Other Immigrants in Urban America* (New York: 1975).

22. This process is in no small measure shaped by the realism and spirit of social reform that characterized those American writers such as William Dean Howells and Hutchins Hapgood who first discovered the New York ghetto, its artists and writers. In tracing lines of influence, one might consider Alfred Kazin's analysis of the

> early realists, with their baffled careers and their significant interest in "local color," cultivating their own gardens, who encouraged in America that elementary nationalism, that sense of belonging to a particular time and a native way of life, which is the indispensable condition of spiritual maturity and a healthy literature.

See also his discussion of the evolution of the documentary mode in imaginative literature and the centrality of the camera as instruments of a new social consciousness (Alfred Kazin, *On Native Grounds: An Interpretation of Modern American Prose Literature* [New York: 1942], 17 and passim).

23. For a very enlightening discussion of the bifurcation of the narrative voice in *Call It Sleep* into the "experiencing self" and the "narrating self," see Naomi Diamant, "Linguistic Universes in Henry Roth's *Call It Sleep*," *Contemporary Literature* 27 (1986), 336–355.

24. Irving Howe defines and qualifies what replaced the traditional Jewish "internal bilingualism of Hebrew and Yiddish" in American Jewish fiction as "a precarious substitute, a half-internal and half-external bilingualism of Englished Yiddish and Yiddished English, from which there sometimes arises a new and astonishing American prose style" (*World of Our Fathers* [New York: 1976], 588). Murray Baumgarten, in his *City Scriptures: Modern Jewish Writing* (Cambridge, Mass.: 1982), makes bolder claims for

> modern Jewish writing [as] a chapter in what Max and Uriel Weinreich called the history of Jewish interlinguistics. . . . If these works [from Henry to Philip Roth, from Malamud to Kazin] are written in English, it is a language with Yiddish lurking behind every Anglo-Saxon character. . . . Yiddish transforms the modern language in which the Jewish writer functions (10, 28).

25. There is a two-line, untranslated Yiddish dialogue at the end of the Prologue between Genya Shearl, who has just disembarked at Ellis Island with her young son, and her husband Albert, who has been living in America for some months (" 'Gehen vir voinen du? In Nev York?' 'Nein. Bronzeville. Ich hud dir schoin geschriben' "). Its lonely status only underscores its absence in the rest of the narrative and the radical nature of the "translation" that is being enacted throughout. (Henry Roth, *Call It Sleep* [New York: 1962], 16.)

26. *Ibid.*, 213, 227.

27. Following Mikhail Bakhtin's model, much work has been done on heteroglossia and polyphony in American subcultures (black, Chinese, Hispanic). Its value for a new hermeneutics of American Jewish culture is demonstrated in Hana Wirth-Nesher's illuminating analysis of bi- or multilingualism and diglossia in Roth's novel ("Multilinguilism in *Call It Sleep*," *Prooftexts* 10, no. 2 [May 1990], 297–312). She argues that throughout the narrative, though written in English, the American language and culture are present in their alterity (it is the English element that "appears to be foreign, as 'other' within the rest of the *English* text"), and that only in the final scene, where David "dies" and is "reborn" through his self-induced electrocution at the train tracks, where the allusions to a presumed Hebrew/Yiddish culture recede and are replaced by an intertextual dialogue with English and European literature, does he "die out of his immigrant life and [become reborn] . . . into the world of English literacy and culture, the world of Henry Roth's literary identity, but at the cost of killing both the father and the mother" (305, 309). I would argue that, whereas such a reading may account for the dramatic nature of the transaction taking place between the experiencing self and its environment, and that it may indeed be a kind of recapitulation of the writer's own *rite de passage,* the presence from the beginning of the narrative self with its fully articulated poetic voice enacts this process throughout the text, both in the Joycean flow

of intrapsychic dialogue and in the luxuriating, almost overwritten metaphoric passages interspersed throughout ("trinkets held in the mortar of desire, the fancy a trowel, the whim the builder. A wall, a tower, stout, secure, incredible, immuring the spirit from a flight of arrows, the mind, experience, shearing the flow of time as a rock shears water" [35]). I would endorse Wirth-Nesher's conclusion that this book both represents the culmination of the immigrant narrative with its multilinguistic resonances—and marks its demise. ("It is no wonder that Roth could write no second book" [311].)

28. S. Y. Agnon, "Tehila," in *'Ad hena* (Jerusalem: 1972), 183, trans. by Walter Lever in *Firstfruits,* ed. James A. Michener (Greenwich, Conn.: 1973), 62.

29. See David Sopher's discussion of the American and English resonances of "home" in his essay "The Landscape of Home," in *The Interpretation of Ordinary Landscapes: Geographical Essays,* ed. D. W. Meinig (New York: 1979), 130:

> The rich meaning of the English lexical symbol is virtually untranslatable into most other languages. The distinguishing characteristic of the English word, which it shares to a certain extent with its equivalent in other Germanic languages, is the enormous extension of scale that it incorporates. . . . It can refer with equal ease to house, land, village, city, district, country, or, indeed, the world. . . . The Romance word for "house" . . . takes on some of the warmth associated with "home" in English, but it remains a symbol for a firmly bounded and enclosed space, which "home" is not.

See also Gaston Bachelard, *Poetics of Space,* trans. Maria Jolas (Boston: 1964), where the author's exploration of the *house* ("life begins well, it begins enclosed, protected, all warm, in the bosom of the house") confirms a French orientation toward physically defined space as primary or maternal; "without it, man would be a 'dispersed being,'" he adds (7). The Hebrew *bayit* carries the same connotation of physical specificity—and within the Zionist vocabulary, a similar defense against dispersion—as the French *maison.*

30. Harold Bloom, *A Map of Misreading* (Oxford: 1975), 17.

31. See, for example, recent encounters with the Scriptures collected in David Rosenberg's anthology, *Congregation: Contemporary Writers Read the Jewish Bible* (San Diego: 1987).

32. Marcus Klein, *Foreigners: The Making of American Literature 1900–1940* (Chicago: 1981), x. See also Higham's discussion in *Send These to Me* (3ff.) of the debate between those who, harking back to John Jay's argument in the Federalist papers, claim that Americans are descended from a monolithic culture and population, and those who, following Tom Paine in *Common Sense,* argue that pluralism is endemic to the American definition of self. This struggle, embodied in the competition between the "melting pot" and the "social fabric" as icons of socialization, provides some depth to the current debate over multiculturalism.

33. Kazin himself, although a contributor to *Partisan Review,* is more closely affiliated during these years, as writer and editor, with *The New Republic.*

34. Kazin, *On Native Grounds,* vii–xii.

35. Mark Shechner, *After the Revolution: Studies in the Contemporary Jewish-American Imagination* (Bloomington: 1987), 47.

36. "America" emerges in the work of Sacvan Bercovitch and others as a sociocultural reality created by primary texts such as the sermons of Jonathan Edwards, the Declaration of Independence, the Gettysburg Address, "The American Scholar" (see his Afterword to *Ideology and Classic American Literature* and *American Jeremiad*). Jews born in America with dim memories of specific Jewish texts may nevertheless have retained enough *text-mindedness* to become engaged in the literature and the law of the land as conduits into the American spirit. Harold Bloom records the attenuation of that "Jewish love for a text" in America of the later twentieth century and concludes his essay on "Free and Broken Tablets: The Cultural Prospects of American Jewry" in his *Agon: Towards a Theory of Revisionism* (1982) with the dim hope that "an American Jewry that has lost its love for a text like the 102nd Psalm might recover, in time, such a love, if it were capable first of loving some text, any text" (329).

37. Kazin, *On Native Grounds*, ix. There is a delightful sense throughout this early work of the deliberate but somehow inevitable nature of the American literary enterprise of discovering a past, the "unabashed recovery of an American mythology. . . . The past now lay everywhere ready to be reclaimed, waiting to be chanted and celebrated," he writes in the chapter "America! America!" (*ibid*, 508–509). The title of this chapter could be an ironic redefinition of the territory of Delmore Schwartz's story by the same name, which, published two years earlier in *Partisan Review*, explores the life of the immigrant as subject of a more authentic, more usable, past. In an entry from his journal of 1942, published only some fifty years later, Kazin acknowledges the complex sources of his own passionate engagement with American literature:

> I have never been able to express the pleasure I derive from the conscious study of Americana. . . . I love to think about America, to look at portraits, to remember the kind of adventurousness and purity, heroism and *salt,* that the best Americans have always had for me. Or is it—most obvious supposition—that I am an outsider; and that only for the first American-born son of so many thousands of mud-flat Jewish-Polish-Russian generations is this need great, this enquiring so urgent? Yet the most extraordinary element in all this is something it is difficult, perhaps hazardous, to express; that is, the terrible and graphic loneliness of the great Americans. . . . Each one that is, began afresh—began on his own terms—began in a universe that remained, for all practical purposes, his own.

In his journals written over the next few decades, one detects the unraveling of that package. Commenting, on 23 July 1957, on his *A Walker in the City*, published in 1951, he speculates: "Can it be that *Walker* was written out of nostalgia for my poor old revolutionary home. . . . I feel more and more that what happened to me during the war years . . . came from the loneliness of having lost one's instinctive, true, spiritual home." Finally, on 8 September 1963, the journal entry made after a visit to Edmund Wilson's "wonderful 'old' house" in Wellfleet is a kind of melancholy return to the gabled houses he had appropriated in the 1930s and 1940s with the vigor of the young explorer:

> Everything in this house is passed down or acquired by someone who could recognize immediately its historical application to himself. By contrast everything I own I have bought for myself or have had to decide its merit in relation to an entirely new situation. . . . I have *never* felt like an American. But that's because I've given up trying to feel like an American. . . . The lack of tradition is the lack of familiarity in many basic associations, and I know that I am outside them, trying to figure out what to do, what to think in relation to many basic American traditions ("The Journals of Alfred Kazin" [excerpts], ed. Richard M. Cook, *American Literary History* 2, no. 2 (Summer 1990), 243, 245, 250).

See Bachelard's exploration of attics and cellars as enclosing and contextualizing different layers of consciousness (in his *Poetics of Space*, 6ff.). In a Yiddish poem entitled "Cellars and Attics," American Yiddish poet Malka Heifetz-Tussman invokes and explores the ancestral home, with its nooks and crannies, its treasures and mementoes—as an effaced presence ("Indeed, where is my grandfather's house?") (Harshav and Harshav [eds.], *Yiddish Poetry in America*, 611).

38. The distance between the shtetl and the American Jewish ghetto as "mythic space" should not be minimized; it can be measured in terms of access. That Kazin can walk in the streets where "Alfred" grew up and Bashevis Singer cannot, relegates the streets of Bilgoray or Frampol entirely to the status of memory, even, paradoxically, freeing it from certain historical constraints. Because, as Judd Teller writes in *Strangers and Natives,* "the bearded generations . . . decimated by German genocide . . . are remote and unreal, like the weightless, levitating figures of Chagall's canvases, one may vaguely relate to them, without the risk of being mistaken for them" (262). Recent Jewish "pilgrimages" to the sites of former

shtetlakh in Poland only dramatize their obliterated presence in the physical landscape of postwar Europe.

That the process by which the Lower East Side was appropriated as mythic space was fairly self-conscious is attested to in Kazin's essay *A Walker in the City*, written in 1986; seeking to write a very ambitious "personal epic" about the city of New York, he recalls that he "suddenly opted for a small country, my natal country"—Brownsville. ("My New Yorks: Writing *A Walker in the City*," *The New York Times Book Review*, [24 Aug. 1986], 29). The negotiation of place is one of the chief privileges and burdens of immigrant and first-generation native writers. "For as a midwesterner, the child of immigrant parents, I recognized at an early age that I was called upon to decide for myself to what extent my Jewish origins, my surroundings (the accidental circumstances of Chicago) . . . were to be allowed to determine the course of my life," writes Saul Bellow in his forward to Allan Bloom's *The Closing of the American Mind* (New York: 1987), 13. For a discussion of the "place of place" in fiction generally and in "regional literature" in particular, see Eudora Welty, "Place in Fiction," *The South Atlantic Quarterly* 55, no. 1 (January 1956), 57–72. In his analysis of Carson McCullers, Flannery O'Connor and other southern writers in *The Literature of Memory: Modern Writers of the American South* (Baltimore: 1977), Richard Gray invokes the "triangular relationship between personal feeling, regional landscape, and moral reference" (268).

39. Irving Howe, "On Jewish American Writing," *Tel-Aviv Review* 2 (Fall 1989/Winter 1990), 344; *idem*, "Strangers," in *Celebrations and Attacks: Thirty Years of Literary and Cultural Commentary* (New York: 1979), 19.

In Delmore Schwartz's story "America, America," a mother's memories of immigrant culture are captured, on the very edge of oblivion, to provide grounding for the restless imagination of her native-born son. But it is the double voice, predicated on the ironizing distance of the narrator from his subject, that rescues not only the writer from a paucity of cultural resources but also the immigrant story from its inherent banality.

40. Quoted from Norman Podhoretz's *Making It* in Shechner, *After the Revolution*, 18.

41. In February 1944, the editors of *The Contemporary Jewish Record* conducted a symposium of Jewish writers "under forty" whom they placed in the "front ranks of American literature." Suggesting that "American Jews have reached the stage of integration with the native environment . . . [no longer as] spectators . . . but [as] full participants in the cultural life of the country," they may have touched on one of the central, spatial, metaphors of American Jewish culture in the second half of the twentieth century. In turn, rather than embracing such "integration," several of those who participated in the symposium delineated a peripheral space for the Jewish writer that was to be understood as somehow central to the cultural enterprise. Isaac Rosenfeld stated that the Jew is a "specialist in alienation, . . . the outsider [as] . . . perfect insider," and Delmore Schwartz affirmed that "the fact of being a Jew became available to me as a central symbol of alienation." ("Under Forty: A Symposium on American Literature and the Younger Generation of American Jews," *Contemporary Jewish Record* [Feb. 1944], 3, 35, 36, 14). See also Schwartz's 1951 essay on the "Vocation of the Poet," in which he writes that "the Jew is at once *alienated* and *indestructible; he is an exile from his own country and exile even from himself, yet he *survives* [sic!] the annihilating fury of history. In the unpredictable and fearful future that awaits civilization, the poet must be prepared to be alienated" (reprinted in *Selected Essays of Delmore Schwartz*, ed. Donald A. Dike and David H. Zucker [Chicago: 1970], 23, emphasis added). It may be useful to recall that "alienated" and "indestructible" are the mythical attributes of the Wandering Jew. The place and function of Jew, exile and poet converge for Schwartz at the very center of American civilization in the middle of the twentieth century. Isaac Rosenfeld was one of the only writers to begin in the late 1940s to come to terms explicitly with the devastation of Jewish civilization in Europe; see his essays on "Terror Beyond Evil," published in the *New Leader* (Feb. 1948), and "The Meaning of Terror," published in *Partisan Review* 1949), both reprinted in *An Age of Enormity*, ed. Theodore Solotaroff (Cleveland 1962), as well as his allegories of terror that were collected posthumously in *Alpha and Omega* (New York: 1966).

In translating Isaac Bashevis Singer's "The Little Shoemakers," he also helped to establish the modern Jewish narrative of exile (in Howe and Greenberg [eds.], *A Treasury of Yiddish Stories*, 523–544).

42. Shechner, *After the Revolution*, 7.

43. Daniel Bell, "A Parable of Alienation," *The Jewish Frontier*, Nov. 1946, 16.

44. Saul Bellow, *The Adventures of Augie March* (New York: 1953), 3.

45. On the imagination of America as an "integrated whole," as a continental "home" beyond regional loyalties, see Sopher, "The Landscape of Home," 144ff.

46. Bellow, *Augie March*, 536.

47. Bellow, *Herzog*, 248.

48. Sidra DeKoven Ezrahi, "Agnon Before and After," *Prooftexts* 2, no. 1 (January 1982), 78–94. The key as metonymy of access to sacred as to private space is as ancient in Jewish literature as the aggadah of the priests who, claiming they were no longer worthy custodians, threw the keys to the burning Temple heavenward (Pesikta Rabati: 131a). David Roskies recalls the legend of the keys to ancestral homes in fifteenth-century Spain and Portugal retained by Moroccan Jews into the twentieth century (*Against the Apocalypse: Responses to Catastrophe in Modern Jewish Literature* ed. David Roskies, [Cambridge, Mass: 1984], 1). Herzog's multiple key ring finds its counterpart in the "broken key" as exemplum of the estrangement of the Jewish refugee in New York in I. B. Singer's story "The Key" (in his *A Friend of Kafka* [Harmondsworth: 1972]).

49. For a fascinating study of the urban odyssey in American literature, of the "compassionate walker . . . [on the] sidewalk as a source of moral as well as aesthetic perspective" in contrast to the "skyscraper [or airplane] experience" that helps to "revivify an epic perspective on human possibilities in the modern world," see Michael Cowan, "Walkers in the Street: American Writers and the Modern City," *Prospects* (Fall 1981), 288, 285, 291, and passim. It might be interesting to compare "walking in the city" and "lighting out" as tropes of American mobility.

50. Bellow, *Herzog*, 266, 285.

51. *Ibid.*, 316.

52. Tenancy, occupancy and ownership are more than signs of the upward mobility and the *embourgeoisement* of the Jew in America. Tenancy as an expression of a provisional foothold in America—haunted by the fear of eviction—is explored by nearly every immigrant and proletarian writer, from Yezierska to Fuchs and Odets. In Bernard Malamud's *The Tenants* (New York: 1971), a condemned tenement is the no-man's-land of an urban encounter between the footloose black and the footloose Jew. (Most of Malamud's characters are ungrounded, closer to the European than the American figure of the Jew as wanderer, as shlemiel. See "The Jewbird" in his collection *Idiots First* [New York: 1964]). In his biography *Delmore Schwartz: The Life of An American Poet* (New York: 1977), James Atlas quotes from Schwartz's (endless) poem, "Genesis," in which he writes of a character very much resembling his own father, who " 'knew well that they had brought with them from Europe / The peasant's sense that land was the most important thing and the owner of land / A king!' Real Estate was a strategic line to be in," Atlas continues, "and Harry Schwartz [Delmore's father] had made himself a wealthy man by the time he met" Delmore's mother (6). Finally, Mordecai Richler's title character in *The Apprenticeship of Duddy Kravitz* (Boston: 1959) is a Canadian caricature of the Jew as landlord.

53. Bellow, *Herzog*, 317, 347.

54. It was probably Irving Howe who first introduced the notion that the work of Jewish writers who came of age in the 1940s and 1950s may constitute a "version of American regionalism" (*World of Our Fathers*, 585ff.). In subsequent articles he has redefined that phenomenon as more transitory: see Howe, "Strangers," and *idem*, "On Jewish American Writing." See also Robert Alter on American Jewish writing as a transitional phenomenon in "Sentimentalizing the Jews" (1965), reprinted in his *After the Tradition: Essays on Modern Jewish Writing* (New York: 1971), and "The Jew Who Didn't Get Away: On the Possibility of an American Jewish Culture," in *The American Jewish Experience*, ed. Jonathan D. Sarna (New York: 1986); Harold Bloom, "Free and Broken Tablets: The Cultural Prospects of

American Jewry" in *Agon*, 318–329; John Hollander, "The Question of American Jewish Poetry," *Tikkun* 3, no. 3 (May–June 1988).

55. Gilles Deleuze and Felix Guattari, *Kafka: Toward a Minor Literature*, trans. Dana Polan, in the *Theory and History of Literature* series (Minneapolis: 1986), 16, 17, 19.

56. The term is Hannah Arendt's own; see her essays from the 1940s on the Jew as refugee and as pariah, reprinted in *Hannah Arendt, The Jew as Pariah: Jewish Identity and Politics in the Modern Age*, ed. Ron H. Feldman (New York: 1978).

57. "In the 'thirties and 'forties," writes Henry Pachter,

> the exiles achieved their stature not in spite of their alienation but because of it. America, deeply shaken by the Great Depression, was passing through a moral and cultural crisis. With intellectuals now the 'in' thing is to be 'out,' and conformism now expresses itself in conforming with the non-conformists. In such a situation the ideal-type exile can be very effective as a model; he represents alienation in his person and he describes it in his work. But a deep misunderstanding occurs here. To him, dissent from society is radical and total; to his audience, dissent is only partial . . . the meaning of alienation has become so fuzzy that the final effect of so much pseudo-alienation is no alienation at all.

Pachter goes on to say that "Arendt had the unfortunate intuition that America needed Kafka, and people who lived quite comfortably in the world he had scorned, assured each other gleefully that they were living in a Kafkaesque world; . . . perhaps it was meant to epatez les bourgeois, but it only tickled them" (Henry Pachter, "On Being an Exile," in *The Legacy of the German Refugee Intellectuals*, ed. Robert Boyers [New York: 1969], 27, 43). *Partisan Review* devoted an entire issue to the new French thinkers in 1946, and William Barrett translated Arendt's essay entitled "What Is Existenz Philosophy?" Recounting his "adventures among the intellectuals," Barrett locates Arendt in her "chosen role as interpreter of European culture to Americans." (William Barrett, *The Truants: Adventures Among the Intellectuals* [New York: 1982], 100.) For a somewhat dissenting view see Walter Kaufmann, "The Reception of Existentialism in the United States," in Boyers (ed.), *Legacy of the German Refugee Intellectuals*. Kaufmann claims that the impact in America of intellectuals who had emigrated from or been expelled from Central Europe was less than one would expect:

> The most important way in which the Nazi regime promoted existentialism and the literature associated with it was not by compelling many people to emigrate but rather by killing so many more. As fear and trembling, dread and despair, and the vivid anticipation of one's own death ceased to be primarily literary experiences and, like the absurd visions of Kafka, turned into the stuff of everyday life, the originally untimely Kafka and Kierkegaard became popular along with Jaspers and Heidegger, Sartre and Camus, who were fashionable from the first (85).

58. Howe, "On Jewish American Writing," 347. See also *idem*, "Strangers," 19.

59. In his critique of the social and political implications of the transformation of the Jewish American intellectual from "champion of maladjustment" with his contempt for all "ideal constructions" to champion of the "affirmative imagination" (a shift monitored over the years in the pages of *Commentary*), Shechner also offers a eulogy to the "so-called Jewish novel": "If it is true, as some believe . . . that the so-called Jewish novel is dead, that is partly so because [of the attenuation in America of] the tension between the self and the world, the knot of unregenerate trouble at the heart's core that once supplied the traction and drive of the imagination in *galut*" (*After the Revolution*, 22).

Value Added: Jews in Postwar American Culture

Stephen J. Whitfield
(BRANDEIS UNIVERSITY)

Americans are "descended from the same ancestors, speaking the same language, professing the same religion, attached to the same principles of government, very similar in their manners and customs," John Jay wrote in *The Federalist* No. 2, in defense of the new Constitution.[1] At least he got the politics right: All the basic political institutions of the United States had been created by the end of the eighteenth century, and none since then. But the Framers could scarcely have imagined how the culture would keep shifting into new configurations. Regional and ethnic customs would vary widely, new languages would get injected (at least for one or two generations) and religious pluralism would become legitimated, largely because Americans increasingly did *not* have the same ancestors.

In this kaleidoscope, virtually no minority has been more colorful than the Jews, whose integration into a culture that they themselves have helped to transform has been especially conspicuous in the postwar era. The argument of this essay is entangled in paradox, however, for the distinctiveness of the Jewish impact—which has extended the contours of American culture over the past half century—has also weakened the sense of difference that has historically defined Jewish identity itself. The value system of the majority has become so open and variegated that the Jews themselves are now less conscious of their own beleaguered status as a minority. So successfully have they become included in American society, so impressively have they contributed to its democratic spirit, that it has become problematic what remains of their own subculture, what still separates the Jews as a singular people, an *'am eḥad*.

One of their ancestors, Benedict Spinoza, was the first Western thinker to uncouple church and state and thus divide the sphere of values from the apparatus of power, in his *Tractatus Theologico-Politicus* (1670). More than a decade earlier, twenty-three Dutch Jews—they could not quite be classified as his "coreligionists"—became the first to disembark in what became the United States, where his principles would be pushed to their furthest point even as its citizenry continued to think of itself as pious. By certain indices, the Americans are more devout than any Western nation other than the Irish; and yet the American public culture has now become almost

68

completely secularized, even surpassing the imagination of seventeenth-century skepticism. So complete is this triumph, for example, that Irving Berlin's "God Bless America" (1918, rev. 1938) could never conceivably replace "The Star Spangled Banner" as the national anthem, despite the fact that it is easy to sing and remember. The principle of separation of church and state is simply too much of an obstacle.[2]

Until the early 1960s, however, the full implications of secularization as well as pluralism were unrealized. Although the election of a Roman Catholic to the presidency has not recurred, John F. Kennedy's victory in 1960 meant that it was no longer necessary for the holder of the nation's highest office to be a Protestant. Two years later, another symbolic defeat was inflicted on the traditions of religious conformity with the landmark U.S. Supreme Court decision of *Engel* v. *Vitale*. Though Protestantism had long unofficially dominated public education in most of the country, the Supreme Court banned the recitation of prayer after the parents of five New York children challenged its compulsory feature. (One of these sixth-graders was eleven-year-old Joe Roth, the son of two Jewish Communists. Until his graduation, he later recalled, some of his classmates would cross themselves in fear before talking to him.) The shock waves caused by the ruling reverberated beyond Long Island and across the country. About 80 percent of the citizenry disagreed with the Supreme Court's ruling, and liberal as well as conservative clergy expressed their outrage. Two years later, the Republican candidate for the presidency doubted whether 1964 was "the time for our Federal government to ban Almighty God from our school rooms"; and a conservative Catholic, William F. Buckley, Jr., warned of increasing antisemitism if the Jews weren't "careful."[3]

Nonetheless, the *Engel* decision remained in force, and the pluralist ideal was thus not only vindicated but was also widely applied in practice. No single faith—not even Christianity itself—achieved a privileged status in the public culture, antisemitism continued to decline dramatically, and society became increasingly accommodating to minorities. Roth himself, who also survived "the theological reverence of Communism in my house," became a Hollywood film director and then head of the Twentieth Century Fox studios,[4] as though personally warranting President Richard M. Nixon's contempt for "the arts," as he told an aide in 1972, because "you know—they're Jews, they're left-wing—in other words, stay away!"[5]

Such antisemitic outbursts, especially when originating with intelligent people, can illuminate the impact of the Jews in American life, and in this sense they deserve at least as much scholarly attention as the claims of communal defense agencies. The florid exaggerations must be discounted, of course, but even the rancid complaint of Henry Adams, who was the grandson and great-grandson of earlier U.S. presidents, should not be dismissed: "We are in the hands of the Jews," he wrote in 1896. "They can do what they please with our values." Nearly two decades later, Adams amplified his sense of a cultural shift:

> The atmosphere really has become a Jew atmosphere. It is curious and evidently good for some people, but it isolates me. I do not know the language, and my friends are as ignorant as I. We are still in power, after a fashion. Our sway over what we call society

is undisputed. We keep Jews far away, and the anti-Jew feeling is quite rabid. . . . Yet we somehow seem to be more Jewish every day.[6]

Such anxieties were ugly, but they were not utterly misplaced. Indeed, they corresponded to the rise of an inescapable new system for the creation, packaging and marketing of the popular arts in which Jews were intimately involved. A revised edition of H. L. Mencken's *The American Language* noted, for instance, that "the most fruitful sources of Yiddish loans [into English] are the media of mass communications—journalism, radio and television."[7] Yet that lowly "jargon," which Henry Adams had found so "weird" when he heard it "snarled,"[8] is well-known to two recent American Nobel Prize laureates in literature: Isaac Bashevis Singer and one of his translators, Saul Bellow. In the family of a third laureate, Joseph Brodsky, Yiddish had already evaporated (though he was born in Russia itself, in 1940). But it is the mother tongue of still another writer holding U.S. citizenship to have won a Nobel Prize: Elie Wiesel. In Hollywood, meanwhile, newspapermen-turned-scenarists such as Ben Hecht (an urbane cynic whose Jewish nationalism became so ardent in the Second World War era that the Irgun later named an illegal immigrant ship after him) and Herman Mankiewicz (an atheist who kept a kosher home) helped make American movies in the 1930s and 1940s talk at a frenetic, witty pace. Hollywood's off-screen talk is still subject to ethnic fields of force. In a recent David Mamet play about movie deal makers, for example, "hiding the *afikomen*" is the double entendre for sexual "scoring" with the blonde secretary, whose own phoniness—Madonna played her on Broadway—one seedy character contrasts unfavorably with the Baal Shem Tov.[9] And when a new film monthly listed the most powerful figures in Hollywood, the first thirteen names already included enough for a minyan. Among them was Steven Spielberg, who is as rich as a brace of Bronfmans. The most successful director in history has *mezuzot* on the doorposts of his own ministudio.[10]

At one time Jews also headed all three private television networks, whose programs were noted in the most widely read magazine to be invented in the postwar era: *TV Guide*. From 1953 until 1989, its publisher was Walter H. Annenberg, the chief legatee of a family that savored a spectacular comeback from the New Deal era. (His father, who published the *Racing Form* and the *Inquirer,* had become so embroiled in anti-Roosevelt politics that the president growled to his secretary of the treasury: "I want Moe Annenberg for dinner." The cabinet officer's reply was reassuring: "You're going to have him for breakfast—fried." The publisher was convicted of income tax evasion and was jailed from 1940 until 1942, when he died of a heart attack. In 1969, Moe Annenberg's son got the satisfaction of becoming ambassador to the Court of St. James—a post to which John Jay had earlier been accredited.)[11]

And even Christian religious festivities have not been immune to Jewish influence, what with Irving Berlin strutting at the head of "The Easter Parade" (1933) and "Dreaming of a White Christmas"—the hit from *Holiday Inn* (1942) that may be the best-selling song ever. No wonder that an immigrant born with the name of Israel Baline grew up invoking the Deity to bless America.

Not only was the Jewish romance with America lavishly expressed in the postwar era; perhaps more importantly, it was reciprocated. Scholarly histories on the Jewish condition in the United States, though their titles may refer to "unease," very rarely draw divisions as do books about "Germans" and "Jews" (as though Jews could not *really* be Germans).[12] Or consider another contrast. A classic history of racism in the American colonies and early republic, Winthrop D. Jordan's *White over Black* (1968), is curiously subtitled "American Attitudes Toward the Negro" (when the author clearly means *white* attitudes). But the equivalent error that has assumed "American" to be synonymous with "gentile" is uncommon. Though the birth certificate of modern Jews is written in German, they were, in Solomon Liptzin's phrase, never more than "Germany's stepchildren." The "world of our fathers," however, for all of its poignant confusions and ferocious tensions, has become thoroughly implanted in America, where the children and grandchildren of Jewish immigrants have felt very much at home.

Millennia of martyrdom do not weigh heavily on the shoulders of most American Jews, who seem to bear no special historical burden of suffering and exhibit little sense of living in *galut*. At the dawn of the postwar era, Diana Trilling praised Isaac Rosenfeld's autobiographical novel *Passage from Home* for "its ability to use its Jewish background as a natural rather than a forced human environment." Rosenfeld had managed, she wrote as early as 1946, to "avoid the well-established emotions of Jewish separateness—the emotions of specialness, embattledness, social over-determinism, self-pity and self-punishment." *Passage from Home* would thus help revise a paradigm that, to Trilling, had become a familiar minority sensibility:

> Unable to believe that his environment really belongs to him, the Jewish novelist cannot envision a valid personal drama of development within it. At best he writes a fiction of dignified resistance or acceptance, at worst a fiction of fierce personal aggression and of the individual effort to rise above the restrictions of Jewish birth.

But Rosenfeld, she felt, had managed to handle "the fact of being Jewish . . . as simply another facet of the already sufficiently complicated business of being a human being."[13]

The naturalness of the American environment was shown in an oddity associated with the historical understanding of the 1960s, the decade that most severely tested the national attachment to John Jay's "same principles of government." The most influential analyst of Lyndon B. Johnson's political failure in Vietnam was David Halberstam (*The Best and the Brightest* [1972]), and LBJ's preeminent biographer has been Robert A. Caro (*The Years of Lyndon Johnson* [1982, 1990]). Their huge and important books on Johnson's policies and career betray no special Jewish sensibility or angle of vision, though Halberstam is a descendant of Rabbi Meir Katzenellenbogen, a famed halakhic authority in sixteenth-century Padua, and Caro is a probable descendant of Yosef Karo, the sixteenth-century codifier of the Shul-ḥan Arukh.[14] In their effort to fathom the complications of modern American history, such writers have typified the indifference of most of their fellow Jews to the further complexities and demands of their ancient heritage.

A formal Jewish culture in America is thin, and except for some immigrant intellectuals, has added little to the rejuvenation of Judaic thought. No native-born Americans have become canonical figures in the evolution of the Jews' religious and moral ideas.[15] Although all the great works of Judaism were composed in exile (except for the Bible itself), none has been written by an American. A cohesive and internally consistent Jewish culture in the United States now consists mostly of memories that are fading, its husk battered in the transmission to succeeding generations, its custodians and most sophisticated legatees generally found in academe and in museums.

The postwar reference points of Jewish culture have not been indigenous to the United States but have been defined instead by the two events that have irrevocably altered Jewish history itself: the extermination of two-thirds of European Jewry and the rebirth of Israel. The significance of the Holocaust and of Zionism has dwarfed whatever has happened in the United States. But the Jews who were so enmeshed in American culture nevertheless had to come to terms with that catastrophe and that hope, however vicariously, and in doing so enlarged and transformed the boundaries of that very culture. How those two events were absorbed and accommodated merits illustration.

The most poetically effective of all subjects, Edgar Allan Poe once theorized, is the death of a beautiful woman.[16] Yet even this morbid seer did not consider for literary purposes a more haunting and terrible death, the sort that brutally forecloses a natural emergence into maturity. Nor did any nineteenth-century writer, no matter how darkly penetrating, foresee that such a violent denial of life would be multiplied, under conditions of maximal suffering, by six million. That is a statistic too numbing to contemplate, too staggering for the ordinary moral intelligence to confront without flinching. But the fate of Anne Frank brought the pain inside.

The diary of her adolescence in the secret annex in Amsterdam was written in Dutch and published in abbreviated form in Holland only two years after she died in Bergen-Belsen. In 1950, translations of *Het Achterhuis* appeared in both French and German, but to little effect. The posthumous power of her words to give concreteness to the Holocaust began only with the publication of *The Diary of a Young Girl* in the United States in 1952.

The catalyst was Meyer Levin, an American novelist who first read the French translation. But he was told by Otto Frank, the only survivor among the eight Jews who had hidden at 263 Prinsengracht, that several distinguished American and British publishers had already rejected his daughter's diary: "Unfortunately, they all said, the subject was too heartrending; the public would resist, the book would not sell." Levin persisted: "I sent the Diary to a half dozen editors whom I knew. The reactions were uniform: they were personally touched, but professionally they were convinced that the public shied away from such material." Then, in the annual literary issue of the American Jewish *Congress Weekly,* Levin urged publication and was eventually persuasive. *Commentary* serialized it, and Levin designated it a classic on the front page of the *New York Times Book Review* after Doubleday published it. Brandished with Eleanor Roosevelt's introduction, *The Diary of a Young Girl* has been translated into fifty-one languages and has sold more than sixty million copies.[17]

Levin went on to write a theatrical version of the diary, even though producer Herman Shumlin warned him: "It's impossible. You simply can't expect an audience to come to the theater to watch on the stage people they know to have ended up in the crematorium. It would be too painful. They won't come."[18] A play other than Levin's, written by Albert Hackett and Frances Goodrich, opened on Broadway in 1955. It won a Pulitzer Prize but also provoked a court battle, initiated by Levin, concerning alleged distortions of the original work.[19] The stage adaptation led to the republication of the *Diary* in German and, according to one historian, "caught the imagination of the German reading public." Attending a performance of the *Diary* in West Berlin in 1956, the British critic Kenneth Tynan recorded "the most drastic emotional experience the theatre has ever given me. It had little to do with art, for the play was not a great one; yet its effect, in Berlin, at that moment of history, transcended anything that art has yet learned to achieve." After it was over,

> the house-lights went up on an audience that sat drained and ashen, some staring straight ahead, others staring at the ground, for a full half-minute. Then, as if awakening from a nightmare, they rose and filed out in total silence, not looking at each other, avoiding even the customary nods of recognition with which friend greets friend. There was no applause, and there were no curtain-calls.

Tynan acknowledged that his report was "not drama criticism. In the shadow of an event so desperate and traumatic, criticism would be an irrelevance. It can only record an emotion that I felt, would not have missed, and pray never to feel again."[20]

Though the Broadway production had, in his opinion, "smacked of exploitation," the emotional force of the New York version was also overwhelming. Pivotal to its effect was director Garson Kanin, who also directed films. (Indeed, when he visited Anne's tiny cubicle in Amsterdam, Kanin quickly noticed a Dutch movie poster on the wall above her bed, among the photos of Hollywood stars that she had collected. The poster announced: "*Tom, Dick and Harry*—starring Ginger Rogers, directed by Garson Kanin.") Among the ten actors Kanin picked for the New York production was Joseph Schildkraut, an Academy Award winner for his portrayal of Captain Dreyfus in Warner Brothers' *The Life of Emile Zola* (1937). Schildkraut's 1,068 performances as Otto Frank, over the course of three years,

> were probably the most important and decisive of my whole life. Because I did not merely act a part, but had to live as Otto Frank through the whole terrible and shattering experience of an era which can never be erased from the memory of my generation. . . . It was, I believe firmly, not accidental that *The Diary of Anne Frank* became the culmination of my professional life.

Himself the son of a leading stage actor who had come from the Balkans to revive for German audiences a love of their own classics, Schildkraut had "never before . . . felt such an intimate relationship to a play, never such an identification with a part." For Anne Frank's diary "actually wrote the epitaph to a whole period of the history of Europe, the history of Germany, [and] the tragedy of the Jews."[21]

The play next became a George Stevens film (1959), in which Schildkraut also starred as Otto Frank, and has gone through other permutations as well. At one Bonds for Israel rally in New York's Madison Square Garden in New York, for example, a torch was brought from the new state and used to light a menorah on stage. Schildkraut lit it and said the prayer just as he had done in the final scene in

Act I on Broadway. "Thirty thousand people filled the arena, a sea of humanity," he recalled. "And like powerful waves the murmurs, sighs, prayers of that mass rose up to me, engulfed me, carried me away. I felt sorrow and exultation. My eyes burned, my heart ached in pride and grief." And in a March 1990 UNICEF benefit concern in New York, Michael Tilson Thomas conducted the New World Symphony in a concert piece he wrote entitled "From the Diary of Anne Frank." (As the grandson of the Yiddish theatrical pioneer Boris Thomashefsky, Thomas was a living link to the culture that the Nazis destroyed.) No wonder that Anne Frank's biographer could claim that "her voice was preserved out of the millions that were silenced, this voice no louder than a child's whisper. It has outlasted the shouts of the murderers and has soared above the voice of time."[22]

The last sentence in her diary was written only three days before the murderers came, and that whisper could not be unmediated. In the United States, her words could only be heard resonating inside a culture not known for its appreciation of the tragic—or of the suffering for which no grief or retribution is sufficient, the kind of loss with which no vengeance or restitution is commensurate. In an era when not even the term "Holocaust" was in use, when not even a name was available to summarize the evil of the Third Reich, when neither knowledge of nor interest in the Nazi genocide was conspicuous, morally serious artistic impulses were frustrated. It was exceedingly difficult to make sense of the senseless, to make mass murder intelligible to a mass audience. Some American moviegoers found *The Diary of Anne Frank* baffling, apparently not realizing that the film was based on one family's actual experience and assuming that what they were viewing was fictional. One early cut of the film ended at Bergen-Belsen, which so vexed a preview audience that it was changed, as in the Broadway play, to conclude on the more optimistic note of Anne's proclamation that "in spite of everything, I still believe that people are really good at heart." Otto Frank himself realized that audiences responded as much to the pathos of adolescent yearning as to the horror outside the secret annex.[23]

But what generated the greatest controversy was the evasion of the distinctively Jewish character of the family's ordeal. Meyer Levin himself blamed the playwrights Hackett and Goodrich, a husband-and-wife team of scenarists who had previously won an Oscar for *Seven Brides for Seven Brothers*. They were not Jewish, though the head of production at M-G-M assured Levin that, in researching the Hanukah scene, the team had "gone to the most prominent Reform rabbi in Hollywood."[24] Their distortions, which Levin also attributed to the editorial influence of playwright Lillian Hellman, had provoked his lawsuit. But the failure to underscore the uniquely Jewish dimension to the *Diary* was also cultural. In the early 1950s, audiences were still uneasy with particularism and peoplehood, with facing the lethal implications of diaspora history. The awful terminus of the Holocaust, it was widely assumed, had to be shown instead under the auspices of universalism: what happened to Anne Frank might have happened to anyone.

For example, the diarist herself wondered:

Who has made us Jews different from all other people? Who has allowed us to suffer so terribly up till now? It is God who has made us as we are, but it will be God, too, who will raise us up again. If we bear all this suffering and if there are still Jews left, when it is over, then Jews, instead of being doomed, will be held up as an example. Who knows, it might even be our religion from which the world and all peoples learn good, and for that reason and that reason only do we have to suffer now. We can never become just Netherlanders, or just English, or just . . . representatives of any other country for that matter, we will always remain Jews, but we want to, too.

This echo of the covenant is posthumously twisted into something quite different in both the play and the film. "We're not the only people that've had to suffer," Anne is made to say. "There've always been people that've had to . . . Sometimes one race . . . Sometimes another."[25]

Meyer Levin therefore asked:

Why had her Jewish avowal been censored on the stage? It is an essential statement, epitomizing the entire mystery of God and the Six Million, a pure and perfect expression of the search for meaning in the Holocaust, for all humanity, Jewish or not. Nowhere in the substitute drama is this touched upon. This brazen example of the inversion of a dead author's words epitomizes the programmatic, politicalized [sic] dilution of the Jewish tragedy. Millions of spectators the world over were unaware they were subjected to idea-censorship.[26]

Nor were the actors in the Hanukkah scene to sing in Hebrew because, as the playwrights explained to Otto Frank, "it would set the characters in the play apart from the people watching them . . . for the majority of our audience is not Jewish. And the thing that we have striven for . . . is to make the audience understand and identify themselves. . . ." According to *Het Achterhuis,* Anne's sister Margot wanted to be a nurse in Palestine if she had survived the war, but neither on stage nor on screen is her Zionist sentiment mentioned.[27] And although Susan Strasberg had drawn raves for her Broadway portrayal of Anne Frank, Twentieth Century Fox honored earlier Hollywood custom by casting a non-Jewish actress named Millie Perkins instead.

It is interesting to contrast the reception of the *Diary* with that of Elie Wiesel's *La Nuit* (1958), which did not appear in an English translation until 1960 (after twenty publishers had already rejected it), but it is doubtful that the mass audience would have been prepared for his unsparingly bleak memoir of the camps—before which the *Diary* of course stops short. As Peter Novick has pointed out, American culture in the 1950s was not yet ready for Wiesel, who was born a year before Anne Frank. He was East European, poor, observant and unassimilated. She had been Western, middle-class, of Reform background, so assimilated that she was pleased that in December 1943 Hanukkah occurred so close to Saint Nicholas's Day and Christmas.[28] Anne Frank was therefore a more endearing icon of violated innocence. For most American Jews as well as non-Jews, identification was thus made easier, reinforcing an interpretation of the Holocaust that generalized it into the signature event of universal suffering.

Though Anne had dreamed of visiting the holy places in Eretz Israel, what she really wanted to do was to travel all over the world and become a writer.[29] That is the very sort of life that Philip Roth has led. In his novella *The Ghost Writer,* the twenty-three-year-old deutero-Roth named Nathan Zuckerman visits an older and more austere Jewish writer and imagines that Amy Bellette, a young researcher who is also staying in the house, has survived Bergen-Belsen and is really Anne Frank. Roth's tale is both a gesture of imaginative resistance to the Holocaust—wondering, as many undoubtedly have, whether something so unbearable and incomprehensible might just possibly not have been so truly awful as it was—as well as a melancholy acceptance of its finality. Amy Bellette is only herself. For "when the sleeve of her coat fell back," Zuckerman "of course saw that there was no scar on her forearm. No scar; [and therefore] no book" after all.[30]

For Anne Frank could *not* still be alive, and hers are only the words of a ghost writer. She can "live" only in memory, only in representation. In the United States she can also live as a fragile symbol of Jewish identification, as an inspiration to sustain *ahavat yisrael*. Zuckerman, for example, stands accused of disgracing the Jewry of New Jersey with his scandalous fiction. But redemption is still possible, according to Judge Leonard Wapter, a distant family friend. "If you have not yet seen the Broadway production of *The Diary of Anne Frank,*" Wapter writes the errant young novelist, "I strongly advise that you do so. Mrs. Wapter and I were in the audience on opening night; we wish that Nathan Zuckerman could have been with us to benefit from the unforgettable experience."

Zuckerman refuses to reply, and tells his father:

> "Nothing I could write Wapter would convince him of anything. Or his wife."
> "You could tell him you went to see *The Diary of Anne Frank.* You could at least do that."
> "I didn't see it. I read the book. *Everybody* read the book."
> "But you liked it, didn't you?"
> "That's not the issue. How can you *dis*like it?"[31]

And in fact her diary eludes such categories of judgment. Though its theatrical and cinematic distortions must be set in the context of the 1950s, when a vigorous and various pluralism was still subdued to a consensus that emphasized social stability, the *Diary* was virtually unique in the attentiveness to the Holocaust that it commanded. In American thought and expression, that subject was at first only slowly and rarely broached. In films, for example, even Stanley Kramer's moralistic *Judgment at Nuremberg* (1961) managed to depict the evil of Nazism without including any major or even minor Jewish characters. Not until Sidney Lumet's *The Pawnbroker* (1965) did Hollywood directly tackle the subject of the Holocaust again;[32] and even then the protagonist, a Jewish survivor named Sol Nazerman (Rod Steiger), was presented as a Christ figure, bearing stigmata. But the trickle of films soon became a flood that has helped shape the sensibility of American Jews—and of many of their neighbors.

While still struggling to restore Anne Frank's authentic voice, Meyer Levin did some research on the history of the Yishuv in Palestine, considering the possibility of giving the topic fictional treatment. Then he saw the galleys for "a novel of Israel" that Doubleday was about to publish, and realized that he would have to pursue another theme. The novel was *Exodus*.

Its author was Leon Uris, a former high school dropout from Baltimore, where he had flunked English three times before joining the U.S. Marines at the age of seventeen. *Exodus* proved to be one of the publishing sensations of the era. For more than a year it remained on the *New York Times* best-seller list (including nineteen weeks perched at the top) and was a Book-of-the-Month Club alternate selection. The hardcover edition has never gone out of print, having sold to date more than half a million copies in some forty printings; the Bantam paperback was quickly reordered at a rate of two thousand per month, reaching almost seven million copies after sixty-three printings. Although propaganda novels have occasionally punctuated the history of U.S. mass taste, *Exodus* was unprecedented. For it was not intended to arouse indignation over a domestic issue, such as the moral horror of slavery (*Uncle Tom's Cabin*), the ugliness of urban working conditions (*The Jungle*) or the plight of migrant farmers (*The Grapes of Wrath*). *Exodus* was published when American Jewish interest in Israel was slight and levels of philanthropy and tourism were—by later standards—low,[33] and when ethnicity was suppressed or disdained as an embarrassing residue of the immigrant past. It was therefore astonishing that an American could write a Zionist epic that would virtually fly off the shelves of American bookstores. The year that it was published, ex–Prime Minister David Ben-Gurion asserted: "As a piece of propaganda, it's the greatest thing ever written about Israel."[34]

Though no political repercussions were immediately discernible, the political value of *Exodus* was unmistakable. Its popularity was not only a tribute to the expanding hospitality of the majority culture, however. It was also evidence that the Jewish people was now permitted to view their own experience through American mythology, to think of themselves not only as virtuous but as courageous, tough and triumphant. Uris pulled off such a feat by outflanking or evading the customary concerns of the ethnic novel—the tension between Old World authority and tradition versus New World promise and freedom. Ignoring such conventional issues as the peril posed to the family or the crises of belief, he drew heavily on the exploits of Yehudah Arazi, a Mossad agent who operated illegal Zionist ships in the Mediterranean under the British Mandate and who had drawn considerable press attention to the plight of Jewish refugees.[35] Uris transposed to the Middle East the adventure formulas that middlebrow American readers already expected. In making Jewish characters into heroes skillful with weapons, the ex-marine who had scripted the Western film *The Gunfight at the O.K. Corral* (1957) knew how to keep the action flowing. Indeed, the scene in Chapter 16, in which the Haganah frees Irgun prisoners from the British, might have been called "the gunfight at the Akko jail."

The critic Leslie Fiedler therefore felt compelled to lodge a protest against "stereotype-inversion . . . [which] merely substitutes falsification for falsification, sentimentality for sentimentality."[36] The courage of Uris's Israelis seemed designed to contradict General George S. Patton's denigrating remark (made after he slapped a couple of hospitalized U.S. soldiers in 1943) that "there's no such thing as shell shock. It's an invention of the Jews."[37] In Uris's novel, "the Jewish military heroes are presented as Jews already become, or in the process of becoming, Israelis." The book thus represented "a disguised form of assimilation, the attempt of certain Jews to be accepted by the bourgeois, Philistine gentile community on the grounds that, though they are not Christians, they are even more bourgeois and philistine."[38]

This interpretation now seems mistaken, however. *Exodus* tapped a subterranean

Jewish nationalism when the path toward full assimilation seemed utterly unob-
structed, and represented an unexpected detour for countless readers. "I have received thousands of letters in the last quarter of a century telling me that *Exodus* has
substantially changed their lives," the author claimed, "particularly in regard to
young people finding pride in their Jewishness. Older people find similar pride in
the portrait of fighting Jews in contrast to the classical characterization as weak-
spined, brilliant intellects and businessmen."[39]

Exodus was Doubleday's third "Jewish" blockbuster in six years (after *Diary of a
Young Girl* and Herman Wouk's *Marjorie Morningstar*) and won the National
Jewish Book Award, a year before the same National Jewish Welfare Board gave its
award to Roth for *Goodbye, Columbus* (1959). With its very different stereotypes,
Exodus was thus wedged between the two novels that established the image of "the
Jewish American princess"—a stereotype that eventually superseded "the Jewish
mother" that Roth himself so giddily pilloried a decade later in *Portnoy's Complaint*
(1969).

The romance between a *sabra* and a gentile nurse (the only important American
character in the novel) was in the foreground of this sage of the genesis of the Third
Jewish Commonwealth. The love story seemed to reiterate the staples of earlier
popular works, stretching back to Israel Zangwill's *The Melting-Pot* (1908) in
imagining how interethnic or interreligious love might surmount the primordial
hatreds that history had nurtured. But *Exodus* shattered that convention when the
nurse, the incarnation of the American majority culture, casts her lot at the end with
the Jewish independence fighters; and the enormous appeal of the novel suggested a
certain deceleration of the assimilationist impulses that previous American Jewish
fiction had registered. (The effect on Otto Preminger, who adapted the novel to the
screen in 1960, was admittedly less impressive. While on location in Israel, the
director wanted to marry an Episcopalian. Because the Weizmann Institute's Meyer
Weisgal, who was cast in a brief scene, was willing to testify to the rabbinate that
the bride was Jewish, the couple was married in Haifa rather than in Cyprus.)[40]

The popularity of Preminger's movie was unaffected by the picket lines of neo-
Nazi George Lincoln Rockwell and his followers in eastern cities. From the film
score, crooner Pat Boone quarried a hit song notable for its egocentric arrogance
("This land is mine/God gave this land to me"), undoubtedly boosting a successful
packaged tour organized in 1960 that traced the route of events in Uris's novel. The
following year, El Al airlines announced a sixteen-day tour that would cover the
very places where Preminger and his crew had shot scenes for *Exodus*.[41] Jewish
ethnicity became a segment of the market.

The breadth of the appeal of *Exodus* was revealed in its impact upon a versatile
black teacher and writer named Julius Lester. The son of a Methodist minister, he
recalled that, while attending all-Negro Fisk University in Nashville, Tennessee, a
classmate thrust the novel at him. Its effect "on me was so extraordinary that I
wanted to go and fight for Israel, even die, if need be, for Israel." Lester added that
"Israel spoke to the need I had as a young black man for a place where I could be
free of being an object of hatred. I did not wish I were Jewish, but was glad that
Jews had a land of their own, even if blacks didn't."[42] By the late 1980s Lester had
become a Jew and even a cantor in a Conservative shul in western Massachusetts.

Though the passions that he felt and enacted were rarely as spectacular among his new coreligionists, one sociologist claimed it was "virtually impossible to find a Reform home in the 1950s without a copy of Leon Uris's *Exodus.*" His novel undoubtedly awakened pride in the fulfillment of a dream that was both democratic and humane as well as nationalist.[43]

Though literary critics ignored *Exodus* (except to spray it with buckshot), it has appeared in more than fifty translations (most importantly, Russian);[44] and even hostile reviewers might be hard put to challenge Uris's assertion that "it has been among the most influential novels in history."[45] Uris himself insisted on a standard of aesthetic judgment that would privilege psychic health and affirmation. In an interview in the *New York Post,* he denounced

> a whole school of American Jewish writers who spend their time damning their fathers, hating their mothers, wringing their hands and wondering why they were born. This isn't art or literature. It's psychiatry. These writers are professional apologists. Every year you find one of their works on the best-seller list. Their work is obnoxious and makes me sick to my stomach. I wrote *Exodus* because I was just sick of apologizing— or feeling that it was necessary to apologize.[46]

When Uris added that, contrary to the diaspora stereotype, "we have been fighters," Roth was provoked to retort, "So bald, stupid, and uninformed is the statement that it is not even worth disputing." Having published a hilarious short story about quite unheroic Jews in military uniform, "Defender of the Faith" (1959), Roth saw little "value in swapping one simplification for the other." Saul Bellow's judgment was more measured:

> It may appear that the survivors of Hitler's terror in Europe and Israel will benefit more from good publicity than from realistic representation, or that posters are needed more urgently than masterpieces. Admittedly, some people say, *Exodus* was not much of a novel, but it was extraordinarily effective as a document and we need such documents now. We do not need stories like those of Philip Roth which expose unpleasant Jewish traits. . . . [But] in literature we cannot accept a political standard. We can only have a literary one.[47]

Politics could not be easily excluded, however, especially when novelists themselves incorporated large historical and political themes in their work. Uris's subsequent *Mila 18* (1961), which was number four among best-sellers that year, counterposed an episode of desperate heroism—the Warsaw ghetto uprising—to the passive victimization that the *Diary of a Young Girl* represented. And in one of his most complex fictions to date, *The Counterlife* (1986), Roth rewrote *Exodus* as ambivalence, putting Nathan Zuckerman, the sort of assimilated novelist whose real-life counterparts Uris had attacked, in the Holy Land. There Nathan confronts his brother Henry, a dentist from suburban New Jersey, now Hanoch, who has chosen to relive on the West Bank the vigilant and embattled Zionism that Ari Ben-Canaan had projected. It is as though the safely suburban professional man whom Marjorie Morningstar had married at the end of Wouk's novel was suddenly thrust, in *The Counterlife,* into a condition of radical insecurity, falling under the sway of the brilliant, fanatically right-wing Mordecai Lippman. *The Counterlife* may be the most dramatic and sophisticated novel that an American has yet written on the moral and political dilemmas facing Israel and of Israel's meaning for American Jewry.

With the news that Roth's *Portnoy's Complaint* would become the first foreign novel translated into Czech under a post-Communist regime,[48] the story of the Jewish impact upon American culture was elevated into a different and even mysterious dimension. The multiple ironies associated with minority life in America could no longer be confined to the United States. For if Czech readers could find engrossing the struggles between Alex and Sophie Portnoy, then even Jewish particularism had lost its specificity, its hermetic pungency, its implosive force. Thus the distinctly postwar phase of the Jewish involvement in American culture—especially mass culture—may be over.

This has been a story that might begin with *The Jolson Story* (1946), starring Larry Parks, a Kansan playing a Jew who was famous for singing in blackface. This cinematic envoi to vaudeville was released when the unrivaled power of the film industry was about to yield to television. The coda of that story might be a videocassette made in 1984 of a one-woman Broadway show, *Whoopi Goldberg*, written by and starring a black comedienne—who was raised as a Roman Catholic but who has given herself a Jewish surname—playing (among other roles) a black, streetwise junkie who visits the Anne Frank House in Amsterdam, and then breaks down and cries while meditating on vulnerability. The supervisor of the Broadway production was Mike Nichols, born Michael Igor Peschkowsky in Berlin in 1931, who had arrived in New York in 1939 knowing two English sentences: "I don't speak English" and "Please don't kiss me."[49] Yet the Jewish embrace of America was about to be fully consummated—and reciprocated.

The romantic tales that Broadway, Hollywood and publishers' row once chose to narrate tended to locate impediments to love in ethnicity, religion and "race"— though, except for race itself, these were hurdles that could be overcome. After the Second World War, the credibility of such impediments crumbled in an increasingly tolerant and diverse America. Hollywood's leading men in its golden age of the 1930s and 1940s tended to be handsome WASPs (Cary Grant, Gary Cooper, Clark Gable, John Wayne) and, somewhat later, their occasional Jewish facsimiles such as John Garfield (né Julius Garfinkle), Tony Curtis (né Bernard Schwartz) and the half-Jew Paul Newman. But while Jewish actresses (unless named Barbra Streisand) are still expected to conform to Anglo-Saxon conventions of what a good profile is, the requirement has now been waived for Jewish actors. The seismic shift in sexual attractiveness can be discerned in *Play It Again, Sam* (1972), when a businessman guesses that his wife (Diane Keaton) must be having an affair with "some stud." The camera suddenly focuses on his guilty, self-conscious best friend (Woody Allen),[50] whose imaginary romantic adviser is Humphrey Bogart. Instead of ridiculing himself as a *nebbish* (as in earlier Woody Allen comedies), he proves himself capable of winning Keaton (off-screen, too).

Director Woody Allen can of course give Actor Woody Allen his pick of women, whether played by Keaton, Charlotte Rampling, or Mia Farrow; but it is noteworthy that audiences have not rebelled. Nor is there widespread puzzlement—much less disapproval—when short, nasal Dustin Hoffman wins Katherine Ross (in *The Graduate* [1967]) and then Jessica Lange (in *Tootsie* [1982]), or when Hoffman, like Allen himself in *Manhattan* (1979), plays the former husband of the ethereal Meryl Streep (in *Kramer vs. Kramer* [1979]). Art Garfunkel (rather than Jack Nicholson) marries Candice Bergen in *Carnal Knowledge* (1971), Jeff Goldblum gets to keep Michelle Pfeiffer as well as a bundle of cash in *Into the Night* (1985), Ron Liebman attracts Sally Field in *Norma Rae* (1979), and Billy Crystal gets to be more than friends with Meg Ryan in *When Harry Met Sally . . .* (1989). If un-prepossessing and even unglamorous Jews can play romantic leads without the novelty of such casting attracting notice—or popular resistance—then Jews and gentiles may have become so comfortable with one another in American society that the historic distinction between them matters less than ever.

Because Jewish values and images have nicked the nation's postwar culture, making it less monochromatic and more variegated, the critical detachment that this marginal people once felt has largely dissipated, and the case for pronounced Jewish separation has been decisively weakened. Thanks to the disproportionate Jewish contribution to the popular arts, the traditional bifurcation between "them" and "us" is blurring into irrelevance. In so benign a setting, where neighbors are more accessible than ancestors, what "we" have left to defend and cultivate cannot be articulated with the same confidence as in the past. The explanation for assimilation that is herein proposed is therefore paradoxical: The very Jewish enlargement and invigoration of American culture that has enabled Jews to identify so fully with it has made Jewish identity under such conditions problematic. That national culture is not so much a distant threat as a distorted mirror, but the Jewish faces that it reveals are coming to resemble everyone else's.

Notes

1. Alexander Hamilton, John Jay and James Madison, *The Federalist: A Commentary on the Constitution of the United States,* ed. Edward Mead Earle (New York: 1937 [1788]), 9.

2. Margaret Carlson, "Oh, Say, Can You Sing It?," *Time* 135 (12 Feb. 1990), 27. "If winning were everything," Carlson claims, "'God Bless America' might carry the day. Anyone can belt out a respectable version."

3. Stanley I. Kutler, *The School Prayer Controversy in America: Constitutionalism, Symbolism, and Pluralism* (Tel-Aviv: 1984), 12–17; Aljean Harmetz, "Has Joe Roth Got the Key to Success at Fox?" *New York Times,* 4 March 1990.

4. Harmetz, "Has Joe Roth Got the Key."

5. "Newly Released Tapes," in Staff of the *Washington Post, The Fall of a President* (New York: 1974), 222.

6. Henry Adams to Charles Milnes Gaskell, 31 July 1896 and 19 February 1914, quoted in *The Jew in the Modern World: A Documentary History,* eds. Paul R. Mendes-Flohr and Jehuda Reinharz (New York: 1980), 370.

7. H. L. Mencken, *The American Language: An Inquiry into the Development of English in the United States,* rev. ed., ed. Raven L. McDavid and David W. Maurer (New York: 1963 [1919]), 253–256, 260–264.

8. Henry Adams, *The Education of Henry Adams,* rev. ed., ed. Ernest Samuels (Boston: 1973 [1918]), 238.

9. Pauline Kael, "Raising Kane," in *idem,* Herman J. Mankiewicz and Orson Welles, *The Citizen Kane Book* (Boston: 1971), 17–20, 51; David Mamet, *Speed-the-Plow* (New York: 1987), 34, 72.

10. "The Most Powerful People in Hollywood," *Premiere* 3 (May 1990), 63–65; "Maker of Hit After Hit, Steven Spielberg is Also a Conglomerate," *Wall Street Journal*, 9 Feb. 1987.

11. Henry Morgenthau Diaries, 10 April 1939, quoted in Ted Morgan, *FDR: A Biography* (New York: 1985), 555–556; John Cooney, *The Annenbergs* (New York: 1982), 20, 125–138.

12. Consider Leonard Dinnerstein's *Uneasy at Home: Antisemitism and the American Jewish Experience* (New York: 1987) and Arthur Hertzberg's *The Jews in America: Four Centuries of an Uneasy Encounter* (New York: 1989), as well as Jacob Neusner's *Stranger at Home: "The Holocaust," Zionism, and American Judaism* (Chicago: 1981).

13. Diana Trilling, *Reviewing the Forties* (New York: 1978), 167–168.

14. Neil Rosenstein, *The Unbroken Chain: Sketches and the Genealogy of Illustrious Jewish Families from the 15th–20th Century* (New York: 1976), 312; Israel Shenker, "Now, Jewish Roots," *New York Times Magazine* (20 March 1977), 42–44; Fred A. Bernstein, "In an Explosive Biography, Robert Caro Portrays L.B.J.'s Path to Power as the Low Road," *People* 19 (17 Jan. 1983), 31–32.

15. Stephen J. Whitfield, *American Space, Jewish Time* (Hamden, Conn.: 1988), 60–64.

16. Edgar Allan Poe, "The Philosophy of Composition" (1846), in *The Portable Poe*, ed. Philip Van Doren Stern (New York: 1945), 557.

17. Sander L. Gilman, *Jewish Self-Hatred: Anti-Semitism and the Hidden Language of the Jews* (Baltimore: 1986), 345; Meyer Levin, *The Obsession* (New York: 1973), 34; Harry Mulisch, "Death and the Maiden," *New York Review of Books* 33 (17 July 1986), 7.

18. Quoted in Levin, *Obsession*, 36.

19. A full account of the legal battle is given in Levin, *Obsession*.

20. Gilman, *Jewish Self-Hatred*, 345; Kenneth Tynan, *Curtains* (New York: 1961), 450–451.

21. Joseph Schildkraut (as told to Leo Lania), *My Father and I* (New York: 1959), 2–3, 233, 236, 237.

22. *Ibid.*, 237–238; Ernst Schnabel, *Anne Frank: A Portrait in Courage* (New York: 1958), 192.

23. Judith E. Doneson, *The Holocaust in American Film* (Philadelphia: 1987), 69, 76, 80–81; Anne Frank, *The Diary of a Young Girl*, trans. B. M. Mooyaart-Doubleday (Garden City, N.Y.: 1952, paperback ed. 1953), 237.

24. Levin, *Obsession*, 152; Doneson, *Holocaust in American Film*, 74.

25. Frank, *Diary of a Young Girl*, 186–187; Frances Goodrich and Albert Hackett, *The Diary of Anne Frank* (New York: 1956), 168; Levin, *Obsession*, 29–30; Doneson, *Holocaust in American Film*, 69–70, 82.

26. Levin, *Obsession*, 30.

27. Quoted in Doneson, *Holocaust in American Film*, 70; Levin, *Obsession*, 126.

28. Frank, *Diary of a Young Girl*, 108–113; Gilman, *Jewish Self-Hatred*, 349.

29. *Diary of a Young Girl*, 177, 206, 210; Levin, *Obsession*, 121.

30. Philip Roth, *The Ghost Writer* (New York: 1980), 207.

31. *Ibid.*, 128, 135.

32. Stephen J. Whitfield, *Voices of Jacob, Hands of Esau: Jews in American Life and Thought* (Hamden, Conn.: 1984), 30–41; Annette Insdorf, *Indelible Shadows: Film and the Holocaust* (New York: 1983), 6–10, 23–28.

33. David Biale, *Power and Powerlessness in Jewish History* (New York: 1986), 184.

34. Quoted in Edwin McDowell, "*Exodus* in Samizdat: Still Popular and Still Subversive," *New York Times Book Review*, 26 April 1987, 13.

35. Herbert Agar, *The Saving Remnant: An Account of Jewish Survival* (New York: 1960), 204–215.

36. Leslie A. Fiedler, *Waiting for the End: The American Literary Scene from Hemingway to Baldwin* (New York: 1964), 91.

37. Phillip Knightley, *The First Casualty: The War Correspondent as Hero, Propagandist, and Myth Maker* (New York: 1975), 320.

38. Fiedler, *Waiting for the End*, 91.

39. Leon Uris, letter to author, 16 April 1985.

40. Otto Preminger, *Preminger: An Autobiography* (New York: 1978), 225–226; Meyer Weisgal, . . . *So Far: An Autobiography* (New York: 1971), 313–315.

41. Patricia Erens, *The Jew in American Cinema* (Bloomington: 1985), 217, 219; David H. Bennett, *The Party of Fear: From Nativist Movements to the New Right in American History* (Chapel Hill: 1988), 325; Daniel J. Boorstin, *The Image, or What Happened to the American Dream* (New York: 1962), 107.

42. Julius Lester, "All God's Children," in *Jewish Possibilities: The Best of Moment Magazine,* ed. Leonard Fein (Northvale, N.J.: 1987), 28; *idem, Lovesong: Becoming a Jew* (New York: 1988), 29–30.

43. Norman Mirsky, "Nathan Glazer's *American Judaism* after 30 Years: A Reform Opinion," *American Jewish History* 77 (December 1987), 237; William A. Novak, "Twenty Important Jewish Books Written Since 1950," *The Jewish Almanac,* ed. Richard Siegel and Carl Rheins (New York: 1980), 425.

44. Even the enormous impact of the novel in America was overshadowed by its Russian version, *Ishkod,* circulating illegally in the Soviet Union. An Israeli embassy official stationed there from 1959 until 1962 has disclosed that he and other staffers gave away numerous copies of the Bantam (U.S.) edition, which had arrived through the diplomatic pouch. The former official, who remains anonymous, recalled that "the book went from hand to hand. Remember, this was before the Six-Day War, when the Russian people were told Jews were bad, Jews were cowards. The book allowed them to identify with the Jewish national movement." The 599 pages of the Bantam paperback were translated and then typed page by page, using as many legible carbon copies as possible in a nation where "private" citizens were denied access to Xerox machines. Four different translations were done by groups of people who were unaware that others were also producing a *samizdat Exodus.* A unit of "ideological Zionists" did some censorship of its own by eliminating the love affair between Ari Ben-Canaan and Kitty Fremont—the very convention that made it formulaic for American readers. As Jerry Goodman, the executive director of the National Conference on Soviet Jewry, explained: "They couldn't see a Jew having an affair with a non-Jew" (McDowell, "*Exodus* in Samizdat," 13). "There were dozens of such translations done in every city in Russia with Jews and by prisoners in the Gulag," the novelist later claimed. "Many of these translations had eight or ten translators working on them, and other times a family would read it aloud during one entire night so that they could pass it along" (Leon Uris, letter to author, 16 April 1985).

Here was a novel that was to change lives—such as Eliahu Essas's. In 1966 the mathematician read a seventy-page digest of *Ishkod,* of which roughly sixty pages consisted of historical background. "But the other ten were involved with the personalities, and they were digested so well that the hero became our hero." Four years later, Essas received in Moscow a two-volume translation that Aliyah Library in Israel also produced. "I read it once, then again the next year, and I participated with many others making typewritten copies" (McDowell, "*Exodus* in Samizdat," 13; Martin Gilbert, *The Jews of Hope* [New York: 1985], 169–173). Natan Sharansky's autobiography records how the appeal of Zionism grew stronger while he was still a student: "Friends began giving me books about Israel, including the novel *Exodus,* which was circulated in *samizdat* form and had an enormous influence on Jews of my generation" (Natan Sharansky, *Fear No Evil,* trans. Stefani Hoffman [New York: 1988], xv). Though it was a work of fiction uninfected by any explicitly anti-Soviet propaganda, the distribution of *Ishkod* was manifestly illegal (see McDowell, "*Exodus* in Samizdat," 13). At the trial of Leonid (Ari) Volvovsky in 1985, evidence was presented that he had given Uris's novel to a woman who was asked to pass it on to others. The computer expert was charged, among other crimes, with distributing "anti-Soviet propaganda." A few months earlier, a similar accusation had been brought against Yakov Levin, a Hebrew teacher in Odessa; he too was sentenced to three years in prison for slander. Both he and Volvovsky were released early in 1987. A year later, at an emotional Action for Soviet Jewry benefit in Boston, Volvovsky met Uris for the first time, along with Senator Edward M. Kennedy.

"When my wife Jill was photographing in a reception center in Israel," Uris has recalled, "people came up and showed her letters saying that, when they started reading *Exodus,* that was the first step for applying for a visa to come out of Russia." In a transfer center for Soviet Jews in Vienna, he met a woman who was among the typists of *Ishkod.* In the fall of 1989, Uris went to Moscow, where he accepted a twenty-six-year-old, first-edition *samizdat* of *Exodus.* Weeping, he responded: "This means more to me than a Nobel Prize. I thank you all in this hall tonight, and I thank B'nai B'rith for bringing me here." During Simhat Torah services in the synagogue, the worshipers roared and applauded loudly upon hearing the announcement from the *bimah* that Uris was there. The Muscovites mobbed the author when he carried a Torah scroll through the sanctuary, kissing the Torah cover—and Uris as well (Michael Neiditch, "Uris in the USSR," *Jewish Monthly* 104 [Jan. 1990], 35–37).

No Jewish book was ever more cherished in the U.S.S.R. than *Ishkod.* "For Soviet Jewish activists," Jerry Goodman asserted, "it was probably more meaningful than even the Bible. Most of the Jewish activists in the late 1960s and early 1970s always cited to me the importance of the book. They didn't treat it as a literary experience; it was history—the only knowledge they had of the Jewish experience." "Its impact was enormous," Essas explained after settling in Israel in 1986, thirteen years after his first application for an exit visa. "It was our first encounter with Jewish history. It gave us inspiration, and turned almost everybody who read it into more or less convinced Zionists." He added: "It gave us hope and pride when we needed it. It was the first book to teach us about the Jewish tradition, which is very different from what the Government said it was" (McDowell, *"Exodus* in Samizdat," 13).

45. Leon Uris, letter to author, 16 April 1985.

46. Quoted in Philip Roth, "Some New Jewish Stereotypes" (1961), in *Reading Myself and Others* (New York: 1975), 138.

47. Roth, "Some New Jewish Stereotypes," 138; Saul Bellow, Introduction to *Great Jewish Short Stories* (New York: 1963), 14.

48. *New York Review of Books,* 37 (12 April 1990), 2.

49. Cathleen McGuigan, "The 'Whoopie' Comedy Show," *Newsweek,* 103 (5 March 1984), 63; Steve Erickson, "Whoopi Goldberg," *Rolling Stone* (8 May 1986), 39–42, 90, 92, 94; Rex Reed, *Do You Sleep in the Nude?* (New York: 1969), 61.

50. *Woody Allen's Play It Again, Sam,* ed. Richard J. Anobile (New York: 1977), 162.

The Postwar Economy of American Jews

Barry R. Chiswick

(UNIVERSITY OF ILLINOIS, CHICAGO)

Introduction

Jews in the United States are a distinctive population. They are primarily the descendants of turn-of-the-century (1880–1924) immigrants from Eastern Europe and Russia, reinforced after the Second World War by displaced persons. They have ascended from economic deprivation to impressive achievements in cultural and economic matters. These achievements have often been cited and frequently celebrated in articles and books, both fiction and nonfiction, that recount the struggles and achievements of individual Jews in the arts, business, the professions, academia and public service. Even writings that do not focus on the high achievers, such as Ande Manner's *Poor Cousins* (1972) and the turn-of-the-century study by Hutchins Hapgood, *The Spirit of the Ghetto* (1902), are largely anecdotal and celebratory rather than analytical and dispassionate.

This paper presents a picture of the state of the economy of American Jews, using quantitative techniques and the most reliable data available. In so doing, it follows in the tradition established by Arthur Ruppin, Simon Kuznets and Arcadius Kahan in their important research on the immigrant and mid-twentieth-century experience of American Jews.[1]

For a population that has been so thoroughly analyzed in the literary world and anecdotal accounts, there is remarkably little systematic quantitative research on its economic and labor market status.[2] This is surely not due to the scarcity of Jewish social scientists (either sociologists or economists). Jews are well represented in these fields and have been at the forefront of scholarly research on other American minorities, including blacks, Hispanics, immigrants and women. One explanation often advanced is the fear that revealing Jewish economic success would invite anti-Jewish sentiment. Another possible explanation is that the focus of research on minorities is on disadvantaged groups, including groups perceived to suffer current disadvantage because of deprivations in the past. Thus, Jews, Mormons, the descendants of the American Revolution patriots and those of northwest European origin are "less interesting" to study.[3] A more compelling explanation is that Jews are a difficult group to study, not because of any characteristic inherent in the Jews themselves but because of the virtual absence of the key ingredient for such an analysis—the data.

On the whole, Americans are perhaps an "overmeasured" population. Government and private data-collection efforts have produced an inordinate amount of
statistics describing various facets of the population. Teasing out data on Jews from
the wealth of data, however, is extraordinarily difficult for several reasons. First, the
most important data collection agency in the United States, the Bureau of the
Census, has not and will not include a question on religion or code a response (such
as to an ethnic-ancestry question) that would reveal the respondent's religion. The
one exception to this rule provides an important source of data for this study.
Second, Jews constitute a small proportion of the population (about 2.5 percent), so
that even surveys that include a question on religious preference and retain a separate code for Jews generally have too few identifiable Jews for a meaningful statistical analysis. Third, Jewish communal surveys, which clearly identify Jews, typ-
ically ask numerous detailed questions about Jewish religious practice and
community involvement; designed for comparisons among Jews, they lack a parallel
sample of non-Jews for comparative purposes. As a result, the research to date
comparing American Jews with others has relied on a variety of indirect methodologies for identifying Jews (such as a Yiddish mother tongue or Russian ancestry) and on special surveys.

The discussion in this paper relies primarily on three independent sets of data.
Although each data set taken separately has either methodological or sample size
problems, the fact that they all paint the same picture greatly enhances our confidence in the results. A description of the data sets is followed by analyses of
Jewish/non-Jewish differences and trends in educational attainment, labor supply,
occupational and self-employment status, and earnings. The summary and conclusion tie together what has been learned from the analysis.

The Data

The Current Population Survey (CPS) has been conducted every month since the
late 1940s by the Bureau of the Census for the Bureau of Labor Statistics, U.S.
Department of Labor. In March 1957, in addition to the usual questions on demographic and labor market characteristics, the CPS asked for the first and last time the
respondent's religion. The sample consisted of about 35,000 households. Jews
constituted 3.2 percent of the population aged 14 and over, and were nearly all
urban residents (96.1 percent), with few living in the South (7.7 percent). Unfortunately, only two very limited reports were released by the Census Bureau in which a
variety of socioeconomic variables were cross-tabulated by religion.[4]

The long questionnaire administered to 15 percent of the population for the 1970
Census of Population affords another, albeit indirect, opportunity to study Jews. A
mother-tongue question was asked of the respondent: Was there a language other
than or in addition to English spoken in the home when you were a child? With the
data limited to second-generation Americans (those born in the United States with at
least one foreign-born parent), those reporting Yiddish, Hebrew or Ladino can be
identified as Jews, while non-Jews are identified as those raised in a home in which
only English or some other language was spoken. The study population is limited to

second-generation Americans because non-English mother tongues virtually disappear by the third generation. It has been shown elsewhere that, although this procedure underestimates the number of Jews, it provides a reliable first approximation for the characteristics of second-generation American Jews around 1970.[5]

The third data set is the General Social Survey (GSS). Conducted by the National Opinion Research Center, the GSS is a random probability sample conducted nearly every year since 1972 of about fifteen hundred independently selected individuals. The data file studied here (1972–1987) is centered on 1980. In addition to asking the respondents numerous questions about their own demographic and socioeconomic characteristics, they were asked their religious preference currently and at age 16. This provides a wealth of data on adult Jews and non-Jews in the U.S. labor market for the period around 1980.[6] A major limitation of the GSS, however, is the small sample size for adult Jewish men (about 150 observations). Religion at age 16 is used to identify Jews, as this is less likely than current religion to be influenced by current economic status.

Finally, the GSS also asked the respondents numerous questions regarding the demographic and socioeconomic characteristics of their parents when they, the children, were age 16. Since the sample is centered on 1980 and the average age of the adult respondents was 42, the reports regarding their fathers and mothers refer to the early 1950s. Because the respondents in the GSS include an equal number of males and females, the sample of fathers is about double that of the male respondents (about three hundred observations), as is that of the mothers.

Taken together, these data permit an analysis of the patterns of Jewish economic achievement over the course of the post–Second World War period. Unfortunately, the data are not strictly comparable, as there are subtle and perhaps not-so-subtle differences in methodologies, definitions and the manner in which the data were made available by the survey agency. Yet they can be used to present a picture, not previously available, of the patterns of American Jewish achievement relative to non-Jews over this long interval.

Educational Attainment

Educational attainment is a complex concept involving both the quality of a unit of schooling and the number of units acquired. Quality differences are particularly difficult to measure, as are the differences in characteristics that students bring to the classroom that can greatly influence the extent to which they acquire productive skills in school.[7] For these reasons, this study follows the tradition of using "years of schooling completed" to measure individual and group differences in educational attainment.

In spite of disadvantages associated with immigrant parents or grandparents, and discrimination against Jews in access to higher education and many professions requiring higher education, American Jews had achieved a remarkably high level of educational attainment by the early postwar years.[8] Among adult men in the early postwar years (the GSS fathers), American Jews had an average of 11.6 years of schooling, compared with 9.7 years for white non-Jews (Table 1). This schooling

Table 1. Distribution of Schooling of the Adult Male Population (Jews and Non-Jews)

Schooling (Years)	GSS Fathers[a]		1957 CPS[b]		1970 Census[c]		GSS Respondents[d]	
	Jews	Non-Jews	Jews	Non-Jews	Jews	Non-Jews	Jews	Non-Jews
0–7	15.0	24.7	10.6	18.6	1.5	7.1	2.0	5.3
8	9.7	20.5	11.2	17.1	3.6	13.3	1.3	5.3
9–11	12.6	12.3	10.6	19.4	12.4	21.5	2.7	13.8
12	30.0	24.0	24.3	26.5	28.5	32.0	12.7	30.9
13–15	8.9	7.9	14.9	8.4	17.5	11.7	16.7	20.2
16	12.1	6.2	28.5	9.9	14.8	7.1	28.0	12.5
Over 16	11.7	4.3			21.6	7.3	36.7	12.0
Total	100.0	100.0	100.0	100.0	100.0	100.0	100.0	100.0
Median	12	10	12.7	11.2	13	12	16	12
Mean	11.6	9.7	NA	NA	13.7	11.5	15.7	12.8

Sources: U.S. Bureau of the Census, "Tabulations of Data on the Social and Economic Characteristics of Major Religious Groups, 1957" mimeo, n.d., Table 12; U.S. Bureau of the Census, 1970 Census of Population, Public Use Sample, 1/100 sample (15 percent questionnaire); and National Opinion Research Center, *General Social Surveys, 1972–1987, Cumulative Data File* (Chicago: 1987).

Notes:

NA = Not available in source.

Figures may not add up to 100 percent because of rounding.

[a]Educational attainment of the fathers of adult (aged 25 to 64) white male and female respondents at age 16. Sample size: 247 Jews and 9,043 non-Jews.

[b]Employed males aged 18 and over for Jews and all (Jews and non-Jews). Sample size: about 35,000 households.

[c]Adult white men not enrolled in school and born in the United States with at least one foreign-born parent. Jews defined as those raised in a home in which Yiddish, Hebrew or Ladino was spoken instead of or in addition to English. Based on a 1/100 sample of the 1970 Census of Population (15 percent questionnaire).

[d]Adult (aged 25 to 64) white male respondents. Sample size: 150 Jews and 5,199 non-Jews.

difference of 1.9 years increased over time to a 2.9-year advantage among the GSS respondents.

Perhaps more telling are the differences in the proportion with at least four years of college education. Among the Jewish men, the proportion increased continuously over the time period, from 24 percent in the early postwar years to 29 percent in 1957, to 36 percent in 1970 and to 65 percent in the 1980 period. By contrast, the proportions for non-Jews increased only from about 10 percent in the early postwar years and 1957 to 14 percent in 1970, and was still only 25 percent in 1980.

The pattern among women is similar. As shown in Table 2, Jewish women have a higher level of education than non-Jewish women, and the difference in educational attainment has increased over time. For example, the Jewish mothers in the GSS had 11.4 years of schooling, and 13 percent had 16 or more years of schooling, in contrast to the 10.2 years and 7 percent, respectively, for non-Jews. By about 1980, the Jewish women averaged 14.4 years of schooling (40 percent with 16 or more years), in contrast to 12.3 years (16 percent with 16 or more years).

Table 2. Distribution of Schooling of the Adult Female Population (Jews and Non-Jews)

Schooling (Years)	GSS Mothers[a]		1957 CPS[b]		1970 Census[c]		GSS Respondents[d]	
	Jews	Non-Jews	Jews	Non-Jews	Jews	Non-Jews	Jews	Non-Jews
0–7	9.1	17.0	6.5	13.0	1.4	6.7	0.0	3.8
8	9.5	18.8	9.2	13.6	4.5	12.8	0.0	4.7
9–11	10.9	14.5	11.3	18.4	11.4	21.1	2.4	16.1
12	45.8	34.4	40.1	36.9	51.3	41.6	28.3	41.7
13–15	11.6	8.8	16.4	9.3	15.5	10.5	29.5	18.0
16	8.4	5.0 }	16.4 }	8.5 }	8.7	4.4	24.1	9.5
Over 16	4.7	1.6 }			7.2	2.9	15.7	6.2
Total	100.0	100.0	100.0	100.0	100.0	100.0	100.0	100.0
Median	12	11	12.6	12.1	12	12	14	12
Mean	11.4	10.2	NA	NA	12.5	11.1	14.4	12.3

Sources: U.S. Bureau of the Census, "Tabulations of Data on the Social and Economic Characteristics of Major Religious Groups, 1957" mimeo, n.d., Table 12; U.S. Bureau of the Census, 1970 Census of Population, Public Use Sample, 1/100 sample (15 percent questionnaire); and National Opinion Research Center, *General Social Surveys, 1972–1987, Cumulative Data File* (Chicago: 1987).

Notes:

NA = Not available in source.

Figures may not add up to 100 percent because of rounding.

[a]Educational attainment of the mothers of adult (aged 25 to 64) white male and female respondents at age 16. Sample size: 275 Jews and 10,067 non-Jews.

[b]Employed females aged 18 and over for Jews and all (Jews and non-Jews). Sample size: about 35,000 households.

[c]Adult white women not enrolled in school and born in the United States with at least one foreign-born parent. Jews defined as those raised in a home in which Yiddish, Hebrew or Ladino was spoken instead of or in addition to English. Based on a 1/100 sample of the 1970 Census of Population (15 percent questionnaire).

[d]Adult (aged 25 to 64) white female respondents. Sample size: 166 Jews and 6,358 non-Jews.

It is interesting to note that the gender difference in favor of males is larger for Jews than for non-Jews. In the most recent period, Jewish men had 1.3 years more schooling than Jewish women, an increase over the virtual equality in schooling in the early postwar years. Among non-Jewish men, however, the recent male advantage is only 0.5 years, in contrast to an earlier male disadvantage (comparing GSS mothers and fathers) of 0.5 years. Does this mean that Jewish parents sacrificed the educational attainment of their daughters to enhance that of their sons? Apparently not, as adult Jewish women in the 1980 period had a schooling level that substantially exceeded that of non-Jewish men, with this differential not changing over the four time periods (compare Tables 1 and 2).

A question can be raised, however, as to whether the high level of Jewish educational attainment is attributable to where Jews live (predominantly in the urban areas and states outside of the South), and to their parents' higher level of education.[9] An analysis of the Jewish/non-Jewish difference in educational attainment in the early postwar years indicates that the observed 1.9-year schooling difference declines to a still statistically significant 1.0-year difference when father's residence (when the respondent was age 16) and the respondent's age (a proxy for the father's age) are held constant. Among the GSS respondents (around 1980), controlling for age and residence at age 16 reduces the educational advantage from 2.9 to 2.5 years for men and from 2.1 to 1.6 years for women, with all of these differences statistically significant. Adding an additional control for father's education reduces the differentials, but they are still large and significant—2.1 years for men and 1.3 years for women.

In summary, the data on educational attainment for the four postwar time periods indicate that American Jews have a substantially higher level of schooling, whether measured on average or as the proportion with 16 or more years of schooling, that this differential is greater among the men than among the women, and that the gap appears to have increased over time. Some of this higher level of schooling is attributable to Jews living predominantly in areas with higher schooling levels in general, and some is due to their greater parental education. Yet even after adjusting for these factors, the patterns remain (although the differences are reduced in magnitude). Indeed, even where other variables are the same, there has been an increase in the Jewish educational advantage from the fathers' to the sons' generation.

Labor Supply

The labor supply of a population is an important dimension of the economic characteristics of the group. A greater labor supply by men or women enhances family money income, on the one hand, thereby expanding the family's ability to purchase goods and services. On the other hand, a greater labor supply reduces the time available for engaging in "home production" and leisure-time activities. Home production activities include providing child care. Parental time—and for most families in practice this means predominantly mother's time—is an important "input" in children's developing a greater potential for success in schooling and, ultimately, in the labor market. Thus, greater female labor supply does not unambiguously enhance a group's economic situation. This depends instead on several factors, including the timing of this labor supply with respect to the number and age of children in the group.[10]

There are several dimensions of labor supply. This study focuses on the labor force participation rate, that is, the proportion of the adult (noninstitutionalized) members of a group who are either employed (i.e., wage, salary and self-employed persons) or are unemployed (i.e., looking for a job).

The labor force participation rates of adult "nonaged" men (25 to 54 years) are very high, vary but slightly across ethnic and religious groups, and have shown little change over time. Among younger men (aged 18–24), participation has declined over time as a result of increased college attendance, while among older men (aged 55 and over), earlier retirement has reduced participation.

The 1957 CPS data indicate that Jewish men aged 25 to 34 years had a participation rate of 97 percent, the same as for non-Jewish men (U.S. Bureau of the Census, no date, Table 11). Even for those aged 45 to 64 years there was little difference—

Table 3. Labor Force Participation Rates By Age Among Women
(Jews and Non-Jews) (percent)

Age	1957 CPS[a]		1970 Census[b]		GSS Respondents[c]	
	Jews	Non-Jews	Jews	Non-Jews	Jews	Non-Jews
14–17	NA	17.7	30.6	26.1	NA	NA
18–24	57.2	45.5	58.5	57.5	54.5	58.3
25–34	25.5	34.8	39.7	42.2	66.1	60.6
35–44	33.5	42.6	48.8	47.4	68.6	63.6
45–64	38.2	41.1	53.3	49.2	60.7	49.8
65 and over	8.5	11.5	19.7	10.7	26.2	9.8
All women	30.7	35.1	46.8	30.0	53.3	48.0

Sources: U.S. Bureau of the Census, "Tabulations of Data on the Social and Economic Characteristics of Major Religious Groups, 1957" mimeo, n.d., Table 11; U.S. Bureau of the Census, 1970 Census of Population, Public Use Sample, 1/100 sample (15 percent questionnaire); and National Opinion Research Center, *General Social Surveys, 1972–1987, Cumulative Data File* (Chicago: 1987).

Notes:

NA = Not available in source.

[a]Women aged 14 and over for Jews and all (Jews and non-Jews). Sample size: about 35,000 households.

[b]White women born in the United States with at least one foreign-born parent. Jews defined as those raised in a home in which Yiddish, Hebrew or Ladino was spoken instead of or in addition to English. Based on a 1/100 sample of the 1970 Census of Population (15 percent questionnaire).

[c]White women respondents. Sample size: 242 Jews and 9,228 non-Jews.

96 percent for the Jews, compared with 93 percent for non-Jews. The lower Jewish male labor supply among men aged 18 to 24 years (54 percent compared with 79 percent) is due to their higher college enrollment. The greater Jewish labor supply among men aged 65 and over (47 percent compared with 37 percent) is due to the greater proportion of Jews who are self-employed and in professional and other white-collar occupations.

Variations in labor supply are far more interesting among women. As shown in Table 3, labor force participation rates in the postwar period have increased for both Jewish and non-Jewish women in nearly every age group.[11] Except for the college-age population, the increase in labor supply was greater for the Jewish women. Although Jewish women had a lower participation rate in the 1957 CPS, the rate was higher among the 1980 GSS respondents. The greater increase in Jewish female participation rates may be attributed, in part, to the larger increase in their educational attainment and their lower fertility.[12]

Detailed analysis of the 1970 Census of Population reveals important differences between Jewish and non-Jewish women in the impact or effect of schooling and children on labor supply.[13] Jewish women's labor supply is more sensitive to the positive effect of schooling, thereby reinforcing the favorable effect on labor supply of the growth in the schooling differential. In addition, the labor supply of Jewish women is more sensitive to the presence of children in the home. That is, Jewish female labor supply declines relatively more than the non-Jewish female labor

Table 4. Female Labor Force Participation Rates for Married Women
by Presence and Age of Children (Jews and non-Jews)

	1957 CPS[a]		1970 Census[b]	
	Jews	Non-Jews	Jews	Non-Jews
Total	27.8	29.6	51.7	46.8
No children under 18	30.0	35.6	55.4	50.2
With children 6–17, none under 6	28.6	36.7	49.2	44.7
With children under 6	11.8	17.0	25.1	31.1

Sources: U.S. Bureau of the Census, "Tabulations of Data on the Social and Economic Characteristics of Major Religious Groups, March 1957," n.d., Table 13. U.S. Bureau of the Census, 1970 Census of Population, Public Use Sample, 1/100 sample (15 percent questionnaire).

Notes:

[a]Women aged 18 and over for Jews and all (Jews and non-Jews).

[b]White women aged 25 to 64, second-generation Americans. Jews defined as in Table 3, footnote b.

supply when there are school-age and especially preschool children in the family (see Table 4). The decline in Jewish fertility has therefore increased the Jewish female labor supply by more than would a similar decline in non-Jewish fertility.

An analysis using the 1970 Census of differences in labor supply (holding constant age, schooling, other family income and location of residence), suggests a more "optimal" pattern of labor supply on the part of Jewish women. They are more likely to work before children are born and after the youngest attains age 18, and are less likely to work when the children are of preschool or school age. Among mothers with school-age children who work, the Jewish mothers are more likely to work part-year and part-time.

The greater labor supply of Jewish women is enhancing family income. The greater labor supply is also associated with low fertility, which eventually has implications for an aging Jewish population that is a smaller proportion of the total population. It is less clear what is happening to parental investments of time and other resources in the next generation of young Jews. If there is a decline in direct parental investments, and if high-quality alternatives (e.g., schooling) are not acquired, there may be negative implications for these children.

Occupational and Self-Employment Status

Occupational Status

A person's occupational status is one of the most commonly used measures of the level of economic attainment.[14] Occupation reflects skills previously acquired through schooling, apprenticeship programs and on-the-job training, as well as the myriad of unmeasured and more subtle characteristics that an individual brings to the labor market. It is a measure of the outcome of the labor market process.

Comparisons of achievement across time are facilitated by an examination of occupation, as distinct from earnings, since the latter are more sensitive to temporary or cyclical factors and need to be adjusted for changes in the overall price level.

Much of the analysis of occupational attainment will be presented in terms of the frequency distribution of workers by occupational status. Occupation is by definition a categorical variable—unlike age or earnings, which are quantitative and continuous variables. To convert the categorical occupational distribution into a quantitative variable, sociologists have developed occupational prestige scores. These scores reflect the evaluation by individuals as to how "good" a given occupation is, converted into an index number that is a linear combination of the average level of schooling and income of workers in the occupation. [15] The GSS includes the prestige scores for the occupational status of the respondents and for their fathers when the former were age 16. This permits an examination of a quantitative measure of occupation at the start and end of the interval under study.

Table 5 reports the occupational attainment for adult Jewish and non-Jewish men for the four time periods, using the three data sets. These data show a dramatic increase in the professionalization of the Jewish labor force. Professionals increased from 13.8 percent of the male Jewish labor force in the early post-Second World War period (GSS fathers) to 20.3 percent in 1957, 27.2 percent in 1970 and 43.0 percent in the 1980 period (GSS respondents). The increase was spread among a wide range of professional occupations, including medicine, law and academia.

This professionalization was counterbalanced by a decline in managerial employment from nearly half of the Jewish men in the early postwar period to a quarter in the more recent period. Blue-collar employment also declined. The proportion of Jews in craft, operative, transportation, laborer and service jobs declined continuously over the period, from 25 percent in the early postwar years to 22 percent in 1957, 18 percent in 1970 and 9 percent in the recent period. Farming was and remained a negligible occupation among the Jews.

In each of the time periods, there is a higher level of occupational attainment among the Jews than among the non-Jews, and although non-Jews have also experienced a rapid improvement in occupational status, the gap has widened. For example, in Table 5, the proportion of professionals among the Jews exceeded that of the non-Jews by 5.0 percentage points for the early postwar period: 10.4 percentage points in 1957, 11.8 percentage points in 1970 and 24.7 percentage points in the period around 1980. In contrast, blue-collar employment (craft, operative, laborer, transportation and service) declined much more sharply among the Jews, from 26 percent in the early postwar period to 9 percent around 1980, in contrast to 53 percent and 50 percent, respectively, among the non-Jews. (Among non-Jews, the farm owner and farm manager category declined from 15.6 percent to 3.1 percent.)

The occupational prestige scores in the GSS can also be used to document the higher level and greater improvement over time in occupational status among the Jews. Table 5 reports the frequency distribution of the occupational prestige scores of the male respondents and the fathers in the GSS separately for Jews and non-Jews. Typical occupations are listed for each of the prestige score categories to provide a better sense of the substantive interpretation of these values. About two-thirds of the Jewish male respondents had occupational prestige scores of 50 or

Table 5. Occupational Distribution and Self-Employment of Adult Men
(Jews and Non-Jews) (percent)

	GSS Fathers[a]		1957 CPS[b]		1970 Census[c]		GSS Respondents[d]	
	Jews	Non-Jews	Jews	Non-Jews	Jews	Non-Jews	Jews	Non-Jews
A) *Occupation*[e]								
Professional	13.8	8.8	20.3	9.9	27.2	15.4	43.0	18.3
Medicine (MDs, DDS)	2.5	0.9	NA	NA	6.1	1.4	8.3	0.8
Law	3.5	0.6	NA	NA	3.6	0.7	5.6	0.9
Col. & univ. teach.	1.1	0.4	NA	NA	1.3	0.6	4.9	1.0
Other P, T & K	6.7	6.9	NA	NA	16.2	12.7	24.2	15.6
Managers (nonfarm)	44.9	14.8	35.1	13.3	26.5	13.4	26.4	16.7
Sales	12.0	4.7	14.1	5.4	19.7	7.0	13.2	6.2
Clerical	3.9	3.6	8.0	6.9	8.3	8.1	8.3	5.8
Craft	13.1	24.6	8.9	20.0	8.4	23.5	4.2	24.0
Operatives (excl. transp.)	6.7	12.4	10.1	20.9	2.9	12.5	0.0	10.1
Transport	3.2	4.6	NA	NA	3.3	5.3	1.4	5.1
Laborers	1.1	7.1	0.8	10.2	1.1	5.4	0.0	5.3
Farm managers & farmers	0.0	15.6	0.1	7.3	0.2	2.3	0.0	3.1
Service	1.4	4.0	2.3	6.1	2.4	7.2	3.5	5.6
Total	100.0	100.0	100.0	100.0	100.0	100.0	100.0	100.0
B) *Self-employed*[f]	55.6	36.2	31.8	8.5	31.9	14.1	35.1	16.3

Sources: U.S. Bureau of the Census, "Tabulations of Data on the Social and Economic Characteristics of Major Religious Groups, 1957" mimeo, n.d., Table 15; U.S. Bureau of the Census, 1970 Census of Population, Public Use Sample, 1/100 sample (15 percent questionnaire); and National Opinion Research Center, *General Social Surveys, 1972–1987, Cumulative Data File* (Chicago: 1987).

Notes:

NA = Detail not available.

Figures may not add up to 100 percent because of rounding.

[a]Fathers of adult (aged 25 to 64) white male and female respondents, when respondent was age 16. Sample size: 283 Jews and 10,191 non-Jews.

[b]Employed males aged 18 and over for Jews and all (Jews and non-Jews). Sample size: about 35,000 households. Percent self-employed refers to self-employed managers (excluding farm) and professionals as percentage of all employed males. Self-employment not reported for other occupational groups. Operatives include transport workers.

[c]Adult (aged 25 to 64) white men not enrolled in school who worked in 1969 and were born in the United States with at least one foreign-born parent. Jews defined as those raised in a home in which Yiddish, Hebrew or Ladino was spoken instead of or in addition to English. Based on a 1/100 sample of the 1970 Census of Population (15 percent questionnaire).

[d]Adult (aged 25 to 64) white male respondents. Sample size: 144 Jews and 5,186 non-Jews.

[e]Professional refers to professional, technical and kindred workers; laborers includes farm laborers; service includes private household workers. Operatives excludes transportation workers except for the 1957 CPS.

[f]Percent self-employed is self-employed as a percentage of all workers except for 1957 CPS, where it is self-employed (and unpaid family workers) in professional and managerial occupations as a percentage of all workers.

more, in contrast to less than one-third of the non-Jews. Among the fathers, the proportions were more than half of the Jews and only one-fifth of non-Jews with scores of at least 50. Although the mean occupational prestige scores increased from fathers to sons from 40.5 to 41.9 among non-Jews, the increase was larger among the Jews, from 46.6 to 53.2.

It is known, however, that occupational status varies systematically with certain characteristics. On average, it increases with the level of education and is higher in urban rather than in rural areas. Both of these characteristics favor high Jewish occupational attainment. One of the releases from the 1957 CPS recomputes the occupational distribution for urban men by standardizing for the educational attainment of employed adult males (U.S. Bureau of the Census, no date, Table 15). That is, it shows what the occupational distribution of urban Jews would be if they had the same distribution of years of schooling as all urban men. When this is done, the proportion of Jewish professionals is below that for non-Jews, 10 percent compared with 12 percent (compare with Table 4, columns 3 and 4). The proportion of Jewish blue-collar workers increases under this experiment, becoming 30 percent compared with 59 percent for non-Jews. Jews still have a high proportion in the nonprofessional white-collar occupations (60 percent compared with 30 percent), especially as managers and sales workers. This exercise suggests that much of the Jewish occupational advantage in 1957 was attributable to their urban location and especially their higher level of schooling, but that with the exception of professionals they still had on average a higher occupational attainment.

Fortunately, far more can be done analyzing the occupational prestige scores for the respondents and fathers in the GSS, using as well such variables as age and marital status, education and place of residence.[16] Among the male workers in the early postwar period (the GSS fathers), the Jews had a statistically significant higher occupational prestige score, 46.6 versus 40.5, a difference of 6.1 points. Holding constant differences in their education, age and place of residence reduces this advantage to a statistically significant 3.1 points, or about half of the observed differential.

The observed difference in occupational prestige scores between Jewish and non-Jewish respondents in the GSS is a statistically significant 11.3 points. Controlling for the above-mentioned variables, the Jewish occupational prestige advantage is reduced, but Jews still have a statistically significant advantage of 3.8 points. Perhaps Jews do well because their fathers had a high occupational status, and occupational status is transmitted from father to son independent of schooling and other measured variables? After holding constant the father's occupational status, the result is only a small reduction in the Jewish occupational advantage, from 3.8 points to a still statistically significant 3.5 points.

The analysis indicates that, among employed adult males, Jews had a higher occupational status throughout the postwar period. Although diminished in value, this differential persists even after controlling for other readily measured variables such as age, schooling, urban residence and father's occupation. Moreover, there has been an increase in the relative Jewish occupational advantage over the period, even after controlling for other variables.

Self-Employment Status

There are three main occupational avenues for self-employment in the United States: as managers of nonfarm enterprises, as farm owners or as self-employed professionals. Most men working in agriculture in the United States are self-employed. For the United States as a whole, self-employment has decreased with the decline in the proportion of the agricultural labor force. Among the fathers in the GSS, 36 percent were self-employed, in contrast to the 16 percent self-employed among the respondents, reflecting the decline in the farm manager and farm owner occupational category from 16 percent to 3 percent.

In spite of the fact that a negligible number of American Jews are engaged in farming, Jews have a very high rate of self-employment—a rate that substantially exceeds that of non-Jews (Table 5). Jewish self-employment decreased from the early postwar period, when it was 56 percent, to 32 to 35 percent in the later time periods. These data mask more substantial movements in the nature of self-employment away from being a self-employed manager (primarily of a manufacturing or retail trade enterprise) to being a self-employed professional (doctor, lawyer, etc.).[17]

In the 1957 CPS data, self-employment status is reported only for those in professional and managerial occupations. Jews have substantially higher rates of self-employment in these two occupations. More than one-third of Jewish professionals were self-employed, twice the ratio for non-Jews. Among managers, more than two-thirds of the Jews were self-employed, in contrast to one-half among non-Jews.

Thus, the entrepreneurial spirit remains strong among Jews, although it is increasingly expressed in terms of self-employed professional activities rather than in the management of business enterprises.

Income

Income or earnings are a measure of both labor market performance and the ability to buy goods and services, that is, the command over resources. As a measure of the labor market outcome, income has the advantage of being a direct quantitative, continuous measure—as distinct from occupation, which is a categorical variable; or the occupational prestige score, which is a constructed value. However, two disadvantages of income are that nominal values may change over time merely because of inflation, and groups may differ in their trade-off between measured and unmeasured dimensions of full compensation. Furthermore, as would be expected, reporting difficulties prevented the collection of data on the income or earnings of the fathers in the GSS survey.

Table 6 reports the mean or median income or earnings among adult Jewish and non-Jewish men in the 1957 CPS, the 1970 Census and among the GSS respondents. In each of the three time periods, earned income is substantially higher among the Jews. In the 1957 CPS data, Jewish median income was 36 percent greater than that of non-Jews. The only standardization or statistical control shown

Table 6. Distribution of Occupational Prestige Scores
for General Social Survey Respondents and Fathers (Jews and Non-Jews)[a] (percent)

Score		Fathers		Respondents	
(Points)	Occupations	Jews	Non-Jews	Jews	Non-Jews
10–19	Construction laborers, baggage porters	3.9	7.4[b]	2.7	6.6
20–29	Sales clerks, taxi cab drivers	7.8	10.9	5.4	11.1
30–39	Restaurant managers, auto mechanics	15.9	24.6	10.9	26.1
40–49	Real estate agents, policemen	17.0	36.0	13.6	25.6
50–59	Librarians, bank tellers	44.5	14.1	36.1	18.8
60–69	Mechanical engineers	3.9	4.3	8.2	8.1
70–79	Lawyers, professors	5.7	2.0	18.4	3.4
80 and over	Physicians	1.4	0.5	4.8	0.3
Total		100.0	100.0	100.0	100.0
Mean score		46.6	40.5	53.2	41.9

Source: National Opinion Research Center, *General Social Surveys, 1972–1987, Cumulative Data File* (Chicago: 1987).

Notes:

Figures may not add up to 100 percent because of rounding.

[a]Respondent refers only to males, while the fathers are for male and female respondents.

[b]Includes one observation with a score less than 10 (bootblack).

in the released data is for urban residence and major occupational category. With these controls, the Jewish median income exceeds that of non-Jews by 6.7 percent (Table 7). That is, even within the same major occupational category, Jews had a higher level of income. Yet controlling in this way may result in "overadjusted" data, if the purpose of the exercise is to ascertain Jewish/non-Jewish income differences controlling for the skills the individual brings to the labor market. Although occupation is in part determined by age (labor market experience), schooling and other characteristics embodied in the person that are brought to the labor market, it is fundamentally a measure of the outcome of the labor market process.

The 1970 Census data on second-generation Americans show much higher mean earnings for Jews. The 55 percent greater earnings is reduced to 16 percent when a set of explanatory variables describing the skills and characteristics workers bring to the labor market is held constant.[18] That is, for the same readily measured inputs into the labor market, the Jews receive 16 percent higher incomes.[19]

The GSS respondent data also permit a comparative analysis of earnings. The observed earnings difference of nearly 40 percent is reduced to 15 percent when there is a statistical control for age (experience), schooling, marital status and place of residence. Within the nearly fifteen-year interval of the GSS data, there is no trend in the ratio of Jewish to non-Jewish earnings, other variables being the same.

Taken as a whole, these data suggest very high earnings for American Jews relative to non-Jews that are partly attributable to the difference in the skills (e.g.,

Table 7. Income or Earnings of Adult Men (Jews and Non-Jews)

Income or Earnings	1957 CPS (Median Income)[a]	1970 Census (Mean Earnings)[b]	GSS Respondents (Mean Earnings)[c]
Jews	4,900	16,176	27,322
Non-Jews	3,608	10,431	19,750
Ratio (1) to (2)			
Observed	1.36	1.55	1.38
Other variables held constant[d]	1.07	1.16	1.15

Sources: National Opinion Research Center, *General Social Surveys, 1972–1987, Cumulative Data File* (Chicago: 1987); U.S. Bureau of the Census, "Tabulations of Data on the Social and Economic Characteristics of Major Religious Groups, 1957" mimeo, n.d., Table 15; and U.S. Bureau of the Census, 1970 Census of Population, Public Use Sample, 1/100 sample (15 percent questionnaire).

Notes:

[a]Income in 1956 of males aged 14 and over with income for Jews and all (Jews and non-Jews). Sample size: about 35,000 households.

[b]Adult white men not enrolled in school who worked in 1969 and were born in the United States with at least one foreign-born parent. Jews defined as those raised in a home in which Yiddish, Hebrew, or Ladino was spoken instead of or in addition to English. Based on a 1/100 sample of the 1970 Census of Population (15 percent questionnaire).

[c]Earnings of adult (aged 25 to 64) white male respondents with earnings. Sample size: 124 Jews and 4,169 non-Jews.

[d]Statistical controls are for urban residence and occupational distribution for the 1957 CPS and for age (experience), schooling, location, marital status and weeks worked for white men in the 1970 Census (second-generation Americans) and the GSS.

schooling) and other characteristics (e.g., location) they bring to the labor market. Yet even after adjusting for these other characteristics, Jews have about 15 percent higher mean earnings. It is not obvious that there is a trend over time in this differential.[20] The earnings differential in favor of Jews appears to vary by level of schooling. It is small for those with very low levels of schooling and increases with schooling level.[21]

Summary and Conclusions

This paper has examined several dimensions of the economy of American Jews compared with white non-Jews in the postwar period by a study of census and survey data at four time periods.

American Jewish men had higher levels of schooling, occupational attainment and earnings in the 1950s than non-Jewish men. During the course of the postwar period, their levels of attainment increased sharply. For schooling and occupational status, the differential between Jews and non-Jews widened over this period. Even after holding constant several important determinants of attainment—such as age, place of residence, parental characteristics and, for occupation and earnings, also the person's level of education—Jews had more schooling (by about 2.1 years) and higher occupational status, and they earned more (by about 15 percent) than non-Jews.

There are interesting differences for women in some of these patterns. The Jewish educational attainment exceeds that of non-Jews by a smaller magnitude overall, and also when other variables are the same. For example, other variables being the same, Jewish women have only 1.3 years more schooling than non-Jews. The labor supply of Jewish women appears to have increased over time more rapidly than for non-Jewish women. This may be the result of the favorable effects of the higher level of education and smaller family size (lower fertility) of Jewish women. Furthermore, the pattern of labor supply with respect to age of the respondents appears to differ—Jewish women are less likely to work when there are young children at home, and they are more likely to work at other times. This suggests a greater sensitivity to the optimal allocation of parental time between child care and the labor market.

The entrepreneurial spirit remains strong among Jews. Throughout the period under study, Jews have had a much higher rate of self-employment, although its nature has changed. Jews are now less likely than previously to be self-employed managers and are more likely to be self-employed professionals. Within either occupational category, however, Jews have a much higher rate of self-employment than non-Jews.

There has been a concern that from generation to generation American Jews would "regress to the mean," that is, to the American norm. This concern appears to be without foundation. Jews retain a strong commitment to educational attainment and labor market advancement, and they continue to display a strong entrepreneurial spirit. The differentials in attainment in favor of Jews have not narrowed in the postwar period; in important instances, they even appear to have widened. Thus, although there are serious problems facing the American Jewish community, including issues of self-identity, intermarriage and an aging population, the American Jewish economy is doing well.

Notes

1. Arthur Ruppin, *The Jews of To-Day* (New York: 1913); Simon Kuznets, *Economic Structure of U.S. Jewry: Recent Trends* (Jerusalem: 1972); *idem*, "Immigration of Russian Jews to the United States: Background and Structure," *Perspectives in American History* 9 (1975), 35–126; Arcadius Kahan, *Essays in Jewish Social and Economic History* (Chicago: 1986).

2. Some additional notable exceptions include Barry R. Chiswick, "The Earnings and Human Capital of American Jews," *Journal of Human Resources* (Summer 1983), 313–336; *idem*, "The Labor Market Status of American Jews: Patterns and Determinants," *American Jewish Year Book 1985* (New York: 1984), 131–153; *idem*, "Labor Supply and Investment in Child Quality: A Study of Jewish and Non-Jewish Women," *Review of Economics and Statistics* (November 1986), 700–703; *idem*, "Jewish Immigrant Skill and Occupational Attainment at the Turn of the Century," *Explorations in Economic History* 28 (Jan. 1991), 64–86; *idem*, "The Skills and Economic Status of American Jewry: Trends Over the Last Half Century," in *A New Jewish World: Continuity and Change 1939-1989*, ed. Robert Wistrich (Jerusalem: forthcoming); Sidney Goldstein, "Socioeconomic Differentials Among

Religious Groups in the United States," *American Journal of Sociology* 74, no. 6 (May 1969), 612–631; William M. Kephart, "Position of Jewish Economy in the United States," *Social Forces* 28, no. 2 (Dec. 1949), 153–164; Thomas Kessner, *The Golden Door: Italian and Jewish Immigrant Mobility in New York City, 1880–1915* (New York: 1977); and Joel Perlmann, *Ethnic Differences: Schooling and Social Structure Among the Irish, Italians, Jews and Blacks in an American City, 1880–1935* (Cambridge: 1988). For studies that address the achievement of Jews in other diaspora countries, see Mordechai Altshuler, *Soviet Jewry Since the Second World War: Population and Social Structure* (New York: 1987); Daniel J. Elazar with Peter Medding, *Jewish Communities in Frontier Societies: Argentina, Australia and South Africa* (New York: 1983); and S. J. Prais and Marlena Schmool, "The Social-Class Structure of Anglo-Jewry, 1961," *Jewish Journal of Sociology* 16 (June 1975), 5–15.

3. In addition to the studies of Jews noted above, a notable exception is the analysis of "Euroethnics" in Stanley Lieberson and Mary C. Waters, *From Many Strands: Ethnic and Racial Groups in Contemporary America* (New York: 1988), and the U.S. Commission on Civil Rights, *The Economic Status of Americans of Southern and Eastern European Ancestry*, Clearinghouse Publication 89 (Washington, D.C.: Oct. 1986), both of which include analyses for those of Russian ancestry—a proxy for Jews.

4. These data, released in the U.S. Bureau of the Census, "Religion Reported by the Civilian Population of the United States: March 1957," *Current Population Reports, Population Characteristics*, Series P. 20, no. 79, 2 February 1958, and *idem*, "Tabulations of Data on the Social and Economic Characteristics of Major Religious Groups," mimeo (undated), have previously been studied by Chiswick, "Labor Market Status of American Jews"; Goldstein, "Socioeconomic Differentials"; and Kuznets, *Economic Structure of U.S. Jewry.*

5. See, e.g., Chiswick, "Earnings and Human Capital of American Jews"; Frances E. Kobrin, "National Data on American Jewry, 1970–71: A Comparative Evaluation of the Census Yiddish Mother Tongue Subpopulation and the National Jewish Population Survey," in *Papers in Jewish Demography, 1981*, ed. U. O. Schmelz, et al. (Jerusalem: 1983), 129–143; and Ira Rosenwaike, "The Utilization of Census Mother Tongue Data in American Jewish Population Analyses," *Jewish Social Studies* (April/July 1971), 141–159.

6. For a detailed technical analysis of Jewish/non-Jewish differences in economic characteristics using these data, see Chiswick, "Skills and Economic Status of American Jewry."

7. The apparently larger return from schooling for Jews than for non-Jews may reflect a higher quality of schooling or the unmeasured characteristics that enhance the productivity of schooling for Jews. See Barry R. Chiswick, "Differences in Education and Earnings Across Racial and Ethnic Groups: Tastes, Discrimination and Investment in Child Quality," *Quarterly Journal of Economics* (Aug. 1988), 571–597.

8. See, e.g., Leonard Dinnerstein, "Education and the Achievement of American Jews," in *American Education and European Immigration, 1840–1940*, ed. Bernard J. Weiss (Urbana: 1982).

9. For the technical detail, see Chiswick, "Skills and Economic Status of American Jewry." In addition, an examination of educational attainment within the time period (1972–1987) for the respondents' and fathers' samples reveals a significant relative improvement over time among the Jewish fathers, and a small, nonsignificant relative improvement among the Jewish respondents.

10. For the most comprehensive analysis of the economics of family formation and decision-making, see Gary S. Becker, *A Treatise on the Family* (Cambridge, Mass.: 1981).

11. Comparable data on the labor force participation of the mothers of Jewish respondents are not available in the GSS.

12. A lower labor supply for Jewish women, especially when there were children at home, appears to be emphasized by commentators at the turn of the century. See Nathan Glazer, *American Judaism* (Chicago: 1957), 80–81, and Gretchen A. Condran and Ellen A. Kramarow, "Child Mortality Among Jewish Immigrants to the United States," *Journal of Interdisciplinary History* 22, no. 2 (Autumn 1991), 223–254.

13. For the detailed analysis, see Chiswick, "Labor Supply and Investment in Child

Quality." Similar patterns emerge in an analysis of Jewish/non-Jewish differences in labor supply using data from Jewish communal surveys. For the United States, see Paul Ritterband, "Jewish Women in the Labor Force." Report prepared for the American Jewish Committee, March 1990; for Canada, see Byron G. Spencer, "Child Quality and Female Labor Supply: How Different Are Jewish Women?" (unpublished paper). Canadian Jewish women had a lower labor supply in the 1981 Census, similar to the 1957 CPS pattern.

14. See, e.g., Peter M. Blau and Otis Dudley Duncan, *The American Occupational Structure* (New York: 1967); David Featherman and Robert Hauser, *Opportunity and Change* (New York: 1978); and Albert J. Reiss with Otis Dudley Duncan, Paul K. Hatt and Cecil C. North, *Occupations and Social Status* (New York: 1961).

15. See Reiss, *Occupations and Social Status,* for further detail on the construction of the occupational-prestige scores.

16. See Chiswick, "Skills and Economic Status of American Jewry."

17. This shift has been less intense among non-Jews, as they have experienced a small increase in managerial employment from their previous low level (in contrast to the sharp decline for Jews), along with a less dramatic increase in professional occupations.

18. The Jews are older, have more schooling, are more likely to be currently married and are more likely to live in urban areas outside of the South. Each of these characteristics is associated with higher earnings among both Jews and non-Jews.

19. As a test, what happens if the broad occupational categories—in addition to the other explanatory variables—are held constant in the 1970 Census data? In this case, the Jewish earnings advantage falls to 10 percent. This is not very different from the 7 percent advantage in the 1957 CPS when the group differences in occupational structure are held constant.

20. The lower ratio in the 1957 CPS may arise from the statistical control for occupation, as well as from using medians rather than means if there is a greater "positive skewness" in the distribution of Jewish incomes.

21. In the 1970 Census data, for example, earnings increase by 8.0 percent per year of schooling for Jews and by 6.8 percent for non-Jews.

Jewish Migration in Postwar America:
The Case of Miami and Los Angeles

Deborah Dash Moore

(VASSAR COLLEGE)

The Second World War and its aftermath ushered in a period of enormous changes for American Jews. The destruction of European Jewry shattered the familiar contours of the Jewish world and transformed American Jews into the largest, wealthiest, most stable and secure Jewish community in the diaspora. American Jews' extensive participation in the war effort at home and abroad lifted them out of their urban neighborhoods into the mainstream of American life.[1] In the postwar decades, internal migration carried Jews to new and distant parts of the United States. Occurring within the radically new parameters of the postwar world—the extermination of European Jewry, the establishment of the state of Israel and the United States' achievement of unrivaled prominence on the world political scene—Jewish migration nonetheless represented a response to domestic pressures. These migrations gradually changed American Jews, influencing the character of their culture, the structure of their organizations, their pattern of kinship relations, the style and substance of their politics.

This essay offers a historical perspective on the migration process that created new American Jewish communities. It indicates some of the dimensions of internal Jewish migration, its sources, motivations and consequences. By focusing on the extraordinary growth of two Jewish urban populations, the essay suggests some categories for analyzing the communal dynamic of postwar American Jewry. It also explores a number of parallels between immigration and the establishment of indigenous American Jewish communities. Given the historic dependence of the United States upon immigration for its social formation and the critical role of immigration in the growth of the American Jewish community, study of internal migration provides a useful framework to assess certain postwar changes.[2] Specifically, *it encourages an emphasis upon the creation rather than the transformation of communities.*[3] Observing the postwar migrations, Oscar Handlin, the eminent historian of immigration, noted that immigrants differed only in degree from native-born Americans who migrated within the United States. Where the newcomer came from was less important than that the migrant had turned his back upon home and family, abandoned the way he had earned a living, and deserted his community.[4]

Handlin's trenchant reflections not only linked immigration with internal migration, seeing them as a continuum, but made the problem of community central to both.

The mobilization of the war years drew young Jewish men out of the insular urban neighborhoods of their childhood and sent them to distant bases scattered throughout the South and West. Most of the Jewish servicemen, like their gentile peers, had not strayed far from their home towns during the difficult years of the Great Depression.[5] Now, en route to the Pacific war theater, they discovered the West. Thousands of them passed through Los Angeles and were amazed by the apparently prosperous and easy way of life that they saw. Others who joined the Army Air Corps often found themselves stationed in one of the Miami Beach hotels requisitioned for the war. When their wives came down to visit, they, too, took in the beauty of the resort city.[6] Smaller numbers went to bases near such Texas towns as Houston and Dallas. Even a small city such as Tucson, Arizona, attracted Jews who discovered it because of its base for training bombardiers and pilots.[7] Often the opportunities these cities offered excited them. "You betcha, I loved it!" Leon Rabin recalled. "I wrote to my friends in Philadelphia and said there's no way for me to tell you what's going on down here and anything I'd tell you wouldn't make you come down here. But now that I'm here there's no way that I'll ever come back."[8] Rabin was true to his word. He married a native Dallas Jew and spent the rest of his life building a Jewish community that reflected some of the values he had learned growing up in Philadelphia. He also understood how limited was the vision of most East Coast Jews and how reluctant they were to venture beyond the suburbs of their cities until propelled by the war. Once word spread of the opportunities available, however, especially in a large city such as Los Angeles, which had a substantial Jewish population even in 1940, the numbers of Jews who migrated quickly reached substantial proportions.

Jewish migration to these southern and western cities—ones that would subsequently be counted as part of an emerging Sunbelt—reflected a response shared by millions of other Americans to federal initiatives and policies. Not only did the war years lead the government to funnel enormous sums for economic development into southern and western states—California alone received 10 percent of all federal war monies—but these funds often went to provide the capitalization for defense-related industries.[9] From airplane construction in Los Angeles to aluminum manufacturing in Miami to medical and communications research in Houston, entire industrial and postindustrial infrastructures were established. The subsequent eruption of the Cold War sustained the economic growth of these cities.[10] The postwar socioeconomic changes produced regional convergence, with the outlying regions of the South and West growing more rapidly than the developed sections of the country. This rapid social change brought the South and West's economies, social patterns and cultural styles closer to national norms.[11] Federal postwar policies, especially the GI bill, with its low-cost mortgage provisions and college loans, also encouraged a generation to seek its fortunes far from home and family. These portable benefits loosened the ties that bound individuals to networks of kin and friends. No longer needing to rely upon relatives and neighbors to find work, to finance an education or even to buy a house, Jews and other Americans were free to pursue their dreams of the good life. For many Jews particularly, the attractions of the apparently affluent and relaxed style of living of the Sunbelt cities proved irresistible.[12]

The term *Sunbelt* is designed to link fundamentally different parts of the United States that share the characteristics of rapid social change and regional convergence. Nicholas Lemann, executive editor of *Texas Monthly,* argues persuasively that journalists invented the Sunbelt concept in order to speak about new political and economic trends. When the word first acquired popular usage in the mid-1970s, "millions of people were living in the Sunbelt without one of them realizing it," wrote Lemann. "They thought of themselves as Southerners or Texans or Los Angelenos."[13] Of course, the particularisms Lemann mentions, the sense of identity derived from being rooted in a city, state or region, had salience largely for old-timers, not for migrants. They just as often thought of themselves as ex-New Yorkers or former Philadelphians. "I am a refugee from Chicago of several years standing," announced Leonard Sperry, a wealthy migrant to Los Angeles.[14] Sperry's self-definition after close to a decade of living in the City of Angels suggests the extent to which a migrant's identity derived from the home of his childhood. Similarly, the death notices of longtime Miami residents that announced burial in Detroit, or Chicago, or Rochester, appear symptomatic of the unwillingness of Jews to identify Miami as "home."[15] By linking a wide variety of locales, the notion of a Sunbelt helped to smooth away these differences in self-identification between the newcomers and the old-timers.

As the United States became a "nation of strangers," in the words of a popular journalist's account of one out of five Americans' propensity to move every year,[16] Jews developed an ethnic variation on the American theme of internal migration. Federal policies drew Jews out of their old homes, but ethnic networks guided them to new ones. Not only did Jews come disproportionately from large cities where they previously had concentrated, most also settled in only a handful of southern and western cities. Ninety-six percent of Jews lived in urban places in 1957, compared with 64 percent of the total U.S. population—and 87 percent of American Jews lived in cities of 250,000 or more inhabitants. In other words, Jews not only lived in cities, they lived in big cities. Although Jews constituted only 3.5 percent of the American population, they made up 8 percent of the nation's urban residents. The high concentration in the New York City area, which held approximately 40 percent of American Jewry, contributed to the distinctive Jewish demographic profile.[17] Aggregate data reveal the shift away from the Northeast and Midwest to the South and West, yet Jewish patterns of migration remained highly distinctive.[18] Despite significant postwar migration, 75 percent of America's Jews lived in only five states in 1960, as they had prior to the Second World War. When these data are disaggregated, the particularities of Jewish migration appear. Enticed by the vision of easy living under perpetually sunny skies, Jews favored certain Sunbelt cities over others. In these cities the rate of Jewish population growth often exceeded that of the general white population.[19] Above all, Jews went to two coastal cities: Miami in the East and Los Angeles in the West. These cities account for 80 percent and 70 percent, respectively, of the total postwar Jewish migration to the South and West.[20] Thus they provide the best case study of the impact of the postwar Sunbelt migrations on American Jewish ethnic culture.

Miami and Los Angeles: Magnet Cities

The postwar Jewish migration put Los Angeles and Miami on the Jewish map of the United States. Miami and Los Angeles received new settlers in record numbers after the war. Both cities had grown during the war, but neither anticipated the postwar influx. In 1946, observers estimated that each month 16,000 newcomers were arriving in Los Angeles. Of these, slightly more than 2,000 were Jews.[21] The new arrivals more than doubled the substantial Jewish population estimated at 100,000 before the war. By 1950, there were almost 300,000 Jews in the City of Angels. Seventh largest in Jewish population in 1940, Los Angeles displaced Chicago a decade later to rank second behind New York City. The number of Jews in Los Angeles continued to grow throughout the 1950s at an impressive rate of just under 50 percent. The rate of growth of the Jewish population exceeded that of the general population, such that the percentage of Jews in Los Angeles rose steadily. By the end of the decade, there were close to 400,000 Jews living in the City of Angels, roughly 18 percent of the total population. So many newcomers had arrived within such a short time period that only 8 percent of adult Jews living in the city in 1950 were native Angelenos and only 16 percent could be considered old-timers who had settled there before the Second World War. Continued migration in the 1960s and 1970s increased the city's Jewish population to more than half a million Jews, a Jewish city of enormous proportions.[22]

Nowhere near Los Angeles initially in the size of its general or Jewish population, Miami grew at an even more rapid rate. Although the number of Jews doubled from 1940 to 1945, from a mere 8,000 to 16,000, the population increased more than threefold to 55,000 by 1950. This astonishing rate of increase far outstripped the 57 percent growth in the general Miami population. Five years later, the Jewish population doubled yet again to reach 100,000. Thus, within a decade after the war, Miami had zoomed from a small and insignificant concentration of 16,000 Jews to a major urban Jewish center of 100,000 Jews. Thereafter, the rate of growth slowed, but Jewish migration to Miami continued to outstrip general migration until the Jewish proportion of the population had increased to 15 percent. By 1970, Miami contained approximately the same number of Jews as Chicago's greater metropolitan area, roughly 250,000. Miami now ranked among the top five American cities in terms of its Jewish population. Even more than Los Angeles, it was a city of newcomers. A mere 4 percent of the Jewish population had been born in the city; virtually everyone had come from someplace else.[23]

Those who chose to move to these cities charted a different path from the majority who made the more modest and popular move to the suburbs. "They came for several reasons," Bernard Goldstein explained,

> but all of them add up to economics. You had young people who were stationed in the army camps here. And they realized the opportunities—this was an open economic frontier. And as soon as the war was over, if they were single they just stayed here and if they had families they went back to New York or Chicago or wherever, packed their bags and came right back.[24]

A move to the suburbs rarely involved the pursuit of economic opportunity, although it often reflected increased affluence and the pursuit of status. For Jews, moving to the suburbs meant choosing a residence within the city's expanding boundaries. For some, however, the suburbs were a "dress rehearsal" for the big move.[25] "When you grow up in New York City—all the world is Jewish," explained Nathan Perlmutter. "When all the world is Jewish, nobody is Jewish, really." Perlmutter moved to Miami from New York City in 1956 to head the office of the Anti-Defamation League. "You've got to leave major metropolitan areas to fully understand what I mean about a sense of a Jewish community—of a 'we' and a 'they'—in New York, it's all 'we'."[26] Miami and Los Angeles represented alternatives to suburbanization.

The growth of Jewish suburban areas stemmed from a different but related set of federal postwar policies that had promoted internal migration within the United States. The scarcity of adequate housing in the cities, the rapid building of modestly priced single-family houses, the extensive program of highway construction and the easy availability of mortgages all encouraged young families to seek homes on the expanding peripheries of the nation's cities.[27] Although energized by these policies, suburbanization represented a postwar continuation and extension of the movement out of older and poorer city neighborhoods into new and more affluent ones that had started as early as the First World War.[28] Jews who moved to the suburbs did not lose touch with the city, its institutions and culture.[29] Many returned daily to work and more visited on occasion. Nor did suburbanization disrupt the family network; it simply extended the reach of the intergenerational family. Similarly, although suburban Jews organized Jewish life anew, they also imported Jewish institutions.[30] Synagogues frequently followed their more wealthy congregants to the suburbs.[31] Such decisions provided suburban Jews with a significant measure of continuity and reaffirmed deference to established leaders. No changing of the guard took place, in contrast with internal migration, which shattered patterns of deference and disrupted structures of collective continuity.

Alongside the mass internal migration to Sunbelt cities of Jews seeking economic opportunity, one should also note a smaller but steady stream of migrants who moved specifically for occupational reasons.[32] This pattern did not radically change the distribution of the Jewish population, although it did contribute a significant number of newcomers to many established Jewish communities. For example, in Toledo, Ohio, the expansion of the university and the centering of several large national retail chains in the city drew many aspiring Jewish academics and managers there. Toledo, however, experienced no overall growth in Jewish population because 45 to 60 percent of the young Jews raised there abandoned the city after college, seeking opportunity elsewhere.[33] Similarly, Kansas City's relatively static Jewish population since the 1950s disguised both a substantial in-migration of Jewish professionals and managers—approximately 37 percent of Jewish household heads in 1976—and a sizable out-migration of adult children of Kansas City Jewish household heads. In the 1970s, fully half of those sons and daughters who grew up in Kansas City no longer lived there.[34] The data on Omaha, Nebraska, reveal a similar pattern.[35] Sidney Goldstein argues that migration of these young, ambitious Jewish professionals and managers indicates the strength of economic motives over the salience of kinship ties. It points to the predominance of the nuclear family among American Jews. It suggests that the residential clustering so characteristic of eastern and midwestern cities no longer appeals to these Jewish migrants, who have discarded an earlier preference for areas of high Jewish concentration. It reveals the extent to which Jews have come to resemble other Americans in social and cultural behavior, even as their distinctive occupational concentration propels them across the continent in search of jobs.[36]

Given the urban choices, especially the rapid growth of such southwestern cities as Houston and such southern cities as Atlanta, it is worthwhile asking why so many more Jews migrated to Miami and Los Angeles.[37] A different dynamic appears to be at work in the rapid emergence of these two cities in comparison with other patterns of migration, either to the suburbs or for occupational mobility. These two cities attracted Jewish newcomers not only through their climate and leisure style of life and their promise of economic abundance, but also through the substantial and visible Jewish presence in a major city industry. Although it would be unfair to compare the Los Angeles–based motion picture industry's enormous assets and glamour with the much smaller Miami Beach tourist trade, Jewish hoteliers in the latter city compensated in part by catering to Jews, advertising for their patronage and encouraging them not only to visit but to settle in Miami.[38] Such encouragement required Jewish efforts to change southern mores—specifically, to eliminate visible signs of antisemitic bias in Miami.

In 1945, as part of an effort by the Anti-Defamation League to remove discriminatory signs on the beach, seventeen ex-servicemen "paid quiet calls on managers of hotels and apartment houses displaying or advertising 'gentiles only' policies," according to the historian Gladys Rosen. "The tactics and its timing proved effective," she concluded, because more than half of the signs disappeared.[39] Jewish residents of Miami Beach, eager to attract Jewish visitors, then urged the local city council to outlaw antisemitic advertising. Although the Florida courts invalidated the council's 1947 law on the grounds that the municipality lacked jurisdiction, by 1949 the state legislature had enacted enabling legislation that granted the city council the power to prohibit discriminatory advertising. The Miami Beach council then forbade "any advertisement, notice or sign which is discriminatory against persons of any religion, sect, creed, race or denomination in the enjoyment of privileges and facilities of places of public accommodation, amusement or resort."[40] Given the widespread acceptance of legal segregation in Florida—as in the rest of the South—the modest action of the Miami Beach City Council reverberated as a loud rejection of discrimination. By passing the law, the council hung out a welcome sign for Jews, at least on Miami Beach. The law did not eliminate antisemitic discrimination and did not affect resorts outside of the council's jurisdiction, but it made Miami Beach's public milieu more accommodating to Jews and set an important precedent.[41]

Despite their comparable attractions for Jewish migrants, Miami and Los Angeles appealed to slightly different Jews. Once they decided to move, Jewish migrants often allowed ethnic networks to influence their choices. These networks channeled postwar internal migration and sorted Jews.[42] Miami drew a more geographically representative sample, including a sizable number of southern Jews, than did Los Angeles. In 1959, approximately 43 percent of Miami Jews came from New York

City, a proportion that slightly exceeded the percentage of American Jews living in New York after the war.[43] By contrast, only 24 percent of the migrants to Los Angeles in 1950 had left New York City. Los Angeles attracted a disproportionate number of Jews from the cities of the Midwest, especially Chicago. An estimated 17 percent of the newcomers hailed from Chicago (45 percent of all midwestern migrants to Los Angeles came from Chicago), although its Jewish population constituted less than 10 percent of American Jewry. Far more Jewish northeasterners moved to Los Angeles, however, than was true among the general white migrant population, which consisted largely of people arriving from states west of the Mississippi.[44]

If Los Angeles attracted Jews disproportionately from the cities of the Midwest, it drew a representative selection of migrants in terms of age. Most Jewish newcomers were young people seeking work, although some came to the city for health reasons or to retire. Miami initially appealed to a similar age spectrum, but by the mid-1950s an ever-growing percentage of elderly retirees had settled in the city.[45] The mass migration of elderly Jews to Miami Beach, which accelerated in the 1960s, received an impetus from the steady decay of the inner cities, accompanied by the rising rate of crime, the high cost of housing and the arrival of new, poor immigrants. The portability of federal social security benefits and union pensions encouraged mobility among retirees in the way that the GI bill had aided a migration of young men after the Second World War. By 1959, the median age of Jews in Miami had risen to 46 from 33 years, while in Los Angeles it had dropped from 37 to 33 years.

The large number of elderly Jews migrating to Miami contributed to a third difference between the two cities. Most Jews moving to Los Angeles settled down and confined any subsequent moves to different sections of the city. Jews migrating to Miami, however, included in their ranks a sizable contingent of "snowbirds." These restless settlers resided in the city anywhere from one to eight months in the course of a year, spending the rest of their time back "home." Many eventually stayed year-round in Miami. Often the difference between an eight-month "snowbird" and a new resident was more a state of mind than a reflection of behavior.

Jewish migrants to Los Angeles and Miami also adopted different residential strategies. The large contingent of New Yorkers in Miami replicated the familiar pattern of dispersed concentration. The newcomers settled initially in two sections: in the South Beach section of Miami Beach and in the Shenandoah and Westchester areas of the city of Miami. By 1955, these two districts held 75 percent of the Jewish population. As more migrants continued to arrive, they drifted northward to North Miami and North Miami Beach.[46] These patterns of concentration reflected in part a response to the restrictive housing covenants in several of the incorporated cities of Dade County that were part of metropolitan Miami. Jewish entrepreneurs in real estate and the hotel and building industry also influenced Miami Jewish residential patterns. The number of apartment houses constructed soared during the 1950s and on into the 1960s. Miami boosters noted that a new house or apartment was completed in Miami "every seven minutes of the working day for an annual average of more than 16,000 units."[47] The migrants' decision to concentrate in certain sections of the city pointed as well to their immigrant and second-generation origins. The move to Miami represented less a decision to leave the familiar urban world of their past than an attempt to radically extend its boundaries. Jews dubbed Miami "the southern borscht belt" and joked that it had become a suburb of New York City.[48] Their humor underscored the sense of connectedness that the newcomers felt with their old homes, which denied the radical character of their relocation.

In contrast, Jews moving to Los Angeles knew that they had left the old neighborhood behind; few sought to replicate the residential strategies of Chicago or New York. When the newcomers arrived in Los Angeles they settled in newly developing sections of the city, especially on the west side and in the San Fernando Valley. Although significant concentrations of Jews appeared in the Wilshire-Fairfax, Beverly-Fairfax, Beverly Hills and Westwood districts, these sections, with the possible exception of Fairfax, did not resemble eastern and midwestern urban neighborhoods.[49] The intensity of public urban life characteristic of eastern and midwestern cities faded under the California sunshine. Yet an awareness of ethnicity persisted. Growing up in Beverly Hills, one knew that it wasn't 100 percent Jewish, "but it felt like it was," a resident recalled. The big ethnic distinctions were culinary. "All of my Jewish friends ate rye bread with mustard and there was one non-Jewish boy in the group that I went around with and he . . . used mayonnaise on white bread, and we used to call him 'mayo.' "[50] The urban character of Los Angeles also muted distinctions between city and suburb, though residents recognized a difference in cultural style between city Jews and valley Jews.[51] One resident who grew up in Los Angeles during the 1950s never understood what a suburb was until she traveled east to settle in Minneapolis.[52] The migrants reversed the perception, thinking that all of Los Angeles was one big suburb.

A Community of Strangers

Despite their differences in age, motivation for leaving the familiar and their diverse residential strategies, the migrants turned to peer group organization to forge the rudimentary bonds of community. Like the immigrants, they broke intergenerational family ties to reconstitute a voluntary community of peers. The new migrants similarly relied upon shared memories of the past or common values to unite them. Unlike the immigrants, the newcomers to Los Angeles and Miami did not convert their impulse to peer group solidarity into social welfare and mutual aid. The new *landsmanshaftn* remained essentially centers of secular ethnic sociability, anchoring their members in unfamiliar urban territory through nostalgic evocations of the well-known world that had been abandoned. By 1950, several dozen of these social clubs organized around city of origin flourished in Los Angeles, as did a smaller number in Miami.[53] They held monthly meetings and hosted annual picnics. A few engaged in charitable endeavors. In 1947, the five hundred members of the Omaha Friendship Club of Los Angeles decided to raise money for a memorial to Henry Monsky, the recently deceased head of B'nai B'rith, who had lived in Omaha.[54] But the clubs' main purpose was social. Most of the Los Angeles clubs limited membership to adults aged twenty-one to thirty-five. Those who didn't join could use the services of the many introduction clubs that sprang up, but often it was preferable to touch base with fellow *landslayt* whose identity with "home" was linked to the neighborhood of their youth. New York City Jews, for example, founded high school alumni associations in Miami and Los Angeles that encouraged contact between former classmates of the Thomas Jefferson or Abraham Lincoln high schools in Brooklyn, or of the DeWitt Clinton or Morris high schools in the Bronx.

The migrants also swelled the ranks of the handful of established American Jewish organizations. By the early 1950s, the one B'nai B'rith group of 1945 in Miami had multiplied into twenty other lodges with a membership exceeding twenty-five hundred.[55] Labor Zionists, General Zionists, Hadassah and the American Jewish Congress rapidly founded local chapters. Often, "even before a new apartment building is fully occupied," observed a Jewish communal worker, "there is already formed (with officers) a Men's Club, B'nai B'rith Lodge, Hadassah Chapter, etc."[56] The newcomers' visible presence encouraged national organizations to refocus their activities. In 1952, the American Jewish Committee established a chapter in Miami and moved its southern headquarters from Atlanta to the new branch.[57] Miami was rapidly becoming the Jews' new headquarters of the South.[58] In Los Angeles, a similar process of recruitment added thousands to the membership rolls of national organizations already established in the city.

The burst of communal activity also affected religious life. In Miami, migrants joined the half-dozen established congregations—which offered special monthly or even weekly memberships to accommodate the "snowbirds"[59]—while those who found the synagogues inconvenient, undesirable or inaccessible initiated new congregations. By 1947, there were twenty-four congregations in Miami, nineteen of them with rabbis. Given the still modest size of the Jewish population, these figures represent significant communal ferment.[60] Los Angeles, with ten times the Jewish population, supported only seventy-three synagogues, or three times the number in Miami.[61] The newcomers found few precedents impeding their efforts to introduce a wide array of communal activities and organizations. Rabbis could, and did, build congregations that became personal fiefdoms unconstrained by an entrenched laity.[62] These communities, a true frontier, were open to individual and collective entrepreneurship; both also contained significant numbers of exceptionally wealthy Jews.

The "snowbird" phenomenon, however, had a significant influence on Miami's communal development. Although it soon overshadowed Atlanta as the major Jewish city of the South, Miami attracted far fewer colonizers from New York than did Los Angeles. When local leaders tried to interest New York institutions in setting up branches in Miami, they more often encountered resistance. Irving Lehrman, rabbi of the Miami Beach Jewish Center (later Temple Emanu-El), grasped the high visibility potential of his synagogue for visitors and made arrangements to establish a branch of the Jewish Museum in the Center as early as 1950. "It will not only bring prestige to, and raise the cultural level of the community, but will afford an opportunity to the thousands of residents, as well as visitors, to see the vast storehouse of Jewish artifacts and learn more about our cultural heritage," he explained.[63] But Lehrman's vision was rarely shared by eastern leaders. Instead, Miami Beach became the campaign capital for national Jewish fund-raising.[64]

Despite its size and diversity, the Los Angeles Jewish community lacked entrenched interests and thus held enormous potential, especially for an elite of ideologically committed easterners. They came to the Southland after the war to establish branches of their institutions and solicit support among Hollywood's moguls. In a brief five-year period after the war, these committed individuals transplanted an institutional range of ideological diversity that had developed in the East. When the American Jewish Committee sent its field-worker for the West to Los Angeles to start a branch in 1945, he emphasized the unique Committee ideology to overcome the reluctance of older residents to join the organization.[65] Four years later, a young communal worker arrived in Los Angeles and dreamed "the vision of establishing a '92nd Street Y of the West' " in the new Westside Jewish Community Center.[66] In 1946, Moshe Davis, a young professor of American Jewish history at the Jewish Theological Seminary, arrived in Los Angeles to recruit supporters for a new branch of the Seminary, the University of Judaism.[67] As Simon Greenberg, the university's first president, recalled, "We had to overcome the feeling on the West Coast that here was a new community. Why did it have to import the divisions (Orthodox, Conservative, Reform) of the East Coast? Why can't we have one school for the Jews of the West Coast?"[68] Eastern leaders' ability to colonize Los Angeles Jews successfully obviated the need to answer such questions. Of course, not all efforts to transplant ideological institutions succeeded.[69] Los Angeles provided a receptive environment largely to a middle range of organizations in the immediate postwar decade. Their success established the foundation for subsequent colonizing efforts.[70]

In the new urban milieu, Jewish self-perceptions gradually changed. "Jews are now free to be Jewish in a new way as an act of personal choice rather than imposition," writes the sociologist Neil Sandberg.[71] The self-selection that lay behind migration reinforced the principle of personal choice of identity. As the Los Angeles lawyer and communal leader Howard Friedman explained, Jews felt able to innovate, experiment, indulge, in short, "to cultivate ourselves . . . in a context of complete freedom."[72] However, according to Moses Rischin, a historian of Jewish immigrants in New York City, the Jewish way of life in Los Angeles was problematic. "Post-Judaic" and "post-secular," he wrote, the life-style was "remote even from an earlier sub-culture of Jewishness" and sustained neither by traditional religious patterns nor by a vigorous secular ethnicity.[73] Others rejoiced in the absence of traditions. According to Charles Brown, the head of the Jewish Community Council in 1952, "here [in Los Angeles] there are no vested interests, here there are no sacred cows, here there is no cold hand of the past. There is an opportunity to develop new forms of Jewish communal living geared in a realistic fashion to the actual needs of the Jewish community."[74] These new forms included such eclectic institutions as the Brandeis Camp Institute, pioneered by Shlomo Bardin. Constrained neither by traditions nor by vested interests, Bardin orchestrated moments of Jewish solidarity designed especially to appeal to a community of strangers, recruiting both old-timers and newcomers for weekend celebrations/explorations of the Sabbath that often inspired the participants to incorporate elements of Jewish study and observance in their lives. The heart of Bardin's program, however, was a month-long innovative leadership training program that raised the Jewish consciousness of the college youth who attended.[75]

Outsiders to the dominant Protestant communities of Los Angeles and Miami, Jewish newcomers introduced additional ethnic diversity to their new homes. Rabbi Edgar Magnin, a fixture of the Los Angeles Jewish scene for decades as the leader of the Wilshire Boulevard Temple, the most prestigious Reform congregation in the city, deplored the new ethnicity introduced by the newcomers in an interview conducted in 1978. "This is a different ballgame today—you've got another Brooklyn here. When I came here, it was Los Angeles. Now it's a Brooklyn."[76] Magnin exaggerated, of course, but other native-born Californian Jews also expressed unease at the changes introduced (mainly in the 1950s) by the newcomers.[77] Often identifying themselves as white ethnics, despite the absence of other such comparable groups as Italians, some migrants used religious symbols to define their collective identity. Foremost among these symbols was Israel: Zion, homeland, state. The migrants' support for the establishment of the state and their subsequent identification with Israel as the vehicle of Jewish idealism helped to make sentimental Zionism the collective glue uniting American Jews.[78] Their numbers overwhelmed the pockets of anti-Zionist commitment among the old-timers, while the attacks on Communists inspired by McCarthy undermined the organizational viability of the internationalist radicals.

Jewish migrants selected themselves to move to Sunbelt cities—to take advantage of the economic opportunities, to bask in the balmy weather and to escape from the constraining intergenerational intimacies of parents and kinfolk. In the process they elevated the principle of self-selection that initially had guided them as migrants into the grounds for collective action. Thus they influenced the character of American Jewish life by creating new patterns of Jewish communal life that upheld the centrality of the consenting individual. Long before converts to Judaism adopted the label "Jews by choice," newcomers to the Sunbelt cities had transformed Jewishness into a matter of one's choosing. The migrants posited a Jewishness rooted in the future, in peer group sociability, in common values and in personal choice, all linked to powerful but distant surrogates—the old home that had disappeared and the Jewish state of Israel that rose like a phoenix on the ashes of the Holocaust. The newcomers created a loosely knit community that supported these possibilities, that allowed for eclectic Jewish styles and symbols of ethnicity, that provided fertile ground for individual entrepreneurship.

"In the past, Jewishness was absorbed by young people as they grew up in Jewish community and family environments," argues Sandberg. "No parental decision was involved in the creation of a sense of Jewish identification in the young person's growing identity and self-image. They were immersed in a culture where Jewish language, behavior, and symbolism developed as automatic responses. . . . Today," he concludes, referring specifically to Los Angeles, "most Jews have grown up without the support of such a community."[79] Under the bright sunshine of Miami and Los Angeles, Jewishness gradually lost its ineluctability. If Jewishness was "not a matter of natural inheritance," then an individual Jew had to develop a number of interlocking networks to sustain a Jewish identity that meant more than self-definition. In Los Angeles, such networks emerged primarily within occupations and politics. In the postwar period, a majority of Los Angeles Jews shared their workplace largely with other Jews. Political lobbying for Israel also served to define the ethnic identity of Miami and Los Angeles Jews. Ironically, work and politics—the two public arenas that originally generated most intra-Jewish conflict—now provided a sense of shared Jewishness for the migrants. For decades Jewish workers had fought Jewish bosses over the conditions of the workplace, and the scars of the past's bitter political battles among Jews had only begun to heal. Yet in the new golden land, work and politics became sources of ethnic continuity helping to define the collective parameters of Jewishness.

In many ways, the Jewish worlds of Los Angeles and Miami and other Sunbelt cities can be seen as the offspring of the large urban Jewish settlements of New York, Chicago, Philadelphia and Boston, and of the more modest communities of such cities as Omaha, Milwaukee, Cleveland and Detroit. As Jewish New York, Chicago and Philadelphia represent continuity with a European past because they were created by immigrants from the cities and towns of Eastern Europe, so Jewish Miami and Los Angeles are creations of the midwestern and northeastern cities, representing continuity with an American past. American Jews produced in the postwar era a second generation of cities, offspring of the first generation. It was, perhaps, a very American thing to send off the sons and daughters—and even the grandfathers and grandmothers—to colonize the new golden land, to build cities, to plant congregations, to forge symbolic bonds of ethnic identity. Borrowing from America's Puritan past, one might see these internal migrations as American Jews' own errand into the wilderness.

Notes

I am grateful to the National Endowment for the Humanities for a research grant, to Cindy Sweet for help conducting interviews, to Gladys Rosen for generously sharing materials collected on Miami Jews, and to Arthur A. Goren and Paula Hyman for criticism of an earlier draft of this essay.

1. There have been few studies of the impact of wartime participation on American Jews. A pioneering early study is Moses Kligsberg, "American Jewish Soldiers on Jews and Judaism," *YIVO Annual of Jewish Social Science* 5 (1950), 256–265.

2. John Bodnar, *The Transplanted: A History of Immigrants in Urban America* (Bloomington: 1985), is a valuable study of the relationship between immigration and social formation in the United States. Lloyd P. Gartner, "The History of North American Jewish Communities: A Field for the Jewish Historian," *The Jewish Journal of Sociology* 9 (June 1965), 22–29, offers a thoughtful analysis of the relationship between Jewish immigration and secondary migration.

3. For a focus on transformation, see Calvin Goldscheider, *Jewish Continuity and Change: Emerging Patterns in America* (Bloomington: 1985), and Steven M. Cohen, *American Modernity, Jewish Identity* (New York: 1983).

4. Oscar Handlin, "Immigration in American Life: A Reappraisal," in *Immigration and American History: Essays in Honor of Theodore C. Blegen,* ed. Henry Steele Commager (Minneapolis: 1961), 8–25.

5. For comparative mobility statistics by state, see "Series C 25-73," *The Statistical History of the United States from Colonial Times to the Present* (Stamford: 1965), 44–47.

6. Interview with Rabbi Murray Alstet, June 1966; interview with Rabbi Joseph Narot, n.d.

7. Leonard Dinnerstein, "From Desert Oasis to the Desert Caucus: The Jews of Tucson," Moses Rischin and John Livingston, eds., *Jews of the American West* (Detroit: 1991).

8. Interview with Leon Rabin by Cindy Sweet, 19 September 1986.

9. Gerald Nash, *The American West Transformed: The Impact of the Second World War* (Bloomington: 1985), 14, 35–36.

10. Ann Markusen, *Regions: The Economics and Politics of Territory* (New York: 1987), and *idem, The Rise of the Gunbelt* (New York: 1990).

11. Otis L. Graham, Jr., "From Snowbelt to Sunbelt: The Impact of Migration," *Dialogue* 59 (1983), 11–14.

12. Interviews with "the Mavens," Jewish migrants to Los Angeles from New York City, Los Angeles, 14 July 1989.

13. Nicholas Lemann, "Covering the Sunbelt," *Harper's Magazine* (February 1982), rpt. in *Dialogue* 59 (1983), 24.

14. Leonard Sperry, "The Development of Programs in the Los Angeles Chapter." Papers presented at Chapter Leaders Workshop, 16 April 1959, American Jewish Committee MSS (California/Los Angeles Chapter, 52–62), YIVO.

15. Memo from Arthur Rosichan, 2 March 1967, with covering memo probably from Robert Forman, Greater Miami Jewish Federation.

16. Vance Packard, *A Nation of Strangers* (New York: 1972), 7–8.

17. Sidney Goldstein, "American Jewry, 1970: A Demographic Profile," *American Jewish Year Book* 72 (New York: 1971), 37–38.

18. Both the prewar (1937) and postwar (1960) distribution of Jews by state and region produce a consistent rank of 4 on an index of dissimilarity. Figures from *ibid*.

19. Ira M. Sheskin, "The Migration of Jews to Sunbelt Cities" (unpublished paper in author's possession), 9–11, 26–27.

20. The Jewish population in the South rose from 330,000 in 1937 to 486,000 in 1960; Miami's growth accounted for 132,000 of the increase. Similarly, Los Angeles accounted for 300,000 of the increase of Jews in the West, from 219,000 in 1937 to 598,000 in 1960. In the following decade, Los Angeles accounted for 64 percent of the western regional increase, while Miami accounted for only 29 percent of the southern regional increase. Computed from Tables 1, 3 and 5 in Sheskin, "The Migration of Jews to Sunbelt Cities."

21. Max Vorspan and Lloyd Gartner, *History of the Jews of Los Angeles* (Philadelphia: 1970), 225. See 225–237 for a good, concise treatment of Jewish migration to Los Angeles—its sources, motivations and impact.

22. Bruce Philips, "Los Angeles Jewry: A Demographic Portrait," *American Jewish Year Book* 86 (New York: 1986), 141, 160; Fred Massarik, "A Report on the Jewish Population of Los Angeles," Jewish Federation-Council of Greater Los Angeles (1959), 18–19.

23. Ira M. Sheskin, *Demographic Study of the Greater Miami Jewish Community: Summary Report* (Miami: 1984), 4–7.

24. Interview with Bernard Goldstein by Cindy Sweet, 20 September 1986.

25. Interview with Michael Wiener, 14 July 1989; comment by Selma Berrol at Columbia University Urban History Seminar, March 1987.

26. Nathan Perlmutter, Oral History Memoir, 15, Oral History of the American Jewish Committee, William E. Wiener Oral History Library.

27. Robert Fishman, *Bourgeois Utopias: The Rise and Fall of Suburbia* (New York: 1987), 174–179; Kenneth T. Jackson, *Crabgrass Frontier: The Suburbanization of the United States* (New York: 1985), 196–217.

28. Erich Rosenthal, "This Was North Lawndale: The Transplantation of a Jewish Community," *Jewish Social Studies* 22 (April 1960), 67–82.

29. Marshall Sklare, *Jewish Identity on the Suburban Frontier* (New York: 1967). Also see Sidney Goldstein and Calvin Goldscheider, *Jewish Americans: Three Generations in a Jewish Community* (Englewood Cliffs, N.J.: 1968), who indicate continuities as well as changes.

30. Herbert Gans, "Park Forest: Birth of a Jewish Community," *Commentary* 11 (April

1951), 330–339; *idem*, "Progress of a Suburban Jewish Community," *Commentary* 23 (February 1957), 113–122.

31. Paula Hyman, "From City to Suburb: Temple Mishkan Tefila of Boston," in *A History of the American Synagogue*, ed. Jack Wertheimer (Cambridge, Mass.: 1987).

32. Interviews with "the Mavens" (14 July 1989) reveal a fairly consistent pattern of job changes that occurred upon arrival in Los Angeles. Very few moved for occupational reasons; most had to hunt for jobs when they arrived. Many often entered completely different lines of work from their training or previous experience.

33. Goldstein, "American Jewry, 1970," 50.

34. Avron C. Heligman, "The Demographic Perspective," in *Mid-America's Promise: A Profile of Kansas City Jewry*, ed. Joseph P. Schultz (1982), 389–391.

35. Murray Frost, "Analysis of a Jewish Community's Outmigration," *Jewish Social Studies* 44 (1982), passim.

36. Goldstein, "American Jewry, 1970," 37, 44, 51.

37. Jews did migrate after the Second World War to both Houston and Atlanta, but not at a rate that exceeded the growth of the general population. On Houston, see Elaine H. Mass, *The Jews of Houston: An Ethnographic Study* (Ph.D. diss., Rice University, 1973), 66, 79, 82; and Sam Schulman, David Gottlieb and Sheila Sheinberg, *A Social and Demographic Survey of the Jewish Community of Houston, Texas* (Houston: 1976), 7–9, 13. On Atlanta, see *Metropolitan Atlanta Jewish Population Study: Summary of Major Findings* (Atlanta: 1985), 2–4, 16. The Jewish population of Atlanta grew at a more rapid rate than did the general population in the 1980s.

38. In 1939, there were more movie theaters (15,115) than banks (14,952). Box office receipts totaled $673,045,000. More than fifty million Americans went to the movies each week every year. Movies were the nation's fourteenth-biggest business in terms of volume ($406,855,000) and eleventh-biggest in terms of assets ($529,950,000). Hollywood was bigger than office machines and supermarket chains. See Otto Friedrich, *City of Nets* (New York: 1986), 14. Statistics on Miami Beach's tourist industry are impressive but do not approach the motion pictures; see Miami Beach Chamber of Commerce, Statistical Review, 1955.

39. Gladys Rosen, "Community Relations: 1945–1960 Post-War Period" (unpublished paper in author's possession), 2.

40. *Jewish Floridian*, 24 June 1949; Polly Redford, *Billion Dollar Sandbar: A Biography of Miami Beach* (New York: 1970), 222.

41. The neighboring town of Surfside passed a similar ordinance in 1951. *Jewish Floridian*, 29 June 1951. Enforcement was another problem. Signs remained on the Beach through the 1950s, as noted in the Survey of Resort Discrimination by the Anti-Defamation League, reported in the *Jewish Floridian*, 29 April 1960. In 1953, 20 percent of the Miami Beach hotels barred Jews; by 1957 this figure had declined to only two percent.

42. Interviews with "the Mavens," 14 July 1989.

43. Manheim Shapiro, "The Bayville Survey," American Jewish Committee, Greater Miami Chapter (1961), summary statement, n.p.

44. Fred Massarik, *A Report on the Jewish Population of Los Angeles* (Los Angeles: 1953), 22; *idem*, "The Jewish Population of Los Angeles: A Panorama of Change," *The Reconstructionist* 18 (28 November 1952), 13.

45. Many of the elderly settled in Miami Beach. The median age of Miami Beach rose from 43 years in 1950 to 54 years in 1960, when there were more than 17,000 people aged 65 and over. By 1965, there were more than 28,000 people in this age category, a very rapid increase of 11,000 in only five years. The elderly made up 28 percent of the Beach population in 1960 and 38 percent in 1965. Jews were estimated to constitute close to 80 percent of the Beach population. Memo from Arthur Rosichan, Greater Miami Jewish Federation, 2 March 1967, 2–3.

46. Letter from Arthur Rosichan to Gladys Rosen, Greater Miami Jewish Federation, 23 May 1968.

47. "Key to Growth: Metropolitan Miami" (brochure of Dade County Development Department), 5.

48. A significant number of Catskill hotel owners purchased or built hotels in Miami Beach, starting with the Grossinger family, which purchased the formerly restricted Pancoast in 1945. Grossinger's Pancoast not only changed the hotel guest policy but installed a kosher kitchen.

49. Philips, "Los Angeles Jewry," 133–137.

50. Dena Kaye, American Jewish Committee Annual Meeting (14 May 1977), Oral History Library Panel Session, 6, William E. Wiener Oral History Library.

51. Interview with Judith Kantor, Robin Hudson and David Hudson, 20 July 1989.

52. Remarks of Riv-Ellen Prell, YIVO Annual Conference, 1988.

53. Vorspan and Gartner, *History of the Jews of Los Angeles*, 228; Irving Lehrman and Joseph Rappaport, *The Jewish Community of Miami Beach* (New York: n.d.), 24.

54. *California Jewish Voice*, 19 December 1947.

55. Harry Simonoff, *Under Strange Skies* (New York: 1953), 313.

56. Memo, probably of Robert Forman, 2 March 1967, Greater Miami Jewish Federation.

57. Background material for Miami chapter, American Jewish Committee, n.d., n.p.

58. Daniel Elazar, *Community and Polity: The Organizational Dynamics of American Jews* (Philadelphia: 1976), 140.

59. Gladys Rosen, "The Rabbi in Miami: A Case History," in *Turn to the South: Essays on Southern Jewry*, ed. Nathan M. Kaganoff and Melvin I. Urofsky (Charlottesville: 1979), 35–37.

60. Memo to Morris Klass from M. C. Gettinger, 16 January 1951; Greater Miami Federation; Census of Greater Miami file (1950–1960), 1.

61. Los Angeles Jewish Community Council, *1950 Jewish Community Directory of Greater Los Angeles*, American Jewish Archives, Nearprint Box, Geography, 1–13.

62. For example, consider the careers of Rabbis Irving Lehrman, Leon Kronish and Joseph Narot in Miami, and Edgar Magnin, Aaron Wise, Isaiah Zeldin and Jacob Pressman in Los Angeles.

63. *Jewish Floridian*, 29 December 1950.

64. Elazar, *Community and Polity*, 244.

65. See correspondence between John Slawson and Maurice Karpf, 19 June and 18 July 1945, American Jewish Archives, Maurice J. Karpf MSS 196, Box 1.

66. Letter from Nathan Hurvitz to Charles Mesnick, 1 October 1956, American Jewish Archives, Nathan Hurvitz MSS, Box 100/4, Jewish Centers Association, 1955–1957.

67. Moshe Davis, conversation with Arthur Hoffnung, June 1985, 3–12, Oral History Interview, University of Judaism.

68. Simon Greenberg, "Some Reflections," *Women's League for Conservative Judaism* 58 (Summer 1988), 22.

69. Both the Reconstructionists and YIVO initially failed to establish viable branches of their movement, although Yiddish was subsequently introduced as a regular language at UCLA and the Reconstructionists did build a number of impressive congregations, e.g., Abraham Winokur's in Pacific Palisades. See letter from Sol Liptzin (recipient's identity unknown), 6 July 1947, YIVO, Max Weinreich MSS, Box 263; Samuel Dinin, "Reconstructionism and the Future of Jewish Life in Los Angeles," *The Reconstructionist* 18 (28 November 1952), 15–16.

70. For example, the University of Judaism and the College of Jewish Studies (later the California School of Hebrew Union College–Jewish Institute of Religion) established the precedent followed by Yeshiva University when it started its branch.

71. Neil Sandberg, *Jewish Life in Los Angeles: A Window to Tomorrow* (Lanham, Md.: 1986), 19.

72. Howard I. Friedman, Oral History Memoir, 58–59; Oral History of the American Jewish Committee, William E. Wiener Oral History Library.

73. Moses Rischin, "Foreword," in *The Jews of Los Angeles, 1849–1945: An Annotated Bibliography*, ed. Sara G. Cogan (Berkeley: 1980), viii.

74. Quoted in Vorspan and Gartner, *History of the Jews of Los Angeles,* 267.

75. Bardin regularly solicited testimonies; there were also unsolicited reflections on the effects of Brandeis Camp Institute. See, for example, Walter Hilborn, "Reflections on Legal Practice and Jewish Community Leadership: New York and Los Angeles, 1907–1975," Oral History Interview, Bancroft Library, University of California, Berkeley, 217–219; and interview with Shlomo Bardin by Jack Diamond, pts. 3–5, Library of Brandeis–Bardin Institute.

76. Quoted in "The Jews of Los Angeles: Pursuing the American Dream," *Los Angeles Times,* 29 Jan. 1978.

77. For example, see interview with Rabbi Paul Dubin, American Jewish Historical Society, Interview Folder, Los Angeles, *I-75, Box 24.

78. Sandberg, *Jewish Life in Los Angeles,* 64, 86; Gladys Rosen, "The Zionist Movement" (unpublished draft essay in author's possession), 2–8.

79. Sandberg, *Jewish Life in Los Angeles,* 131.

Understanding Jewish Communal Involvement: Theoretical Issues and Policy Implications

Gary A. Tobin and Gabriel Berger
(BRANDEIS UNIVERSITY)

Organizational structure is one of the most distinctive features of American Jewish life in the contemporary era. No other diaspora community rests on an institutional network of such breadth and scope that involves so many individuals as either members, professional staff or volunteer leaders. Not surprisingly, participation in Jewish organizations is assumed to be a critical factor in ensuring continuity of the community. The assumption is that Jewish organizations not only facilitate social contacts but also generate further ties and networks among Jews, in addition to socializing and educating them in various aspects of Jewish life. It follows that the vitality and quality of the American Jewish community depend to a large extent on the capacity of its institutions to generate loyalty and participation; and the actual level of participation can serve as a measure of the community's general state of health.

With this in mind, it is somewhat surprising that research and analysis of the patterns of communal involvement have been relatively meager in recent years. Most studies have focused on identifying what are defined as affiliated, unaffiliated or marginally affiliated Jews, in the hope of finding ways to reach the latter two groups.[1] We will argue that attention might fruitfully be shifted away from the *fact* of organizational affiliation and directed instead toward the *level* and *quality* of that participation. As we will show, most Jews already are, will be, or used to be formally affiliated to the community in some way—but are all but invisible within the Jewish communal structure. As a result, many communities expend a good deal of resources unsuccessfully seeking such unaffiliated Jews when such resources might be better spent in locating and encouraging the vast majority who are already connected, but *underinvolved,* to participate more actively in Jewish institutional life.

This article focuses both on the different ways in which Jews connect themselves with communal institutions and on the level of organizational participation in such institutions. Throughout this article, a distinction will be made between two aspects of organizational participation. On the one hand, there is the *connection* or *affilia-*

tion with Jewish organizations—the linkage established with a Jewish institution through formal membership, utilization of services or programs, or contributions of time or financial resources. This terminology follows much of the empirical research on organizational participation, which has used affiliation as the sole measure of participation. On the other hand, we will refer to *involvement* in Jewish organizations—that is, active participation and support.

The distinction between the concepts of affiliation and involvement corresponds closely to David Horton Smith's differentiation between analytical membership, involving at least some minimal level of participation or provision of services, and official or nominal membership.[2] The utilization of these two concepts—whatever way they are measured—results in dramatically different portraits of the level of organizational participation in a particular society or community. For example, in their seminal work on political participation in the United States, Sidney Verba and Norman N. Nie[3] reported that, while 62 percent of adults in the United States reported *membership* in voluntary associations, only 40 percent indicated some type of *activity* in these organizations.

This article applies the same distinction to the analysis of participation in Jewish organizations. The changing patterns of affiliation and involvement are set against a radically altered American Jewish landscape in terms of demography, religious identity and institutional structure. Each of these factors has a marked effect on the relationship of members to their organizational and institutional activities. We will also analyze a number of structural impediments to greater involvement in Jewish organizations, and conclude with a discussion of some policy implications.

The Demographic and Religious Context of Institutional Participation

Most demographic change in the United States today militates against involvement in Jewish organizations. First, interregional mobility exerts a powerful negative influence. The regional shift of Jewish populations from the Northeast and Midwest to the Southeast, Southwest and West has redistributed the Jewish population into less dense concentrations in such communities as Phoenix, San Francisco, Denver and San Diego. The lack of cohesive ethnic neighborhoods in the emerging metropolises of the West and Southwest makes it difficult to locate institutions centrally, such that many Jews are no longer within short driving distances of Jewish community centers, synagogues and other Jewish agencies. There has also been an unprecedented movement of Jews, many of near-retirement or retirement age, from the Northeast and Midwest to southern Florida. Upon relocating to the new communities of West Palm Beach, Hollywood, Fort Lauderdale, Boca Raton and elsewhere, these individuals do not necessarily join Jewish organizations and institutions, even if they were previously involved.

Second, changing patterns of neighborhood living have a negative effect on Jewish institutional life. In the more established communities in the Northeast and Midwest, the suburbanization of Jews (first to the inner suburbs, then to the outer suburbs and now to the exurbs) has also resulted in lowered population densities.

Even in communities such as Cleveland, Detroit and Saint Louis, where Jews are concentrated and not distributed at random, they no longer live in the close neighborhood networks that were characteristic of one generation back, and institutions and organizations tend to be less centrally located than they once were.

Both the interregional and intraurban patterns of mobility have decreased the likelihood that Jews will be active participants in the organizational life of the community, notwithstanding their "paper" membership. This is because access is the key to involvement; when people move within a community, or move from one metropolitan area to another, the proclivity to reestablish institutional and organizational ties tends to weaken. During periods of adjustment that accompany such moves, many Jews are likely to be either reluctant or unwilling to invest large amounts of time or money, or both, in unfamiliar institutions. Furthermore, if the move is viewed as temporary, because of employment mobility, further educational goals, or other such factors, the desire to become attached is not likely to be strong, since any new ties would soon be broken.

A third demographic change involves the generational structure of American Jewry at the end of the 1980s. A majority of Jews in this country are now third- or fourth-generation, and an increasing number are even fifth-generation. Religious and cultural patterns that were often part and parcel of daily life for first- and second-generation Jews—the synagogue as the center of religious life, a commitment to *zedakah* (philanthropy), support for Israel and for Jewish organizations—frequently have only a tenuous hold on, or are even completely unknown to, third- and fourth-generation Jews. Involvement, active support for Jewish organizations and institutions, must therefore become a "learned" behavior.

The final significant demographic change affecting communal involvement is the transformation of Jewish family structure. Over the past generation, Jews have tended to marry and form families later in life. Thus, the single status has come to occupy a longer period in the life cycle of more Jews. Singles, however, are less likely to become involved with Jewish organizations and institutions. Moreover, many more Jewish women than in the past are today part of the labor force, with the result that the pool of potential volunteers for Jewish organizations and agencies has substantially contracted. In double-income families, the demands on both parents with regard to child care are much greater, so that there is less leisure time to spend with their families—a situation that militates against volunteering. Finally, substantially increased divorce rates over the past generation have resulted in proportionately more single-parent households, usually headed by women. They, too, are less likely to find time to spend in Jewish organizations.

While demographic changes have created an environment in which it is more difficult to develop organizational loyalties, changing religious realities have also played a major role. Most Jews are no longer bound by common ritual observances. Involvement in the life of the Jewish community as a function of religiosity, once a significant factor, has declined as many Jews have abandoned formerly common religious practices. Even if the synagogue remains the center of religious life, it is not the center of everyday life for most Jews. Neighborhood, career, other voluntary organizations, recreation and many additional involvements now compete with, or replace, religion as the focus of their attention and energies. Thus, lack of Jewish organizational involvement is a direct outcome of the diminished importance of religion in the lives of individuals and families.

Involvement is also a function of in-group cohesion—that is, Jews associating primarily with other Jews, in terms of either friendship circles or marriage. Data consistently show that third- and fourth-generation Jews are much less likely than first- or second-generation Jews to socialize exclusively or even primarily with other Jews. Since friendship circles and peer groups reinforce institutional attachments and involvement—and vice versa—such changes are bound to weaken the links to Jewish organization.

Marriage is, of course, one of the primary religious and ethnic group bonds. Increasingly, however, whether measured by age, generation or date of marriage, Jews are currently more likely to marry non-Jews than at any other time in American Jewish history. In particular, the intermarriage rates among third- and fourth-generation Jews married in the 1980s are very high compared both to those that prevailed among first- and second-generation Jews and to those who married in the 1950s or 1960s. As a growing proportion of the Jewish population consists of intermarried couples, the tendency to become involved exclusively, or at all, with Jewish organizations is diminished.

Prevailing Scholarly Analysis and Policy Prescription

During the last few years, observers of the Jewish community have been using the term "marginally affiliated" to describe those who are underinvolved in the Jewish community but still have *some* attachment to Jewish organizational life. Several analysts have argued that communal effort should be targeted to reach this group. For example, Steven M. Cohen, using data from the 1981 Greater New York Jewish Population Study, found that the large majority of Jews were in the middle ranges of Jewish involvement: A full 64 percent of the New York Jewish community were defined as belonging to the group of marginally affiliated or semicommitted Jews, 27 percent were seen as heavily involved in Jewish life and the remaining 10 percent were located on the periphery of the Jewish community. Cohen suggests that "sooner or later, almost all Jews affiliate with some Jewish agency," and concludes that the problem is not simply one of promoting affiliation but how to reach, inspire, involve and educate those Jews in the large group of marginally affiliated.[4]

From another theoretical orientation, Calvin Goldscheider suggests that policies should be targeted toward the very marginal sectors of the Jewish population—the intermarried, the migrants, and those in areas of low Jewish density—in ways that would lead to their greater integration. According to Goldscheider's analysis, those on the margins do not reveal desires for assimilation or actual disengagement from the Jewish community. He considers group cohesion to be based on the frequency and intensity of the interaction among Jews. Therefore, Jewish communities should concentrate on increasing such interaction and providing the appropriate organizational contexts.[5]

Obviously, the assessment of such policy options rests upon a critical analysis of how the concepts of Jewish affiliation and involvement have been defined and measured: in other words, what criteria have been used to differentiate the "core" from the "margins" and to categorize Jewish affiliation and involvement. Affiliation has generally been conceptualized in the context of Jewish identification. Multidimensional analyses of Jewish identification have consistently included, inter alia, elements of institutional and organizational affiliation. However, since their primary aim has been to develop scales summarizing the multiple aspects of Jewish identification, these attempts have not provided an articulated set of concepts regarding Jewish affiliation and involvement. More important, when communal participation is explored in this analytical context, those measures of affiliation that are used inevitably miss other important ways in which people connect themselves to the organized Jewish community: using community-sponsored social services, for example, or participating in recreational and educational programs, or volunteering time for Jewish organizations (see Appendix).

Admittedly, whichever scale of Jewish identification or involvement is used, decisions on what to include and the weight to be attached to each item are bound to be arbitrary in many respects. Moreover, the particular conceptual framework employed, the nature of available data and the requirements of the statistical techniques utilized all interact to define the analytic strategy of the study (see Appendix). Nevertheless, in what follows below, we seek to minimize these obstacles and deficiencies in measurement by focusing solely on those variables that pertain to organizational affiliation and involvement, omitting other dimensions of Jewish identification.

Our study of the patterns of affiliation and involvement in the Jewish community utilizes data from demographic studies conducted by two Jewish communities: Baltimore and San Francisco.[6] Although they do not constitute a representative sample of the American Jewish community, they serve as useful case studies that display (in addition to regional variations) very different demographic, institutional and religious profiles. Baltimore is a geographically compact Jewish community. It has a high proportion of Jews who identify themselves as Orthodox. It has a well-developed institutional network and relatively high level of philanthropic activity. Intermarriage in this community tends to be less frequent than in the Jewish communities of the West and Southwest. San Francisco, in contrast, has a highly assimilated Jewish community. Jews there tend to have been born someplace else, having migrated to the community in the past twenty years. There are relatively low levels of synagogue membership and attendance, and rates of intermarriage are among the highest in the United States. Baltimore tends to represent the more traditional and conservative Jewish community, and San Francisco the more loosely knit and less identified Jewish community. The data were collected between 1985 and 1986 from these representative communities. Table 1 provides an illustration of the distribution of key variables used in this study.

The criteria that we have employed to define and measure formal connection to and involvement in Jewish organizations were determined largely by the nature of the available data. The dimensions used to build the scales presented below were restricted by the variables included in the demographic studies on which this analysis is based. Data collection designed for direct study of affiliation and involvement is rare, and it would require the employment of more specific survey instruments.[7]

Table 1. Percentages of Institutional Participation Variables

	Baltimore	San Francisco
Contribute to Jewish philanthropies	65.7	60.3
Volunteer time for Jewish organizations	23.1	24.1
Belong to a Jewish organization	52.0	37.5
Synagogue member	53.9	32.7
Adult receiving Jewish education	4.2	3.8
Child receiving Jewish education	37.3	30.8
Used Jewish Federation during last year	49.1	40.3
Received help from Jewish-sponsored service	7.6	7.7

Nevertheless, the Jewish community studies are not only the best empirical material available at this time but, as we shall see, can also produce significant findings when the organizational variables are isolated and analyzed separately.

For our analysis, different types of connections with Jewish organizations were used to measure the extent to which Jewish households are linked to the organized Jewish community. Eight such connections are listed in Table 1: contribution to Jewish charities or causes, volunteer time for Jewish organizations, membership in Jewish organizations, membership in a synagogue, participation of an adult in Jewish education classes, any child in the household receiving Jewish education, utilization of Jewish-sponsored social services and use of Jewish agencies. These variables reflect the ways in which a given household was linked to Jewish organizations during the year previous to the survey.[8] An index of connections to Jewish organizations based on these variables assigns a score ranging between 0 and 8 to Jewish households, depending on the number of ways in which they are connected with Jewish organizations. The index of connections provides a descriptive measure of the extent to which Jewish households are currently connected in some way to the formal structure of Jewish organizations. It differs from other measures of communal affiliation (see Appendix) in that it eliminates those identification and affiliation factors not related to institutional connections, such as number of Jewish friends, readership of Jewish newspapers, and visits to Israel—all of which do not necessarily reflect formal connections to Jewish institutions. Our measure also excludes the frequency of synagogue attendance, a statistic more related to religiosity than to formal institutional affiliation.

The index of connections to Jewish organizations in Baltimore and San Francisco is shown in Table 2. This index shows that at the time of the survey the vast majority of Jewish households (88 percent in Baltimore and 77 percent in San Francisco) had some type of current connection with formal Jewish organizations. Although these findings clearly challenge the prevailing notion that the rate of institutional participation in the Jewish community is low, they only provide a scale on which the level of association of Jew to the organized community can be represented: They do not provide any assessment of the quality and strength of the involvement.

It also should be noted that this index records a high level of institutional par-

Table 2. Number of Current Connections
to Jewish Organizations

	Baltimore	San Francisco
0	12.0%	22.8%
1	15.8%	19.4%
2	19.1%	18.6%
3	21.2%	15.0%
4	18.1%	11.6%
5	9.4%	7.1%
6 or more	4.4%	6.5%
Reliability coefficient		
Standardized item alpha	.65	.69
Unweighted cases	1,117	2,422

ticipation despite the fact that it excludes past connections to Jewish organizations. Other studies have shown that religious and communal affiliation is significantly affected by the life cycle and family status.[9] Households consisting of married couples with school-age or older children have been found to have higher levels of participation, which indicates that at some point during their life cycle most Jews have some formal linkage to the Jewish community. Therefore, a study that adjusted for life cycle effects would in all likelihood show even higher affiliation rates.

Factor analysis was completed to assess the index of current connections for theoretical cohesiveness. (This type of analysis is a statistical technique that attempts to represent relationships among sets of interrelated variables; it allows for an examination of the underlying dimensions that explain the conceptual relationship among the eight variables included in our model.) The factor analysis resulted in the isolation of two factors from the eight variables included in the index (see Table 3). The first six variables (synagogue membership; organizational membership; contributions to Jewish philanthropies; time volunteered for Jewish causes; current participation of an adult in Jewish education; and current Jewish schooling for a child) are closely related to the first factor, while the other two variables (services received from a Jewish-sponsored agency and usage of program and services from Federation agencies) are closely related to the second factor.

These results suggest that the eight variables included in our analysis of formal connections to the Jewish community express two very different spheres of formal communal participation. The first one represents variables related to affiliational connections: time commitments; philanthropic contributions; dues paid to synagogues; membership in Jewish organizations; enrollment (or enrollment of one's children) in Jewish educational programs. The second factor refers to connections generated by consumer needs: the use of Jewish services and programs. The fact that our eight variables are summarized by two factors rather than by one has a number of implications that we will now examine.

Table 3. Factor Analysis of Institutional Participation Variables

	Baltimore		San Francisco	
	Factor A	Factor B	Factor A	Factor B
Synagogue membership	.67		.75	
Organizational membership	.64		.65	
Contrib. to Jew. charities	.59		.66	
Volunteer for Jewish causes	.52		.74	
Adult in Jewish education	.54		.29	
Child in Jewish education	.52		.62	
Received help from Jewish-sponsored services		.83		.84
Used Jewish Federation agencies		.65		.69
Eigenvalue	2.43	1.14	2.80	1.11
Percentage of variance explained	30.4	14.2	35.0	13.8
Unweighted number of cases	1,117		2,422	

Levels of Involvement in the Jewish Community

Thus far, we have explored the variety of ways in which Jewish households are connected to Jewish organizations. We have found that in two very different communities the percentage of households with no current connections to Jewish organizations is quite low. However, this pattern of connections to formal Jewish organizations does not inform us about the quality of that participation.

When we shift the focus from *affiliation* (the formal connection or association with an organization) to *involvement* (that is, commitment to its activities), we confront an entirely different problem. What does being "involved" in Jewish organizations mean? What are the standards by which it should be assessed? Both questions are difficult to answer.

Voluntary "citizenship" is a basic characteristic of Jewish life in America, where Jews often define their religious or ethnic identity in communal activity. Defining the criteria for "active" citizenship thus becomes a matter of prime importance for understanding the organized Jewish community.[10] Jewish organizations must secure members' commitment in order to hold members and channel their efforts toward organizational goals. Members' commitment is particularly crucial for voluntary associations such as Jewish organizations that derive most of their necessary inputs from the contributions and activities of members but do not pay members for that input. A critical expression of organizational commitment is the degree to which members provide the continual infusion of resources necessary to the survival and efficacy of organizations: participation, money, time and efforts. Members' support for organizations is thus a critical factor in sustaining the organization's capacity to mobilize resources for collective action. We suggest that central to the concept of

Table 4. Factors of Communal Involvement

	Baltimore Factor A	San Francisco Factor A
Synagogue membership	.70	.73
Organizational membership	.74	.71
Amount contributed to Jewish charities	.67	.71
Hours volunteered for Jewish causes	.65	.73
Eigenvalue	1.91	2.07
Percentage of variance explained	47.8	51.8

involvement will be not only joining but also contributing time and resources to Jewish organizations.

We measured *involvement* in Jewish organizations through an ordinal scale that included only those variables that reflected active participation and support for Jewish organizations: membership in a Jewish organization or a synagogue; the level of financial contributions; and the amount of time volunteered for Jewish organizations. Although the first two items were also included previously in the index of formal connections to Jewish organizations, we now substituted for general categories the *amount* of money contributed and the *hours* volunteered. This makes it possible to give expression to different degrees of involvement. The results of the factor analysis presented in Table 4 give additional empirical support to our contention that these variables are positively linked.

The first category of involvement includes those who belong neither to a Jewish organization nor to a synagogue, do not volunteer time for Jewish causes and do not make contributions to Jewish charities. The second, which we call the "partially involved," refers to those households that do belong to a synagogue or to a Jewish organization but contribute less than one hundred dollars annually or volunteer less than four hours a month. Finally, there is the "involved" group, which includes those households that belong to a synagogue or to a Jewish organization, contribute one hundred dollars or more to Jewish philanthropies and volunteer at least four hours per month for Jewish organizations.[11]

The portrait that emerges from Table 5 differs sharply from our previous analysis of institutional connections to the Jewish community. Previously, we observed that the majority of households (88 percent in Baltimore and 77 percent in San Francisco) have some type of current formal connection to Jewish organizations. When we focus our attention on variables that denote institutional *involvement* or active *support* for Jewish organizations, however, we find that the largest category is formed by those households partially involved in institutional Jewish life. The percentage of those not involved in the life of Jewish organizations increased slightly compared with the percentage of those households that have no connections to Jewish institutions. The percentages of households having no current formal connections to Jewish organizations are 12 percent in Baltimore and 23 percent in San Francisco, while

Table 5. Level of Organizational Involvement
in the Jewish Community

	Baltimore	San Francisco
Not involved	17.6%	30.5%
Partially involved	70.9%	59.9%
Involved	11.5%	9.7%
Reliability coefficient		
Standardized item Alpha	.63	.69
Unweighted number of cases	1,117	2,422

the percentage of households not involved in the life of Jewish organizations are 18 percent and 31 percent, respectively. The most interesting finding, however, is the small percentage of households actively involved in the life of the Jewish community: Between 9.7 percent and 11.5 percent in both communities, in spite of the intentionally minimal criteria used to define active involvement.

Although the high rates of Jewish households with present connections to Jewish communal organizations constitute grounds for cautious optimism, the low rates of active involvement raise some serious questions for Jewish policymakers. It appears that, while Jewish organizations are successfully serving some needs of the Jewish community, they may be failing to generate a minimum level of commitment and loyalty—a problem we will now examine in some detail.

Institutional and Organizational Barriers

Although it is difficult (if not impossible) for Jewish communal initiatives to alter the demographic and social factors that negatively affect the level of institutional involvement, another set of negative factors—institutional and organizational barriers—may directly or indirectly derive from the manner in which Jewish organizations currently operate. These, clearly, may be within the capacity of the Jewish community to change.

One such institutional factor relates to the increasing role of professionals in voluntary organizations. Many tasks previously undertaken by volunteers are now the province of salaried executives and staff who are often trained in fund-raising, social work or other similar fields. The growing dominance of professionals in the voluntary sector brings with it attempts to delineate separate roles for volunteers and professionals. Since involvement often leads to increased commitment or to larger financial contributions, the need to define volunteer roles wisely is of critical concern.

Low levels of active involvement may result partially from the lack of interesting, rewarding or meaningful tasks assigned to volunteers. Since much of the voluntary sector is now professionally managed, some of the more interesting and challenging roles are no longer filled by volunteers. Jewish organizations have not necessarily been very creative in the face of this challenge. Often, volunteers are relegated to committee or board work that many find either repetitious or unproductive. Moreover, as Jews have gained more open access to non-Jewish organizations and agencies, rewards for civic and voluntary work are no longer to be obtained solely from Jewish organizations. Many universities, museums, symphonies and other organizations that previously did not welcome Jewish involvement now actively compete for Jewish contributions, volunteers and commitments. Indeed, as more Jews find greater satisfaction and status in non-Jewish organizational and institutional networks, a severe burden will be placed on Jewish organizations, institutions and agencies. Unless more creative volunteer roles are developed with specific and meaningful ends, many Jews will simply not become involved.

Again, many individuals become impatient with the way in which voluntary organizations work. Volunteers who have professional or executive occupations tend to be accustomed to a more expeditious process of decision-making and more efficient managerial methods. The cumbersome and time-consuming pattern of consensus-building common to many Jewish organizations deters many potential volunteers.

Yet another organizational barrier derives from the tendency of many Jewish institutions to produce leadership cadres with long years of tenure in office. To the extent that cadres of this type appear to those on the outside to be too closed, cliquish, or tight-knit, the incentive for voluntary involvement will be dampened.

Jewish organizations and institutions would be well advised, likewise, to examine their internal structures. For example, many synagogues and temples still maintain separate sisterhoods and brotherhoods, men's clubs and women's auxiliaries. For younger people who are hard-pressed by the multiple demands of two-career families and by the desire to spend more time with their children, the idea of separate-gender activities may not be as appealing as joint couple programs.

Finally, Jewish organizations and agencies must also begin to examine their rewards. Very often these are structured on the old model of bestowing titles upon outstanding volunteers or feting donors at dinners within the Jewish institutional and organizational orbit. Such recognition may no longer offer as much status as it once did, and different reward structures may have to be established that involve both the Jewish and non-Jewish worlds in a way that confers status in both.

Policy Implications

A basic assumption of communal policy is that the provision of social services and recreational programs encourages greater communal involvement. Our data, however, suggest that this assumption is questionable. Through which processes or channels do receipt of Jewish-sponsored social services or participation in Jewish recreational programs lead to more active involvement in Jewish organizations? When do services, programs and organizations interact in order to achieve their potential as real springboards, increasing involvement in the institutional life of the

Jewish community? Do programs designed to meet the needs of different social groups, or strategies formulated to provide specific services tailored to segments of the community, transmit a clear message regarding the type of active participation and commitment desired from community members?

It has not been the goal of this study to answer these questions and we are unable to judge the impact of such programs and services on increasing institutional involvement: This cannot be achieved by community population studies but rather requires the design of complex evaluation studies. However, the findings of this study do show that variables related to use made of Jewish-sponsored social services and recreational programs do not necessarily go hand in hand with those variables that reflect affiliation to Jewish organizations (see Table 3). Therefore, we suggest, they refer to distinct *dimensions* of Jewish communal participation that are related neither empirically nor conceptually. These findings suggest at the least a need for further studies concerning the validity of the assumptions that are central to much of Jewish communal policy in the United States.

Expanding the delivery network of human services could be one means of increasing communal involvement. The provision of valuable services such as day care or housing for the elderly, for example, may link people to the Jewish community. However, it must be stressed that since most people use these services as consumers, such a result is not likely to occur unless mechanisms are structured to bring service users into another level of involvement. In other words, Jewish-sponsored services may be a reasonable mechanism to elicit people's interest in the organized Jewish community, but they will encourage organizational involvement only if they are strongly associated with efforts to promote activity in other areas of Jewish organizational life as well.

Unfortunately, the data do not allow for differentiation between leaders—those most active in the Jewish community—and the Jewish public. Likewise, the data provide no information about what kinds of volunteer roles people engaged in, or for which organizations, other than to differentiate between Jewish and non-Jewish organizations. Questions about the nature of volunteer work; how one enters the volunteer world; how leadership roles are determined; or how certain organizations or titles prove attractive are beyond the scope of this discussion.

Much of the research and policy development in the Jewish community has focused on the various levels of Jewish affiliation in an attempt to uncover the factors that account for those different levels. It has also sought ways to describe the patterns of relationship to the Jewish community—who is inside, who outside and who on the periphery—with the aim of defining the priorities to be set in outreach programs.

This paper suggests that the research and policy focus be moved from communal affiliation to *involvement* in the Jewish community at its various levels. A change of direction would then follow. Research on social involvement and organizational commitment in voluntary organizations suggests that the two key determinants are, on the one hand, positive motivation and, on the other, the removal of barriers to active participation. Motivation and barriers—as functions of perceived benefits and costs—interact to activate or discourage active participation.[12] In addition to social incentives, the primary determinants of willingness to participate are individuals' attitudes toward the goals and values of organizations and their expectations about the efficacy of organizations in achieving their goals.

Research on successful voluntary organizations shows that these organizations offer their members widespread opportunities for decision-making and influence. When members feel able to affect organizational policy decisions, they are likely to exhibit higher levels of commitment.[13] Lack of involvement and active participation in Jewish organizations is partly due to the competition from secular society but also may be based on members' perceptions that they do not have a major stake in the life of those organizations.

Hence, the critical questions become: (1) What kind of incentives do Jewish organizations offer in order to motivate participation and commitment? (2) What are regarded by the organizations themselves as acceptable levels of involvement, participation and commitment? (3) How do Jewish organizations make their expectations and incentives known? (4) How is the efficacy of Jewish organizations assessed by the community members? (5) What are the obstacles to increased levels of involvement among the underinvolved? Federations, synagogues, Jewish centers and other Jewish organizations must ask themselves these questions as a first step in considering new policies.

Jewish community organizations throughout the United States are confronted with a vital challenge as they approach the twenty-first century: how to strengthen the level of active participation in, and commitment to, Jewish institutional life. We have discussed a number of demographic and religious factors that militate against this goal. Changing demographic and religious characteristics of Jews in the United States require that Jewish organizations adapt to this new environment, as they have done in previous decades. As large number of Jews have adopted a consumer approach toward Jewish organizations and institutions, the tasks of cultivating organizational loyalty and commitment become increasingly difficult. How well the Jewish community responds to this challenge will increasingly depend on its capacity to create vibrant and flexible structures and contexts in which new and transformed expressions of Jewish identity can be cultivated and developed.

Appendix

Measuring Jewish Identification and Involvement: Methodological Issues

Harold Himmelfarb has suggested that the various dimensions of Jewish identification can be categorized by the objects of their orientation: supernatural, communal, cultural and interpersonal. In Himmelfarb's analysis, the communal orientation of Jewish religious involvement (that which focuses upon the people as a collective) includes affiliational and associational dimensions, such as extent of membership and participation in formal Jewish organizations.[14]

In a more recent analysis of Jewish identification among American Jews, Bernard Lazerwitz distinguishes between items related to Jewish religious involvement and indicators of Jewish communal involvement. The former includes Jewish education of adults, religious denomination, synagogue membership, frequency of synagogue attendance and religious practices observed, while the latter embraces number of memberships in Jewish organizations, number of Jewish best friends and visits to Israel. While the distinction between indicators of Jewish religious involvement and those of Jewish communal involvement permits us to differentiate these domains or arenas of activities, together they account for just two types of connections to formal Jewish organizations: synagogue membership and number of memberships in Jewish organizations. Such an approach misses other important types of formal ties to the Jewish community.[15]

In developing his typology of Jewish communal involvement, Steven M. Cohen groups together variables measuring formal affiliation and variables related to social and religious involvement, on the assumption that these various behavioral dimensions represent different expressions of Jewish identity, connection and commitment. For example, the communal affiliation index includes the following variables: synagogue membership, Jewish organizational membership, contribution of one hundred dollars or more to a Jewish charity, travel to Israel and reading a Jewish newspaper. The interpersonal index draws upon the number of the three closest friends who were Jewish, as well as the religion of the spouse, when applicable. Because different dimensions are used to create this typology of Jewish involvement, specificity in regard to organizational involvement is lost. For example, financial contributions to Jewish organizations are not a requirement in this typology for high level of involvement (those belonging to the "Activist" or "Observant" types): 25 percent of the group called "Activist" and 49 percent of the "Observant" do not make financial contributions to Jewish charities.[16]

In an analysis of interrelationships of community participation in the Philadelphia Jewish community, William Yancey and Ira Goldstein initially included seven measures of social participation: synagogue membership, organizational membership, volunteering for at least five hours a week, having at least half of one's friends Jewish, receiving the local Jewish newspaper, use of the Jewish community center and visiting Israel. In order to present responses to individual variables in a single scale measuring the overall pattern of participation in the local Jewish community, they created a Guttman Scale of community participation. However, since synagogue membership, visits to Israel and use of the Jewish community center did not conform to the criteria required by this statistical technique for inclusion, they had to be excluded from the scale. As a result, those who had visited Israel, belonged to a synagogue or attended activities at a Jewish community center, but did not participate in the community in any of the ways included in the scale, were considered as having no communal participation.[17]

Notes

1. Steven M. Cohen, "Outreach to the Marginally Affiliated: Evidence and Implications for Policymakers in Jewish Education," *Journal of Jewish Communal Service* 62 (1985), 147–157.

2. David Horton Smith, "Altruism, Volunteers, and Volunteerism," *Journal of Voluntary Action Research* 10 (1981), 21–36.

3. Sidney Verba and Norman N. Nie, *Participation in America* (Chicago: 1972).

4. Steven M. Cohen, *American Assimilation or Jewish Revival?* (Bloomington: 1988), 130. For further discussion of Cohen's typology, see Appendix.

5. Calvin Goldscheider, *The American Jewish Community: Social Science Research and Policy Implications* (Atlanta: 1986), 19.

6. These two samples were drawn using sampling methods that are accepted practice in Jewish population studies. The Baltimore study used a two-frame sampling methodology: Two samples were drawn using random digital dialing and distinctive Jewish names techniques, and were combined so as to produce an unbiased representative sample of the Baltimore Jewish community. The San Francisco study's sample used a three-frame sample methodology: random digital dialing, distinctive Jewish names and a list sample. Utilization of these different sampling frames ensures the inclusion not only of Jews living in areas of low Jewish density but of intermarried households, while keeping sampling costs to an affordable amount. For additional explanation of sampling methodology in Jewish population studies, see Gary Tobin, "Jewish Perceptions of Antisemitism and Antisemitic Perceptions About Jews," in *Studies in Contemporary Jewry*, vol. 4, *The Jews and the European Crisis, 1914–1921*, ed. Jonathan Frankel (New York and Oxford: 1988), 227. For further details regarding sampling and methodologies used in these population studies, see *idem*, "A Population Study of the Jewish Community of Greater Baltimore," Associated Jewish Charities and Welfare Fund, Baltimore, Maryland, 1986; *idem* and Sharon Sassler, "Community Development Study of the Bay Area Jewish Community," Jewish Community Federations of San Francisco, the East Bay and San Jose, 1988.

7. Robert Nash Parker, "Measuring Social Participation," *American Sociological Review* 48 (1983), 864–873; David Knoke, "Incentives in Collective Action Organizations," *American Sociological Review* 53 (1988), 311–329.

8. Some of the questions were asked for each member of the household, while others were asked only for the respondent. When at least one of the members of the household answered positively to a question, that household was counted as a "yes" answer for that question.

9. Cohen, *American Assimilation or Jewish Revival?*, 103–104; Steven Huberman, "Understanding Synagogue Affiliation," *Journal of Jewish Communal Service* 61 (1985), 295–304.

10. Jonathan S. Woocher, "How the Community Governs Itself," *Face to Face—An Inter-religious Bulletin* 9 (Fall 1982).

11. In spite of the desirability of having more categories within our ordinal variable in order to reflect a continuum of involvement, the distribution of the variable and the small number of cases that fell into higher levels of involvement (for example, those having some Jewish institutional membership, making contributions of at least five hundred dollars and volunteering eight hours per month or more account for 2.4% of Jewish households in Baltimore and 3.9% in San Francisco) precluded our original intention. This, of course, reveals much about current levels of involvement for most Jews.

12. Bert Klandermans and Dirk Oegema, "Potentials, Networks, Motivations, and Barriers: Steps Towards Participation in Social Movements," *American Sociological Review* 52 (1987), 519–531.

13. David Knoke and James R. Wood, *Organized for Action: Commitment in Voluntary Associations* (New Brunswick, N.J.: 1981).

14. Harold Himmelfarb, "Research in American Jewish Identity and Identification: Progress, Pitfalls, and Prospects," in *Understanding American Jewry*, ed. Marshall Sklare (New Brunswick: 1982); *idem*, "Measuring Religious Involvement," *Social Forces* 53 (1975), 606–618.

15. Bernard Lazerwitz, "Trends in National Jewish Identification Indicators: 1971–1985," *Contemporary Jewry* 9 (1987–1988), 87–103.

16. See Cohen, *American Assimilation or Jewish Revival.*

17. William Yancey and Ira Goldstein, *The Jewish Population of the Greater Philadelphia Area,* Pamphlet of the Federation of Jewish Agencies of Greater Philadelphia, 1985.

All in the Family:
American Jewish Attachments to Israel

Chaim I. Waxman

(RUTGERS UNIVERSITY)

No other ethnic group in American history has so extensive an involvement with a foreign nation; no other nation relies upon a body of private individuals who are neither residents nor citizens of their land to underwrite a major portion of their budget. American Jews buy Israel bonds, give generously to the United Jewish Appeal, lobby governmental representatives to pursue a pro-Israel policy, travel extensively to Israel (where they are greeted by "Welcome Home" signs), respond immediately to every crisis in that part of the world, and yet maintain passionately that they are Americans first and Jews afterward. It is a curious, puzzling, and yet totally logical arrangement.[1]

In this article, that "totally logical arrangement" will be analyzed by means of an examination of American Jewish support for Israel on the institutional, individual and denominational levels. A second focus is the issue of whether this support has undergone any significant change since the late 1970s, and whether it is likely to erode in the near or long-term future. Finally, attention will be paid to the *familial* aspect of American Jewish-Israeli relations—that which is symbolized by the "Welcome Home" signs noted by Melvin Urofsky. As will be discussed, the nature of the American Jewish attachment to Israel is, in large measure, a consequence of the group self-definition of American Jews as well as of their status in U.S. society.

Viewed from the perspective of the institutional structure of American Jewry, Israel undoubtedly plays a central role in American Jewish life. In the *American Jewish Year Book*'s annual listing of "National Jewish Organizations," for example, more than eighty organizations specifically devoted to Zionist and pro-Israel activities are listed, and for many others, objectives and activities such as "promotes Israel's welfare," "support for the State of Israel" and "promotes understanding of Israel" appear with impressive frequency. There is, moreover, the fact that fifty-five of the largest and most active of these national Jewish organizations are affiliated with the Conference of Presidents of Major American Jewish Organizations, for which Zionist and pro-Israel activity is the major emphasis. The Conference of Presidents shares an address with the U.S. headquarters of the Jewish Agency and World

134

Zionist Organization, and virtually all of its chairmen have had long records of extensive previous activity on behalf of Israel.

There is no substantive evidence of any erosion of support for Israel among the leadership of the American Jewish community. A 1989 survey conducted by Steven M. Cohen that included "key professionals and top lay leaders from some of the most influential organizations in American Jewish life"[2] as well as a small number of academics who are involved with Israel found that 99 percent of the respondents had been to Israel at least once and 84 percent had been there three times or more. Moreover, 78 percent identified themselves as "Zionists," and 54 percent had "seriously considered living in Israel." When asked, "How close do you feel to Israel?" 78 percent responded "very close" and 19 percent "fairly close." Only 2 percent stated that they feel "fairly distant" and none stated "very distant."[3]

Not only do most Jewish leaders feel close to Israel and identify with Zionism in the American sense of that term—that is, pro-Israelism[4]—they also appear to subscribe to the Zionist tenet of the centrality of Israel. Thus, in response to the statement "Jewish life in America is more authentically and positively Jewish than Jewish life in Israel," 81 percent of Cohen's sample disagreed and only 10 percent agreed.[5]

The ways in which Jewish organizations have been strongly involved in defense activity for Israel have been amply documented.[6] Israel has also become increasingly central in the realm of American Jewish education. If, in 1968, Alvin Schiff found that Israel was taught as a separate subject in 48 percent of all Jewish schools, including all-day, weekday afternoon and one-day-a-week schools under Orthodox, Conservative, Reform, communal and secular auspices,[7] Barry Chazan found by 1974 that 63 percent of the school curricula listed Israel as a separate subject, with "a general increase of attention paid to Israel in all subject-areas as compared with 1968."[8]

Indeed, Israel has become so central to American Jewish institutional life that some observers tend to confuse symbols with substance. Yakir Eventov and Cvi Rotem, for example, offered a sweeping panoramic view in the *Encyclopaedia Judaica* of the extent to which Israel has become central within the American Jewish community since the Six-Day War, arguing not only that "American Jews showed themselves more willing and ready to be identified as Jews, to affiliate with Jewish organizations and institutions, and to send their children to Jewish schools," but that Israel now occupied "an important place in synagogue activities, sermons, and various religious celebrations," including Israel Independence Day. They continued,

> The Israel flag is frequently displayed in synagogues and community centers. In many synagogues, prayers for the welfare of the State of Israel and world Jewry are recited on Sabbaths and holidays following that for the welfare of the United States. . . . Hebrew songs and Israel folk dances have become American Jewish popular culture: at weddings, [bar mitzvah ceremonies], and on many college campuses.[9]

In short, the traditional Yiddish-based East European Jewish culture has been largely supplanted by the forms and symbols of modern Israel.

American Jews, however, are not as interested or knowledgeable about it as is frequently assumed. On the contrary, as Steven Cohen has found in a number of surveys of American Jewish attitudes toward Israel, most of them are quite ignorant not only of Hebrew but of basic aspects of Israeli society and culture. For example, while two-thirds of the respondents in his 1986 national sample were aware that "most major Jewish religious holidays are also legal national holidays in Israel," only one-third were aware of such elementary facts as that Menahem Begin and Shimon Peres are not from the same political party, that Conservative and Reform rabbis cannot officiate at weddings in Israel, and that Arab Israeli and Jewish Israeli children do not generally go to the same schools.[10]

Such ignorance notwithstanding, individual support for Israel remains consistently high within the American Jewish community, as shown in the extensive analysis of surveys by Eytan Gilboa, an Israeli political scientist.[11] This attachment is strong enough to have weathered severe challenges such as the Israeli war in Lebanon and outright Israeli rejection of various U.S.-sponsored Middle East peace proposals. Gilboa has found no indications that there is likely to be any decrease in the intensity of the American Jewish attachment to Israel in the foreseeable future.[12]

In Cohen's 1986 survey of American Jews, approximately 85 percent of the respondents declared themselves supporters of Israel. On the basis of this survey, Cohen proposed an "attachment index" of American Jewry comprised of three different groups: (1) those who are intensely involved with or attached to Israel, constituting about one-quarter to one-third of the American Jewish population; (2) those who care deeply about Israel but do not have strong personal ties with either Israel or Israelis, constituting one-third of the population; (3) a remaining third, most of whom are probably pro-Israel but do not express the kind of deep concerns of those in the first two groups.[13]

More specific findings in this "attachment index" concerned age. Cohen found the lowest level of attachment among those aged thirty to thirty-nine years—which did not correlate with age differences in religious belief and practice—and the highest level of attachment among those aged sixty-five and above. Cohen offered no explanation for this finding, although it may derive in part from the relationship between intermarriage and attachment to Israel, about which there is conflicting evidence.[14]

Significantly, Cohen finds a very strong relationship between denomination and level of attachment to Israel. Specifically, the extent of Orthodox Jews' attachments to Israel—however measured—greatly exceeds those among other denominations. At the same time, Conservative Jews consistently score higher than do Reform or nondenominational Jews. Moreover, differences between Orthodox and non-Orthodox are sharpest with respect to the most demanding measures of involvement with Israel, be it receptivity to aliyah rather than pro-Israel feelings, having closer ties with individual Israelis or having fluency in Hebrew rather than just a rudimentary knowledge.[15]

In addition, when Cohen compared his 1986 findings with those of his earlier 1983 study, he found that the Orthodox had become more intensely attached between 1983 and 1986, that there was virtually no change in the percentage of Conservative Jews who were highly attached (despite an increase in the percentage of those with low levels of attachment), and that among Reform Jews there was a decline in the percentage of those who were highly attached and a concomitant sharp rise in the percentage of those with only low levels of attachment. In sum, while Orthodox attachments, which were intense initially, intensified even more during those years, the attachments of the Reform Jews and some of the Conservatives, both of which are larger groups than the Orthodox, weakened somewhat.[16] Nevertheless, the vast majority of America's Jews remained staunch supporters of Israel.

In a 1989 update of his survey of American Jews, Cohen found no evidence of any significant weakening of American Jewish attachments to Israel as a result of the Palestinian Arab *intifada*. On the contrary, the responses to most of his questions indicate the rather firm stability of American Jewish pro-Israelism, with some responses even showing an intensification of attachment from 1983 to 1989.[17] It should be pointed out, however, that Cohen did find evidence that younger Jews— those under thirty-five years of age—are less pro-Israel than older Jews. The reason for this pattern is as yet unclear.[18]

One other post-*intifada* survey is that of the *Los Angeles Times* of March–April 1988, based on a national sample of American Jews. When asked to indicate the quality most important to their Jewish identity, half of the respondents answered "social equality" and the other half were equally divided between various other options—among them "support for Israel," which was cited by a full 17 percent of the respondents as the *most important* aspect of their Jewish identity. It seems reasonable to assume that many of the other respondents considered such support to be part of their Jewish identity as well, even if not its most important part.[19] Indeed, 85 percent of those sampled, as contrasted with only 27 percent of non-Jewish Americans, favor strong U.S. support for Israel.[20]

As is the case with the community-at-large, there are also denominational variations in the level of Zionist attachment of American Jewish institutional leaders. These variations are clearly evident in a 1989 survey of rabbis and communal workers conducted by Cohen and Gerald Bubis. One of the statements in that survey, "It is easier to lead a fuller Jewish life in Israel than in the U.S.," met with a 10 percent positive response and a 73 percent negative response among American Jews in general. Among Orthodox rabbis, however, approximately 70 percent agreed with the statement, as did 60 percent of the Orthodox communal workers. Among Conservative rabbis and communal workers, the figures were 50 percent and 33 percent, respectively. But less than 20 percent of Reform rabbis and communal workers agreed.[21] This last finding corroborates the results of a recent study of Reform Jewry's national leadership. When participants in this study were presented with a similar statement ("A Jew can live a more authentic Jewish life in Israel than in America"), 81 percent disagreed and only 10 percent agreed. And in response to the statement "Israel is the center of contemporary Jewish life," 74 percent disagreed and 11 percent agreed.[22]

Beyond the quantitative data, there is a good deal of history regarding the form and depth of Orthodox, Conservative and Reform Jewish attachment to the Jewish homeland. Interesting changes, moreover, have occurred over the years in the way each of these movements relates to Israel.

In contrast to East European Orthodoxy, which was characterized in the prestate era by its anti-Zionism, American Orthodoxy was always highly supportive of the establishment of the Jewish state. Mizrachi, the religious Zionist movement, was one of the major forces in American Orthodoxy, more influential by far than the non-Zionist Agudath Israel.[23] During the interwar period, Yeshiva Torah Veda'ath, one of the first higher yeshivahs in the United States, was strongly Zionist.[24] And as late as 1949, *Hapardes* (the oldest extant Torah journal in the United States) contained regular reports on religious Zionist developments, both within Mizrachi and beyond it. Among the features in the April 1949 issue, for example, was a detailed report on an address delivered by Rabbi David Lifshitz to the annual convention of the Union of Orthodox Rabbis of the United States and Canada (*Agudath Harabanim*), in which strong sentiments of religious Zionism were expressed.[25]

Today, much of that picture has changed dramatically. American Orthodox Judaism is now heavily influenced by Agudath Israel. Religious Zionism, when not loudly condemned, is rarely mentioned in the aforementioned Torah journal; the leadership of Agudath Harabanim is wholly of the Agudath Israel persuasion; and the *yeshivishe velt,* the "world of the yeshivah," is virtually synonymous with the world of non-Zionism. This is a result, in large measure, of the post–Second World War immigration to America of the survivors of East European Orthodoxy—including those of the scholarly elite who headed the higher yeshivahs in Russia, Lithuania and Poland, as well as a number of Hasidic grand rabbis and their followers, most of whom came from Hungary, Czechoslovakia and Poland.[26] Establishing a network of day schools and yeshivahs in America that socialized a new generation in accordance with their non-Zionist version of Orthodoxy, these new arrivals soon took over the ideological leadership of the Agudath Israel of America and provided it with a following from within the rank and file of yeshivah students and hasidim. By the 1950s, Agudath Israel had grown to be one of the largest and most influential organizations of American Orthodoxy, whereas Mizrachi's leadership had stagnated and its membership and significance had declined markedly.

Not only within "the world of the yeshivah,"[27] but within much of American Orthodoxy in general, the ideology of religious Zionism is now much less frequently espoused. Indeed, when ArtScroll, a highly successful publisher of traditional Judaica that caters to the Orthodox public, put out a new edition of the traditional prayer book, it omitted the prayer for the welfare of the state of Israel. Although the organization of Modern Orthodox rabbis, the Rabbinical Council of America, issued its own special edition of the ArtScroll siddur that included this prayer, it appears that the regular edition has become the standard one for the Orthodox public in the United States.[28] Likewise, there seems to have been a decline in the *religious* celebration of Israel Independence Day within Orthodox congregations across the United States.

Such developments, however, do not indicate a decline in support for Israel within American Orthodoxy. Rather, there seems to have been a *transformation* in the role of Israel within American Orthodoxy, although its precise nature is not yet quite clear. It may be that there is a decline in the tendency to define the state of Israel within the context of modern (albeit religious) Zionism and an increasing tendency to define Israel traditionally, as Eretz Israel—a trend that has also manifested itself within Israel, especially since the Begin era.[29] Alternatively, the transformation may be characterized as the secularization of Israel. Perhaps because

Israel has become so modernized, American Orthodox Jews increasingly relate to it as a modern secular society to which, nevertheless, strong allegiances are attached because it is a state in which Jews are sovereign.[30]

In all, religious Zionist ideology that defines Israel in religious terms has lost influence, so much so that today most American Orthodox Jews no longer overtly conceive of Israel in ritualistic-religious terms. They remain strongly attached to Israel as the state of the Jewish people and therefore deserving of high communal priority, but the state per se is not part of the specifically religious realm.[31] In any event, even the traditional Orthodox can now openly express their attachments to Eretz Israel and the people of Israel without being tainted by secular Zionism.

Founded in the nineteenth century by moderate traditionalists, Conservative Judaism appealed to large numbers of young immigrants and, later, children of immigrants from Eastern Europe who found Orthodoxy too confining and inhibiting and Reform too lacking in tradition.[32] Given their strong ethnic self-definition and the fact that many of them were familiar with Zionist groups in Eastern Europe (even if they themselves had not been members), it was natural for many Conservative Jews to join the American Zionist movement that was beginning to take form. Here, too, they opted for the mainstream. Mizrachi was for the religious Zionists and Poale Zion was for the socialists, but for the majority of recently arrived immigrants who were ethnic rather than ideological Zionists, the much less ideologically sophisticated General Zionism, embodied first in the Federation of American Zionists and later in the Zionist Organization of America, was the logical choice.

These tendencies were reinforced by the fact that the leaders of Conservative Judaism were virtually all self-proclaimed Zionists who defined Zionism as an integral part of Judaism. As Moshe Davis aptly put it,

> Zionism was an integral part of the program of thought and action which the Historical School developed in the closing decades of the past century and which it transmitted to the Conservative Movement. Conservative Judaism and Zionism developed separately, but their interaction was constant. As a result, both were stimulated conceptually and organizationally.[33]

Given the deep interconnections between Conservative Judaism and American Zionism and the explicit definition of Zionism as integral to Judaism, it is not surprising that Conservative Judaism came to be seen as the most Zionist branch of American Judaism.[34] The depth of Conservative Jewry's Zionist commitment was apparent in its staunch support of the Zionist movement as well as the state of Israel.

Officially, it would appear that this commitment to Zionism and Israel remains unattenuated. Indeed, in *Emet Ve-Emunah,* its recent statement of principles, the movement's leadership extensively reiterates its deep—albeit not unequivocal—commitment to Zionism and Israel:

> This zealous attachment to *Eretz Yisrael* has persisted throughout our long history as a transnational people in which we transcended borders and lived in virtually every land. Wherever we were permitted, we viewed ourselves as natives or citizens of the country of our residence and were loyal to our host nation. Our religion has been land-centered but never land-bound; it has been a portable religion so that despite our long exile

(*Galut*) from our spiritual homeland, we have been able to survive creatively and spiritually in the *tefutzot* (Diaspora). . . . We staunchly support the Zionist ideal. . . . The Conservative movement is a member of the World Zionist Organization. We have undertaken major efforts in Israel. . . . Increasing numbers of Conservative rabbis and laypersons have gone on *aliyah,* and we cherish and encourage *aliyah* to Israel as a value, goal, and *mitzvah.* . . . Both the State of Israel and Diapora Jewry have roles to fill; each can and must aid and enrich the other in every possible way; each needs the other. It is our fervent hope that Zion will indeed be the center of Torah and Jerusalem a beacon lighting the way for the Jewish people and humanity.[35]

The fact that the statement does not endorse the classical Zionist notion of the centrality of Israel is neither surprising nor a deviation. Neither Conservative Judaism nor American Zionism has ever sincerely supported it.[36] What is more noteworthy is the fact that the statement goes on both to decry existing conditions in Israel and to distance the Conservative movement from Israeli government policies. For example, it emphasizes that "the Conservative movement has not always agreed with Israel's positions on domestic and foreign affairs."[37] If such statements are seen as representative of the movement as a whole, a certain subtle shift has in fact taken place among Conservative Jewry.[38]

Of the three major branches of American Judaism, it is unquestionably Reform Judaism that has made the most radical strides in coming to terms with Zionism and Israel, from Classical Reform's early antipathy to Zionism to the movement's acceptance of Israel's statehood on the eve of its creation.[39] It is true that some outposts of Classical Reform opposition remained into the 1950s (as Marshall Sklare and Joseph Greenblum found in the "David Einhorn Temple" in "Lakeville"), but even there most of the community professed a sense of attachment and concern for the Jewish state.[40]

By the end of the 1960s, it was already hard to imagine that only a relatively short time earlier there had been such strong opposition to Zionism and Israel within the movement. In 1897, the Reform rabbinic body, the Central Conference of American Rabbis (CCAR), had issued a declaration stating "that we totally disapprove of any attempt for the establishment of a Jewish state. Such attempts show a misunderstanding of Israel's mission."[41] In 1917, in response to the Balfour Declaration, the CCAR had demurred, "We do not subscribe to the phrase in the declaration which says, 'Palestine is to be a national home-land for the Jewish people.' . . . We are opposed to the idea that Palestine should be considered the home-land of the Jews."[42] But fifty years later, in June 1967, the CCAR declared its "solidarity with the State and the people of Israel. Their triumphs are our triumphs. Their ordeal is our ordeal. Their fate is our fate."[43]

An extensive study of the Reform movement reported that by 1970, 82 percent of Reform adults and 67 percent of Reform youth found it either essential or desirable to support Israel, and more than 40 percent of both groups found it either essential or desirable to support Zionism.[44] And by the 1980s it was found that 81.6 percent of Reform Jews living in communities in which Jews are at least half of the population, and 67.2 percent of those living in communities with only some or a few Jews, agreed with the statement that "the existence of Israel is essential for the continuation of American Jewish life."[45]

Despite all the data pointing to continuing solid American Jewish support for Israel, there is also evidence that American Jews strongly defend the propriety of publicly voiced criticism of Israel and Israeli government policies. The Conservative movement's statement of principles is one striking example. And on the individual denominational level, Bubis and Cohen found wide agreement with the statement "Jews who are severely critical of Israel should nevertheless be allowed to speak in synagogues and Jewish Community Centers" in their 1989 survey. Among the Orthodox, 42 percent of the rabbis and communal workers agreed; among the Conservative, 62 percent of the rabbis and 63 percent of the communal workers agreed; and among the Reform, 82 percent of the rabbis and 74 percent of the communal workers agreed.[46] Cohen also found widespread criticism of Israel among American Jewish leaders on a number of specific issues, including Israel's stance toward the P.L.O., the settlements on the West Bank and the issue of "Who is a Jew?"[47] For example, a clear majority (59 percent) stated that the Arabs on the West Bank are being treated unfairly, and "as many as 77 percent affirmed that they have privately criticized 'Israel's handling of the Palestinian uprising.' "[48]

Tempting as it might be, it would be an oversimplification to attribute the increasingly critical stance of American Jewry solely to the change in the Israeli government since the fall of the Labor Alignment coalition in 1977. It is true that American Jews are much more comfortable with the Labor party than they are with the Likud. The political liberalism of American Jews is well-documented,[49] and thus it is understandable that the democratic socialism of the Labor party is much more appealing than the nationalism of Likud. In addition, when the Labor Alignment was in power, it strongly discouraged public criticism by diaspora Jewish leaders of Israeli policy. Since the accession of the Likud to government leadership, however, some key Labor Alignment figures have reversed their stance, asserting an *obligation* on the part of American Jewry to be publicly critical of the Israeli government when they disagree with its policies and bemoaning the fact that such criticism is not more pronounced. Nonetheless, changes in the American Jewish stance toward criticism of Israel do not appear to be tied exclusively to political trends within Israel or the changing attitudes of some Israeli leaders toward the public expression of criticism of Israeli policies. Rather, they seem to be primarily the consequences of a basic change in the self-definition of American Jews.

Until the late 1960s to early 1970s, Jews in the United States were defined by American society as a religious group; they defined themselves in this way as well. Since then, however, American Jews have increasingly defined themselves as an ethnic group. As a result, American Jewish attachment to Israel has found new and much more public expression.[50] Whereas the connection with Israel was defined in religious terms when U.S. Jewry defined itself primarily as a religious group—as Charles Liebman observed, Israel was part of their religious behavior[51]—there is now an increasing tendency to assert the extended kinship character of the Jewish people. Israel within this context now has an overt extended familial dimension because American Jews increasingly define their relationship with Israel as one of *mishpaḥah,* or family, with all of the emotions and obligations implicit in that term.[52]

An understanding of the extended familial nature of the American Jewish attachment to Israel helps in explaining a number of otherwise anomalous aspects of that relationship—for instance, the fact that American Jews seem to hold to political positions regarding Israel that are somewhat different from those concerning other countries. The reason for this is that American Jews do not relate to Israel solely in political terms but rather in extended familial, ethnic terms. Even though they refer to it as the "state of Israel," it is not solely or even fundamentally the state as a political entity to which American Jews are so attached. True, the political autonomy of Israel is a matter of enormous importance, but the real significance of Israel is much deeper: it is also the *land* of Israel, Eretz Israel, and it is this aspect of Israel that has so much meaning.[53]

Liebman has argued that Israel has importance for American Jews as a *"heim,"* the Yiddish word for "home," with all of the nostalgia that surrounds that concept. (The meaning of *heim* may actually be captured more accurately if it is translated "the old home.")[54] Thus, American Jews who subscribe to the basic tenets of political liberalism do not apply the same rules to Israel. Being perceived more as a "home," what Christopher Lasch termed a "haven in a heartless world,"[55] Israel is not subject to all of the same rules that apply to political entities, but rather to what may be termed "family rules." Just as the family does not always necessarily operate according to the rules of democratic procedure or in accordance with rational or legal-rational rules—being instead the place where "they'll always take you in"—so do many American (and other) Jews relate to Israel as a nonpolitical entity. Israeli leaders, moreover, frequently reinforce this perception of Israel when they speak, for example, of the obligations that world Jewry has to Israel.[56]

The extended familial character of Israel may also explain the strong reaction by so many American Jews (even those who otherwise had little to do with Israeli domestic politics) to attempts made in 1988 to amend the Law of Return so that it would define as Jews only those born of a Jewish mother or those who had converted according to halakhic procedure. Asked why they were so taken aback by the Law of Return issue, members of a group of UJA leaders in Westchester, New York, responded that they wanted to be sure that Israel would be open to their children and grandchildren, should they need it. In other words, they wanted to make sure that Israel would take *them* in, that it would remain a haven, a home, not only for them but for their children and grandchildren as well.[57]

Similarly, the notion of Israel as home helps to clarify what at first blush may seem a puzzling contradiction in American Jewish attitudes. As previously noted, most American Jews—despite their strong support for Israel—do not view it as the most important factor in their Jewish identity. Nor are most familiar with spoken Hebrew or the most basic facts of Israeli society. But such a contradiction fits in precisely with the nature of a nostalgic home. As Charles Liebman put it,

> Now, the characteristic of the *heim* . . . is that one doesn't live there. It is the parents' home, or in the case of Israel the surrogate parents' or surrogate grandparents' home. One visits it on occasion, one sends money . . . and one wants very much to feel that

life goes on there as it always has. . . . This is the Jew who is quite certain he would be completely at home in Israel, though he knows very little about the country and makes no special effort to learn anything.[58]

Liebman attributes this nostalgic longing for the *heim* primarily to poor, elderly American Jews. It can be argued, however, that a large segment of American Jewry is in fact "homeless" in the United States, in the ethnic as opposed to material sense of the word, such that their pro-Israel sentiment is rooted in a sense of extended familism and nostalgia for "the home."[59]

What is the basis for this suggestion that U.S. Jews—who, according to some, are "at home" as never before[60]—may actually be "not quite at home"?[61] One manifestation is the contrast between how non-Jewish and Jewish Americans view antisemitism and the condition of Jews in the United States today. Despite a wide variety of studies showing a steady decrease in antisemitic attitudes in American society since the end of the Second World War[62] and other studies indicating that the structural barriers to Jewish participation in the society are crumbling,[63] America's Jews are still uneasy. Paradoxical as it may appear, American Jewish concern about antisemitism is in fact intensifying. Whereas in 1983, about 50 percent of American Jews in Steven Cohen's survey disagreed with the statement "Virtually all positions of influence in America are open to Jews," by 1989, 66 percent disagreed with it. And whereas in 1983, about 50 percent disagreed with the statement "Anti-Semitism in America is currently not a serious problem for American Jews," by 1989, 73 percent disagreed.[64] Apparently, there is a relationship, perhaps even a correlation, between concern with antisemitism and attachment to Israel.

Beyond their anxieties concerning antisemitism and the subsequent focus on Israel as a haven for themselves, American Jews have a number of functional bases for their support of the Jewish state. As outlined below, Israel's functions include far more than "mere" physical (or psychological) sanctuary for U.S. Jewry:

Haven for Jews worldwide. Israel has traditionally had meaning for American Jews as a haven for downtrodden Jews around the world. Indeed, this is the most common American Jewish conception of Zionism—that there should be a Jewish state so that there will be a refuge for Jews who are persecuted in their native countries—and it is probably subscribed to by the overwhelming majority of American Jews. However, they don't all subscribe to it for the same reason. For some, this commitment derives from a strong sense of commitment to fellow Jews and a belief that a sovereign Israel is the best guarantee for the safety and well-being of persecuted Jews. For others, the commitment may derive from other, somewhat less noble sources, such as resolving a sense of guilt for not doing more. Insisting on Israel as a haven may be a convenient way of avoiding the direct confrontation with the problems of the persecuted and downtrodden. Directing such "Jewish problems" to Israel is, in this context, not very different than those American Jewish parents who were ready to ship their problem teenagers off to Israel in the hope that this would "cure" them. Israel, in these instances, is like an "easy fix." What will happen to the Israel commitments of those who come to learn that there rarely are easy fixes—and Israel, in any event, is not one of them—remains to be seen.

Legitimation for the American Jewish organizational structure. As indicated previously, Israel is central to that structure. In fact, many American Jewish organizations now need Israel to legitimate their own existence. Although these organizations may have been established for the purpose of enhancing and strengthening Israel, today Israel is vital for their continued viability. This is another manifestation of the classical process of organizational goal displacement, wherein the original goal for which an organization was created is displaced, once the organization comes into existence, with the goal of maintaining the organization itself.[65]

Outlet for the expression of Jewish identity. For the majority of America's Jews, including the religiously nonaffiliated and those who are religiously affiliated but for whom religion is very compartmentalized, Israel provides an outlet for the expression of Jewish identity within the ethnic sphere. By reading about Israel, by participating in organizational activities involving Israel, by donating time and money and by being involved with Israel in a variety of other ways, American Jews are able to express their Jewish identity without necessarily participating in formal religious activities. For many of those who also identify religiously, Israel serves as the tangible location and manifestation of much that is found in Jewish history, folklore and prayer, and thus provides those with a much deeper sense of meaning.

Source of ego strength. When Israel is strong in positive ways, American Jews feel good about being Jewish. In particular, Israel as the hero disproves the negative stereotypes about weak, cowardly Jews. This was probably most obvious immediately after the Six-Day War and after the Israeli rescue in Entebbe. For example, shortly after the Six-Day War, journalist Robert Silverberg recounted his thoughts and emotions:

> How splendidly "we" had fought, I told myself; how fine it was that "we" had once
> again foiled the Arabs. *We!* I, no Zionist, hardly even a Jew except by birth, was
> amused by an audacity in identifying myself with the Israeli warriors.[66]

Silverberg goes on to quote a Brooklyn College graduate student, who put it succinctly: "I really do feel prouder today. There is new meaning in being Jewish."[67]

It should be noted that one consequence of this kind of identity and identification is that it is contingent on Israel's being viewed as the hero. If, however, Israel ceases to be viewed by Americans as hero—as has already widely occurred—and American Jews no longer identify with Israel's policies, then both American Jewish support for Israel and the Jewish identity of many of America's Jews will invariably weaken. This is probably as much a challenge for Jewish communal leaders, especially rabbis and Jewish educators, as it is for Israel.

Outlet for status-inconsistency frustrations. Many American Jews find themselves in an incongruous situation—that of attaining high educational, occupational and income status without necessarily acquiring an equal measure of social prestige. Although the existence of a Jewish state cannot, of course, change the status of U.S. Jews as a sometimes unloved minority, it may serve as an outlet for some of the resulting frustration.

An extreme example is the support many Jews have given to controversial figures such as the late Meir Kahane. It may be that through their support of Kahane's "Kach" movement some Jews are able to retain their own sense of self-esteem and self-worth in the face of daily rejection on the part of both the dominant U.S. culture and those of other minorities in the United States.[68] A much more benign example is the way in which Israel serves as a parallel social and political structure for Jews, otherwise successful, who are lacking in American political clout. Through membership and activity in national Jewish organizations, these people have a chance to meet and socialize with prominent Israeli figures, either in the context of organization "study missions" to Israel or in meetings arranged with visiting Israeli statesmen.[69]

Israel, in short, may represent the ultimate dream of being fully "at home"—even though the home is not necessarily one that is culturally familiar to most American Jews. Culturally, they are far more at home in the United States. But their "at-homeness" can never really be complete. U.S. Jews are too much aware of their minority status, not that of a deprived minority, it is true, but a minority nonetheless. And with this perception, perhaps by definition, they can never be completely at home. It is only in Israel that Jews, even many American Jews, can feel that they are no longer minority group members but part of a dominant extended family.[70]

With this, of course, comes the freedom to be critical of family affairs. As American Jewry increasingly defines itself as an ethnic group and relates to Israel ethnically, its criticism is apt to become ever more vocal. As long as Israel was predominantly part of the American Jewish religion, it had a sacred character, and criticism amounted almost to sacrilege. But now that the relationship has moved from the religious to the familial-ethnic sphere, American Jews are more likely to strike a new balance between their profound sense of attachment to Israel and their opposition to some of its policies.

Notes

1. Melvin I. Urofsky, *American Zionism from Herzl to the Holocaust* (Garden City, N.Y.: 1975), 1.

2. Steven M. Cohen, *Israel-Diaspora Relations: A Survey of American Jewish Leaders* (Ramat-Aviv: 1990), 14.

3. *Ibid.*, 26–28.

4. Chaim I. Waxman, *American Aliya: Portrait of an Innovative Migration Movement* (Detroit: 1989), 105–118.

5. S. Cohen, *Israel-Diaspora Relations*, 28. If it were based solely on this statement, Cohen's interpretation of the responses to this question as a measure of Zionism would be somewhat questionable. Those who responded negatively may not have been affirming the centrality of Israel. Perhaps they merely do not subscribe to the "centrality" of America; that is, they may hold Israel and America as of equal importance. This would be in line with the findings of a study of Reform Jewry's national leadership in which an almost identical percentage disagreed with the statement "It is easier to lead a fuller Jewish life in Israel than in the U.S." (See p. 137). However, in light of the responses of Cohen's sample to other Israel-related questions, his interpretation does seem appropriate for the majority.

6. See, e.g., Daniel J. Elazar, *Community and Polity: The Organizational Dynamics of American Jewry* (Philadelphia: 1976), 288; Jonathan S. Woocher, *Sacred Survival: The Civil Religion of American Jews* (Bloomington: 1986), 76–80.

7. Alvin I. Schiff, "Israel in American Jewish Schools: A Study of Curriculum Realities," *Jewish Education* 38, no. 4 (Oct. 1968), 6–24.

8. Barry Chazan, "Israel in American Jewish Schools Revisited," *Jewish Education* 47, no. 2 (Summer 1979), 10.

9. *Encyclopaedia Judaica*, vol. 16 (Jerusalem: 1971), 1147.

10. Steven M. Cohen, *Ties and Tensions: The 1986 Survey of American Jewish Attitudes Toward Israel and Israelis* (New York: 1987), 36–39.

11. Eytan Gilboa, "Israel in the Mind of American Jews: Public Opinion Trends and Analysis," *Research Report*, no. 4 (London: 1986), 17.

12. *Ibid.*, 18.

13. S. Cohen, *Ties and Tensions*, 6–8.

14. *Ibid.*, 8–10. For a review of the evidence and a discussion of its implications, see Chaim I. Waxman, "Is the Cup Half-Full or Half-Empty: Perspectives on the Future of the American Jewish Community," in *American Pluralism and the Jewish Community*, ed. Seymour Martin Lipset (New Brunswick, N.J.: 1990), 71–85. One aspect of the overall debate about intermarriage is the strength of the ties to Israel of converts and those in mixed marriages. With respect to converts, the available empirical evidence is conflicting. In his 1978 study of Reform converts, Steven Huberman found that 52 percent of those aged twenty to twenty-nine and 32 percent of those aged forty and older disagreed with the statement "It is my duty to support the State of Israel" and do not feel any strong association with the country. They feel no more strongly about Israel than they do for any other humanitarian cause, because their identification as Jews is religious, not ethnic (Steven Huberman, *New Jews: The Dynamics of Religious Conversion* [Ph.D. diss., Brandeis University, 1978], 141–144).

However, a more recent study of 407 converts by Brenda Foster and Joseph Tabachnick found strong support for Israel among them. They found that 71 percent feel that support for Israel is important; 70 percent include visiting Israel as important, and two-thirds plan to visit Israel at least once (F. Brenda Foster and Joseph Tabachnick, *Your People Shall Be My People: A Study of Converts to Reform and Conservative Judaism* [Hoboken: 1991]). The study was based on a sample of those who had participated in an introductory course on Judaism offered by the Chicago Association of Reform Rabbis and the Chicago Region of the Rabbinical Assembly (Conservative) between 1973 and 1987. Not surprisingly, less than half (43 percent) deemed aliyah for others as important, and only 29 percent deemed it important for themselves.

Such conflicting evidence might be resolved by further research. In the meantime, the major problem with regard to the whole issue of the relationship between intermarriage and ties to Israel is that currently there are virtually no data about the attachments to Israel among those in *mixed* marriages, which today constitute the vast majority of Jewish intermarriages.

15. S. Cohen, *Ties and Tensions*, 17.

16. *Ibid.*, 19–21.

17. Steven M. Cohen, *Ties and Tensions: An Update—The 1989 Survey of American Jewish Attitudes Toward Israel and Israelis* (New York: 1989), 5–10.

18. *Ibid.*, 11–14.

19. Robert Scheer, "Serious Splits: Jews in U.S. Committed to Equality," *Los Angeles Times*, 13 April 1988.

20. Robert Scheer, "The Times Poll: U.S. Jews for Peace Talks on Mideast," *Los Angeles Times*, 12 April 1988.

21. Gerald B. Bubis and Steven M. Cohen, "What Are the Professional Leaders of American Jewry Thinking About Israel?" *Jerusalem Newsletter* 107 (15 March 1989), 4. The sample of "Jews in general" is from Cohen's *Ties and Tensions: An Update*.

22. Mark L. Winer, Sanford Seltzer and Steven J. Schwager, *Leaders of Reform Judaism: A Study of Jewish Identity, Religious Practices and Beliefs, and Marriage Patterns* (New York: 1987), 63–64.

23. Menahem Kaufman, *Lo-ẓiyonim beamerika bemaavak 'al hamedinah, 1939–1948* (Jerusalem: 1984), 7. For a historical overview, albeit somewhat romanticized, of the Mizrachi in the United States, see Aaron Halevi Pachenik, "Haẓiyonut hadatit bearẓot haberit," in *Sefer haẓiyonut hadatit*, ed. Yitzchak Raphael and S. Z. Shragai (Jerusalem: 1977), vol. 2, 226–241.

24. Jenna Weissman Joselit, *New York's Jewish Jews: The Orthodox Community in the Interwar Years* (Bloomington: 1990), 17.

25. *Hapardes* 23, no. 7 (April 1949), 12–15. See also p. 10, which contains a report of the New York visit of Rabbi Yoseph Kahanman, "one of the great heads of yeshivahs, of Ponivezh, and now of the state of Israel." The last phrase in Hebrew is "*medinat yisrael,*" not "*eretẓ yisrael.*"

26. Somewhat surprisingly, there is still no thorough study of the American Orthodox, especially since the Second World War.

27. William B. Helmreich, *The World of the Yeshiva* (New York: 1983). This is the "world" known as the *haredi*, "black-hat," "right-wing" or "ultra-Orthodox" community. Helmreich includes Yeshiva University's Rabbi Isaac Elchanan Theological Seminary (RIETS) in his analysis. However, RIETS is clearly peripheral to the world of the yeshivah and not considered as part of it by the overwhelming majority of that world. As he suggests, it "is viewed by many in the other major yeshivas as not being part of the community because it not only permits secular education but maintains a college on its campus that is a required part of study for all undergraduates" (36). Although Helmreich makes no mention of it, there is every reason to suggest that the religious Zionism espoused in RIETS only confirms its "deviant" status. On the growing influence of the *haredi* perspective within Orthodoxy, see Menachem Friedman, "Life Tradition and Book Tradition in the Development of Ultra-orthodox Judaism," in *Judaism Viewed from Within and from Without: Anthropological Perspectives*, ed. Harvey E. Goldberg (Albany, N.Y.: 1987), 235–255; Chaim I. Waxman, "Toward a Sociology of *Psak*," *Tradition* 25, no. 3 (Spring 1991) 12–25.

28. It is perhaps even more revealing that ArtScroll Publishers blatantly omitted a phrase implying religious Zionist sentiments from its translation of Rabbi S. Y. Zevin's *Hamo'adim behalakhah*. See Reuven P. Bulka, "Israel and the State of the Religious Mind," *Morasha: A Journal of Religious Zionism* 2, no. 2 (Spring–Summer 1986), 30–34. For another critique of the ArtScroll phenomenon, see B. Barry Levy, "Judge Not a Book by Its Cover," *Tradition* 19, no. 1 (Spring 1981), 89–95, and the response by Emanuel Feldman, *Tradition* 19, no. 2 (Summer 1981), 192. For a more extensive version of Levy's critique, see his article, "Our Torah, Your Torah and Their Torah: An Evaluation of the ArtScroll Phenomenon," in *Truth and Compassion: Essays on Judaism and Religion in Memory of Rabbi Dr. Solomon Frank*, ed. Howard Joseph, Jack N. Lightstone and Michael D. Oppenheim (Waterloo, Ont.: 1983), 137–189.

29. Cf. Charles S. Liebman and Eliezer Don-Yehiya, *Civil Religion in Israel: Traditional Judaism and Political Culture in the Jewish State* (Berkeley: 1983), 123–166.

30. Such an approach is somewhat similar to the religious Zionism espoused by Rabbi Jacob Reines, rather than that of Rabbi Abraham Isaac Kook. See Michael Zvi Nehorai, "Harav Reines veharav Kook—shetei gishot leẓiyonut," in *Yovel orot: haguto shel harav Avraham Yiẓhak Hacohen Kook,* ed. Binyamin Ish Shalom and Shalom Rosenberg (Jerusalem: 1985), 209–218.

31. For evidence that there is a correlation between religiosity and national Jewish identity and identification, see Simon N. Herman, *Israelis and Jews: The Continuity of an Identity* (New York: 1970); John E. Hofman, "Hazehut hayehudit shel no'ar yehudi beyisrael," *Megamot* 17, no. 1 (Jan. 1970), 5–14; Rina Shapira and Eva Etzioni-Halevy, *Mi atah hastudent hayisraeli* (Tel-Aviv: 1973); a series of surveys conducted in Israel in 1974 by Shlomit Levy and Louis E. Guttman and published in Jerusalem during that year in four parts by the Israel Institute of Applied Social Research (Part IV, *Values and Attitudes of Israeli High School Youth*, contains an English summary); Eva Etzioni-Halevy and Rina Shapira, "Jewish Identification of Israeli Students: What Lies Ahead," *Jewish Social Studies* 37, nos. 3–4, (July–Oct. 1975), 251–266; Simon N. Herman, *Jewish Identity: A Social Psychological Perspective*, 2nd ed. (New Brunswick, N.J.: 1989); Eva Etzioni-Halevy and Rina Shapira, *Political Culture in Israel: Cleavage and Integration Among Israeli Jews* (New York: 1977), 157–178.

32. See Marshall Sklare, *Conservative Judaism: An American Religious Movement,* aug. ed. (New York: 1972). For a Conservative ideological perspective, see Mordecai Waxman (ed.), *Tradition and Change: The Development of Conservative Judaism* (New York: 1958).

33. Moshe Davis, *The Emergence of Conservative Judaism* (Philadelphia: 1963), 268.

34. Naomi W. Cohen, *American Jews and the Zionist Idea* (Hoboken: 1975), 10.

35. *Emet Ve-Emunah: Statement of Principles of Conservative Judaism* (New York: 1988), 38–40.

36. Waxman, *American Aliya,* 65–76.

37. *Emet Ve-Emunah,* 38.

38. See S. Cohen, *Ties and Tensions,* 18–21, in which he notes a growing percentage of low levels of attachment to Israel on the part of Conservative Jews.

39. A good analysis can be found in Howard R. Greenstein, *Turning Point: Zionism and Reform Judaism* (Chico, Calif.: 1981).

40. Marshall Sklare and Joseph Greenblum, *Jewish Identity on the Suburban Frontier* (New York: 1967), 214–249.

41. W. Gunther Plaut, *The Growth of Reform Judaism: American and European Sources to 1948* (New York: 1965), 153.

42. *Ibid.,* 154.

43. *Central Conference of American Rabbis Yearbook* 77 (New York: 1967), 109.

44. Leonard J. Fein et al., *Reform Is a Verb: Notes on Reform and Reforming Jews* (New York: 1972), 65–73.

45. Gerald L. Showstack, *Suburban Communities: The Jewishness of American Reform Jews* (Atlanta: 1988), 89–92.

46. Bubis and Cohen, "Professional Leaders of American Jewry," 6, Table 3.

47. S. Cohen, *Israel-Diaspora Relations,* 37, 48–59; idem, *Ties and Tensions: An Update,* 19–32, 47–52.

48. S. Cohen, *Israel-Diaspora Relations,* 67–70.

49. See, e.g., Chaim I. Waxman, *America's Jews in Transition* (Philadelphia: 1983), 98–103, 107–112, 147–151.

50. Many of the changes are analyzed in *ibid.,* 204–234.

51. Charles S. Liebman, *The Ambivalent American Jew* (Philadelphia: 1973), 88–108.

52. See Melvin I. Urofsky, *We Are One!: American Jewry and Israel* (Garden City, N.Y.: 1978), 392. Steven Cohen found that 60 percent of his sample of American Jews agreed with the statement "I see the Jewish people as an extension of my family," and only 23 percent disagreed (*Ties and Tensions,* 15). Interestingly, Mina Zemach's findings were very similar when she presented an almost identical statement to her sample of Israeli Jews in her *Through Israeli Eyes: Attitudes Toward Judaism, American Jewry, Zionism and the Arab-Israeli Conflict* (New York: 1987), 13–14.

53. Chaim I. Waxman, "Religion and State in Israel: The Perspective of American Jewry," in *State and Diaspora: The State of Israel and Jewish Diaspora—Ideological and Political Perspectives,* ed. Eliezer Don-Yehiya (Ramat-Gan: 1991), 97–107.

54. Liebman, *Ambivalent American Jew,* 105.

55. Christopher Lasch, *Haven in a Heartless World: The Family Besieged* (New York: 1977).

56. In fact, it was suggested, the very existence of the Law of Return supports this notion of Israel as the home of the extended family. See Waxman, "Religion and State in Israel."

57. The responses were given by a number of participants in a series of lectures in the "University Day" program sponsored by the Westchester Women's Campaign for UJA-Federation, 18 January 1989. Obviously, no claim is being made herein about the statistical representativity of the expressions.

58. Liebman, *Ambivalent American Jew,* 106.

59. It with within a similar context that, at the outbreak of the Six-Day War, Arthur Goldberg, then U.S. ambassador to the United Nations, rejected the accusations made by the Syrian ambassador that American Jews were guilty of dual loyalty because of their support for Israel. Goldberg responded that in the United States attachment to one's *"ancestral home"* is not taken as "a sign of double loyalty or lack of attachment to our American institution." He then made reference to President John F. Kennedy's visit to his ancestral home and the degree to which that trip was applauded. Thus, according to Goldberg, Jewish

support for Israel is part of a comparable attachment to the ancestral home (USUN-81, 6 June 1967, 8, emphasis added). See also Waxman, *American Aliya.*

60. Charles E. Silberman, *A Certain People: American Jews and Their Lives Today* (New York: 1985).

61. The phrase is borrowed from the study by Marshall Sklare, Joseph Greenblum and Benjamin B. Ringer, *Not Quite at Home: How an American Jewish Community Lives with Itself and Its Neighbors* (New York: 1969).

62. Waxman, *America's Jews in Transition,* 151–158. See also Silberman, *A Certain People.*

63. Richard L. Zweigenhaft and G. William Domhoff, *Jews in the Protestant Establishment* (New York: 1982). Also see Samuel Z. Klausner, *Succeeding in Corporate America: The Experience of Jewish M.B.A.'s* (New York: 1988).

64. Cohen, *Ties and Tensions: An Update,* 41–43. See also Gary A. Tobin with Sharon L. Sassler, *Jewish Perceptions of Anti-Semitism* (New York: 1988).

65. For a discussion of another kind of goal displacement in a somewhat different context, see Robert K. Merton, *Social Theory and Social Structure,* enlarged ed. (New York: 1968), 353–354. On the connection between ethnic politics, antisemitism and the American Jewish attachment to Israel, see Peter Y. Medding, "Segmented Ethnicity and the New Jewish Politics," in *Studies in Contemporary Jewry,* vol. 3, *Jews and Other Ethnic Groups in a Multi-Ethnic World,* ed. Ezra Mendelsohn (New York: 1987), 26–48.

66. Robert Silverberg, *If I Forget Thee O Jerusalem: American Jews and the State of Israel* (New York: 1970), 18.

67. *Ibid.,* 19.

68. Chaim I. Waxman, "An American Tragedy—Meir Kahane and Kahanism: A Review Essay," *American Jewish History* 78, no. 3 (March 1989), 429–435.

69. For an analysis of the role of status inconsistency in the development of the American Jewish communal structure, see Waxman, *America's Jews in Transition,* 76–79.

70. Ironically, many American *olim* find that with their aliyah there is a heightening of their identities as Americans; that is, they feel more American in Israel than they did prior to their aliyah. See Waxman, *American Aliya.* Also see Kevin Avruch: *American Immigrants in Israel: Social Identities and Change* (Chicago: 1981).

Essays

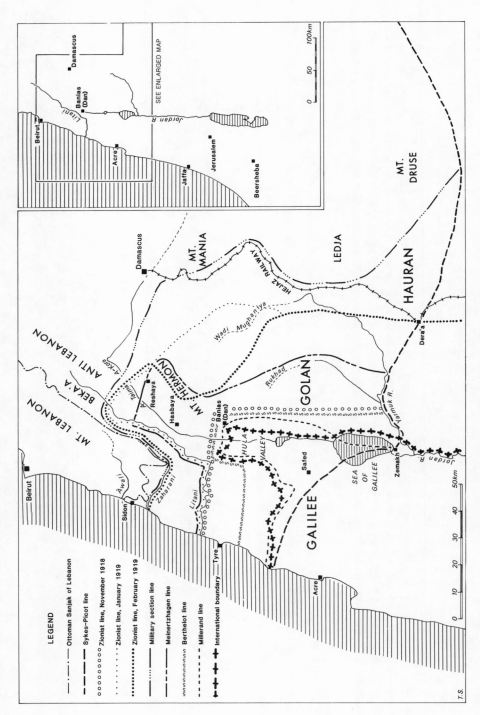

LEGEND

Ottoman Sanjak of Lebanon
Sykes–Picot line
Zionist line, November 1918
Zionist line, January 1919
Zionist line, February 1919
Military section line
Meinertzhagen line
Berthelot line
Millerand line
International boundary

Figure 1. Proposals for the Northern Border of Palestine (1916–1923)

Zionist Policy at the
Versailles Peace Conference:
Setting the Northern Border of Palestine

Yitzhak Gil-Har

(THE HEBREW UNIVERSITY)

Chaim Weizmann is often credited by historians with raising Zionist diplomacy to an entirely new level. He did not have to stand at the roadside to receive the kaiser's good wishes, nor go hat in hand to ministers and heads of state. It was he who succeeded in placing Zionism on the agenda of the major powers. The Zionist question thus became one of the issues to be resolved within the context of political reconstruction at the end of the First World War.

Weizmann, in this scheme of things, emerges as a consummate politician and skilled diplomat. In what is considered his major coup, he persuaded the foremost power of the time to lend its aegis to the Zionist movement, as expressed in the Balfour Declaration. He is portrayed as a man who won free entrée into the world of diplomats and heads of state. It is for this reason that Weizmann has been singled out as the true founder of the Jewish National Home in Palestine, a man whose leadership and personality are held up as models of modern diplomacy.[1]

As against this, though, others have pointed out that the Balfour Declaration was hardly the single-handed victory of Weizmann himself but rather the fruit of the cumulative efforts of many Zionist leaders and advocates.[2] Moreover, it has been argued that the Balfour Declaration was simply an expression of policy in principle, which then required definition in real political terms. To a great degree indeed, it was in this period of transition from general theory to the details of the new order in Palestine that Weizmann confronted his true test as a statesman. Yet the great disparity between the grandiose plan submitted by the Zionists to the Versailles Peace Conference of 1919 (also known as the Paris Peace Conference) and the modest attainments achieved in the terms of the Palestine Mandate permits us to ask whether the final result can in fact be considered a real triumph for Weizmann.[3]

The guiding assumption of the strategy pursued by Weizmann was that Britain and the Zionists needed each other in order to realize their respective ambitions in Palestine. The first order of the day, then, ought to have been to draft a mutually agreed British-Zionist proposal. Was such a partnership achieved?

It may also be asked whether the Zionists correctly assessed the shift in the realities of the situation when France renounced its political claims on Palestine (within the terms of the Sykes-Picot Agreement of 1916). This development, in which the Zionists played no active role, considerably enhanced the British position in advance of the peace conference.

Then, too, there is the question of how the Zionists were expected to answer British opposition to their plan, as stated to Nahum Sokolow by the British foreign secretary, Lord Curzon:

> Lord Curzon said that sentimental reasons were largely responsible for the original issue of the [Balfour] Declaration. Mr. Sokolow pointed out that there were political reasons also. Lord Curzon suggested that the political reasons had been altered by the lapse of time. Lord Curzon talked about the Arab opposition, and also about the opposition of [Emir] Feisal.[4]

The Zionists submitted to the peace conference a maximalist plan based on a broad geographical definition of Palestine. They assumed, however, that only the northern border would be problematic—involving, as it did, outside interests—while the eastern border would be settled between the Zionists, the English and the Arabs as an internal British concern.[5] In this, too, they were to be vastly disappointed.

The British suggested to the Zionist movement that it frame its territorial demands in terms of economic arguments,[6] although they themselves tended to favor the biblical description "from Dan to Beersheba"—a formula that could not accommodate the Zionist map. The British position was stated in an aide-mémoire of September 13, 1919, that was submitted two days later by Prime Minister David Lloyd George to the peace conference.[7] Should not this serious discrepancy have prompted a fundamental reassessment of Zionist goals and strategy?

Weizmann regarded himself, as did many Zionist historians after him, as primarily a pragmatist whose policy was crafted to suit his own particular, practical brand of Zionism. But this policy must be judged historically by the criteria of modern diplomacy.[8] Did he grasp the different interests at work in the international arena; adopt an approach that admitted of negotiation, flexibility and compromise; and properly assess political developments and the dynamics of policy in its formative stage?

The basic political goals of the Zionist movement were crystallized during the First World War. These aims included the assignment of authority over Palestine to Britain; the maximal geographical definition of that country's boundaries in order to ensure its economic viability; and the adoption of government mechanisms that would allow the Jewish National Home to develop as a political entity. This was the position formulated during the war by the political committee of the Zionist office in London and subsequently revised by an advisory council, headed by Herbert Samuel, on the eve of the peace conference. This policy was approved by the conference of Zionist organizations from the Allied and neutral countries that took place in London during February–March 1919.[9]

The preliminary draft of the Zionist proposals was first shown on November 15,

1918, to W. Ormsby-Gore (a senior Foreign Office official), who, together with other prominent figures in British public life, participated in the opening discussion of Herbert Samuel's advisory council.[10] The hope was that the involvement of top Foreign Office officials at an early stage would facilitate the coordination of policy. Several days later the draft was officially submitted to the foreign secretary, Arthur J. Balfour.[11]

Ormsby-Gore expressed reservations regarding both the legal and administrative provisions in the draft and the map presented by the Zionists. The northern border as envisaged by the advisory council extended from the mouth of the Litani River, following its course eastward until the bend northward, and then proceeding to Banias, including the sources of the Jordan (see Figure 1, p. 152). From that point the line turned southward. This line no longer met with the approval of Ormsby-Gore, who now preferred the "Dan to Beersheba" idea, including the Jordan rift, despite the fact that he himself had suggested the Litani-Banias line to the Zionist political committee a few months earlier.[12]

Conversely and ironically, it was Weizmann himself who had referred to the historical formula when asked by Mark Sykes in 1918 to describe what constituted Palestine—"from Dan to Beersheba, and from the sea to the desert, as far as possible."[13] At that time, Weizmann had not had in mind any exact boundary line, but with the peace conference fast approaching, the historical formula stood in clear contradiction to the recently finalized Zionist plan.

Balfour did not comment directly on the details of the Zionist proposal. He agreed in principle to have the plan submitted to the peace conference by the British delegation, warning, however, that the Zionists would still have to arrive at a political arrangement with Feisal. Weizmann did not believe that such an arrangement would be difficult to achieve.[14] The Zionists were under the impression that a British-Zionist understanding existed regarding their proposals, despite British reservations on specific aspects of the Palestine administration and the proposed boundary lines.[15]

However, in reality the British had their own, differing, interpretation of the significance of the Zionist proposals. Moreover, there was a measure of disagreement about what had been concluded at the talks between Weizmann and Balfour. "I fully recognize," Balfour told Weizmann, "that all the most interesting and important portions were contributed by yourself. Such a procedure is almost certain to lead to misunderstanding and controversy."[16]

Weizmann's activities in London were paralleled by Nahum Sokolow's work in Paris. The two men together had shaped and conducted Zionist policy during the war, although they differed over diplomatic tactics. In particular, Sokolow disagreed with Weizmann's approach to France, contending that despite the priority that Britain ought to enjoy in Zionist thinking France and the other Allies should not continue to be disregarded.[17] Sokolow believed that the French could come to constitute a major obstacle to the achievement of Zionist goals, and that the Zionists thus had to attempt to reach an understanding with them. Weizmann realized the difficulty posed by France, particularly by the Sykes-Picot Agreement of 1916, but disagreed with Sokolow's operative conclusion. Weizmann was in favor of openly ignoring the French factor and concentrating instead on Britain as the vehicle for implementing Zionist aims. (Concluded in 1916 between Britain, France and Russia, the Sykes-Picot Agreement on the future of the Middle East had, inter alia, envisaged the northern border of Palestine as running from the Ladder of Tyre down to the Sea of Galilee and thence along the Yarmuk valley to Dera'a—thus cutting off northern Galilee from the rest of Palestine.)

Sokolow explained to the French foreign ministry and to French political figures that the Zionists were committed to the British route in seeking a Great Power umbrella for the Jewish National Home. The French, for their part, voiced concern for their own interests in the region, especially the Catholic holy places.[18] Sokolow was persuaded that Britain's projected role as the sole mandatory power for Palestine was the main stumbling block in his search for an understanding with the French. He believed that omitting the name of the proposed mandatory power from the document to be submitted by the Zionists to the peace conference might remove this obstacle.[19] The French, who were loath to see Britain in the role of the mandatory power, suggested that the Zionists turn to the Americans instead.[20]

Under the circumstances, Sokolow felt, the Zionists ought to ask Britain for clear guarantees, not simply general statements of principle, regarding the Zionist proposals.[21] Weizmann, however, rejected both the French suggestion and Sokolow's approach, hinting that he would resign and thus create a major crisis at that critical moment if his viewpoint was not accepted. Weizmann was adamant that the Zionists give up any prospect of an accommodation with the French, preferring that the movement voice its unequivocal support for a British mandate for Palestine.[22] It was his opinion that confrontation with the French was actually a factor in the Zionists' favor,[23] an opinion apparently based on the positive attitude of the Americans toward the Zionist position.[24]

Weizmann's differences with Sokolow extended to the personal level as well as to matters of tactics and diplomacy. Sokolow was Weizmann's senior within the Zionist hierarchy. Weizmann only became a member of the Zionist Executive on January 22, 1919, when he was named to fill the seat left vacant by the death of Yehiel Chlenov.[25] It was in Weizmann's interest to emphasize the differences between himself and Sokolow while playing down the latter's role in achieving Zionist diplomatic successes.[26]

There was some internal opposition in the Zionist movement to the draft proposals to the peace conference. The Dutch Zionist Federation demanded a northern boundary that would more or less follow the line between Beirut and Damascus, without actually including either city.[27] The American Jewish Congress approved resolutions defining the Zionist goal as the establishment of a sovereign Jewish republic in Palestine.[28] In Palestine itself, the Jewish Palestine Council formulated an "Outline for Provisional Rule in Palestine."[29] In London, Harry Sacher, despite his close association with Weizmann, also expressed a degree of dissatisfaction with the draft proposals.[30]

Weizmann, whose leadership of the Zionist Organization was not yet assured, felt under pressure to accommodate his critics; as a result, the advisory council together with the political committee now drew up alternative proposals. The new draft was completed during the second half of January 1919,[31] and it turned out to be territorially more ambitious. The northern boundary of Palestine was now to include both banks of the Litani up to the 33°35' parallel, and to proceed from there in a southeasterly direction to the outskirts of Damascus.[32]

The new Zionist document, submitted to the British delegation at the peace conference on January 20, 1919,[33] aroused immediate British opposition. Ormsby-Gore and Sir Louis Mallet (a senior official of the Foreign Office) strenuously objected to several features of the new draft: the proposal to name a Jew to the post of governor; the proposed composition and powers of the executive council; the concept of a legislative assembly; the designation of the country as a Jewish state; and the proposed lands policy. Thus, British objections centered around the attempts to put a Jewish cast on the country and its government and the favorable status to be granted the Jews in relation to that of non-Jews.

For their part, the British diplomats argued that the plan ought to allay Arab fears as much as possible. They envisioned the role of the mandatory power as that of a mediator between the various national and ethnic groups in Palestine, and the Zionist proposals did not correspond to such a view. Naturally, they appreciated the explicit mention of Britain as the proposed mandatory power, but they could hardly agree to the many delimiting conditions envisaged by the Zionists.[34] Lord Curzon, then deputy foreign secretary, felt that the Zionist movement was simply seeking to use the mandate as a facade for the establishment of a Jewish state.[35]

As for the new northern border, Ormsby-Gore believed that it lay too far to the north.[36] Mark Sykes was also convinced that such a line was bound to lead to conflict between the Zionists and the Arabs.[37] Ormsby-Gore was part of a group of officials who sought to define the territory of Palestine within as limited an area as possible, taking into account the political and demographic difficulties involved in attempting to include a large Moslem population within its boundaries.[38] Nevertheless, the British did not reject the new draft outright, counseling the Zionists instead to couch their demands in economic terms.[39]

The British response caused consternation within the Zionist leadership. It seemed as if one of their chief goals was threatened with collapse. The policy coordination with the British that had seemed so much assured in December 1918 suddenly appeared most unstable by January 1919. Lloyd George was asked to receive a delegation of senior Zionist figures, led by Weizmann and Samuel, but he declined, pleading an overburdened calendar.[40] There were those within the Zionist leadership who now argued that a reassessment of the Zionist position had become essential and that the reference to Britain as the preferred mandatory power be removed from the document to be submitted to the peace conference.[41] Weizmann, however, firmly rejected any hint of a break with England.

He blamed Sokolow for the crisis, although it had been the latter who had advocated a more moderate document and was not directly involved in writing the second Zionist draft proposal.[42] Weizmann and Samuel conducted discussions with the British delegates and produced a new understanding, on the basis of which the British would be willing to accept the mandate for Palestine.[43] Mutual interests still made a measure of collaboration desirable to the two sides, despite the differences in their positions. A new Zionist statement of political goals was thus drafted on February 3, 1919,[44] and was directly submitted to the secretariat of the peace conference, though without official British approbation.

The boundary line as depicted in this latest plan had been formulated in late December 1918 according to recommendations submitted by two experts familiar with the topography, Samuel Tolkowsky and Aaron Aaronsohn.[45] This time the line ran from the outskirts of Sidon on the Mediterranean eastward toward the southern heights of Mount Lebanon; moved from that point northward to the watershed between the A-Taima and A-Kora rivers; along the divide between the eastern and western slopes of Mount Hermon and reached the northern divide of Wadi Mughar-niya, lying to the southwest of Damascus. From there it continued to Sheikh Mis-khin, along the western edges of the Ledja area and the Druse mountains to De-ra'a.[46] The western section of the line thus coincided with the southern and eastern limits of the independent Sanjak (province) of Lebanon, as it had existed under the Ottoman administration.[47]

In the Ottoman period it had generally been accepted that historical Palestine extended as far as the administrative boundary of the Lebanon province.[48] The Zionists decided, however, not to rest their case on this historical claim, preferring instead, as the British urged, to base their territorial conception on economic grounds. This primarily meant that the territory now claimed contained the water resources arguably needed to enable the Jews to develop a normal economic and social existence.[49] They were aware of the demographic and political problems that would result from the inclusion of these areas within the Jewish National Home, and for that reason decided against including the city of Sidon in their map[50] (even though Sidon had also been located south of the administrative lines of the Sanjak of Lebanon). Weizmann was quite prepared to accommodate the rights of the existing inhabitants.[51] As for Feisal and the national movement he led, Weizmann believed it was incumbent on the Zionists to negotiate a compromise with him. But Feisal's weakening position in Syria, he felt, was likely to favor the Zionist proposal for the northern border of Palestine.[52]

Not everyone within the Zionist camp was comfortable with this latest boundary proposal. The American Zionists were worried about the demographic and political implications of incorporating a large and hostile population into the area of the Jewish National Home and therefore preferred expanding the boundaries of Palestine southward toward the sparsely populated Sinai.[53]

The Zionist proposal was based on a geopolitical conception that had two aspects: First, it sought to avoid the situation that had generally existed in ancient times when the Jewish people had not controlled all the highlands and passes that served as invasion routes from the north and the east.[54] And second (as already suggested), there was the economic issue. The success or failure of the Zionist enterprise seemed to depend, above all else, on a single geographical factor: control of the water sources in northern Palestine and the Beka'a in Lebanon that fed the Jordan, the Litani and their tributaries.[55]

However, the British remained dissatisfied with this new Zionist proposal, with Balfour making note of his objections. True, they found one improvement in the latest document: The Zionists had given up their demand concerning their paramount position in Palestine and had moderated their portrayal of the country as a Jewish one.[56] As for the northern border in this latest proposal, the British noted that in some places it was even more northerly than the previous line they had already rejected.[57] Regardless of these reservations, the British maintained their special link with the Zionists. Ormsby-Gore instructed Weizmann regarding the appearance of the Zionist delegation before the Council of Ten (which consisted of two delegates from each of the principal Allied powers: Great Britain, the United States, France, Italy and Japan), scheduled for February 27, 1919. In his opinion, the Zionists would do well to drop all political arguments from their presentation and to emphasize purely economic considerations.[58]

The Zionists did not accept his advice. They were, after all, warmly supported by U.S. Secretary of State Robert Lansing; at the same time, the French delegate, André Tardieu, had even expressed publicly his government's acceptance of a British mandate for Palestine.[59]

Political developments at the peace conference should have taught the Zionists that a new power balance existed between the British and the French. On the one hand, it was true that the French prime minister, Georges Clemenceau, in his meeting with Lloyd George in early December 1918, had permitted alterations to be made in the Sykes-Picot Agreement and had renounced any claims on Palestine in Great Britain's favor.[60] The French announcement that it had no objections to assigning the mandate for Palestine to Britain removed the last psychological and political obstacle from full British control of the country. On the other hand, the French objected strongly to the northern boundary as it was proposed by the Zionists; for their part, the British were interested in separating the question of the border—an international issue—from the question of the detailed elaboration of the mandate, which they viewed as a matter for discussion between themselves and the Zionists.

Despite the differences in conception between themselves and the British, the Zionists decided not to change their position on the boundary issue. It may be that they were encouraged by the fact that the military section of the British delegation favored a strategic line that approximated the Zionist proposal. One member of the British delegation, Eric Forbes-Adam, indeed worried that Britain could be blamed for the ultimate failure of the Jewish National Home if the Zionists did not receive the borders they were asking for.[61] He favored finding ways to compensate the French elsewhere in return for concessions in this area. His proposal was rejected, however, by Lloyd George and Lord Curzon.[62] There is little doubt that Forbes-Adam's favorable attitude influenced Zionist thinking and reinforced their intention to insist on the boundary they had drawn.

Weizmann, who had good personal relations with British personnel in Paris, was nonetheless caught unprepared in September 1919 by the meeting in Deauville, where the British politicians and military experts gathered to examine the issue of the withdrawal of their armed forces from Syria. He was concerned that Britain, in seeking an accommodation with the French in the Middle East, would disregard Zionist interests. He tried unsuccessfully to contact the prime minister, after which he contacted French diplomatic figures who were themselves waiting to hear the results of the British deliberations in Deauville. Weizmann was pleased to find the

French quite flexible. One of their advisers, Robert de Caix, stated his readiness to propose a new line for Palestine's northern border that would place all the Jewish settlements in the Hula Valley within the territory of Palestine.[63] The French were also willing to include a Zionist representative on the boundary delimitation committee.[64]

The immediate consequence was that Weizmann entertained the illusion that the French had been impressed by the strong Zionist position.[65] The French, for their part, also profited from their talks with Weizmann. They learned, for example, that the Zionists were not interested in the Golan and Hauran so much as the sources of the Jordan and the lands associated historically with the biblical Israelite tribes. The French therefore began to frame a proposal to give up the Safed district and the Hula Valley in exchange for the Golan and Hauran, which were to remain in the area assigned to the French mandate for Syria.[66]

If Weizmann was pleased with these signs of French flexibility, he could only have found the direction taken by Britain to be disquieting. Lloyd George specifically mentioned the biblical formula in the aide-mémoire that he had submitted to the peace conference, even though (as explained earlier) it stood in contradiction to the Zionist map. He explained to Weizmann that he could not demand more than the historical boundary but that the door remained open for the Zionists to demand the economic boundaries. In that case, however, the burden of proof would fall on the Zionists themselves.[67]

From the Zionist perspective these were alarming developments. Lloyd George had now clearly come to distinguish between the borders of Palestine that were sufficient for Britain and those demanded by the Zionists. Britain would indeed be willing to raise the Zionist map for discussion and negotiation, but only in the Zionists' name, not in the name of His Majesty's government. What this meant, in effect, was that the British were not prepared to make a serious effort to gain for the Zionists what they were asking for.

No less negative was the fact that the salvation expected by the Zionist leadership to arrive from Washington did not materialize. The Americans refused to take a position until Britain and France had settled the differences between them.[68] Moreover, one of their advisers rejected the northern border proposed by the Zionists, arguing that its acceptance would provoke an Arab revolt.[69] Thus, although the political scenario that the Zionist movement had envisioned had been fundamentally transformed, it maintained its position. It drew some hope from the fact that Foreign Secretary Balfour was personally interested in the northern border issue.[70] (Lord Milner, the colonial secretary, was also interested in seeing Jewish settlement in Transjordan.)[71]

At the same time, however, confusing signals continued to emanate from official British circles. Lloyd George and Balfour's successor as foreign secretary, Lord Curzon, refused to receive a high-level Zionist delegation or to issue a new public statement in support of the proposed Jewish National Home.[72] And yet it turned out that Lord Curzon was nonetheless prepared to submit the Zionist map to the peace conference and to support it. Or, as Lloyd George had put it, if the Zionists could extract further territory from the French, there was no reason to refuse it. In consequence, Weizmann turned to Colonel Richard Meinertzhagen, General Sir Edmund

Allenby's chief political officer in Egypt, with the request to redraw the desired borders for Palestine. The resulting "Meinertzhagen Line" extended from the mouth of the Litani; followed the river up to Jisr Karoun; then turned eastward to include Reshaya and Mount Hermon; and crossed the Golan Heights going south about twenty-five kilometers west of the Hejaz railway.[73] Both Allenby and Herbert Samuel backed this proposal, which as a result was now adopted by the Zionist leadership as its own. For a moment it thus appeared that coordination between the British and the Zionist movement had been restored.

In December 1919 the British presented the "Meinertzhagen Line" to the French as a compromise proposal. The French rejected the idea and insisted on the line agreed on in Sykes-Picot,[74] noting that they would not be budged unless they were given suitable political or territorial compensation elsewhere. Curzon objected to any sort of compensation. As far as he was concerned, there was no reason why Britain should pay the price for concessions made by the French to the Zionist movement.[75] This argument was consistent with Lloyd George's view that the Zionist demands were not essential to British interests.

At this stage, very belatedly, the Zionist leadership concluded that France held the key to their success in obtaining the desired "economic" borders of Palestine and therefore sought to negotiate with the French without British intermediaries. Sokolow accordingly met with Leon Bourgeois, the French representative to the League of Nations. He also met with Alexander Millerand, the new prime minister and foreign minister of France, as well as with the president, Paul Deschanel.[76] Weizmann, for his part, met in London with the French ambassador, Paul Cambon, and with the director general of the French foreign ministry, Philippe Berthelot.[77]

The French expressed sympathy for the position of the Zionists regarding the Jewish question and for the solution that they were proposing. In return for the satisfaction of French territorial demands, they were willing to support Zionist claims. France felt that its international standing was being placed in question by the new balance of power created by the war and was not reassured by the system of collective security established under the League of Nations. The balance of power in colonial terms had also changed to the detriment of French interests and in Britain's favor. France was therefore ready to be flexible regarding the northern borders of Palestine as long as it received compensation.[78] In the course of the bargaining, the French raised the moral obligation that they had to safeguard the rights of the Arabs as a counterweight to Zionist claims based on the urgency of finding a solution to the Jewish question.[79]

Weizmann had become well aware by now that his political leverage with the British was limited. He therefore made friendly overtures to the French, offering them good neighborliness, the benefits of a positive press and the chance to appoint a French Jewish representative to the Zionist commission for Palestine.[80] (There had been no representative of French Jewry on the commission since the resignation of Silvian Levy at the end of 1918.)

Simultaneously, the Zionists sought to activate their contacts in the American administration. The French were impressed by American diplomatic interventions in London and Paris in favor of the Zionist proposals.[81] The Syrian-Arab revolt against French rule in Syria and Lebanon also influenced French thinking. As a result, French policy had softened by the eve of the San Remo conference, which convened on April 18–26, 1920. Berthelot proposed new alterations in the Sykes-Picot line, suggesting that Palestine's border be extended northward (though not as far as the Litani).[82] During the conference itself, French delegate Albert Kammerer offered to reconcile the "Berthelot Line" with the "Meinertzhagen Line" in the area east of the Sea of Galilee.[83]

The British were prepared to accept the latest French proposals on condition that the French state their willingness to allocate water surpluses from the Litani to Palestine, and on the further condition that the French permit them to build a rail line through the Yarmuk River valley.[84] The Zionists expected further concessions to be forthcoming, taking the "Berthelot Line" as a fait accompli.[85] Instead, other developments during the San Remo conference upset British and Zionist plans entirely.

While Berthelot sought to resolve the boundary question, it now emerged that Curzon did not wish to reach a definitive and detailed decision for fear that publication of the results would provoke angry Arab reactions. Lloyd George, for his part, stated that he would not support the Zionist bid to include Sidon, Tyre and the headwaters of the Jordan within Palestine. Citing the work *The Holy Land* by George Adam Smith, he argued that these areas had never been part of historical Palestine.[86] The French greeted this declaration enthusiastically, and they too now stated their preference for the "Dan to Beersheba" definition. They identified "Dan" with Banias in a document submitted by Millerand on June 29, 1920.[87] This "Millerand Line" constituted a definite retreat from the "Berthelot Line" and in essence reflected the views of Robert de Caix as stated the previous September.

The San Remo conference upheld the French position. France was given the mandate for Syria and proceeded to impose its authority there. The remaining problem for the French was the question of their border with Palestine.

The Zionists, thoroughly surprised and confused, appealed to the British to ask for a suspension of negotiations, during which they hoped to persuade the French to reverse their position. The British agreed to this step.[88] Sokolow and Pinhas Ruthenberg were sent to Paris to do what they could to influence the French, but they failed to score any success there. Personal appeals by American Zionist leaders similarly proved to be fruitless. Weizmann realized the weakness of his position, for America was then absorbed in its presidential election campaign and could not be depended upon to pressure the French. He therefore sought a postponement of negotiations until after the U.S. elections.[89]

An interdepartmental committee was set up in London to weigh various options for compensating the French in return for French concessions on the northern boundary issue. However, Lord Curzon maintained his objections to such a course.[90] He felt that Britain had no card to use in bargaining with the French and was concerned that further delays in settling the issue would damage Anglo-French relations.[91]

At a conference held in London, Lloyd George finally cut the Gordian knot and settled for a northern boundary of Palestine that to all intents and purposes coincided with the "historical" line.[92] This boundary, based on the "Millerand Line," was enshrined in the Anglo-French convention of December 23, 1920. (The final touches were applied to this agreement by the Newcombe-Paulet demarcation committee in the summer of 1921; it was officially ratified in 1923.)

The Zionists had developed a diplomatic approach through which they sought to implement their plans for Palestine in close cooperation with Great Britain. They preferred to see a British mandate for Palestine for reasons that were both ideological and political. Because their approach to the boundary question was rigid, they neither demonstrated flexibility nor reevaluated their policy in light of the fluid diplomatic situation. In the process, they minimized the strength of the other political actors in the arena.

Absolute agreement between the Zionists and the British government was a sine qua non for the success of the Zionist policy. Such an agreement proved elusive, however. Zionist policy was not amended despite disagreements with Britain that arose both over the boundaries question and over the terms of the mandate. Such amendments ought to have been made once the British had achieved their goal—British rule over Palestine—and especially after the Deauville meeting, at which the British government adopted the historical definition of Palestine as the territory between "Dan and Beersheba."

France was perceived as a political rival rather than a diplomatic asset, until the eve of the Deauville meeting in September 1919. But the doctrinaire approach of the Zionists prevented them from reaching a compromise with France on the basis of the "Berthelot Line." The same limited conception prevented them from exploring the possibility of a partial implementation of the Jewish National Home within the areas assigned to the French mandate. The Zionists feared that such a step might allow the British to reduce their commitment to establish a Jewish National Home in Palestine.

Weizmann presented his policy as realistic and pragmatic,[93] but once the Anglo-French convention of 1920 was signed the Zionists had to accept the exclusion of large areas from their own map of the Jewish National Home. In private, Weizmann admitted that the policy he had followed regarding the northern border had failed. "On the boundary question we lost. None of our territorial demands was accepted."[94] However, he would never admit this publicly, pointing the finger of blame instead at his rivals and opponents both within and outside the Zionist movement.[95]

Weizmann did not always exhibit the professional dexterity of a statesman and diplomat. The doors of political leaders did not always open for him. In the episode described here, he did not act as a master of modern diplomacy.

Notes

1. C. Webster, *The Art and Practice of Diplomacy* (London: 1961), 5–6, 113–132.
2. M. Vereté, "The Balfour Declaration and Its Makers," *Middle Eastern Studies* 6, no. 1 (Jan. 1970), 48–76.
3. "Statement of the Zionist Organisation Regarding Palestine, third day of February Nineteen-hundred and Nineteen," London, 1919.

4. H. Sacher to Dr. V. Jacobson, 13 November 1919, Central Zionist Archives (hereafter, CZA), London Office Z4/124/11.

5. Chaim Weizmann to Winston Churchill, 1 March 1921, Public Records Office (hereafter, PRO), Colonial Office (hereafter, CO) 733/16.

6. Nahum Sokolow to Chaim Weizmann, 25 January 1919, CZA Z4/16009.

7. Great Britain, Foreign Office, *Documents on British Foreign Policy*, vol. 1 (London: 1952), 685–701.

8. Webster, *Art and Practice of Diplomacy*, 4–5.

9. Decision of 9 March 1919. See: *Protokolim shel hava'ad hapo'el haẓiyoni, 1919–1929*, vol. 1: Feb. 1919–Jan. 1920 (Tel-Aviv: 1975), 80.

10. Minutes, World Zionist Organization (WZO) Political Committee, 2 November 1918, CZA Z4/1720.

11. Minute written by W. Ormsby-Gore, 19 November 1918, Foreign Office Archive (hereafter, FO) 371/3385.

12. Minutes, WZO Political Committee, London, 16 August 1918; addendum to the report by Ormsby-Gore, 22 August 1918 (following his return from Palestine), FO 371/4354.

13. Samuel Tolkowsky, diary entry for 25 February 1918 in his *Yoman ẓiyoni medini, london, 1915–1919* (Jerusalem: 1986), 280. The original ms. is in CZA, file A248.

14. Aide-mémoire of Weizmann, report of his meeting with Arthur J. Balfour on 4 December 1918. Balfour did not agree with the gist of what was said and with some of the particular points made. Balfour to Weizmann, 18 December 1918, CZA Z4/1933/II.

15. Weizmann to M. D. Eder, 4 December 1918, Zionist Commission Archive, Jaffa, CZA L4/60.

16. Balfour to Weizmann, 18 December 1918, CZA Z4/1933/II.

17. Sokolow to Weizmann, 12 June 1918, Zionist Commission Archive, Jerusalem, CZA L3/370.

18. Sokolow to Weizmann, 13 and 14 December 1918, CZA Z4/305/2; CZA Z4/62.

19. *Ibid.*

20. Weizmann to Sokolow, 22 December 1918, *The Letters and Papers of Chaim Weizmann* (Series A—Letters), vol. 9, no. 81 (81).

21. Sokolow to Weizmann, 25 December 1918, CZA Z4/61/II.

22. Weizmann to Sokolow, 8 December 1918, *Letters,* vol. 9, no. 54 (56); Weizmann to A. Aaronsohn, 16 December 1918, *ibid.*, no. 69 (68); Weizmann to Sokolow, 22 December 1918, *ibid.*, no. 81 (81).

23. Weizmann to his wife, Vera, 8 January 1919, *Letters,* vol. 9, no. 100 (93–94).

24. According to Weizmann's report to the Foreign Office about his meeting with President Wilson, 14 January 1919, FO 608/98.

25. Minutes, Zionist Executive Committee, CZA Z4/302/1.

26. Tolkowsky, *Yoman ẓiyoni medini,* entry for 17 December 1918, (399); entry for 22 December 1918, (403); Weizmann to Vera, 8 January 1919, 11 September 1919 and 18 January 1920, *Letters,* vol. 9, no. 100 (93–94); no. 214 (214) and no. 266 (280). For this reason, Weizmann asked Aaronsohn to proceed independently with his activities in Paris: Weizmann to Aaronsohn, 12, 14 and 16 December 1918, *Letters,* vol. 9, no. 61 (62–63), no. 67 (66) and no. 69 (68).

27. Resolutions of the Zionist Federation of Holland, 3 November 1918, CZA Z4/57/I.

28. Sections of the resolutions were incorporated in a paper submitted by Sokolow to Ormsby-Gore and Sir Louis Mallet, leading members of the political section of the British delegation to the peace conference, on 20 January 1919: "Memorandum of the Zionist Organisation Relating to the Reconstitution of Palestine as the Jewish National Home, January 1919," London, 1919.

29. The Palestine Council met from 18 to 22 December 1918 and adopted proposals that were to serve as binding instructions for the Jewish delegation from Palestine to the Peace Conference. See Va'ad Leumi, National Council of Palestinian Jewry Archive, CZA J1/8766.

30. I. M. Sieff to Harry Sacher, 19 November 1918, CZA Z4/120.

31. Weizmann to Sokolow, 19 January 1919, *Letters,* vol. 9, no. 104 (96–97).

32. "Proposals Relating to the Establishment of a Jewish National Home in Palestine" (n.d.), CZA Z4/5040.

33. Aide-mémoire of a discussion between Sokolow and Mallet, 20 January 1919, FO 608/98.

34. Sokolow to Weizmann, 25 January 1919, CZA Z4/61/II; aide-mémoire about meeting between Mallet and Sokolow, 20 January 1919; and note by Ormsby-Gore, 22 January 1919, FO 608/98.

35. Note by N. Curzon, 26 January 1919, relating to G. Kidston's aide-mémoire about a discussion with Weizmann, FO 608/98.

36. "Proposals Regarding the Future Government of the Separate Palestine State," 23 January 1919, FO 608/98.

37. "Appreciation of the Situation in Syria, Palestine and Lesser Armenia," by Col. Sir Mark Sykes, 27 January 1919, FO 608/105.

38. Section 22 in Ormsby-Gore's "Report on the Existing Political Situation in Palestine," 22 August 1918, FO 371/4354; Yitzhak Gil-Har, "Hagevul haẓefoni vehamizraḥi shel ereẓ yisrael," *Yahadut zemaneinu* 2 (1985), 324–325.

39. Sokolow to Weizmann, 25 January 1919, CZA Z4/16009.

40. P. H. Kerr to Sokolow, 1 February 1919, Nahum Sokolow Archive, CZA A18/32/1.

41. Sacher to S. Landman, 30 January 1919, CZA Z4/120.

42. Weizmann to Vera, 31 January 1919, *Letters,* vol. 9, no. 114 (107–108); entry for 9 February 1919, Tolkowsky, *Yoman ẓiyoni medini,* 405; Weizmann to Sokolow, 22 December 1918, *Letters,* vol. 9, no. 81 (81); Weizmann to Herbert Samuel, 3 January 1919, *ibid.,* no. 93 (88).

43. Entry for 9 February 1919, Tolkowsky, *Yoman ẓiyoni medini,* 406 n. 4; report of L. Mallet, 30 January 1919, FO 608/98.

44. "Statement of the Zionist Organisation Regarding Palestine," 3 February 1919.

45. Weizmann to Tolkowsky, 23 December 1919, CZA Z4/108/51; entry for 9 February 1919, Tolkowsky, *Yoman ẓiyoni medini,* 407–408; Tolkowsky, "Memorandum on the Boundaries of Palestine," February 1919, CZA Z4/25052; Aaron Aaronsohn, "The Boundaries of Palestine," CZA Z4/25052.

46. "Statement of the Zionist Organisation Regarding Palestine," 3 February 1919.

47. Weizmann to Tolkowsky, 23 December 1918, CZA Z4/108/51.

48. Gil-Har, "Hagevul haẓefoni vehamizraḥi," 317–319.

49. Weizmann to L. S. Amery, 18 October 1918, *Letters,* vol. 8, no. 282, (279); Weizmann to Balfour, 17 September 1919, CZA Z4/16009; Weizmann to L. B. Namier, 18 September 1919, CZA Z4/1404.

50. Entry for 9 February 1919, Tolkowsky, *Yoman ẓiyoni medini,* 407.

51. Aide-mémoire of discussion between Weizmann and Balfour, 4 December 1919, CZA Z4/56.

52. Weizmann to L. D. Brandeis, 29 October 1918, *Letters,* vol. 9, no. 4 (3–4); Weizmann-Feisal Agreement, 3 January 1919, CZA Z4/2989; Weizmann's statement, 7 March 1919, *Protokolim shel hava'ad hapo'el haẓiyoni, 1919–1929,* vol. 1, 68.

53. Jacob de Haas to Stephen S. Wise, 4 December 1918, CZA Z4/2086/II; Weizmann, in *Protokolim shel hava'ad hapo'el haẓiyoni, 1919–1929,* vol. 1, 68.

54. S. Tolkowsky, "A Note on the Boundaries of Palestine," in *Zionism and the Jewish Future,* ed. H. Sacher (London: 1915), 210; *idem,* "The Boundaries of Palestine," *Palestine* (Manchester), 15 February 1917; *idem,* "Memorandum on the Boundaries of Palestine"; *idem,* "The Hedjaz Railway," 27 February 1917, CZA Z4/1720; H. Sidebotham, "A Memorandum on the Boundaries of Palestine" (Aug.–Sept. 1919), CZA Z4/565.

55. See n. 49; Aaronsohn, "The Boundaries of Palestine," CZA Z4/25052; Weizmann to Lloyd George, 29 December 1919, CZA Z4/25052. Two British hydraulic engineers, L. W. Dane and John Benton, had a certain amount of influence on the outlines of the Zionist map. They stated in a proposal submitted to the WZO in London that "whoever holds the keys to the water—the whole country is his." Entry for 19 August 1918, Tolkowsky, *Yoman ẓiyoni medini,* 371.

56. "Statement of the Zionist Organisation Regarding Palestine. Proposals to be presented to the peace conference, by Dr. Weizmann as amended by the Secretary of State," FO 608/99.

57. *Ibid.;* note by M. D. Peterson, 4 March 1919, FO 371/4170.

58. Ormsby-Gore to Weizmann, 20 February 1919, CZA Z4/16009.

59. "La France et le Sionisme," *Le peuple Juif* (Paris), 13 (4 July 1919).

60. C. M. Andrew and S. A. Kanya-Forstner, *The Climax of French Imperial Expansion 1914–1924* (Stanford: 1981), 161–165.

61. E. G. Forbes-Adam, "Boundaries of the Arab Countries," 9 August 1919, FO 371/4181.

62. Memorandum of discussion between Forbes-Adam and Phillippe Millet, editor of the Paris *Temps,* 9 October 1919; notes regarding the objections of Hubert Young, D. Sperling and N. Curzon, 17 October 1919, FO 608/107; memorandum by Forbes-Adam, "France and the Northern Boundary of Palestine," 30 December 1919; Curzon's objections, FO 371/4215.

63. Robert de Caix to "Cher ami," 11 September 1919, Ministère des Affaires Étrangères (MAE), Paris: Palestine, vol. 14, E312-4, Weizmann at the annual conference of the Anglo-Zionist Federation, 21 September 1919, CZA Z4/1833 II.

64. Weizmann at meeting of the Zionist Executive Committee, 25 September 1919: *Protokolim shel hava'ad hapo'el haẓiyoni,* vol. 1, 232–233.

65. Weizmann to Sokolow (undated: written approximately in the third week of September 1919), CZA Z4/1187.

66. Robert de Caix to "Cher ami" (see n. 63).

67. Weizmann at meeting of the Zionist Executive Committee (see n. 64).

68. B. V. Cohen to Weizmann, 20 September 1919, CZA Z4/565.

69. Statement attributed to Captain William Yale, a U.S. State Department special agent in the Near East, in *ibid.*

70. Weizmann to L. B. Namier, 18 September 1919, CZA Z4/1404.

71. Memorandum of discussion between Sokolow and Lord Milner, 4 November 1919, CZA Z4/565.

72. Sokolow's memorandum of discussion with Curzon, 2 November 1919, CZA Z4/1050; Sacher to V. Jacobson, 13 November 1919, CZA Z4/124/11.

73. Richard Meinertzhagen to Curzon, 17 November 1919, FO 371/4186.

74. Anglo-French Conference in London, 22–23 December 1919, FO 371/4239.

75. See n. 62.

76. Memorandum, 23 January 1920, CZA Z4/565; Sokolow to Millerand, 7 February 1920, CZA Z4/25051; Millerand to Sokolow, 12 February 1920, CZA Z4/25006; "Notes of Interview Between President Deschanel and Mr. Sokolow, 14th February 1920," CZA Z4/1264/I.

77. To Jean Gout, 7 February 1920; Berthelot to Larouche, 27 February 1920, MAE, Palestine, vol. 14, E312–314.

78. See n. 76.

79. Millerand to Sokolow, 12 February 1920, CZA Z4/25006.

80. Berthelot to Larouche, 27 February 1920, MAE, Palestine, vol. 14, 312–314.

81. Zionists (New York) to Weizmann, 11 February 1920, CZA Z4/565; George Graham Paris to Curzon, 10 February 1920, FO 371/4187; Sokolow to Alfred Mond, 11 March 1920, CZA Z4/565.

82. 11 March 1920, FO 371/5032.

83. R. Vansittart to Curzon, 6 May 1920, FO 371/5244.

84. Minutes by Vansittart, Colonel Gribon and Curzon, 13–22 March 1920, FO 371/5032.

85. Weizmann to Vera, 25 April 1920, *Letters,* vol. 9, no. 309, (339); Weizmann to Herbert Samuel, 29 July 1920, *ibid.,* vol. 10, no. 3, (3–4).

86. British secretary's notes of a meeting of the Supreme Council, San Remo, 25 April 1920, FO 371/5244.

87. FO 371/5244.

88. Curzon to the Foreign Office, 11 July 1920, FO 371/5036; after a month passed without any action, the Zionists requested and received a further postponement. Vansittart to Curzon, 2 August 1920, FO 371/5245.

89. Weizmann to Curzon, 30 October 1920, FO 371/5246; B. V. Cohen on behalf of Weizmann to Curzon, 10 November 1920, FO 371/5247.

90. Interdepartmental committee, 12 October 1920; notation of Curzon's objection, 24 October 1920, FO 371/5247. The subject was raised again at the session held on October 29, 1920, by General W. Thwaites, the director of military intelligence in the War Department, FO 371/5277.

91. Vansittart to Curzon, 13 November 1920, FO 371/5247; Weizmann, on the strength of Vansittart, at the Zionist political committee in London, 24 November 1920, CZA Z4/1281/IV.

92. London Conference, 4 December 1920, FO 371/5247.

93. Weizmann to his critics, in meetings of the Zionist executive of 24 February 1919 and 8 January 1920: *Protokolim shel hava'ad hapo'el haẓiyoni*, vol. 1, 18 and 272–275, respectively.

94. Weizmann at meeting of the Zionist political committee, London, 7 December 1920, CZA Z4/1281/III.

95. "Dr. Weizmann et les Juifs Francais," *Le Peuple Juif*, 5 November 1920; "Le 12e Congres Sioniste," *L'Univers Israelite*, 16 September 1921; "Hakongres bekarlsbad," *Haaretz*, 26 September 1921.

Ahad Ha'am in Historical Perspective

Yossi Goldstein

(UNIVERSITY OF HAIFA)

In the summer of 1926, the Tel-Aviv municipal council decided by majority vote that the carriages traveling toward Herzl and Allenby streets and from time to time crossing Ahad Ha'am Street would take an alternate route between 2:00 and 4:00 P.M. A desire to allow Asher Ginzberg—universally known as Ahad Ha'am—to enjoy his daily siesta undisturbed occasioned this decision; since settling in Tel-Aviv, he had complained bitterly about the noise and tumult around his house. In the meantime, his illness had taken a turn for the worse, and the council's symbolic and highly unorthodox resolution was intended to placate him and alleviate his suffering. There is no question that their action also reflected a feeling of great respect for a figure who, while admittedly controversial and highly opinionated, was universally acknowledged to symbolize the development of Tel-Aviv.[1]

Yet another aspect of the public's feelings toward the founder of spiritual Zionism was evinced by the vast throng that followed Ahad Ha'am's casket at his funeral in January 1927, the numerous eulogies and the many mourning assemblies[2] held to mark his passing. Hardly a superlative was omitted in the steady stream of panegyrics. According to Meir Dizengoff,[3] "[Ahad Ha'am] infused all the workers of Zion with happiness by providing them with a moral foundation." David Yellin called him "the heir to Maimonides. . . . He was the one who forged the harmony within us between the universal and the Israeli."[4] And Hayim Nahman Bialik, who had returned from the United States to be with him, considered Ahad Ha'am's passing an irreparable loss to the Yishuv. "Ahad Ha'am possessed a stately nobility," he said during the funeral procession:

> He seemed to possess a golden scale that enabled him to weigh every statement and utterance. He brought to mind the responsibility that was shown by the members of the Great Assembly when they set about arranging the books of the Bible, and by *rabeinu hakadosh* [Judah Hanasi] who arranged the Mishnah. From [Ahad Ha'am] we all learned the meaning of a sense of honor and responsibility. For the task of the writer is not to amuse: the writer creates the image of God that informs the nation.[5]

With Ahad Ha'am's death, Bialik wrote later, "the sun set on a great hope of Israel."[6]

Ahad Ha'am's death did not spell the end of the almost mythic reverence accorded him by part of the Jewish national community as expressed in eulogies such as these or the resolution of the Tel-Aviv municipal council. Ten, twenty, even thirty years after his death, his teachings were still considered a guide for the perplexities of the times,[7] and some continued to regard him as the successor of Moses and Maimonides.[8] Until the 1970s, every high school student in Israel was required to study Ahad Ha'am's writings, and his name adorns hundreds of streets, institutions and cultural projects.

The extraordinary veneration that Ahad Ha'am received from the Jewish people in Israel and in the diaspora, a feeling that was powerfully seconded by the Jewish intellectual elite, undoubtedly derived from both his philosophy and his personality. At the same time, however, the lavish praise showered upon Ahad Ha'am seems at times to be incommensurate with the historical record. The explanation for this phenomenon, as suggested here, may be found in the contemporary social and psychological needs of East European Jewry.

In the last third of the nineteenth century and the first part of the twentieth, Jewish society experienced a social, economic and cultural revolution that radically altered its essence. Fifty or a hundred years earlier, it had seemed that nascent modern European values, as expressed in the Emancipation and the Enlightenment, would leave the Jewish people untouched. The typical Jewish reflex action of self-enclosure within the confines of the ghetto and a recoil from dependence on the surrounding society was actually intensified during this period. Although some individuals within the Jewish society had begun to assimilate the revolutionary European ideals of enlightened education and nationalism in order to become part of the European mainstream, the fact that they were so few in number demonstrated the tenacity of Orthodoxy's hold on Judaism. The same pattern was evident in Hasidism: For a brief moment it appeared that the movement was about to foment a cultural and social revolution of its own, but then its proponents took a different route, and Hasidism's subsequent entrenchment within Jewish society actually set reactionary processes into motion.

This picture changed dramatically at the end of the nineteenth century. The emancipation of the Jews in most European countries (with the exception of Russia and Rumania), which occurred simultaneously with their growing integration into diverse economic sectors and a mass movement to the large cities, accelerated the process of secularization in Jewish society. These developments necessitated socio-economic solutions and contributed to unprecedented cultural change.

The transformation of Central European Jewry affected, perforce, the Jews of Eastern Europe. However, the acute disparity in political conditions, compounded by social and demographic differences, created a cultural lag. When Western social and cultural processes eventually reached the East, they were adapted to fit the distinctive conditions prevailing there. Since the authorities in Russia, under both Tsar Alexander III (1881–1894) and Tsar Nikolai II (1894–1917), continued to believe that the granting of emancipation would adversely affect the regime, Jewish community leaders sought ways to alter their situation that were not always acceptable to their brethren in Central and Western Europe. The unprecedented population growth experienced by East European Jewry, which intensified socioeconomic problems, also spurred the Jewish leadership in the East to seek social and cultural solutions.

Zionism was one of these solutions to the physical distress of the Jewish community—offering as well, perhaps, a cultural, social and psychological rationalization for accelerated secularization. For its proponents, Zionism was both a means of resolving problems related to national identity and a possible instrument of suppressing antisemitism, which had been exacerbated since the 1870s. But the Zionist solution was practicable only for a small minority. It was obvious to the Jews that Eretz Israel could not yet constitute a viable alternative to their present home—it was not at that time a place where Jews could be secure, develop their own economy, cultivate their national aspirations and be free of antisemitism. True, many considered Zionism to be better than such alternatives as national autonomy ("autonomism") or full integration into the Christian society. Its advocates, nonetheless, were well aware that their program was still unfeasible.

The impossibility of expeditiously fulfilling Zionist aspirations as they were conceptualized by Moses Lilienblum, Leo Pinsker, Samuel Mohilever and the leaders of the Hibbat Zion movement perhaps accounts for the success of Ahad Ha'am's ideas among activists in the Jewish national movement. His notion of creating a spiritual and cultural center for the Jewish people in Eretz Israel as a means of preparing the nation to realize its national identity was seized upon by those who espoused Zionism but who knew that its implementation was not possible. Many found in his ideas a way of resolving the dilemma of believing in a vision without being able to realize it in practice. For Ahad Ha'am's ideology proposed remaining in the diaspora in the first stage. Even supporters of Hibbat Zion could utilize these ideas as a bulwark against feelings of powerlessness caused by inactivity and the nonfulfillment of their national aspirations. In contrast to the views of Lilienblum and others, Ahad Ha'am argued that the existence of a Jewish diaspora was a legitimate phenomenon. The first step was to work in the diaspora in order to prepare the people for nationalism. The national-cultural center to be established in Eretz Israel was meant primarily to serve a national vanguard—only at a later stage, Ahad Ha'am believed, would it be possible to fulfill the yearnings of Hovevei Zion and create a political entity for Jews in Eretz Israel.

Another explanation for the success of Ahad Ha'am's philosophy lies in the secular Jewish aspect of his ideology, which provided a psychological solution for those in Jewish society who were affected by the secularization process but felt that they had to rationalize their behavior. Many Jews who had been brought up according to the rigid code of Torah now desired to be free of its burden. But this desire, in turn, led to mental anguish and pangs of conscience: Their forefathers had consecrated themselves to divine works, whereas they were discarding the Torah and its precepts. In such a situation, Ahad Ha'am's nationalist doctrine seemed to provide an honorable way out. His assertion that the Torah of their forebears had become fossilized and needed to be revivified through the agency of Jewish nationalism, and that secularization was a legitimate process provided that it did not entail a deviation from Jewish-nationalist principles, was an ideal solution to their dilemma. No longer were Jewish religious precepts to be upheld as a supreme value: By and large they belonged to an archaic worldview. The current agenda, Ahad Ha'am felt, called for the emergence of a Jewish nationalism informed by modern secular values that would retain an affinity for the Jewish historical past. Such a doctrine enabled a simultaneous release from Jewish tradition—particularly from the fulfillment of religious precepts—and a continuing attachment to a Jewishness centered on nationalist principles.

The appropriateness of Ahad Ha'am's ideology and principles for his contemporaries, together with his unique personality and his activity in Hibbat Zion, largely account for his political success until Theodor Herzl's arrival on the scene. Indeed, there is no doubt that in the first half of the 1890s, Ahad Ha'am, until then a publicist espousing original ideas that attracted only marginal public support, became a central figure in the Jewish national movement. In this period, his public standing was solid and he wielded considerable political power. In the face of Hovevei Zion's failure to register any enduring achievements beyond the establishment of a few *moshavot,* Ahad Ha'am's success in creating a political force (Bnei Moshe) and leading it to key positions in the national movement was all the more striking. If a few years earlier the author of "This Is Not the Way" and "The Truth from Eretz Israel" had been known for his criticism of Hibbat Zion and his adversarial stance toward the movement's leaders, the period from 1894 to 1896 saw a turnabout: To many in the Jewish national movement, the ideas of those in the "Odessa Committee"—Lilienblum and Pinsker, Mohilever and Mordechai Eliasberg—had become almost irrelevant, whereas Ahad Ha'am's tripartite national doctrine (one that defined the goals of the Zionist movement, the place of Eretz Israel and the relationship between religion and nationalism) seemed better suited to the actual situation of Jewish society.

To some among the *maskilim,* Ahad Ha'am's call for the national movement to view its cardinal task as "preparing the hearts" of the people seemed more practicable than the alternative proposed by the founders of Hibbat Zion. Indeed, in 1894 to 1896, the "practical" reality as conceived by Hibbat Zion was largely irrelevant even to the leaders of the Odessa Committee. They too had to admit that the movement had become merely another charitable society, one among many, that looked after the farmers in its dozen colonies in Eretz Israel. Another element in the thought of Ahad Ha'am that gradually penetrated the consciousness of the Hibbat Zion leadership was the idea of transforming Eretz Israel into a "spiritual center" that would constitute the cultural core of the Jewish people. This idea seemed more realistic than the concept that took shape at the first Conference of Hovevei Zion, held in Kattowitz in 1884. Similarly, Ahad Ha'am's treatment of religion in its national context, an idea that evolved between 1893 and 1896, seemed more apt than other current solutions to the problems of secularization. His emotional call for the creation of a dynamic system that would effect changes in religious values, customs and rituals (which to a certain degree conflicted with his former stance concerning the place of religion in the national movement; clarifying his views, he explained that he had no wish to derogate the principles of Jewish ritual but rather sought to adapt Judaism to the flux of modern life) was readily welcomed by many *maskilim.* Thanks to the popularity of these ideas, a transformation was wrought in

Ahad Ha'am's public image. From being the head of a "fraction" espousing a socio-political platform, he became the leader of an ideological stream that aspired to bring about radical changes, a figure whose ideas the *maskilim* of Odessa, Warsaw and Saint Petersburg—not to mention Rabbi Eliasberg and the Lubavitcher Rebbe—were eager to hear, even if they did not always agree with what he said. Half of the wall posters of the Jerusalem *haredim* and of the "Defenders of the Faith" in Kovno were aimed at Ahad Ha'am and at Bnei Moshe, but this only testified to the enthusiastic reception that his program was enjoying among the public at large.

Yet just when it appeared that nothing could stand in the way of his accession to the political leadership of the national movement, Ahad Ha'am reverted, in 1896, to his role of opposition figure and national preacher—more the sounder of warnings than the leader. Paramount among the reasons for this turnabout was Herzl's appearance on the national political stage. The young and dynamic journalist from Vienna had succeeded in instilling in those around him the hope that the aspiration of Hovevei Zion would soon be realized and that the Jewish state was about to be established. For more than two years, all eyes were focused on Herzl. Only a few (such as Ahad Ha'am) found the courage to criticize him. The center of national activity shifted from Odessa to Vienna and Central Europe. Herzl's ideas and even more his deeds appealed to the overwhelming majority of Zionists. The fact that his doctrine bore an amazing resemblance to the ideas of his precursors in Hovevei Zion did not bother his multitude of followers. In their eyes, he was a leader capable of rendering the Zionist vision a reality. The convening of the Zionist Congress, Herzl's meetings with Abdul Hamid and other world leaders, the establishment of the bodies that formed the Zionist Organization—all these helped affirm Herzl's preeminence.

Herzl's meteoric rise had the effect of supplanting Ahad Ha'am, along with other Hibbat Zion leaders, from Eastern Europe. Suddenly, Zionist activity was directed from Central Europe. The *Ostjuden* whose situation was most urgently in need of amelioration looked to Vienna, of all places, for salvation. Personalities from the East, notably Ahad Ha'am, were shunted aside; during Herzl's seven active years, they were compelled to either swim in his current or serve as his opposition.

As Ahad Ha'am and his coterie in Odessa were being dislodged from their positions of influence in the national movement, the order of Bnei Moshe entered its final stages of disintegration. Founded by eight of Ahad Ha'am's followers in 1889, Bnei Moshe had become a political body numbering some two hundred persons, the cream of Hibbat Zion; through it, Ahad Ha'am had achieved his own position of prominence in the movement. With Herzl's initial successes, however, Bnei Moshe appeared to undergo a process of self-dissolution. It is thus not surprising that when Herzl achieved his decisive successes in the First Zionist Congress, Ahad Ha'am described Bnei Moshe as "an experiment that failed" and ordered its liquidation.

Herzl's ascendancy notwithstanding, it was not only his arrival that shattered the vision of Bnei Moshe's transformation into a vanguard that would lead the national movement to its manifest destiny. A major contributing factor to the erosion of

Ahad Ha'am's standing and his ouster from the movement's political leadership was his own complex psychological makeup.

From his youth, Ahad Ha'am had suffered from lengthy periods of severe mental depression in which he was gripped by pessimism and at times ceased to function altogether. These depressions were interspersed with brief periods of euphoria in which his perception of reality was no less flawed: At such times the world seemed to be at his disposal.

Ahad Ha'am's pessimism proved on occasion to be beneficial to his political aspirations—for example, in his early days in Hibbat Zion. As the movement's leading opposition figure, his piercingly critical intellect (exemplified in "This Is Not the Way" and the two articles titled "Truth from Eretz Israel") was a definite boon. This was again the case in 1903 to 1914, a period in which his influence had faded and he was subjected to numerous and frequent critical attacks. His acute perceptiveness was here a clear advantage. Ultimately, however, such a trait was self-destructive; instead of seeing events in their real light and then endeavoring like a politician to achieve the possible, Ahad Ha'am's dark vision often condemned him to inaction.

Even in his euphoric periods, Ahad Ha'am was prone to self-delusion in his reading of the political map—when the Odessa Committee was established (1890), during the Warsaw Conference (1898), in the period of the Russian Revolution (1905–1906) and even in the elections for the Tel-Aviv municipal council (1924). At such times his euphoria bordered on a feeling of omnipotence that was projected as well to those around him. Inevitably, however, Ahad Ha'am would find himself defeated and downtrodden politically, with euphoria giving way to severe depression.

Having succumbed to depression and its accompanying blanket pessimism, Ahad Ha'am was unable to take advantage of convenient political situations that would allow him to achieve desired positions of power. On many occasions, for example, he failed to exploit the strength of Bnei Moshe. He did not grasp the potential latent in the Zionist movement in Russia, was unable to mobilize his supporters in the Democratic Fraction (1902–1903) or the enthusiasm of the proponents of the Hebrew language (1913–1914), and could not even strengthen his political standing after being accorded the honorary title of "Elder" of the Zionists in Britain. In retrospect, a clear pattern was discernible: Whenever his supporters were yearning for a struggle—either behind him or for him—he cooled their ardor with rational arguments. But the impulse underlying these arguments generally derived from his unstable and pessimistic mental state.

After Ahad Ha'am entered political life, a myth sprang up around him that was closely bound up with the irrational aspect of his behavior. Admirers and opponents alike consistently refrained from even a mention of his unstable personality. Instead (with his full encouragement), they cited his exemplary character in explaining some of his actions: He did not wish "to dirty his hands" in "petty politics"; he stood "above" or "to the side"; his was a "prophetic voice." And yet Ahad Ha'am's supporters knew full well that the object of their adulation had given his energies and best years to political activity of virtually every stripe. He was constantly a member of bodies such as the Odessa Committee, the Technion Curatorium, the

Zionist Political Committee (in Britain) and dozens of other similar groups that afforded him the opportunity to intervene in the minutest details of nationalist politics.

This also accounts in part for the myth. With the exception of his close friends, few people were fully aware of Ahad Ha'am's erratic personality. His actions, some of which appeared illogical in retrospect, were explained as those of a man almost saintly in character. No wonder, then, that more than others Ahad Ha'am was regaled with superlatives that knew no bounds.

Beginning in 1896, Ahad Ha'am's political standing gradually declined. Nevertheless, he retained his stature as a morally authoritative political figure whose opinions could not be ignored. Occasionally his associates proposed him as a possible alternative to the existing leadership. In the period when the Democratic Fraction was being founded (1901–1902), during the Minsk Conference (1902), at the Cultural Congress (1909) and even when Chaim Weizmann's star began to rise, Ahad Ha'am was elected as a political leader—although as compared with the preceding period (1894–1896) his supporters now recognized that he was not made of the stuff that could lead the national movement.

However, it was precisely after his political fortunes had faded that Ahad Ha'am became the leader of a distinctive literary school and an authoritative literary arbiter. In the period in which he edited *Hashiloah* (1896–1902), the group of artists that formed his immediate circle—along with others outside that circle—regarded Ahad Ha'am, along with Mendele, as the premier literary authority not only of content but of form.

Ahad Ha'am's literary standing predated his editorship of *Hashiloah*. The literary principles he stressed in his articles and in the almanac he edited (*Kaveret*) would subsequently be dubbed the "Odessa Formula" and become a virtual guidebook to Hebrew literature. During the first seven years of his political activity, however, Ahad Ha'am's thought was devoted largely to power struggles in the movement. True, his essays were focused on the "Jewish problem" and some of them lacked the relevant political contexts, but he was not considered a philosopher or an intellectual sitting aloof and tutoring the nation. His public image was more closely associated with nationalist politics, and during this period his pronouncements generated reverberations because of the political controversies that attended them. A striking case in point: His attitude toward religion and its place in Israel was said to derive primarily from the fierce debate that raged between himself and the critics of Bnei Moshe and, later, the authors of the wall posters.

Another example, perhaps the outstanding one of this period, was his running dispute with Lilienblum. For three years (1890–1892), the two were engaged in a debate over the place and aims of the national movement. The controversy bolstered Ahad Ha'am's public image as a political leader who wished to revise the goals of Hibbat Zion and take his rightful place in the movement's leadership. It was only in retrospect that the public saw the controversy as an ideological polemic:[9] These two political figures had in fact been engaged in a struggle for control of the Jewish national movement via an appeal to public opinion.

Even at the height of his success, in the period in which he published his eight

"Peirurim" articles (1892–1894), the public's perception of Ahad Ha'am was not so much that of an articulator of a distinctive literary-philosophical school as of a political figure espousing original ideas who wished to radically change the Hibbat Zion movement. Furthermore, the East European *maskilim* accepted his positivist-nationalist doctrine as his own creation, even though the majority of his ideas had been borrowed from other thinkers of his generation from Russia and elsewhere, particularly Herbert Spencer, Joseph Ernest, Alex Renan and Michael Dobrlyuvov. Ahad Ha'am did not deny having drawn on these philosophers for many of his ideas, but it is likely that many of his contemporaries were unfamiliar with these European philosophers and therefore accorded him full honors for the positivist-nationalist ideology articulated in his articles. Another possibility is that credit was given to Ahad Ha'am not because his contemporaries were ignorant of the philosophy of Spencer or Renan, but because his was the first serious attempt to translate the positivist European national ideology into Hebraic terms. Hence the great enthusiasm and approbation for Ahad Ha'am's essays on the concept of a nation being an organic unit possessing a "soul" and "consciousness," and his argument that in periods of tension and crisis a people behaves in accordance with its character and the character of its surroundings. Ahad Ha'am applied these principles to the unique nature of the Jewish people and its place among the surrounding nations, presenting the concept in a form that was lucid, concise and logical.

As previously noted, Ahad Ha'am's literary standing came to its peak at a time when his political strength had begun to decline. As editor of *Hashiloah* between 1896 and 1902, he laid down a literary "formula" that was viewed by many as the definitive precept for *Haskalah* writers and poets of the time. At its heart the formula prescribed an almost exclusive preoccupation with Jewish subjects and an emphasis on the "afflictions of Judaism," a clarity of style and description with a thrust toward brevity and an almost mystical negation of all things romantic, with the stress placed instead on the rational, the logical and the judicious. Ahad Ha'am's tireless labors during this period gave *Hashiloah* its reputation as the greatest Hebrew journal of its time (it is still, perhaps, unrivaled). He edited the journal with infinite assiduousness; in his hands, the craft of editing became an art that some critics regarded as a creative work in itself. The finest writer of the generation, from Mendele and Bialik to Shalom Aleichem and Mordecai Zev Feuerberg, spared no effort to be published in *Hashiloah*. So immense was its success that at times only about a tenth of the manuscripts that reached the editor were actually published.

Yet just as Ahad Ha'am was being adulated as the supreme authority in Hebrew literature he once again withdrew, resigning as editor of *Hashiloah* in 1902. Once again, two reasons can be adduced for this withdrawal. The first is connected with his weariness with editing; the other—involving manifestations for which no rational explanation presents itself—derived, as in the past, from his mental problems.

In his own explanation, Ahad Ha'am pointed to the difficulties he had faced in constantly fighting for the journal's survival. However, there was also a less rational cause for his resignation that stemmed from his concern about the inroads made by his literary rivals, above all the supporters of M. Berdyczewski. Since the start of the century a growing preference had been discernible for the universalist ideas represented by the author of *'Orvah Paraḥ*. Gradually the attacks on Ahad Ha'am became more aggressive and his defenders dwindled in number. At the outset of the dispute between the two (1897), Ahad Ha'am was at the height of his powers, considered the exponent of a literary school, and gave little thought to his responses. Six years later, however, he already felt himself under attack and to some degree even defeated. His only desire was to get out of the business of literature.

The termination of his editorship of *Hashiloaḥ* coincided with the conclusion of Ahad Ha'am's period of prolific and influential creative output—just as seven years earlier, his political influence had waned. True, he continued to write and publish a number of important articles ("Moses," "The Summation"), some of which generated public discussion; all told, however, his image seemed to owe more to the myth that had been forged around him than to any concrete political or intellectual influence he still possessed. For this reason, it is not particularly surprising that in a letter to Ahad Ha'am written by Simon Dubnow (in July 1926!), the latter wrote that an entire generation had been educated in "his school, which stood 'at the crossroads' " and that under his guidance it had "found the road to our national revival."[10] Thus, the mythic, almost superhuman aura that had enveloped Ahad Ha'am even before 1902 was enhanced and took on ever-greater proportions as the years passed.

The dimensions of the myth can be grasped even in their most negative form: in the allegation of *The Protocols of the Elders of Zion* that Ahad Ha'am was the leader of the supposed "Elders of Zion"; and in the further accusation that he was the actual author of the *Protocols*.[11] The compilers of the tract depicted Ahad Ha'am as a demonic figure, hostile to world morality, whose word was law to the Israelites.

All this notwithstanding, Ahad Ha'am left his doctrine unsystematized. It was presented in his books in fragments, without order or continuity. After he organized his writings it was widely expected that he would systematize his ideas to form a clear and complete picture. But as the years went by, the very non-completion of his philosophical system became part of the Ahad Ha'am myth. Even his closest associates, such as Zalman Epstein and Simon Dubnow (who, from the beginning of the century, had frequently urged him to write his "great" book on Judaism so that the nation would see that he was the heir to Moses and Maimonides) changed their thinking ten or twenty years later when the myth was at its height, contending that there was no need for him "to complete the magnificent edifice" he had constructed. Others, Dubnow wrote Ahad Ha'am, would fill in what was missing and "it will eternally be called by your name."[12] Thus, according to Epstein, "our generation was privileged that you brought comfort to the whole nation," and thus "the generations to come will derive great pleasure from this rare and noble phenomenon, and it will be accorded an important place in the annals of the Jewish people."[13]

The myth of Ahad Ha'am was largely related to his public standing, his moral influence and the role that he played in the spiritual development of the time. As previously noted, both his lofty standing among the Jewish people and the legend that evolved around him were related to his ideology, combined with an extraordinary and not always explicable charisma that made Ahad Ha'am (in the words of Yehezkel Kaufmann) "a teacher, creator of a new philosophy, heir to the dynasty of the masters of Jewish thought, felt by his contemporaries to be an original and innovative thinker and guide."[14]

The Ahad Ha'am myth encompassed not only political behavior but his personal life, which was often depicted unrealistically—almost as if the mere perception of him as a moral and sublime figure was enough to prove his personal greatness.[15] It has already been noted that Ahad Ha'am's supporters not only virtually ignored his mental afflictions but usually found ways to explain them in a positive light. Similarly, his personal image, assiduously promoted both by Ahad Ha'am and by his supporters, was that of an unimpeachable personality, a veritable model for human morality whose ideological tenets were absolutely consistent with his domestic life.[16] There is no doubt that for the most part Ahad Ha'am's behavior and personality were truly unimpeachable, but like every human being, he had weaknesses. In his case, however, these were frequently concealed and obscured.

For this reason, the public never heard about Ahad Ha'am's serious problems with his children. If something nevertheless leaked out—such as the fact that his daughter had married a gentile—he tried to gloss over the situation to maintain his positive image, even at the expense of harming those closest to him. He followed the same pattern of behavior regarding other aspects of his domestic relations. A case in point was his use of Hebrew. At home, Ahad Ha'am rarely spoke Hebrew. His family correspondence was conducted mostly in Russian and Yiddish (alongside Hebrew). Yet he demanded that the public speak Hebrew, arguing that it was absolutely essential to cultivate the language.[17] When it became public knowledge that he himself spoke Russian in the streets of Tel-Aviv or wrote in English to a (Jewish!) government official, he had to come up with various, rather hypocritical excuses.[18]

The year 1902, a turning point in Ahad Ha'am's public life, paralleled a sharp change in East European cultural life that had a profound effect on Odessa. Until then the southern port city had been an influential center of the uniquely Russian form of *Haskalah*. But by the start of the new century, the synthesis that was articulated by Odessa's *maskilim,* one that emphasized the heritage of the Jewish past while binding it to the modern ethos, proved inadequate for the secular revolution experienced by the Jewish society. True, the values of Judaism remained deeply ingrained, but growing numbers desired reforms and modernization that were far more radical than anything contemplated by the Odessa *maskilim.*

For about ten years, Ahad Ha'am had been the luminary of the earlier cultural development. He set its norms and determined its parameters, delineated related spheres and vested them with ideological validity. Hence his importance to his contemporaries. Once this ideology filtered down to diverse popular strata, however, additions and revisions were called for. The demand was for a synthesis between the "Odessaite" *maskilic* philosophy and the cosmopolitan Jewish culture that called for a further diminishment of religion (which would leave only the faintest hints of the new culture's affiliation with Judaism). In this state of affairs, it was incumbent on Ahad Ha'am to make way for other luminaries. Such persons were in fact at hand; Berdyczewski and his coterie would henceforth influence the nationalist perceptions in Hebrew literature.[19] The creative Jewish cultural center shifted from Odessa to Warsaw, Berlin, even New York. Slowly "Odessa" and its secular "formula" became obsolete. Here, perhaps, is a further explanation for Ahad Ha'am's abandonment of direct involvement in literature. Consciously or not, he understood that he must leave the stage to others. He had already made his contribution; others would now have their turn.

Following his departure from *Hashiloah*, Ahad Ha'am devoted most of his time to administrative work in the Wissotzky tea company, first as a controller and later as a company official in London. Most of his waking hours were spent in the company's offices, and in his leisure time he served on a number of public and political committees, most notably the Technion's Curatorium. Yet the public's impression was that he was still engaged in creative endeavors. This phenomenon can perhaps fully explain the "scandals" and controversies of which he was the center during the period from 1903 to 1912. Those involved in the disputes over Ahad Ha'am's publicistic writing constituted a broad spectrum of writers, journalists and functionaries who considered Ahad Ha'am an authoritative and extremely influential figure in the national movement; as time passed, his detractors seemed to grow ever more furious. An observer of these disputes might well have had the fleeting thought that they did not involve an exhausted, elderly man who had long lived with his frustrations to the point where he had almost ceased writing, but rather someone young, full of energy and eager for a good fight.

The "Altneuland affair" (1902) marked the onset of this period in Ahad Ha'am's life. This episode, in which Max Nordau set out (at Herzl's behest) to settle accounts with the person who had dared criticize the Herzlian utopia, was the first controversy in which Ahad Ha'am found himself in a clearly defensive position. If until then he had felt that he enjoyed broad support and that his adversaries (such as Lilienblum and Berdyczewski) were in large measure wary of denigrating him, henceforth it seemed as though everyone wanted to undermine his position. Most of the "scandals," as mentioned, developed as a result of his articles; a few revolved around his political activity. The peak was reached in the "scandal" that erupted after he demanded the cessation of support for the publication *Hapoel haza'ir* because of the publication of an article by Yosef Hayim Brenner—the "Brenner affair," as it was later dubbed.

Yet in retrospect it appears that, despite the scathing criticism, even these "scandals" worked to strengthen the myth surrounding Ahad Ha'am. From around the time of the First World War's final stages, Ahad Ha'am seems to have become a near-superhuman figure. Near the end of his fifties, just when he felt his days were numbered, his public image was of a person with a magnificent record of achievements. In time the harsh criticism was forgotten, and only the legend remained. Its zenith came in the honor that was accorded him during his residence in Tel-Aviv, most notably in the celebrations of his seventieth birthday;[20] the eulogies at his funeral and the panegyrics of ten and twenty years later;[21] the monuments erected in his memory; and the fact that virtually every political group that took itself seriously—from the moderate Brit Shalom[22] to Hapoel Hazair[23]—inserted "Ahad Ha'amist" motifs into its platform. Activists such as Joseph Klausner[24] and Zev

Jabotinsky[25] also adopted part of Ahad Ha'am's doctrine and identified their own groups with him.

Yet as the years passed, the myth of Ahad Ha'am was gradually chipped away. The generation that had proudly declared itself to be the bearer of his philosophy disappeared. Few and far between were the intellectuals (such as Gershom Scholem),[26] statesmen (such as Chaim Weizmann),[27] poets (such as Bialik) or philosophers (such as Martin Buber[28] or Hugo Bergman)[29] who would now assert with pride that Ahad Ha'am had, for example, been "a teacher who shows the way and carves out the path, a man of truth and a master of erudition."[30] Neither could there be found an Israeli government department to aver that "Ahad Ha'amism in its supremely pure form" would henceforth serve as the "basis for [Hebrew] education."[31] From about the mid-1960s, "Ahad Ha'amism" became almost a negative concept, or at best another slogan in Zionist terminology. Thus, from being a figure around whom a myth had been forged in his own lifetime—a myth that had grown even more powerful in the first decade or so after his death—Ahad Ha'am's very name had all but disappeared for the generation of the 1970s and 1980s. Some vague, lingering memory perhaps remained of his image, into which a handful of historians, intellectuals and sometimes politicians occasionally tried to breathe life.

Paradoxically, however, at the very time that "Ahad Ha'amism" has all but been consigned to oblivion and the person and his doctrine have given way to other myths, the ideology he propounded has proven more applicable than most to the existential reality of the state of Israel. Herzl's total Zionism did not prove itself workable in the past, and there is nothing to indicate that it will do so in the future. The same can be said of the other Zionist "isms," from the socialist Zionism propounded by Nahman Syrkin and Ber Borochov, to Jabotinsky's "iron wall," all of which have succumbed to the reality of the Israeli experience. The diaspora in the Herzlian sense has not been liquidated, and neither has an egalitarian Judaism emerged that would ingather the Jewish masses either of their own volition (Syrkin) or through its implacable force (Borochov).

On the other hand, Ahad Ha'am's doctrine had been realized. The image of the state of Israel as a nation and spiritual center for the Jewish people is today an irrefutable fact. The historical reality has proven that "Ahad Ha'amism" is practicable. Even if there are more Jews in the United States than in Israel—and even if the Jews almost universally identify as an integral part of the diaspora country in which they reside—Israel nonetheless constitutes, whether consciously or unconsciously, an additional source of self-identity. Herein lies the explanation, for example, of the commitment of American Jews to Israel and the material, political and psychological support they offer the Jewish state, even though their integration in the American society is now an incontrovertible fact.[32] Hence as well the sudden upsurge of Zionist-national consciousness among tens of thousands of Soviet Jews (and those in other countries) when Israel was endangered during the Six-Day War.

These examples point to the development of an increasing identity between Jewishness and nationality, an identity that Ahad Ha'am perceived to be the primary goal of Zionism in its initial stages. A theory that was propounded in its general lines more than a century ago has been implemented and become almost banal, while its author, by a paradox of history, has been consigned to near oblivion.

Notes

1. Cf., for example, B. Z. Mossensohn, *Ketuvim* 1, no. 23 (6 Jan. 1921).

2. Cf., for example, *Ha'aretz*, 9 Jan. 1927.

3. Mossensohn, *Ketuvim* 1, no. 23 (6 Jan. 1921).

4. *Ibid.*

5. *Hapo'el haza'ir* 14 (1927), 4.

6. Letter from Hayim Nahman Bialik to Simon Rawidowicz, 24 January 1927, in P. Lakhover (ed.), *Letters of Bialik,* vol. 3 (Tel-Aviv: 1938), 177.

7. Ben-Zion Dinur, *Ahad Ha'am and His Historic Enterprise* (pamphlet) (Jerusalem: 1945).

8. Cf., for example, Simon Dubnow, *Kniga zhizni* (Riga: 1934), 238.

9. Cf., for example, S. Braiman's literary-ideological analysis, "Hapulmus bein Lilienblum levein Ahad Ha'am veDubnow," *Shivat ziyon* (annual [1950]), 138–168.

10. Letter from Simon Dubnow to Ahad Ha'am, 28 January 1926, in National and University Library (hereafter NUL) 4-791/103.

11. Cf., for example, *Ha'aretz*, 31 May 1923.

12. Letter from Dubnow to Ahad Ha'am, 28 July 1926 in NUL 4-791/103.

13. I. A. Epstein, "Adam vihudi," *Hashiloah* 27 (1914), 246ff.

14. Y. Kaufmann, "'Ikarei dei'otav shel Ahad Ha'am," *Hatekufah* 24 (1934), 421–439.

15. Cf., for example, S. Schiller, "Ahad Ha'am," *Hagalil* (annual [1939]), 111–137.

16. Cf. S. Rosenfeld, "Reb Asher ba'al hamusar," *Hadoar* 40 (1926), 772.

17. Cf., for example, Ahad Ha'am's article "Revival of the Spirit" in his *At the Crossroads* (Jerusalem: 1965), 167–177.

18. Cf., for example, Ahad Ha'am's letter to *'Al hamishmar,* 13 February 1923, in NUL 4/791/1738.

19. Cf. G. Shaked, *Hamahazeh ha'ivri hahistori bitkufat hatehiyah* (Jerusalem: 1970), 43.

20. Cf., for example, *Hadoar* 40 (1926), 774.

21. Cf., for example, M. Glickson, "Ahad Ha'am," in *Kitvei M. Glickson,* vol. 2 (no ed. named), (Tel-Aviv: 1981), 146–196.

22. Cf., for example, *Sheifoteinu* 2, no. 6 (Fall 1931), 185–186.

23. Cf. *Hapo'el haza'ir,* 5 January 1927.

24. *Avukot,* 7 January 1932.

25. Zev Jabotinsky, "Ahad Ha'am," *Avukot* (1932), 4–5.

26. Gershon Scholem and Walter Benjamin, *Sipurah shel yididut* (Tel-Aviv: 1987), 33.

27. Chaim Weizmann, *Masa uma'as* (Jerusalem and Tel-Aviv: 1927), 42–43.

28. Martin Buber, *Ha'olam* 3 (1927).

29. H. Bergman, "Aharei moto shel Ahad Ha'am," *Moledet* 9, 162–166.

30. Buber, *Ha'olam* 3 (1927).

31. E. Shvadron, "Bimei haahad ha'amiyut," *Moznayim* 36 (165) 49, 1933.

32. For another view, see Chaim Waxman in this volume, 134–149—Ed.

Jewish Scholarship and Jewish Identity: Their Historical Relationship in Modern Germany

Michael A. Meyer

(HEBREW UNION COLLEGE, CINCINNATI)

While the development of modern Jewish scholarship and the formulation of various modes of modern Jewish identity have both been popular subjects of study, they have usually been treated separately.[1] Only a few studies have dwelt on their relationship, and those only within the context of a relatively brief period; as yet consideration has not been given to a longer view. How did these two elements of modern Jewish history relate to one another over a span of time sufficient for the perception of change? This article examines the question by focusing upon the development of *Wissenschaft des Judentums* in Germany from its inception in the early nineteenth century until the eve of the Holocaust. As it will become evident, modern Jewish scholarship was variously perceived as undermining, ignoring or revitalizing Jewish identity. Moreover, not only did Jews recognize the far-reaching significance of the relationship; Christians did as well, and they responded accordingly. To trace the relationship between Jewish scholarship and Jewish identity, then, is to gain a significant perspective from which to view both the external and the internal history of Jews in modern Germany.

Both of the concepts to be dealt with here are modern in origin. Identity, in the psychosocial sense in which it is relevant for the present subject, has become a popular tool of analysis only in this generation, largely through the theoretical work of Erik Erikson. Studies of personal and collective identity have gained popularity at a time when crisis and confusion attend individual maturation and hinder the formation of group self-definition. But for the Jews, the identity question did not await the twentieth century. They were forced to confront it as they emerged from a physical and spiritual ghetto into a non-Jewish environment that was deeply ambivalent about taking them into its midst, and that to varying degrees demanded they alter the identity that had characterized them in the past. Hitherto, turned inward both by exclusionary pressure from the outside and by their own religiously grounded sense of superior worth, Jews had not needed to mark off their Jewishness; they possessed no non-Jewish identifications. Only when they began to feel that they were Europeans or Germans as well as Jews did Jewish identity become problematic.

Even more obviously does scientific scholarship enter Jewish history only in modern times, despite the fact that it has its analogues in traditional Judaism. Jews, of course, have always given great honor and respect to their scholars, and even during medieval times they were characterized by an extraordinary degree of male literacy. But there is a vast difference between study, *talmud torah* (or in Yiddish and German, *lernen*), on the one hand, and Wissenschaft des Judentums, on the other. To study the classical texts is a religious commandment in Judaism; it is *melekhet shamayim* (literally, the work of heaven).[2] Such study was for a clearly defined purpose—to discern the will of God speaking through the text of Torah and Talmud—and thus the sanctity of the house of study, Moses Maimonides noted in the twelfth century, exceeds even that of the synagogue.[3] The truth was understood to reside in the text itself, not in the mind or methodology of the scholar. Modern Wissenschaft, in contrast, brought to Jewish scholarship a critical element that was not inherent within its own tradition. It separated the present from the past and introduced the concept of development. To varying degrees, it also secularized what had previously been regarded as wholly sacred. Not surprisingly, it was soon perceived as a grave threat to the faith of those who were most traditional; a threat that extended, moreover, to their very identity as religious Jews.

For other Jews more receptive to the intellectual world of the nineteenth century, the application of scientific scholarship to Judaism in the form of critical historical research became a necessary means for assuring the survival of Judaism outside a ghetto. These Jews believed that Wissenschaft des Judentums could liberate them from the old ways and suggest new paths more compatible with modernity; while unbinding the old ties, it would rebind with new ones. Yet even among non-Orthodox Jews, Wissenschaft des Judentums raised doubts and fostered disputes with regard to its consequences for Jewish identity. By the beginning of the twentieth century it had become the object of severe critique not only by Orthodox Jews but also by some of the scholars themselves, by proponents of religious revival and by Zionists. As for Christian scholars, with few exceptions they viewed it all along with mistrust, or else sought to use it for the purpose of weakening Jewish identity. The relationship between Jewish scholarship and Jewish identity was thus both complex and ambiguous.

In focusing on Wissenschaft des Judentums, it is important to recall that the initial assault upon the untroubled identity of premodern Jews actually arose from the Haskalah, the Jewish response to the German Aufklärung. It was in the age of Moses Mendelssohn (1729–1786) that the most acculturated German Jews were forced into the realization that their traditional way of life conflicted with their aspirations to be accepted and to feel at home in gentile society. That society was now more willing to accept them into its midst as Jews—provided they would give up most of the ties of solidarity that had bound them together until then. Mendelssohn had argued that Judaism, properly understood, did not conflict with the tenets of the Enlightenment, that it was in fact more rational and tolerant in its beliefs than was Christianity. Therefore, he argued, commitment to the ideals of the Enlightenment need not damage loyalty to Judaism. But Mendelssohn, like most men of the Enlightenment, did not think in historical categories. It was not until two generations later, when historical consciousness came to replace rationalism as the key to understanding human reality, that scientific historical study rather than the reconciliation of Judaism with reason became the crucial task for those who sought a means of justifying the persistence of Judaism in the modern world.

The group of young men who formed the Verein für Cultur and Wissenschaft der Juden in 1819 were convinced that science, broadly conceived, was the principal intellectual characteristic of the modern age. In order to survive in this milieu, Jewish identity had to be made consistent with it. The canons of critical scholarship taught in German universities, where a number of them were students at the time, would have to be applied to the sources of Judaism. One result would be a clearer understanding that Judaism had changed over the centuries: that in its present configuration the pristine idea of Judaism lay hidden beneath later accretions. The overthrow of rabbinism and the emergence of religious reform would be a necessary and important product of Wissenschaft. As Immanuel Wohlwill put it in the opening article of Leopold Zunz's *Zeitschrift für die Wissenschaft des Judenthums* (1822): "The freer, scientific attitude forces its way through the weed-infested underbrush of ceremonialism, grown mechanical and mindless through millenia of habit—and it perceives, still present within, the same divine idea, just as it had once clearly revealed itself."[4] So too, it was believed, the political emancipation of the Jews in Germany, which had been set back during the period of reaction following the defeat of Napoleon, would gain renewed impetus from objective studies of the Jews. But although the members of the Verein thus considered carefully what they regarded as the beneficent practical effects that the new Jewish scholarship would have on Jewish life, what they sought above all else was to show that Wissenschaft and Judaism were not intellectually incompatible—an aim that recalled Mendelssohn's earlier efforts to reconcile Judaism and rationalism.

It was the immediate goal of the Verein to raise Judaism to the level of Wissenschaft, which, according to Wohlwill, was "the standpoint of European life." Only on this level could Judaism survive in the modern world. But Wissenschaft was first of all criticism. To employ its tools meant to undermine the unity and sanctity of Jewish tradition. Its first stage was necessarily demolition. Only once the building, which had been constructed on a foundation that could not withstand critical analysis, crumbled could some of its bricks be used to build a new structure on more durable foundations.

German Jewry, however, was by no means agreed that Judaism required a new lodging built by Wissenschaft. As the seeds planted by the Verein began to sprout in critical studies and in scholarly institutions during the course of the nineteenth century, Wissenschaft des Judentums represented for some a force that shored up Jewish identity and made it viable for modern Jews. But for others it was a force that needed to be severely kept in check. Untrammeled, they feared, Wissenschaft would run rampant over all that Jews held sacred.

At one end of the spectrum stood those modern Jews whose limited internalization of modernity excluded Wissenschaft des Judentums entirely. German Jews who were adherents of the Neo-Orthodoxy of Samson Raphael Hirsch welcomed both the opportunity to become German patriots and the literary culture that Germany and Europe offered them. But they rejected vehemently any and every attempt to apply the tools of historical criticism to those sources that constituted the religious foundations of Judaism. The revelation contained in Torah and Talmud remained by its very nature beyond the reach of literary or historical analysis: It was by definition and unassailably God's word. Hirsch did believe there was a legitimate *jüdische Wissenschaft,* but what he meant by the term when he used it positively was not the application of the same scientific criteria to Jewish sources that others had applied to the sources of ancient Greece or Rome. He meant rather the uniquely *Jewish* Wissenschaft that had been practiced by Jews throughout the millennia; in fact, nothing other than a continuation of *talmud torah,* the reverent study of the sacred texts.

But Hirsch was not one to be satisfied with defending the bastion of tradition. He sallied forth as well to do battle with modern scholarship over its own objectives. He argued that, if Wissenschaft des Judentums had hoped to rescue Jewish identity from the forces of assimilation, it had failed badly. Whereas *lernen* had been everyone's Jewish task (or at least that of male Jews), Wissenschaft des Judentums was necessarily elitist. Its influence was limited to those few who engaged in it and the not much larger circle that read the scholarship they produced. The true Jewish scholarship, Hirsch argued, had been a *Wissenschaft des Lebens,* a living scholarship; it had taught traditional Jews how to lead their lives and it was also the *Wissenschaft der Juden* in the sense that it belonged uniquely to Jews. What modern scholarship might have accomplished—that is, giving new form to the old conceptions—it had failed or refused to do, instead calling the religious conceptions themselves into question and thereby undermining Jewish faith, the only basis for Jewish identity.

But the most pernicious effect of Wissenschaft des Judentums, according to Hirsch, was that it legitimized abandonment of Orthodoxy. He wrote of critical scholars in 1862: "In all of this they see only the all too welcome scholarly legalization of the break with Jewish law that in practice they undertook long ago for themselves and their children."[5] In other words, Wissenschaft des Judentums was a palliative for guilty consciences. Or, put more kindly: Even when Wissenschaft only raised doubts, without drawing conclusions, its effect was to influence parents to withhold their children from traditional Jewish education. Because it suspended commitment it broke the transmission from one generation to another. Or, put yet another way, the new form of study, unlike the old, did not complement religious acts; it replaced them. For some of the scholars, Wissenschaft des Judentums had become the principal basis of their Jewishness. For them the practice of Judaism itself had become secondary to studying *about* Judaism through the alien lens of Wissenschaft. For Hirsch, the result was at best a vicarious Jewish identity. The new scholars no longer recited the religious poetry of the synagogue; they only studied it.

Hirsch and his supporters were especially fearful of Wissenschaft des Judentums at its most conservative, for then its pernicious influence was difficult to detect. In 1859, for example, Zacharias Frankel had published his *Darkhei hamishnah,* an important scholarly work on the ancient rabbis. Though showing great respect for the ancient sages, Frankel had ventured the view that, despite the explicit insistence of the Talmud, there were laws in the Mishnah that did not originate at Sinai but were innovations of the rabbis themselves. From the Orthodox point of view, such questioning of the revelational status of the Oral Law was tantamount to undermining the foundations of traditional Judaism and therefore abetting the erosion of Jewish consciousness.[6] To the eyes of the Orthodox, the Jewish Theological Seminary in Breslau, headed by Frankel since its creation in 1854, was a particularly insidious source of contamination for German Jewry. Its teachers and students were generally observant of the rabbinic commandments no less than of those in the Pentateuch—but in accepting historical criticism of rabbinic texts, they had created a cleft between belief and practice that was bound to widen.[7]

The Orthodox camp itself, however, was not entirely monolithic, and Wissenschaft des Judentums was not rejected out of hand by all Orthodox scholars. Ezriel Hildesheimer, who in 1873 became the first director of the Rabbinical Seminary for Orthodox Judaism in Berlin, believed that Torah and Wissenschaft could exist side by side. Although Hildesheimer and his colleagues never questioned the Sinaitic origins of the Written and Oral Law, they produced scholarly historical writings, published critical editions and compiled bibliographies. Hildesheimer's associate, David Hoffmann, was even willing to cite the work of non-Orthodox scholars and to allow that the form of the Mishnah—though not the content of its laws—was determined by the ancient rabbis themselves. The Orthodox rabbinic seminary in Berlin thus allowed a discipline foreign to Judaism to enter rabbinic training. Much criticized on that account by Hirsch, its faculty represented the most liberal position in German Orthodoxy.[8]

Wissenschaft had a firmer hold at the Jewish Theological Seminary in Breslau. Frankel himself humanized the talmudic literature, while his colleague, the historian Heinrich Graetz, freely emended the verses of Psalms. Yet Frankel drew the line at Pentateuch criticism. The Five Books of Moses remained beyond the grasp of Wissenschaft, a kernel of direct divine revelation that Frankel would not allow to be dissected into disparate sources. Insulated from the more open atmosphere of the university, the Breslau seminary let in as much Wissenschaft as Frankel and his colleagues believed would enhance its status and strengthen Judaism, while shutting it out from the inner sanctum, which they believed had to remain inviolate. The seminary employed on its faculty only men who were in basic agreement with Frankel's conception of Judaism,[9] and its statutes specified that if a teacher left the standpoint of positive and historical Judaism or "taught in a manner that endangered the above mentioned point of view" he was subject to dismissal without compensation.[10] Scholarship without faith, Frankel was convinced, would lead in Germany, as it had in ancient Alexandria, to the complete loss of Jewish identity.[11]

Yet Frankel also believed that Wissenschaft, properly applied, was absolutely essential to Jewish survival in that it could reveal the inner life of the Jews, their spiritual activity through the generations, thus creating a bridge between past and present. Without scholarship, he wrote, there could be no Judaism, for "it decays when the love of its scholarly study disappears."[12] Not surprisingly, Frankel's own writings and those published in the renowned *Monatsschrift für Geschichte und Wissenschaft des Judentums* during the years that he was its editor concentrated on the inner, religious history of the Jews, especially as revealed in the rabbinic literature—an area of research that stressed those elements that made the Jews unique and provided the basis for their continuing religious separateness in Germany.[13]

In focusing on religious history, the Conservative Frankel followed much the same path as did Abraham Geiger, the most important intellectual leader of the Reform movement in Germany and one of the greatest modern Jewish scholars. Like Frankel, Geiger saw himself as a theologian and the task of Wissenschaft des Judentums as principally theological. His research as well sought to reveal the spiritual creativity of the Jews, to rehabilitate the reputation of the Pharisees from the distorted image presented in the New Testament and to provide a more variegated historical basis for a religious Jewish identity.

Where Geiger differed from Frankel was in his willingness to apply Wissenschaft to all Jewish texts, even to the Pentateuch, and in his intentional use of it for the purpose of religious reform. Although he claimed never to depart from the canons of unprejudiced historical scholarship, Geiger freely admitted that, unlike most other scholars, "I was always concerned to study thoroughly the kernel [of Judaism] and to draw results from it for reform."[14] For Geiger, Wissenschaft des Judentums demonstrated the historical flexibility of Judaism and hence the possibility of reshaping it once more in a manner that could sustain Jewish identity in the modern world.[15]

The overtly present-minded religious rationale for Wissenschaft des Judentums, shared by Frankel and Geiger though differently understood by them, is almost absent in the later work of Leopold Zunz, perhaps the foremost of all nineteenth-century Jewish scholars. After his early disappointment with religious reform and a brief failed attempt to serve as rabbi for the progressive segment of the Jewish community in Prague, Zunz increasingly withdrew to Wissenschaft des Judentums as a kind of refuge from the present. He disliked the use of Jewish scholarship for the purpose of advancing particular religious conceptions, whether by Jews or by Christians. In his *Zur Geschichte und Literatur* he wrote in 1845: "Our Wissenschaft therefore needs first of all to emancipate itself from the theologians and raise itself to the level of historical understanding."[16] Jewish scholarship became for Zunz an end in itself: To be a Jewish scholar was his way of being Jewish. Increasingly, as he grew older, Zunz occupied himself with the Jewish past almost to the exclusion of contemporary Jewish affairs. He ceased to read Jewish newspapers. He knew well the work of the medieval Jewish poet Kalir but was not familiar with the poetry of Y. L. Gordon, the leading Hebrew poet of his own time.[17] His most fervent wish was to see Wissenschaft des Judentums gain entry into a German university where it could flourish freely, unaffected by the sectarian purposes of rabbis and seminaries.

Zunz's extraordinarily erudite disciple, Moritz Steinschneider, went even further in dissociating Jewish scholarship from Jewish identity. Steinschneider's scholarly concern was to show the cultural influence of Jews in Islamic lands during the Middle Ages by bringing to light their long-forgotten works. It was recognition of the Jewish contribution to Western civilization by the scholarly world that Steinschneider sought, not any internal Jewish goal.[18] Consisting of dry data, his works lacked historical imagination and were virtually unreadable. But

Steinschneider took pride in the fact that they were wholly untendentious and free of all sentimentality. In an age of positivist historiography, he held high the ideal of objectivity, of "pure" research uncontaminated by present-minded considerations. He refused to join the faculty of any Jewish institution or become a member of any Jewish scholarly association. For him, as for Zunz, Jewish scholarship in a purely Jewish setting meant the creation of a new intellectual ghetto.[19]

However, the German academic establishment would not allow Jewish scholarship to expand from Jewish institutions into the fully public sphere of the university. Not only did it refuse to grant it the status of a recognized discipline, those gentile scholars who dealt with its subject matter did so in a manner that could only discourage Jews from identifying with their tradition. Internal Jewish ambivalences about critical scholarship were thus complicated by the negative verdict upon Judaism passed by leading non-Jewish scholars.

Zunz and Steinschneider both longed for a professorship at a German university. Zunz repeatedly petitioned the Prussian government to create such a position but to no avail. He was especially hopeful in 1848, when he believed that the prevalent liberal spirit would make it possible. But the reply he received used the newly created political situation as an argument against such a position:

> A professorship that would be established with the ulterior motive of supporting and strengthening the Jewish organism in its particularity, in its alienating laws and customs, would contradict the purpose of the new freedom that levels stubborn differences. It would mean a special concession to the Jews, an abuse of the university.[20]

In other words, Jewish scholarship could not be allowed to enter the University of Berlin lest its presence there serve to perpetuate a differentiated Jewish identity in Germany. Zunz, perforce, remained a *Privatgelehrter,* a scholar consigned to working on his own.[21]

Of course, German universities could not ignore Jewish studies entirely. Hebrew and Old Testament were well established in theological faculties, and in the nineteenth century there was also increasing interest in postbiblical Jewish literature. Yet scholars who dealt with the literature of the Jews, such as Julius Wellhausen and Friedrich Delitzsch, denigrated the object of their study—and sometimes also the reputations of Jewish scholars outside the universities whose learning exceeded their own.[22] The most vicious such scholar was the antisemitic orientalist at the University of Göttingen, Paul de Lagarde. Although he and his students perforce drew heavily upon the works of the Jewish scholars, they attacked them for overvaluing the objects of their research. Zunz was a particular target of their venom; according to Lagarde, he and other Jewish scholars demanded "admiration for things that, like the poems of the Jewish Middle Ages translated by Zunz and Zunz's translation itself, fill us either with irresistible sarcasm or with disgust."[23]

Similarly, the German historian Heinrich von Treitschke attacked the last volume of Heinrich Graetz's *History of the Jews* (1870) because its author had evaluated his material by internal Jewish standards rather than by the German criteria Treitschke himself employed when he dealt with such figures as Heinrich Heine and Ludwig Börne. Graetz had indeed written his history to implant deeper identification in his

Jewish readers, just as Treitschke's *German History* (7 vols., 1915–1919) was intended to inspire greater German loyalty. Yet although their romantic historiography was remarkably similar, Graetz could not effectively defend his views against the Berlin professor, and even fellow Jews turned against him for his alleged Jewish chauvinism.[24]

Where antisemitism was absent among Christian scholars of Judaism, missionary intent took its place. Hermann Strack, professor of oriental languages at the University of Berlin, was a friend of the Jews who had defended them against the ritual murder libel. But when he founded the Institutum Judaicum at the university in 1883, his purpose was not only to advance scholarship but also to win Jews over to Christianity. In a lecture he delivered in 1906, Strack attempted to reveal the basis of Jewish loyalty to their faith so that it would be easier to undermine it.[25] The Institutum Judaicum founded by Franz Delitzsch at the University of Leipzig three years earlier served similar purposes.

Thus, Jews who studied at German universities found their religion represented either by antisemites or by missionaries. The German university was prepared to weaken Jewish identity, but in no way to sustain it. The hope of gaining recognition for Jewish practitioners of Wissenschaft des Judentums by the German academic establishment was repeatedly disappointed throughout the nineteenth and early twentieth centuries. Only here and there was a Jewish scholar allowed to give a course or two without benefit of a regular professorship.[26]

By the beginning of the twentieth century Wissenschaft des Judentums in Germany was clearly in decline. Its greatest scholars had passed from the scene. It remained outside the universities and, of most immediate significance, the connection between Wissenschaft and Jewish identity had become ever more tenuous. Jewish scholars were mostly following the paradigm of Zunz and Steinschneider. They dwelt on minutiae at the expense of exploring larger ideas and concepts; an obsession with uncovering new facts had replaced the original scholarly endeavors to discover the Jews' inner spirit. Looking back upon the evolution of Wissenschaft des Judentums even as early as 1879, Ludwig Philippson wrote: "If we look more closely at the course of its development down to the present, we will have to admit to ourselves that in fact it became only historical research and this historical research, in turn, became microscopic."[27] It was felt that Wissenschaft des Judentums was far more concerned with what clothing the medieval commentator Rashi might have worn than with the content of his writings.

Heinrich Graetz's history had been exceptional. Its popular style had won entry for it into thousands of Jewish homes, and in translations its influence had spread throughout the Jewish world.[28] Although deficient in methodology and objectivity, it had linked scholarship with identity more effectively than any other single work. But by the end of the nineteenth century no equivalent works were being produced. Jewish scholarship had become an elite occupation, not in the sense that its practitioners enjoyed a high degree of prestige but because they wrote in such a specialized and recondite fashion that only those few who shared their background and interest could fully appreciate and derive benefit from their work. Jewish scholars had adopted the standard to which Max Weber called attention in a famous lecture:

"Today any truly definitive and sound achievement is always—a specialized achievement."[29] In seeking to meet the standards of scholarship, Wissenschaft des Judentums had almost completely severed its link to Jewish life. It was wholly determined by its object, not by the subjective desires of those who engaged in it.

In the period after the First World War, criticism of this conception of Wissenschaft des Judentums emerged from three independent sources. It came first of all from within its own circle of scholars. The historian Ismar Elbogen, who taught at the Hochschule für die Wissenschaft des Judentums in Berlin—the Jewish institution most open to theologically unconstrained scientific research—fully accepted the universal standards of scholarship, noting that "the special character of our scholarship results only from the material, not from the method or mentality of the scholars." But he also declared of Wissenschaft des Judentums:

> Even though it considers the most careful historical and philological treatment of the sources and determination of the facts among its tasks, it does not engage in these for their own sake nor in order to revive dead literary monuments, but rather to reveal the foundations on which the present can be built. Its goal is and remains *living Judaism*. That must be the focal point at which all the rays are aimed, the leading idea that ties a unifying bond around the multiplicity of sources and scholarly inquiries.[30]

Elbogen argued for what he called a "reorientation of our scholarship,"[31] by which he meant redirecting scholarly endeavor from adducing new (but relatively insignificant) facts to uncovering roots in the Jewish past that would strengthen Jewish identity in the present.

A second source of criticism came from the small circle of Jewish intellectuals who were seeking to revive religious faith and commitment to Judaism among those Jews most estranged from Jewish life. The leading spirit in this group was the Jewish theologian Franz Rosenzweig. Whereas Steinschneider had held the view that the task of Jewish scholarship was simply to recover the Jewish past, scholarship and education being two distinct areas of activity,[32] Rosenzweig argued that "the teacher and the scholar must be the same person."[33] Speaking at the opening ceremony for the Freies Jüdisches Lehrhaus, the institute for adult study that he established in Frankfurt in 1920, Rosenzweig deliberately reintroduced the premodern term *lernen*.[34] In his view, Wissenschaft des Judentums had proven its inadequacy to sustain Jewish identity: Specialized scholarly works would not bring the highly assimilated Jews of Germany back to Judaism. That goal could be achieved only by leading them gradually back to the center, to the basic texts of the Jewish religion.

Lernen, Rosenzweig maintained, was the proper mode of such study, although it had to be informed by Wissenschaft rather than employing the old uncritical method of the yeshivah. Rosenzweig proposed an Akademie für die Wissenschaft des Judentums whose members would be both scholars and teachers. Shortly thereafter, such an academy did come into existence, and although it did not fully correspond to Rosenzweig's concept, the goal of its various scholarly projects was similar. As the historian of Jewish philosophy Julius Guttmann set it forth, the task of the academy was to lead back to the sources of Jewish life: not to indicate a particular direction but to create self-understanding; not to engage in apologetics or edification but to reveal "the force and content of Jewish spirit and life."[35] Jewish scholars increasingly turned their attention to the history of Jewish philosophy, seeking to analyze and interpret the systematized expressions of the Jewish spirit. They repeatedly called upon the Jewish community to support their work, which they saw as serving the purpose of Jewish survival.[36]

The most severe critique of Wissenschaft des Judentums came from the Zionists. As early as 1902, the foremost proponent of cultural Zionism, Ahad Ha'am, had complained that Jewish scholarship had become only a "monument to our spiritual enslavement."[37] Later, a fellow Zionist, the great scholar of Jewish mysticism Gershom Scholem, made a similar point by quoting a remark attributed to Steinschneider: "The only task we have left is to provide the remnants of Judaism with a worthy burial."[38] Rather than erect memorials, the Zionists sought to revive the dead, and Zionism in Germany soon began to make use of Wissenschaft des Judentums for its own ideological purposes.

In 1904, the sociologist and Zionist leader Arthur Ruppin published a book entitled *The Jews of Today*. Expanding the scope of Wissenschaft des Judentums to include statistical demographic studies, Ruppin set out to show that Jewish identity in the diaspora was progressively eroding and would soon disappear entirely. His tables demonstrated that the modern religious identity that Geiger and Frankel had sought to shape through Wissenschaft des Judentums had been unable to withstand the pressures of assimilation. In fact, it had abetted assimilation through its secularization of the sacred literature.[39] Ruppin pointed to the increasing number of apostasies, dissociations from the Jewish community and mixed marriages. Although few Central and West European Jews were willing to admit it, only the influx of Jews from the East had prevented their numbers from diminishing severely. Since few Jews were willing to give up modern culture, the only basis for continued Jewish identity, he believed, was a national one distinguished by ethnic unity and common language. In Ruppin's hands, Wissenschaft des Judentums became diagnosis, prognosis and remedy—all from a Zionist perspective.

Yet Zionism also shared in large measure the positive program set forth by Elbogen and by Rosenzweig. Scholem later defined its purpose as "the recognition of our own character and history," and beyond that "to fathom what is alive in Judaism; in place of antiquarian literary history, to undertake a phenomenologically penetrating, objective examination."[40] In fact, that goal was not unlike the one initially set forth—but not fully achieved—by the founders of Wissenschaft des Judentums in Germany more than a hundred years earlier.

During the Weimar period, Jewish scholarship also enjoyed a slightly more favorable reception in German universities. At the recently founded university in Frankfurt, Martin Buber taught as honorary professor for general religious studies, and Nahum Glatzer received a teaching assignment in Jewish religious studies and Jewish ethics. Other universities employed Jewish scholars on a part-time basis.[41] In Berlin, a most amazing transformation of attitude to Jewish scholarship occurred in 1925 when a prominent biblical scholar at the university, Hugo Gressmann, took over the Institutum Judaicum three years after the death of Hermann Strack. Under its new director the institute was wholly divested of any missionary intent. But Gressmann went further, beyond toleration to an extraordinary respect for the integrity of Jewish tradition. He believed that there were valuable insights regarding the inner spiritual life of the Jews that Jewish scholars, knowing their tradition from within, would be uniquely able to offer students at the university. He was persuaded that "true objectivity always presumes love, and for that reason the Jewish scholar always has an advantage with regard to the Jewish religion; necessarily, he must know it better than the Christian scholar." Moreover, Gressmann insisted, to study Judaism was to deal with a religion that "has proven itself to be a living force down to the present time." Gressmann organized a series of lectures under the auspices of the institute in the academic year 1925/1926 in which leading Jewish scholars were called upon to convey the dynamics of Jewish religious creativity for Christians as well as for Jews. In introducing the series, he explicitly asked that his listeners regard these lectures "as a recognition of Jewish scholarship."[42] Until his early death in 1927, Gressmann was also a member of the governing body of the Pro-Palästina Komitee, a group of Christian supporters of Zionism.

For German Jewry the reassessment of Wissenschaft des Judentums by Jews and by gentiles came late in its history. There was not sufficient time for it to influence Jewish identity. Nazism introduced its own Wissenschaft des Judentums in the form of *Rassenforschung*, and, one by one, the Nazis closed down the institutions of Jewish learning. In 1936, the Zionist Jewish newspaper *Jüdische Rundschau* sent a set of questionnaires to Jewish scholars concerning the state and future of Jewish scholarship in Germany. The replies testified to a state of crisis. One scholar after another was finding refuge outside of Germany; there were "deeply felt gaps." Nevertheless, Viktor Aptowitzer wrote from Vienna: "It is a Jewish obligation to prevent Jewish scholarship from perishing in Germany." And Ismar Elbogen in Berlin replied resolutely:

> It is clear that the severe emotional convulsion that we contemporary Jews have experienced must also affect scholarship. It alters one's mental attitude, pushes certain problems to the fore. But it must not impinge upon the goal of all scholarship, the search for truth.[43]

Only a few years later Wissenschaft des Judentums would come to an end in Germany when the Hochschule (now demoted to the rank of Lehranstalt) für die Wissenschaft des Judentums, the last Jewish scholarly institution allowed to operate, was forced to close in 1942 and its last teacher, Leo Baeck, was deported to Theresienstadt.

Was the German Jewish experience typical for other Jewries? Certainly the erosive effect of historical criticism upon Jewish belief, and hence upon Jewish religious loyalty, affected all Jews who encountered it. What differed was the percentage of Jews exposed to its canons: in Russia, a relatively small proportion during the nineteenth century; in the West, nearly all Jews. Moreover, in Eastern Europe at the turn of the century, the solution for modernizing Jews more frequently entailed the substitution of a secular Jewish identity for a religious one, whereas in Germany, religion and critical scholarship were harmonized in one manner or another. In addition, the especially large role that scholarship played in German culture made the issue of its relationship to Judaism more important than elsewhere; it could not be pushed aside.

The situation of contemporary Jewry in the United States differs sharply. For the first time in the diaspora, Jewish scholarship is amply represented—by Jews—in the universities, and this at a time when upwards of 90 percent of young Jews receive higher education. If Jewish scholarship, as practiced by both Jews and non-Jews in Germany, served to undermine and to alter as well as to sustain Jewish identity, it would seem that in the United States it is now in a position to strengthen it greatly. But if it does so, it will be through those forms of accommodation that emerged in response to the earlier challenges first presented in Germany.

Notes

1. A somewhat different version of this article in the German language was delivered as a lecture in October 1989 at a symposium sponsored by the Hochschule für jüdische Studien in Heidelberg, and is scheduled for publication in a volume of its proceedings.

2. Cf. Isador Twersky, *Introduction to the Code of Maimonides* (New Haven and London: 1980), 170–171.

3. See his *Mishneh Torah,* hilkhot talmud torah 4:9.

4. Leopold Zunz, *Zeitschrift für die Wissenschaft des Judenthums* 1 (1822), 15–16.

5. Samson Raphael Hirsch, "Wie gewinnen wir das Leben für unsere Wissenschaft?" *Jeschurun* 8 (1862), 89.

6. Gottlieb Fischer, "Herrn Dr. Z. Frankel's hodogetisches Werk über die Mischnah," *Jeschurun* 7 (1861), 197–198.

7. Esriel Hildesheimer, "Harav 'Azriel Hildesheimer zaẓal 'al Rav Zekhariyah Frankel zal uveit-hamidrash lerabanim bebraslav," *Hama'ayan,* Tishrei 5713 (1952), 65–73.

8. Mordechai Breuer, "Hokhmat yisrael: shalosh gishot ortodoksiyot," in *Jubilee Volume in Honor of . . . Joseph Soloveitchik* (Jerusalem and New York: 1984), vol. 2: 856–865; idem, *Jüdische Orthodoxie im Deutschen Reich 1871–1918* (Frankfurt: 1986), 168; David Ellenson and Richard Jacobs, "Scholarship and Faith: David Hoffmann and His Relationship to *Wissenschaft des Judentums,*" *Modern Judaism* 8 (Feb. 1988), 27–40.

9. M. Brann, *Geschichte des jüdisch-theologischen Seminars in Breslau* (Breslau: 1904), 48–52.

10. *Statut für das jüdisch-theologische Seminar, Fraenckel'sche Stiftung* (Breslau: 1854).

11. Zacharias Frankel, "Ueber palästinische und alexandrinische Schriftforschung," *Programm zur Eröffnung des jüdisch-theologischen Seminars,* 10 August 1854 (Breslau: 1854), 42.

12. Zacharias Frankel, "Einleitendes," *Monatsschrift für Geschichte und Wissenschaft des Judentums* (hereafter, *MGWJ*) 1 (1852), 5.

13. Ismar Schorsch, "The Emergence of Historical Consciousness in Modern Judaism," *Leo Baeck Institute Year Book* 28 (1983), 429.

14. *Nachgelassene Schriften* 2 (Berlin: 1875), 27.

15. For more detail see Michael A. Meyer, "Jewish Religious Reform and Wissenschaft des Judentums: The Positions of Zunz, Geiger and Frankel," *Leo Baeck Institute Year Book* 16 (1971), 19–41.

16. Leopold Zunz, *Zur Geschichte und Literatur* (Berlin: 1845), 20.

17. Paul Mendes-Flohr (ed.), *Hokhmat yisrael* (Jerusalem: 1979), 26.

18. Moritz Steinschneider, "Die Zukunft der jüdischen Wissenschaft," *Hamazkir: Hebraeische Bibliographie* 9 (1869), 76–78.

19. Gotthold Weil, "Moritz Steinschneider," *Jüdische Rundschau* 8 (Feb. 1907), 53–55.

20. S. Maybaum, "Die Wissenschaft des Judentums," *MGWJ* 51 (1907), 655. The faculty, in its report to the minister, also noted that the presence of a chair for Wissenschaft des Judentums might have the undesirable effect of attracting more Jewish students to the univer-

sity. L. Geiger, "Zunz im Verkehr mit Behörden und Hochgestellten," *MGWJ* 60 (1916), 340.

21. The resentment Jewish scholars felt at their exclusion despite superior knowledge is evident in David Kaufmann, "Die Vertretung der jüdischen Wissenschaft an den Universitäten," in his *Gesammelte Schriften*, vol. 1, ed. M. Brann (Frankfurt: 1908), 14–38.

22. Michael A. Meyer, *Response to Modernity: A History of the Reform Movement in Judaism* (New York: 1988), 202–204.

23. Paul de Lagarde, "Lipman Zunz und seine Verehrer," *Mittheilungen* 2 (Göttingen: 1887), 159–160. So, too, one of Lagarde's students found it necessary to write of Zunz in his doctoral dissertation: "The continual admiration of one's own people seems unjustified." Ludwig Techen, *Zwei Göttinger Machzorhandschriften* (Göttingen: 1884), 17. David Kaufmann came to the defense of Zunz with his "Paul de Lagarde's jüdische Gelehrsamkeit," in his *Gesammelte Schriften*, 207–257.

24. Michael A. Meyer, "Heinrich Graetz and Heinrich von Treitschke: A Comparison of their Historical Images of the Modern Jew," *Modern Judaism* 6 (Feb. 1986), 1–11.

25. See Hermann L. Strack, *Das Wesen des Judentums. Vortrag gehalten auf der Internationalen Konferenz der Judenmission zu Amsterdam* (Leipzig: 1906). Strack also reviewed Techen's work favorably. Excerpts from his review are in Kaufmann, "Paul de Lagarde's jüdische Gelehrsamkeit," 213.

26. Alfred Jospe, "The Study of Judaism in German Universities Before 1933," *Leo Baeck Institute Year Book* 27 (1982), 295–319.

27. *Allgemeine Zeitung des Judentums* 43 (1879), 706–707.

28. Ismar Elbogen, "Hokhmat yisrael: sekirah," in *Devir: Maasaf 'iti lehokhmat yisrael* 2 (annual [1923]), 12.

29. Max Weber, *Wissenschaft als Beruf* (Munich and Leipzig: 1919), 10.

30. Ismar Elbogen, "Ein Jahrhundert Wissenschaft des Judentums," *Festschrift zum 50 jährigen Bestehen der Hochschule für die Wissenschaft des Judentums in Berlin* (Berlin: 1922), 142.

31. *MGWJ* 62 (1918), 84.

32. M. S. Charbonah [Moritz Steinschneider] (ed.), *Herev be-tsiyon oder Briefe eines jüdischen Gelehrten und Rabbinen über das Werk Horev* (Leipzig: 1939), x.

33. Franz Rosenzweig, "Zeit ists . . . Gedanken über das jüdische Bildungsproblem des Augenblicks (1917)," in his *Kleinere Schriften* (Berlin: 1937), 73.

34. Franz Rosenzweig, "Neues Lernen: Entwurf der Rede zur Eröffnung des Freien Jüdischen Lehrhauses," in *ibid.*, 94–99.

35. Julius Guttmann, "Jüdische Wissenschaft: Die Akademie für die Wissenschaft des Judentums," *Der Jude* 7 (1923), 489–493.

36. See, e.g., Hermann Vogelstein, "Das liberale Judentum und die jüdische Wissenschaft," *Liberales Judentum* 9 (1917), 61–65.

37. Ahad Ha'am, "Die Renaissance des Geistes," in his *Am Scheidewege* 2 (Berlin: 1916), 124.

38. Gershom Scholem, "Wissenschaft vom Judentum einst und jetzt," in his *Judaica* (Frankfurt: 1963), 152–153, based on *Jüdische Rundschau* 8 Feb. 1907, 54.

39. Arthur Ruppin, *Soziologie der Juden*, vol. 2 (Berlin: 1931), 185.

40. Scholem, "Wissenschaft vom Judentum einst und jetzt," 148, 163–164.

41. Jospe, "The Study of Judaism in German Universities Before 1933," 311–312.

42. Hugo Gressmann (ed.), *Entwicklungsstufen der jüdischen Religion* (Giessen: 1927), 1–12. On Gressmann and on the participation of Jewish scholars in the second edition of *Die Religion in Geschichte und Gegenwart*, see Leonore Siegele-Wenschkewitz, "The Relationship Between Protestant Theology and Jewish Studies During the Weimar Republic," in Otto Dov Kulka and Paul Mendes-Flohr (eds.), *Judaism and Christianity Under the Impact of National Socialism* (Jerusalem: 1987), 143–147.

43. *Jüdische Rundschau* 41, no. 27/28 (3 April 1936), 9–10.

The Impact of Jewish Education and an "Israel Experience" on the Jewish Identity of American Jewish Youth

David Mittelberg

(UNIVERSITY OF HAIFA)

Introduction

The contribution of Jewish education to Jewish identity is the subject of debate among scholars. Steven M. Cohen,[1] for example, has challenged the conclusions of two earlier researchers, Geoffrey Bock[2] and Harold Himmelfarb,[3] that part-time Jewish education is no better than none, and perhaps even worse, in terms of its impact upon Jewish identity. Cohen's findings are that part-time Jewish education does have a positive influence on its alumni, especially with regard to religious practice, though it has a somewhat lesser influence on levels of community affiliation and none upon friendship patterns. These relationships became stronger, Cohen found, when denomination, gender, home background and the number of hours of education were controlled for.

The primary goal of the present analysis is not to settle this scholarly debate but rather to go beyond it by examining two basic issues: First, the circumstances under which Jewish education (both part-time and day school) has an impact on Jewish identification; and second, the role of a visit to Israel as an independent factor making its own unique contribution to Jewish identity *beyond* both denomination and Jewish schooling.

Research Focus and Methodology

The first part of this present study is based on data derived from the 1985 Demographic Study of the Combined Jewish Philanthropies of Greater Boston (CJP), which surveyed 1,446 Jewish adults over the age of 18.[4] In order to eliminate the confounding effects of age and generation, the analysis presented here deals only with respondents under the age of 35, thus holding these variables constant. An additional reason for the age cutoff is that personal experience of Israel, the major focus of this paper, became a major option for diaspora youth only after the Six-Day War.[5]

In contrast with other studies, those who gave no response to questions about Jewish education, rather than being excluded from the analysis, were regarded as not having received any Jewish education. However, Orthodox respondents *were* excluded from this analysis, on two grounds. First, the subsample of Orthodox Jews under the age of 35 consisted of only eleven cases—far too small a sample for parametric analysis, especially when one wants to control for gender. Second, the use of "Jewish religious practice" as an index of Jewish identity becomes almost tautologous in the case of Orthodox respondents. Following these exclusions, the final sample consisted of 559 Jewish adults aged 18–35, of whom 47 percent were men and 53 percent women.

The data analyzed here are cross-sectional, which limits our ability to establish conclusively causal relationships. Nevertheless, the statistical methods utilized are sufficiently discriminating to establish the relative weights of the factors being analyzed. For the purposes of our study, Jewish education was divided into four types: none; Sunday school; afternoon school; and day school, with respondents classified according to the most intensive type that they had ever received as children. Visit to Israel was recorded by means of a simple dichotomous variable, namely, had the respondents ever visited Israel or not. Finally, as is common among sociologists of Jewish life, two different indexes of Jewish identification were employed, one measuring Jewish religious practice and the other, Jewish community affiliation.

Jewish Education and Jewish Identification

In Steven Cohen's 1988 study, it was found that women generally had less formal Jewish education than men, that those with more intensive Jewish education scored higher on the Jewish identity indexes than those with less education—though to a significant degree such differences paralleled those of home environment and parental observance—and that Jewish education had a more powerful impact on Jewish religious practice than on Jewish communal affiliation. Afternoon school graduates, as a whole, did not score higher on Jewish identity than those with no Jewish education at all. However, when men and women were analyzed separately and when controls were introduced for parental background, Cohen found that afternoon school alumni had higher scores on measures of Jewish identity than those with no Jewish education.[6] These conclusions will now be critically reexamined, controlling for gender and respondents' denomination, the latter a reasonably reliable surrogate for other background variables not contained in the CJP data, such as the level of religious observance and ritual practice in the parental homes of the respondents.

Among Boston respondents under the age of 35, the incidence of Jewish education itself is, overall, somewhat influenced by gender differentiation, with men generally manifesting higher rates of attendance than women (Table 1). However, while gender differentiation is not significant for the Conservative Jews in this sample, it is very significant for Reform Jews and somewhat significant for the nonreligious.

Among the Conservative, men and women report nearly the same rates of atten-

Table 1. Jewish Education by Denomination and Gender

Jewish Education	Conservative (N = 168)			Reform (N = 237)			Nonreligious (N = 135)			All (N = 540)
	All	M	W	All	M	W	All	M	W	
None	4	1	5	17	11	23	31	24	36	16
Sunday school	10	14	7	22	12	32	20	18	19	18
Afternoon school	72	70	74	58	74	43	48	57	43	60
Day school	15	15	14	NS	NS	NS	NS	NS	NS	6
Total (%)^a	100	100	100	100	100	100	100	100	100	100
	Chi Sq. = NS			Chi Sq. = 24.73; D.F. = 3; p < .001			Chi Sq. = NS			

^{a}Totals here and elsewhere may not add up to 100 percent because of rounding.

dance for afternoon and day schools, though the rate of Sunday school attendance is somewhat higher for men (14 percent) than for women (7 percent). For Reform Jews, in contrast, the rate for more intensive afternoon school attendance (day school rates were too low in the sample to be computed) was significantly higher among the men than among the women (74 vs. 43 percent). Gender differentiation was also significant in the rate of Sunday school attendance. Here, however, Reform men showed a lower rate of attendance than did the women (12 vs. 32 percent). Similarly, a higher percentage of Reform women reported receiving no Jewish education at all (23 percent, compared with 11 percent of the Reform men). Among the nonreligious, the rate of attendance at Sunday school was virtually the same for men and women (18 and 19 percent, respectively); however, men were more likely than women to attend afternoon school (57 vs. 43 percent), while women were more likely than men to report having no Jewish education (36 vs. 24 percent).

The results in Table 1 clearly point to denominational differences in addition to gender differences. As previously noted, denomination is being used here as the major independent variable serving as surrogate for home and other background variables not available in the Boston data set.[7] Such a research strategy is further warranted by the relationship between home background as reflected in the denominational affiliation of the respondents' parents and their own denominational affiliation, as shown in Table 2.

While the Boston data do not allow sufficient room for detailed parametric analysis, Table 2 suggests that a high proportion of the parents of Conservative respondents are themselves Conservative (80 percent), to which might be added the 10 percent of children of Orthodox parents. Among the Reform, only two-thirds have Reform parents, with most recruits coming from the Conservative movement. Finally, among the nonreligious, only one-third report having nonreligious parents, though just under 50 percent claim to have Reform parents and another 21 percent report Conservative parentage.

Table 2. Frequency Distribution of Denomination of Respondents' Parents, by Respondents' Denomination

Parent's Denomination	Respondents' Denomination					
	Conservative		Reform		Nonreligious	
	Father	Mother	Father	Mother	Father	Mother
Orthodox	11	10	4	1	1	5
Conservative	81	78	25	26	22	22
Reform	4	8	64	65	46	45
Nonreligious	1	1	3	5	28	23
Other	3	3	4	3	3	5
Total (%)	100	100	100	100	100	100
N =	(165)	(164)	(242)	(241)	(139)	(140)

These figures reflect both considerable intergenerational denominational continuity, on the one hand, and noticeable intergenerational denominational change, on the other hand. Overwhelmingly, the direction of denominational change is "down" the denominational rank order—from Orthodox to Conservative to Reform to nonreligious with very little "upward" movement. In general, any analysis of the degree of variance within denominations with regard to religious practice must take intergenerational denominational change into account. This is somewhat complicated by the absence of background data about the denominational auspices under which the respondents received their Jewish education, of whatever type. If the schooling was within the framework of the parents' denominational affiliation, the effect of intergenerational denominational change might be to heighten rather than weaken the lasting effects of Jewish education, if any, because those who changed denomination received their education in a more highly identified denominational framework. Nevertheless, the impact of denominational change may, in fact, be in the opposite direction—toward the modal pattern of the current denomination rather than that of the respondents' parents.

In addition to level of Jewish education, the Boston survey also measured respondents' Jewish religious practices and level of Jewish community affiliation. (These two indexes, it will be recalled, are used to define the level of Jewish identification.) Tables 3 and 4 show the results, analyzed by denomination.

Table 3, a religious practice index, consists of a constellation of standard ritual practice items that are common to previous studies. The findings shown here are similar to the data reported by others, including Cohen,[8] with the most frequently performed rituals being Passover seder (78 percent), Hanukah candles (73 percent) and Yom Kippur fast (59 percent). Having a mezuzah is less common (40 percent), and kashruth observance (11 percent and 13 percent) and synagogue attendance of at least once a month (10 percent) are low. As might be predicted, for all of these items Conservative Jews have the highest rates of performance, followed by Reform Jews with a lower, but median, score and then by nonreligious Jews.

Table 3. Jewish Religious Practice Index, by Denomination

	All		Conservative		Reform		Nonreligious	
	%	N	%	N	%	N	%	N
Seder	77.5	559	90.3	171	81.0	248	55.7	140
Separate dishes	10.6	555	27.6	170	1.8	247	5.6	138
Kosher meat only	12.7	552	28.8	171	5.6	247	5.3	135
Hanukah candles	73.0	557	92.6	171	79.7	246	37.1	140
Shabbat candles	12.9	553	29.9	171	7.0	242	2.5	140
Mezuzah	40.3	559	74.5	171	33.4	248	10.7	140
(No) Xmas tree	77.8	557	90.4	171	74.2	246	68.7	140
Yom Kippur fast	59.4	557	90.5	171	57.6	246	24.5	140
Attend synagogue at least once a month	9.6	559	19.5	171	6.4	248	2.9	140

Index reliability = .74

Table 4, a community affiliation index, measures the connectedness and commitment of Jews to their community, both in behavior and in attitude. The items include synagogue membership (24 percent), which among all denominations is higher than is attendance, though the pattern of membership follows the same denominational order as attendance. Jewish community center membership, which is especially low (12 percent), probably as a result of the respondents' relatively young age, also follows the same denominational pattern. However, the percentage of those contributing to the CJP is identical for Conservative and Reform Jews (19 percent), compared with only 5 percent among nonreligious Jews. The proportion of those having mostly Jewish friends is similar among Conservative and Reform Jews (33 percent and 27 percent, respectively) but much lower for the nonreligious Jews (10 percent). The greatest difference between Conservative and Reform Jews is that of attitude to

Table 4. Jewish Community Identification Index, by Denomination

	All		Conservative		Reform		Nonreligious	
	%	N	%	N	%	N	%	N
Synagogue member	24.4	599	49.0	171	18.7	248	4.2	140
JCC member	11.6	559	21.1	171	7.3	247	7.5	140
Most friends are Jewish	25.4	557	27.9	171	32.6	246	9.7	140
Very or somewhat negative feelings if child would intermarry	42.5	545	74.7	166	37.1	241	13.4	139
Contribution to CJP	15.8	551	19.3	165	19.5	246	5.3	140

Index reliability = 0.67

Table 5. Jewish Education and Level of Religious Practice

Jewish Education	Low	Medium	High	Total (%)	N
None	59	37	4	100	84
Sunday school	37	58	5	100	98
Afternoon school	22	62	17	100	316
Day school	7	63	30	100	33
All	30	57	13	100	531

Chi Sq. = 64.67; D.F. = 6; p < .001

a child's intermarriage. While 75 percent of Conservative Jews under the age of 35 express negative feelings toward such a prospect, only 37 percent of Reform Jews and 13 percent of nonreligious Jews similarly object.

The frequency distribution of these computed indexes, while controlling for Jewish education, is found in Tables 5 and 6. Overall, the indexes indicate a higher rate of religious identification than of community affiliation—though with regard to the latter, responses tend more toward a bipolarity (i.e., more responses at the extremes). The data presented in Table 5 show clearly that Sunday school has a greater effect on Jewish ritual practice than no Jewish education, afternoon school has a greater effect than Sunday school and day school the greatest effect of all (despite the small N of day school alumni throughout the analysis, it is presented here because it conforms to the pattern). The percentages are statistically significant. Those without any Jewish education score the lowest on this index—59 percent with a low level of religious practice compared with 30 percent of all respondents—and this ratio is reversed as the degree of Jewish education increases. In the Jewish community affiliation index of Jewish identification (Table 6), exactly the same pattern repeats itself: Although only 17 percent of the total score high on this index, afternoon and day school alumni have high levels of 22 percent and 30 percent, respectively.

In Table 7, the relationship between Jewish education and level of religious practice is examined within each denomination. While this analysis is somewhat limited by the small N's of the Jewish education subsamples in each denomination,

Table 6. Jewish Education and Level of Jewish Community Affiliation

Jewish Education	Low (%)	Medium (%)	High (%)	Total (%)	N
None	57	38	5	100	85
Sunday school	45	48	7	100	97
Afternoon school	36	43	22	100	312
Day school	15	55	30	100	31
All	39	44	17	100	525

Chi Sq. = 34.4; D.F. = 6; p < .001

Table 7. Jewish Education and Level of Jewish Religious Practice, by Denomination

Jewish Education	Conservative					Reform					Nonreligious				
	Low (%)	Med. (%)	High (%)	Total (%)	N	Low (%)	Med. (%)	High (%)	Total (%)	N	Low (%)	Med. (%)	High (%)	Total (%)	N
None	—	—	—	—	4	44	48	8	100	40	79	20	1	100	40
Sunday school	6	73	21	100	17	39	59	2	100	52	52	47	1	100	29
Afternoon school	6	60	34	100	122	27	66	8	100	132	42	56	2	100	62
Day school	4	57	39	100	25	NS	NS	NS	—	6	NS	NS	NS	—	2
					168					230					133

Chi Sq. = NS   Chi Sq. = NS   Chi Sq. = 15.86; D.F. = 6; p < .05

Table 8. Jewish Education and Level of Jewish Community Affiliation, by Denomination

Jewish Education	Conservative					Reform					Nonreligious				
	Low (%)	Med. (%)	High (%)	Total (%)	N	Low (%)	Med. (%)	High (%)	Total (%)	N	Low (%)	Med. (%)	High (%)	Total (%)	N
None	—	NS	—	—	6	38	56	6	100	41	86	9	1	100	39
Sunday school	17	54	29	100	15	44	51	5	100	52	61	39	0	100	28
Afternoon school	10	57	33	100	115	41	38	21	100	130	71	26	3	100	67
Day school	12	62	26	100	22	NS	NS	NS	—	6	NS	NS	NS	—	2
					158					229					136

Chi Sq. = NS (Conservative)

Chi Sq. = 18.37; D.F. = 6; p < .01 (Reform)

Chi Sq. = NS (Nonreligious)

the relationship between the degree of intensity of Jewish education and higher levels of religious practice is preserved within all three denominations, although the actual percentages cover a wide range. For example, the percentage of afternoon school alumni with a medium score varies from 56 percent of the nonreligious to 66 percent of the Reform. Moreover, 34 percent of the Conservative are at the high end of the scale, while 42 percent of the nonreligious are at the low end. In the overall analysis, there is no statistically significant relationship between Jewish education and religious practice for the Conservative and Reform. Thus, it can be hypothesized that Jewish education reflects *denominational practice* rather than the other way around.

Similarly, Table 8 shows no statistical difference between different levels of Jewish education on Jewish community affiliation in both the Conservative and the nonreligious subgroups. Only among the Reform (where 21 percent of afternoon school alumni score high on this index) is there a statistically significant relationship.

Table 9 examines the role of gender in mediating between Jewish education and religious practice. Within both genders, alumni of afternoon and day schools score higher on religious practice than do alumni of Sunday school and those without Jewish education. Among women only, the incremental difference between Sunday school and no Jewish education is negligible. This finding seems likely to be affected by home life or denomination, a hypothesis that will be considered below.

It has just been demonstrated that, when denomination is held constant, a relationship between Jewish education and Jewish religious practice was found only in the case of the nonreligious (Table 7); with respect to community affiliation, it was found only in the case of the Reform (Table 8). By way of contrast, Table 9 demonstrates that there *is* a statistically significant relationship between Jewish education and the indexes of Jewish religious practice when men and women are analyzed separately, a finding that confirms Cohen's analysis.

As seen in Table 10, Jewish education seems to have a far weaker influence on the community affiliation scores of men than of women: The bare statistical significance that holds for men derives from the positive high extremes of afternoon and

Table 9. Jewish Education and Level of Religious Practice, by Gender

	Men					Women				
Jewish Education	Low (%)	Med. (%)	High (%)	Total (%)	N	Low (%)	Med. (%)	High (%)	Total (%)	N
None	82	18	0	100	27	45	49	6	100	54
Sunday school	27	70	3	100	37	40	54	6	100	57
Afternoon school	26	65	9	100	174	15	58	26	100	143
Day school	0	80	20	100	15	11	47	42	100	19
					253					273

Chi Sq. = 41.2; D.F. = 6; p < .001   Chi Sq. = 37.02; D.F. = 6; p < .001

Table 10. Jewish Education and Level of Jewish Community Affiliation, by Gender

Jewish Education	Men					Women				
	Low (%)	Med. (%)	High (%)	Total (%)	N	Low (%)	Med. (%)	High (%)	Total (%)	N
None	44	51	5	100	27	58	37	5	100	56
Sunday school	45	53	2	100	37	47	42	11	100	57
Afternoon school	40	42	18	100	168	31	44	25	100	145
Day school	6	66	28	100	13	21	48	31	100	18
					245					276
		Chi Sq. = 15.11;					Chi Sq. = 21.84;			
		D.F. = 6; p < .05					D.F. = 6; p < .001			

day school alumni. Among women, however, there seems to be a strong and significant relationship between the level of Jewish education and the level of community affiliation. Is this really a gender issue? The answer is only partly yes, since in Tables 11 and 12, where denomination is controlled, the effects of gender are once again limited. As seen in Table 11, 35 percent of Conservative women have a high score on the Jewish community affiliation index as compared with 7 percent of Reform women and 1 percent of nonreligious women. However, overall differences between the genders tend to be somewhat narrower—indeed, there is no statistical difference between the genders among Reform and Conservative respondents, though there is a slight difference among the nonreligious respondents on the community affiliation index (Table 11), where 35 percent of the men have a medium or high score, compared with 17 percent of the women.

With regard to religious practice (Table 12), more Conservative women than men have a high score (44 percent vs. 17 percent). In other denominational subgroups, however, the differences between genders is negligible, indeed statistically insignificant. It may be of some interest to report that of the 44 percent of Conservative women with a high level of religious practice, 16 percent had Orthodox fathers and 13 percent Orthodox mothers, a fact that may also account for their higher level of observance.

To date, the evidence analyzed here generally supports Cohen's thesis that Jewish school education does have some impact on Jewish identity. But we are also in a position to go beyond Cohen's analysis and examine evidence on an additional important question, namely, the educational impact of a visit to Israel and its relative weight among the various elements of Jewish education that have been dealt with so far.

The Israel Experience

In June 1984, leaders and educators from thirty-one countries met at the First World Leadership Conference on Jewish Education held in Caesarea, Israel. The con-

Table 11. Gender and Level of Jewish Community Affiliation, by Denomination

	Conservative					Reform					Nonreligious				
	Low (%)	Med. (%)	High (%)	Total (%)	N	Low (%)	Med. (%)	High (%)	Total (%)	N	Low (%)	Med. (%)	High (%)	Total (%)	N
Men	8	68	24	100	68	44	41	15	100	113	65	30	5	100	67
Women	12	53	35	100	92	28	65	7	100	124	83	16	1	100	65
					160					237					132

Chi Sq. = NS   Chi Sq. = NS   Chi Sq. = 6.54; D.F. = 2; $p < .05$

Table 12. Gender and Level of Jewish Religious Practice, by Denomination

	Conservative					Reform					Nonreligious				
	Low (%)	Med. (%)	High (%)	Total (%)	N	Low (%)	Med. (%)	High (%)	Total (%)	N	Low (%)	Med. (%)	High (%)	Total (%)	N
Men	5	79	17	100	70	35	61	4	100	119	50	48	2	100	67
Women	6	50	44	100	99	28	65	7	100	117	55	44	1	100	61
					169					236					128

Chi Sq. = 15.00; D.F. = 2; p < .001

Chi Sq. = NS

Chi Sq. = NS

205

ference affirmed that Jewish identity was in crisis and that Jewish education was the appropriate response to that crisis. It was also agreed that the "Israel experience" was a central means by which diaspora Jewish education could be enriched on a large scale, both in quality and in scope.

"Israel experience" refers to a plethora of educational programs—formal and informal—that are based primarily in Israel. The duration of any given program is from less than a month to up to a year or more. In 1985, it was estimated by Annette Hochstein that some 41,500 participants were enrolled in approximately four hundred Israel experience educational programs. "These participants," she notes, "divided up into three main categories: 19,000 participants in informal programs and study; 15,000 participants in formal educational Yeshiva, high school, and universities; and 7,600 participants in work or other volunteer programs. Sixty percent of participants were aged 18–30."[9] These participants came to Israel with a plurality of motivations, the most important of which were (in order) the desire to visit Israel's historical and archaeological sites; spend time with Israelis; and study (in decreasing order of importance) Hebrew, Judaism and politics. The Boston data do not deal with the Israel experience per se, but rather with *any* visit to Israel. In the Boston survey, 30 percent of the respondents under the age of 35 reported having visited Israel at least once, a figure that is in line with the national data cited by Cohen.

In Table 13 responses to the question "Have you been to Israel?" were analyzed by denomination and gender. Among the Conservative, 40 percent reported at least one visit to Israel, compared with 25 percent of the Reform and nonreligious. However, gender is much less relevant. Among Conservative Jews, both men and women visit Israel at the same rate. Among Reform and nonreligious Jews, women were slightly more likely than men to have visited Israel, but even here, the differences are not statistically significant.

The data found in Tables 14 and 15 reflect the finding that any visit to Israel, even one, is correlated with a higher score both on Jewish religious practice and on Jewish community affiliation. Although a causal relationship between visits to Israel and heightened level of Jewish identity cannot be conclusively derived from this cross-sectional data, the possibility of such a relationship is certainly indicated. More specific findings, by denomination, are shown in Tables 16 and 17. Concerning religious practice (Table 16), a visit to Israel is shown to have no statistically significant effect on Conservative Jews; among the Reform and nonreligious, how-

Table 13. Israel Visit, by Denomination and Gender

Any Visit to Israel	Conservative			Reform			Nonreligious			All
	All	M	W	All	M	W	All	M	W	
No	61	61	60	75	77	73	75	79	74	70
Yes	39	39	40	25	23	27	25	21	26	30
Total (%)	100	100	100	100	100	100	100	100	100	100
		N = 171			N = 248			N = 140		N = 559
		Chi Sq. = NS			Chi Sq. = NS			Chi Sq. = NS		

Table 14. Israel Visit and Level of Religious Practice

Any Visit to Israel	Low (%)	Medium (%)	High (%)	Total (%)	N
No	36	53	11	100	377
Yes	13	69	18	100	162
					N = 539

Chi Sq. = 30.53; D.F. = 2; p < .001

ever, there are statistically significant differences in the rate of medium and high scores between those who had been to Israel and those who had not. This overall pattern is quite different from that found in the earlier discussion on the monotonous relationship between Jewish education and religious practice and denomination. As can be seen from Table 7, once denomination is held constant, Jewish schooling does not have a significant impact on religious practice among either Conservative or Reform Jews.

For the second index of Jewish identity, namely Jewish community affiliation, the relationship between a visit to Israel and a high score is pronounced in all *three denominational groups.* Among the Conservative, 45 percent of those who had visited Israel had a high score, compared with 21 percent of those who had not. Similarly, for the Reform, 27 percent of those who had been to Israel had a high score, compared with 11 percent of those who had never visited there. Indeed, even among the nonreligious, 56 percent of those who had been to Israel had a medium score on this index, as compared with only 14 percent of those who had not. Is the relationship between a visit to Israel sustained for both indexes of Jewish identity for both genders? The answer is clearly yes, as can be seen in Tables 18 and 19. On each index, and for both men and women, those who have been to Israel score high on the religious practice index (especially and interestingly women) as well as on the community affiliation index. All of these relationships are both statistically significant and substantive: For example, while only 9 percent of the men and 14 percent of the women who had never been to Israel scored high on the index of Jewish community affiliation, the figures for those who had visited Israel were 31 percent (men) and 29 percent (women).

Table 15. Israel Visit and Level of Jewish Community Affiliation

Any Visit to Israel	Low (%)	Medium (%)	High (%)	Total (%)	N
No	47	41	12	100	383
Yes	19	52	29	100	153
					N = 536

Chi Sq. = 45.35; D.F. = 2; p < .001

Table 16. Israel Visit and Level of Jewish Religious Practice, by Denomination

Any Visit to Israel	Conservative					Reform					Nonreligious				
	Low (%)	Med. (%)	High (%)	Total (%)	N	Low (%)	Med. (%)	High (%)	Total (%)	N	Low (%)	Med. (%)	High (%)	Total (%)	N
No	8	61	31	100	102	39	56	5	100	175	59	40	1	100	101
Yes	2	63	35	100	67	10	83	7	100	61	39	58	3	100	34
					169					236					135

Conservative: Chi Sq. = NS

Reform: Chi Sq. = 17.53; D.F. = 2; $p < .001$

Nonreligious: Chi Sq. = NS; $p < .09$

Table 17. Israel Visit and Level of Jewish Community Affiliation, by Denomination

Any Visit to Israel	Conservative					Reform					Nonreligious				
	Low (%)	Med. (%)	High (%)	Total (%)	N	Low (%)	Med. (%)	High (%)	Total (%)	N	Low (%)	Med. (%)	High (%)	Total (%)	N
No	15	64	21	100	98	44	45	11	100	179	82	14	4	100	106
Yes	4	51	45	100	62	23	50	27	100	59	42	56	2	100	33
					160					238					139

Conservative: Chi Sq. = 13.38; D.F. = 2; p < .001

Reform: Chi Sq. = 13.37; D.F. = 2; p < .01

Nonreligious: Chi Sq. = 23.73; D.F. = 2; p < .0001

Table 18. Israel Visit and Level of Jewish Religious Practice, by Gender

Any Visit to Israel	Men					Women				
	Low (%)	Med. (%)	High (%)	Total (%)	N	Low (%)	Med. (%)	High (%)	Total (%)	N
No	38	54	8	100	188	33	53	14	100	186
Yes	10	85	5	100	69	40	54	6	100	57
All	30	63	7	100	256	26	55	19	100	277
	Chi Sq. = 20.49; D.F. = 2; p < .0001					Chi Sq. = 18.44; D.F. = 2; p < .001				

The major finding presented here is that a visit to Israel affects *both* indexes of Jewish identity for both men and women—unlike Jewish education, whose frequency and intensity are mediated by gender. Moreover, a visit to Israel has considerable positive effects on both indexes for both genders.

Multiple Regression Analysis of Findings

In order to determine the relative weight of all these factors—denomination, Jewish education and a visit to Israel—on the two indexes of Jewish identity, multiple regression analysis was performed on the Boston CJP data. In this analysis, the two indexes of Jewish identity were treated as dependent variables, while denomination, gender, Jewish education and prior visit to Israel were entered as independent variables in the form of dummy variables. In the case of each index, the analysis was first performed for all the respondents and then separately for each gender. Results are presented successively in Tables 20 and 21.

The most striking finding of the overall regression analysis is that denomination has a powerful role in explaining the variance on both indexes. Both Conservative and Reform background are found to influence the variance in religious practice,

Table 19. Israel Visit and Level of Jewish Community Affiliation, by Gender

Any Visit to Israel	Men					Women				
	Low (%)	Med. (%)	High (%)	Total (%)	N	Low (%)	Med. (%)	High (%)	Total (%)	N
No	50	41	9	100	185	44	42	14	100	195
Yes	11	58	31	100	64	25	46	29	100	86
All	40	45	15	100	248	38	44	18	100	281
	Chi Sq. = 34.69; D.F. = 2; p < .0001					Chi Sq. = 13.34; D.F. = 2; p < .001				

Table 20. Multiple Regression Analysis of Factors
Explaining Level of Jewish Religious Practice

Dependent Variable: Level of Jewish Religious Practices	All N = 525 Beta	Men N = 252 Beta	Women N = 272 Beta
Independent Variables			
Conservative	.52***	.47***	.55***
Reform	.25***	NS	.36***
Gender	NS	NA	NA
Visit to Israel	.15***	NS	.18***
Sunday school	NS	.14***	−.12***
Afternoon school	.11***	.38***	NS
Day school	.10***	.23***	NS
F =	55.34***	33.5***	47.80***
R Sq. =	.35	.35	.42

***p < .0001

though the latter less than the former. Gender per se makes no contribution to either equation, while afternoon school and day school attendance make modest contributions only. What *is* critical is the independent and statistically significant contribution of a visit to Israel, which has an incremental effect above and beyond both denomination and afternoon and day school Jewish education. In contrast, Sunday school education did not in any way explain the variance on this index.

In the separate analyses of men and women for religious practice, a visit to Israel

Table 21. Multiple Regression Analysis of Factors
Explaining Level of Jewish Community Affiliation

Dependent Variable: Level of Jewish Community Affiliation	All N = 519 Beta	Men N = 244 Beta	Women N = 274 Beta
Independent Variables			
Conservative	.38***	.34***	.43***
Reform	.31***	.23***	.38***
Gender	NS	NA	NA
Visit to Israel	.19***	.27***	.13***
Sunday school	NS	−.11***	NS
Afternoon school	.08	NS	NS
Day school	NS	NS	NS
F =	49.93***	17.98***	35.9***
R Sq. =	.25	.22	.28

***p < .001

does *not* contribute to the explanation of religious practice variance among men; however, all three forms of Jewish education do so, and to a significant extent. For women respondents, *none* of the educational frameworks are a positive influence— and Sunday school is actually negative. But a visit to Israel once again appears as a positive factor contributing incremental and independent explanation of variance in the degree of religious practice of women, above and beyond that provided by denomination.

For the second dimension of Jewish identification, community affiliation, a different and even more interesting pattern emerges. As can be seen in Table 21, denomination again accounts for the major share of variance explanation, but in a less powerful way than was the former case of religious practice. Moreover, the gap between Conservative and Reform is smaller on this table. Gender per se, Sunday school and day school are all insignificant contributors to variance explanation, while afternoon school is only barely significant. Once again, it is a visit to Israel that serves as an independent factor explaining the variance in the degree of community affiliation above and beyond the denomination of respondents. For the separate gender analysis, it can be noted that, with regard to Jewish community affiliation, in contradistinction to Jewish religious practices, the weight of a visit to Israel is stronger for men than for women, but statistically significant for both.

When an identical analysis was repeated with Reform excluded but nonreligious included, the same general pattern was preserved.[10] However, the nonreligious Beta was negative on each index ($-.17$ for religious practice and $-.28$ for community affiliation), while a visit to Israel was positive in both (0.17 on religious practices, 0.23 on community affiliation). In sum, a visit to Israel is a factor that makes a positive and statistically significant contribution to the variance on both indexes of Jewish identification for *all* respondents, irrespective of denomination and its well-documented correlates. It significantly contributes to the level of religious practice of women (more than men) and the degree of community affiliation of men (more than women). Thus, for all respondents, it contributes in one way or another to the strengthening of Jewish identity.

The data presented here confirm Cohen's general thesis that Jewish education does have an impact on Jewish religious practice. However, unlike Cohen's sample, afternoon school alumni in the Boston survey always score higher on both indexes of Jewish identification than do those with no Jewish education. As with Cohen, a statistically significant relationship was found between Jewish education and Jewish identification scores only when the genders were analyzed separately. Moreover, whereas Cohen reported a far lower impact of Jewish education on Jewish community affiliation, the data presented here indicate that Jewish education does explain differences in community affiliation, albeit more powerfully for women than for men.

Finally, in contrast to these mixed findings concerning the impact of Jewish schooling on Jewish identity, the factor of a visit to Israel explains the differences in religious practice for the Reform and nonreligious; the variance in community affiliation in all three denominations; and variance for both genders, analyzed separately, on both indexes of Jewish identification.

Otzma: An Israel Experience Program

Cross-sectional data, as is well known, are limited in their capacity to demonstrate the existence and direction of causal relationships. An alternative approach (albeit with its own methodological problems) is that of longitudinal analysis. The analysis that follows[11] is based on questionnaires given to participants in the "Otzma" program, which is cosponsored by the Israel Forum and participating member federations of the CJF. Otzma is a yearlong program in Israel for selected young adults, aged 18 to 30, aimed specifically at fostering stronger ties between Israel and the future leaders of the diaspora community. The major components of the program are a three-and-a-half-month stay in a kibbutz ulpan/work framework and an additional period of time working on kibbutzim and moshavim in the Arava desert. Otzma also includes service in youth villages and Project Renewal neighborhoods.

Questionnaires were presented both before and after the program, with the aim of determining whether changes in Jewish identity and behavior could be measured and explained in terms of this particular Israel experience. An analysis of the data leads to the basic thesis that the Israel experience has a positive impact on participants, irrespective of formal Jewish educational background.

The following four figures compress a great deal of data. In Figures 1, 2 and 3, three sets of histograms are presented. Each histogram shows the respondents' answers on the given dimension at three points in time: before the program begins; about a third of the way into the program (after the kibbutz ulpan); and ten months into the program, when it is near conclusion.[12] In each figure, the first histogram reports the changes over time in all 178 respondents. The second histogram records responses of those for whom Otzma was their first Israel experience, while the third reports the responses of those who had been there previously.

Figure 1 deals with responses to the question "How important is being Jewish in your life?" This figure reports the percentage of participants who respond "very important" or "important" to this question. It should be noted that Otzma participants were a scholarship-funded and carefully selected elite group that was clearly very Jewishly committed even at the outset of the program, and Jewish commitment was particularly pronounced in the case of those who had been to Israel before. In the course of the program, changes were greatest for those who had not previously been to Israel. The figures here clearly illustrate the "ceiling effect," whereby high initial scores had little room to advance in order to reach a 100 percent maximum score. This maximum score was recorded, at the third point in time, by two groups—day school alumni on their first Israel experience; and those with no Jewish education who had had a previous Israel experience.

In Figure 2, participants' responses are recorded for the question "To what degree is your fate and future bound up with the fate and future of the Jewish people?" Here, too, a similar though more dramatic effect of the Israel experience can be seen, especially among day and afternoon school alumni who are first-timers. Responses of veteran participants who either had no Jewish education or who were Sunday or afternoon school alumni showed radical increments over time. The

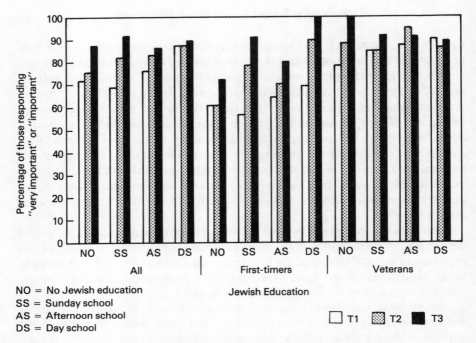

Figure 1. Personal importance of being Jewish.

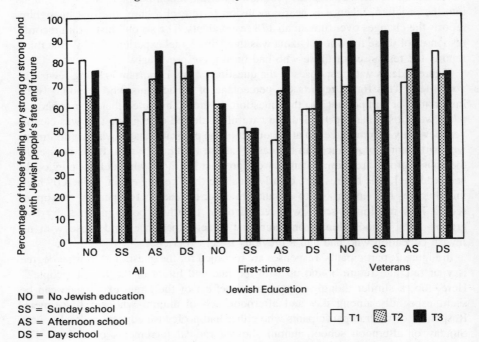

Figure 2. Personal fate and future linked with the Jewish people.

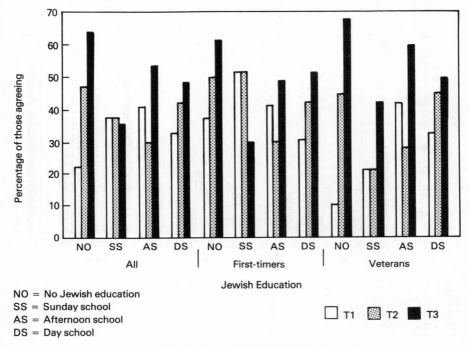

Figure 3. Fuller Jewish life in Israel.

absolute score was higher overall for those for whom Otzma was a second Israel experience. Among the first-timers, alumni of afternoon and day schools registered important positive changes; Sunday school alumni, in contrast, had higher levels of response over time only when they were veterans of a previous Israel experience.

Do the Otzma participants feel, after a year in Israel, that they can "live a fuller Jewish life in Israel"? (Figure 3) Between 22 percent and 42 percent of all Otzma participants gave an affirmative response to this question prior to the program (a response that can be compared with the 10 percent positive response reported by Cohen in his 1986 and 1989 national Jewish surveys). By program's end, the range of positive responses was from 37 to 65 percent.

Sunday school alumni are once again the exception in their pattern of responses. Over time, there is virtually no change in their level of positive response (though it is still far higher than that of the national sample). This is in clear contrast to all the other groups—especially those with no Jewish education at all, who start with a lower positive response (22 percent vs. 39 percent among Sunday school alumni) and end with a far higher score (65 percent vs. 37 percent). When the data on Sunday school alumni are broken down into two groups—first-timers and veterans of a previous Israel experience—two contradictory trends emerge. Sunday school alumni on their first Israel experience come to Israel with a relatively high score on this item (53 percent), which then falls by the end of the year to 31 percent. The veterans, however, begin with a far lower score than their Sunday school peers (21 percent) yet finish the year with a far higher score (43 percent). This suggests that

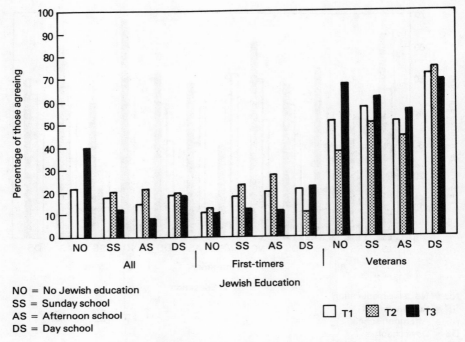

NO = No Jewish education
SS = Sunday school
AS = Afternoon school
DS = Day school

Figure 4. Threat to Jewish survival of assimilation.

the veterans may be giving a more realistic declaration of expectations at the outset (compared with the highly charged expectations of first-time visitors to Israel), while still being subject to the cumulative impact of multiple visits to Israel. In the other three groups, the Israel experience has a uniformly positive impact, most markedly among those with no Jewish education and those with afternoon school experience.

Figure 4 focuses on the problem of Jewish identity viewed from a diaspora perspective, namely, the degree to which "assimilation is seen as a threat to group survival." Two elements deserve particular attention. The first is the universally low rate of concern felt on this issue upon the participants' arrival in Israel. No more than 20 percent of participants from each level of Jewish education (including day school) consider assimilation a threat to Jewish survival. By the end of the year, however, there is a universal change on this variable—between 50 and 70 percent of the participants consider assimilation a threat. The most radical change is found among those with no Jewish education, although the highest scores are found, not surprisingly, among day school alumni.

Conclusion

This paper has utilized two radically different methodologies and two quite different data sets to address the following questions:

1. Does Jewish education have an impact on key aspects of Jewish identification, and if so, for whom and to what degree?
2. Does the Israel experience independently and aggregatively contribute to the Jewish identity of its participants, both while in Israel and on their return to the diaspora?

Utilized together, it appears that the cross-sectional and longitudinal analyses present two powerful points. First, all forms of Jewish education in the diaspora are only a basis for the development of the Jewish identity of the young adult. Second, interventions such as a focused, "quality" Israel experience are shown to have a statistically significant and considerable positive impact on the various components of participants' Jewish identity.

Those seeking to foster deeper Jewish identity and fuller Jewish community involvement might be well advised to focus on ways both to increase the number of educational programs in Israel and to deepen their quality (a factor left unexplored in this paper). For if Jewish education and its consequences are a function of denominational practice, then intervention with the goal of strengthening Jewish identity of North American young adults would require a transformation of the denominations themselves, in the absence of the Israel experience option. Whatever the desirability or chances of such a project might be, this paper has demonstrated that intervention at the level of the Israel experience is not contingent on such a burdensome prerequisite. On the contrary, it can be implemented by all the denominations and benefit all their members, indeed all Jews, wherever they may be.

Notes

I gratefully acknowledge all those who granted me access to the CJP Boston demographic study and who aided me in its analysis: Dr. Sherry Israel, senior planning associate at the Boston CJP; Dr. Motti Rimor, Center of Modern Jewish Studies, Brandeis University; Nancy Williamson and Cherie Minton, Harvard Institute for Social Research; Richard Primus, Project for Kibbutz Studies, Harvard; and Lilach Lev Ari, Moira Blekoff and Miri Sarid, Institute for the Research of the Kibbutz, University of Haifa.

1. Steven M. Cohen, *Ties and Tensions: The 1986 Survey of American Jewish Attitudes Toward Israel and Israelis* (New York: 1987).

2. Geoffrey Bock, *The Jewish Schooling of American Jews: A Study of Non-Cognitive Educational Effects* (Ph.D. diss., Harvard University, 1976).

3. Harold Himmelfarb, *The Impact of Jewish Schooling: The Effects of Jewish Education on Adult Religious Involvement* (Ph.D. diss., University of Chicago, 1974).

4. See Sherry Israel, *Boston's Jewish Community: The 1985 CJP Demographic Study* (Boston: 1987) for major findings, methodology, interview and sampling techniques, etc.

5. Cf. David Mittelberg, *Strangers in Paradise: The Israeli Kibbutz Experience* (New Brunswick, N.J., and Oxford: 1988).

6. Steven M. Cohen, *American Assimilation or Jewish Revival?* (Bloomington: 1988), 91–95.

7. This procedure conforms to accepted practice in the literature. Mary C. Waters, for example, in her analysis of white, non-Jewish ethnicity based on 1980 U.S. Census data (*Ethnic Options: Choosing Identities in America* [Berkeley: 1990]), demonstrated that denominational homogeneity in families tended to strengthen the socialization of religious values.

8. See Cohen, *American Assimilation.*

9. See Mittelberg, *Strangers in Paradise,* 171–172.

10. For the sake of brevity, the data are not presented here; they are available from the author.

11. See Mittelberg, *Strangers in Paradise,* 177–178.

12. Still to be completed is a follow-up study of Otzma alumni in North America and Israel.

The Question of Jewish Identity

Anthony D. Smith

(LONDON SCHOOL OF ECONOMICS)

Few subjects arouse so much passion and misunderstanding as the identity and status of the Jewish people. What follows cannot claim to be exempt from these limitations. At the same time, the comparative approach presented here may lead to new understanding of these age-old problems. The perspective offered here differs from others in distinguishing between different kinds of Jewish ethnicity and relating them to the emergence of Zionism and an Israeli nationality. By comparing the Jewish people with other diaspora communities, this analysis highlights the persisting unique elements of Jewish identity.

Received Views of the Jewish People

Broadly speaking, there have been two main schools of thought regarding Jewish identity. On the one hand, the Jews have been seen as a religious community, a "holy people," a "nation of priests." This is the traditional self-understanding of Orthodox Judaism: In a world of idolatry, the Jews have been singled out to live a sanctified life according to the Torah.[1] There are, of course, more external and critical accounts of Jewish religious identity. Critics have represented the chosen people variously as a "fossil," "pariah people" or *Gegentypus*—an anomaly standing in the way of progress, civilization or the master race.[2] Less hostile observers have been struck by the dense network of rituals, liturgies and beliefs that guard Jewish identity. Like Rousseau, they have defined that identity in terms of "its mores, laws and rituals," features that have preserved the Jewish community through persecution and dispersion.[3] In this reading, Judaism becomes the prototype for all those religioethnic communities—Sikhs, Druse, Copts, Armenians—whose identity is defined in terms of ritual and religion.[4]

On the other hand, Jews have long been viewed as a nation more or less like other nations. The term "nation" is used here in the sense of a territorially demarcated human population possessed of a common culture, a single economy and shared legal rights and duties. Such a conception of the Jews naturally served the cause of nationalists everywhere, Jewish and non-Jewish, philosemites and antisemites. In the Jewish case, however, such a reading poses a genuine problem of interpretation as to how far we may be guilty of a retrospective nationalism in arguing that it was always impossible to separate national from religious identity, the Jews as nation from Judaism.[5]

Neither of these approaches to Jewish identity is completely convincing. Both are guilty of simplifying a many-sided phenomenon and exaggerating certain of its features at the expense of others. The idea that "Jews" are coterminous with "Judaism" and that the Jewish people is really only a "community of faith" ignores the genealogical aspect present from the outset—the fact that Jews define themselves also as a community of (matrilineal) descent. There is, furthermore, a strong territorial element in Jewish identity that sets it apart from a universal faith community. Thus, the Book of Ruth can be read in two ways: as emphasizing both the religious openness of a faith community and the ethnic closure of the convert.[6]

Moreover, Jews in recent history have referred to themselves as the Jewish "people," not the Jewish "faithful." Their intense concern for Jewish survival is reflected in demographic anxiety, and the centrality of Israel for most Jews today reflects their concern for national rather than purely religious survival.[7]

But can the Jews be usefully defined as a nation in the sense outlined above? Arguably, from the Davidic kingdom to the captivity in Babylon they did possess some of the features of a nation: a definite territory, a common religious culture and some common legal rights and duties, though rather less in the way of a single division of labor and economy. But after the Bar Kokhba uprising, it becomes increasingly difficult to think of the scattered Jewish communities as constituting a nation in anything but a symbolic sense, even where some of the larger communities in Babylon or Poland enjoyed a measure of internal autonomy. It does not really aid understanding or further the interests of clarity to designate such communities as nations in the same way that the French or Polish nations are spoken of today; and further confusion results if we confine ourselves to an umbrella use of the term "nation" in attempting to clarify the nature and status of the Israeli Jewish community vis-à-vis other Jewish communities.[8]

The Jews as a Demotic *Ethnie*

A starting point for a more comparative understanding of Jewish identity—one that tries to do justice to the multifaceted nature of the phenomenon—is the concept of *ethnie,* and more specifically, of "demotic" *ethnie.*[9]

An *ethnie* may be defined as a named human population with a shared myth of descent, shared memories and culture and a sense of attachment to a "homeland." Such communities are found in the historical record from the period of the Bronze Age, starting with the ancient Sumerians and Egyptians, and they appear in every epoch and continent from antiquity to the modern era.[10]

Ethnic communities, or *ethnie,* are both mutable and durable. That is to say, they are subject to processes of formation and dissolution like every other historical phenomenon; but they can also endure in similar or changed form for centuries, even millennia. They must be seen as communities of culture and history based on a fictive kinship, summed up in a powerful myth of descent that binds and legitimates the community. It is neither actual descent nor historical events that bind the members of *ethnie;* what count are the myths of ancestry and what successive generations remember. An ethnic community is a population cluster that shares distinctive memories, symbols, myths and values. The "core" feature of such memories, myths and symbols is their point of reference in the past, in myths of origin and memories of liberation and a golden age. This feature is what marks the community as an "ethnic" one.[11]

But who exactly, it may be asked, are the ones who hold these values and share these myths and memories? In preindustrial societies, there was often a social and cultural gulf between rulers and ruled, between the tiny urban elites and the vast mass of peasants and tribesmen. How widely and how far down the social scale did these collective symbols, myths and memories penetrate?

Clearly, the answer will vary from community to community, and each area and period will throw up different patterns of ethnic penetration and solidarity. However, it is possible to distinguish two kinds of *ethnie,* the one "lateral" and extensive, the other "vertical" and intensive. Lateral *ethnie* are usually upper-class, aristocratic, clerical and urban in character. Their boundaries tend to be ragged, and the barriers to outsiders of the appropriate status are low. Such communities may exhibit a certain esprit de corps among themselves but may be quite indifferent to other strata and classes, making little attempt to disseminate their ethnic culture to outlying areas or to lower strata. This is very much the picture gleaned from records of the aristocratic Philistine pentapolis and of the "feudal" Hittite nobility, both of whom conquered large areas of the eastern Mediterranean littoral in the latter part of the second millennium B.C.E.[12]

In contrast, vertical *ethnie* tend to be more exclusive and demotic. A greater cross-class solidarity is found in these communities, along with higher barriers against out-marriage and external cultures. There is a correspondingly greater emphasis on indigenous culture and values, a greater attachment to participation in native rituals and customs. *Ethnie* of this type also tend to experience more enthusiastic modes of mass mobilization, whether for war or through zealous religious movements. Though here, as in the case of lateral *ethnie,* priests, scribes and bards occupy a central role as guardians and augmenters of the communal traditions, the ethnic heritage in vertical, demotic communities tends to be the possession of *all* members of the community, no doubt with regional and class variations, but nevertheless with almost equal intensity. We have only to recall the strength of Galilean traditions of Jewish piety—particularly among the lower classes—to appreciate the difference in the role of ethnic culture between lateral, aristocratic *ethnie* and those that are vertical and demotic.[13]

Vertical and demotic communities, moreover, often exhibit a special sense of ethnoreligious mission and a powerful myth of ethnic election, both of which help to bind the members into a spiritually (and sometimes also territorially) compact ethnic community. This has been true, at different moments in their ethnohistories, of such communities as the Armenians, medieval Greeks and the Irish under British rule.[14]

The distinction drawn here between lateral and vertical *ethnie* is not a hard-and-fast one, any more than most distinctions in social life and history. The longer a community survives, the more it becomes influenced by outside forces and the more likely it is that internal divisions will emerge. In such circumstances, even the most vertical and demotic of *ethnie* may begin to manifest opposite tendencies toward hierarchy and aristocratization. Conversely, defeat in war and exile may "decapitate" an ethnic hierarchy, as happened to the Czech nobility in the battle of the White Mountain in 1620, leaving behind a more cohesive community as the basis for later ethnic revival. This is also, to some extent, what happened to the Greek community under Ottoman rule, despite the continuing influence of the Orthodox Patriarchate and the growth of Phanariot economic power.[15]

How can the categories and distinctions outlined previously throw light on the millennial—and contemporary—Jewish experience?

Historically, we can distinguish between the oscillating trends toward a more demotic or aristocratic type of community among the Jews, first in ancient Palestine and later in Babylon, Egypt and other centers in the Roman empire. The original tribal confederation of Israelites who entered Canaan from Egypt can be characterized as a vertical and demotic *ethnie* molded at the same time by Moses and his successors into a religious congregation. By the time of the Solomonic kingdom, however, social divisions had reached a point where two kingdoms and communities of a distinctively lateral and semiaristocratic kind proved the eventual outcome. The return from Babylon witnessed the rebirth of a small demotic community focused physically and spiritually around Jerusalem, re-formed by Ezra and Nehemiah into a community of faith as well as a cultural community, only to be once again rent by social divisions and political turmoil that culminated in the Jewish revolt of 66 to 70 C.E. Thereafter, Jewish identity is that of a diaspora *ethnie*, a series of more or less demotic enclaves segregated in varying degrees by and from their several host societies and bound together by a Hebraic liturgy, decentralized rabbinic authority and the study of the Torah in home and synagogue. In this respect, the closest parallel is with the Armenian diaspora enclaves. Both of these "archetypal" diasporas became increasingly demotic communities in exile, with specific trading and middlemen roles in an ethnic division of labor and a scriptural religion playing the decisive part in ensuring the survival and cohesion of the communities. In both cases, religious education and the clergy occupied a central place in the reproduction of ethnic consciousness in successive generations, with the decentralization of clerical authority going further in Judaism to match the conditions of prolonged exile from spiritual and territorial homelands.[16]

The Zionist Revolution

It was these conditions that the national revolution of Zionism sought to transform. For the Zionists, the Jews constituted a nation like any other nation. True, the national character of the Jewish nation had been stunted and its economic development deformed. But this was a temporary development, the result of exile and dispersion among the nations. The Zionists rejected the "diaspora nationalism" of Simon Dubnow, who proposed a system of cultural enclave nationalities along the lines suggested by the Austro-Marxists Karl Renner and Otto Bauer. Instead, they demanded a swift evacuation from a Europe once again in the grip of rising antisemitism, and a return of the Jewish people to its ancient homeland in Palestine. This, they believed, was the only radical and practical solution to the political, cultural and economic needs of the scattered Jewish communities; only in their homeland would each Jewish community and every Jew come to feel himself a member of a revived Jewish nation.[17]

Of importance here is the fact that Zionism, though it found its mass base in the Russian and Polish Jewish communities (especially in the wake of the pogroms of 1881), was founded as a political movement in the West by half-assimilated Western Jews such as Theodor Herzl and Max Nordau. For this reason, it revealed a pronounced Western orientation—and not only in the way that Zionists mainly appealed to Western governments and public opinion, or in the way that they employed Western modes of reasoning and discourse. The imitation of the West went deeper than this: It involved a conceptual revolution, the revolution of a nationalism born in the West and imbued with Western concepts and ideals.[18]

Four processes were, and are still, involved in this nationalist and westernizing revolution. The first and most obvious is the territorialization of the Jewish people, their restoration to their homeland—which substitutes for the scattered Jewish enclaves a single, compact and clearly demarcated national unit on its own soil. The second process emerges from the first: economic unity and even autarchy—the cultivation of the nation's territorial resources, the creation of a single occupational system and a single market for the nation's produce and for its labor resources and skills. The third process is cultural—the need for each Jew to communicate through a single, distinctive medium and acquire similar values, memories and ideals. The only distinctive language that could be shared by Jews of such different backgrounds and customs was a modernized version of liturgical Hebrew, and the only way of teaching it to immigrants of such varied backgrounds (and thus disseminating the new national culture) was through a common, public and standardized education system. The schools were to turn ethnic Jews into Hebrew-speaking Israelis, that is, national Jews. Finally, as in the West, a new type of citizen had to be formed through the process of legal unification and the extension to all members of a common legal code of rights and duties. Such rights and duties soon extended, as they had done in the West, beyond the civil and political spheres. The creation of a civic, as opposed to an ethnic, nation also entailed the provision of social welfare to less privileged classes and to all citizens of the new nation-state, which had some problematic consequences in the new Israeli democracy.[19]

All four of the processes described above—territorialization, economic unification, the creation of a common mass culture and legal standardization with common rights and duties—define the concept of a modern nation, but in a very Western or "civic" conception of the term. It is not the only conception. A rather different one emerged in Central and Eastern Europe (though one should not exaggerate the differences), where the emphasis fell on what may be called the "ethnic" or cultural features of the nation: myths of descent, a common vernacular language and culture and a strong popular or folk element. Ethnohistory, the history remembered and retold by successive generations of the community, was also given pride of place; though it must be added that such ethnohistories also played a vital role in the burgeoning of French, English and American nationalism.[20]

Not surprisingly, this more ethnic conception of the nation appealed to many nationalists from demotic *ethnie,* such as those of Eastern Europe and the Middle East; equally unsurprisingly, it had greater appeal for Jewish nationalists from the centers of Jewry in Russia and Eastern Europe. The difference in conception and orientation between Western and Eastern types of Zionist and Zionism were to bedevil national debates about the identity and status of the Jewish people for decades.[21] But even the more ethnic and less Western conception of the Jewish nation posed fundamental problems for traditional religious self-conceptions of the Jewish people. This is because the Zionist revolution placed the "people" and their heroes at the center of Jewish history instead of the Deity, requiring them to emancipate themselves for citizenship in a national homeland and exhorting them to live and work on the soil, to become members of a modern nation, to communicate in a modernized version of the sacred language and to obey the laws of a secular nation-state. How were such Zionist conceptions to be harmonized with the traditional religious ideas of a "chosen people" and a "nation of priests"? The Zionists were separating the old ethnoreligious community into its constituent parts, and the religious part was now increasingly subordinated to the ethnic aspect. Jews were no longer to be seen mainly as carriers of Judaism; rather, Judaism was to be regarded as the vehicle and expression of Jewishness, of a living Jewish community.[22]

And yet the old linkage of religion and people was not wholly obliterated. The very choice of Zion as the homeland of the Jewish people, rather than Uganda or Argentina, testifies to the continuing strength of tradition within the new ethnic conception of a Jewish nation. The return to a golden age of Sages and Rabbis in the Roman period, which served to inspire religious Zionists, suggests a persisting identification of the nation with its faith.

As with other nationalisms, the appeal by middle-class intelligentsia to the lower classes has required important modifications of the Western "civic" ideal of the modern Israeli nation.[23] The process of transforming the balance between religious and ethnic components of the Jewish people, as the early Western-oriented Zionists sought, was achieved in ways characteristic of national revivals everywhere, particularly among demotic *ethnie.* One such method, used by Zionists and others, was to create "poetic spaces" in the homeland by endowing it with human and poetic meanings. Another involved a revolution in ways of viewing nature. The Swiss, for example, began to view their Alpine landscape in an entirely new light: as an intrinsic element in their survival as a small people against encroaching tyrants, as a symbol of ancient virtue and purity, as the scene of epic national dramas such as the Oath on the Rütli meadow and William Tell's struggle with Gessler.[24] For the Jews newly arrived in their ancient homeland, no such radical rethinking was needed. The land of the Bible, the divine history of their origins and development in their own land, had already become humanized enough in the long years of exile. Archaeology and excursions in nature—both popular passions of the restored inhabitants—were simply new modes of confirming the human and poetic heritage of the Eretz Israel landscape. Mountains such as Carmel, Gilboa and Tabor, rivers such as the Yarmuk and Jordan and famous *tells* such as Hatzor, Megiddo and Lahish—and especially the rock fortress of Masada—these were already part of the ancient divine history, and they were now appropriated as settings and events in a *national salvation drama*.[25]

Another way of transforming demotic *ethnie* into ethnic nations is through the uses of history, more specifically the cult of heroes and golden ages. In other cases, this entailed a considerable secularization of traditional religious images of the ethnic past. The Gaelic revival, with its cult of the pagan past enshrined in the Ulster cycle of ancient epics and of such heroes as Fin Mac Coil and Cuchulain, implicitly challenged the rival Catholic cult of a monastic golden age after Ireland's conversion by Saint Patrick in the fifth century.[26] Early nineteenth-century Greek nationalists sought a secular version of their country's ethnic past in the golden age of ancient Athens under Pericles, with its great artists and philosophers, in opposition to the rival cult of Orthodox Byzantium and its imperial glories.[27] Even in early twentieth-century Egypt, a pharaonic cult appeared—secular, liberal and westernizing—to challenge the Arab Islamic heritage of the majority.[28]

Similar divisions in the choice of ethnohistory and myths of origin and golden ages surfaced among the European Jewish communities at the beginning of the nineteenth century. One such vision, the cult of a commonwealth of farmers, herdsmen and traders in the ancient Davidic kingdom of Israel, appeared in the writings of some early *maskilim* in Berlin. Other golden ages and their heroes soon followed: Judah the Maccabee and the Hasmoneans; the era of Sages, from Hillel to Akiva and Judah Hanasi; and backward in time to the original tribal covenant forged by the quasi-Nietzschean figure of Moses.[29] In the twentieth century, these epochs and heroes were supplemented by more overtly nationalist figures, notably Bar Kokhba and Eleazar ben-Yair, the commander of the Zealot garrison on Masada in 73 C.E., whose heroic act of self-sacrifice marked the culmination of the nationalist political interpretation of Jewish history and Jewish identity. For a nation at war, such leaders appeared the natural and truly national heroes.[30]

In many ways, the Zionist revolution succeeded in fulfilling its goals and in reinterpreting Jewish history in its own terms. However, such reinterpretation led to a number of major problems. In the sections that follow, attention will be focused on two of the most vexing problems of the new Jewish nation-state—the status of its non-Jewish inhabitants and the problem of relations with Jewish communities in the diaspora.

The Arabs in Israel

The ambiguous status of Israel's non-Jewish inhabitants is a direct consequence of the contradictions between the civic and ethnic concepts of nationality, exacerbated by Israel's geopolitical situation. Were a truly civic and Western ideal of an Israeli nation to be realized, all permanent residents in the country would become full and legally equal citizens, with common rights and duties. Arabs, Druse and other non-Jewish permanent residents would thus be entitled to full citizenship and its benefits and obligations, including military service, office-holding, social welfare benefits, public education and the like. But they would also be expected to share in the political culture of the Israeli nation, its founding myths and memories and Hebrew culture. In contrast, were an ethnic ideal and definition of the nation to be realized, the *Jewish* character of the Israeli nation would be underlined. Though the ideal posits equality before the law for non-Jewish inhabitants, these would nonetheless be kept at arm's length, since they would not and, more to the point, *could* not, share in the millennial Jewish heritage. In Israel today, this distinction is in fact underpinned by the prominence of the criterion of Jewish descent that plays a key role in the Law of Return and in definitions of Jewishness that grant those Jews who so desire immediate access to Israeli citizenship. Thus, even where security concerns do not require vigilance, the status of non-Jewish Israeli citizens in a state that seeks to be simultaneously Israeli and Jewish is bound to be uneasy and somewhat marginal.[31]

There are, indeed, points of comparison here with ethnic relations in other new polyethnic states. Dominant *ethnie* and governments in states such as Burma, Sri Lanka, Ethiopia and Kenya, despite many differences, have to wrestle with problems posed by the existence of significant minority cultures and deep ethnic cleavages; they too have experienced ethnic discontent and even secession bids. Israel finds itself in a similar situation vis-à-vis its Arab minority. But here the problem is compounded by Israeli Arabs' geocultural and geopolitical relations with the populations in surrounding Arab states that are still technically in a state of war with Israel. For the Arab minority within Israel, there are sharp and painful problems of identity and loyalty: On the one hand, there is a conflict between citizen loyalty to the Israeli state and ethnic solidarity with Arabs everywhere; on the other hand, within this solidarity, there is a problem of identification with an emergent Palestinian Arab *ethnie* as a fragment of a much wider "Arab nation."[32]

It must also be remembered that Palestinians, and more generally Arabs, are experiencing a similar arduous transformation from a former demotic *ethnie*—the Arab tribes in Arabia, whose communal bonds had been frayed by Mongol and later Ottoman conquest—into a series of compact Arab nations based on rival states in the Western mold. There are quite a few parallels both in the Jewish and Arab starting points and in the transitions they are undergoing. Thus, it is not surprising that neotraditionalist religious rivalries are now redefining and intensifying Israeli Jewish and Palestinian Arab identities, despite the appeals of some for a secular pluralism. Such nationalization of Islam and Judaism can only sharpen the dilemmas of Israel's relations with its Arab minority.[33]

If in the much more secular and secure Western states there is now something of an ethnic renascence, for example, among the Quebecois, Scots, Flemish, Bretons and Basques, and if the "national question" has so swiftly reappeared in the wake of Communism's collapse in Eastern Europe and the Soviet Union, we can hardly be surprised at the intensity and intractability of ethnic cleavages in the Middle East and more particularly in Israel, where there has been so little time for a civic and territorial conception of the nation to take root. Given both the size and the potential power of Israel's Arab minority, together with its strong cultural links with Arabs on the West Bank and Israel's Arab neighbors, and the continuing Arab-Israeli conflict, the problems created by the Zionist revolution and a concomitant Arab nationalism are but more intense and explosive variations on a common contemporary theme, that of the dilemmas of polyethnic states all over the world.[34]

The Problem of the Diaspora

The ambiguous success of the Zionist revolution is manifested in a second important area, Israel's relations with diaspora Jewish communities. To the extent that the ethnic conception of a Jewish Israel retains its hold, Israelis will continue to see themselves as part of a wider Jewish people, albeit the only part able to exercise sovereignty in its homeland. The question for Israelis is one of direction: whether they will continue to see themselves as the leading Jewish community, and the only one residing in a sovereign Jewish state, or whether they will increasingly view themselves as a new nation of *Israelis,* increasingly divergent from Judaism, Jewishness and the Jewish diaspora—and hence a radical departure from the millennial pattern of Jewish history and identity.[35]

The wider question, however, concerns the fate of the Jewish people as a whole. How far has the current transformation of one part of that people in its ancient homeland changed the character and status of the other parts and of the people as a whole? After all, most Jews live, and will probably continue to live, outside Israel, which is unlikely ever to contain more than a large minority of the Jewish people as a whole. Nor can the experience and weight of two thousand years of Jewish dispersion be undone, and with it the identification of many diaspora Jews as survivors and successors of the lost generations of the Holocaust.

This is the real problem of Jewish identity, and it is one that Israelis share as Jews. This is also the focal point of conflict between the two conceptions of the modern nation, civic and ethnic, that is as deeply embedded within Zionism as within any other form of nationalism. Despite the necessity to incorporate components of the Western civic ideal, ethnic conceptions of the Jewish nation remain powerful, and they are likely to increase their hold within Israel to the extent that Israeli public education incorporates diaspora experiences and Holocaust memories. Continuing antisemitism in Europe and elsewhere is also expected to reinforce the ethnic conception of Israel as a Jewish nation and a haven for persecuted Jews. Israel's raison d'être as a sovereign state depends on the survival of large numbers of self-identifying Jews inside and outside Israel; hence the drive to liberate and protect all Jews. Thus, the dream of a small band of "Canaanites" to create a new, non-Jewish Israeli nation is likely to be postponed *sine die.*[36]

It is reasonably certain that, despite continuing conflicts between Orthodox and secularist Jews and between Ashkenazic and Sephardic Jewish communities over the character and shape of Israeli Jewishness, the Jewish character of Israel will persist and become institutionalized. Systematic socialization of new generations through study of the biblical heritage, archaeology and public education in Jewish history will instill a renewed Jewish consciousness and a revaluation of the diaspora experience. Perhaps most important, the profound connection between the Holocaust and the birth of Israel is likely to sink deeper into the consciousness of many

Israelis (despite fears to the contrary). Although the character of Israeli Jewishness may diverge somewhat from others in the diaspora, as has happened before, Israelis will continue to see themselves as children of the miraculous rebirth of the Jewish people in the shadow of its darkest hour.[37]

What of the Jewish communities in the diaspora? Will they suffer rapid attrition through assimilation and intermarriage—or else reshape their Jewishness to suit their post-Holocaust situation? As for Israel, what are the consequences of attempts to create a society that is both civic in character and ethnic in its Jewish spirit?

It is not necessarily the case that Israel and diaspora Jewry must increasingly diverge, spelling the dissolution of the Jewish people. Such a fear seems to be based on a lack of historical and comparative perspective. Following their dispersion, the Jewish people were divided into a series of geographical and cultural centers, becoming a network of demotic ethnic enclaves. Despite the destruction of most of the European enclaves and one-third of the Jewish population, this characterization of the Jewish people has not basically altered. If anything, rapid global communications have increased the interlocking networks of these ethnic enclaves, as have the mass media and the emergence of a secular Jewish intelligentsia.[38]

This is in line with recent ethnic and national trends. We live in a world of multiplying ethnonational demands and conflicts, where the spread of nationalism has politicized formerly quiescent ethnic communities. World Jewry is no exception. The sheer scale and suddenness of recent events in Jewish and world history have thrust a number of Jewish enclave-communities more directly into the political arena from which they had been formerly excluded. Various social, cultural and political bodies have sprung up to represent the interests of world Jewry and/or its constituent communities, quite apart from existing religious and Zionist organizations. Concern for Israel's survival and its material and moral welfare has become the central issue for many Jews around the world, providing both a focus and a link for community and organizational efforts; at the same time, the Arab-Israeli conflict spills over, often with tragic results, into the lives of diaspora Jews and their communities, feeding into the revival of European antisemitism and racism. In such a situation, opting out of the Jewish people may be feasible for individual Jews, but could only prove self-defeating for Jewish communities.[39]

Conclusion

What, then, is the nature of Jewish identity today, and how may the analysis offered here aid in its elucidation?

The image of the Jewish people today is that of an identity in transition. Neither a purely religious community nor yet a nation, the network of Jewish communities around the world forms an increasingly politicized, demotic *ethnie* around a dense, compact, sovereign and Hebrew-speaking "ethnic core" in Israel. In Israel itself, the Jewish community seeks to create a nation both like other nations and culturally distinctive in its Jewishness—with incalculable consequences for other Jewish communities. At the same time, growing interdependence in communications and in economic and political structures has politicized the main Jewish communities outside Israel, notably the major concentration of Jews in the United States. Hence, in the short term, the future of Jewry will be shaped both by the links between the major Jewish communities in Israel and the United States, and by global developments.[40]

The fate of the Jewish people over the longer term will be conditioned by its continuing overall diaspora situation and by the more general trends indicated above. For, contrary to earlier analyses such as those of Karl Deutsch and Daniel Lerner, which predicted the supersession of nationalism as societies became fully modern and regionally interdependent, economic interdependence and global information and communications networks have in fact encouraged denser ethnolinguistic clustering, and engendered deeper ethnoregional cleavages. The overall result has been an intensification and proliferation—not a diminution—of ethnic nationalisms across the globe.[41]

The example of the Jewish people, however, highlights the deeper roots and the longer-lasting effects of modern ethnic nationalisms. Unlike most recent theories of ethnic identity and nationalism that emphasize its modernity and malleability, the analysis presented here underlies the continuing power and relevance of premodern ethnic ties in the development of modern nations. For many scholars, the modern nation is a product of peculiarly modern conditions and a construct of modern, usually secular, intelligentsia. Ernest Gellner, for example, locates nationalism in the dislocations of the transition to an industrial type of society and credits the public, mass education system with the creation of mass citizen-nations.[42] Similarly, Elie Kedourie views the Enlightenment as the intellectual matrix of nationalism—despite its parallels with medieval Christian millennialism—and regards the non-Western nation as a peculiarly modern and Western-inspired innovation of secular intellectuals.[43] This view is echoed by Eric Hobsbawm, who places the birth of mass democratic nationalism in the 1780s and that of mass-mobilizing ethnic and linguistic nationalisms from 1870 to 1914.[44] The upshot of these approaches is to limit the life span of nations and nationalism to a specific historical period, the "modern" period of the last two centuries in Europe (and later elsewhere), and to emphasize the abstract and constructed, even "invented," quality of the modern nation.[45]

In contrast to such views, this analysis of Jewish identity seeks to ground the Zionist revolution and the birth of Israel as a modern nation in the millennial diaspora situation of the Jewish people. This is not to minimize the modernity of Zionism or that of its creation, an Israeli Jewish nation. Such a "creation," however, took place within limits dictated by the premises of diaspora Jewish history and the continuing significance in the modern period of a dispersed but self-aware demotic Jewish *ethnie*. Like the Armenians and Greeks, so many of whom were also dispersed as a result of conquest and enforced poverty and exile, the Jewish diaspora testifies to the durability and resilience of diaspora *ethnie*, especially those whose solidarity is undergirded with a religious myth of ethnic election and a scriptural religion, liturgy and clergy to give it daily practical expression. More broadly, the millennial Jewish diaspora and its continuing vitality today reveals the

need for a more historical and comparative approach to modern nations and nationalisms—one that gives greater weight to symbolic and cultural elements than do
many of the current economic and political perspectives and theories.[46]

It may be true that nations, in the sense defined at the outset, are in fact modern
and require certain conditions found only in this era to bring them into being. At the
same time, however, particular nations are the products of specific collective ethnohistories as remembered and recounted by later generations of the same or closely
related community. The memories, myths, symbols, values and traditions of this
ethnohistory, often preserved in liturgies, chronicles and artifacts, provide the material but also prescribe the limits of the new nation-in-the-making. Through the uses
of poetic landscapes and the cults of heroes and golden ages (which always have
resonance only for particular ethnic communities), modern nationalists are able to
evoke a vision of the nation-to-be *as if it had always been there* from time imme-
morial. There is no need to charge nationalists with self-deception or fabrication;
how else could ancient, often scattered, demotic *ethnie* become fully modern nations commanding the allegiance of the designated population?[47]

The role of ethnic memory has been particularly salient in the case of the Jewish
people. If the testimonies of the past have played a vital role in the survival of a
number of demotic *ethnie* down the centuries, they have been of particular significance for Jewish identity and survival. Today, the vast increase in the scale of ethnic
memory in terms of witnessing, recording, investigating and cataloging the Jewish
past in genealogies, reports, books, broadcasts, films and trials—especially of
events concerning the Holocaust—has opened up the varieties of Jewish experience
and identity to a much greater Jewish public and thereby kept alive the cultural chain
of the generations at a time when extermination and assimilation threatened to break
it. The experience of the Holocaust has also served to inspire in many Jews a need
for long-term political mobilization; in this sense, the Holocaust, for all of its
tragedy, has become the charter of Jewish power.[48]

Both the return to the Jewish past as encouraged by present global trends of
ethnonationalism and the need to grasp the meaning of Jewish history, especially the
Holocaust, have reinforced the demotic character of Jewish ethnic identity and
destiny. By retelling that past and seeking to grasp its many meanings in each
generation, the Jewish people are likely to renew their identity as a politicized
community of culture centered in its ancient homeland and its national heritage.

Notes

1. See, for example, Ex. 19:5–6; Isa. 42:6; for the original covenant, see Irving Zeitlin,
Ancient Judaism (Cambridge: 1984), 94–95.

2. Toynbee dubbed Judaism a "fossilised" religion, although he recognized the survival
capacity of the diaspora; Max Weber regarded the Jews of the European diaspora as a "pariah
people." See Max Weber, *The Sociology of Religion,* trans. Ephraim Fischoff (London:
1965). For German Romantic and proto-Nazi stereotypes of "the Jew," see George Mosse,
The Crisis of German Ideology (New York: 1964).

3. J. J. Rousseau, cited in Salo Baron, *Modern Nationalism and Religion* (New York:
1960), 26–27.

4. For several of these Middle Eastern ethnoreligious communities, see Aziz Atiya, *A History of Eastern Christianity* (London: 1968).

5. For the view that Jews have always constituted a nation, see Benjamin Akzin, *State and Nation* (London: 1964); for the definition of "nation" given here, see Hans Kohn, *The Idea of Nationalism*, 2nd ed. (New York: 1967), ch. 5; and Anthony D. Smith, *Nationalism: A Trend Report and Annotated Bibliography, Current Sociology* 21, pt. 3 (1973), sec. 1.

6. See Ruth 1:16; on conversion to Judaism, see Alan Unterman: *The Jews, Their Religious Beliefs and Practices* (Boston, Henley and London: 1981), 8–18.

7. For these concerns, see the title and contents of Georges Friedmann, *The End of the Jewish People?* (London: 1967). For a sociology of Judaism, see Stephen Sharot, *Judaism, A Sociology* (Newton Abbot, London and Vancouver: 1976).

8. It is also true that in the Second Temple period there were sharp cultural divisions between the Jewish upper class in Jerusalem and the rest of the population, the upper class being permeated with Greek culture; see Raphael Patai, *The Jewish Mind* (New York: 1977), chs. 4–5. For the role of contemporary diaspora *ethnie*, see *Modern Diasporas in International Politics*, ed. Gabriel Sheffer (London: 1986).

9. The French word "*ethnie*" is used here as a convenient shorthand expression referring to the "ethnic community" and "ethnic identity" of a collectivity. "Demotic" conveys in a single word the sense of "folk" and "popular" vernacular culture and society.

10. For the concept of *ethnie*, see Donald Horowitz, *Ethnic Groups in Conflict* (Berkeley and Los Angeles: 1985), ch. 2, and Anthony D. Smith, *The Ethnic Origins of Nations* (Oxford: 1986), ch. 2.

11. This is the briefest of summaries of Anthony D. Smith, "Ethnic Myths and Ethnic Revivals," *European Journal of Sociology* 25 (1984), 283–305.

12. For the Hittites, see Sabatino Moscati, *The Face of the Ancient Orient* (New York: 1962), ch. 5; for the Philistines, see K. A. Kitchen, "The Philistines," in *Peoples of Old Testament Times*, ed. D. J. Wiseman (Oxford: 1973). For a fuller discussion of these "lateral" *ethnie*, see Smith, *Ethnic Origins of Nations*, ch. 4.

13. For a fuller discussion of "vertical" *ethnie*, see *ibid.*, chs. 4–5; for Galilean Jewish piety in the Second Temple period, see Irving Zeitlin, *Jesus and the Judaism of His Time* (Cambridge: 1988).

14. For the Armenians, see Atiya, *History of Eastern Christianity*, pt. 4; on the medieval Greeks, see John Armstrong, *Nations Before Nationalism* (Chapel Hill: 1982), 178–181; for the Irish, see John Hutchinson, *The Dynamics of Cultural Nationalism: The Gaelic Revival and the Creation of the Irish Nation State* (London: 1987), chs. 2–3.

15. For a brief description of the Greek *millet* on the eve of independence, see John Campbell and Philip Sherrard, *Modern Greece* (London: 1968), ch. 1.

16. For some perceptive observations on this parallel between the Jewish and Armenian diasporas, see Armstrong, *Nations Before Nationalism*, ch. 7; for a general history of the Jewish diaspora, see Robert Seltzer, *Jewish People, Jewish Thought* (New York: 1980).

17. For the conceptions of diaspora Jewish nationalism, see Simon Dubnow, *Nationalism and History*, ed. Koppel Pinson (Philadelphia: 1958). For the origins of Zionism, see David Vital, *The Origins of Zionism* (Oxford: 1975); see also Baron, *Modern Nationalism and Religion*, ch. 7.

18. On the Western orientation and ideals of Herzl and Nordau, see Arthur Hertzberg (ed.), *The Zionist Idea: A Reader* (New York: 1960), Introduction.

19. For the links between westernizing "civic" nationalism and legal enfranchisement and civil rights, see Reinhard Bendix, *Nation-Building and Citizenship* (New York: 1964); and Anthony D. Smith, "State-making and Nation-building," in *States in History*, ed. John Hall (Oxford: 1986). For language revivals and nation-building, see Joshua Fishman (ed.), *Language Problems in Developing Countries* (New York: 1968); for the revival of Hebrew, despite the Yiddish renascence of the period, see David Patterson, *The Hebrew Novel in Czarist Russia* (Edinburgh: 1964).

20. For the contrast between the two kinds of nationalism in paradigmatic cases, i.e., France and Germany, see Hans Konn, *Prelude to Nation-States: The French and German*

Experience, 1789–1815 (New York: 1967); cf. the criticisms of Kohn's dichotomy in Hutchinson, *Dynamics of Cultural Nationalism,* ch. 1. The populist or folk elements accord well with doctrines of self-rule and collective participation, as shown in Israel's proportional representational system of parliamentary democracy.

21. These differences in conceptions also bedeviled Zionist policies; see Ben Halpern, *The Idea of a Jewish State* (Cambridge, Mass.: 1961).

22. Elie Kedourie (ed.), *Nationalism in Asia and Africa* (London: 1971), Introduction; and for the Arab parallel of religious reform, see Anthony D. Smith, "Nationalism and Religions: The Role of Religious Reform in the Genesis of Arab and Jewish Nationalism," *Archives de sociologie des religions* 35 (1973), 23–43.

23. For an Indian parallel, see Charles Heimsath, *Indian Nationalism and Hindu Social Reform* (Princeton: 1964). For the mishnaic ideal, see Jacob Neusner, *Max Weber Revisited: Religion and Society in Ancient Judaism,* Eighth Sacks Lecture, Oxford Centre for Postgraduate Studies (Oxford: 1981).

24. For the Swiss uses of medieval heroes and settings, see Jonathan Steinberg, *Why Switzerland?* (Cambridge: 1976), especially ch. 2; see also Hans Konn, *Nationalism and Liberty: The Swiss Example* (New York: 1957).

25. The passion for archaeology (and not only in Israel) combines military nationalism with the enthusiastic excavation of "roots"; see, e.g., Yigal Yadin, *Masada* (London: 1966), and *idem, Hazor* (London: 1975); see also the brief discussion in Eric Chamberlin, *Preserving the Past* (London: 1979).

26. On this pagan Celtic past, see Nora Chadwick, *The Celts* (Harmondsworth: 1970), 83–88, 100–109; for a detailed discussion of the Gaelic revival, see Hutchinson, *Dynamics of Cultural Nationalism.*

27. For the role of the secular Greek intelligentsia, see C. Koumarianou, "The Contribution of the Greek Intelligentsia Towards the Greek Independence Movement, 1798–1821," in *The Struggle for Greek Independence,* ed. Richard Clogg (London: 1973).

28. This is discussed by J. P. Jankowski in "Nationalism in Twentieth Century Egypt," *Middle East Review* 12, No. 1 (Fall 1979), 37–48.

29. For early visions of the Haskalah, see Isaac Eisenstein-Barzilay, "National and Anti-National Trends in the Berlin Haskalah," *Jewish Social Studies* 21 (1959), 165–192; for Ahad Ha'am's essay "Moses," see *Achad Ha'am: Essays, Letters, Memoirs,* ed. and trans. Leon Simon (Oxford: 1946), 102–115.

30. Hence the popularity of books such as Yigal Yadin's *Bar-Kochba* (London: 1971). For the Zealots, see S. G. F. Brandon: *Jesus and the Zealots* (Manchester: 1967), ch. 2.

31. It is not only the Orthodox who opt for ethnic concepts of Israeli nationality. Most Jews accept the underlying Jewish rationale for the state and the choice of Zion as the homeland. For the influence of Orthodox interpretations and for the growth of Gush Emunim, the ultranationalist movement of settlement in Judea and Samaria, see Emanuel Gutmann, "Religion and Its Role in National Integration," *Middle East Review* 12, no. 1 (Fall 1979), 31–36; Dan Segre, *A Crisis of Identity: Israel and Zionism* (London: 1980).

32. For the ethnic problems of new polyethnic states, see Donald Horowitz, *Ethnic Groups in Conflict* (Berkeley and Los Angeles: 1985). For the position of Arabs within Israel, see the earlier study by Jacob Landau, *The Arabs in Israel: A Political Study* (Oxford: 1969); and the more general study of Israeli society and ethnic relations by Sammy Smooha, *Israel: Pluralism and Conflict* (London: 1978), esp. 65–69, 120–123, 197–202.

33. For some of these parallels, see Smith, "Nationalism and Religion," 23–43; cf. Shlomo Avineri, "The Social Background of Jewish and Arab Nationalism," in *Nationalism: The Nature and Evolution of an Idea,* ed. Eugene Kamenka (London: 1976).

34. The ethnic revival in the West is examined in Milton Esman (ed.), *Ethnic Conflict in the Western World* (Ithaca: 1977), and in Anthony D. Smith, *The Ethnic Revival in the Modern World* (Cambridge: 1981). For an analysis of recent ethnic conflicts in the Soviet Union, see Valerii Tishkov: "*Glasnost* and the Nationalities Within the Soviet Union," *Third World Quarterly* 11, no. 4 (1989), 191–207.

35. This is the question posed, for example, in Friedmann, *End of the Jewish People?*; cf. Amos Elon, *The Israelis: Founders and Sons* (London: 1971).

36. For the impact of the Holocaust on Israeli consciousness and for the dreams of this tiny coterie of "Canaanites," see Elon, *Founders and Sons*.

37. This is why Friedmann's pessimism in this regard is misplaced. For some theological views of the links between the Holocaust and Israel's rebirth, see Eliezer Berkovits, *Faith After the Holocaust* (New York: 1973), and Emil Fackenheim, *The Jewish Return into History* (New York: 1978).

38. For the current position of the Jewish diaspora communities, see Howard Sachar, *Diaspora: An Inquiry into the Contemporary Jewish World* (New York: 1985).

39. For an analysis of the centrality of Israel in the contemporary Jewish diaspora, see Daniel J. Elazar: "The Jewish People as the Classic Diaspora: A Political Analysis," in Sheffer (ed.), *Modern Diasporas in International Politics;* on material support for Israel, see Gabriel Sheffer, "Political Aspects of Jewish Fundraising for Israel," in *ibid.*, 258–293.

40. For the "symbolic" nature of ethnicity in the United States today, see Herbert Gans: "Symbolic Ethnicity," *Ethnic and Racial Studies* 2, no. 1 (1979), 1–20; for the American Jewish community, see Steven M. Cohen, *American Modernity and Jewish Identity* (London and New York: 1983).

41. See Karl Deutsch, *Nationalism and Social Communication,* 2nd ed. (Cambridge, Mass.: 1966), and Daniel Lerner, *The Passing of Traditional Society* (New York: 1958); for a critique, see Walker Connor, "Nation-building or Nation-destroying?" *World Politics* 24 (1972), 319–355. For recent "postindustrial" trends, see Anthony Richmond, "Ethnic Nationalism and Post-Industrialism," *Ethnic and Racial Studies* 7 (1984), 4–18.

42. An early statement of his position is found in Ernest Gellner, *Thought and Change* (London: 1964), ch. 7; a much-revised exposition of his theory is contained in *idem, Nations and Nationalism* (Oxford: 1983).

43. For Kant and the Enlightenment as the immediate sources of nationalist ideologies, see Elie Kedourie, *Nationalism* (London: 1960); for the parallel and filiation with Christian medieval millennialism and the impact of imperialism on non-European forms of nationalism, see *idem* (ed.), *Nationalism in Asia and Africa,* Introduction; cf. Anthony D. Smith, *Nationalism in the Twentieth Century* (Oxford: 1979), ch. 2.

44. See Eric Hobsbawm and Terence Ranger (eds.), *The Invention of Tradition* (Cambridge: 1983), Introduction and ch. 7; and more recently, Eric Hobsbawm, *Nations and Nationalism Since 1780* (Cambridge: 1990). Hobsbawm nevertheless sees the period 1830–1870 in Europe as the first great epoch of nationalism.

45. This abstract and "imagined" quality of modern nations is the main theme of Benedict Anderson, *Imagined Communities: Reflections on the Origins and Spread of Nationalism* (London: 1983). For a critique of these "modernist" approaches to nationalism, see Anthony D. Smith: "The Myth of the 'Modern Nation' and the Myths of Nations," *Ethnic and Racial Studies* 11, no. 1 (1988), 1–26.

46. The durability of these "archetypal" diaspora *ethnie* is underlined and discussed by John Armstrong, "Mobilized and Proletarian Diasporas," *American Political Science Review* 70 (1976), 393–408. For a full statement of the perspective adopted here, see Smith, *Ethnic Origins of Nations*, especially chs. 2–5; and *idem, National Identity* (Harmondsworth: 1991).

47. For a discussion of these issues, see the essays in *History and Ethnicity*, ed. Elisabeth Tonkin, Maryon McDonald and Malcolm Chapman (London and New York: 1989); and Smith, *Ethnic Origins of Nations*, ch. 8.

48. See, for example, the record of Jewish witnesses of the Holocaust in Isaiah Trunk (ed.), *Jewish Responses to Nazi Persecution* (New York: 1979).

Review Essays

"Not of Pure Aryan Stock": The Jewish Impact on the Economic Transformation of Modern Germany

Werner E. Mosse, *Jews in the German Economy*. Oxford: Clarendon Press, 1987. 420 pp.

Werner E. Mosse, *The German-Jewish Economic Elite 1820–1935: A Socio-Cultural Profile*. Oxford: Clarendon Press, 1989. 369 pp.

Perhaps the most spectacular economic development of the nineteenth century (which can be conveniently regarded as covering the years 1815 to 1914) was the transformation of Germany from a backward, fragmented and poverty-stricken territory into an advanced industrial society second only to the United States.[1] And even after the defeat and losses of the First World War and the trauma of hyperinflation, Weimar Germany before the onset of the Great Depression had regained European economic preeminence in a number of directions.[2]

This economic transformation was the consequence of several interrelated factors, including the growth of commercial and political unity, the impact of new modes of transport (especially the railway), the acquisition through conquest of important sources of industrial raw material—coal and potash from Alsace, iron ore from Lorraine—and the spread of improved methods of business organization and finance, including commercial banking.[3]

Less obvious but nonetheless significant as a major influence on the economic modernization of Germany—with an impact to a greater or lesser degree on all the factors mentioned above—was the role of Jewish entrepreneurial initiative. More than any other group in German society during the nineteenth and early twentieth centuries, the Jews were responsible for the creation of a sophisticated industrialized economy increasingly able to challenge Britain, the original pioneer of the industrial revolution.

The part played by Jewish businessmen in the modernization of German economic life was recognized by German scholars before the outbreak of the First World War,[4] and in recent years a great deal of specialized work in this field has been undertaken.[5] Until now, what had been lacking was an overall assessment of that role within the broad context of German economic history. Such an analysis has now been produced by Werner E. Mosse (professor emeritus in the School of European Studies, University of East Anglia, Norwich) in his *Jews in the German*

Economy, which covers the period from the 1820s to the advent of Adolf Hitler and which is likely to become the definitive general text on the subject.

Mosse's approach in this volume is to concentrate attention on what he calls "the German Jewish economic elite"—that is, the several hundred prominent businessmen who played leadership roles in the various sectors of the German economy—comparing and contrasting their activities wherever feasible with their gentile counterparts. This procedure is made possible by the Prussian, and later imperial, penchant (especially during the nineteenth century) for both classifying individuals into groups or "estates" according to their socioeconomic role and conferring official recognition on those of high standing by means of titles such as *Kommerzienrat* and (even more coveted) *Geheimer Kommerzienrat*. The criteria for the selection of such title-bearers were rigorous and comprehensive; in addition to yardsticks such as wealth and income, account was taken of economic services to the state, charitable activities and business innovations. Thus, the official archives dealing with this "honourable merchant estate" provide a wealth of relevant data for interpreting German Jewish economic activities. Significantly, they yield little evidence of antisemitic discrimination in the awarding of such titles. In fact, between 1819 (the date of the first recorded conferment on a Jew) and 1901 (by which time these honors had lost much of their prestige), some 250 men of Jewish extraction had been awarded such titles, amounting to about 20 percent of the total (pp. 2–6), although Jews over the whole of this period constituted less than 1.2 percent of the population.

Of course, exact comparative quantifications are impossible, but Mosse suggests that this Jewish elite performed a more prominent role in German economic development over a period of four generations than its counterparts in other Western industrial societies such as Britain, France, the Netherlands or even the United States; it was only in the adjoining Hapsburg monarchy and its successor states, he argues, that Jewish enterprise could be said to have played a comparable part (p. 23).

An underlying causal factor here was the underdeveloped nature of entrepreneurship in post-Napoleonic Germany: In its fragmented state, the territory remained an economic backwater where feudalism, serfdom and other surviving medieval practices such as guild privileges continued to retard the forces of growth and innovation. Commercial activity of any sort was regarded with disdain and contempt by peasant and aristocrat alike (pp. 24–26). In brief, there was a vacuum that became filled by minority "outsiders,"[6] of whom the Jews were the most important. In particular, there was an incessant demand for the specialized services of war contractors, which reached unprecedented heights during the revolutionary and Napoleonic wars when Jews such as the Frankfurt branch of the Rothschild family became indispensable to the public finances of the multiplicity of German principalities.[7]

Jewish involvement in war contracting by no means ended in 1815. During the military campaigns for political unification (1864, 1866 and 1871) new Jewish fortunes were made,[8] and the trend continued in the First World War, when Jews were responsible both for the distribution of critical raw materials,[9] food imports and marketing and for negotiations with neutrals.

Mosse suggests four special reasons why Jews became so prominent in military contracting (pp. 387–389). First was the traditional prominence of Jews in the agricultural produce trade, where they enjoyed almost a quasi monopoly in the grain, cattle, meat, horses, fodder and wool trades. Before the railway age, Jewish involvement in rural transport meant that they were the only group in a position to organize the mobilization of massive quantities of farm produce, which was the essence of effective war contracting. Second, there is much evidence to indicate that Jewish entrepreneurs went out of their way to cultivate close ties with those responsible for awarding such contracts—princes, generals and, above all, commissariats—strengthening their indispensability by offering generous credit facilities. Third, Jews traditionally had been prominent, again almost to the point of monopoly, as scrap-metal dealers—a field that assumed great importance during wartime. Finally, in the second half of the nineteenth century, Jewish armament manufacturers (the Loewe family in particular) pioneered the mass production of weaponry as well as precision machinery.[10]

War contracting led naturally to involvement in the financial transactions of government. This served as a springboard for the growth of German Jewish banking activities; and it was private and joint-stock banking that gave the Jewish elite its special importance in German economic life.

In some chronological detail, Mosse explains that by virtue of their history, cultural background, minority status and ethnicity the Jews enjoyed certain advantages not shared to anywhere near the same degree by their gentile counterparts (ch. 6 and pp. 380–384).

Unlike their Christian neighbors, Jews for many centuries had been earning their living within a monetary framework: At whatever level, Jewish commercial activities had been concerned not only with the exchange of goods but with cash and credit transactions. Conditioned to think in monetary terms, they formed by the early nineteenth century a capitalist enclave within a still predominantly pre-capitalist economy. As possessors of liquid and mobile wealth, they were the ideal partners for impecunious princes—partnerships that often led to the founding of court and state banks. Moreover, such moneylending conferred both respectability and status: Under the aegis of the Rothschilds (and of their enormous wealth), the mystique of banking offered for those of more modest backgrounds a promising avenue of upward mobility. This developing Jewish banking network operated through a strong element of mutual trust and remained largely self-perpetuating,[11] strengthened further by extensive and sustained contacts with fellow Jewish bankers on an international level.[12]

After the Franco-Prussian War, Germany's economic transformation was made possible by the rapid growth of a sophisticated joint-stock commercial banking sector[13] in which the Jewish influence was predominant. This development by no means meant the eclipse of the private banking houses, though they thenceforth tended to concentrate on more specialized financial services, especially of an international character.

As in Britain somewhat earlier, there was a continual tendency toward absorption and amalgamation in the German banking sector, such that by the close of the nineteenth century, joint-stock banking was dominated by the "Four Ds," the Darmstädter Bank (founded by Abraham Oppenheim and given its leadership role by Jakob Riesser and Bernhard Dernburg),[14] the Diskontogesellschaft (guided by three generations of the Salomonsohns), the Deutsche Bank (which Ludwig Bamberger—descended from a Jewish banking family in Mainz—helped to establish in 1870, and which was to be run by a series of Jewish financial specialists, including Hermann Wallich, Max Steinthal and Paul Mankiewitz) and the Dresden Bank (the creation of Eugen Gutmann in 1872, who was to remain its unchallenged head until his retirement in 1920).[15]

Almost without exception, these joint-stock banking pioneers were self-made men who were not drawn from the ranks of the traditional private banking families. Nor were they particularly wealthy individuals; in contrast to the Rothschild generation, the joint-stock bankers managed the investments of others rather than their own (pp. 235–236).

Besides making a major contribution to every aspect of banking activity, Jewish financiers continued to play a leading role in the field of public finance, developing public credit and floating and subscribing to government issues. They also promoted the process of capital mobilization, since Jewish brokers played a prominent part in the growth of the Berlin stock exchange (pp. 383, 396).

In one particular field of development the Jewish financial role proved to be decisive—the construction of railways. Private Jewish banks were well placed to mobilize the necessary venture capital during the crucial middle decades of the century, and Jewish entrepreneurs had a particular interest in the potentialities of steam-driven transport, given their earlier involvement in the business of moving bulky cargoes over considerable distances. While Abraham Oppenheim of Cologne, the Mendelssohn family of Berlin and Gerson Bleichröder take pride of place as railway promoters, many other Jewish provincial bankers were prominent in regional railway construction, and a good deal of Jewish capital came to be invested in the production of railway equipment and rolling stock. In no small degree, Jewish enterprise and foresight may be said to have pioneered much of the German railway system (pp. 10, 101, 108ff., 113ff.).

Among more traditional fields of Jewish enterprise was textile production, led by Valentin Grünfeld (woolen fashionwear in Upper Silesia), Philip Lieberman (pioneer of calico printing in Berlin) and the Simon brothers (the leading wholesalers) (pp. 118–129). But Jews were also to be found in "heavy industry" on a substantial scale. The Caro dynasty of iron merchants hailing from Breslau was to evolve in the course of the nineteenth century into a giant metalworking conglomerate, while Albert Hahn was instrumental in the transfer and adaptation of the latest British steel technology. At the same time, during the 1860s and 1870s, British coal imports were gradually ousted by the growing output from the Silesian mines as organized by Emanuel Friedlander (subsequently joined by his son Fritz) and Caesar Wollheim (pp. 131–137). The development of the armaments industry by the Loewe brothers has already been alluded to. Mosse points out that the Kuznets thesis of Jewish concentration in "light" consumer-oriented ventures (typical perhaps of Eastern Europe, South Africa and the United States)[16] hardly applies to the industrial revolution in Germany, where Jews were in the forefront of large-scale, capital-intensive enterprises.

The most striking example of this trend was to be found in a completely new field, the electricity industry. In 1883, the German Edison company was set up by a consortium of Jewish banks to support Emil Rathenau's project for producing electric bulbs and a central generating plant; a year later Rathenau concluded an agreement with the city of Berlin to supply electric current at an agreed price after laying a network of subterranean cables. From these beginnings was to emerge the mammoth Allgemeine Elektrizitäts-Gesellschaft (AEG), which was to dominate the German electrical industry until Hitler's rise to power (pp. 244ff., 254ff., 296–300, 395–396).

The modernization of German industry, then, was in considerable measure the product of Jewish entrepreneurship; and AEG—the cherry on the top, as it were, of these initiatives—created an infrastructure of power stations and transmission systems that brought a new source of energy to public utilities, manufacturing industry and domestic households while at the same time contributing to German exports worldwide.[17]

In commerce, the departmental chain store was a unique Jewish innovation that was to transform the entire pattern of retailing. Having its origins in Paris and New York (with Jews very much involved in both cities), the technique was transferred to Germany during and after the 1880s by astute businessmen who recognized the emergence of a middle-class mass market in the major urban centers. The new stores were characterized by the sale of a large variety of goods under one roof at fixed and clearly marked prices, and they were kept highly competitive by economies of scale and a rapid turnover. This retailing revolution, generated by families such as the Tietzes, Wertheims and Grünfelds, was an altogether Jewish phenomenon—there were no gentile counterparts (pp. 124–126).

The advent of the department store was accompanied by the modernizing of sales techniques, including advanced methods of quality and stock control, after-sales service to customers, the nationwide distribution of mail-order catalogs and the generation of demand by systematic advertising (the specialist advertising agencies that appeared as a result were also in the main Jewish-owned and operated). This Jewish flair for imaginative and innovative retailing altered German shopping habits and influenced public taste in many directions (pp. 389–390).

Another major feature of Jewish commercial activity was the opening of markets for German products and services across Central, Eastern and Southeastern Europe. In these relatively underdeveloped areas during the decades before the First World War, German Jewish businessmen were able to develop investment areas (notably for railway construction and heavy industry) and create markets for German manufactures in return for raw materials, often through contacts with fellow Jews in Vienna or Budapest, Lodz or Warsaw, Saint Petersburg or Kiev. Mosse suggests that these compatriots were the natural protagonists of German "commercial imperialism" in the East (p. 391).

Finally, mention must be made of the unique role of Albert Ballin (1857–1918),

who converted the ailing Hamburg-Amerikanische Paketfahrt into the world's largest and most prestigious shipping line (with technical innovations such as combined
passenger and cargo vessels propelled by twin-screw engines) and who was described as a charismatic "past-master in the art of negotiation," inspiring such
confidence that his gentile British competitors refused to attend the international
shipping "conferences" (negotiations to pool traffic and fix rates) unless Ballin
could preside.[18] Although Ballin's contribution was sui generis, he was by no
means the only Jewish figure involved in Germany's maritime commerce (p. 393).

In the important concluding chapter of *Jews in the German Economy,* Mosse emphasizes two broader issues, the significant Jewish contributions to German capitalism and economic integration.

Not only did Jewish banks mobilize capital resources to advance the techniques
and scale of government borrowing, but by the late nineteenth century they had
become a major source of funds for private industry; it was chiefly Jewish financiers
who initiated moves toward "rationalization" (industrial concentration)[19] through a
variety of fusions and associations. In short, almost to the end, Jews played a
considerable role in the evolution of German capitalism.

The contribution of Jewish enterprise in building up a single German national
economy as a prelude to political unification is evident both in the development of a
communications network between the eastern and western halves of the Prussian
monarchy and in the establishment of regional banks that were to become coun-
trywide in scope, thereby promoting economic integration between north and south.

Even more significant was the integrative role of Jewish enterprise on an international level, where a heretofore parochial Germany was thrust into the world economy. As members of a widely dispersed and commercially articulate minority, the
German Jewish elite deliberately cultivated close personal and economic ties across
frontiers, and they were thus more attuned than their gentile counterparts to the
potentials of foreign markets and investment opportunities. AEG had three hundred
foreign sales offices, Ballin pushed his luxury liners' appeal for American tourists,
and the Mendelssohns developed complex financial dealings with Russia; nor was it
accidental that a Jew became cofounder and the only German member of the
London metal exchange. Technology transfer was also part of this process: By
buying up foreign patents and closely studying new industrial and commercial
techniques abroad, Jewish businessmen helped to raise German standards to advanced world levels. Eventually, Jews became the principal medium for the export
of German know-how to less developed regions both in Europe and in the rest of the
world.

It is hardly surprising, then, that these same Jews were strongly opposed to
protectionism of any kind. This made the German Jewish economic elite a target of
attack from right-wing circles in agriculture and heavy industry, who stigmatized
their attitude as "cosmopolitan," "un-national" and even unpatriotic. Given the
prominence of Jews in capitalist enterprise, these arguments were reinforced by
virulent attacks on the way in which pristine preindustrial values had been upset by
modern capitalism, which was portrayed as something "alien" and "un-Ger-

man."[20] Nor were such attitudes confined to right-wing conservative groups; Marx himself had regarded the terms "Jew" and "capitalist" as synonymous.[21]

While the onset of the Great Depression in 1929 and particularly the banking crisis of 1931 hit many firms in which Jews were prominent, the evidence suggests that the Jewish component within the German economy was not disproportionately weakened (pp. 362–373). Thereafter, the impact of increasing antisemitic agitation and political instability was diffuse and delayed, partly because the leading Jewish private banks remained an irreplaceable economic asset as a result of their international standing[22]—a factor clearly recognized by Hitler's finance wizard, Hjalmar Schacht. Hence, the forced removal of Jews holding prominent positions was a relatively slow and uneven process until 1938. But from then onward, the personnel files of major firms carried the following cryptic entry opposite Jewish "resignations": *als nichtarisch ausgeschieden,* "not of pure aryan stock."

In his most recent work, *The German-Jewish Economic Elite,* Mosse skillfully makes use of published memoirs, unpublished reminiscences, surviving correspondence, monographs on individuals and families and a miscellany of other primary and near-primary sources to construct a sociocultural profile of this distinctive group within German Jewry. Building on the economic foundations provided in *Jews in the German Economy,* Mosse presents an absorbing analysis of the German Jewish elite's attitude toward Judaism and its Jewish identity, on the one hand, and the degree of its integration into the broader society, on the other.

Until the mid-nineteenth century, the question of self-identification among German Jews was resolved in religious terms only. However, as secular education and German acculturation alienated members of the elite from traditional religious observance, Jewish identity was increasingly expressed in terms of social action—the formation of organizations for the relief of refugees (mainly from Russian pogroms), endowments and foundations to care for orphans, holiday homes for the underprivileged, scholarships for aspiring students.[23] Such charitable giving, mandated by Jewish tradition, grew in scope and variety with the increasing prosperity enjoyed by members of the elite and flowered into the remarkable pattern of welfare organizations that had come to characterize German Jewish life by the early twentieth century.

But identity and integration, as Mosse is at pains to stress, are fluid processes rather than static conditions, such that individuals and families were in a state of constant flux. Unmistakably, however, the trend was for German Jews to strive more toward integration into the broader society; in this process, there was little prospect of reaching a stable equilibrium. During the second half of the nineteenth century, the cultural aspect of the elite's social activity expressed itself in lavish patronage of theaters, concerts and art galleries, with the group playing a unique role in the cultural development of Wilhelmine Germany (though possibly somewhat less so during the Weimar aftermath). In the public sphere proper, however, the elite's part was far less significant and was limited mainly to municipal or, at the most, regional political affairs, with virtually no active participation in public life at the national level.[24]

In trying to draw inferences from the often-fragmented evidence assembled in his second volume, Mosse argues that two radically different sets of conclusions can be reached. On the one hand, the elite's history represents an outstanding success story: Within a short time span a succession of Jewish merchants, bankers and industrialists had reached the pinnacle of economic achievement. They exerted a marked influence on German modernization, lived in opulent style and were able to guide their offspring, in a majority of instances, in following successful business or professional careers. On the other hand, it can equally well be demonstrated that members of the elite remained outsiders in gentile society, officially tolerated for their undoubted economic expertise but the victims as well of widespread disdain that was not unmixed with envy. As a consequence, many of their children would develop an inferiority complex compounded by Jewish self-hatred. The wider German atmosphere was extensively poisoned by antisemitism, from which neither economic achievement nor philanthropy or cultural activities could insulate the Jew (pp. 351–355).

These contrasting interpretations are not mutually exclusive; each contains substantial elements of truth. Complete escape from the dilemma was impossible. Baptism often did not bring acceptance, and intermarriage (which was surprisingly rare) only deferred the issue to a generation that would be starkly confronted with an identity problem after 1933. Moreover, there also were instances in which wholly assimilated Jews were driven back into an attitude of ethnic solidarity as a result of rising antisemitism (pp. 58–59).

While Mosse's first volume is a path-breaking study in the much-neglected field of German Jewish economic history, his second constitutes a pioneering group biography that makes a major contribution to our understanding of the changing nature of "Jewishness" in an increasingly hostile environment. Together, these two works constitute a signal contribution to German Jewish history.

MARCUS ARKIN
University of Durban-Westville

Notes

1. J. H. Clapham, *Economic Development of France and Germany, 1815–1914* (Cambridge: 1961), passim.

2. K. S. Pinson, *Modern Germany: Its History and Civilization* (New York: 1954), ch. 18.

3. An excellent summary of German economic unification is to be found in A. Milward and S. B. Saul, *The Economic Development of Continental Europe, 1780–1870* (London: 1973), 365–431.

4. Werner Sombart's *Die Juden und das Wirtschaftsleben* (Leipzig: 1911) was the most influential of these works.

5. Marcus Arkin, "Some Recent German Studies," *Jewish Affairs* (Feb. 1978), 37–38.

6. As early as the seventeenth century (after the Thirty Years' War), German princes anxious to develop their territories were forced to offer all kinds of inducements to foreign immigrants, including Protestant refugees from Catholic persecution and Jews fleeing the Inquisition, because of the lack of any indigenous entrepreneurial class.

7. Marcus Arkin, "The Rise of the Rothschilds During the Napoleonic Wars," *Jewish Affairs* (Nov. 1960), 23–29.

8. See, for example, Fritz Stern's study of the relationship between Gerson Bleichröder and Bismarck, *Gold and Iron* (New York: 1977).

9. See Ernst Schulin, *Walter Rathenau* (Göttingen: 1979).

10. The brothers Ludwig and Isidor Loewe had branched out into armaments from the manufacture of sewing machines; see Georg Tischert, *Aus der Entwicklung des Loewe-Konzerns* (Berlin: 1911).

11. The histories of prominent banking families such as the Landaus, Salomonsohns, Gutmanns and Fürstenbergs contain many examples of dynastic intermarriage; some details are to be found in Daniel Bernstein, *"Wirtschaft II: Handel und Industrie,"* in Siegmund Kaznelson (ed.), *Juden im deutschen Kulturbereich* (Berlin: 1962).

12. For instance, the collection and transfer of French war indemnity payments after the Peace of Frankfurt in 1871 was so complex and involved such enormous shifts of funds (5 billion francs) that only the network linking major Jewish banking houses in Germany, France and Britain was capable of carrying it out. See Ellis T. Powell, *The Evolution of the Money Market, 1385–1915* (London: 1966), 494–499.

13. Jacob Reisser, *The German Great Banks and Their Concentration in Connection with the Economic Development of Germany*, 3rd ed. (Washington, D.C.: 1911); P. Barrett Whale, *Joint Stock Banking in Germany* (London: 1930).

14. For Dernburg's career, see W. Schiefel, *Bernhard Dernburg* (Zurich: n.d.).

15. For Eugen Gutman, see Kurt Huscha, *Aus der Geschichte der Dresdner Bank, 1872–1969* (Frankfurt: 1969).

16. Simon Kuznets's argument is to be found in Louis Finkelstein (ed.), *The Jews: Their History, Culture and Religion*, vol. 2, 3rd ed. (Philadelphia: 1966), ch. 39.

17. By 1907, the AEG, under Emil Rathenau's able leadership, had grown to be a huge concern of ten thousand employees; six years later, Germany's exports of electrical goods were valued at nearly 220 million marks. See W. O. Henderson, *The Industrial Revolution on the Continent* (London: 1961), 72. For more details on the Rathenau era, see Felix Pinner, *Emil Rathenau und das elektrische Zeitalter* (Leipzig: 1918).

18. There is a considerable bibliography on Ballin's career; two particularly useful contributions are Lamar Cecil, *Albert Ballin: Business and Politics in Imperial Germany, 1888–1918* (Princeton: 1967); and Eduard Rosenbaum, "Albert Ballin: A Note on the Style of His Economic and Political Activities," *Leo Baeck Institute Yearbook* 3 (1958), 257–299.

19. For some details of the pre-1914 trend toward rationalization, see Alfred Marshall, *Industry and Trade*, bk. 3, 3rd ed. (London: 1920), chs. 9 and 10.

20. For Sombart's equivocal views, see the discussion by Wanda Kampmann, *Deutsche und Juden* (Frankfurt: 1979), 427ff.; for pre-Nazi antisemitic views about Jewish "domination of commerce," see Bernt Engelmann, *Germany without Jews: A Balance Sheet* (New York: 1984), 228–235.

21. Marcus Arkin, "Marx's Writings and Jewish Enterprise," in his *Aspects of Jewish Economic History* (Philadelphia: 1975), pt. 3, ch. 16.

22. Such was the prestige of some of these firms that even after they were "aryanized" in 1938, the Nazis continued to operate them under their old names (e.g., M. M. Warburg & Co.).

23. Benjamin Hirsch of Halberstadt (1840–1911) typifies this form of "Jewishness in action," but Mosse (66–90) also provides examples drawn form the Tietz and Simon families of Berlin and of Wilhelm Merton and Charles Hallgarten in Frankfurt-am-Main (66–90).

24. Mosse notes (349) that the assassination of Walter Rathenau in 1922 "was final proof—if proof was needed—that Jews had no substantial role to play on the German public stage" (*ibid.*, 349).

Walking the Tightrope:
Jordan and the Middle East Conflict

Uri Bar-Joseph, *The Best of Enemies: Israel and Transjordan in the War of 1948*.
London: Frank Cass & Co., 1987. 254 pp.

Samir A. Mutawi, *Jordan in the 1967 War*. Cambridge: Cambridge University
Press, 1987. 228 pp.

Mary C. Wilson, *King Abdullah, Britain and the Making of Jordan*. Cambridge:
Cambridge University Press, 1987. 289 pp.

Jordan's domestic stability and essentially stabilizing effect on the central Arab-
Israeli equation acquired almost universal endorsement after 1970–1971 from academic authorities and policymakers alike. They constitute two pillars of a strategy
for resolving the Palestinian problem through a two-state territorial compromise
known generically as the "Jordanian option"; they are also a cornerstone of the
strategic consensus between Jerusalem and Washington. So traditional and uncon-
tested did this view become of King Hussein's confident mastery over the internal
affairs of the Hashemite kingdom, combined with his moderate diplomatic orientation and commitment to peace with Israel, that each of these premises enjoys the
status of Middle East conventional wisdom.

Of late, however, this web of assumptions and unquestioned answers spun around
Jordan—king and country—if not in tatters, has certainly unraveled. A major cause
for the challenge to fundamental assumptions is Hussein himself in his own unset-
tling words and deeds. Reaching backward several years, there is Hussein's nationwide televised address of July 31, 1988, in which he renounced all claims to the
contested West Bank; his mismanagement of structural economic, social and political disorders on the kingdom's East Bank heartland; and his conscious affiliation
with Iraq's Saddam Hussein during the Persian Gulf war, to the undisguised consternation of U.S. and Israeli officials.

Whatever else, such developments have served two useful functions. In the first
instance, they have put an end to complacency and "groupthink" toward Jordan, its
basic capabilities and intentions. In the second instance, there has been renewed
interest—and in some quarters, unprecedented concern—over Jordan as a pivotal
actor whose government's staying power and future prospects seem increasingly
uncertain. Earlier premises can no longer be taken for granted, but if greater political realism prevails, the result may be some fresh, if belated, thinking about the
intricate Israeli-Palestinian-Hashemite triangular relationship.

With this objective in mind, the books under review, by offering a larger historical perspective, make an important contribution—individually and collectively—to understanding Jordan. Each study focuses upon one of the three major signposts in Jordan's political evolution: Mary Wilson on its formative years between 1921 and 1948; Uri Bar-Joseph on the controversial 1948 partitioning of Palestine between Israel and Jordan; and Samir Mutawi on events preceding and immediately following the Six-Day War.

While of uneven quality and scholarship, these three books complement one another, each providing a fragment of the broader tapestry that is Jordanian history. Those reading all three works will be rewarded with a deeper sense of the process of consolidation, expansion and contraction that has seen the country transformed from a small emirate (Transjordan from 1921 to 1948) to an East Bank/West Bank kingdom during its annexationist phase (1949–1967) to the present, more restricted Jordan of the East Bank. All three authors also underscore just how critical is the role of personality in Jordan, offering comparisons between the two monarchs, Abdullah and Hussein—grandfather and grandson, respectively. Moreover, each work makes it clear how disproportionate an impact Jordan has always had on the circumstances of war, peace, or no-war no-peace vis-à-vis Israel.

This latter realization leads us, in turn, to a final insight afforded by these studies. They hint at some of the motivating forces and political dynamics that underlie the extraordinary Amman-Jerusalem connection inaugurated in the pre-1948 era by Abdullah and Zionist leaders. What amounts to a secret understanding among cobelligerent states has been nurtured for many years by King Hussein and a succession of Israeli governments—surviving basically intact any number of military confrontations, crises, regional tensions and misunderstandings. This unique relationship, truly that of "the best of enemies," is all the more remarkable for being de facto and tacit, discreet rather than codified. Being limited to functional cooperation, however, it is also susceptible to sudden defection by either one of the two parties. This is what occurred in June 1967 when, disregarding two urgent Israeli entreaties, Hussein made the worst mistake of his long career in committing Jordan to the Arab war option, forfeiting as a result the principal West Bank legacy bequeathed him nineteen years earlier by Abdullah.

The explanation for Hussein's 1967 fiasco, as indeed for all actions by Jordan, may be traced back to what Bar-Joseph terms the "limited strategy" dictated by the country's geopolitical realities. Hussein, like Abdullah before him, has had to plot each of his moves with the utmost prudence, calculating every act of commission or omission for its possible impact on as many as five different (and often competitive) sets of political onlookers: his own subjects, the Palestinian national movement, fellow Arab world leaders, watchful Israelis and, not least, Jordan's current Great Power patron, the United States (a replacement for Great Britain). It is this broad interplay of rival forces, competing interests and counterpressures that makes leadership of Jordan at once so challenging and so perilous.

The origins of this structured Jordanian dilemma, like the history of the kingdom itself, go back to 1921, when there was a momentary convergence of British expediency and the wiliness of a young Hashemite tribal prince, Abdullah. A "temporary" agreement worked out between him and Colonial Secretary Winston

Churchill for preserving calm on the eastern frontier wilderness of Palestine became tantamount instead to its first partitioning as the arrangement gradually assumed permanence. The 1920s and 1930s—as carefully traced by Mary Wilson through the use of archival sources and private British papers—constitute the phase of consolidation, during which Abdullah was preoccupied with building a personal power base on the East Bank through the indispensable assistance of his patrons in London. The latter appreciated, in Wilson's words, the fact that Transjordan was "an artificial creation with little meaning beyond its importance to British strategy and imperial communications" (p. 213).

Abdullah's isolation in a desert kingdom dominated by Britain may have suited British purposes. Yet Abdullah had his own personal agenda. Indeed, as Wilson notes insightfully, "His awareness of Transjordan's limitations was the springboard of his ambition" (p. 85), which was further whetted by formal independence in 1946. The goal was unambiguous: an economically and politically weighty throne. Two geographical frameworks existed: "greater Syria," or expansion westward. Blocked by Arab rivals on the "greater Syria" scheme, Abdullah concentrated on the growing struggle over Palestine, waiting patiently for an opportune moment and a favorable balance of forces.

Both came for him in 1948–1949. Domestically, the structure of Transjordan allowed Abdullah to pursue his objectives in Palestine with little regard for popular opinion. The Palestinian community disintegrated, creating a political and military vacuum into which Abdullah was prepared to insert his Arab Legion, moving swiftly to occupy and then annex those West Bank areas designated by the 1947 United Nations resolution for an independent Palestinian state. But what facilitated yet another act of boldness on the part of Abdullah, not unlike his 1921 gamble, was once again the timing, and also the convergence of interests and weaknesses, by the other three concerned parties. Inter-Arab divisiveness prevented rival Arab countries from deterring Abdullah's unilateral land grab. The British, too, silently acquiesced, deciding to support an expansive Transjordan rather than a separate Palestine. The key factor, however, was tacit consent on the part of Israel; or, more precisely, that of David Ben-Gurion on behalf of the Jewish state-in-the-making.

This dramatic turn of events, and how the gentleman's agreement partitioning Palestine anew evolved in behind-the-scenes secret negotiation, is the theme of Uri Bar-Joseph's book. While not as exhaustive as Avi Shlaim's *Collusion Across the Jordan* (1988), this competent analysis has the virtue of being more focused. It is limited to the critical transitional period from November 1947 to March 1949, with the author patiently taking us through the maze of calculations, maneuvers and bargaining positions on respective sides of the river, along with the series of quiet diplomatic exchanges that ultimately led to a bilateral accord advantageous to both parties. Israel managed to safeguard its most immediate security concerns, while Abdullah succeeded in outflanking his Palestinian, Egyptian, Saudi and other Arab opponents to extend his Hashemite domain.

Given the hard constraints upon his freedom of action, Abdullah emerges as a shrewd bargainer who parleyed his few assets and an extremely fluid situation in and around Palestine to his advantage. Nevertheless, Bar-Joseph, reflecting a talent for conceptualizing considerable historical detail, correctly portrays Ben-Gurion and

Abdullah as equals. Both men were supreme pragmatists, masters of the art of the possible and of the fait accompli. In the author's own words, each leader demonstrated the ability "to appreciate the stakes involved, define that fine line beyond which demands exceeded the necessary minimum for each side, and thereby achieve the maximum possible, without breaking the rules of the game" (pp. 236–237)— rules no less operative or compelling for being unwritten. The 1947–1949 phase of Hashemite expansionism, in short, owed less to collusion than to geopolitics.

Enduring geopolitical realities, eventually reinforced by a predisposition toward stability mutually shared by elites in Amman and Jerusalem, are what thrust the two vulnerable states together. Facts on the ground led Israel to sanction Abdullah's annexation of the West Bank; they enabled the Israeli-Jordanian relationship to survive his assassination in 1951; and they encouraged his young successor, Hussein, not only to maintain but even to widen the scope of this bilateral understanding. Not least important, they also enabled Israeli-Jordanian ties to recover from Hussein's major miscalculation in 1967.

According to Bar-Joseph, it is no exaggeration to state that "if any Arab ruler contributed positively to the existence of the State of Israel, it was Abdullah" (p. 242). Without finding fault with this argument, it only tells half the story: Israel has more than paid its "debt of thanks" by maintaining a tolerant policy toward Hussein's indiscretions. Indeed, there are political grounds for widening Bar-Joseph's quotation—if any Middle East country contributed positively to the existence and security of the Kingdom of Jordan during the past twenty years, it was Israel.

This fact, in retrospect, makes Hussein's judgment in 1967 all the more inexplicable. In Samir Mutawi's book, there is a good deal of background provided on the policy process, institutions and foreign affairs of Jordan. Unfortunately, however, Mutawi contributes little to the historical record. The author, a journalist and broadcaster who at the time of writing served as chief of press, research and studies at the Royal Hashemite Court in Amman, benefited from interviews with high Jordanian government and military figures and had access to the ultimate decision maker, King Hussein himself. His book, however, is a thinly veiled and altogether unconvincing effort to exonerate Hussein and Jordan from any direct responsibility for gross crisis mismanagement in June 1967. According to Mutawi's self-serving interpretation, we are to believe that the usually astute and resolute monarch chose to ignore his own personal misgivings and those of his army advisers in the name of Arab unity. It is for this reason, Mutawi claims, that Hussein threw caution and national-dynastic self-interest to the wind, allowing Israeli provocations (together with Egyptian dictates and Syrian warmongering) to determine Jordan's stance against Israel.

In Mutawi's words, Jordan thus offered "the ultimate sacrifice." Be that as it may, Hussein violated two rules: He disobeyed the basic strictures set down by Abdullah to avoid excessive risk-taking and Arab entanglements in favor of prudence and extreme caution, and he acted contrary to the fundamental guidelines of maintaining tacit coexistence with Israel—a mistake he took pains not to repeat in 1973. What matters in terms of the crisis denouement and in geopolitical terms is that Jordan after June 1967 was once again the Transjordan of King Abdullah. Or, as Mutawi puts it, "the nation which gave the most, lost the most" (p. 185). Far more dubious is the consolation of gaining "Arab recognition of the depth and sincerity of Jordan's commitment to Arab unity and the Palestine cause" (p. 185). Small balm; or has the author, writing in the 1980s, possibly forgotten the backhanded slap given the Hashemites by the Rabat Arab summit in 1974, which declared the P.L.O. to be henceforth and forever more "the sole legitimate representative" of the Palestinian cause?

Hussein and Jordan, both restricted and resigned to the East Bank, were thus fully reengaged in the earlier, far from completed task of consolidation when the crisis over Kuwait erupted in August 1990 and threatened to upset the delicate political balances that lie at the heart of the kingdom's stability and security.

In the course of the previous decade, Hussein could point with pride to his regime's success in reordering and stabilizing relationships with at least four of the five omnipresent political onlookers, the four external parties. At the inter-Arab level, Jordan appeared to be fairly safely within the Arab consensus; at a minimum, its territorial integrity was not too directly challenged by any neighboring would-be Arab predator. So, too, the fundamental strategic mixed-adversarial relationship with Israel seemed likely to endure, barring any rash move by Amman, such as creating a flagrant casus belli by opening its borders to Iraqi or other Arab armed forces. In the aftermath of the 1982 Lebanon intervention, Israel had neither the inclination nor the will to interfere in the domestic affairs of another neighboring country, least of all Jordan. Similarly, Hussein had been careful to maintain correct relations with the P.L.O., even as he continued to receive a sympathetic audience in the United States and the West.

Mary Wilson is useful in establishing the pattern of Jordan's patron-client relationship. Bar-Joseph supplements her analysis by providing sources for the enduring (and durable) Jerusalem-Amman axis. And Mutawi, despite his ex post facto rationalization for 1967, is of help in squaring the circle by viewing Jordan in an inter-Arab context.

Yet the next scene in the Jordanian tapestry could well be woven by the one political force least dealt with by the three works under review. For the great "unknown" in the Jordanian equation is likely to be the domestic determinant. Either still during Hussein's reign or following his departure, there looms the long-averted confrontation in Abdullah's "dual monarchy" between, on the one hand, the Hashemite state and, on the other hand, the Palestine nation that has proven the single greatest casualty of Jordan's successive creation, expansion, contraction and consolidation of power.

AHARON KLIEMAN
Tel-Aviv University

Book Reviews

Antisemitism, Holocaust and Genocide

Thomas Albrich, *Exodus durch Österreich: Die jüdischen Flüchtlinge 1945–1948.* Innsbrucker Forschungen zur Zeitgeschichte, herausgegeben von Rolf Steininger, Institut für Zeitgeschichte der Universität Innsbruck, Band I. Innsbruck: Haymon Verlag, 1987. 265 pp.

The history of Austrian Jews and the interrelation between Austrian and Jewish history have for several years received the attention of Austrian academia. Thus, it is not surprising that this new Innsbruck University series begins with a pioneering work relating both to Jews and to Austria: the post-Holocaust Jewish migration in Europe, in which Austria occupied a central position.

When Europe was liberated from the Nazi yoke, those Jews who survived in concentration camps, in underground groups or in hiding were faced not only with devastation but with an unknown future. The response of many, especially in Eastern Europe, was to get up and leave—to turn their backs on Europe's bloodstained soil and begin new lives across the sea. These first postwar migrants turned southward and westward, primarily to the Mediterranean ports from which they hoped to sail for Eretz Israel.

Once the first migration wave had subsided, the Jews continued to move, for two main reasons. First, many of the initial group who had wished to leave Europe were unable, as a result of restrictive immigration policies, to reach the two most favored destinations of Palestine or the United States. Consequently, they began to gather in DP camps, both those near the Italian and French ports and the German and Austrian camps set up by the American, British and French occupying forces. Second, new migration waves emerged during the postwar years. The Russian-Polish repatriation agreements had provided for the return of some one hundred seventy thousand Polish Jews who had found refuge in Soviet Russia during the war, but an outbreak of murderous antisemitism in Eastern Europe—particularly in Poland—caused many to leave their countries. Jews also suffered from economic distress, to the point of starvation, in several countries (especially Rumania and Hungary). Finally, many Jews were anxious to leave the Soviet sphere of influence in Eastern Europe.

In their search for a permanent refuge, postwar Jewish migrants gathered in three principal countries: Germany, Austria (both of these Allied-occupied) and Italy. The circumstances and refugee populations in each country were distinctive. Jews who concentrated near the Italian ports saw them as the penultimate stop, the stepping-stone to rescue by means of illegal immigration to Palestine. Predominant in this group were the young and those determined to reach Eretz Israel at any cost; the turnover depended on the varying rate of success in finding means of transport. Far more static was the situation of displaced persons in Germany who could not reach the southern European ports or who awaited other migration alternatives. In contrast, the description of Jews in postwar Austria is far more dynamic, a tale of restless wandering and constant movement either southward to Italy or to the German camps. Such shifting precludes any precise estimate of the number of Jews who spent any length of time in postwar Austrian DP or transit camps. Albrich cites a total figure of some two hundred thousand. As the chief way station to both the south and the west, Austria played the major role in the drama of the postwar Jewish exodus from Europe—a saga of displaced persons that would end only with the establishment of the state of Israel and the opening of the American gates to increased immigration in the late 1940s.

This entire epic, with a focus on its Austrian aspect (hitherto shrouded in obscurity), unfolds in Albrich's book. Incorporating a variety of British, Jewish and Austrian sources as well as numerous pertinent studies of such related issues as the *briḥah* (flight) and Britain's Palestine policy, Albrich weaves his findings on the Austrian role into an intricate historical fabric. He does not overlook a single migration wave or any of the acts and policies affecting movement to and from Austria: those of the East European countries from which most of the migrants came, as well as those of the Soviet Union, the Allied occupying powers, Italy and, not least, Austria itself. Albrich deals with the way Austrian citizens responded to the displaced Jews in their midst and provides a vivid—and rather shocking— depiction of the lives of the migrants as they struggled toward a permanent home, usually in Eretz Israel.

Like Germany, Austria remained under occupation for several years after Europe was liberated from the Nazis, with independence restored only gradually. Both countries were divided into occupation zones: Soviet Russia in the East; Britain, the United States and France in the West. Despite a certain degree of cooperation (mainly among the Western powers), the occupying regimes differed greatly. Albrich contributes decisively toward our understanding of how markedly these differences affected the displaced Jews in the various zones of occupation—of the factors that brought the greatest concentration of displaced persons to Germany, of all places, and the ways in which the DP issue figured within the policy constellations of the various occupying powers. The generally accepted picture of a harsh British regime acting to avert immigrant pressure on Palestine is mitigated here; what emerges instead is a clear disparity between the humanitarian aims of the local British administration and the policies of the government back home. As to the "permissive" American regime, certain questions arise regarding both its motives and, more importantly, the social and economic effects of its policy on the displaced persons.

The author's thorough grasp of the Austrian sphere gives him an edge over students of American or British policy in general, whose attention is directed more toward other issues such as the Cold War or the Middle East. But the soundness of Albrich's interpretation of American (as well as French, Italian and Soviet) policy is undermined to some extent by its reliance on British and Austrian sources alone, rather than on those of the countries in question. Indeed, the most compelling portions of the book are those that address the roots of British policy and its many-faceted implications for the Jewish DPs in Austria and elsewhere.

The key determinants of Austria's role in Jewish migration were its geographical location and its postwar political status. Yet the book does not make even brief mention of either the major stages of Austria's economic and political reconstruction or the country's apportionment among the occupying powers. Nor is there a map showing the chief transit routes that led southward and westward from Austria. Since these transits (including those between occupation zones) constitute the essence of the book, such fundamental omissions are hard to understand, as is the conspicuous absence of material about some seven thousand Jews who eventually settled in Vienna, except for mention of the role of the Viennese Jewish community in offering assistance and refuge to Jews in transit.

A final point: The lives of the migrant Jews are depicted only sketchily. There is ample information on their difficult material circumstances and on the assistance and rehabilitation they were offered, but such descriptions rely largely on outside, chiefly British, sources. The lack of internal Jewish reports—most of which were written in Yiddish—translates into a lack of information regarding the migrants' cultural and political lives. The few descriptions of the Irgun's intensive activity among the DPs, for example, serve mainly to whet the reader's unsatisfied curiosity.

Such points, however, do not detract from the substantial value of this book, which includes as well indexes, scientific documentation and illuminating illustrations. It is unfortunate that this useful work is currently accessible only to readers of German; translation would ensure a larger audience for a work worthy of wider attention.

HAGIT LAVSKY
The Hebrew University

Shmuel Almog (ed.), *Antisemitism Through the Ages*. Jerusalem: The Hebrew University, Vidal Sassoon International Center for the Study of Antisemitism, 1988. 430 pp.

Antisemitism Through the Ages is a difficult book to assess. Edited by Shmuel Almog for the Vidal Sassoon International Center for the Study of Antisemitism of The Hebrew University, this collection of essays spans Jewish history from the Hellenistic period to the present. It is not, as I had hoped, a text that might be used in place of works by Leon Poliakov, George Mosse, Malcolm Hay, Norman Cohn, Sabato Morais or even Jacob Marcus. As with any anthology, the writing is uneven, ranging from very good to pedestrian. Some contributions in fact are gratuitous lecture pieces no more than three to five pages in length that contain few, if any, citations.

While a number of essays (in particular Shmuel Ettinger's opening piece, Almog's assessment of Ernest Renan, and Yisrael Gutman's discussion of Nazi antisemitism) read like excellent historiographic exercises, often as not there are major glosses within and among other essays. Various scholars debate whether animosity toward Jews and their religion should be labeled antisemitism or anti-Judaism (could not Leon Pinsker's term of Judaeophobia serve to adequately describe bigots who simultaneously have contempt for and fear of the "unlike"?), but there is no real discussion of animosities that antedated the Hellenistic period, such as those chronicled in the Old Testament. Other notable omissions include the role of Julius Caesar or Julian the Apostate in Jewish-Roman relations, the various pseudo-messiahs of the Middle Ages, and the seventeenth-century Chmelnicki massacres. Talmud burnings and charges of host desecration are mentioned, but only in passing.

Sometimes important questions are raised but are answered either superficially or not at all. Jacob Barnai correctly attributes most of the blood libels in the Ottoman Empire to Christian sources, but unfortunately, his discussion of the position of the Turkish government is extremely brief, consisting of just one paragraph. Haggai Ben-Shammai states that Christians enjoyed a "clear priority" over Jews in the Islamic world, without pointing out that the advantage they enjoyed stemmed from a "balance of terror"—potential reprisals by Christians against Muslims resident in the European countries. Avraham Grossman blames the excesses of the Islamic world upon the "profligate," "ostentatious" Jews with "extravagant life styles" rather than the villainy of pogrom-makers. Similarly, Kenneth Stow's essay attributes papal outbursts against Jews to the Jews themselves not keeping within the traditional bonds of servitude to the Holy See.

Like Lloyd Gartner, who contributes an uninspiring essay on America, Zefira Rokeach suggests that the history of antisemitism in England is yet to be written. And yet other works, regarded as standards, come readily to mind while reading through this volume. Robert Bonfils's terse essay on the Devil and the Jews makes one long for Joshua Trachtenberg's timeless study of the same name. Joseph Kaplan rejects Spinoza's contention that antisemitism disappeared in Spain with the expulsion of the Jews by stressing the importance of the *limpieza de sangre* (blood certificate) for centuries after. But a nonscholar, Simon Wiesenthal, did a more thorough job in *Sails of Hope,* and Cecil Roth and A. A. Neumann are still the benchmarks of Hispanic Jewish history. In like manner, the studies on Islam leave one recalling works by S. D. Goitein, Bernard Lewis, Norman Stillman and Miriam Bat Yeor.

Having said all of this, I do not want to leave the reader with the idea that *Antisemitism Through the Ages* is an unsubstantial volume. There are good, solid, scholarly pieces such as Haim Avni's study of the Buenos Aires pogrom of January 16, 1919, Nathaniel Katzburg's piece on Hungary under Miklos Horthy, Moshe Zimmerman's fascinating essay on Wilhelm Marr, and Jacob Katz's equally captivating essay on the obscure journalist Otto Glagau. Several chapters are markedly superior. Mordechai Breuer makes three crucial observations in his discussion of the Black Death: (1) however popes or monarchs tried to rationalize their social situation, Jews were in fact chattels by the fourteenth century; (2) there were no incidents of *kiddush hashem* after 1348 because Jews were given no choice of converting during persecutions associated with the plague; and (3) the masses did believe the libels attributed to the Jews.

Shalom Bar-Asher is unique in relating how Jews coped with the pressures of antisemitism. His essay on Morocco in the seventeenth century tells of internalized insecurities and fears, of curses leveled against Muslims, of the yearning for Eretz Israel expressed in *piyutim;* and it explains as well the loyalty that most Jews felt for the king, who was their only protector. Shmuel Almog's study of Ernest Renan is necessary reading for those who have lumped the French scholar with racists of the nineteenth century. While Renan did subscribe to Eurocentric notions of racial superiority (Semites allegedly were inferior), he was, as Almog points out, a mass of contradictions who, like Heine, saluted Jews and Hellenes as the principal sources of European civilization. I would also salute Yisrael Gutman's "On the Character of Nazi Antisemitism," which quickly dispenses with such bogus issues as whether the Holocaust is metahistory and goes on to examine Hitler through his speeches and writings.

Two essays merit special commendation for their didactic nature. Not surprisingly, Yehoshafat Harkabi's discussion of Arab antisemitism raises one of the crucial points in this book. While Jews, Zionism and Israel have undergone a propaganda barrage for the past forty years, very little has been done by Jewish scholars to publicize anti-Jewish persecution or diatribes in the Arab world. Some eight hundred thousand Jews who had suffered every form of discrimination before 1948 dwindled to twenty-five thousand currently living on the brink of terror, while Israeli scholars fantasized that Arabs one day would become more "mellow." Harkabi chides both free world governments and historians for this "almost forgiving stance."

Surprisingly, the other instructive piece is one that deals with a familiar subject. Richard Cohen's "The Dreyfus Affair" is fairly straightforward in its recitation of the roles of Bernard Lazare, Zola and Leroy-Beaulieu. But just as Anatole France did in *Penguin Island,* Cohen condemns the "pusillanimity" of Jews in France at the end of the nineteenth century. Governed by insecurity and fear of backlash, many counseled silence ("to think of it, always; never to speak of it").

How much or little was done by the free world to assist the Jews of Europe during the Holocaust is a matter for debate elsewhere. The important point to note is that the worth of a book, especially a book dealing with an ongoing issue like antisemitism, lies in its utility. To whom is the book addressed, and how effectively will it be used? My guess is that scholars will applaud the appearance of *Antisemitism Through the Ages.* However, it cannot be used as a principal text in courses of Jewish history because it presumes too much knowledge on the part of the reader. It may prove helpful as a reference guide or source of a quick quotation for some researchers. My hope is that it will not be lost in the pedantic quagmire of what is or is not antisemitism but that it will provoke discussion and, more importantly, action concerning the issues touched upon here.

SAUL FRIEDMAN
Youngstown State University

Randolph L. Braham (ed.), *The Tragedy of Hungarian Jewry: Essays, Documents, Depositions*. New York: Columbia University Press, 1986. viii + 328 pp.

The Holocaust in Hungary continues to engage the attention of historians, undoubtedly because of its uniqueness and later repercussions, which included extensive political and historical debate in the postwar years. Some of the major issues in the tragedy of Hungarian Jewry are freshly examined in a volume of studies edited by Randolph L. Braham, whose *The Politics of Genocide* (2 vols. [1981]) is the definitive history of the subject.

The opening study by John S. Conway, "The Holocaust in Hungary: Recent Controversies and Reconsiderations," criticizes prevalent trends in research that, in his view, aim to focus attention on the failure of the Allies to take effective steps to save Hungarian Jewry. According to Conway, historians have not considered the internal Jewish factors that also played a major role in the events of the tragic summer of 1944, particularly the attitude of the leaders and the suppression of information on the true nature of the deportations. Conway also argues that historians have not appreciated the real difficulties involved in the Brand mission and in the requests to bomb Auschwitz: "Instead, those authors seek to present a picture of realistic plans to save Jewish lives, which were 'sabotaged' by the inertia or deliberate obstruction of Allied officials" (p. 15). In Conway's view, "The conclusion is inescapable that the story of the Holocaust in Hungary is not immune to what can only be described as the deliberate forging of alibis" (p. 4). This is indeed a grave accusation against some historians of the Holocaust in Hungary, and attempts will undoubtedly be made to refute them. Perhaps new material may also come up, or fresh insights may emerge, which may place the Holocaust in Hungary in a new perspective.

Two documents by Fulop Freudiger, a leader of Hungarian Orthodoxy, illustrate some of the points raised by Conway. In his testimony, "Five Months," written in 1972, Freudiger discusses the period from March to August 1944, when he and his family fled to Rumania. This is of course a strictly personal reflection. Its value lies in being a complementary piece to Rezso Kasztner's well-known report of 1946. The second Freudiger document is closely related to the first. It is a letter written to Kasztner in August 1944, in which Freudiger attempts to clarify the circumstances of his departure from Budapest. At the time it greatly perturbed the Orthodox community, which now felt abandoned to its fate.

Three hitherto unpublished depositions augment that part of the volume which deals directly with the Holocaust: those of Gendarmerie Lieutenant Colonel L. Ferenczy, who was in charge of the ghettoization and deportation of provincial Jewry; Shulem Offenbach, a member of the Budapest Relief and Rescue Committee (headed by Kasztner); and Lajos Stockler, a member of the Jewish Council in Budapest from August 1944. In two of these depositions, grave accusations are leveled against the leaders of the council. Ferenczy believes that the deportations from the provinces could have been stopped if the leaders had intervened with the regent. Stockler judged the leadership as unsuitable, and he is convinced that their first obligation should have been to warn the masses: "If this had happened, the [lives] of many Jews would have been saved" (p. 322). He further accuses them of taking advantage of their position for their personal benefit. Stockler's testimony, given in 1946, reflects the then-prevailing views among the survivors. Historical research since then has not basically altered this view.

The pre-Holocaust period is represented in this volume by the study of Yehuda Don, "Anti-Semitic Legislations in Hungary and Their Implementation in Budapest —an Economic Analysis." Don concludes that "the second Anti-Jewish law was not, in fact, implemented in a systematic fashion" (p. 59). While the middle and lower middle classes were considerably affected and suffered much misery, on the whole the effects were not as disastrous as previously feared. Consequently, it was felt that the Jewish laws, harsh as they were, could be lived with, under the circumstances. This, together with other factors such as the uninterrupted continuity of Jewish life, accounted for much of the feeling of complacency among Hungarian Jews up to 1944. With this in mind, we may perhaps appreciate better their behavior and attitudes under the sudden impact of the events of the summer of 1944.

Dennis Silagi in his "A Foiled Jewish Political Venture in Hungary 1939–1942" deals with a hitherto little-known venture of Jewish political activism launched by a group of Revisionist Zionist activists (though not under the auspices of that organization as such). The basic tenet advanced by this group was that the Jewish-Magyar partnership should be dissolved, the Jews recognized as a national minority and preparations be made for the organized exodus of Hungarian Jews to the Jewish state after the war. These ideas, the results of a sober analysis of the Hungarian Jewish situation at the end of the 1930s, were forcefully advanced in the group's publications. They not only propagated their ideas among Jewry but also reached out to the non-Jewish political and social establishment.

The post-Holocaust period in Hungary produced new forms of assimilation among the survivors, or to put it more precisely, adaptation to the new conditions created by the forceful emergence of the Communist party and its strengthening hold on political and economic life. It was one of the characteristics of assimilationist Hungarian Jews that they always tended to adjust to the current political conditions. Thus, it was not surprising that among those who chose to remain in Hungary there were many who seized the opportunities offered by the new regime and integrated into its structure. This situation is analyzed by Victor Karady in his piece, "Some Social Aspects of Jewish Assimilation in Socialist Hungary 1945–1956." Another article, Peter Vardy's "The Unfinished Past—Jewish Realities in Post-War Hungary," examines the new realities in Jewish life in Communist Hungary. The scene described by Vardy, however, has changed during the past few years, and is now becoming part of the Hungarian Jewish past.

NATHANIEL KATZBURG
Bar-Ilan University

Christopher Browning, *Fateful Months: Essays on the Emergence of the Final Solution*. New York and London: Holmes & Meier, 1985. 111 pp.

There is an exhaustive—and often exhausting—debate among scholars about whether it was ideological intent or systemic functioning that was the decisive factor determining the early course of the Nazis' search for a solution to what they called the Jewish problem. Recently, the focus of that debate has come to be shifted toward what Christopher Browning in this book of essays identifies as the "fateful months" of 1941, those months during which the Nazis decided to prepare their murderously final solution.

Although scholars are largely in agreement that the Final Solution took shape in the months of March to July 1941, they differ on the role that Adolf Hitler played in the chain of decisions that eventually culminated in the building of the gas chambers at Auschwitz. There exists no single document bearing Hitler's signature that orders the Final Solution, and thus there are a wide range of explanations regarding how this solution came into being. The most extreme of these explanations, although it cannot be sustained by the available evidence, denies Hitler any role at all in the plan: Proponents of this theory argue that the murder of European Jews came about in contradiction to his wishes, in contrast to those who maintain that Hitler was intimately involved in every small step of the process. In the debate between the intentionalist and functionalist schools of thought, Browning identifies himself as "a moderate functionalist," arguing that Hitler was indeed a critical player during the "fateful months" of 1941 but also warning against an "overly Hitlerocentric interpretation" that "focuses exclusively on the intentions and decisions at the top while ignoring the attitudes and behavior of those at the bottom" (p. 4).

In the first and most authoritative essay in this book, "The Decision Concerning the Final Solution," Browning directly addresses the question of Hitler's role at the top of the Nazi hierarchy. The remaining three essays explore more tentatively the roles of those "at the bottom" in setting the Final Solution into motion.

Browning argues brilliantly and convincingly in his opening essay that the notion of murdering European Jewry did not crystallize in Hitler's mind until 1941, when the prospect of conquests in Russia promised to add greatly to the number of Jews in the Nazi clutches and thereby render unworkable the less extreme solution to the Jewish problem then being carried out. Even then, Browning argues, it was not a single decision but rather a series of decisions that gave final shape to this solution-through-murder. The first decision in this series came in the spring of 1941, when Hitler ordered the making of preparations for the murder of the Jews of Russia; the second in the summer (probably July, according to Browning), when Hitler, still confident of victory in Russia, instigated an expanded plan to include the killing of all the Jews in Europe. This "instigation," as Browning calls it, may have been no more formal than Hitler nodding his head or winking his eye in the direction of a receptive Heydrich, Himmler or Goering. They understood what was meant. Elsewhere Browning uses the term "green light" to characterize Hitler's authorization to prepare a program of mass extermination.

The fact that there were no plans of any sort in place for carrying out a program of mass extermination when Hitler˙ gave his green light becomes the lynchpin of Browning's argument that Hitler did not know all along exactly where his persecutions were heading. Of course, Hitler's willingness to choose murder as the solution to certain problems had already been amply demonstrated in the cases of the euthanasia program and the murder of the Polish intelligentsia. Whereas the unworkable Madagascar Plan of forced deportation, as Browning points out, was backed by elaborate charts, maps and plans to facilitate its implementation, the Final Solution had to be improvised.

The clumsiness of this improvisation, Browning demonstrates effectively, is traceable to the suddenness with which the decision for mass extermination was taken. Solving the myriad of technical and administrative problems connected with designing and then supplying the actual machinery of destruction made it necessary to draw upon the energies and ambitions of people ranging from antisemitic ideologues such as Heinrich Himmler and Reinhard Heydrich to the likes of obscure and nonideological chemical technicians, motor-pool superintendents and truck mechanics. An ever-widening circle of people was enlisted in this process of destruction as it progressed in efficiency from the *Einsatzgruppen* shootings in Russia to the use of the mobile gas van and, finally, to the assembly-line factories of death established in Poland.

Browning shows how even at the upper levels this enlistment came not so much from explicit orders as it did through the self-recruitment of ambitious servants of the Third Reich who responded "to the impulses and hints they perceived emanating from the centers of power" (p. 36). How this recruitment worked at the lower levels is a main theme of the other three essays in this volume, which demonstrate how petty careerism played a critically important role in keeping the machinery of destruction in motion. Evil, it seems, may be supremely destructive in effect, even when it is genuinely banal.

The second of Browning's essays treats the mass murder of Jewish males in Serbia during the late months of 1941, an extermination that took place not at the behest of Hitler or S.S. zealots or any of the newly established machinery of destruction but quite independently as a consequence of the German army's retaliation against Serbian partisans for their attacks on German soldiers. Frustrated by its inability to end these attacks, the army decided upon a policy of brutal reprisal: the shooting of fifty to a hundred Communist partisans for every German soldier killed. Why would this decision lead to the murder of Jews? Because, Browning explains, after years of Nazi propaganda Jews had come to be identified not only with Communists but also as Germany's prime enemy. The result was the shooting of virtually the entire male Jewish population of Serbia. The surviving women and children, about seventy-five hundred of them, were carried off to the Semlin *Judenlager* on the outskirts of Belgrade.

A third essay deals with "The Development and Production of the Gas Van," the instrument that delivered death during that stage of the murder process following the shootings in Russia and preceding the assembly-line gassings in Auschwitz. More than any of the others, this essay shows how easy it was to harness the petty

ambitions of ordinary people—be they mechanics, motor-pool supervisors or tox-
icological specialists—to help solve the technical problems surrounding the design
of the mobile gas van.

Browning's fourth essay picks up where his second one left off, with the Germans
in Serbia confronting the problem of what to do with the Jewish women and children
who had survived the massacres of late 1941. The answer of the RHSA in Berlin
was to send the newly designed gas van to the Semlin *Judenlager*. There is no more
chilling account of the horrors of the Holocaust in this work than Browning's
laconic recital of how the gas van took the Jews of the Semlin camp on their final
journey.

The range and depth of the research undergirding these essays, as well as the
clarity and sophistication of their exposition, make them major contributions to the
understanding of the Holocaust, placing their author at the forefront of those scholars currently promoting this understanding.

KARL A. SCHLEUNES
University of North Carolina at Greensboro

Shalom Cholawski, *Besufat hakhilayon: yahadut bilorusiyah hamizraḥit bemilḥemet ha'olam hasheniyah* (*In the Eye of the Hurricane: The Jews in Eastern
Belorussia During World War II*). Jerusalem and Tel-Aviv: The Hebrew
University Institute of Contemporary Jewry, Moreshet and Sifriat Poalim,
1988. 318 pp.

Shalom Cholawski is practically the only scholar working in an area fraught with
difficulties and daunting obstacles. Until this year, a historian researching the Holocaust as it took place in Belorussia did not have access to the Soviet archives that
contain both Soviet and captured German documents; what is more, he faced a
formidable language barrier. Cholawski's command of the necessary languages,
especially Yiddish, Hebrew, Russian and German, together with his intimate knowledge of the region and his training as a historian, make him well qualified to tackle
this difficult subject. The result is an informative and valuable history of the Holocaust in eastern Belorussia, the only book of its kind.

Cholawski defines the region in question as what had been Soviet Belorussia until
1939, an area that he estimates had a Jewish population of 405,000 on the eve of the
war. His aims and perspective, as in his previous work on the Holocaust in western
Belorussia, are to provide a profile of the Jews on the eve of destruction and to
describe that destruction through Jewish eyes. His central questions concern what
befell the Jews and how they reacted to the annihilation policies of the Nazis. To
answer these questions, he makes extensive use of survivors' memoirs and testimonies, especially those filed at Yad Vashem, the Moreshet Archive, and the Oral
History Division of the Institute of Contemporary Jewry in Jerusalem. Other
sources, German and Russian primarily, are brought to bear insofar as they can shed
light on the process, places, dates and methods of destruction, as well as on the
internal Jewish dynamics in responding to the murders.

In view of Cholawski's approach, the book's title is somewhat misleading. Not only is the book devoted mostly to Minsk and not to all of eastern Belorussia, but it also concerns the Holocaust rather than the Second World War. That is, the discussions of the battles on Soviet soil and how these related to the Jewish policies of the Germans and the Soviets are both limited and peripheral. Cholawski makes no claim to be offering the final word on the Nazi murder apparatus in the region. This is reflected in the relative space devoted to German policies and murder operations as opposed to Jewish life, suffering and underground work. Of 243 pages of narrative (aside from the foreword), 42 deal directly with the Germans (Chapters 2, 3 and 8), whereas 169 (the Introduction and Chapters 4–7) constitute an excellent overview on the various Jewish communities of the region, the Judenrat, Jewish resistance and Jewish accounts of life in the ghetto and murder operations. This approach is also reflected in the absence from the bibliography of several important works on the Second World War in the Soviet Union, such as those of Alexander Werth and Alexander Dallin. Given this fact, it is hardly surprising that Cholawski did not consult German documentation beyond the partial (though large) holdings at Yad Vashem. Cholawski is clearly part of the Israeli tradition of historiography on the Holocaust, which insists on treating the Jews as a subject of history—the main subject—and not merely as an object of Nazi policies.

The book's structure is chronological through the first third, followed by an extensive discussion of events in Minsk and the Jewish underground there in the next third. The last third deals briefly with a number of issues: the fate of the Jews in the smaller cities and towns of the region; the fate of the German Jewish deportees to Minsk; a description of the main murderers; a few words on the aftermath of the war and concluding remarks.

Within this structure, Cholawski succeeds in clarifying and substantiating a number of points regarding the Soviets, the Germans and the Jews. There is no evidence, argues Cholawski, that the Soviet authorities gave Jews preferential treatment in the eastward evacuation of civilians. Rather, those Jews who could be of use were evacuated, since the Soviet ideology did not recognize Jews as a particular nation or as the particular potential victims of the Nazis. Regarding the Germans involved in the murder, Cholawski offers convincing evidence that the Wehrmacht was intimately involved in defining racial policy in the region. He also documents the fact that 140,000 of the 190,00 Jews killed in the region were dead by the end of 1941: Most Jews had no opportunity to react to the Nazi threat. But Cholawski also describes how leading figures in the Judenrat in Minsk were closely linked to the founding and operation of the Jewish underground, which was the first and most effective underground in that city.

There are a number of problems in the book that should be mentioned. The maps at the end of the book are singularly unhelpful. They would be more useful if they were integrated into the text as a means of highlighting the major places, roads and rivers mentioned. Maps photocopied in black and white are also visually confusing. Even worse, three of the five maps (of *Einsatzgruppe* activity, the Minsk ghetto and the Trostiniets killing center) are amateurish hand drawings with handwritten placenames. Even a low-budget book should be able to include typed street names and proper maps in order to avoid appearing comical. Similarly, the editors seem to have

264

missed a not-insignificant number of typographical errors, such as the June 28, 1949 (should be 1943) German report on the occupied eastern territories (p. 62), or the *810* (should be 810,000) Soviet POWs murdered in Belorussia (p. 64) or an incomplete sentence regarding the conclusions of the Soviet War Crimes Commission concerning the fate of the 209 cities and ninety-two hundred villages under Nazi rule (p. 67). The editors seem also to have missed quite a few redundancies both within and between chapters.

From an editorial point of view, the individual biographical sketches of nearly 100 of the 450 members of Minsk's Jewish underground should have been placed in an appendix, rather than in Chapter 5. As it is, the sketches of numerous middle-level members become very tedious and detract from the author's point, which is that this underground was relatively large, popular, well-organized and effective.

More serious than these editorial quibbles, which could be attended to in a second edition or translation, are several of Cholawski's unsubstantiated underlying assumptions. For example, Cholawski sets out to demonstrate the presence of widespread and institutionalized antisemitism in Minsk and the rest of eastern Belorussia. He cites instances of Belorussian officials relating to Jews gruffly and unsympathetically; such examples, however, do not *ipso facto* indicate official antisemitism. Similarly, Cholawski tries to demonstrate the antisemitism of the Soviet partisans. For this he contrasts the partisans' reception of tens of thousands of Belorussians to their ranks with open arms in 1944, when the outcome of the war was clear, with their rejection of many Jews who had escaped to the forests in 1942 and 1943 (pp. 162–163). Cholawski also alludes to the partisans' refusal to accept any unarmed Jew (p. 167). Yet such a presentation begs the question of whether we can compare the partisans' policies toward the Belorussians in 1944—when they were near victory—with their policies toward the Jews at a time when they were in a much more precarious position. Moreover, Cholawski does not say if non-Jews were also required to bear arms in order to be accepted by the partisans. This is not to say that there was no antisemitism in government or partisan circles. Many of Cholawski's examples clearly do show antisemitism, but the above questions, together with the absence of uniform antisemitism in the incidents he cites, leaves this reviewer wondering if Cholawski should consider obtuseness and myopia in addition to possible antisemitism as an explanation of local official attitudes toward Jews.

Finally, comparison with other areas (save western Belorussia, the only other area Cholawski has researched as extensively) is lacking in much of the discussion. This leaves the reader uninformed regarding a number of key issues, such as why it was clear to members of the Minsk underground that they must flee to the forests, whereas similar organizations in other ghettos faced a dilemma in deciding between flight to the forests and remaining with family and community in the ghetto.

As with any historical work, there is much room in Cholawski's book for disagreement and not a few places where the research seems to be wanting. However, the book is meant to be mainly descriptive, not analytical, and it is meant as the first word on the subject, not the last. Perhaps the apparent new Soviet willingness to allow Western researchers access to captured German documents will help fill in some of the many gaps in this and other Holocaust research. In the meantime,

Cholawski's book is a valuable addition to our knowledge of the Holocaust in its being the first work to deal with this specific region.

DAVID SILBERKLANG
The Hebrew University

Abraham J. Edelheit and Hershel Edelheit, *Bibliography on Holocaust Literature.* Boulder and London: Westview Press, 1986. 842 pp.

With the seemingly exponential proliferation of titles on the Holocaust, the aims of a comprehensive bibliography such as this are bound to be both justified and frustrated. In the authors' attempt at exhaustiveness, they have compiled a volume of unusual heft, defining "Holocaust literature" as all critical and historical, theological and imaginative responses to this period. At the same time, the sheer length of such a bibliography demands an extremely precise and self-critical set of canonical categories by which readers might make their way through more than nine thousand entries. Given the fact that all the works listed here are in English, one can only wonder at the size of a Holocaust bibliography also encompassing works in Yiddish, Hebrew, German and French.

The result is, therefore, double-edged: On the one hand, this collection is a necessary bibliography of essays, papers, books and even newspaper articles on topics related to the Holocaust; on the other hand, in its sheer voluminousness, the book is a little unwieldy and so demands patient and careful reading. Finally, as must be the case with any such compilation in the face of hundreds of new works on the Holocaust every year, the most recent research (that published after 1985) is necessarily absent from these pages.

This bibliography is broken into four basic sections, each with a number of subheadings: I. "Before the Storm," which includes entries on Jewish life in prewar Europe, modern Europe as a "seedbed for destruction" and antisemitism; II. "The Perpetrators," with headings under fascism, the S.S.-state and the Nazis; III. "The Crucible," comprising sections on the Second World War, Europe under Nazism (country by country), the concentration camp system, the Shoah (including diaries, memoirs and testimonies), resistance, bystanders and "the free world reaction"; and IV. "Aftermath," with parts on "from Holocaust to rebirth," reflections on the Holocaust (theological, memorial and pedagogical), Europe after the Second World War, literary responses, *Yizkor bikher,* distortions of history and historiography. Each of these sections is preceded by a short introductory essay, outlining what the editors feel to be the essential issues surrounding these topics.

The compilers of this work are both editors and archivists, who inevitably organize and define the canon around their own conceptions of this time and literature. In this light, it would be easy to question the assumptions underlying the categories that order this bibliography (e.g., literary responses as distinct from memoirs). But in fact, such assumptions are a necessary hazard of any such catalog; at best, therefore, bibliographers formulate their organizing criteria as self-reflexively as possible. To this end, the remarks prefacing each of the sections of this bibliography serve two purposes: to orient the reader, making the entries comprehensible, and to draw into the reader's view a sense of the logic organizing this list. In sum, no matter how quickly a bibliography such as this falls out of date, it remains extremely valuable both as a compendium for researchers and as a basis for future, updated bibliographies.

JAMES E. YOUNG
University of Massachusetts at Amherst

Gerhard Hirschfeld, *Nazi Rule and Dutch Collaboration: The Netherlands Under German Occupation, 1940–1945*. Trans. from the Dutch by L. Willmot. Oxford, New York and Hamburg: Berg Publishers, 1988. 360 pp.

Jacques Presser, *Ashes in the Wind: The Destruction of Dutch Jewry*. Trans. from the Dutch by A. Pomerans. Detroit: Wayne State University Press, 1988. 556 pp.

Both books under review here, although published in 1988, are not new. Presser's book on the Holocaust of Dutch Jewry is a reprint of the abridged English version (1968) of *Ondergang* (1965), while Hirschfeld's book on Dutch collaboration with the Germans is a slightly adapted version of his *Fremdherrschaft und Kollaboration. Die Niederlande unter deutscher Besatzung 1940–1945* (1984). Both books will be useful to English readers as a means of becoming acquainted with the situation in the Netherlands during the German occupation of the Second World War. However, there are significant differences in quality between the two.

Presser's study, initially commissioned by the Dutch government in 1950, is divided into two parts that in the original Dutch version were two separate volumes. The first part deals chronologically with the development of German anti-Jewish policies in Holland, which Presser divides into three stages: from May 1940 to fall/winter 1941–1942 ("isolation"); from winter 1941 to July 1942 ("from isolation to deportation"); and from July 1942 to September 1943 ("deportations"). In the second part, Presser examines the period as a whole, focusing on Jewish society (prominent individuals, significant groups, the Jewish Council), aspects of persecution (resistance, escape, "protected groups," the relationship between Jews and gentiles, economic persecution) and the two transit camps on Dutch soil, Westerbork and Vught. The last chapter ("Murder") deals with the fate of Dutch Jews outside Holland.

When first published, Presser's study was widely hailed by the Dutch press and public. His sensitive and captivating, almost literary, narrative and his personal involvement gave the book a special dimension, and it became a best-seller in Holland. Among scholars, however, including some of his senior collaborators and sponsors, serious criticism was raised from the outset, although most of it was muted at the time.[1]

Herman von der Dunk (at that time still a young scholar but afterward one of Holland's leading historians), wrote such a harsh review that the historical periodical for which it was written refused to publish it. He finished his analysis with the following sentence: "Remembering, remembering personally—and writing history are two different things."[2] And indeed, from a scholarly point of view this book has many deficiencies. Many key issues are totally neglected—the background of Dutch Jewry; attitudes toward the Jews in Dutch society before the occupation; synchronization of the developments in Holland with those in the Third Reich in general; an in-depth analysis of the functioning of the German and Dutch administration, and so on. Additionally, Presser's book lacks a scholarly apparatus; on the basis of the few notes it contains, it is almost impossible for scholars to trace original documents back in the archives.

This does not mean that *Ashes in the Wind* is of no importance. Presser has done a good deal of research, and one can find many important details in this study. The readability of the book is also an important virtue. However, from the point of view of historical research, it is a pity that the book was reprinted. Since 1965, research on the period has been extensive; among other works, there have been two comprehensive and well-documented analyses of the fate of Dutch Jewry,[3] although there is still need for an up-to-date English-language account of the Netherlands and the Holocaust. In the meantime, scholars who do not read Dutch or Hebrew will have to be satisfied with Presser and the much better but far shorter entries on Holland in the recently published *Encyclopedia of the Holocaust* (1990).

Hirschfeld's study, though not primarily dealing with "the Jewish question," is a useful and insightful study of the background of the Holocaust in Holland. His subject, as the title indicates, is Dutch collaboration with the Nazi occupiers—a delicate topic often couched in black-and-white terms only. Because of the loaded and pejoratively generalizing meaning of the term "collaboration," scholarly research on Nazi-era collaboration has to attempt to (1) analyze its forms during various stages of occupation and (2) introduce a meaningful and dispassionate terminology of the phenomenon.

Concerning the first task, Hirschfeld presents a well-documented and clearly constructed picture of the situation. Following a chapter on the history and structure of the "Reichskommissariat Niederlande," we learn about the conservative bourgeoisie and "the Netherlands Union" that emerged from this social group several weeks after the occupation, whose purpose was to lead Dutch society in new paths in which the preservation of Dutch national feelings and Dutch society could be combined with the "New European Order." Hirschfeld examines collaboration on the part of social organizations (parties, trade unions), the press and state institutions, most notably the Committee of Secretaries-General (the highest level of state officials left after the escape of government and queen, who acted as a second-level government), the Supreme Court and the police. Another chapter is devoted to the economic collaboration of state institutions and Dutch employers. Finally, Hirschfeld devotes a chapter to collaboration by Dutch Fascists.

Although much of the information and conclusions of this work is not entirely new, Hirschfeld has succeeded in presenting a clearly focused and coherent study that furthers the path of comparative research on collaboration. This does not mean that Hirschfeld's study has no weaknesses. For example, every successive chapter is longer than the former; thus the chapter on the Fascists is the longest, which gives the reader the feeling that this constituted the most important collaborationist group. This is doubtful, however, given the facts brought forth by Hirschfeld himself in previous chapters. Hirschfeld also misses the chance here to point out the fundamental differences between fascism as a general phenomenon and hard-core National Socialism, which was Germanocentric. Since Hirschfeld deals only briefly with Dutch society before 1940, such an omission is perhaps understandable. More puzzling is the absence of any discussion either of the role of Dutch churches during the occupation, or that of the Jews.

Perhaps Hirschfeld felt that the Jews, as "enemies" of National Socialism, simply could not be taken into account. But if one includes "accommodation" within the framework of collaboration—as Hirschfeld does—some (naive?) Jewish groups could certainly be included, such as the "Jewish Council," which was indeed accused of "collaboration" by many Jews during and after the Holocaust.[4] It would have been interesting to have Hirschfeld's view of "Jewish collaboration." I believe that a comparison of the collaborating Jews with the groups that Hirschfeld examines would have contributed to a more proper understanding of the real meaning of this phenomenon among Jews as well as pointing to the uniqueness of the Jewish situation under Nazi rule. Most of the members of the European nations had an opportunity to *choose* between collaboration of different colors, various sit-and-wait policies or outright resistance of several types. Collaboration was an option that could bring long-term benefits. But Jews could not benefit from the first two choices; even full collaboration could not save a Jew from the final death sentence.

Hirschfeld's introduction and summarizing chapter are devoted to the aforementioned second task of defining terminology. In the original German version of this book, Hirschfeld introduced the term *Attentismus* (i.e., the "politics of waiting" or, in German, "ein versichtiges Abwarten, eine Auf-Zeit-Spielen"). This term was criticized by the Dutch historian J. C. H. Blom as not fitting many of the examples brought forth in this study.[5] Hirschfeld has apparently accepted this criticism, since he now uses the term "accommodation" in place of "attentism." However, the boundaries of the concept are still not entirely clear; this is an area that requires more comparative research. I believe that it might be useful for scholars to consider together, rather than separately, the two extreme poles of attitudes toward the occupying forces—collaboration and resistance. During the last fifteen years, much has been published on the theoretical aspects of resistance, especially in Germany, Israel and the United States.[6] As with collaboration, resistance has in the past been viewed as a black-and-white phenomenon. More recent research, which indicates its variegated hues, might be fruitfully applied as well to the topic of collaboration.

Finally, two remarks concerning proofreading and translation. There are too many printing mistakes, mainly in Dutch names and in footnotes. Additionally, the generally well-done translation was not always checked. Thus we find, for example, on p. 258 that the Dutch National Socialist Rost van Tonningen "worked as a financial advisor for the Voelkerbund"—an institution known, of course, in English as the League of Nations!

DAN MICHMAN
Bar-Ilan University

Notes

1. See, for example, the recently published interview with L. de Jong, the former director of the Netherlands State Institute for War Documentation, in M. Pam, *De Onderzoekers van de Oorlog: Het Rijksinstituut voor Oorlogsdocumentatie en het werk van dr. L. de Jong* ('s Gravenhage: 1989), 60–62. Says de Jong: "When it [i.e., Presser's study] was finished, we [B. Sijes and I] . . . had a critique on the whole of his study: on the scholarly approach, on the methods and on the structure. We held some lengthy conversations [with Presser]. Finally, Presser told us that our critique was just, and that he wanted to think about it. . . . After a week he came back and said: "I'm sorry, you're right, but I don't have the [spiritual] strength to change it; it has to be published the way it is."
2. H. von der Dunk, *Kleio heeft Duizend Ogen* (Assen: 1974), 52.
3. L. de Jong, *Het Koninkrijk der Nederlanden in de Tweede Wereldoorlog,* vols. 1–14 ('s Gravenhage: 1969–1988), devoted about 15 percent of his general study on the Netherlands during the Second World War to the fate of Dutch Jewry; in J. Michman, H. Beem and D. Michman, *Pinkas hakehilot: Holland* (Jerusalem: 1985), a major part of the Introduction and the entries on the communities deals with the Holocaust period.
4. For this aspect in Eastern Europe, see also I. Trunk, *Judenrat* (New York and London: 1972), 570–575.
5. J. C. H. Blom, in *Bijdragen en Mededelingen betreffende de Geschiedenis der Nederlanden* 100, no. 4 (1985), 732–733.
6. For a most illuminating article, see R. J. Gottlieb, "The Concept of Resistance: Jewish Resistance During the Holocaust," *Social Theory and Practice* 9, no. 1 (1983), 31–49.

Stefan Korbonski, *The Jews and the Poles in World War II.* New York: Hippocrene Books, 1989. viii + 136 pp.

Stefan Korbonski served during most of the Second World War as head of the Directorate of Civil Resistance (Kierownictwo Walki Cywilnej) of the Polish underground organization affiliated with the Polish government-in-exile in London. In this capacity, among other activities, he transmitted a number of radio messages to the West concerning the systematic murder of Polish Jewry—including news of the onset of mass deportations from the Warsaw ghetto in July 1942, the uprising in the ghetto in April 1943 and the operation of gas chambers at Auschwitz. Korbonski was also responsible for arranging the trial and execution of collaborators, including some of those who had blackmailed Jews in hiding or revealed their hiding places to the German authorities. In recognition of these activities, in 1980 he was honored by Yad Vashem as a Righteous Gentile.

Viewed against such a background, Korbonski's book on *The Jews and the Poles in World War II* appears especially disturbing. Though ostensibly written "to clear the clouded atmosphere of Polish-Jewish relations" (p. viii), it is in fact primarily a protest against a supposed Jewish "campaign of slander against the Poles" (p. viii)—a campaign that allegedly charges the Polish people with "sharing responsibility for the Holocaust by not preventing the slaughter of the Jews" (p. vii). In response to this purported accusation, Korbonski has produced what amounts to a brief for the defense, replete with material calculated to impeach the credibility of the plaintiff. The book is predictably one-sided, and if, in the words of the dust jacket copy, "Mr. Korbonski sets the record straight," he does so only in the non-Euclidean sense.

Thus, Korbonski argues that although "the Poles were utterly powerless to stop the extermination" (p. vii), "the Polish masses . . . tried to save as many Jews as possible" (p. 66). If more Jews were not saved, he suggests, this was not for lack of trying. Rather, the Poles themselves were subject to a reign of terror at the hands of the German occupiers, including the threat of death for any Pole caught aiding a Jew; while the Western Allies—the only source from which effective succor could be obtained—were indifferent to the Jews' plight.

There is, of course, nothing new about this argument, nor is there anything new about the evidence that Korbonski adduces in its support. Indeed, most of the material devoted specifically to the Jewish situation during the war has been copied almost verbatim from some of Korbonski's previous writings. But be that as it may, this case rests upon a number of facts and inferences that at first glance appear quite telling. For example, by estimating the number of Jews who survived the Holocaust at Poland at anywhere between fifty thousand and two hundred thousand (the higher figure provided by his own Directorate of Civil Resistance) and surmising that "the hiding of one person over a period of four to five years required changing the site every few months and consequently would mean the involvement of at least ten families, each comprising several members" (p. 43), Korbonski suggests—though he never says so explicitly—that literally millions of Poles must have risked their lives to save Jews. They were encouraged to do so, he claims, by the underground leadership, which is said both to have published information about the Jewish situation on a daily basis and to have called upon the Polish population "to render the Jews all possible assistance" (p. 45). Korbonski also maintains that the Polish underground was in active contact with Jewish organizations in the ghettos, noting that both the Home Army and the Government Delegacy maintained special sections to deal with Jewish affairs. He highlights the operation of *Zegota* (a Polish code name for the Council for Assistance to the Jews), established with the approval of the Government Delegacy in December 1942. And he calls special attention to the mission of the emissary Jan Karski, who carried an eyewitness report about the murder of Jews to the West in 1942–1943, only to have it fall upon the deaf ears of Allied leaders.

Now much of this information is true, albeit considerably exaggerated. The problem is that Korbonski's material does not come close to representing the whole truth. Yes, Poles who helped Jews did so under threat of death, but this fact was adduced by Polish spokesmen as the primary explanation for the behavior of Poles toward Jews only after the war had ended, not during the war itself. Yes, the underground leadership did from time to time condemn German actions and praise the rendering of assistance to the Jews, but on other occasions—as, for example, in March 1943—it specifically declined to do so. Yes, both the Home Army and the Government Delegacy maintained bureaus for Jewish affairs, but both were established only in 1942, staffed by one person each and limited mainly to gathering information. Yes, *Zegota* operated under the auspices of the Government Delegacy, but the delegacy did not initiate its establishment and funded it only partially, and *Zegota* leaders frequently noted a cool attitude toward their activities on the delegacy's part. And yes, Jan Karski did witness the murder of Jews in a German camp, but that was not the reason that he was sent to the West, and Jewish matters played only a peripheral role in his mission.

Noting this additional information raises questions of interpretation. Does, for example, the fact that the Home Army established a bureau of Jewish affairs actually mean that the body assigned high priority to the rescue of Jews, as Korbonski seems to suggest? After all, the United States government has maintained a Bureau of Indian Affairs since 1924, but few would argue that the United States was vitally concerned with the well-being of American Indians throughout this entire period. Does the publication in the underground press of periodic condemnations of German anti-Jewish atrocities really prove that the underground leadership as a whole was constantly prepared to do everything in its power to help Jews escape the sentence of death? In August 1941, the United States and Great Britain issued the Atlantic Charter, which, among other things, abjured "territorial changes that do not accord with the freely expressed wishes of the people concerned"; but it is doubtful that Korbonski, in particular, would hold that the sum total of those two governments' actions throughout the war indicates that that statement was made for anything more than propaganda purposes. And even if as many as three million Poles (a doubtful figure) helped the Jews in any way, does this justify Korbonski's claim that "the Polish masses . . . tried to save as many Jews as possible"?

Such questions are among the many that must be addressed forthrightly if Korbonski's stated objective is to be pursued in earnest; in answering them, researchers must take into account the full range of available evidence, even when this is scanty, contradictory and susceptible to multiple interpretations. And based upon such an accounting—for example, that the Government Delegacy and the Home Army did not regard the rescue of Jews as a major focus of their activities—a historian's argument does not necessarily have to read as implying a moral argument that things should have been different. So long as writers on Polish-Jewish relations attach greater value to self-image (whether Polish or Jewish) than to the objective insight that can result from honest confrontation with the subject—and this, ultimately, is what Korbonski appears to do—their writing will continue to be cast in the strident moralistic tone of adversarial briefs.

It is also worth noting that the majority of the book's text (84 out of 134 pages) does not deal directly with the period ostensibly in question but rather with such subjects as the role of Jews in Polish life before and after the Second World War and the behavior of American Jews toward Poland and the Poles. In these pages Korbonski argues that, although for more than seven centuries Jews had found shelter from persecution in Poland and enjoyed full freedom and opportunity for upward mobility in the prewar Polish state, they consistently refused to identify with their country and its people, an attitude made manifest after the war when the Communist government, in which Jews held leading positions, imposed "ten years of Jewish rule in Poland" (p. 86). Furthermore, he charges American Jews with deliberately promoting "hatred of Poland" (p. 89) and with withholding assistance from any Polish Jewish refugee arriving in the United States "who dared to contradict [the] theory" that the Poles were "co-responsible for the Holocaust" (p. 90), though he offers no evidence for this patently absurd accusation.

Mr. Korbonski will never have to deal with the problems raised by his book; he passed away shortly before it was released. How sad that the final work of a man with so much to his credit is a splenetic diatribe, falling at times far below acceptable scholarly standards to the level of gutter literature.

DAVID ENGEL
New York University

Deborah E. Lipstadt, *Beyond Belief: The American Press and the Coming of the Holocaust, 1933–1945*. New York: Free Press, 1986. xi + 370 pp.

We are enjoined to remember the past, George Santayana warned, lest we repeat it. But sometimes the price of avoiding such a repetition may be far too high. That is the lesson, the tragic twist on the philosopher's apothegm, emerging from *Beyond Belief*, which shows how American journalists, having disseminated First World War stories of German atrocities that proved to be either exaggerations or hoaxes, refused to be "duped" again—even when the stories proved to be true. The Holocaust was possible, Deborah E. Lipstadt implies, not only because it was considered impossible but because it was so unprecedented and hence unimaginable. In this case, not even seeing was believing; thus the tyrants and killers carried on for years without outside interference. In illuminating the passivity of the American bystanders, Lipstadt's invaluable account not only contributes to the literature of the Holocaust but also darkens the history of U.S. journalism.

"The press may not determine what the public thinks, but it does influence what it thinks *about*," Lipstadt writes (p. 3), and from the Nazi ascent to power until the surrender little more than a dozen years later, American newspapers failed to inform their readers of the centrality of the Jew in the demonology of the Third Reich. With some exceptions, such as Edgar Ansel Mowrer (who was forced out of the Third Reich) and William Shirer, American reporters on the scene erred on the side of minimizing the extent of the atrocities similar to those for which Germany had been blamed two decades earlier. The warning signals from the victims were discredited: Jews who had been released from concentration camps were considered interested parties who brought back little proof of the horrors they described. Yet official assurances of peaceful intentions and Nazi replies to the "unfair" propaganda stemming from biased Jewish sources were accepted. The aim of most U.S. journalists based in the Third Reich was to provide balanced reporting that idealized "objectivity." Getting expelled for telling the truth about antisemitism was considered no badge of honor but rather an outcome of unprofessional behavior. It is true, Lipstadt acknowledges, that the intensity of Nazi hatred of the Jews diverged radically from the sort of antisemitism with which journalists were familiar, thus complicating coverage of the barbarism. However, only the Final Solution itself was intended to be concealed; as early as 1933, the astute Mowrer was able to infer that National Socialism sought "the extermination, permanent subjugation or voluntary departure of the Jews from Germany" (quoted on p. 57).

Lipstadt devotes half of her chronicle to the period in which the brutality was openly conducted and the noose was tightening on German (and then Austrian) Jewry, and the second half to the dissemination of news of the genocide itself. Until the outbreak of the Second World War, Hitler was fairly successful in winning the propaganda battle whose goal was the inclusion of his regime in the community of civilized states. The Berlin Olympics were especially useful in inducing such myopia, which was seriously but only temporarily dispelled by *Kristallnacht*. Editorials in American dailies reinforced the general opposition to relaxation of immigration quotas, thus confirming the Nazi assumption that the world was divided between governments trying to get rid of Jews and countries refusing to accept them. The skepticism of the press was directed more at Jewish fears than at the Roosevelt administration's claims of compassion, a skepticism that was reflected in the limited space—often on the back pages—granted to what became the most formidable moral test that modern Western civilization would face. That test was flunked, in part because the press did not understand that after 1939 the Third Reich was fighting not one war but two. The result was that the news of the annihilation of European Jewry was treated as an extension of prewar discrimination and cruelty (hence it was "old" news), or else was placed in the context of general civilian suffering (where, admittedly, the Jews were worse off). Only during the final year of the war—with the impending destruction of Hungarian Jewry, the official confirmation of the Holocaust through the establishment of the War Refugee Board, and after the publicity that the Peter Bergson group (associated with the Irgun) generated—did the overwhelming and awful evidence finally pierce the disbelief.

Lipstadt's book is impressively and extensively researched, drawing heavily upon those newspapers throughout the United States that were conveniently clipped and digested for Roosevelt's use in a daily *Press Information Bulletin* (now available at the presidential library at Hyde Park, New York). Her examination of magazines is limited, confined primarily to the often grotesque views of the *Christian Century*. Even less evidence is presented from radio, where documentation was far more limited. Hence, the subtitle of this book should more properly have referred to "newspapers" instead of "press."

Beyond Belief is more satisfactory as a complement to histories of the Holocaust—especially in Germany—than as an analysis of the problematics of newsgathering. The author pays little attention, for example, to the variations in news emphasis and editorial opinion among newspapers, nor in how those differences might be explained. The ideological orientation and ownership of even the major dailies are rarely mentioned, and the special anxieties of the Jewish publishers of the *New York Times* are confined to an intriguing footnote (pp. 170n–171n). Lipstadt's

inattention is unfortunate, because the unrivaled prestige of the *Times* signaled to
other forums of opinion the weight to be attached to the stories from Europe, and
because its admirable refusal to let the scarcity of newsprint reduce its overseas
coverage gave it an unmatched opportunity to trace the destruction of a people.
Surprises emerge, but these are too often left dangling by the author. In editorials on
the subject of rescue efforts, for instance, Lipstadt shows that highly reputable
organs such as the *Times* behaved worse than the vulgar tabloids owned by the
reactionary William Randolph Hearst. Perhaps the two most widely syndicated
columnists of the era could not have been more contrasting: the sophisticated intellectual Walter Lippmann and the dyspeptic guttersnipe Westbrook Pegler. Lippmann, the brilliant pundit, was eerily silent on the great challenge that Nazi antisemitism posed (to civilization as well as to his fellow Jews), while Pegler on
several occasions sharply attacked such bigotry.

Lipstadt also fumbles the larger cognitive question that her book frequently
raises, which is how public opinion—and the press that helped shape it—could so
seriously misapprehend the calamity that befell European Jewry. Often she blames
cynicism (or thinks that it is synonymous with skepticism), seeing in the hard-boiled
stance of wizened reporters and editors a shock resistance to reports from the Third
Reich. Yet on occasion *Beyond Belief* confusingly attributes disbelief to something
very different, which is innocence. Americans found it inconceivable that human
beings, especially the legatees of Goethe and Beethoven, could sink to a level lower
than the beasts. Lipstadt does not clarify how contradictory causes can produce the
same blindness—but at least she is careful not to overestimate the historical failure
of the press, which "did not have the power to stop the carnage or to rescue the
victims. The Allies might have remained just as committed to inaction, even if they
had been pressured by the press" (p. 277). But in not alerting readers to the sort of
world they inhabited (or could make more habitable), U.S. newspapers failed to
fulfill their own constitutional mandate.

STEPHEN J. WHITFIELD
Brandeis University

Abraham J. Peck and Uri D. Herscher (eds.), *Queen City Refuge: An Oral History
of Cincinnati's Jewish Refugees from Nazi Germany.* West Orange, N.J.:
Behrman House, 1989. 270 pp.

Works of oral history are usually intended to fill in the gaps in the written documentation of a given historical period. Since books recording numerous recollections of
a single set of historical events are rare, *Queen City Refuge* is an exceptional
example of its genre. The editors have gathered the testimonies of twenty-two
Jewish residents of Cincinnati, Ohio, who had lived under the Nazi regime in
Germany or Austria and managed to escape its death machine. Also included are
two interviews with members of the second generation, the children of survivors,

and three interviews with members of the Cincinnati Jewish community who helped absorb the refugees in their new home.

The interviewees are not a representative sample of the German Jewry of the 1930s and early 1940s, nor even of those who were able to escape the inferno. Nevertheless, these edited interviews are valuable evidence both for scholars of the period and for general readers interested in the events that led to the Nazi extermination of German Jewry.

The editors' introduction is no less valuable than the interviews themselves. We learn, for example, that of the 140,000 German Jews who reached the United States, approximately 1,000 settled in Cincinnati. Fearing an increase in anti-semitism, American Jews showed little enthusiasm for the immigration wave. This attitude was responsible for the tremendous difficulties the German Jews encountered in obtaining affidavits, those desperately sought guarantees signed by Americans of means without which it was impossible to receive a visa, even within the restricted framework under which emigration permits were granted.

Some of the interviewees testify in their accounts that Jewish millionaires who had financed statues to decorate American cities refused their desperate pleas for a signature on an affidavit. As noted in the Introduction, articles in the American Jewish press, such as the local *American Israelite*'s February 1933 piece stating that Hitler did not intend to actually implement his antisemitic plans, may have salved wealthy American Jews' consciences and buttressed their refusal to offer a lifeline in the form of an affidavit. The *American Israelite* even gave a voice to Joseph Goebbels, allowing him space to explain the Nazi program to the Jews of Cincinnati.

In the category of little-known details, one of the interviewees relates that the father of the family was able to gain release from a concentration camp after *Kristallnacht* thanks to connections with well-placed government persons. There were instances of S.S. members, even in 1939, warning "their Jews" of imminent arrest. But these were exceptions; the attitude of most Aryan "good friends," as revealed in many interviews, was an immediate and total severing of all ties. One of the most instructive interviews is with Inge Friedman, who tells of the West European Jews' deportation, by regular railroad, to Riga. According to Friedman, members of the Latvian S.S. were much crueler than their German counterparts. She reports the immediate murder of the weak, who were transported in buses that were no better than gas chambers on wheels; the hanging of her father for the "crime" of selling old clothes to the Latvians; and her own long odyssey through various concentration camps until she reached the northern German city of Kiel on May 1, 1945, from whence she was transferred to Sweden at the last minute by the Red Cross.

The possible pitfalls of relying on personal testimony are demonstrated by the interview with Anne Spiegel, who recalls no antisemitism during her girlhood in Vienna, although hatred of the Jews was rampant in this city well before the Anschluss. Until 1938, her father did not believe that what had befallen the German Jews could happen in "beautiful Vienna." It was only when the Nazis forced Anne to clean filthy barracks occupied by German soldiers that she became hysterical and understood that "they mean it." Even then, her father, clinging to the belief that "this will blow over," remained unconvinced (p. 75).

Of great documentary value is the testimony of Paul Heiman, the son of a propertied family from the Nazi capital of Munich and now a well-to-do leader of the Cincinnati Jewish community. Despite the persecution, which touched the young Paul, it was only the events of *Kristallnacht* that convinced the family that there was no hope. He reports that a non-Jewish friend who was not a Nazi, "but in order to be able to survive as a non-Jew you had to join the Nazi party" (p. 113), came to his mother—his father was in a concentration camp—and said, " 'Pack up. Get ready. I'll get him out. I'll get you a visa. Just get ready to leave' " (p. 113). The visa was quickly obtained; the family traveled to Switzerland, then to France and England, and finally to the United States. (Persons of means were apparently able to escape Germany in 1938 and 1939, even at the last minute.) Yet while America has been good to Heiman, he has drawn his conclusions from history. An active Zionist, he maintains today that without the state of Israel the Jews have no chance to survive.

The interview with Werner Coppel is one of the longer ones in the book. It may have been worth extending it even further to extract more detailed information, since Coppel is a rare witness: one who experienced each stage of the Final Solution and survived. The son of an Orthodox family whose members viewed themselves as "German citizens of the Jewish religion," Coppel was thrown out of his public school and lived at a fairly well-protected kibbutz training farm in Germany until 1941. From there he was sent to a forced labor camp, then to Riga in the deportation action of 1942, and from there to Auschwitz 3, to the I. G. Farben factory, where he worked turning coal into liquid fuel; as a Jew, he was not allowed to take shelter when the Americans bombed the factory. Coppel notes that on June 20, 1944, an American pilot accidentally photographed the death camp, yet it was not bombed. He also took part in the infamous death march from Auschwitz until the Russian army caught up with the marchers near the city of Gleiwitz.

While this book is not a monograph but rather a collection of personal testimonies, several important generalizations nevertheless emerge. It was easier for the well-to-do to find safety; some even traveled to the United States in advance of their escape to prepare their new homes. It is thus not surprising that many of the interviewees are from prosperous homes. The interviews also indicate that, at least until 1938, the Jews were not affected in the same ways or to the same degree in all parts of Germany. In general, Jews living in small towns and villages began to suffer considerably as soon as Hitler came to power, and many moved to larger cities to escape persecution. But in some cities, such as Nuremberg, life had become a hell for the Jews as early as 1933. Most interviewees, moreover, testify that until *Kristallnacht* their fathers believed that things could not get any worse and that the wave of violence and persecution would pass. This theme, repeated in most of the interviews, may explain why the young people usually emigrated before their parents. Finally, regarding present-day Germany, most express their negative or skeptical feelings. For those who have visited Germany since the war (returning primarily to visit the remaining cemeteries), the experience has usually been traumatic. Some of the interviewees still will not set foot on German soil, even after fifty years.

In general, the interviewees experienced little empathy on the part of their fellow

Jews in the United States. As noted, the widespread unwillingness to sign the affidavits left a bitter impression. But here, too, there were exceptions. Rabbis such as the Orthodox Eliezer Silver and the Reform Zionist James Heller did whatever they possibly could to help, and there were families who served as guarantors for Jews they did not know. Nevertheless, the prevalent refusal to sign, combined with the American government's maneuvers to delay Jewish immigration, rankle to this day. Most of the immigrants had to work hard for their livelihood, and apparently did not always receive much help from the Jewish communal boundaries. While the evidence presented here does not warrant all-inclusive generalizations, such personal testimony cannot be ignored.

Although not all of the interviews are of equal historical value, *Queen City Refuge* provides an important oral photography of Jews' memories of a traumatic period of their lives. Like all records of this kind, the picture is susceptible to the distortions that can creep in during the course of forty years; in order to live normal lives, the survivors have often had to repress painful memories. Yet the editors have managed to present a partial delineation of the terrible tragedy that befell Jews who considered themselves "patriotic German citizens of the Mosaic persuasion" but suddenly found themselves, in the words of interviewee Oscar Dewald, "thrown out, hated, pursued like animals and treated like animals" (p. 111). It is fitting that, rather than languishing in an archive, these testimonies have been published in a book that will be an instructive document for future generations.

MENAHEM KAUFMAN
The Hebrew University

Rivka Perlis, *Tenu'ot hano'ar heḥaluẓiyot befolin hakevushah* (*Pioneering Youth Groups in Occupied Poland*). Tel-Aviv: Beit Lohamei Hagetaot and Hakibbutz Hameuhad, 1987. 608 pp.

Since the end of the Second World War, intense interest has been focused on the youth movements active during the Holocaust. While Rivka Perlis's work belongs to this broad trend, it differs from its predecessors. Most previous works have dealt with a particular movement or a certain aspect of their activities, often with apologetic or other nonacademic objectives. Perlis's book is unique in its systematic, comprehensive exploration of youth movements wherever they played a central role in Jewish underground fighting groups.

The book, sixteen chapters in all, is divided into two parts, with an afterword, notes and indexes of places and persons. The first part presents a panoramic view of the activities of Hashomer Hazair, Dror, Gordonia, and the Akiva movements between the late 1930s and the Nazi invasion of the Soviet Union.

This period was characterized by a gradual transition from the movements' prewar methods and values to those demanded by a new and quickly changing reality. Central to their organizational, education and ideological work during this period was the goal of helping young people maintain their essential humanity and movement values under circumstances of underground activity and persecution under the Soviets, and in the face of hunger, humiliation, oppression and terror under the Nazis. The author stresses the youth movements' successful efforts to recover from the shock of the war and systematically renew their ideological-educational activities in response to new conditions, even when traditional Jewish and universal sociocultural constraints had disintegrated. This success was further highlighted by contrast with the adult world and its social and communal parties and organizations, most of which fell apart with the outbreak of the war and in many cases failed to be rehabilitated afterward.

With Nazi Germany's invasion of the Soviet Union and the onset of systematic mass extermination of Polish Germany, the youth movements began to focus on a single goal: preparation for armed rebellion in the ghettos of Poland. In describing the transition to training for revolt, the author exchanges her broad, panoramic approach for a detailed, point-by-point study of preparatory action in those places where rebellion was attempted.

One of the most fateful decisions made by the youth movements was that of sending some of their members back from Vilna to the German zone. By 1940, some fifteen hundred youth movement members under the aegis of Hehalutz had concentrated in Vilna, which was then briefly under Lithuanian rule. Yitzhak Zuckerman, Mordechai Anielewicz, Zivia Lubetkin, Yosef Kaplan, Mordechai Tenenbaum-Tamaroff and Tosia Altman were among those who returned to Warsaw to lead their movements and who crystallized the rebellion idea, inculcated it in their followers (not only in Warsaw but throughout occupied Poland) and brought it to fruition. The author is right in emphasizing that these actions affected not only the youth movements themselves but also their distinctive status within the Jewish community at large. Strikingly, no party or organization, either Zionist or non-Zionist, followed the Hehalutz lead. This significantly affected the complex relations between the youth movements and those few communal leaders who did remain in Vilna, who were joined by former party and organization functionaries of the second and third rank.

This new reality undoubtedly strengthened the youth movement leaders' sense of their uniqueness and even their superiority over the veteran communal functionaries, although the two groups may have agreed ideologically. Indeed, tension between the pioneering youth movements and establishment Jewish parties such as Poale Zion (C.S.) and Hitahdut had predated the war, a tension that may be characterized as a conflict between an elite who realized their ideas and those who preached without drawing personal conclusions regarding their own lives. This conflict took on new forms during the Holocaust—due, inter alia, to the youth movements' heightened status that resulted from their wide-ranging social and educational activity. Such activity enhanced the movements' sense of responsibility for the Jewish community at large; as the primary organized Jewish communal force, they filled the vacuum left by the absence of a veteran leadership. Perlis presents an extensive survey of the movements' pan-Jewish activities that strengthened their ties with elements of the Jewish community from which they were formerly alienated.

Beginning in late 1941 and more so in 1942, the idea of rebellion took precedence over the movements' other areas of activity. But an ever-growing gap between the formation of the idea and preparation for its realization soon became apparent; among the many reasons was the Jewish communal leadership's inability to digest the terrible truth of the Nazis' determination to exterminate all the Jews. The veteran leaders at first refused to believe the news of extermination that came from the east. Even when the truth could no longer be ignored, they voiced other forms of denial—for example, that the Nazis would not dare perpetrate such crimes within Europe proper. Some of the Judenrat heads in such places as Bialystok and Zaglembie maintained that a significant portion of the community could be saved by working for the Germans. And there was of course tremendous fear that any outburst on the part of Jews would bring German retaliation and the destruction of the entire community. Such views, supported by the majority of the Jewish population, intensified the youth movements' sense of isolation—as well as the conviction that, since they were the only ones with the courage to face reality, they were the natural leaders of an effort to steer the entire community toward armed revolt.

Viewed from today's perspective, the young people's understanding of the wartime reality seems to have surpassed that of the older generation, whose assessments were rooted in a sociocultural heritage that did not include the concept of genocide in the name of a racist ideology. Weighed down by fewer cultural and psychological inhibitions, the younger Jews could grasp the situation as it was with greater clarity and draw far more radical conclusions. In addition, the young people's freedom from family responsibilities made it easier for them to demand revolutionary action.

Almost everywhere, however, most Jews chose to heed the pleas of the Judenrat members, especially when they pointed to the dangers inherent in the young people's "lawlessness." Perhaps the most tragic (though not the only) instance of the rift between the Jewish resistance movement and the community at large occurred in Vilna, when the commander of the "United Partisan Organization" gave himself up to the Gestapo after Yaakov Gans, the head of the Judenrat, had gathered around himself the few survivors of the ghetto and incited them against the fighting organization.[1] The idea of rebellion, in short, did not ignite the hearts of the masses; the book presents numerous examples of this tragic gap. In this respect, the Jewish Fighting Organization did not succeed, except in Warsaw. In most cases the young people fought and died alone.

Perlis's thesis is that the youth movements played a decisive role both in creating the Jewish Fighting Organization and in the Warsaw ghetto rebellion itself, and that they drew in their wake such political elements as the Bund and the Communists. This development was not coincidental, she maintains. First, unlike other Jewish communal groups, the youth movements were able to preserve their unity throughout the entire period in question, primarily because some of their leadership returned to occupied Poland. Second, the dire view of diaspora life held by the pioneering youth even before the war helped them understand the new wartime reality. The collective group experience in the kibbutz training programs fostered the social and ideological cohesiveness that was a necessary condition for successful underground activity. Finally, the youth movements' leadership in Warsaw maintained a well-developed communications network with their colleagues in outlying areas that allowed them to chart similar courses of action.

This discussion has focused on only a few of the important issues discussed in the book, which include as well the youth movements' ties with Polish underground groups, the negotiations with the non-Zionist parties toward unifying the United Jewish Fighting Organization, the attempt in Warsaw to integrate the Revisionist fighting organization, and other matters too numerous to even mention.

I have certain reservations about the brief and necessarily superficial survey of the history of Hehalutz and its member youth movements during the years just prior to the outbreak of the war. It would have been preferable to either expand this section somewhat or omit it completely. Moreover, the appendix includes a table numbering the prewar membership of the youth movements, with the figures based on internal movement sources. My familiarity with the material indicates that the movements have padded these figures, for reasons of their own that are too lengthy to discuss here. In any event, the data given cannot serve as a reliable index of the youth movements' status, either individually or as a totality.

These minor cavils are in no way intended to minimize the value of this book. Some of the author's conclusions may of course be challenged. But even those who disagree with the author will not be able to ignore her intellectual effort and determination to base each conclusion on a firm factual foundation, an effort that has resulted in an impressively accurate and original work.

YISRAEL OPPENHEIM
Ben-Gurion University of the Negev

Note

1. See also Yitzhak Zukerman, *Begeto uvemered* (Tel-Aviv: 1985), 24ff.

Menachem Z. Rosensaft and Yehuda Bauer (eds.), *Antisemitism: Threat to Western Civilization*. The Vidal Sassoon International Center for the Study of Antisemitism. Jerusalem: The Hebrew University of Jerusalem, 1988. 116 pp.

Gary A. Tobin with Sharon L. Sassler, *Jewish Perceptions of Anti-Semitism*. New York: Plenum Press, 1988. xv + 325 pp.

Why has antisemitism in America, which often reflects European origins and parallels European stereotypes, not attained the severity of European bigotry? Why, though exposed to social, economic and literary abuse, has the American Jew so infrequently been touched by physical antisemitism? Modern Jewish European history has been marked by ghettoization, expulsion and extermination, but only very rarely have American Jews been murdered by mob violence. Why was the travesty of justice that took the lives of Leo Frank, Andrew Goodman and Michael Schwerner so unusual in America? In short, what is unique about American antisemitism? These questions and others like them have been the subject of essays, surveys, pamphlets and media attention, but no conclusive answers have resulted. Important full-length books, such as Arthur D. Morse's *While Six Million Died: A Chronicle of American Apathy* (1968) and Saul Friedman's *No Haven for the Oppressed: United States Policy Toward Jewish Refugees 1938–45* (1973), deal with only a limited aspect of the problem, or with a circumscribed historical period. Charles Silberman, in his *A Certain People: American Jews and Their Lives Today* (1985), has presented evidence (both statistical and narrative) to suggest that the negative attitudes of non-Jews toward Jews are changing for the better, but Nathan and Ruth Perlmutter in another recent book *The Real Anti-Semitism in America* (1982) argue that abusive, hard-sell, anti-Jewish stereotypes have merely been replaced by moderate, soft-sell antisemitism. And Yehuda Bauer's essay in *Antisemitism* (one of the two books reviewed here) ponders the thought that millions of European Jews were not murdered by "ideologically convinced antisemites"; he reaches the disturbing conclusion that antisemitic acts, or even genocide, may occur even in the absence of popular, overt or violent hatred.

In light of the Holocaust, can Jews feel secure in America? Gary Tobin of Brandeis University, whose published work has been mainly in the areas of urban planning and Jewish demography, approaches the problem by seeking to pin down the "reality" of antisemitism in the United States by measuring and assessing polling data about Jews, Israel and antisemitism; analyzing extremists and hate groups; appraising the dual identity of American Jews and the external charges of dual loyalty; evaluating the Jewish press and its coverage of antisemitism; and measuring institutional responses. The final chapter details ways of combating and containing stereotypical projections of Jews in politics, in the media and in society.

Tobin concludes that what Jews need and freely choose to preserve in seeking to insure distinct minority status—namely, support both for Israel and for Jewish communities in distress across the world—contributes to individual, group and governmental antisemitism on the part of many in the majority. Yet the American sense of fair play and its constitutional democracy, which was created in the age of enlightenment that had become free of medieval state religion, have provided Jews and others with legislative immunity from attack.

There are cracks in the constitutional process, however. Tobin concurs with the view of G. Selznick and S. Steinberg, who state that

> simplistic beliefs and authoritarian attitudes, ignorance and disregard of democratic norms, a low threshold of tolerance for social and political diversity, insensitivity to the suffering of others—these are tendencies that characterize large numbers of Americans. Given a crisis situation and political leadership, they constitute a potential threat to the democratic order. [1]

Signs of political reaction in the United States (including, for example, the success of the Moral Majority at the polls, which threatens the separation of church and state; or the accusations made by far Right organizations such as the Liberty Lobby and the Aryan Nations in the Great Plains–Midwest, alleging that Jewish bankers were to blame for the farm crisis in 1985) suggest that this may be so.

Further, it can be argued that the most far-reaching threat to Jews in America is constituted not by the traditional neo-Nazi/Ku Klux Klan and far Right fundamentalist hatred (though that, too, is important) but rather a less tangible form of passivity or apathy: for instance, the standing by in silence when Zionism is condemned as racism. Or, to take another case, when Secretary of State James Baker declared to leaders of the American Israel Public Affairs Committee (AIPAC) in a much-publicized address in May 1989 that it was high time to abandon the vision of a greater Israel, many Jews concluded that American foreign policy was about to move in an anti-Israel direction, and they sought the political maneuverability to counteract any such trend. This reaction produced in turn a negative response from certain groups within the administration, the media and the public, who implied that these American Jews were loyal to a foreign power and were meddling irresponsibly in American foreign policy. In the face of such realities most Jews nonetheless remain vigilant, actively expressing the fear that persistent hostility to Israel is linked to antisemitism.

Anti-Semitism: Threat to Western Civilization is made up of selected papers from a conference on this theme held at the New York University School of Law in 1985. The titles give the impression of high theory and grand research. However, with one exception, the essays are actually minutely crafted and concentrated on a single idea: namely, that antisemitism is a malignant and chronic disease endemic to Western culture. It is up to humankind to uproot this virus lest it once again reach epidemic proportions.

Several essays speak out against the trivialization of the Holocaust and the misuse of the imagery of the Shoah. Other pieces analyze the ways in which international institutions have identified themselves with the new anti-Jewishness, made respectable by the United Nations resolution of 1975 ("Zionism is racism") that sought to delegitimize Israel and the Jewish people. William Korey's well-researched survey of Soviet antisemitism at the United Nations is particularly effective in exposing how, until very recently, the U.S.S.R. systematically equated Zionism with Nazism and antisemitism. This canard is repeated throughout the Arab world; it was not officially repudiated even in the era of *glasnost,* and it surfaces from time to time in the attacks of radical Jewish Left against the Jewish state.

The Jewish emergence from powerlessness often presents the churches with something of a dilemma, given many of their traditional attitudes. The Jews' new status can be seen as negating the characteristic pity with which the liberal Protestant views the Jews as a weak people; the demands of conservative Protestantism that the Jews play a confessional role in Christian eschatology, and, of course, many of the basic tenets of Roman Catholic theology. The comments of Franklin H. Littell and Harry James Cargas, respectively, on Protestant and Catholic views of antisemitism—what has been done and what needs to be done—are instructive, as is Hubert G. Locke's empirical appraisal of black attitudes toward Judaism and antisemitism. Locke finds that the black-Jewish alliance in the struggle for civil rights no longer exerts significant influence on public opinion and that the vulgar antisemitism of Minister Louis Farrakhan, as well as Jesse Jackson's acerbic remarks during the presidential campaign of 1984 concerning Jews, the Holocaust and Zionism, proved to be attractive to the younger generation of blacks. Nonetheless, he believes that the positive relationship between blacks and Jews remains intact for the majority of black Americans.

Both books are recommended. The generally reliable quality of *Jewish Percep-tions of Anti-Semitism* will make it a useful reference work in its field, while the warning signals and active agenda mentioned in *Antisemitism* help identify Chris-tian guilt, Jewish pain and the evil of indifference, as well as suggesting ways to respond. Together, these books speak out against racial and religious defamation from whatever source and in whatever place or time.

ZEV GARBER
Los Angeles Valley College
and University of California, Riverside

Note

1. Gertrude Selznick and Stephan Steinberg, *The Tenacity of Prejudice: Anti-Semitism in Contemporary America* (New York: 1969), 185.

David Roskies (ed.), *The Literature of Destruction: Jewish Responses to Catastro-phe*. Philadelphia: Jewish Publication Society, 1989. 652 pp.

If it is paradoxical to find creative genius, even creative joy, stirring and sometimes surging in a literature of destruction, then that paradox must be grounded elemen-tally in the human interchange between history and art. And if the Jewish people persistently exemplify this paradox, that must be because they, more than others, have been vulnerable to destructive force and given to literary response.

"What shall I take to witness for thee? What shall I liken to thee, O daughter of Jerusalem? What shall I equal to thee, that I may comfort thee, O virgin daughter of Zion? For thy breach is great like the sea, who can heal thee?" This remarkable outcry from the book of Lamentations (2:13) seems to question the virtue of meta-phor vis-à-vis utter duress. Yet the very question personifies a solitary wasted city, *bat yerushalayim* and *bat ẓiyon,* who is "become as a widow" and "weepeth sore in the night."

This passage, then, at once challenges and endorses figurative language, the stuff of poetry, by its quintessential feminine metaphor as well as its formal modula-tion—incremental questions leading through varied invocations to a mixed note of expectation and despair. And add to this the virtuosic nature of Lamentations, which is composed in an alphabetic acrostic. What is more, the passage implies a further question no less radical than that of literary commensurability. Can bearing witness, can mere verbal likening, act to comfort and even to heal? Touching on the destruc-tion of the Temple and the Babylonian exile, these questions from Lamentations— partly because of their content and context, and partly because they *are* questions— stand at the source of Judaic Shoah literature.

At the near end of that tradition, in our own time, we might locate Yitzhak Katznelson's *Song of the Murdered Jewish People* (1944), an epic (originally written in Yiddish) with powerfully desperate recourse to Scripture. In Katznelson's eyes, a people has perished—"Never will the voice of Torah be heard." As it happened, the poet and his son were gassed, but his manuscript survived, hidden in bottles underground.

We also have Uri Zvi Greenberg's fierce Hebrew elegy *To God in Europe* (1951): "Where are there instances of catastrophe / like this that we have suffered at their hands? / There are none—no other instances." For Greenberg, the Shoah of his own days is incomparable, in itself a new standard of comparison. Yet this very cry, David Roskies shows, is itself traditional—though God forbid it should ever be evoked again! Moreover, Greenberg's mere use of Hebrew in the reborn state of Israel offers a form of redemptive consolation.

Both these poems, along with Lamentations and scores of other writings, make up the anthology that Roskies has devotedly, scrupulously, pointedly compiled. Torah, the Prophets, Psalms, midrash, martyrs' prayers, chronicles, songs, stories, poems, proclamations, ghetto parodies, epic, archives, diaries, sermons, jokes and more poems—from its evocation of the first *ḥurban* and the Second Temple through Ashkenaz and Spain to revolutionary Russia, Nazi-ridden Poland, and Israel in 1948, *The Literature of Destruction* (like Roskies's earlier study, *Against the Apocalypse* [1984]) demonstrates not a lachrymose but a resilient Jewish temper, the covenant persisting through and despite its violent ruptures.

All of the hundred writings here, except Babel's Russian stories and Szlengel's Polish poems, were originally written in either Hebrew or Yiddish. This deliberate choice brings out an archetypal and allusive continuity of engagement with covenantal Judaism, promoting a body of literature, much of it translated here for the first time, that acutely deserves a wider readership.

At the same time, it is not exactly correct to claim that "Glatshteyn and Alterman have never before rubbed shoulders in any anthology" (see *Voices Within the Ark* [1980] and *A Treasury of Jewish Poetry* [1957]), or that Singer and Agnon have not (see *The Penguin Book of Jewish Short Stories* [1979] and *Great Jewish Short Stories* [1963]). The editor might also have delved somewhat more into the question of what identifies a "Jewish" response to catastrophe. Two works that come to mind are Paul Celan's *"Todesfuge"* (1944–1945) and Primo Levi's *"Se questo è un uomo"* (January 1946)—German and Italian lyrics that are both biblically resonant and compellingly collective, and thus closer to the thrust of this anthology than Babel's fine stories that appear in it. But including even great European Jewish writers such as Celan and Levi might have distracted attention from the volume's high points—to cite just one, S. Y. Agnon's "The Sign," a luminous, elegiac prose hymn to Jewish language.

With intelligent introductions, good translations of many little-known writings, and useful glosses, David Roskies has (re)claimed a vital inheritance in this holistic, if not ultimately healing, book.

JOHN FELSTINER
Stanford University

Salomon W. Slowes, *Ya'ar Katin—1940* (*Katyn Forest—1940*). Tel-Aviv: Sifriyat Ma'ariv, 1986. 230 pp.

When the Red Army overran eastern Poland in September 1939, about a quarter of a million officers and men were taken prisoner by the Soviets. Most of the soldiers were freed after undergoing a screening procedure, but some fifteen thousand prisoners remained, of whom approximately two-thirds were officers and the remainder an assortment of doctors, lawyers and other professionals who served as reserve officers (including fourteen generals and three hundred general staff officers). These prisoners were herded into the three POW camps inside Russia—Kozielsk, Starobielsk and Ostashkow—where they were kept behind barbed wire under harsh conditions of internment until April 1940, when most of them were dispatched to an unknown destination.

In May 1943, the corpses of about forty-five hundred men with bullet holes in their skulls were discovered by the Nazi occupation forces in the Katyn Forest, near Smolensk, and identified as the Polish officers who had been held in the Kozielsk camp. An international commission of forensic experts set up at German initiative determined that the massacre had taken place about three years earlier, that is, in 1940, about a year before the region was occupied by the Wehrmacht. Somewhat later the Russians also set up a commission of inquiry, which concluded that the prisoners had been shot by the Germans at the end of 1941. But in the early 1950s, additional evidence came to light implicating the NKVD in the massacre. This was also the unanimous conclusion of a commission of inquiry set up after the war by the U.S. Congress, which heard hundreds of witnesses and checked various documents and exhibits throughout Europe. Even with the passage of several decades, however, the question of who was "responsible" for the Katyn massacre has not yet been totally answered.

This enigmatic affair has a significant Jewish component as well, which is the theme of Salomon Slowes's recently published volume. Slowes, a physician from Vilna, was one of ninety-six prisoners who survived the Kozielsk camp. According to Dr. Slowes, on April 26, 1940, he and another ninety-five officers were suddenly led out of a secret postern of the camp and hustled onto waiting trucks. After a long journey, they reached the Pavlishchev-Bor camp, where a stunning surprise awaited them: dining tables covered with starched linens, laden with carefully arranged baskets of freshly sliced white bread. The men were seated, whereupon they were served hot vegetable soup (obligingly ladled out by aproned sentries) that had been brought in fresh from the nearby kitchen. A similar reception awaited those officers who were brought to Pavlishchev-Bor from the Ostashkow and Starobielsk camps. Subsequently, all of these officers were transferred to the Griazowietz camp, which was also a sort of "holiday village." All in all, 394 prisoners, including 40 Jews, were brought to the camp.

In Pavlishchev-Bor (a "showpiece" POW camp—in his words), the Griazowietz camp, and later, in various camps assigned to Anders's Army in the Soviet Union and other locations in Asia and Europe, the author enjoyed the friendship and patronage of the elderly professor Boleslaw Sharecki, who before the war had been commander of the Center for Medical Training and Specialization of the Polish Army. Unlike many Polish officers who treated their Jewish counterparts—even under POW conditions—with scorn and hostility, Sharecki stood out in the officers' corps for his liberal outlook and his opposition to antisemitism. In both the POW camps and in Anders's Army he held senior positions in the medical corps. It was thanks to him that the author was able to find a niche in this service, practicing dentistry and stomatology—his profession before the war.

The author contrasts this outstanding humanitarian with General Wolkowicki, the elderly mentor of the antisemitic junior officers and cadets, who defended their criminal behavior toward their Jewish neighbors. Cases of extreme antisemitism are cited in the chapters dealing with his service in Anders's Army (from autumn 1941), in the Totskoye camp, in the headquarters at Buzuluk and even following the army's departure from Russia in the summer of 1942. The author is not sparing in his examples of antisemitism, which was increasingly prevalent in the formation of the Fifth Division in the "Koltubanka Ghetto" camp and later in Iraq, Palestine and Italy.

A special chapter is devoted to the anti-Nazi plans of the Jewish Legion within the Polish army. Two of its main proponents, attorney Marek Kahan, one of the owners of the Warsaw *Der Moment,* and Miron Szeskin, the former commander of Brit Hahayal (the Jewish Ex-Servicemen's Alliance) in Poland, even addressed a detailed memorandum to General Anders on this issue. A translation of the memorandum, dated October 10, 1941, can be found in the appendix to the book, which also contains "A Report of General Anders' Talk with Representatives of Polish Jews in the Soviet Union." These two documents, in particular the second, complete the picture drawn in the chapter on the Jewish Legion's plan and add a novel note to a rather well-worn theme.

The volume also includes a number of facsimiles of the author's personal papers, and pictures (sketches by artist friends) both from his stay in the POW camps at Griazowietz and Starobielsk and from his period of service in Anders's Army in and outside the Soviet Union. Of special interest is the rare photograph from that time showing the Kozielsk camp in the background and an accurate and detailed plan of the camp in the foreground. This plan, which remains extremely rare even today, was drawn by Slowes himself in 1940 and hidden in the sole of his boot. There is no doubt that these appendixes further enhance the value and importance of this book—as does the fact that the Soviets, after so many years, have finally begun to acknowledge their role in the Katyn massacre.

Dov Levin
The Hebrew University

Nechama Tec, *When Light Pierced the Darkness.* Oxford and New York: Oxford University Press, 1986. 261 pp.

It is axiomatic to observe that in virtually no area of Holocaust studies is there much "good news" to leave one with a sense of hope or faith in the actions of humanity.

There is one exception: the behavior of the righteous gentiles, those who risked their own lives and those of their families to aid Jews. For a variety of reasons, this is an area that was long left unexplored by scholars and researchers. When it was discussed, it was usually in a purely anecdotal fashion and in terms of a few well-known cases, for example, those in Holland who hid Anne Frank and her family. While Yad Vashem tried assiduously to document as many cases as it could and to honor those who had performed these incredible acts, there was relatively little serious and systematic study of who these people were and what led them to act in such a unique and heroic fashion.

The topic of righteous gentiles has also not occupied a prominent position in broader Jewish circles; all too often, it has been ignored, shunted aside or even belittled. Increased attention to this subject, it was said, might give the world the impression that more people helped than actually did. It might make it seem that things were not really "that bad." It would take the focus off the horrible acts of the perpetrators and place it on a few people whose behavior in no way characterized that of the majority.

In the past few years, however, a number of scholars have brought serious sociological and historical methodology to bear on the subject of righteous gentiles, thus rescuing from oblivion a critically important aspect of the entire story of the Holocaust. Rather than take the focus off the horrible acts of the perpetrators, such research has given the lie to the oft-repeated claim that "there was nothing anyone could do to help these hapless people." There was something some could do to help—and many, far more than ever imagined, did so.

Nechama Tec's book *When Light Pierced the Darkness* is an exploration of the Christian rescue of Jews in Nazi-occupied Poland. These were people who were engaged in autonomous altruism, selfless help that was neither reinforced nor rewarded by the society in whose midst they dwelt.

The basic question Tec seeks to answer in her book is what influenced the decision to rescue: Was it social class, political beliefs, the degree of antisemitism or philosemitism expressed by the rescuer, the extent of religious commitment, the role of previous friendships or the prospect of receiving a monetary award? In interviews with those who rescued and those who were rescued, she finds that none of these factors are fully reliable predictors of who would attempt to rescue and who would not. Rescuers came from all social classes and political beliefs. Some had close Jewish friends and some had none.

She does, however, find certain important predictors that corroborate previous research carried out by Perry London. Both find that those who engaged in this form of altruism shared certain characteristics: a strong identification with a parental mode of moral conduct and a sense of being socially marginal or, as Tec calls it, a sense of individuality. These were often people who in one way or another did not blend into their environments, for example, the Huguenots in France. They were people who possessed a high level of self-reliance; consciously or unconsciously, they were freer from social constraints than were their neighbors. Tec adds certain other characteristics. Virtually all the rescuers had an amazingly matter-of-fact attitude toward what they did. They repeatedly deny that they acted in a heroic or extraordinary fashion. Most of the rescuers did not plan to become rescuers, they "merely" opened their doors to those Jews who knocked on them. Moreover, the vast majority of the rescuers had a universalistic perception of the needy. The fact that the victims were Jews was essentially irrelevant to them. They were simply helpless people in desperate need, as one rescuer explained:

> By saving the Jewish girl I simply did my duty. What I did was everybody's duty. Saving the one whose life is in jeopardy is a simply human duty. One has to help another regardless of who this human being is as long as he is in need, that is all that counts (p. 165).

Given the unique and heroic aspects of their behavior, why is it that the rescuers insist that what they did was ordinary behavior, unworthy of special notice? This attitude, Tec believes, may in fact be traced to the fact that they were people who had a long history of aiding those in need. It is this tradition of standing up for the needy that Tec finds to be the most significant factor in predicting who would rescue. In addition, they were characterized by deep-seated individuality.

There were a few exceptions to these rules, including rescuers who were committed antisemites. While there were relatively few of these, the fact that there were any at all is quite striking. Antisemites who engaged in rescue were generally deeply religious, prominent people who were quite nationalistic. They had no compunctions about admitting that they wanted Poland to be rid of Jews, but they did not believe that murder was the way to go about this. Some were concerned that their antisemitic attitudes had helped foster the conditions that allowed the Holocaust to blossom, and in certain cases their acts of rescue were a form of atonement—not for the attitudes themselves but for what these had helped spawn. In fact, recent research has shown that some of the antisemitic rescuers continued to express antisemitic beliefs even after the war.

The story of individual rescue efforts is a strikingly important aspect of Holocaust studies, one that deserves to find its way not only into the scholarly literature but into the communal and popular aspects of Holocaust commemoration. It is interesting that far more attention has been paid in these circles to the liberators—who, in most cases, rode into camps that had already been abandoned by the Germans—than to the rescuers.

Tec has written an impressive book. She has meshed serious scholarship with moving renditions by both rescuers and those they aided. It is the tale of an amazing group of people, who are all the more amazing because they are convinced that what they did was so unextraordinary.

DEBORAH E. LIPSTADT
Occidental College, Los Angeles

Gerhard Vilsmeier, *Deutscher Antisemitismus*. Frankfurt: Peter Lang, 1987. 317 pp.

The exact relationship between the antisemitic movements of the nineteenth and early twentieth centuries and the genocidal policies of the Third Reich has been a matter of much dispute. On the one hand, it can be argued that German National Socialism could hardly have made the headway that it did had Germany not had both a long tradition of Christian anti-Judaism and more modern, but still widely accepted, hostile stereotypes. Hitler and the Nazis, after all, did not invent antisemitism, racialism or doctrines of Aryan superiority: Everything they said had already been said by somebody else. What the Nazis contributed to the craft of politics was a uniquely successful formula for mobilizing and intensifying existing prejudices. Non-Nazi antisemitism was unsystematic, producing a great deal of abuse, some discrimination and spasmodic violence. But no movement other than National Socialism would ever have implemented, as opposed to dreaming of, enforced emigration—and no other movement would ever have conceived of outright genocide. There is a line to be drawn, in short, between the friendly neighborhood antisemite and Adolf Eichmann.

A comparison between the policies of the Third Reich and other antisemitic regimes in Europe lends some support to the proposition that Nazism represented a unique form of antisemitism. Although Vichy France, Hungary, Rumania and Slovakia were willing to deport foreign Jews and appease the Third Reich in general, and though there were some fanatical antisemites among their officeholders (such as Xavier Vallat in France), a sizable proportion of the Jewish populations of these countries was saved, at least so long as the Germans were not in direct occupation. An examination of the reactions of world opinion to events in the Third Reich between 1933 and 1938 shows that others, too, saw Nazi Germany in the light of a more virulently antisemitic regime.

A number of such investigations exist already, though each is limited to specific case studies, for example, Andrew Sharf's on Britain, David Wyman's on the United States and Meir Michaelis's on Italy.[1] Gerhard Vilsmeier's work features a somewhat broader examination as he compares press reactions to Nazi government measures from the 1933 boycott of shops to *Kristallnacht* in several Central European countries, focusing on Austria in detail and Czechoslovakia, Hungary, Rumania and Yugoslavia somewhat more summarily.

Perhaps because it is more thorough, the section on Austria is the most successful. Vilsmeier concentrates on the right-wing and centrist press, a self-evident choice since the socialist press was banned after 1934; pro-Nazi papers such as the *Deutsch-Osterreichische Tageszeitung* were predictably apologetic, and specifically Jewish newspapers such as *Die Stimme* were predictably critical. Among the periodicals examined are those connected with the Catholic Church; what emerges is a sense of how close they were to the spirit of Nazi antisemitism, despite their strong disavowal of racial doctrines. The *Reichspost,* for example, saw the 1933 boycott as emerging from "the deepest soul of the German people," and the *Linzer Volksblatt,* whose views generally reflected those of the city's bishop, criticized the boycott's premature end, noting that "even the National Socialists are not capable of standing up to international Jewry." The Nuremberg Laws, which inter alia forbade marriages between Catholics if one of them was of Jewish descent, were criticized only insofar as they affected the rights of the Church. Of the middle-of-the-road papers, only the *Neues Wiener Tagblatt* was consistently critical; the *Neue Freie Presse,* once the archetypal "Jewish-liberal" mouthpiece, carried discretion to extremes.

Given the censorship exercised by the Dollfuss regime and the general desire not to offend a hostile and powerful neighboring state, the predominant note of restraint is not surprising. What is significant is the extent to which most Catholic papers saw nothing wrong in persecution per se. The moral framework for the pogroms that followed the *Anschluss* was well set. It is difficult to dissent from the author's conclusion that Austrian claims of having been the victim of Nazism lose a good deal of their credibility when one surveys the tone in which much of the press reported pre-1938 Nazi policies.

The overlapping factors of self-censorship and pro-Nazi sympathies are equally in evidence in the four papers of Habsburg successor states that Vilsmeier examines: namely, the *Prager Tagblatt*, the *Pester Lloyd*, the *Bukarester Tageblatt* and the Zagreb *Morgenblatt*. Each of these reported Nazi policies much as might be expected. The Czech *Prager Tagblatt*, in accordance with its liberal tradition and the democratic environment in which it operated, was cautiously critical while the *Bukarester Tageblatt*, reflecting the political atmosphere in Rumania, became increasingly supportive of Nazi policies. The Zagreb *Morgenblatt*, true in turn to the relatively tolerant climate of Yugoslavia, printed the earliest and most detailed accounts of Nazi measures, although its coverage became briefer and more bloodless as Yugoslavia was drawn into the German orbit. The most difficult position was that of the Hungarian *Pester Lloyd*, which addressed a predominantly liberal and Jewish clientele but which also came under growing pressure from the regime not to offend Hitler.

It is difficult to know what this part of the book proves. Vilsmeier tells us little here about the real opinions of the editors or of their readers concerning Nazi antisemitism. In fact, reporting of Nazi policies over time became more and more a function of what the governments of these four states wanted their papers to say about a Germany of which they were increasingly afraid, and on which they felt a growing economic dependence: A survey of press coverage of Nazi foreign or economic policy would presumably have yielded similar findings.

Except in its Austrian section, therefore, this book is more about government-press relations in the relevant period and only secondarily about antisemitism.

PETER PULZER
All Souls College, Oxford

Note

1. Andrew Sharf, *The British Press and Jews Under Nazi Rule* (London: 1964); David Wyman, *Paper Rescue: America and the Refugee Crisis, 1938 to 1941* (New York: 1985); Meir Michaelis, *Mussolini and the Jews: German-Italian Relations and the Jewish Question in Italy* (Oxford: 1978).

Jewish Communal and Social History

Eugene C. Black, *The Social Politics of Anglo-Jewry 1880–1920*. Oxford: Basil
Blackwell, 1988. xi + 428 pp.

What is this sizable, thickly documented book actually about? The author explains
that it "examines the ways in which a small, highly acculturated, London-based
elite developed a variety of institutions to socialize the Jewish community [mainly
East European Jewish immigrants]," by seeking "to create patriotic Britons and to
preserve Jewish culture" (p. x). The last term appears to refer to Jewish identity,
which the elite sought to mold in a specific form through its educational and
philanthropic institutions.

Black divides his book into three parts. In the first part, he examines the purpose
of Anglo-Jewish institutions and their effectiveness. Following this, he deals with
the elite's response to the problems of poverty and immigration. He also discusses
what the immigrants did for themselves, not infrequently in open opposition to the
elite. The final part deals in detail with the elite's diplomatic endeavors, especially
during the First World War.

It must be said that the book as a whole, while easy to read, is difficult to grasp
because it is diffuse and intensely detailed. Black pays little attention to chronology
in the main part of his work, so that the substantial difference between communal
conditions and institutional activity during the 1880s and the 1910s does not achieve
sufficient clarity. He becomes attentive to chronology later on, when discussing the
aliens issue in British politics and in his treatment of the diplomatic efforts of British
and French Jewry during the First World War. Lucien Wolf was then the principal
Anglo-Jewish diplomatic figure, and Black's account is based mainly on Wolf's
papers. Important as his activity was, however, the much-studied diplomatic efforts
of the Zionists whom Wolf sought to counter need more attention in order for the
reader to obtain a balanced picture. It should be added that the author's account of
Anglo- and French Jewish diplomacy during the Balkan War of 1912 is, so far as I
know, the first substantial account in English.

But the main substance of *The Social Politics of Anglo-Jewry* is in its first part,
which the author begins by presenting a gallery of the arresting individuals who
directed the affairs of Anglo-Jewry—the grand dukes, as they were called later
during less deferential decades. The most doughty appears to be Samuel Montagu,
while Nathan S. Joseph is featured as the planner and strategist. Less significant in
Black's view, it would seem, was the Cohen clan, apart from their domination of the
Jewish Board of Guardians. However, when Black turns next to the communal

291

activities that these men together with a few women directed, the reader may lose his way in the great profusion of data concerning individual institutions and dozens of charitable societies. The author would gain in conciseness and thrust were he to sacrifice some of the data he has assiduously gathered from archives, the press and obscure annual reports.

Black's work stirs reflections that suggest additional areas of research. The reviewer would have liked to see a fuller analysis of what was meant by self-help, that tirelessly championed goal of charitable organizations. Perhaps he might have gone beyond V. D. Lipman's pioneering attempt in *A Century of Social Service* (1959) to determine what were the long-term effects of Jewish charitable assistance on its recipients and their children. Black rather casually observes that some Jewish charitable policies influenced those that the state adopted—could we not have had more on this important point? He does, however, make clear how the increasing role of the state in providing for the needy rescued Jewish charities from responsibilities for which they did not have enough money. Comparison with American Jewry would bring to the foreground a question yet to be clearly answered: The most typical and expensive philanthropy maintained by the American Jewish elite was hospitals. Some Jewish hospitals became vast institutions, among the finest in the United States. In England, however, the Jewish community satisfied itself with arrangements for kosher food and Jewish chaplains in general hospitals, as it did not support attempts to set up Jewish hospitals. One wonders why this difference between the two communities.

Black pays attention to an interesting congeries of small, native Jewish charities, and to many friendly societies, Jewish trade associations and small synagogues that supported favorite small charities of their own. The elite's Jewish Board of Guardians functioned as the instrument for coordinating them and bringing these policies into harmony with those of the elite.

Black's chapter on immigration is valuable for its attention to East End economics, including that area's industrial decline and its chronic, accelerating shortage of housing. One of the more stimulating passages in the book is Black's contention (p. 232) that neo-Puritanism and religious revival are to be found among the lower middle classes throughout Western Europe in the late nineteenth and early twentieth centuries. However, he only hints at the presence of such phenomena among the Jews. Most historians, the present reviewer included, find instead widespread secularization among masses of recent Jewish immigrants, somewhat offset by a competing conservative religious effort. But historians' views are, or should be, open to conversion. Can Black prove his point for the Jews? At any rate, he has produced a striking, readable book crammed with information, even if it is too often diffuse and requires sharper focus.

LLOYD P. GARTNER
Tel-Aviv University

David Cesarani (ed.), *The Making of Anglo-Jewry*. Oxford: Basil Blackwell, 1990.
    222 pp.

Not very long ago, Anglo-Jewish history was justifiably considered a poor relation of the Jewish academic world. For one thing, it possessed no solid professional base. Advances in the field were largely dependent on the spasmodic exertions of individual enthusiasts, few of whom were full-time historians. Furthermore, Anglo-Jewish developments seemed devoid of any specific identity of their own. In intellectual, political, economic, social and demographic terms, they appeared to be little more than pale reflections (sometimes imitations) of those evident in the larger and more illustrious diasporas of Eastern and Central Europe and North America.

The past thirty years have witnessed a transformation. With a growing cadre of trained students now selecting Anglo-Jewish history as their main field of research, the subject has come of age. Present scholarship is notable not only for its standard but also for its range and sophistication. No longer does the chronology of modern Anglo-Jewry appear to be a rather bland and monodimensional record in which phases of immigration are inevitably followed by almost painless communal acculturation and pronounced economic improvement. Instead—and far more realistically—what have become apparent are the twists and turns in that record and the degree to which "modernization" was experienced at varying paces and with diverse results.

This volume of essays reflects the new wave of Anglo-Jewish historiography, to which it makes a substantial contribution. The editor is to be particularly commended for arranging his nine contributions in a way that itself proclaims the heterogeneity of the book's contents. He has opted for a thematic rather than a strictly chronological approach. Two of the papers (generically headed "Class and Community") illustrate degrees of class consciousness among Anglo-Jewish communities in Leeds and Manchester prior to the First World War; one (under "Gender") contains Rickie Burman's analysis of "Jewish Women and the Household Economy in Manchester, ca. 1890–1920"—which I personally found to be the most stimulating essay in what is altogether a very stimulating collection; two more ("Culture") discuss matters as diverse as the acculturation of children of Jewish immigrants in Manchester between 1890 and 1930 and aspects of Anglo-Jewish fiction between 1875 and 1905; the final four ("Politics") are concerned with matters as far apart as changes in Anglo-Jewish leadership between 1914 and 1940; Jewish involvement in East End Jewish politics during the interwar period; Anglo-Jewish interventions on behalf of refugees during the 1930s; and "The Impact of British Anti-semitism, 1918–1945." True, and as is immediately apparent, the time frame is limited; next to nothing is said about developments prior to the last quarter of the nineteenth century. Within these limitations, however, the book contains something for almost everyone, with the history of the community being approached from the bottom up as well as from the top down. All of the articles are solidly researched, using oral testimonies as well as conventional source materials. To the best of my knowledge, all are also original contributions.

Confronted with such a praiseworthy effort, it might seem churlish to object to its overall title. But "The Making of Modern Anglo-Jewry" is surely too comprehensive a choice for a book in which large areas of the communal map receive no attention at all. At the very least, the reader expects some mention of (for instance) the proliferation and polarization of Anglo-Jewish institutions; changing patterns of philanthropic activity; and—perhaps most striking of all by its omission—diversifications in ritual observance.

There is more to this complaint than the request for either a larger book or an alternative title. More fundamentally, it calls into question the continued applicability of the terms of historical reference still being used in analyses of recent Anglo-Jewish phenomena. Put another way, are not the new wave of historians becoming the victims of their own success? Having demonstrated the diversity of their subject, they have undermined the assumption that it might be considered a conglomerate unit of analysis. We must now ask whether, during the past 150 years, there has in fact existed a single "Anglo-Jewry." If not, how can its "making" be usefully described? Or the membership of its various components be identified and classified?

To be fair, in his introductory essay, David Cesarani does allude to some of these questions. One can only hope that, in their future publications, he and his fellow historians will furnish at least some of the answers.

STUART A. COHEN
Bar-Ilan University

Neil M. Cowan and Ruth Schwartz Cowan, *Our Parents' Lives: The Americanization of Eastern European Jews*. New York: Basic Books, 1989. 305 pp.

Our Parents' Lives: The Americanization of Eastern European Jews is a well-organized, sensitively written portrayal of ethnicity, immigration and the process of assimilation. In focusing specifically on the Americanization of "Eastern European Jews born, either here or abroad, between 1895 and 1915" (p. xv), Neil M. Cowan (a public affairs consultant) and his wife Ruth Schwartz Cowan (a professor of history at the Stony Brook campus of the State University of New York) present a familiar story with little original material or analysis. However, they have succeeded in refashioning this tale of Jewish life in the old country, immigration and assimilation in America into an engaging and readable book.

Although based primarily on "hundreds of hours of interviews," this book is really a skillful weaving together of the authors' voices, "documents of the period . . . newspaper accounts, advertisements, a reformer's polemics, a physician's advice" and "the most important voice . . . the men and women we interviewed" (p. xxi). In this, the authors have achieved a rare goal: that of producing a work of oral history that never becomes tedious or ambiguous but rather presents the reader with a textured and contextualized picture of history. That picture is made even more vibrant by the inclusion of a number of well-chosen photographs. And yet the book's organizational strengths—its smooth, seamless quality, its direct thematic simplicity—are also the symptoms of serious weaknesses.

In their attempt to show why and how East European Jews assimilated so quickly, which is the book's underlying theme, Cowan and Cowan focus on the daily patterns of these people's lives. Thus, the book's eight chapters (sample titles: "Dangerous Just to Be: Life in the Old Country," "It's a Free Country: Remaining Jewish in America") are devoted to what the authors describe as "mundane matters" such as child care, schooling, health care and sexual mores. This is a valuable exercise in social history that seeks the roots of the Americanization process from the bottom up. However, the two most promising chapters—those dealing with the ways in which changing views of sexuality and changing modes of childbirth and child care affected the process of assimilation—prove rather disappointing in their lack of unusual or unexpected material. The thesis that children of European immigrants were for the most part more progressive with regard to sexual mores and more likely to raise their children in a popular American, rather than traditional East European, manner is not particularly shocking, and the suggestion that these changes facilitated the "Americanization process" is a fairly obvious one.

Indeed, the book's entire premise and organizing theme is that the speed and success of the Americanization process resulted from nineteenth-century progressive reforms combined with the compatibility of certain aspects of Jewish culture and the dominant American culture, and that the process also led to the creation of a unique form of Jewish American culture. This interpretation is hardly new. The authors, in short, have used potentially original material to bolster a hackneyed theme. The fact that the materials' unique qualities are realized only rarely—for example, when used to question stereotypes of education and sexual behavior—is not surprising. For the most part, new sources are consulted only to lend weight to an already established point of view.

Perhaps the key to this problem can be found in the authors' decision to create composite characters by "defining types of people and then merging several individual voices into one character who represents the type—a professional who was born in the United States, for example, or a factory worker who was born and lived abroad until her teens" (p. xxiv). Such an approach certainly helps explain the book's chief virtue, its readability. Unfortunately, it also suggests that individual lives may have been shuffled about to service a theme. Editing oral histories is a difficult and challenging task. The interviewer/author must always seek to balance his or her theme and the interviewee's story, never letting one overwhelm the other—a feat that is only rarely achieved. Consequently, more often than not, books of oral history exhibit a great deal of tension. Sometimes they appear to be poorly organized, disjointed reminiscences that have no coherent theme. Here, however, the authors have gone to a different extreme by making one individual out of many, "creating composites" and "defining types." No matter how well intentioned, such an approach upsets the balance of oral history and may lead to a work in which one author's theme overwhelms what should be a collaborative effort between "authors."

Our Parents' Lives is a tribute to the possibilities of careful organization, while at the same time disappointing analytically and disturbing methodologically. In their quest to create a readable book, Cowan and Cowan have too closely monitored the voices in it and thereby missed the opportunity of either challenging an old tale or presenting it from a new perspective. They have simply told us once again, in a clear and entertaining manner, the things we already knew.

DAVID LEVIATIN
Harvard University

Daniel J. Elazar and Harold M. Waller, *Maintaining Consensus: The Canadian Jewish Polity in the Postwar World.* Lanham, Md., New York and London: University Press of America/The Jerusalem Center for Public Affairs, 1990. xiv + 501 pp.

Only a few years ago, I suggested in these pages that Canadian Jewry was terra incognita for most scholars of modern Jewry. Today that statement can no longer be made. In recent years, a number of scholarly and popular works on Jewish life in Canada have appeared, bringing the diaspora's fifth (perhaps fourth) largest community into the mainstream of Jewish scholarship. This volume, essentially a guidebook to the political organization and operation of Canada's Jewish communities, is one of those works. It appears in a series that resulted from a study, undertaken over the course of two decades by the Jerusalem Center for Public Affairs, of Jewish polities around the world; and it represents another milestone in the efforts of Daniel Elazar and his colleagues at the Center to put political studies on the Jewish scholarly map.

If Elazar, Harold Waller and their collaborators are right, there is no little irony in Canadian Jewry's emergence from the scholarly closet. It seems that the community is becoming known to outsiders just as it is beginning to lose its uniqueness. In contrast to their U.S. cousins, Canada's Jews have long had a strong, central representative organization, the Canadian Jewish Congress. (Earlier, the Zionist Organization of Canada had served the same purpose.) In contrast to British and French Jews, the Canadians endeavored to keep their central organization democratic. Congress included the wealthy but never surrendered totally to them, not even to the overpowering Samuel Bronfman. Most Congress leaders, moreover, were committed and sometimes observant Jews (Reform made little headway in Canada until the 1960s), unlike those assimilationists who often rose to power in other countries.

In recent years, however, according to *Maintaining Consensus,* Canadian Jewry has suffered creeping Americanization. Local communities, increasingly dominated by charitable federations and welfare funds, have usurped many of the traditional powers of Congress and robbed it of budgetary independence. As in the United States, Canadian welfare funds tend to be controlled by wealthy Jews who lean to assimilationism. Moreover, the Canadian funds are active constituents of the (American) Council of Jewish Federations and Welfare Funds. To a degree, as noted by the authors, the balkanization of Canadian Jewry reflects the centripetal forces at work in the general Canadian polity. To a greater extent, however, it reflects the powerful American influences to which all Canadians are subject, as well as the plutocratization of the community.

The decline of Congress and the rise of money power and assimilationism are also furthered by the Israel-centeredness of Canadian Jews. Money is the most important means of supporting Israel, and the federations are the effective fund-raisers. If Israel is central to Jewish life, an organization such as the Canadian Jewish Congress, which focuses on Canadian affairs and Jewish life at home, naturally becomes overshadowed by Israel-oriented groups, most of which are connected to the welfare funds. And for a variety of reasons, Israel has an appeal for community leaders, especially those not strongly rooted in Judaism, that local institutions find hard to match.

Maintaining Consensus is actually a series of communal studies varying in length, style and insightfulness. Among the most interesting are those that deal with the smaller cities, each of which seems to have some unusual characteristics. Winnipeg, for example, in many ways the most vibrant Jewish community in Canada and the best integrated into the general community, is in the fastest decline. (It deserves a full-length monograph of its own.) In Ottawa, the community council, or Va'ad Ha'Ir, was originally formed by the city's synagogues, which still maintain a strong say in community affairs, in contrast to the anticlericalism manifested in other places. In Hamilton, leftist, Yiddishist secularists gained control of the community more than half a century ago and still retain some power, yet an extraordinary 80 percent of the city's Jews are synagogue members. Calgary, only half of whose Jews belong to synagogues (although the community is about the same size as that of Hamilton), supported two day schools back in the 1920s—before most of the larger communities had even one. Its sister city, Edmonton, has a community of similar size that barely supports one day school today, despite Alberta government assistance (the authors mention provincial aid to day schools in Quebec but fail to take note of it in Alberta)—and yet subsidizes kosher meat. In Vancouver, where about half the members of the Jewish Community Center are not Jewish, Zionism exerts a particularly strong influence in the community.

Despite their differences, all these communities, as well as those of Montreal and Toronto, have in recent years adopted similar forms of communal political organization. Waller and Elazar are not unfriendly observers of the change, although they are aware of some of the resulting problems. One of the outcomes of the ascendancy of wealth indicated in the book, although not explicitly articulated by the authors, is growing insensitivity to the needs of the disadvantaged. The essay on Vancouver speaks of the city's "alleged Jewish poor" and readily admits that criminals and other "marginal" people "claiming" to be Jewish are spurned by the community. The concluding essay, "Canadian Jewry Since 1975," which is by far the most cogent and best written of all the chapters, hints at the difficulties on the horizon for a community whose leaders are increasingly drawn from the ranks of the Jewishly untutored and even uninvolved.

Maintaining Consensus raises a number of substantive and methodological questions for future researchers. Perhaps the most important is whether the present form of political organizations serves its constituents well. Data for the book are drawn from dozens of interviews conducted all over the country. Only community "leaders" were interviewed, however, and these people may be presumed to have had a strong bias in favor of the organizations they head. Another question has to do with community budgets and the political power that is their concomitant. The authors draw major conclusions from the concentration of community expenditures in the hands of the secular welfare funds. They do not consider in their calculations, however, the budgets of synagogues and a variety of organizations not connected to the central communal budgeting process, or the portion of school, community center and health care institution budgets covered by tuition, dues and fees. In terms of Israel-directed money, Israel Bonds and the "Friends" of Israeli universities and other public institutions are in some cases overlooked, although these groups raise substantial sums and their leadership is often not the same as that of the UJA or the federations. The issues of the efficacy of Canadian Jewish political institutions, the size of budgets and the loci of money-connected power may thus be somewhat more complex than this generally useful and informative volume suggests.

MICHAEL BROWN
York University

Heinz Moshe Graupe, *Die Enstehung des Modernen Judentums. Geistesgeschichte der Deutschen Juden 1650–1942* (Hebrew edition, *Hayahadut hamodernit behithavutah*). Tel-Aviv: Schocken, 1990. 396 pp.

Let me divide my comments into two parts—the first, a general value judgement; the second, critical and suggestive.

The importance of this study lies in its general descriptive approach. Although the philosophical language seems at times too condensed and difficult, the intellectuality of German Jewish life is vividly exposed. This is especially the case with Chapters 18 and 19, which offer an attempt to analyze a new kind of self-understanding of German Jewry as the result of changing attitudes toward the Jews in the nineteenth century. What is missing in Graupe's analysis is the general background dealing with the rise of nationalism. For example, the important article on nationalism by Lazarus is mentioned only superficially here (261ff.). The new intellectual self-understanding of German Jewry would be better understood, I believe, if it were explained against the background of the new sociopolitical trends in nineteenth-century German history.

What we gain from Graupe's survey is the essence and importance of Jewish cultural activity and its contribution to Western civilization in general, and to Germany in particular. My critical remarks should not minimize the importance of this contribution. Few studies have been presented that try to give a descriptive overview of German Jewish intellectual history. Seen from this angle, Graupe's work should be praised.

Much of my criticism focuses on the author's ambitious aim of covering a range of time from 1650 to 1942, almost three hundred years. This period is termed by the author as "modern." And yet a historian who chooses to examine a particular period has to justify his choice. In our case, the author should have been obliged to explain why the year 1650 was chosen to mark the beginning of modern times. It does not suffice to elaborate the changes in Jewish history only. After all, Jewish history is to be understood, and therefore to be analyzed, within the framework of general history. Consequently, the question to be posed should be: What were the specific presuppositions for determining the year 1650 as the beginning of the modern area in general history? An answer to this question would help to clarify the particularity of the Jewish aspect being dealt with in this study. Unfortunately, Graupe provides no introductory chapter discussing the seventeenth century in terms of general European history. Moreover, two phenomena in Jewish history have been chosen to be analyzed in this work: the emergence of modern Jewry and the intellectual history of German Jews. "Modern Jewry" is a very broad concept, one that has not been scrutinized systematically in this book. A considerable number of points are missing here, and thus the question may be asked why the author did not focus on the intellectual history of German Jewry alone.

On the subject of German Jewry, it seems that the author has based his method of research on the biographical approach. The reader is made acquainted with ideas, thoughts and concepts of individuals who are presented in chronological order. Such a method is certainly historical; its disadvantage, evident in Graupe's work, is that it neglects sociopolitical developments. For example, Chapter 13 deals with the new historical consciousness, Chapter 14 with the *Wissenschaft des Judentums*. Herder, Humboldt, Hegel and Ranke, the dominant figures in German Historicism, are mentioned occasionally. Neither has the interrelation between German philosophy of history and Jewish thought been elaborated, and hence remains unclear. If indeed a new Jewish historical consciousness developed during this era, we have to understand the general background, motives and reasons for such a development at this specific time.

In surveying the cultural contributions of German Jewish intellectuals to general civilization, Graupe distinguishes between two groups. One group he terms "Jews by accident" (*Zufallsjuden*); the other, Jews who wanted their part and activity in German culture to be acknowledged and valued as a *Jewish* contribution. *Zufallsjuden* are defined by the author as Jews who had no ties whatsoever to their Jewishness. Formally, without great awareness of their Jewishness, they remained Jews. Graupe chose not to place any emphasis on this large group, even though he recognized that most Jewish intellectuals did belong to this group of *Zufallsjuden* (p. 237). From Sigmund Freud to Max Liebermann, the list of persons belonging to this category is long and impressive. It is surprising that a treatise dealing with the intellectual history of German Jews barely mentions the major portion of German Jewish intellectuals. Dedicating three sentences to Sigmund Freud (p. 236) seems to be unsatisfactory, especially given Freud's own feelings about the impact of his Jewishness upon his lifework, as we can learn from his own memoirs: "Because I was a Jew, I found myself free from many prejudices which limited others in the use of their intellect, and, being a Jew, I was prepared to enter opposition and to renounce agreement with the 'compact majority.' "[1]

At the end of Chapter 9, Graupe denies the possibility of comparing European pietism with Jewish Hasidism. He believes that only an external common denominator, an emotional component (*Gefuehl*), exists between these two currents of thought. I wonder, though, why *Gefuehl* should be conceived of as "external" (p.

120). Even if one agrees with the author that completely different phenomena cannot be compared, we may still presuppose the impact of the Zeitgeist on the course of history at a certain period. The shifting of importance from the outward to the inward factors of human behavior was characteristic of the seventeenth century, and this shift in concept influenced both Christianity and Judaism. Therefore, such analogies should not be ruled out. Finally, concerning the "race-theory," Graupe chooses to categorize it under the "objective" characteristics of nationalism (p. 261). But in Germany "race" meant the expression of a subjective, inner feeling of belonging—not an objective attitude.

To sum up, I believe that the interrelation between general and Jewish history should have been more stressed. Had Graupe done this, his important study would have been more comprehensive.

ZWI BACHARACH
Bar-Ilan University

Note

1. Ernest Jones, *Life and Work of Sigmund Freud,* vol. 1 (New York: 1953), 235.

David Leviatin, *Followers of the Trail: Jewish Working-Class Radicals in America.* New Haven and London: Yale University Press, 1989. 298 pp.

Based on interviews conducted in 1980, this book presents the memoirs of a small group of American Jewish Communists and pro-Communists who in 1929 established a summer camp in upstate New York called "Followers of the Trail." The author, the grandson of several members of this by now venerable band, has provided a brief introduction that includes basic facts on the history of the American and American Jewish Left and on the great Jewish immigration from Eastern Europe to the New World. The memoirs, unannotated and preserving the Russian- and Galician-born radicals' special variety of English, are divided into three parts: reminiscences of the old country; experiences in America; and material on the camp itself, which the author calls "a shtetl on a hill." There are also a number of photographs, some of them (to my eye) unflattering and even grotesque portraits of great old age.

It was undoubtedly a very good idea to publish this oral history project on a group of forgotten foot soldiers of American Communism "whom historians have written around," as Leviatin puts it (p. 5). These people, we are informed, "attempted to change the course of history with dreams and with sweat" (p. 8). Their stories are certainly interesting. Most came from little towns and emigrated rather late to America, shortly after the Great War and right before the end of the mass immigration in 1925. This would seem to be of importance, since a number of them lived through the Russian Revolution in its most hopeful and idealistic, even messianic phase but had no experience with the subsequent oppression. Most were very poor, and there is no sentimentalization of the wretched conditions of their *shtetlakh*. Some describe the all-pervasive antisemitism of the time and place. Among many of them, we discover that old religious ties had already begun to loosen in the Old World, where new currents of thought and the Russian language had penetrated even the shtetl.

The "followers" were proletarianized in America. They went straight from the ship into the workshops, just like Sholem Aleichem's characters in his American novel *Motl paysi dem khazens*. The reader is given some fascinating glimpses of the Americanization process and the encounter with the baffling *goldene medine:* the refusal on the part of youngsters who had been in the New World for a few years to speak Yiddish with the new arrivals; the problem of how to eat a banana, a fruit unknown in Jewish Eastern Europe; and riding on a train that "goes above houses" (the el). There are some enlightening comments on Jewish geography in New York, on the decline of religious practice in the big city, and details on the sanitary conditions (or rather the lack thereof) in the tenements. And we learn as well that these working-class people actually went to concerts at Lewisohn stadium and to the Metropolitan Opera, places probably not frequented by Irish and Polish workers.

Most of the "followers of the trail" were radicalized in America, most commonly through their experience in the socialist and Communist-run Jewish unions. Some became fanatic Communists. "At first we accepted everything, we didn't question. That was the way it was, that's the way it should be. Stalin was our leader. Nobody questioned, that's the theory of Marxism-Leninism and you accept it" (pp. 143–144). "At first, not only I but to people who were in high positions of the working class and high positions of the Communist Party, Stalin was like a God to everybody. Some people used to say, 'How could the Soviet Union be wrong?' " (p. 201).

True, by the 1950s disillusion had begun to set in, and sympathy for Israel and the Zionist venture, partly a result of the impact of the Holocaust, had begun to surface. And yet some of the "followers" remained loyal to the "ideals" of Communism well into the 1960s and beyond. One interviewee informs us that even after a trip to the Soviet Union, "I still am not against the system, I am against the people that are running it" (p. 238). Another comments, "I think the life in the Soviet Union—the politics of the Soviet Union—is the future of the world" (p. 247).

Now here is a problem that the editor of this book does not quite face up to, perhaps because he likes his subjects too much. How could a group of decent, gentle, cultured Jewish workers—the kind of people who would not harm a fly—have unhesitatingly supported the tyrannical regime of a mass murderer? Neither Leviatin nor his interviewees present a satisfactory answer. Hints are provided: the exposure to raw capitalist exploitation in the shops; the Russian connection; the fact that the entire social life of the "followers" was inextricably tied to the subculture of the Left; ignorance of conditions "over there"; the rise of fascism in Europe; a refusal to believe the capitalist press; and so forth. And yet we are still left wondering at the blindness of these people—a blindness they shared, of course, with many brilliant intellectuals. It may well be that the historian simply lacks the tools to solve this riddle, and should leave it for the psychologist or the novelist with the powers of a Joseph Conrad.

It is clear from reading these accounts that the Jewishness of the "followers" has always been something perfectly natural, something that one cannot and does not wish to deny. But it is also the case that they did not develop any kind of ideology for Jewish survival. Was the secular but undoubtedly Jewish radical culture of these immigrants handed down to the next generation? Or was the radicalism handed down without the Jewishness? Perhaps Leviatin should publish another volume based on interviews with the followers' children. Meanwhile, we can be grateful to him for making available to us revealing texts from what seems to be, in this period of the collapse of European Communism, the ancient past.

EZRA MENDELSOHN
The Hebrew University

Dov Levin (ed.), *Pinkas hakehilot: Latviyah veestoniyah* (*A Guide to the Communities of Latvia and Estonia*). Jerusalem: Yad Vashem, 1988. 396 pp.

This book is termed an encyclopedia of Jewish communities in Latvia and Estonia. Indeed it is—but it is actually much more than that. The guide is divided into two sections—one on Latvia (pp. 1–297) and the other on Estonia (pp. 299–374). Each section is introduced by a full survey of the history of the Jews in that country. The survey of Latvian Jewish history is forty-seven double-columned pages; that of Estonia, seventeen pages. A long list of sources accompanies each survey and serves in effect as a bibliography of primary and secondary sources on the history of the Jewish community. The bulk of the book consists of entries on the histories of individual communities in Latvia and Estonia. The standard entry consists of three sections: the history of the community before the First World War, the interwar period and the Holocaust period. Where possible, there is also a section on the postwar Jewish community. The volume comes with maps of the Jewish communities in each country, one of the Riga ghetto and one of Jewish population density in interwar Latvia. The book is very well indexed, with separate indexes for names of individuals and place-names for both Latvia and Estonia.

This volume thus serves not only as a guide to the characteristics and fate of individual Jewish communities but also as a regional history. While many of the communities involved were small in population, some, such as Riga and Dvinsk, had quite significant roles in Jewish history. Moreover, the special sociopolitical conditions prevailing in these countries both in the interwar period and even earlier make Latvia and Estonia ideal choices for comparative studies on the impact of different environments and political systems on the development of Jewish communities. Until now, very little has been written on the history of Latvian and Estonian Jewry. Since the editor and assistant editors could not rely on secondary sources, they provide a convenient summary. A great deal of effort went into the collection and analysis of primary sources in the preparation of both the general surveys and the entries on individual cities. The resulting articles on the larger cities are thus more in the nature of scholarly monographs than encyclopedia entries.

The high level of scholarship of the authors and the utility of the indexes make this volume a must for anyone interested in East European Jewry. What should be given consideration at this stage is the possibility of translating the *Pinkas* series into English. No such geographical guide exists in English, and the articles on individual cities in the standard English-language Jewish encyclopedias are either nonexistent or, at best, much shorter than in the *Pinkas*. Such a translation should appeal not only to Jews who originated in the Baltic states but also to the wide body of non-Jews interested in the history of the region. It is a pity that such a fine reference book is available at this time only to the Hebrew reader.

SHAUL STAMPFER
The Hebrew University

Ezra Mendelsohn and Chone Shmeruk (eds.), *Studies on Polish Jewry: Paul Glikson Memorial Volume.* Jerusalem: The Hebrew University, Center for Research on the History and Culture of Polish Jews/Institute of Contemporary Jewry, 1987. English section, 73 pp.; Hebrew section, 183 pp.

The late Paul Glikson (b. Warsaw, 1921; d. Jerusalem, 1983) served as secretary of the Division of Jewish Demography and Statistics in the Institute of Contemporary Jewry at The Hebrew University. Among his publications in that field were seven volumes of the *Jewish Population Studies* series that Glikson edited. Alongside his professional work in Jewish demography he retained an ongoing interest in Polish Jewry, its history and culture, and he was an enthusiastic participant in the early activities of the Center for Research on the History and Culture of Polish Jewry at The Hebrew University.

The present volume, dedicated to Gilkson's memory by his friends and colleagues, offers to the general reading public a wide variety of essays in both these fields. The essays by U. O. Schmelz (in English) and Sergio DellaPergola (in Hebrew) discuss the development of Jewish demographic studies, outline some of the conceptual and methodological difficulties involved in such studies and attempt to evaluate Glikson's contribution to the field. But as its title indicates, studies on Polish Jewry take up the lion's share of this memorial volume.

In recent years we have witnessed an unprecedented growth in publications and periodicals on this topic in Israel, Poland, Western Europe and North America. Seen in this context, the Glikson memorial volume well illustrates the achievements already made in this field as well as indicating the potential for further growth. This volume reflects research by two generations of scholars: those born in Europe and trained in either European or Israeli universities, and those born more recently in Israel or North America, who were raised in a different cultural environment and trained in different scholarly traditions. It also presents a representative cross-section of current research concerning Polish Jewry. Finally, it demonstrates the ever-widening circle of source material utilized by scholars to further our understanding of this most fascinating and once vibrant of diaspora communities.

For the purposes of this review, we can roughly divide the articles into four major categories: literature and folklore (Chone Shmeruk, Yechiel Szeintuch, Richard Low, Olga Goldberg-Mulkiewicz); demography (Shaul Stampfer, B. Bloch); archival and documentary studies (Jacob Goldberg, Gershon Hundert); and synthetic and comparative studies (Mordechai Altshuler, Shmuel Krakowski, Ephraim Urbach, Ezra Mendelsohn). Within the confines of this short review, we note only some of the highlights of this rich volume.

Among the literary studies, Chone Shmeruk focuses on performances in Polish of a comic play by Sholem Aleichem on the Warsaw stage in 1905 and 1910, offering some suggestive comments on the interaction between Yiddish and Polish literary circles, theaters and audiences.

In the realm of folklore, Olga Goldberg-Mulkiewicz offers a fascinating comparative analysis of the symbolism of the book in the Jewish and Polish folk milieu. Calling on a wide variety of sources, including folk art, toys, proverbs and the texts of village nativity plays, she describes the book as one of the major aspects of the Jewish stereotype as conceived by the Polish peasant.

The demographic studies in this volume provide interesting new perspectives on some longstanding matters of dispute. Complaints about the ill effects of early marriage on Jewish young men and women are well known from the autobiographies and literary works of East European *maskilim*. In the past, the influence of this extant literary evidence led historians of nineteenth-century Russian Jewry to conclude that the practice of early marriage was widespread. Shaul Stampfer takes a fresh look at statistical and literary evidence from the period, concluding that early marriage was actually limited to affluent circles and that even there it died out by the end of the nineteenth century as upper-class values changed.

At their best, archival studies publish hitherto untapped sources along with appropriate introductory and explanatory material, thus aiding the process of constructing a new historical consensus. The present volume includes two such studies. Jacob Goldberg looks at Jewish retail trade in eighteenth-century Poland in the light of a series of interesting documents relating to the cities Zaslaw and Brody. From the material there emerges a detailed picture of the difficulties faced by Jewish petty traders. For the use of future researchers, Goldberg appends to his study a list of items traded by Jewish merchants, giving the Polish and Yiddish names for those items, as well as a Hebrew explanation of the terms. In his study of the Jewish community of Opatow, Gershon Hundert draws on rich collections of archival data to reexamine the changes in Jewish communal life in Poland in those areas where Jews came under the authority of the magnate aristocracy. Hundert's essay represents a short introduction to his much-awaited full-length study of Opatow Jewry.

In the category of synthetic studies, Ezra Mendelsohn adds to his long and impressive series of ruminations on the political and communal life of Polish Jewry with a comparative look at the German and Jewish minorities in the European successor states between the two world wars. Mendelsohn finds extensive room for comparison of these two nonterritorial minorities in the interwar period, while remaining sensitive to their divergent fates under the Nazis.

In his essay on Jews in the Polish army in the September 1939 campaign, Shmuel Krakowski reopens the painful and controversial issue of the Polish army and the Jews. Making skillful use of oral testimonies preserved in archives as well as printed sources, he sketches the fate of Jewish soldiers and civilians against the backdrop of the general collapse of the Polish armed forces in the face of the onslaught of the German army from the west, followed by the Russian invasion from the east.

Ephraim Urbach finds portrayals of interwar Polish Orthodoxy too much influenced by Western approaches and models. He calls for a new approach that utilizes the largely untapped Polish rabbinic literature, first and foremost the corpus of responsa literature. His article in the Glikson volume presents a case study showing how Polish rabbis understood and responded to Western Jewry of the period.

Finally, Mordecai Altshuler offers a short but intriguing look at a little-known aspect of the peace negotiations following the Polish-Soviet war of 1920–1921.

In addition to the essays here surveyed and abstracts of each article in either Hebrew or English, the volume also includes a bibliography of works edited or written by Paul Glikson.

Paul Glikson's colleagues have erected for him a most fitting memorial in *Studies on Polish Jewry*, which presents in capsule form much of the promise and the achievements of Polish Jewish studies.

GERSHON C. BACON
Bar-Ilan University

Robin Ostow, *Jews in Contemporary East Germany: The Children of Moses in the Land of Marx*. London: Macmillan, 1989. 169 pp.

Unification of the two Germanys brought together two groups whose history has received scant attention—the Jews who after the end of the Nazi period remained in, or returned to, the German Democratic Republic (East Germany) and the Jews who lived in the Federal Republic (West Germany). This is an interesting book about the small Jewish community of East Berlin. Written before the dismantling of the Wall, it reveals the enormous diversity of experience and assessment among Jewish professionals in what was once the G.D.R., and it gives us a good sense of the transformations that took place even before reunification. The twelve interviews that form the core of Robin Ostow's book make it very clear that for the Jews of East Germany—whether inside or outside the official Jewish community, and whether openly sympathetic to the state of Israel or hostile—both the experience of being Jewish and the state of Israel have increasingly become deeply felt reference points and catalysts for changing political orientations.

The two hundred or so members of the official Berlin Jewish community and the approximately two thousand other Jews in East Germany come from quite different backgrounds. Many children are from mixed parentage or have been married to non-Jews themselves. Unlike Jewish communities in other East European countries, the Juedische Gemeinde has, until recently, represented an exclusively Orthodox tradition. Its orientation did not meet the needs of secular Jews, who for many years identified with those Jews (and non-Jews) who were engaged antifascists and who had been imprisoned or were forced into emigration during the Nazi period. Before the dramatic impact of the Slanksy trial in the early 1950s, these Jews anticipated increasing integration in a developing Communist society and some believed in this goal even later. Ostow suggests that it was during this period that the Jewish community came to be completely under the control of party and state, with its members joining other veteran antifascists in receiving special benefits such as private health care and good housing.

Readers unfamiliar with the two Germanys would have benefited from a description of the two German Jewish communities, the different patterns of emigration and remigration, and some assessment of the occupational and social integration of the Jews who lived in East and West Germany. Which part of Germany was more successful in overcoming National Socialism remains an intensely debated issue, an issue perhaps more complex than Ostow's discussion admits. Increasing access to G.D.R. data and press coverage of sporadic incidents among East German youngsters indicate that these problems have not been completely eradicated, despite the official promulgation of antifascist values during the period before reunification.

Increasing integration of the G.D.R. into the international community during the 1980s was accompanied by some exchange of visitors to and from Israel, an American rabbi for the Gemeinde (who soon left because of tensions with the Jewish community) and an increase in the number of activities aimed at integrating Jewish nonmembers and greater contact with the Jews of West Berlin. Many Jews in East Germany at this time (in common with other citizens who had once been committed to socialism) were deeply frustrated with the lack of real reform in the political system. As a result, they looked for new ideals and for new social and cultural identities. This book documents their search with a number of moving interviews that reveal an uncovering and an acceptance of a previously latent Jewish identity.

Following the collapse of the Berlin Wall, East German Jews have been extensively exploring the Jewish community in West Berlin. Whether the community in the East will retain what its members considered a somewhat special character is still an open question. And whether Jews in both parts become really integrated in a united Germany depends on, as Ostow rightly suggests, a continuing commitment to democratic values and institutions. As of now, it seems this is what most people in both parts of Germany hope for as well.

MARILYN RUESCHEMEYER
Rhode Island School of Design
Brown University

Abraham J. Peck (ed.), *The German Jewish Legacy in America, 1938–1988: From "Bildung" to the Bill of Rights.* Detroit: Wayne State University Press, 1989. 257 pp.

This work constitutes a written symposium of forty intellectuals, thirty-seven of them living in the United States. Approximately half the participants are historians or social scientists, and many deal, or have dealt, with academic areas related to German or European history and culture. Most of the contributors reached the United States before the outbreak of the Second World War, largely in 1938 and 1939.

The book's focus is Abraham Peck's juxtaposition of two concepts: *Bildung*, the belief in education held by the nineteenth- and early twentieth-century German Jewish intellectual elite, and the American Bill of Rights. Optimists among the German Jews believed that the Jews' integration into German society would be fostered by education and its molding of individual character, the acquisition of universal scholarship and the cultivation of general humanist values—all this without forfeiting Jewish tradition. It was only when they completely despaired of this aspiration (and some of the contributors, or their parents, needed *Kristallnacht* to convince them of its utter futility) that they fled for their lives to the land of the Bill of Rights.

The participants were asked to address the issue of whether there is a recognizable German Jewish heritage in the American diaspora and what manifestations, if any, are apparent in their own value systems as Jews and as Americans. Was their former heritage incorporated in its entirety into the American Jewish system of values? Or are there still traces of it left, and if so, which components can and should be passed on to future generations?

Some of the contributors, in particular the historians, chose to view the topic as a subject for study or even analytic research. Others offered biographical family sketches, emphasizing the autobiographical elements. A third group related their positions on current social issues to certain aspects of their own or their parents' German Jewish heritage. The result is a broad spectrum of responses to the questions posed. The editor has rightly stressed that these essays do not form a representative sample of the 140,000 German Jews who emigrated to the United States during the period in question; given the choice of academics as contributors, there is little to indicate how the masses of German Jewish immigrants may have experienced their former heritage in the new land.

Few of the contributors directly address the question of how they view their current national-ethnic identity, and to what extent this identity was shaped by their own or their parents' German Jewish past. While most may define themselves as American Jews, many seem to have had difficulty in forging a new and balanced identity; some perhaps still do. They seem unwilling to ignore or forget the past, the personal trauma they experienced when they were uprooted from the German people and culture and, in many cases, forced to run for their lives. Many of the respondents note, either directly or indirectly, that it was not easy for them to give up their German Jewish identity.

The historian Henry R. Huttenbach is perhaps most explicit in his account of the difficulties in forging a new identity. Calling himself "a deracine" (one that is uprooted), he describes himself as "a man who thinks German but speaks American with a British accent, a man more at home with Dostoyevsky and Bartok than with Bellow and Gershwin, . . . a historian poignantly aware that his past will fade but never enough to make the future welcome" (p. 134).

A central issue in the symposium is the contribution of the 140,000 immigrants in question to American Jewry and society at large. According to George Mosse, whose piece opens the symposium and whose views the editor seems to endorse, the essence of the German Jewish heritage is *Bildung*. Judging by much of the testimony offered here, however, Henry Feingold is more likely to be correct in stating that there is no "German Jewish spirit in exile" as a distinct, established trend in the United States today. While a number of participants stress the German Jewish contribution to the American Jewish institutional structure, most of this organizational development occurred in the nineteenth century. The impression gleaned from almost all of the essays is that of individual, rather than collective, contributions of German Jewish immigrants of the late 1930s and 1940s. Also stressed are the German Jews' key roles in today's American Jewish religious movements, particularly Conservativism and Reform. It is apparent that this group's greatest contribution was of numerous persons of stature in various areas of modern life —Albert Einstein, Kurt Lewin, and other scientists, thinkers, and cultural personalities who fled from Hitler and contributed vastly, each in his field, both to American society and to humanity at large. (Contributions in the area of government policy were more limited; even Henry Kissinger, the prime example here, came to government via the academic world.) The roots of these achievements seem to lie in the impressive intellectual development that had become the norm for German Jews, particularly in the Weimar Republic period, and in the parent generation's ceaseless and vigorous efforts toward their children's advancement in all areas of modern life.

The most striking indication of the absence of an institutionalized German Jewish tradition in the United States is that the editor of the *Aufbau*, the newspaper of the German Jewish immigrants, is now Gert Niers, a non-Jew. Niers writes that the *Aufbau* readership is shrinking in the United States but growing in Germany. The newspaper is thus returning, in a sense, to the country from which its original readers were expelled, which may in itself constitute a kind of continued Jewish existence in Germany.

The level of the forty essays is not uniform. One senses that Peck, in initiating the symposium and soliciting the participation of each contributor, had no choice but to include even those who barely addressed his questions or who retold twice-told tales. Another problem is that the historians, in particular, do not always distinguish between the conclusions drawn from their own subjective experience and their later research findings. It sometimes seems as though the writers arranged the data to fit conceptual conclusions derived from their own research. This criticism, however, does nothing to alter the fact that Peck has compiled an engrossing and often compelling book, one that has contributed significantly to describing and documenting the final chapter of the history of German Jewry and its surviving representatives.

MENAHEM KAUFMAN
The Hebrew University

Ada Rapoport-Albert and Steven J. Zipperstein (eds.), *Jewish History: Essays in Honour of Chimen Abramsky*. London: Peter Halban, 1988. 700 pp.

Chimen Abramsky is the acknowledged doyen of Jewish historiography in England. Now retired from University College in London, he is known both for his extraordinary knowledge of Jewish history and as a bibliographer, a legacy of his earlier career as a book dealer in Judaica. Born in Minsk in 1917, Abramsky came to England in the 1930s. After studying at The Hebrew University he held faculty appointments at Oxford and London.

Abramsky's fields of specialization include East European Jewish history and the history of the Jews of England, both subjects nicely represented in the present festschrift. The wide range of scholars from Israel, England and North America who have contributed to this volume testifies to the international esteem in which Abramsky is held. Beyond his scholarship, Abramsky has played a singular role in creating the academic field of postbiblical Jewish scholarship in England. Indeed, the contributions to this volume by those who are either presently working or who studied or spent time in England add up to persuasive evidence of Abramsky's institutional achievements.

This is a massive festschrift of some seven hundred pages, containing twenty-eight entries on subjects as diverse as the Romans and the Maccabees, medieval Jewish sexual behavior, Hasidism, and communal conflict in Palestine. As with any such eclectic collection, some essays are of greater moment than others, but the editors are to be praised for their selection of generally outstanding material. This work is not only a tribute to the man it honors but a book that can be read with interest by historians working in a wide variety of fields.

Given the diversity of the essays and present lack of space, I should like to draw attention to a number of contributions that seem particularly remarkable. Three essays deal with aspects of the history of Jewish women and the family. Avraham Grossman analyzes the ordinances against polygamy and divorce without a wife's consent attributed to Rabbenu Gershom and sets them against the social background of the mercantile activity of the German Jews, analyzing records from the Mediterranean communities with which these traders dealt that show how it was not uncommon to marry second wives far from home. Yom Tov Assis has contributed an exhaustive catalogue of the sexual misdeeds of medieval Spanish Jewish society, including rape, premarital and extramarital sex, concubines and prostitution. According to Assis, the sexual laxity of the Jewish community was primarily a product of the influence of Spanish society: In intimate matters, the Jews often resemble their neighbors far more than the apologetic literature admits. Finally, Ada Rapoport-Albert's essay challenges S. A. Horodecky's tendentious view of the Maid of Ludmir story as an overly positive distortion of the image of women in Hasidism. Although framed around a rather narrow historiographical question, this essay provides extensive material for understanding the status of women in Hasidism as it actually was.

Two other excellent pieces deal with aspects of the doctrine of the tzaddik. Rachel Elior focuses on one of the founders of Polish Hasidism, Jacob Isaac, the Seer of Lublin, showing how he reversed the philosophical antagonism toward the material world then prevalent among disciples of the Maggid. Although the tzaddik continued to strive for spiritual detachment, he was also now charged with bringing material benefits to earth for his disciples by converting the *ayin* (nothingness) of God to the *yesh* (somethingness) of the material world. Elior suggests that this new affirmation of materiality may have resulted from the desperate economic conditions in late eighteenth-century Galicia in addition to a perceived need to have Hasidism expand from an elite pneumatic circle into a mass movement.

Naftali Loewenthal writes on the doctrine of self-sacrifice (*mesirat nefesh*) of the tzaddik in the teachings of Dov Ber, the son of Shneur Zalman, the founder of Habad Hasidism. The most fascinating aspect of this study is its portrayal of the way in which Dov Ber appropriated the language of *kiddush hashem* for entirely spiritual purposes. *Kiddush hashem,* which traditionally refers to a physical forfeiting of life, was reinterpreted by Dov Ber as the tzaddik's spiritual sacrifice on behalf of his followers. This transformation of the medieval doctrine of martyrdom into a metaphor, Loewenthal shows, may reflect the fact that Hasidism arose at a time when East European Jews were generally not in physical danger, as they had been a century earlier.

Special mention ought to be given as well to Arnaldo Momigliano's essay on "The Romans and the Maccabees." This was Momigliano's last full-length essay before his death, and it demonstrates once again how a command of the Roman sources can shed new light on Jewish history. Momigliano shows that a complex alliance existed between Jews and Romans during the Maccabean period, which consisted of an interplay between political and religious factors.

Beyond these very strong contributions, there are several others especially worthy of mention. Among them are Steven Z. Zipperstein on "Transforming the Heder: Maskilic Politics in Imperial Russia," Eleazar Gutwirth on "The Expulsion from Spain and Jewish Historiography," Chava Turniansky on "Yiddish Song as Historical Source Material: Plague in the Judenstadt of Prague in 1713," and Antony Polonsky on "The Bund in Polish Political Life, 1935–1939." But there is really something for every reader in this excellent volume, and it is indeed a fitting tribute to a scholar with such catholic interests as Chimen Abramsky.

DAVID BIALE
Center for Jewish Studies
Graduate Theological Union, Berkeley

Monika Richarz (ed.), *Bürger auf Widerruf. Lebenszeugnisse deutscher Juden 1789–1945*. Munich: C. H. Beck, 1989. 609 pp.

At the start of the nineteenth century, the Jews living in the German *Länder* accounted for no more than about eight percent of European Jewry. During the following hundred years, this percentage constantly declined. In 1933, the half million Jews living in Nazi Germany constituted only some five percent of all European, and little more than three percent of world, Jewry. In the light of such small numbers, one wonders why the history of the German Jews, specifically in the nineteenth and twentieth centuries, is today so intensively investigated, presenting an impressive body of scholarly research that in recent years has almost become an academic subspecialty at many universities.

The reasons for this are to be found not only in the laudable, well-funded efforts of institutions such as the Leo Baeck Institute and others. German Jewry and its history obviously continues to arouse the interest and fascination of Jewish as well as non-Jewish scholars and the educated public. In the spiritual sphere, Germany in the eighteenth and nineteenth centuries was the cradle of the Haskalah, the religious Reform, and the modernized Jewish Orthodoxy. Politically, Germany's Jews lagged behind the United States, France and England in the process of emancipation. But probably because emancipation was protracted and subject over many decades to public disputes and virulent opposition in legislative bodies, the press, and popular scientific literature, the German *Judenfrage* attracted disproportional attention beyond the country's borders.

The German Jews in the 1870s were probably not more economically advanced than those in West European countries, where relatively smaller Jewish communities existed at the time. But their situation strongly contrasted with the desperate position of the East European Jews. Furthermore, starting around 1830, German Jews paved the way for the Jewish mass emigration from Europe to America. Up until 1880, American Jewry can justly be regarded as a branch of the German, which laid the first institutional and spiritual foundations of Jewish life in the New World. When the East European mass emigration started after 1880, German Jews on both sides of the ocean ambivalently faced the task of integrating the newcomers while coping with the problems of their own Jewish identity.

It was also in Germany that modern, secular and racist antisemitism was ideologically formulated and, from the 1870s on, found its most substantial and lasting political expressions. Last, though not least, German Jews were also the first victims of Nazi persecution, and played a fateful involuntary role in the gradual realization of the Holocaust.

This wide spectrum of Jewish life in Germany is reflected in these memoirs. They are a selection from three volumes, also edited by Richarz, that were published between 1976 and 1982. The title of the original three-volume edition, *Jüdisches Leben in Deutschland, Selbstzeugnisse zur Sozialgeschichte,* is a more precise indication of the editor's scientific approach and the publisher's intentions. These are the memoirs of mostly unknown and common, not prominent, people. Accordingly, "Jews from all social strata, from town or countryside, of different vocations, and diverging political and religious groups come to word" (p. 7). All of the memoirs are from the archives of the Leo Baeck Institute in New York, and most of them have not been published before. The selection covers the whole period from 1789 to 1945, though close to half the volume describes the period from 1918 to 1945. This is, however, a fair representation of the institute's constantly growing collection, of which more than two-thirds was written after 1945.

Richarz is well aware of the value, as well as the pitfalls and shortcomings, of these sources. As the lower social strata hardly ever wrote diaries or memoirs, the educated middle class is overrepresented. One may add that the growing importance of youth movements, the agricultural and other *hakhsharah* centers, and internal Jewish political discussions—especially during the last years of Jewish existence in Germany—are not sufficiently illuminated. This is probably a result of the original limitation to those memoirs deposited specifically in the New York Leo Baeck archives. A more representative picture could probably have been gained by the inclusion of additional collections such as those of the Central Zionist and other archives in Israel. The editor has, however, tried to compensate for probable distortions with a concise introduction that covers the history of social, political and internal Jewish developments. Though this is declared to be a shortened version of the three introductions in the earlier volumes, it is actually much more. Richarz has now been able to integrate the research of the last decade or so in a precise overview that makes valuable reading on its own.

Because it is a popular edition, and one limited in space, this selection lacks most of the scientific apparatus of the earlier three volumes. It contains a short bibliography and two indexes of persons and locations. It is, however, regrettable that the excellent indexes of subjects included in the former edition have been omitted. We may hope that this omission may be reconsidered for the forthcoming English and Hebrew translations of this valuable book.

AVRAHAM BARKAI
Kibbutz Lehavot Habashan

Moses Rischin (ed.), *The Jews of North America*. Detroit: Wayne State University Press, 1987. 280 pp.

Based on the proceedings of a conference sponsored by the Multicultural History Society of Ontario (April 1983), this volume incorporates fifteen original essays on the meaning of Jewish immigration and ethnic experience in both the United States and Canada. Collective books very rarely attain cohesiveness; the present one, the highly learned and sensitive editing notwithstanding, is no exception to the rule. The book's strength derives chiefly from the importance of most of the articles and from the very refreshing effort to bring together the experience of North American Jewry as a whole.

The first part, "Modern Migration," opens with the astute article by Lloyd Gartner on Jewish migration from Europe to North America. We learn the essentials of the epoch-making phenomenon and are intrigued by the well-put challenge to pursue the research further in a way that will use the records produced by the immigrants themselves. This, according to Gartner, will elevate the "history of immigration into the history of immigrants."

Following Gartner, though not a direct companion piece, is Harold Troper's article on Canadian immigration policy between 1900 and 1950, when immigration of Jews was mercilessly kept to a minimum. Troper's article is authoritative. However, he does not delve into the specific reasons for the immigration to Canada or examine the immigrants' lives in their new country. As Rischin rightly observes in his introductory remarks, these themes are still on the historians' agenda.

The second part, "Continuity and Tradition," is led by Arthur A. Goren's seminal essay on "Traditional Institutions Transplanted." Through the important case of the *ḥevrah kadisha* (burial societies), Goren illustrates the vitality of the traditional values and patterns in the new world and convincingly calls on scholars to develop this thesis more extensively in future research.

Writing on the folk culture of immigrant communities, Barbara Kirshenblatt-Gimblett answers Goren's call to elaborate on the persistence and flexibility of ethnicity. The examples she brings, however, are somewhat marginal. In contrast, Mark Slobin in "Klezmer Music as an Ethnic Musical Style" chooses to emphasize the opposite aspect of ethnicity, that is, the *disjuncture* in material culture, the radical change in the context of expressive repertoires and the dissociation of cultural packages. Examining as well the internal-external dialectic, he concludes that the "neo-klezmer revival movement is not just a rehashing of old ethnic dance tunes. It is a restatement of self-perception by the current generation of Jewish-American musicians," as well as by the audiences that have enthusiastically responded to these bands.

Deborah Dash Moore's analytical discussion, "The Construction of Community: Jewish Migration and Ethnicity in the United States," illuminates the two polar interpretations of American communal life, that is, the "old world traits transplanted" and the famous "frontier" thesis according to which America's physical circumstances radically change its settlers. Moore, however, suggests following a third interpretation, that of Louis Wirth, who regarded *residence* as being of decisive importance. According to Wirth, the source of cohesion of American Jews was located in the spatial relationships of the immigrant community. It is this tradition, contemplates Moore, that guided future generations of Jews in their settlement choices when the achievement of middle-class status made it feasible for them to establish such residential enclaves.

It seems to me that the third part of this collection, "The Fathers of Jewish Ethnic Culture," rightfully belongs at the end. The actual impact of Louis Wirth, Simon Dubnow and Horace Kallen on immigrants and consecutive generations is hardly discussed here. Moreover, those ideas of Dubnow, a Russian Jew, that may have had some influence beyond Europe, are not examined in the North American context at all. Thus, the knowledge gained from exposure to the philosophies of these original thinkers would have been more appropriately placed in an appendix rather than in the body of the book.

The inherent shortcoming of collective works is also demonstrated here in the absence of any material relating specifically to Canada. In the post–Second World War years, the older conception of Canada as a binational, bireligious and bicultural society receded. There arose instead a new vision of the country as an ethnic mosaic, bilingual but multicultural. This "mosaic" theory, (similar to Kallen's), which accorded Jews a legitimate place in Canadian society, is unfortunately not discussed in this book.

The balance between American and Canadian material is retrieved, however, in the book's last section, which is devoted to "Jews, Community and World Jewry." Two penetrating essays on Canadian Zionism, a solid article by Marc L. Raphael on the origins of organized national Jewish philanthropy in the United States and a scholarly expose of antisemitism in Canada in the interwar years by Irving Abella constitute the bulk of this part. An interesting article by Pierre Anctil on the Canadian Jewish poet Abraham Klein describes the change in theme in his poetry from Jewish survivalism (in antisemitic Quebec of the 1930s) to openness toward other minorities in a later, more tolerant French Canada. An intriguing, though very sketchy, article by Gerald L. Gold on the ethnic limits of small-town experience and viability in the United States and Canada is also included.

The editor's thoughtful epilogue, related to the last part of the book, touches upon the enlightened nature of American Zionism; it is the genuine connectedness with Jewish universalist values that gives this Zionism a valid humanistic character, suggests Rischin. But the reader remains somewhat puzzled—does this observation imply that Canadian Zionism is different in this regard? Or perhaps the implication is that there is a challenge here, that is, to explore how this thesis is applicable to the Canadian Jewish ethos as well?

In the epilogue, as in the book all along, there are important new ideas and seminal insights. On the other hand, major themes of ethnicity such as religious life, education, demography and socioeconomic structure are missing. In all, though, this volume is a significant contribution toward the desired comprehensive study of North American Jews and the systematic comparative analysis of U.S. and Canadian Jewries.

ALLON GAL
Ben-Gurion University of the Negev

Emanuela Trevisan Semi, *Allo Specchio dei Falasciá: Ebrei ed etnologi durante il colonialismo fascita*. Firenze: Editirce la Giuntina, 1987. xii + 166 pp.

Despite the existence of a vast and growing literature on the Beta Israel (Falasha) of Ethiopia, no serious attempt has yet been made to chronicle their modern history. Researchers have instead tended to gravitate to opposite extremes of the historical spectrum and have focused their attention upon either the question of "Falasha origins" or (especially in recent years) the phenomena of immigration to Israel and integration into its society. The period from the middle of the nineteenth century until the Ethiopian revolution of 1974, by far the best documented period in Beta Israel history, has been largely neglected by scholars. It is therefore with considerable anticipation that one approaches Emanuela Trevisan Semi's monograph, the first serious attempt to grapple with any aspect of the Beta Israel's history during the Italian Fascist occupation of Ethiopia. In fact, as the subtitle indicates, the book is more a study of foreign attitudes and behavior (both Jewish and Italian) than a detailed examination of the Beta Israel's own experience. Consequently, it may well be of more immediate interest to those interested in the impact of politics (particularly racism and antisemitism) on scholarship than to students of Ethiopian Jewry.

Trevisan Semi begins her work with two chapters, which offer a general introduction to the Beta Israel (pp. 9–24) and a survey of scholarly opinions concerning their origins (pp. 25–40). While both of these are competently executed, neither takes full account of recent scholarly opinion. Thus, for example, on the meaning of the name "Falasha" in the first chapter, Trevisan Semi cities Joseph Halévy and Carlo Conti Rossini, writing in 1896 and 1938, respectively, but makes no mention of the debate engendered by Taddesse Tamrat's suggestion put forward in 1972 that the term originated in the fifteenth century. This omission is significant as well for the second chapter, where she passes over in silence those researchers who have recently argued that the emergence of the "Falasha" is in the main the result of cultural developments in fifteenth-century Ethiopia.

The five succeeding chapters, which form the core of this book, consider the relationship of Italian Jewry and the "Falasha" from 1888–1935, the impact of racism on Italian Jewry, the image of the "Falasha" in Fascist "scientific" literature, the mission to Lake Tana led by the Italian geographer Giotto Dainelli, and the activities of Carlo Alberto Viterbo on behalf of the Jews of Ethiopia. These latter chapters are particularly significant for the utilization of previously unstudied works both from Italian scholars who worked during the Fascist period and from the Italian Jewish community. As Trevisan Semi notes, Italians did not initially introduce any specifically anti-Jewish legislation in Ethiopia beyond the racism practiced with regard to the general population. In this manner, Mussolini apparently hoped to win Jewish support for his policies. Even the idea of a Jewish home in Italian East Africa was discussed. Although the attitude toward the Jews changed after several years, the liberation of Ethiopia in 1939 spared the Beta Israel from the worst period of Italian antisemitism. Characteristic of the Eurocentric focus of Trevisan Semi's books is the absence of any attempt to supplement her sources with oral histories gathered from the Beta Israel themselves. Although early in her notes (p. 135 n. 1) she mentions that she visited with Beta Israel in an absorption center in Ashkelon in 1984, this does not appear to have offered her the opportunity to complement her Italian and other sources with indigenous traditions.

In summary, Trevisan Semi's monograph should be judged less as an attempt to reconstruct the history of Ethiopian Jewry during a particularly dramatic period in their history than as a study of the manner in which political ideologies and events influence research and, in particular, ethnography. Although there are enough minor errors to cause some concern (for Ullendorf on pp. 37, 38, 136, 142 and 166, read Ullendorff as on p. 10; Yael Kahana's popular Hebrew book is called 'Aḥim shehorim, not 'Ahinu shehorim [p. 138]), *Allo Specchio dei Falasciá* succeeds in providing much of the background information necessary for a proper understanding of the experience of Beta Israel under Fascist occupation.

STEVEN KAPLAN
The Hebrew University

David Sorkin, *The Transformation of German Jewry, 1780–1840*. New York and Oxford: Oxford University Press, 1987. 255 pp.

This book is surely one of the most challenging, thought-provoking and indeed brilliant among recent studies in modern Jewish history. In an original and profound manner, David Sorkin has reconceptualized the critical period during which German Jews in significant numbers first integrated into non-Jewish society. He has provided a distinctly new way of understanding that process. His work both deserves and requires serious consideration and evaluation.

Sorkin's book has its beginnings in a doctoral dissertation done at the University of California, Berkeley, under the guidance of Martin Jay. But its chief influence is George Mosse, with whom Sorkin also studied. From Mosse, Sorkin adopted the concept of *Bildung* (a hard-to-translate term whose approximate meaning is self-attained culture) as the ideal of German Jewry that replaced the earlier one of textual Jewish learning. Perhaps the most derivative aspect of Sorkin's study, therefore, is the role he assigns to *Bildung* in the process of transformation. However, even here there is originality of application, since Mosse has especially called attention to the continued prevalence of the original *Bildungsideal* among German Jews long after others had dropped it or changed its meaning. Sorkin, by contrast, focuses on how that cultural ideal first developed among German Jews against the background of the emergence of a class of *Gebildeten* among non-Jews. Moreover, he shows just how prevalent the ideal was, recurring as it did in the popular Jewish literature of the period examined here: the periodicals (especially *Sulamith*) and the sermons. In the earlier Enlightenment, moral virtue (*Tugend*) was the ideal striven for, the one that Mendelssohn sought to incorporate as a Jew; by the end of the eighteenth century, it was eclipsed by *Bildung*.

Sorkin places the goal of *Bildung* within the context of Jewish efforts for emancipation. For it was precisely *Bildung* that was frequently required of Jews as a prerequisite for political and social equality. With the notable exception of Prussia, German states adopted a "tutelary" approach to their Jewish subjects: They would grant them rights in return for such regeneration as would transform them into cultured Germans. Mendelssohn had rejected such a quid pro quo, arguing that Jews deserved equality on the basis of natural rights alone. However, succeeding generations accepted the bargain. What emerged, according to Sorkin, was an "ideology of emancipation," a determined effort to "improve" the Jews in order that the partial emancipation attained during the years of Napoleonic hegemony would become complete.

According to Sorkin, the ideology of emancipation spawned in turn what he considers to be a German Jewish "subculture," a set of symbols and shared values that was focused on the quest for full emancipation. This subculture rested on continuing Jewish differentiation consisting not only of shared political goals but also of demographic and social similarities that set Jews apart from non-Jews. Sorkin maintains that this culture remained "invisible" to the Jews themselves, though non-Jews may have perceived it. The reason for the invisibility was the Jews' politically determined need to define their identity in religious terms alone. Sorkin believes that this failure to see the obvious was immensely ironic: In seeking emancipation overtly on the basis of being a religious confession alone, the German Jews in fact created a subculture in support of that aim, which had the unintended effect of broadening the basis of Jewish unity. Thus, there was what Sorkin terms an extraordinary "disparity between ideology and social reality."

Sorkin manipulates these concepts deftly throughout his study, shedding a good deal of light on cognate matters. For example, he shows how the Haskalah, the Jewish enlightenment, was not only a reaction to changes in the non-Jewish world but was also internally related to the earlier Musar movement, which had likewise stressed moral reform. The *maskilim,* however, accepted the need for reform out of their particular understanding of Jewish history, an understanding to which Sorkin applies Salo Baron's term—"lachrymose." The *maskilim* believed that European Jewry—sadly—had degenerated, the necessary consequence of the persecution they had suffered, and for this reason they now required regeneration. Although David Friedländer still believed, as did Mendelssohn, that the state was required to take the initiative by granting the Jews equality, he made his argument on the basis of utility rather than natural rights. Those who followed him increasingly accepted the state's contention that Jews must take the initiative by proving themselves "worthy." Internally, Jews justified this projected moral and cultural transformation as no mere assimilation but rather as a return to the pristine Judaism that had preceded the period of degradation.

The subculture was the more easily sustained as Jews became increasingly concentrated in the German bourgeoisie and, like their Christian bourgeois counterparts, formed numerous free associations (*Vereine*) for a variety of beneficent purposes. Synagogues and schools, reformed to differing degrees, were its vehicles as well. Thus, German Jews remained distinct in their political purpose, social separation and common commitment to some expression of the Jewish religion.

Sorkin also examines leading figures in this process: the pedagogues, preachers and earliest modern Jewish scholars who were the main exponents of the ideology. And he concludes with a detailed study of two figures whose activities would seem to lie outside the given framework but, according to Sorkin, in fact lie within it: the popular writer Berthold Auerbach and the founder of neo-Orthodoxy, Samson Raphael Hirsch. Other individuals who figure prominently in the writings of previous historians of the period—Heinrich Heine, Ludwig Börne and Abraham Geiger, for example—here obtain only passing mention.

Sorkin's categories raise some serious questions. Does "ideology of emancipation" really do full justice to German Jewry's concerns? Gabriel Riesser, one of this period's central figures (whom Sorkin mentions only via Auerbach), explicitly rejected the ideology of quid pro quo; moreover, alongside the ideology of emancipation there was also an ideology of Jewish survival. Certainly Jews wanted complete emancipation, but they also wanted to preserve their Jewish identity. What characterizes the period especially, I would suggest, is the conflict between the two. I wonder also whether the subculture was in truth invisible to the Jews themselves. Certainly the official community was there for all to see, and so were the associations Sorkin describes. To be sure, Jews continued to define themselves as a religion alone, but was that because they could not see the broader reality, or was it only that they did not want to admit to it in public? It is not surprising the *Sulamith*, intended for gentile as well as Jewish readers, should have articulated the narrower view. But what did Jews write in letters to one another? I suspect that what Sorkin misses was not so much invisible to the Jews themselves as it was purposefully not articulated in the public sphere.

However, such questions do not detract from the value of the book. Quite the contrary, as with any provocative new thesis, this work invites reflection and further refinement of our thinking. One must be grateful to Sorkin for moving our understanding of this period a giant step forward.

MICHAEL A. MEYER
Hebrew Union College, Cincinnati

Michael Stanislawski, *Psalms for the Tsar: A Minute-Book of a Psalms-Society in the Russian Army, 1864–1867*. New York: Yeshiva University Press, 1988. 64 pp.

The participation of Jews in the nineteenth-century European military, once neglected but now a subject of growing interest among the historians, is of obvious importance. Service in the army inevitably broke down walls between Jews and gentiles, but most armies were bastions of antisemitism. The fate of Europe's most famous Jewish soldier, Captain Alfred Dreyfus, illustrates both the degree to which Jews had succeeded in penetrating into the host society and the potency of the new antisemitism. Generally speaking, Jewish organizations committed to the ideals of integration emphasized and even exaggerated the role of Jews in the armed forces, taking special delight in enumerating the number of Jews who fell in defense of the fatherland. Antisemites, on the other hand, accused the Jews of shirking their military obligations while at the same time profiting from Europe's wars.

As far as Russia is concerned, the partial truth of this accusation has been accepted even in the Jewish camp. Did not our grandfathers lie, emigrate and even disfigure themselves to avoid the tsar's army? And who could blame them? Was not such service on behalf of Europe's most antisemitic country an abomination? The American Jewish writer Delmore Schwartz has given poetic expression to this widely held sentiment:

O Nicholas! alas! alas!
My grandfather coughed in your army,

> Hid in a wine-stinking barrel,
> For three days in Bucharest
>
> Then left for America
> To become a king himself[1]

It is the great virtue of Michael Stanislawski's splendid and beautifully produced little book that it gives us a rather different picture of Jewish military service in Russia. The essence of the book is the publication of a remarkable document—a minute-book (*pinkas*) of a *ḥevrat tehilim* (meaning a society whose members gathered to study and recite the psalms) of Jewish soldiers serving in the army in the 1860s during the reign of Mikhail Gorbachev's predecessor, Tsar Alexander II. The Pinkas contains fascinating information concerning its thirty-two members. It is also a beautiful document to behold, and the ten plates reproduced here from the minute-book—depicting, among other things, a membership list, the rules of the society, and a splendid rendition of two lions holding banners inscribed with the slogan (in Russian) "God protect the Tsar"—are a feast for the eyes. Stanislawski tells us what light this document sheds on the social history of Russian Jewry in the crucial 1860s, and he also provides an excellent historical introduction. What stands out is that even in the land of the tsars many Jews were able to serve in the army with "dignity, loyalty, and courage" (p. 26) while at the same time remaining loyal members of the Jewish community.

Stanislawski is an outstanding historian who has already changed received views on a number of important subjects. His new publication demonstrates his mastery of the sources and his excellent style. I have only two quibbles. The author empha-sizes, correctly, the important differences between the Jewish condition in Russia proper and in Congress Poland, but he is wrong, I think, to imply that this distinc-tion is "often" not made (p. 21). Is there a single serious historian of Russian Jewry who has not insisted on this point? Second, he believes that the special situation prevailing in Congress Poland was one reason for the "much lesser degree of active politicization of the Jews . . . as opposed to those of the Pale, later in the century" (p. 29). I do not think that there was a "lesser degree" but rather that Jewish politicization in Poland took a different course. No matter. This publication, coming hard on the heels of Stanislawski's book on Y. L. Gordon, will only enhance his reputation.

Ezra Mendelsohn
The Hebrew University

Note

1. Delmore Schwartz, "The Ballad of the Children of the Czar," in his *Selected Poems (1938–1958)* (New York: 1967), 21–22.

Language, Art and Literature

David Aberbach, *Bialik*. London: Weidenfeld and Nicolson, 1988. 146 pp.

In his introductory remarks to this monograph, David Aberbach sets out some cogent reasons for undertaking a new study of Hayim Nahman Bialik. A monumental figure in Hebrew literature and one who had a major impact on Zionist history, Bialik is not widely known to non-Hebrew readers. Even those who are familiar with his work in an English version may not fully appreciate Bialik's achievement, since his poetry loses so much in translation and since the age in which he lived is not always adequately understood. Finally, Bialik engaged in a variety of careers (e.g., as editor, publisher and translator) in addition to writing poetry. The cultural ramifications of these multifaceted accomplishments tend to be insufficiently recognized outside of Israel.

Aberbach's book aims to dispel some of this ignorance by providing an overview of Bialik's life and work. In addition, the author sets out to fill a gap in critical commentary by charting connections between Bialik's personal life and his role as Hebrew national poet.

The first of his goals is readily achieved. In lucidly written background chapters, Aberbach offers a concise biographical summary of Bialik and outlines the historical milieu from which he emerged. These sections touch on various social forces that affected Bialik deeply, including Romanticism, the Haskalah, Hasidism, anti-semitism and Zionism. Another section covers literary roots, including Jewish sources, European influences and Bialik's relationship with Ahad Ha'am. Particularly worth noting is the assessment of Bialik as a *Russian* writer. The affinities between his poetry and mainstream Russian literature can be sensed in his intense chiaroscuro moods and in his thematic treatment of the countryside where he grew up. Furthermore, Bialik's skirmishes with Russian censorship helped to ensure the importance of his writing. In places where free speech is restricted, poetry often assumes enlarged moral authority; since poems rely on multivalent or oblique forms of expression, they can easily circumvent official scrutiny. In this way, the poet—as was the case with Bialik—may gain prominence as a social, cultural or political leader. Aberbach's attention to this point is important. Though poets and other writers still attain roles of social and political leadership in East European countries, this phenomenon is alien—and perplexing—to many contemporary American readers.

The chapter on literary antecedents is smoothly written and here, as elsewhere, Aberbach displays a knack for anecdote. Detracting from these strengths, however, is his discussion of individual poems, which at times is disappointingly brief.

Quotations from particular texts do not always clearly illustrate his main points. For instance, almost telegraphic comments on "Ve-Haya ki timtze'u" ("And If You Find") (pp. 45–46) are meant to show the poet's "most sophisticated and brilliant" use of *aggadah*. Such occasional lapses may serve as a reminder that there is a crying need for close readings in English of Bialik's poems. An exemplary approach would be one patterned on *The Modern Hebrew Poem Itself.*[1] That anthology provides poems in Hebrew and in English translation, together with an interpretation of each text, a sketch of the poem's historical and cultural background, an explanation of biblical and talmudic allusions and a transliteration for those readers who do not know Hebrew but wish to appreciate rhyme schemes and meter. Aberbach's monograph would make a fine companion text to a volume such as this that would focus exclusively on Bialik's poetry. Together the two would provide valuable information for newcomers to Hebrew literature.

Bialik's poems are more fully analyzed in Aberbach's longest chapter, "Romantic National Poet," which also provides a psychological analysis to explain the overlap of private and public issues in Bialik's oeuvre. Aberbach contends that Bialik's personal preoccupations—orphanhood, uprootedness, infertility—coincided with national concerns of East European Jewry: collective vulnerability during the pogrom years, geographical and cultural displacements and a devastating alienation from traditional communal continuities. For this reason, Bialik's poetry came to express the mood of his generation, and so he was propelled to the forefront of Hebrew literature. Aberbach's assumptions here lead to some intriguing conclusions. A case in point: The early loss of his parents, through bereavement and separation, is presumed to have yielded both enormous anger and insecurity in the young Bialik. Leaving lasting imprints on his personality, this experience is thought to account for Bialik's unusual ability to portray both prophetic wrath and childlike helplessness. Aberbach also speculates that Bialik's grief over the death of his mother may help explain his prolonged and mysterious silence after 1911.

One awkwardness mars the structure of this book. Two brief chapters, "National Figure" and "Poet of Private Grief," primarily repeat ideas mentioned earlier. The genuinely substantive insights that these chapters do add could have been integrated into the previous, longer essay, "Romantic National Poet." Altogether, though, this volume serves a significant function in Bialik studies. Offering a general introduction for broad audiences and a convenient reference work for students of Hebrew literature, this text is especially attractive as a teaching tool. It includes a bibliography of primary works and English translations as well as a limited number of secondary sources. A fuller, thoroughly annotated bibliography might have made a useful addition to Aberbach's work; this remains a desideratum for future scholarship.

NAOMI SOKOLOFF
University of Washington

Note

1. Stanley Burnshaw, T. Carmi and Ezra Spicehandler (eds.), *The Modern Hebrew Poem Itself* (New York: 1965).

Herbert G. Goldman, *Jolson: The Legend Comes to Life*. New York and Oxford: Oxford University Press, 1988. ix + 411 pp.

While Einstein was based in Zurich, formulating in abstract mathematical terms the notion that energy consisted of mc^2, he might have easily discovered its most ebullient embodiment dominating the vaudeville circuit across the Atlantic. Perhaps no white entertainer in American history has ever exuded the demonic razzle-dazzle and the kinetic force of Al Jolson; probably no one could match his eerie gift for deluding everybody in the audience into believing that "Rock-a-Bye Your Baby with a Dixie Melody" or "Sonny Boy" was being belted out just for them. He was neither physically prepossessing (only five feet seven inches tall) nor handsome, could neither act well nor dance, and his jokes and banter were banal. But at the opening of *Bombo* in New York in 1921, Jolson returned for thirty-seven curtain calls. At a U.S. Army benefit in 1918, it seemed malicious to have billed him after Enrico Caruso. But when Jolson bolted onto the stage and assured the already dazed audience, "Folks, you ain't heard *nothin'* yet," a legend was indeed given life. Booked as "The World's Greatest Entertainer," thrilling standing-room-only crowds from Bangor to Dubuque to Tacoma, Jolson lived up to his own hype.

As his most recent biographer frequently notes, the source of that dynamism is no longer accessible. The ten films in which Jolson starred are, except for his first, forgotten; and even in *The Jazz Singer* (1927), his acting performance is awkward and stilted. Because microphones and recording equipment were too primitive to capture the full timbre of that hell-bent-for-leather voice, he could not make the transition to radio, and Decca has not re-released his records. The BTUs emitted by that first superstar to live audiences can no longer be measured; the power that he could command merely by strutting onto a stage and dropping to one knee to apostrophize "My Mammy" is dimmed. A headliner at the dawn of the century whose spectacular career was already fading by the Great Depression, Jolson can now be appreciated only by an act of faith, only by summoning reliable witnesses from that era such as Zelda Fitzgerald, who once proclaimed Jolson greater than Jesus.

Though no singer could more poignantly evoke the banks of the Swanee, waitin' for the *Robert E. Lee,* he was born in Lithuania, probably in 1886, and came to the United States eight years later. His father, Moshe Yoelson, served as a rabbi in Washington, D.C., where Jolson's mother, Naomi, died soon after immigrating—a shock that Herbert G. Goldman interprets as the key to their fifth child's desperate need for acclaim, his unappeasable appetite for the love of which he was so abruptly deprived. Where the piercing ambition and the relentless drive came from are less easily explained, but no one was more assertive in pursuing the success that he believed his talent merited. Success came quickly, bolstering an ego so huge that General Douglas MacArthur by comparison seems downright self-effacing. At the age of thirty-five, Jolson had a Broadway theater named after him by the Shubert brothers, and Republicans such as Warren G. Harding and Calvin Coolidge were quick to enlist his galvanic presence in their presidential campaigns. Jolson became enormously rich and famous, the personification of all the glowing promises that the

New World might bestow on so charismatic an adopted son. He reciprocated in part by a series of exhausting musical tours during the Second World War and the Korean War, entertaining American troops so endearingly that he enjoyed something of a comeback before succumbing to a fatal heart attack in 1950.

The world's greatest entertainer was, however, a lousy role model for his fellow Jews. Neither the piety of his family background, nor his own fluency in Yiddish, nor the speed with which he replied to antisemitic remarks with his fists immunized Jolson against the lures of assimilation. All four of his wives are gentiles—a record so perfect that the reader is unsurprised to learn that Jolson was incapable of sexual relations with "Jewesses" (the author's gauche term that the publisher let pass). When Jolson once greeted his two-year-old son with the question "Who am I, sonny boy?" Al Jolson, Jr., humiliated his father by responding: "You're the Jew." Although *The Jazz Singer* ends with "Jack Robin" returning to the synagogue from which he had fled as a youth to substitute for his dying father by chanting "Kol Nidre," Jolson himself performed on Yom Kippur until, near the end of the his life, the gossip columnist Walter Winchell shamed him into desisting. Buried in a *tallis* (which he never wore) after a funeral service at Los Angeles' Temple Israel (which he never attended), Jolson was eulogized by comedian George Jessel (whom he detested) as a

> great inspiration . . . to the Jewish people in the last forty years. . . . With a gaiety that was militant, uninhibited and unafraid, [Jolson] told the world that the Jew in America did not have to sing in sorrow. . . . Jolson is the happiest portrait that can be painted about an American of the Jewish faith.

But that faith is precisely what Jolson was so eager to abandon, and his gaiety sprang from his American citizenship, not his Jewish origins—as *The Jazz Singer* itself makes clear. The enduring fascination of that first talkie—in which Jolson was lucky enough to play himself—is how the conflict of generations is adjudicated. Remaining loyal to the primordial love of his mother, the heir to an unbroken cantorial tradition of "Rabinowitzes" betrays no signs of guilt for having repudiated the world of our fathers. It was inadvertent but fitting that Jolson's most famous film accelerated the tempo of Americanization, for silent movies had been popular in immigrant neighborhoods in part because no knowledge of English was required.

Goldman's biography offers little insight into the price of such progress, and thus fails to grasp the symbolic trajectory of the career of "The Sweet Singer of Israel"—the phrase inscribed at Jolson's grave site. Far more pages are devoted to, say, the early show business career of his third wife, Ruby Keeler, than to *The Jazz Singer,* the cinematic achievement by which Jolson is most likely to be remembered. This book is superbly researched, with appendixes ready to burst with details of each of Jolson's vaudeville bookings, plus his other appearances on stage, screen, radio and recordings. The author's extensive reading of newspapers, supplemented by two dozen interviews, make this volume close to definitive, superseding Michael Freedland's excellent *Jolson* (1972) and mitigating the shamelessness of its own self-congratulatory subtitle.

Jolson's life mixed public acclaim and private emptiness, as though the transaction between the performer and the audience was too fulfilling to permit any love to spill over outside of show business. A factotum had to remind Jolson every winter to say kaddish for his mother. Though often impulsively generous, he was virtually friendless. Fanny Brice's reaction to the news of Jolson's death was rare only for its candor, not its sentiment: "I never liked him."

STEPHEN J. WHITFIELD
Brandeis University

Gabriel Josipovici, *The Book of God: A Response to the Bible*. New Haven: Yale University Press, 1988. 350 pp.

Recent interpretations of the Hebrew Bible have emphasized the literary quality of the texts. Robert Alter started the trend with his perceptive close reading of biblical texts in *The Art of Biblical Narrative* (1981). His work was followed by at least two anthologies, David Rosenberg's *Congregation: Contemporary Writers Read the Jewish Bible* (1987) and Robert Alter and Frank Kermode's *A Literary Guide to the Bible* (1987). The most recent literary reading of the Hebrew Bible is Gabriel Josipovici's *A Response to the Bible*.

The literary approach presupposes that we moderns turn to literature for an understanding of existence, in the way our ancestors opened their Bibles to come to grips with the problems of living. Implied in this set of assumptions is the idea that, in our day, literature has replaced the Bible as a source of revelation.

A further presupposition of the literary approach to biblical texts is the notion of privileged, or authoritative, speech. The inherent question in all of these works is: Can the Hebrew Bible be read in light of modern literature? Can the texts be redeemed in a modernist perspective? The stress on the modern is extremely important to the rhetoric and to the apologetics that underpin the literary argument. The redemption of the biblical texts as authoritative is presented in terms of the history of narrative literature. The Bible is juxtaposed with the allegedly normative nineteenth-century novel, with its aggressive absolute linear form. Justification of the Bible begins with an attack on the idea that the nineteenth-century novel sets the standard for narrative literature, since prenovelistic narrative and the literature of modernity both eschew the linear mode. The techniques employed by Pound, Proust, Joyce, Fielding and Cervantes become the new criterion for understanding biblical narrative techniques. In light of these models the biblical texts are not only rehabilitated but deserve to be viewed as literary works of value.

The literary approach has yielded impressive results. Alter and Josipovici remind us how close readings of texts yield fruitful insight and new perspectives in the biblical texts. In many respects their approach is reminiscent of the rabbinic study of sacred texts. Yet for all the analogies to tradition in the literary methodology, we need to take into account Meir Sternberg's provocative critique of the literary hypothesis in *The Poetics of Biblical Narrative* (1987). Sternberg argues that the Hebrew Bible cannot be reduced to merely a work of literature, since in addition to storytelling it also claims an epistemological, historical status.

The literary hypothesis tends to leave unexamined its own presuppositions. Why is literature privileged? And what is the purpose of literature and art? The implicit answer to these questions is that all authentic speech is sacred. Hence an examination of the possible grounds of the significance of literature or art in general transforms the question so that it becomes: Can any literature be read in the absence of the Hebrew Bible? This question is crucial because the literary hypothesis presupposes that literature, if it is not mere decoration, is redemptive and prophetic. If literature is the privileged norm, it must embody the biblical values and assumptions of critique, the structure of historicity and the illumination of the complex paradox of freedom in order to attain legitimacy. Without these cultural motifs, personal and social transformation is impossible. In the absence of these themes, literature as existential communication falls into the contradiction of despair and idolatry. Thus, the literary perspective ironically points away from its own questions and premises.

Gabriel Josipovici comes closest among the literary theorists to recognizing the importance of crucial elements in the Hebrew Bible for literature, without drawing out its ultimate implications. He begins with a provocative and fruitful polemic concerning the difference between the Hebrew Bible and the Christian scriptures. Central to his argument is that the disparate organization of the two canons and the implications that follow from the canonizations provide a strikingly dissimilar view of existence and the meaning of life. Josipovici demonstrates persuasively that the organization of the Hebrew canon leads to an open-ended existential view of reality, while the Christian canon aims for a final closure based on a unity encompassing four levels of interpretation. Josipovici provides very close readings of the opening chapters of Genesis. He demonstrates that the text is not only ambiguous but defies resolution and closure in its stubborn adherence to an authentic, multifaceted view of reality. The text, in fact, eludes all attempts to complete its meaning throughout Hebrew scriptures. Josipovici illustrates his thesis by an examination of the Jacob stories, the Joseph cycle and the role of law in the biblical texts. (This last topic, being embedded within the narrative structure, is read as part of the story.) Law, providing a set of governing rules for human behavior, is at the heart of the Hebrew Bible. Yet the stories themselves are existential in nature, promoting anxiety and ambiguity. Thus the biblical narrative mode yields the liberation of the paradox of freedom, displaying a sophisticated conception of life and death while adhering to a profound sense of the significance of human existence.

Josipovici goes on to demonstrate that closure lies at the heart of the Christian canon. By definition, closure is a process that leads to the finality of dogma and doctrine in the expectation of insuring certitude and security. A corollary of closure is the impulse to certainty and a drive for an authoritarian appropriation of the text. The most provocative aspect of Josipovici's work is his explication and illumination of the ways in which demands for closure, in accordance with the dogmatic dimensions of early Christianity, induce Christian gospel writers to lapse from the stance of authentic narrative into forced and artificial conclusions.

Josipovici's thesis is, on balance, supportable and insightful. His work elucidates the multiplicity of sophisticated narrative techniques employed by the biblical writers. Josipovici is particularly adept at relating various narrative techniques to differing worldviews. On the basis of these distinctions, he shows how the Hebrew Bible is more compatible with the modern worldview, modernist literature and art in general, which are all antipathetic to closure and finality. Modernist literature, in fact, uses many of the devices found in Hebrew scriptures to structure its own narratives.

Because Josipovici's main concern is to justify Hebrew scriptures within the privileged canons of literature, he does not draw out the radical implications of his thesis—which have ramifications for the Christian canon as well. He ignores, for example, various attempts at closure in the Hebrew Bible and moments of real storytelling in the Christian canon. The Hebrew Bible is replete with intratextual expressions of the struggle between the libertarian and authoritarian interpretations. In the Christian context, Josipovici ignores the fact that the Gospel writers are individuals telling stories; even Saint Paul claims only to be writing letters to communities.

It is the ambiguity and uncertainty of Hebrew biblical narrative within a historical context that finally defies either intentional or unintentional closure. Even in the Christian canon, the impulses of Hebrew scriptures break through the demand for completeness. To read the Hebrew Bible as the revelation of the paradox of freedom explains the unity of form and content of the biblical texts. On the one hand, the biblical writers often bracket the tales they tell in a coercive fashion, wishing to impose authoritarian, specific meaning on the text. On the other hand, the logic of biblical narrative is implicitly the logic of freedom; hence the actors literally escape from the control of their creators just as Adam and Eve defy control by God. Indeed, while the biblical writers proclaim that revelation is God's story, what they actually tell, paradoxically, is the existential tale of the human adventure.

BERNARD ZELECHOW
York University

Dovid Katz (ed.), *Winter Studies in Yiddish,* Vol. 2, *Papers from the Second Annual Oxford Winter Symposium in Yiddish Language and Literature, 14–16 December 1986*. Oxford and New York: Pergamon Press, 1988. 123 pp.

Yiddish research centers, touched by Jewish fortunes and exigencies in general, come and go, but their publications—at least potentially—endure. Yiddish Vilna is no more, but the *Filologishe shriftn* (1–5; 1926–1938) are a staple of all serious Yiddish collections. Columbia University's chair of Yiddish may be expiring, but *The Field of Yiddish* (1–4; 1954–1980), which it was instrumental in issuing, is regularly used by students of Yiddish. The YIVO Institute of Jewish Research is noted for many reasons, and two of them are the *Yivo bleter* (1931–) and *Yidishe shprakh* (1941–), periodicals whose rich ore has by no means been exhausted with the passage of half a century (especially now that there is an index volume to the latter for the years 1941–1974!). The United Kingdom as a center of Yiddish studies has now begun to make its presence felt in print. Volumes 3 to 5 of the *Winter*

Studies are in the pipeline; volume 1 of the Yiddish-language *Oksforder yidish* has appeared, and a second is on the way. Given the practical obstacles to issuing a quality publication in a relatively small field, these are impressive achievements.

In his preface to the volume under review, Dovid Katz gives pride of place to Noyekh Prilutski (1882–1941), "the twentieth-century grandmaster of Yiddish dialectology" who, from 1912 through 1940, assiduously collected and published dialect and folklore data whose mapping Katz believes will yield "an astoundingly detailed picture of prewar Yiddish." Both in the preface and in his article "Origins of Yiddish Dialectology," Katz—in the best Weinreichian tradition—shows a fine historical sense regarding the growth and agenda of Yiddish linguistics. Noting first of all the rabbinic contribution to modern Yiddish dialectology (ancillary to the rabbis' legal concerns) that defined two dialect groups within Western Yiddish, and Johann Buxtorf the Elder's cursory perception of a distinction between Western and Eastern Yiddish, Katz focuses on Carl Wilhelm Friedrich's *Unterricht in der Judensprache, und Schrift. zum Gebrauch fuer Gelehrte und Ungelehrte* (Prenzlau: 1784). As Katz notes, the bibliographers knew this book, and Max Weinreich had already dubbed its apostate Jewish author "the first Yiddish dialectologist." But apparently nobody had actually studied it. In the *Algemeyne entsiklopedye Yidn B*, Weinreich referred to Friedrich's work as *"ingantsn nokh nit baarbet un kimat vi nit bavust"* ("completely unworked and practically unknown").[1] Katz uninhibitedly claims for Friedrich two "major contributions . . . (a) the first proposed classification of Yiddish dialects and (b) an outstanding synchronic description of the lost Yiddish of Prussia" (p. 44). Franz Beranek wrote on Friedrich's dialectology[2] (p. 44), but Katz is the first to sound the theme that "Friedrich preserved for posterity the features of a lost Yiddish dialect" (p. 47), the theoretical import of which, he claims, is that it verifies the "major features of modern Reconstruction of Proto Eastern Yiddish" (p. 48). Katz places the lost dialect in the northern regions between Western and Eastern Yiddish, an area he has elsewhere dubbed "Northern Transitional Yiddish."

The notion that after a hundred years of modern Yiddish dialectology vowels are lying about waiting to be discovered seems incredible, but Shmuel Hiley argues reasonably that the double *yod* grapheme in "Polish" (Central/ Mideastern/Western/Southern/Polish-Galician-Marmures) Yiddish has a split realization, as distinct from all other Eastern dialects that have only one. Thus, Polish double *yod* in words of the Germanic component stands for the phoneme /aj/, but in the majority of cases it stands for /Ej/ (let E = vowel in English *mess*). Hiley also raises the interesting possibility that the /Ej/ vs. /aj/ differentiation helps explain spelling confusion in early texts.

In a deeply probing meditation on historical linguistics, Robert D. King responds to a seminal paper by Uriel Weinreich presented almost three decades ago.[3] King explains the problems of loss of vowel length and of final devoicing in Northeastern and Southeastern but not in Mideastern (= Central) Yiddish in terms of both internal and external causation; moreover, he finds a causal relationship between the two phonological changes. Jean Jofen contributes revised excerpts of her 1953 Columbia University thesis in which she tried to prove that an atlas could be constructed from data collected by emigrants who had been far from their native homes for decades, an assumption confirmed by Uriel Weinreich's *Language and Culture Atlas* project.

Roughly speaking, pre-nineteenth-century Yiddish literature, written in what Max Weinreich termed "Written Language A," was based on Western Yiddish. The development of modern Yiddish literature and the shift to Eastern Yiddish are virtually one. Dov-Ber Kerler looks for the origin of Written Language B (which he calls "Modern Literary Yiddish") in works that are chronologically and semantically still part of Old Yiddish Literature. He examines *Derekh tomin* (Zholkve: 1723), discovered by Chone Shmeruk in 1979, and *Derekh khayim* (Zholkve: ca. 1723), both of which are *muser* monographs (actually parts of a single work), and finds in these earliest Eastern-European Yiddish prints orthographic, lexical, morphologic and syntactic evidence of Eastern Yiddish—the origins of modern literary Yiddish. In "Early Yiddish Texts and Western Yiddish Dialectology," Christopher Hutton tries to show how rhyme research impinges on linguistic theory. He hypothesizes the presence of front-rounded vowels in a sampling of Old Yiddish verse texts. In a longer paper, perhaps, the argument might have seemed less abstruse.

In the preface, Katz describes Devra Kay's and David Schneider's articles as examinations of the notion of "literary dialect"—the quotation marks show that *dialect* is meant figuratively here. Though concentrating on a single lexical feature of seventeenth-century *tkhines* by women, namely words for God, Kay throws much light on this subgenre, which she distinguishes from the standard and the male-authored *tkhines*. We learn that "standard *tkhines* have the opening line which has become the phrase most associated with Yiddish *tkhines:* 'Got fun Avrom, fun Yitskhok un fun Yankev' " (p. 59). For many this line conjures up the prayer recited until this day by Ashkenazic women at dusk on the Sabbath night before the *havdole* ceremony (and said to have been recited in the eighteenth century by Rabbi Leyvi-Yitskhok of Berditshev after the late Sabbath afternoon meal). Within the bounds of a certain formulaic sameness there is immense variation in these homely supplications, scores of which are known. Aren't these a kind of oral poetry parallel to the literary *tkhine*?

Schneider asks, "Is There a 'Mystical Dialect' in Modern Yiddish Drama?" and employs lexical analysis to arrive at an answer. He discovers that "the frequency of Aramaicisms proved to be of doubtful worth," that "rabbinical vocabulary *per se* does not necessarily form part of a mystical style of discourse," and that Germanic component items, alongside Hebrew-Aramaic ones, express religious ideas. Resisting simplistic answers, Schneider concludes: "Our findings must now be refined by expanding the corpus, by investigating how the tendencies delimited become the raw materials which are acted upon by the process of poetic mimesis (the use of stageplay, of verse, of silence etc.), thus enabling us to work towards a better understanding of the dramas and even of mysticism itself" (p. 118).

Marion Aptroot finds that, by and large, Dutch influences were not integrated into Dutch Yiddish, but books for local use contain Hollandisms absent in works printed for export, and some genres contain more Hollandisms than others. Moshe N. Rosenfeld directs us to the *Liber Vagatorum,* a source of romanized Yiddish-origin terms that predates Yiddish printing. He lists thirty-eight variants of that sixteenth-century best-seller, and culls from it more than a score of what he regards as Yiddish-origin words.

Katz's claim that "it is evident from the contents of this volume that research in the late 1980s is focusing upon Western Yiddish and the application of Yiddish dialectology to the study of older Yiddish and non-Yiddish moments" (p. 2) needs to be scaled down to apply to the British and perhaps also the German scenes. Unfortunately, as small as the Yiddish research world is, it is fragmented, and various institutions ignore one another. Thus Abraham Novershtern in the *Encyclopaedia Judaica Year Book 1988/9* mentions no Oxford linguistics at all.[4] Katz and Novershtern both refer to the long-awaited *Language and Culture Atlas of Ashkenazic Jewry,* the great project conceived by Uriel Weinreich and, after his death in 1967, continued by Marvin I. Herzog. Katz also mentions the eagerly awaited publication of Uriel Weinreich's *Outlines of a Descriptive Yiddish Dialectology,* a guide to the atlas. As of the date of writing (October 1990), these important dialectological works have not been published. In the history of Yiddish scholarship, unfortunately, there have been altogether too many important projects scuttled, emasculated or at the least drastically delayed. The devotion of a signal part of *Winter Studies* to dialectology and dialect-related subjects confirms the discipline's keen interest in a part of Yiddish studies in which the two works cited are glaringly absent kingpins.

Dialects of the Yiddish Language, as this volume is called, is dedicated to the memory of Sharon Chazan (1963–1987), an art photographer known for her work on the Jews of London's East End. She was the photographer of the Oxford Winter Symposium in Yiddish in 1986.

LEONARD PRAGER
University of Haifa

Notes

1. Max Weinreich, "Yidishe filologye," *Algemeyne entsikopedye Yidn B* (Paris: 1940), col. 103.
2. Franz Beranek, "K. W. Fridrichs [*sic*] Mundartliche Einteilung des Jüddischen," *Mitteilungen aus dem Arbeitskreis fuer Juddistik,* no. 10 (July 1959), 143–148.
3. Uriel Weinreich, "Four Riddles in Bilingual Dialectology," in *American Contributions to the Fifth International Congress of Slavists,* vol. 1 (The Hague: Mouton, 1963) (no ed. named), 335–359.
4. Abraham Novershtern, "From the Folk to the Academics: Study and Research of Yiddish After the Holocaust," *Encyclopaedia Judaica Year Book 1988/9; Events of 1987/8,* (Jerusalem: 1989), 14–24.

Ira B. Nadel, *Joyce and the Jews: Culture and Texts.* Iowa City: University of Iowa Press, 1989. 290 pp.

Most readers of *Ulysses* will probably have wondered why Joyce, in his epic of modern Irish life set in Dublin, chose to make one of his two main protagonists a

Jew. When questioned about this, Joyce replied: "Bloom Jewish? Yes because only a foreigner would do. The Jews were foreigners at that time in Dublin." Study of the novel, however, enables one to go further than that. First, Joyce uses the *Odyssey* as a mythic substructure to his text, setting up analogies between his Dubliners and Homer's Greeks; Bloom, the modern counterpart of Odysseus the epic traveler, stands in for the Wandering Jew. But Odysseus, separated from home and family, is an alien in the lands he travels through; and Bloom, a Jew among Irishmen—taken by them to be Jewish despite his conversion to Christianity, and so exposed to antisemitism—is also characterized by his sense of alienation and estrangement, though in his own country. Furthermore, this view of Bloom enables Joyce to establish a central analogy between his Jew and his other protagonist, the young Irish writer, Stephen Dedalus: At first it seems that the relation between these two characters is one of contrast, the cold, brilliant intellectual being implicitly opposed to the warm, down-to-earth sensualist; but gradually a deeper and more significant analogy is set up, one of the constituents of which is Stephen's own sense of alienation, for he feels as little at home in Ireland as Bloom.

In *Joyce and the Jews,* Ira B. Nadel opts for other explanations of Joyce's interest in Jews and, ranging far beyond a concern with Bloom as Jew, offers a survey not only of Jewish references and influences in all of Joyce's work but also of his involvement with Jews and Judaism in his own life. Nadel, indeed, turns Joyce into a kind of honorary Jew, throughout referring not to his postulated "identification" with Jews but to his "identity" with them, and finally presenting him triumphantly as a super-Jew: "To call Joyce, as Frank O'Connor does, 'the greatest Jew of all' is to identify not just biographical parallels between Joyce and the lives of Jews, but the habits of mind, cultural values, and form of discourse Jewish history created and Joyce projected" (p. 240). To this end Nadel first establishes the parallel between "Joyce and the lives of Jews," asserting that "the overriding historical link between Joyce and the Jews is the exodus, a situation experienced individually by Joyce and universally by Jews" (p. 16), though it would seem more appropriate, despite his protestations, to talk of "exile" in both cases. Thereafter, in successive chapters, he deals with Joyce in relation to Jewish history, to Jewish typology and to the idea of the Jew; finally he describes Jews and Jewish life in various cities in which Joyce lived—Dublin, Trieste, Rome, Zurich and Paris—which he curiously calls "Jewish cities." In all these respects Nadel is a mine of information, bringing to bear an impressively wide range of reading (scrupulously documented in his extensive notes) and a capacity for clear and concise presentation of sometimes complicated material.

Nadel, however, is a sloppy reader of Joyce. He says, for instance, that Bloom "has been baptised as a Protestant twice and converted to Catholicism" (p. 190), but this reveals a strange blindness to Joyce's playfulness, for the supposed second Protestant "baptism" clearly refers to a ducking Bloom has been subjected to: Bloom, we are told in the Ithaca chapter, has been "baptised" three times—"by the reverend Mr. Gilmer Johnston M.A., alone, in the protestant church of Saint Nicholas Without, Coombe, by James O'Connor, Philip Gilligan and James Fitzpatrick, together, under a pump in the vilage of Swords, and by the reverend Charles Malone

C.C., in the church of the Three Patrons, Rathgar." Nadel's response in so straight-forward a matter as this is symptomatic, and points to the quality of comments that are designed to highlight Jewish dimensions of Joyce's work. These are seldom illuminating, often forced, and on occasion ludicrous. A few examples must suffice.

Having asserted that "exodus" is the "overriding link" between Jews and Joyce, Nadel seemingly feels constrained to offer support for this in Joyce's presentation of Jews in his work: "In 'Calypso' Bloom himself undertakes a minor exodus, first to the pork butcher's and then home, parodying the Return" (p. 16). But this view of Bloom's walking down the street to buy a kidney for his breakfast and then going back home to cook and eat it as an "exodus," no matter how minor, is a parody not of "the Return" but of the critical enterprise.

A similar kind of forcing in relation to Bloom comes, in a section on antisemitism in the chapter on "Joyce, Jews and History," after a workmanlike account of the Dreyfus affair. Nadel reports that the affair was extensively covered in the Irish press, particularly in Arthur Griffith's *United Irishman,* which in October 1899 stated that "the Jew capitalist has got a grip on the lying 'Press of Civilisation' from Vienna to New York and further," and then adds: "Bloom's attachment to the press is consistent with the scandalous anti-Semitism linking Jews and journalism which developed in the nineteenth century" (p. 66). But Bloom the Jew cannot be linked to journalism since he is not a journalist. When this belatedly strikes Nadel, he man-fully struggles on: The kind of antisemitism referred to "may have influenced Joyce's choice of associating Bloom with the papers, although his status as a hero and peripheral activity as advertising canvasser rather than journalist make his attachment to the press ironic" (p. 66). That "although" takes some beating, even if read as unintended irony.

Finally, Nadel contrives to turn the robustly Irish Molly Bloom into a Jewess, maintaining that her "Jewish origin *specifically* emerges" (my emphasis) in a number of instances (p. 169). These are: "her concern over whether Bloom is circumcised or not (18.314–15)," the reference being to her sexual curiosity in this regard when Bloom is courting her; "her knowledge of her father-in-law's *Yartzeit* (anniversary of his death) which means Bloom will go to Ennis to visit the grave to say Kaddish," the reference here, significantly not given a line attribution, is to no more than "just as well he has to go to Ennis his fathers anniversary the 27th" (18.349–50); "her effort as a young girl to read the Hebrew inscriptions in the Jewish cemetary [sic] of Gibraltar in the company of Lieutenant Mulvey (18.834)," the reference being to her "pretending to read out the Hebrew" on the gravestones; and "her confidences concerning various positions of intercourse discussed only with a Jewish woman, Mrs Mastiansky" (18.417–19). Is it, we wonder, her confidences that specifically express her Jewish origin—though in the text it is she who is the recipient of Mrs. Mastiansky's confidence in this respect; or the unorthodoxy of the positions she adopts in intercourse; or the exclusiveness of the Jewish lady as *her* confidante (even if manufactured as such for the occasion)?

H. M. DALESKI
The Hebrew University

Religion, Thought and Education

J. David Bleich, *Contemporary Halakhic Problems,* Vol. 3. New York: Ktav Publishing House and Yeshiva University Press, 1989. xv + 415 pp.

David Ellenson, *Tradition in Transition: Orthodoxy, Halakhah and the Boundaries of Modern Jewish Identity.* New York, Latham and London: University Press of America, 1989. 192 pp.

Both volumes being reviewed have two things in common, but besides these two similarities the differences are much more meaningful. In each work, the authors have collected a number of their essays that were written and published during the past few years. More significantly, both volumes are about the responsa literature.

J. David Bleich's *Contemporary Halakhic Problems* is the third volume in a series that summarizes the views of leading contemporary respondents on questions that were posed to them. However, as with the previous two volumes, this is not only a compendium of the opinions of others—Bleich's own personality and halakhic worldview are clearly enunciated and entwined with those of the other leading rabbinic authorities. David Ellenson's *Tradition in Transition* is a different sort of book. The author chooses select responsa in order to glean from them not only their legal content but also their general context within a given historical-sociological setting.

Bleich's halakhic erudition is dazzling, especially if one contrasts his book with the limited scope of halakhic literature referred to in Ellenson's volume. The latter's aim, it is true, is more to analyze select responsa in depth for the purposes set forth by the author. Nevertheless, I am sure that Ellenson would admit that Bleich is one of today's leading *halakhists* and is more knowledgeable than himself with regard to halakhah in general and the responsa literature in particular. Bleich writes not only as an observer of the halakhic process (as does Ellenson) but also as a *molder* of the law, being both scholar and *posek,* or rabbinic decisor, at the same time.

The topics discussed by Bleich are, as usual, varied. A random sampling runs from kashruth to conversion, nuclear warfare to vegetarianism, prostate surgery and artificial heart implantation to women's prayer services, preemptive war to physicians' strikes. Ellenson writes about a much more limited range of subjects, particularly conversion to Judaism and the Orthodox-Reform schism in its historical-sociological perspective. Bleich overwhelms a topic while Ellenson writes in a more scholarly, low-keyed style that attempts to squeeze all that he can out of his comparatively few sources. Compared to Bleich's fortissimo, Ellenson is pianissimo.

Both write on the responsa literature, that is, Orthodox halakhic decisions. However, Ellenson is the detached outsider while Bleich is the epitome of the insider.

In one of his chapters, Ellenson points out that one cannot equate a liberal halakhic policy or decision with those rabbis who were acculturated by Western standards and had a broad secular education, or a restrictive halakhic policy with those who remained solely within the traditional framework. A good example of the aforementioned (who was not, of course, in Ellenson's mind when writing what he did) is Bleich.

Rabbi Bleich, who is also a professor of law at Cardozo Law School and a leader of Modern Orthodoxy—one who is steeped both in Judaic and in Western culture—is indeed a model of the conservative, uncompromising Orthodox rabbi. A number of deceptively unimportant points in the volume before us (e.g., his use of Hebrew dates without their Gregorian counterpart), together with a few statements enunciating his worldview, help corroborate this characterization.

Bleich, for example, never refers to Conservative "rabbis"; they are always called "clergymen." Moreover, he refuses, on principle, to sit together with non-Orthodox clergymen on the Synagogue Council of America and the New York Board of Rabbis. In this volume he explains why such a cooperation is, and should be, prohibited.

After bringing the views of a number of respondents who do not permit the use of a *mikveh* for non-Orthodox conversions, Bleich not only agrees with them but adds two of his own reasons for such a prohibition: It would appear to confer legitimacy to the non-Orthodox conversions, and since the converts may be unaware that the conversion is not valid in the eyes of the Orthodox, the permission to use the *mikveh* constitutes a fraud on the parties concerned. Bleich also takes a one-sided and stringent stand on conversions. He cites the responsa of those rabbis who adopted a restrictive stance on the conversion question but fails to relate to more liberal views of other eminent Orthodox respondents on this question. Bleich could even have referred to some of the responsa brought by Ellenson. I am sure that he did not forget that they exist; he deliberately ignored them in order to reach his own desired conclusion.

Finally, Bleich's strongly worded rejection of womens' prayer groups, even if these are conducted within the framework of halakha, clearly delineates his philosophy of Judaism. As he puts it, "*Kavanah* and the most intense of religious experiences are essentially meaningless if the act itself is deficient in any way, even if only by virtue of inattention to one of the myriad details which constitutes the *sine qua non* of the requisite fulfillment of the *mizvah*" (p. 119).

As is frequently the case with books that are collections of articles published at different times and in various journals, Ellenson's essays are unequal in quality. At times he is too verbose about the obvious. In other instances, however, he can enlighten the reader (even one familiar with the sources) with an insight previously not thought of. The last chapter of the volume shows Ellenson at his best as he leads us through the responsa to demonstrate how the Orthodox rabbinate changed its attitude toward Reform Jewry from one of complete rejection (referring to the new Reform Jews as apostates) to one of recognizing them as part of the Jewish community (i.e., despite their having gone astray).

Sometimes, though, Ellenson's attempt to see development of the halakhah and change from one historical period to another is misconceived. For example, he claims, on the basis of the literature, that from 1840 to 1870 the attitude to conversion was one of stringency, whereas from 1870 to 1930 the attitude changed to one of leniency. This is just not so. There were rabbis who took lenient views on conversion prior to 1870, and those who took more stringent views afterward. There is no historical development here, notwithstanding Ellenson's attempt to show that there was. The author here is either unaware of the decisions of many other respondents written during these ninety years, or else was taken away with the theory he wanted to prove and hence made selective use of the responsa literature to help prove his thesis.

The 1980s have produced a good number of works in English on the halakhah. These books were written by scholars and rabbis connected with the different Jewish religious movements, and they have greatly contributed to the renewed interest in Jewish studies. The two volumes here, both published at the close of the decade, are excellent examples of the literature. The Orthodox Bleich and Reform Ellenson have given us new insights into the halakhah in general and the responsa literature in particular, each in his own way. It is a portent that such intellectual pluralism will be with us well into the 1990s.

SHMUEL SHILO
The Hebrew University

A. Roy Eckardt, *Three Wars for Human Liberation: Black-Woman-Jew.* Bloomington and Indianapolis: Indiana University Press, 1989. 229 pp.

One of the central questions religion seeks to answer is how one can reconcile suffering with the concept of a benevolent and caring deity. If God is all-good and all-powerful, the argument goes, the Holocaust, for example, could not and would not have happened. Therefore, God cannot be all-good or all-powerful. Thus, one either dispenses with or refashions God. Liberation theology is just such a refashioning.

Roy Eckardt is well known for his work on Christian antisemitism. Professor emeritus of religion studies at Lehigh University and visiting scholar at the Centre for Hebrew Studies at Oxford University, Eckardt presents here the best one-volume summation and discussion of North American liberation theology yet published. Additionally, he seeks to do what no one else has done, namely, create a theological coalition between blacks, women and Jews.

Eckardt sees blacks, women and Jews as the three primary groups defined as nonpersons by Western society. The only group excluded from this formulation is white, gentile males. They, and a male God, are the target of liberation theology.

Liberation theology puts forward the position that God must be for "us" (blacks, women and Jews) and against "them" (white people, men, gentiles). Should God not be so aligned politically, He must be "murdered." Liberation theology also rejects as "garbage" (p. 190) any notion of suffering having "moral and spiritual value or virtue":

> God has a lot of accounting to do—no less, and probably much more, than all the human oppressors. What kind of God—or at least what kind of religion about God—would wish blacks, women, Jews, or anyone else to suffer for the sake of others? What kind of God would utilize human beings in this way? (p. 190)

According to liberation theology, suffering is not redemptive; radical political action is. Eckardt contends that "the exercise of politics often proves to be morally superior to the ruminations of spirituality" (p. 166). This is based on the essential principle of liberation theology that "all thought, not excluding theology, is political thought. For all thought sooner or later involves itself in human power relationships and conflicts" (p. 182). Moreover,

> Apart from power and the seizing of power, love is futile; apart from justice, love is kept from loving. Liberation does not come from preaching justice, peace and self-sacrifice; it comes from revolutionary political and economic action (p. 187).

Such thinking was excusable in the 1960s, perhaps, but not today. Liberation theology was a child of the 1960s and it is as flawed as the era that birthed it. Its essential flaw is reducing all of human reality and experience to the realm of the political. Humanity is equated with an Armageddon-like struggle between the oppressor and oppressed, with liberation theology enlisting God on the side of the latter.

Accepting such a formulation leads Eckardt into silliness, as in his statement that "in a sexist culture a man remains a man and is scarcely capable of looking at things the way women do" (p. 85). Such a statement is not only silly, it is dangerous because it assumes that men *should* look at things the way women do. It assumes that a male way of looking at things does not have its own integrity, as necessary as the other point of view.

Eckardt compounds the problem when he writes that "men remain, after all, incomplete human beings, i.e., they are incapable of birthing, of bringing forth and sustaining life, a capability that has essential relevance and power in ministering to and teaching people" (p. 80). Asserting that men are "incomplete" because they lack wombs sounds dangerously like the sort of biological determinism that deems women to be "incomplete" because they lack penises. Eckardt, however, goes so far as to maintain that "the capacity to give birth to life and to nurture it in its all-determinative, forming stages not only represents a fundamental disparity between male and female but also ties the one sex uniquely to the Creator of all life" (p. 101).

While he adds that such a formulation does not mean that "human self-identity" does not "infinitely transcend sex roles and sex differences," the thrust of his writing on women is to wave the banner of women's liberation as if he had found a universal panacea: "No authentic human liberation can transpire until women have been freed—or have freed themselves—from bondage" (p. 74).

After a while, it is difficult to take such oversimplifications seriously. This is not theology; it is not even clear thinking. It is "The Return of the 60s," as if enough damage was not done the first time around.

What is missing from liberation theology and, thereby, Eckardt's account of it is any sense of the complexity, mystery and awe of human existence. In other words, what is missing is any sense of religious experience. Religion is confused with its institutional manifestations. Liberation theology aims for a rational construct in which human existence can be understood. Religion is the effort to find ways in which we can learn to live with that which can never be understood.

Liberation theology is the attempted radical politicization of religion and, as such, is no different from the ultra-Orthodox theology found in Israel or Christian fundamentalism in America. Those who subscribe to such theologies have their own religiopolitical vision of what humanity and societies should be like, and they seek to impose it on us all.

It is unfortunate that Eckardt cannot see how much his thought is like the very ideas he seeks to depose.

JULIUS LESTER
University of Massachusetts at Amherst

Simon Greenberg (ed.), *The Ordination of Women as Rabbis: Studies and Responsa, A Centennial Publication*. New York: The Jewish Theological Seminary of America, 1988. 223 pp.

When Henrietta Szold moved to New York in 1903, "The Jewish Theological Seminary accepted her request for admission to some classes only after she had assured its administration that she would not use the knowledge thus gained to seek ordination."[1] Nearly eight decades later, the Seminary voted to admit women to its rabbinic program. The present volume is a compilation of responsa by members of the seminary faculty regarding the question of women's ordination. As a book, it is flawed and the essays are uneven. As historical testimony, however, it is both valuable and important in its documentation of what its editor, Simon Greenberg, is quoted on the book jacket as calling "a watershed in American Jewish history."

No historical background is provided to explain how the question of women's ordination first arose within the Conservative movement. It seems to be assumed that readers are conversant with the various and sometimes opposing decision-making bodies within the movement—for example, the Rabbinical Assembly vs. the Seminary faculty. What the book *does* offer are nine statements by Seminary faculty members concerning the ordination of women. Some of the statements are very short—no more than two or three pages—while others, such as the Joel Roth *teshuvah,* are lengthy scholarly treatises. The essays appear in alphabetical order, without editorial comment or evaluation. Combined with the lack of historical background, such omissions make for a book that for many will be difficult to follow.

In 1979, the Rabbinical Assembly's Commission for the Study of Ordination of Women as Rabbis made a positive recommendation on the issue of women's ordination. Only three of the fourteen members of this commission were women, and only one woman faculty member is represented in this volume. Contributors include professors of history and literature in addition to rabbinic and talmudic scholars. This, too, may be seen as problematic: in the words of Joseph Brodie, one of the respondents, "The primacy of halakhah demands that halakhic decisions be rendered by bona fide halakhists, not to be made in effect by broad-based commissions!" (p. 32).

As seen in this work, opposition to ordaining women derives from both sociological and halakhic concerns. Sociological arguments suggest that traditionally committed Jews within the Conservative movement will be alienated and that the ordination of women will further widen the current gap between Conservative and Orthodox Jews. Halakhic objections focus on the fact that, unlike men, women are not obligated to pray in public and thus cannot be counted in a minyan or lead services as a *shaliah zibur*. For other halakhic reasons, they are not considered to be valid witnesses in rabbinic courts or for the signing of legally binding documents such as *ketubot*. Hence the question: Can the Seminary ordain a rabbi with "second-class" halakhic status who might not count in the minyan of her own shul?

While only one contributor, Joseph Brodie, deals with the sociological argument, the halakhic issue receives lengthy treatment, most notably in the piece by Joel Roth. (This article later became the focus of a review essay that appeared in the important Orthodox journal *Tradition*.)[2] The gist of Roth's argument turns on the halakhic status of a woman's "self-obligation." In his view, a women may become the halakhic equal of a man if she commits herself to praying the three daily prayers of *shaharit*, minha and *ma'ariv*, dons tallit and tefillin and performs all positive time-bound commandments from which, halakhically, women are normally exempt. Such a woman, Roth maintains, may not only be counted in a minyan but may indeed lead one. It is important to add that Roth does not advocate the promulgation of a rabbinic ordinance (*takanah*) that would obligate all women equally with men, since, in his words, "that would result in the creation of a large class of sinners where none now exists" (p. 166).

Roth's argument is challenged in this volume by Israel Francus, who argues that self-obligation can never take on the same weight and meaning as either a scriptural or a rabbinic obligation. As Francus puts it:

> Women who voluntarily obligate themselves to observe mitzvot from which they are exempt cannot [carry out the mitzvah for] men whose obligation is imposed by the Torah or the sages. Consequently, a woman cannot act as a cantor or a reader of the Torah at a service, or recite the marriage benedictions, or be counted in a minyan. Without being able to perform the above-mentioned functions, she will not be able to carry out her duties as a rabbi in a congregation (p. 19).

Two other objections to Roth may also be noted. First, if a woman were to enter Roth's shul in order to participate, say, in an afternoon minyan, she would probably be asked if she had put on tefillin that morning and if she regularly recites the *minha* prayer. If her answer was negative, she would have to assume the traditionally passive woman's role in the synagogue. Such interrogation would seem to undermine the basic notion of equality implied in the decision to ordain women. Second, there is no reference anywhere in Roth's *teshuvah*—or indeed, in any of the others—to the possible existence of models for women's spiritual expression other than the traditional male one. As Daniel Gordis has noted, "The subtle message that Roth imparts is that, in order to count, women have to act like men. Nowhere does Roth suggest that women might have something spiritually unique to offer Judaism. Nowhere does he seem concerned that women may feel a loss in trying magically to become male in the world of ritual."[3]

In general, the essays in this volume demonstrate a conscious struggle with the challenge of defining the nature of Conservative Judaism and its parameters. What is less emphasized is the need to reconsider definitions of the rabbinate, its role in the community, and the appropriate training required for the role. Is the model for rabbinic school a yeshivah, a professional training program or a graduate school in Judaic studies? Is the rabbi in fact the *shaliah zibur,* or primarily a teacher, preacher and pastoral counselor? No one seems to have considered a scenario in which there are different kinds of rabbis serving different kinds of functions. I find compelling a throwaway remark by Gordon Tucker that "it is a commonplace to ordain *Kohanim,* even though officiating at a funeral, which can pose halakhic problems for a *Kohen,* is popularly viewed as a rabbinic function" (p. 19).

Theoretically, the Seminary could have empowered women to serve as rabbis without considering the issue of obligation at all. Together with their male colleagues, these women could have embarked on an intensive and halakhically profound consideration of women's roles in Judaism. My own hope is that such a step may now in fact be taken: Women who fought for the right to be ordained as Conservative rabbis are now free to direct their energies and expertise within the halakhic framework to bring about change that may be less radical in the short run—but ultimately, perhaps, more lasting and profound.

DEBORAH WEISSMAN
The Hebrew University

Notes

1. Susan Dworkin, "Henrietta Szold—Liberated Woman," in *The Jewish Woman: New Perspectives,* ed. Elizabeth Koltun (New York: 1976), 168.

2. Gidon Rothstein, "The Roth Responsum on the Ordination of Women," *Tradition* 24, no. 1 (1988), 104–115.

3. Daniel Gordis, "The Conservative Rabbinate: Looking for Men in All the Wrong Places," *Tikkun* 4, no. 2 (March/April 1989), 98.

Norman Lamm, *Torah for Torah's Sake in the Works of Rabbi Hayyim of Volozhin and His Contemporaries.* New York and Hoboken: Yeshiva University Press and Ktav, 1989. 368 pp.

This book focuses on the place of Torah study, in theory and in practice, in the thought and deeds of Rabbi Hayyim of Volozhin and contemporaneous rabbis, notably Rabbi Eliyahu ben Shlomo (the Vilna Gaon) and Rav Shneur Zalman of

Lyady, the founder of Habad Hasidism. As such, it introduces the English reader to the world of the East European rabbinic elite that was previously rather inaccessible. At the beginning of the nineteenth century, all of these figures were active in a culture that was far removed from modern Jewish realities. Nonetheless, as Lamm's book demonstrates, many of the issues that they dealt with, as well as the responses they formulated, remain relevant today. In the contemporary Orthodox world, for example, Rabbi Hayyim's book *Nefesh Haḥayim* is still studied and regarded as a classic text. The ideology toward Torah study that he developed, which emphasized the importance of the study of Torah over all other religious activities, has had a major impact even on those unfamiliar with his written work.

A case in point regarding the influence of Rabbi Hayyim's views is the *kollel,* an institution that has seen a remarkable growth in the post-Holocaust period. A *kollel* is a framework in which married yeshivah students receive stipends in order to study full time for a period of several years—sometimes for an entire lifetime. The institution itself is a relatively modern phenomenon, since the first *kollel* was founded around 1880. However, the number of *kollelim* and *kollel* students has mushroomed in recent years. Moreover, in many Orthodox circles, study in a *kollel* has become the norm rather than the exception. This has had an impact not only on Orthodox educational systems but on marital patterns and fertility, since the *kollel* framework makes earlier marriage possible for yeshivah students.

The ideological basis for the whole *kollel* system and the goal of full-time, lifelong study of Torah rest to a large degree on the issues raised in this book. Lamm clarifies, for example, the way in which the theological underpinnings of the yeshivah movement are based far more on Kabbalah than one might have anticipated. In general, he offers a very useful introduction to a contemporary phenomenon that also merits serious sociological investigation.

Lamm's book is a translation of his 1972 Hebrew study. Considering the difficult and technical Hebrew of the texts Lamm has to deal with, the translation is felicitious. The author has made efforts to update the volume in light of studies written during the last fifteen years, although some gaps still remain. While it lacks a bibliography, the book does contain an index that provides useful information concerning sources.

SHAUL STAMPFER
The Hebrew University

Michael L. Morgan (ed.), *The Jewish Thought of Emil Fackenheim: A Reader.* Detroit: Wayne University Press, 1987. 394 pp.

The purpose of this reader is to expose Emil Fackenheim's thought to interested readers who lack a technical philosophical education. Though it presents Fackenheim's commitment to a systematic philosophical methodology, it does not introduce the methodology itself; rather, it tries to satisfy the readers' curiosity by means of general references to main philosophical sources. Wisely, however, the editor has placed the selections here in a historical-biographical context that emphasizes the great turn in Fackenheim's philosophy after the Six-Day War, with reference to his own biographical experience in the Holocaust.

Fackenheim's creative philosophical work began after the Holocaust, though he paid no philosophical attention at first to this traumatic event. In his first period, his Jewish thought reflects a continuation of German Jewish idealistic theology, combined with a tendency to reorientate Liberal Judaism toward a stronger commitment to traditional Jewish religiosity. Ironically, traditionalism found expression in Fackenheim's thinking not only with regard to faith in the personal "God of our fathers" and the Sinaitic covenant, but also concerning classical philosophical sources. While his seniors—Martin Buber, Franz Rosenzweig and Leo Baeck—based the same reorientation toward tradition on a rejection of classical idealism, adapting instead existentialism and phenomenology, Fackenheim moved halfway back to Hegel in order to justify philosophically his traditional bias. Recognizing in secular scientific rationalism the main source of modernistic alienation from the supernatural personal God, Fackenheim sought a synthesis of Hegelian dialectics and Buberian dialogism that would transcend Hegelian progressive historicism. Thus, he reaffirmed faith in God as the subjective "absolute existential a-priori" of man.

The experience of the Six-Day War from a diaspora perspective led to a dramatic reconsideration. For Fackenheim, the Six-Day War recalled the memory of the Holocaust in a situation that granted him both direct experience and reflective distance. Through it, he suddenly grasped the fact that the Holocaust was a unique turning point in history that does have a significant philosophical meaning—though it is a complete reversal, or rather denial, of the Hegelian progressive understanding of history.

As Hegelian idealism was the main source informing Fackenheim's basic philosophical grasp of reality, and as its historical dimension has been both confirmed and denied by the Holocaust, it is understandable why reflectively experiencing the uniqueness of the Holocaust became for him not only an event worthy of philosophical evaluation but also "an event in philosophy": paradoxically, evaluating the Holocaust as an "unprecedented event" from an idealistic grasp of reality undermined this selfsame grasp of reality. The "unprecedented" in the Holocaust could not be expected, nor understood, on the basis of that philosophy, which had presented itself as humanity's general and ultimate self-understanding.

This was a real philosophical trap. In order to get out of it, Fackenheim had both to defend and to transcend his former philosophy and his former understanding of history. This was also a traumatic theological trap because of the selfsame contradiction: grasping the meaning of the "unprecedented" in the Holocaust on the basis of belief in a personal-supernatural God of the covenant meant a complete denial of that belief. Once again, Fackenheim had to defend and transcend his former traditional understanding of belief and faith in God. On both the philosophical and the religious level, this could be done only through an empathetic reflection on the testimony of those victims of the Holocaust who stood their trial and resisted "radical evil," thus proving the possibility of "mending the world," namely, of "fitting" the world, deformed by radical evil, to its former idealistic and religious destiny.

From the Jewish theological point of view, Fackenheim's way out meant a radical shift in the understanding of the idea of covenant. Fackenheim emphasized the Jewish people's role in underpinning the covenant, a role that makes God utterly dependent on His holy people's faith in His guiding law, and which changes the meaning of belief in God from "absolute existential a-priori" into a symbol, or a projection, of the Jewish absolute will to exist: Only when the Jewish people bear their testimony of faith in Him and in His law—in order to survive Jewishly—does God exist. This is of course the source of Fackenheim's well-known formulation of the "614th commandment," which makes the responsibility of the Jewish people to their own survival the fundamental commitment of Jewish religiosity. But how could one bridge the contradiction between such radical, revolutionary understanding of belief and faith in God with Jewish traditional understanding, which must serve as the basis for the historical continuity of a Jewish identity?

Fackenheim tries to respond to this dilemma through a radical midrash on the meaning and function of the Midrash. According to him, the Midrash always served as a tool for continuation by providing interpretation of Judaism's "root experiences" (Exodus and the Sinaitic covenant) time and again from the perspective of ever-forthcoming, challenging "epoch-making experiences." But one must admit that it becomes completely unclear whether we should consider the Holocaust, in Fackenheim's interpretation, as an "epoch-making experience" or, being evaluated as an "unprecedented event," as a "root experience"—the last term contradicting the one before it, such that the task of continuation by interpretation becomes impossible even for a radically reinterpreted form of a "mad midrash." In fact, Fackenheim's attempts to propose such "mad midrashim," based on Elie Wiesel's testimony of the Holocaust, raise more doubts than convictions.

Be that as it may, Fackenheim's efforts to arrive at some directive conclusions and to draw practical commandments from his philosophical-theological demand "to mend the world" bring him back to classical Zionism and to the belief in the centrality of the state of Israel as the positive "root experience" of Judaism in our era. There is a hidden irony in this move, too. Fackenheim actually discovered after the Holocaust the truth of some basic intuitions of radical Zionism, whose proponents foresaw an approaching huge catastrophe before the Second World War and who urged the people—alas, unsuccessfully—to find means of rescue in due time. This of course does not shake the historical validity of Fackenheim's general claims both about the central position of the state of Israel in Jewish life and faith and about the commandments of aliyah and completion of the task of building Israel as a Jewish state. However, one expects now a new analysis of the inner and outward situation of the Jewish people after the Holocaust, and some more directive reflections on the meaning of a Jewish state, or rather, on how traditional Jewish self-understanding should be continued in a modern Jewish state. Merely restating the "614th commandment" after the Holocaust and after the establishment of Israel without such new reflections leaves us without the means and knowledge to implement this command.

The *Reader* before us is a product of excellent editorial work. The selection of material, made according to the criteria of representing central ideas and those of philosophical clarity and forceful literary expression, is most fortunate indeed. It presents Fackenheim at his best both as a deep thinker and as a brilliant writer who is able to move his readers intellectually and emotionally, making them empathize and share his authentic religious pathos and his deep commitment to the survival of the Jewish people. The short introductory essays are also very helpful: informative, precise and illuminating. It is a work of love done for the sake of a great work of love. As such it is sure to achieve its aim—that of extending Fackenheim's Jewish thought to a wide Jewish public.

ELIEZER SCHWEID
The Hebrew University

David Novak, *Jewish-Christian Dialogue: A Jewish Justification*. New York and Oxford: Oxford University Press, 1989. 194 pp.

Contemporary efforts to provide for and implement Jewish-Christian dialogue often stem from Christian initiative and motivation—in the past, from Christian missionary stratagems; more recently, from reparation for Christian antisemitism. On the Jewish side, commitment to such dialogue—with varied reasons—is often found among more "liberal" Jews. The unique contribution of the volume under review derives from the fact that this "Jewish justification" for dialogue comes from a representative of "the full authority of traditional Jewish law—Halakhah—as God's permanent mandate" for Jews (p. 3), a rendering of Judaism that has many times opposed such interfaith dialogue. In support of his own dialogic advocacy, the author marshals such worthies as Maimonides, for whom Christianity is the only scripturally based non-Jewish faith; Yaakov (Rabbenu) Tam, for whom Christianity is a valid form of non-Jewish monotheism; and Menahem Hameiri, for whom Christianity is (together with Islam) obedient to God's law.

In his introduction, Novak stresses that "neither Judaism nor Christianity . . . can authentically claim the truth as its own original possession. That type of theological arrogance is religiously insufferable." Yet the fact stands that "the doctrine of revelation, which Judaism and Christianity affirm, enables each community to claim that it is *uniquely related* to the truth, that it has received a revelation of the truth from God unlike that of any other community" (p. 17). "It is only when there is the attempt to constitute dialogue as an original religious reality—that is, as a new revelation itself—that halakhic objections can be raised" (p. 23).

In successive chapters, the author builds support for his own "new theology of Jewish-Christian dialogue" (ch. 6). Chapter 1 examines the Noahide Laws as a most essential way of bringing non-Jews "within the purview of Halakhah." That chapter and later pages address the companion question of "whether or not Christianity is a form of proscribed idolatry—even for gentiles." Rather curious is the claim that because the "covenantal relationship between God and Israel is considered by Scripture to be unique, idolatry can only be a sin for Israel." Not only is this difficult to reconcile with the Noahide judgment upon idolatry; it appears to conflict with

Novak's immediate finding afterward that "the great innovation of the new doctrine of Noahide law was that the ban on idolatry was now understood, to a certain degree at least, as being shared by Jews and non-Jews" (pp. 24, 37–38, 39).

Chapter 2 is devoted to the status of Christianity within medieval European halakhah. To Rabbenu Tam and later medieval halakhists, Christianity is simply not idolatry, despite its inferior quality relative to Judaism. In this development, the great influence of the Kabbalah is held, radically, to be decisive, with special respect to the doctrine of the Trinity (which affirms, as does the Kabbalah, strictly interdivine and inner divine relationships). However, European Sephardic communities "followed Maimonides's halakhic thesis about the unequivocal prohibition of any immediacy between God and man as idolatry, whether for Jews or for gentiles" (p. 51).

Maimonides's view of Christianity receives separate attention in Chapter 3. Maimonides eventually came to believe that while Christians "may not be true monotheists in theory, . . . they have accepted practical monotheism in their acceptance of the Hebrew Bible as the word of God." Evidently, Maimonides emerged with the conviction that the "theoretical reason" is subordinate to the "practical reason." Nevertheless, Christianity at best remains a form of derivative Judaism. Novak concludes:

> If it can be shown that the common biblicism of Judaism and Christianity—especially in the doctrines of creation and human nature—provides the basis for a common constitution [see p. 159 for Novak's Husserlian use of this term] of morality, then we have a true basis for the Jewish-Christian dialogue. This is my own appropriation of an essential insight of Maimonides in a way that he would not and could not do (pp. 67, 68, 72).

The "quest for the Jewish Jesus" in the nineteenth century and in Martin Buber and American Reform is attended to in Chapter 4, while Franz Rosenzweig's theology of the Jewish-Christian relation is treated intensively in Chapter 5. On the Rosenzweig view, the necessity of Christianity for Jews and Judaism is that the church "has the capacity to include all nations in the revealed relationship with God. Judaism cannot perform this redemptive function for itself" (p. 108). For Novak, our necessary rejection today of Rosenzweig's Jewish unworldliness largely rules out the latter's constitution of the Jewish-Christian relation.

Novak's final constructive essay (ch. 6) grounds itself upon "the logic of the relation of the singular and the general," terminology he finds much preferable to the more usual "universalism" and "particularism" (p. 115ff.). I shall not deprive readers of the opportunity to grapple for themselves with this climactic chapter. I shall simply report that according to Novak's unique epistemological methodology, there is no such thing as immanent *potentiality;* there is only *possibility*, which waits upon God's revealing will:

> Possibility, unlike potentiality, entails more than one outcome. . . . [This] enables one faith community . . . to recognize that revelation is possible for another faith community without having to constitute what that revelation is in that other community. In other words, it can apprehend it (*an sit*), but it cannot judge it (*quid est*), for any such judgment would require the constitution of a genus including both faith communities as

species. The faith claims of both communities . . . would be lost in any such move (p. 135).

Jewish-Christian Dialogue brilliantly combines philosophical acumen, erudition in Judaica and a plea (pp. 141–156) for theonomous morality (in contrast to all autonomy and heteronomy). As one who lives upon the threshold of Jewishness—never quite inside yet never quite outside—I find Novak's argumentation coherent and compelling. This is not to imply that the work leaves us with no questions: Is it actually the case that secularism is as much the enemy of Judaism as the author finds? Is Christian faithfulness to the law as definitive within the Church, as the author suggests? And is it really convincing to identify the Christian faith as non-idolatrous? Finally, Novak's claim that "at least as many Christians were anti-Nazi as pro-Nazi" (p. 5) is highly questionable.

Finally, readers ought to be aware of printing mistakes. I found typos on pages 40, 43, 101, 114, 135, 138, 143, 145, 181 and 185, and an incorrect spelling of names on pages 160 and 188. On page 109 "at" is missing from line 29.

A. ROY ECKARDT
Oxford Centre for Postgraduate Hebrew Studies

Riv-Ellen Prell, *Prayer and Community: The Havurah in American Judaism*. Detroit: Wayne State University Press, 1989. 335 pp.

Jack Wertheimer (ed.), *The American Synagogue: A Sanctuary Transformed*. Cambridge: Cambridge University Press, 1987. 433 pp.

After more than a century and a half of steady evolution, the quintessential institution of American Judaism—the synagogue—stands at a rare moment of retrenchment and reappraisal. Both of the books reviewed here contribute to our knowledge of that evolution as well as to our appreciation of current trends. But most of all they remind us of how *American* the American synagogue is in its ability to absorb rapid change and to thrive (or not, as the case may be) on individualism, voluntarism and pluralism.

Nowhere else has the synagogue been so uniquely adapted to conditions of institutional independence and legal freedom. Unprecedented freedom from constraint has unquestionably encouraged the freedom to create. Yet at the same time the "finished product" has also clearly depended a great deal on the "raw materials" provided by the environment. The American synagogue may be justly described as being both innovative and imitative, as both of these books abundantly demonstrate.

Riv-Ellen Prell's study of a typical *havurah* locates this most recent phenomenon of American Judaism against the background of the counterculture trends of the 1970s. It makes fascinating reading as an account of community-building and institutional change. Just as important, it is a portrait of one small segment of a generation who chose to reinvent the synagogue of their great-grandparents (as they perceived it), but in so doing stamped it with an aesthetic and a social rationale (Prell terms this a "decorum") that was pure Americana.

Prell's point is that, despite significant differences, there is much deep-structure continuity in the impulses that fed the development of middle-class suburban synagogues in the 1950s and 1960s and those that produced the *havurot* of the 1970s and 1980s. Both organized their Jewishness around prayer and community (hence the book's subtitle); indeed, the very word *organize* is a key to understanding them as parallel social phenomena. And neither the one nor the other abandoned the basic premise of a synthesis between Jewish tradition and American modernity. It is pertinent to remember the non-Orthodox background of most *havurah* members and the fact that the *havurah* idea, in modified form, has made inroads mostly in the liberal Jewish denominations, where it has become institutionalized in some mainstream synagogues.

Plus ça change, plus c'est le même chose? It is tempting to look for functional equivalents in the way that War-on-Poverty and civil rights liberalism of "the Sixties" was scoffed at but actually reappropriated by antiwar activism, the presidential campaign for Eugene McCarthy, affirmative action, "pro-choice" and pro-ERA forces—all of which focused on government as the key to all social issues.

Prell successfully avoids the pitfalls of oversimplification. Her book documents the very real distinctions of style, vocabulary, and purpose that set the *havurah* or minyan community apart from its parent model. She merely reminds us, in the process, just how much parentage counts, even among rebellious children.

Unlike Prell's book, which will be read with most profit by those who already have some background in the sociology of religion, Jack Wertheimer's anthology *The American Synagogue* readily lends itself to use as a college textbook. This admirable collection of historical essays is organized in two sections: the first ("The Denominational Perspective") oriented to developments within specific synagogue movements; and the second ("The Thematic Perspective") devoted to aspects of change and seminal developments that are not denomination-specific. The book is ably introduced by Abraham Karp's essay, "Overview: The Synagogue in America—A Historical Typology."

The first section includes an essay by Jeffrey Gurock on "The Orthodox Synagogue," one by Leon Jick on "The Reform Synagogue," and a third, by Jack Wertheimer, on "The Conservative Synagogue." Each one moves easily from historical analysis to contemporary survey.

The second, much longer section, is both wide-ranging and (like the essays in the first section) well written. It presents portraits of individual congregational development with significant sociohistorical ramifications (Marc Angel on a Sephardic synagogue in Seattle; Paula Hyman on a Boston synagogue's growth "From City to Suburb"; Benny Kraut on ethnic relations in a Cincinnati congregation; Deborah Dash Moore on the flagship synagogue-center of Brooklyn). Other essays address specific issues that transcend the confines of one congregation or look at one seminal period in a synagogue's history: Barry Chazan writes on Jewish education in the synagogue; Jenna Weissman Joselit details the growth and development of synagogue sisterhoods; and Marsha Rozenblit compares two German congregations in Baltimore in the nineteenth century. Robert Liberles's essay on the beginnings of synagogue reform in Charleston is original and illuminating; Jonathan Sarna addresses the debate over mixed seating; and Kay Kaufman Shelemay writes on the use of music in the service, as illustrated by a case study from Houston.

The "thematic" section is thus rich in detailed analysis, varied in subject matter, and drawn from the experiences of congregations in different regions and different types of communities.

After undergoing much ideological turmoil and dramatic social change, the American synagogues—for they are plural, rather than singular, as these essays teach us—retain their primary importance at the grass roots level of the Jewish community. That is their strength but also their weakness, for with their local (not to say parochial) concerns, independent funding structure, and individual style and character, it is difficult for them—even when organized nationwide into "movements"—to rival the nondenominational Jewish organizations for power and influence in Jewish communal policy-making. This point is lost in any study that focuses only on this one institution (however central it is) in American Judaism today. One might also have wished for a deeper comparative perspective than is afforded by the single introductory essay.

Nevertheless, *The American Synagogue* will be a splendid guide for students of American Jewish history and of American religion. I know of no other single work that makes up-to-date, reliable historical research and contemporary analysis on this topic so accessible to the reading public.

ELI LEDERHENDLER
The Hebrew University

Marc Lee Raphael, *Abba Hillel Silver: A Profile in American Judaism.* New York: Holmes & Meir, 1989. xxxiii + 282 pp.

There have been only a handful of biographies of American rabbis, and one on Abba Hillel Silver is long overdue. Rabbi of one of the largest Reform congregations in the country, scholar, communal activist and, above all, leader of American Zionism during and after the Second World War, Silver played an important role on the stage of American Judaism. Yet a generation after his death, he is remembered only by historians and some aging congregants in Cleveland. This biography by Marc Lee Raphael, himself a Reform rabbi as well as a historian, goes a long way toward providing us with a portrait of the man some called the "Jewish lord."

This book has many strong points. Raphael writes clearly and knowledgeably about Silver's beliefs, his scholarship, his work patterns and his management of the Temple. No one could doubt that Silver ran his congregation; members of the board did not tell Silver what they wanted, he told them, and no one got onto the board without his approval. Yet this arrangement worked out well because Silver gave his large congregation what it wanted, above all in his brilliant Sunday morning lectures.

Silver conceived of the rabbinate in almost traditional terms—namely, the rabbi as teacher. He taught every Sunday, using the pulpit to instruct his congregation in Zionism, public affairs, Jewish events and anything else he thought the audience should know. He also taught his confirmation class, and despite a rigorous schedule that took him to New York and Washington almost every week from 1943 to 1948, he would return to Cleveland on Thursday nights to teach his Friday classes and handle the weekend services.

Silver was also a scholar, and his work for both rabbinic as well as lay audiences has stood up well over time. Raphael contrasts Silver with his great rival, Stephen S. Wise, concluding that while both were gifted orators, Silver had more of substance to say. (This is a comment I heard on a number of occasions when doing my own research on Wise.) After being deposed from his leadership of American Zionism, Silver spent the last fifteen years of his life serving, apparently quite happily, as rabbi, teacher and scholar.

Unfortunately—and this is not Raphael's fault—we never get more than a glimpse of Abba Silver the person as opposed to Rabbi Silver the persona. Raphael tells us about how Silver liked Yiddish jokes, how he liked to eat, how he behaved around the house and how he wrote poetry as a young man. A very formal person (his son recalled that his father never left the bedroom in the morning without being fully clothed in tie and suit), he had very few close personal friends. Unlike Wise, who wore his heart on his sleeve, Silver kept his personal life very personal indeed, and there seem to be neither public statements nor private letters in which he bared his soul.

A problem in this book, common to biographers and one that the author would have done well to avoid, is the narrow focus on Silver, often at the expense of giving the reader a more general historical context. By virtue of his position as rabbi of one of the largest Reform congregations in the country, Silver held an influential place in the Reform movement, which was in turmoil during much of his lifetime. Although Silver played a role in that turmoil, we hear very little about it in this work; Raphael tells us, for example, that Silver as a student stood up to the anti-Zionism of Hebrew Union College but does not mention the anti-Zionism of the Reform movement in general and the split during the Second World War regarding the anti-Zionist American Council for Judaism. He also notes that Silver played a role in the civic affairs of Cleveland. But many Reform rabbis played similar roles in other cities, in part because the Reform rabbinate stressed the Jewish version of the social gospel calling upon rabbis to live in the world and to be active in social betterment. Moreover, civic reformers during the early part of this century created a particular climate that invited clerical participation. We would have understood Silver's activity better had it been firmly set in this broader context.

Although it is absorbing to read, Raphael's narrative of Silver's Zionist activities errs similarly in its focus on Silver rather than the various internecine feuds that created the particular Zionist climate in which he operated or the larger context of American politics during this period. The weakness of Raphael's approach is especially apparent in his handling of the post-1948 period in which Silver and his allies, especially Emanuel Neumann, were driven from leadership of the Zionist Organization of American (ZOA). On reading this narrative, one would think that personal jealousies played the key role, and that Henry Montor, aggrieved at Silver's overbearing dominance, plotted with the non-Zionist large contributors to the United Jewish Appeal to wrest control of the organization from Silver. The actual story is far more complicated, and Raphael only partially alludes to the fact that this struggle was part of a larger battle between Israeli and American views of Zionism and the proper relationship between Israel and the diaspora.

That Silver's personality played a role in the drama is indisputable, but one wonders whether the participants, including Silver, saw it as only a personality conflict or were aware of the larger issues involved. Raphael barely discusses the ways in which American Zionism had to grapple with a major change in orientation following the birth of Israel, mentioning in one brief paragraph that Silver was aware of the need for change. Left unexplored is the issue of David Ben-Gurion's deliberate crippling of the ZOA, which went beyond his personal antagonism to Silver, involving as it did his views of what the role of Zionism should be in a post-state world.

Finally, while Raphael acknowledges that many people found Silver's personality overbearing, he himself often skirts this issue with euphemisms. Silver did not just have a powerful personality, he could be downright nasty, and often was, especially with people who did not agree with him or whom he viewed as opponents. I know of one occasion, for example, where Rose Halprin (an American General Zionist leader) tried to mediate between Silver and Wise, pleading with Silver to show some respect and charity to the older Wise. According to Halprin, Silver snorted in response and stomped away. It is only when one recognizes this aspect of Silver's personality that some of Raphael's statements make sense. People resented and opposed Silver not because he had a forceful personality, but because that forcefulness was often expressed in a nasty and mean-spirited manner.

All in all, though, we should be grateful to Raphael for a book that has many more virtues than defects. We need more studies of American Jewish leaders, especially the rabbinic leadership, and I hope Raphael will take a leading role in continuing to provide them.

MELVIN I. UROFSKY
Virginia Commonwealth University

Social Sciences and Politics

Brenda Danet, *Pulling Strings: Biculturalism in Israeli Bureaucracy.* Albany: State University of New York Press, 1989. 374 pp.

As its name suggests, this is a study of the use of personal influence in Israeli citizens' encounters with the bureaucracy—a practice popularly known as *protekziyah* (sometimes jocularly referred to as Vitamin P). The book carries with it a rather heavy baggage of partly superfluous models, typologies and classifications of cultural and personal factors that may influence the practice. But for those willing to work their way through these rather cumbersome conceptualizations, the book has a good deal of thought-provoking information to impart.

Its central argument is that "pulling strings" should be viewed neither as corruption nor as deviance but rather in the framework of biculturalism. This term refers to a hybrid organizational culture in which people simultaneously adhere to two seemingly incompatible codes of bureaucratic behavior. The first is a universalistic code, based on criteria of objective entitlements and fairness. The second is a particularistic code, based on personal relations and solidarity. Although the codes seem to be mutually exclusive, biculturalism implies that people switch quite easily from one to the other.

Danet goes on to argue that such biculturalism is generated by two sets of actors. First, it is created by the difficulties experienced by citizens in obtaining goods and services from the bureaucracy; these difficulties, in turn, are caused by the scarcity of resources and/or the bureaucratic monopoly over them, along with the bureaucracy's rigidity and inefficiency. Second, biculturalism results from the persistence of traditional, premodern forms of legitimizing particularism.

Within this framework the author distinguishes, on the one hand, modern Western societies (such as Britain and the United States) where neither of these factors—or biculturalism—prevails. Apart from some intermediary types that are not particularly relevant for the discussion, she then distinguishes, on the other hand, mainly developing countries where these two factors, and biculturalism, are present. This latter type of country clearly includes Israel, where the bureaucracy is widely seen as inefficient and rigid. Moreover, there is a widespread legitimation of particularistic channels of influence. This is derived from a strong emphasis on familial and other forms of group solidarity, in combination with illegalism, or lack of respect for the law, formal rules and regulations.

On the basis of an empirical study carried out in 1980 on a sample of one thousand Israeli Jews living in Israel's major cities (where the great majority of

Israel's Jewish population resides), the author demonstrates that biculturalism is in fact prevalent in Israel. A large majority (nine out of ten) of the respondents adhered to the universalistic norm that it was wrong to use *protekẓiyah*. Yet of those who had had some contact with the bureaucracy and who had felt a need for *protekẓiyah*, the majority (51 percent) had used it at least once. The study replicated the major finding of a previous research project—conducted by the author in 1968—which showed that while most people oppose *protekẓiyah* in principle, given need and opportunity, most will use it.

Another finding of Danet's study is that the strings are pulled not only in initial bureaucratic encounters but also as a means of redress: The single most frequently used channel in response to perceived bureaucratic injustice was not the ombudsman but *protekẓiyah*. Thus, far from dying out, the use of personal influence in confronting the bureaucracy has been flourishing in Israel in recent years.

Who, then, uses *protekẓiyah*? Almost everyone, says Danet. But some use it more than others. Those people who are best integrated into Israeli society, the most highly educated, the most knowledgeable on the workings of bureaucracy, are also most likely to be bicultural. That is, they are most likely to combine use of universalistic (formal, objective) channels of redress with particularistic ones that involve the utilization of personal connections.

Ostensibly, by showing that *protekẓiyah* is still rampant in Israel, the study merely confirms what anyone who has any acquaintance with Israeli society knows already. And on the face of it, the finding that those who are best integrated into Israeli society and most knowledgeable about bureaucracy are most likely to use *protekẓiyah* also appears simply to validate the popular saying that you need to know the ropes in order to pull the strings. In fact, however, these findings are of considerable sociological interest. For they fly in the face of the earlier conceptions of some of Israel's most prominent students of bureaucracy, including Shmuel Eisenstadt, Elihu Katz, Rivka Bar-Yoseph and, at some stage, even the author herself.

As Danet reminds us, some of these scholars had shared the belief that the particularistic patterns of bureaucratic behavior that had been pervasive in Israel in the 1950s and 1960s were a response to the large waves of immigration from Middle Eastern countries. Thus, as the immigrants were absorbed, so the reasoning went, those who came from Western countries would impose their own modern patterns on the host society, and those from Middle Eastern countries would simply adopt these Western patterns. Hence, Israel would shortly be well on the road to becoming universalistic not only in its bureaucratic norms but in its bureaucratic practices as well.

The results of Danet's study show that this absorption-modernization paradigm did not predict Israeli reality as it emerged in the 1970s and 1980s. In fact, it turned out that the immigrants from Western countries have changed the most in adapting to Israel's hybrid organizational culture. For it was they—who also tended to be the best educated and the best integrated into Israeli society—who most prominently adopted both universalistic and particularistic channels of redress in the face of bureaucratic injustice.

Contrary to what was previously thought to be the case, then, biculturalism in Israel's bureaucracy is not merely a remnant of the large-scale immigration of the 1950s. It is not merely the characteristic feature of new immigrants from Middle Eastern countries placed, as it were, on the edge of two cultures: a more traditional and a more modern one. Nor is it merely the characteristic pattern through which Israeli bureaucracy deals with such immigrants. Indeed, it may be said with only a slight degree of exaggeration that if *protekẓiyah* is still rampant in Israel today, this is not *despite* the fact that previous waves of immigration (especially from the Middle East) have been well absorbed into Israeli society but *because* of this fact.

Interestingly, and paradoxically, these findings raise some questions with regard to the author's own framework of analysis. For if, as the author claims, biculturalism in Israel is the combined result of blocked access to bureaucratic resources and remnants of legitimation of premodern particularism, how can one explain that it is precisely the best-educated—and thus the most modernized and Westernized—who are also the best socialized into Israel's double-bind bureaucratic culture?

Could it not be argued instead that even in modern Western societies there are certain elements of a hybrid organizational culture—that, in some respects, universalistic and particularistic norms and practices coexist and inform organizational behavior? This is the conclusion that could be reached, for instance, on the basis of the famous study by Rosabeth Moss Kanter in *Men and Women of the Corporation* (1979). This study of a large American corporation has shown, inter alia, that where promotions to top managerial positions are concerned not only are universalistic criteria of talent and aptitude taken into account, but also particularistic criteria such as similarities to present incumbents, gender and personal trust.

In this context, Danet herself cites various studies that clearly show how norms of particularism take their place alongside criteria of universalism and are well entrenched in the organizational culture of a variety of Western societies. Significantly, these societies include Britain and the United States, two countries that Danet herself, in her analytical framework, had presented as the prototype of cultures in which universalistic norms predominate. As the author correctly points out, routine goods and services in these countries can be easily obtained by universalistic criteria alone. However, this merely signifies that particularistic criteria have moved up a notch in the hierarchy and are applied only where scarce goods and services—such as high-level appointments—are concerned.

Could it be, then, that the hybrid organizational culture that Danet correctly identifies as characteristic of Israel is not a remnant of premodernism, but a certain version of modern organizational culture? This is a question that cannot, of course, be answered on the basis of Danet's study. But it certainly counts in the book's favor that the author's work provokes thought on questions such as these.

In conclusion, the book is somewhat cumbersome to read, and its presentation could have been simplified and streamlined without incurring any significant loss in message and meaning. It is nevertheless well worth the effort to master its contents. This is so not merely because of the interesting factual information it imparts but also because of the broader issues on bureaucratic culture in modern society that it raises. Because of these, it will doubtless be an invaluable aid not only to scholars of Israeli bureaucracy but to students of bureaucracy in general as well.

EVA ETZIONI-HALEVY
Bar-Ilan University

Daniel J. Elazar (ed.), *The New Jewish Politics*. Lanham, Md.: University Press of America, 1988. 76 pp.

This slim, useful volume is the first in a series of "American Jewish Policy Agenda Resource Books," a project initiated in 1984 by the Jerusalem Center for Public Affairs and the Center for Jewish Community Studies at Temple University, Philadelphia. The establishment of the project was in itself of some significance: Leading academic students of American Jewry teamed up with voluntary and professional community leaders to identify issues likely to be of concern to the American Jewish community at the end of the twentieth century.

The series is not intended to be heavily academic but rather presents what might be termed the distilled essence of university-based research and informed public discussion for the benefit of a wide (and, it might be noted, more or less exclusively American) audience. In the volume presently under review, Daniel Elazar has assembled contributions from leading American Jewish political scientists and communal leaders on the theme of political activism in the contemporary life of American Jewry: how it developed, how it is expressed and what its future direction (and, to a lesser extent, its agenda) might be.

In his own introductory chapter, Elazar reminds us that "the Jewish community as an active and powerful bloc in American politics is a relatively recent phenomenon." *Shtadlanim* (Jewish political intermediaries in the gentile world—a term too often used pejoratively) there have always been: The tensions between the older American Jewish Committee and the American Jewish Congress earlier this century were in an important sense nothing more or less than rivalries between two segments of American Jewry who were determined to achieve the goal of becoming the paramount *shtadlanic* group. Since the entry of Zionism onto the American Jewish stage new organizations have emerged: the American Israel Public Affairs Committee (AIPAC), the Conference of Presidents of Major American Jewish Organizations, the Jewish War Veterans, the Anti-Defamation League, the Council of Jewish Federations, and so on. Each of these groups has tried to define and defend its own political territory; between them, however, there is an unmistakable tension, which derives in part from the wider world of American public life and from international considerations.

The blacklash against the Vietnam War, for example, weakened the position of the Jewish War Veterans, and the breakdown of the so-called alliance between Jews and blacks caused major—and inevitable—problems for the American Jewish Congress. Similarly, the salience of Israel as a unifying force in American Jewish life strengthened the position of AIPAC. Meanwhile, Jews began to run for and win public office, and the development and exploitation of political action committees has ensured that even congressmen with few Jewish constituents have come to feel the weight of Jewish political pressure.

Above and beyond these developments, however, two facts stand out: First, the Anti-Defamation League continues to flourish—a living testimony to the insecurity still felt by the diaspora's largest and most powerful community; second, a majority of this community still votes for the Democrats, even though economic self-interest, it might be argued, should have long ago propelled them into the Republican camp.

I would suggest that these two facts are connected. Much has been written about black antisemitism. I vividly recall how, at the end of a Sabbath morning service in a packed synagogue in Queens, New York, in the summer of 1988, the rabbi asked the congregation to stay behind and then delivered a mighty verbal onslaught against the presidential candidacy of Governor Michael Dukakis; behind Dukakis (the rabbi reminded his enthusiastic audience) stood the figure of Jesse Jackson, whom Jews could not trust. But this was a right-wing Orthodox house of worship in a neighborhood full of right-wing Orthodox Jews, who are a clear minority in American Jewry. In general, attempts by powerful elements within the Republican party to undermine religious pluralism were profoundly disturbing to the majority of non-Orthodox American Jews and (it should be said) to many as well within the Orthodox camp. New Testament–thumping Republicans did much to keep most American Jewish voters loyal to the Democratic ticket, even in the Reagan era.

Will this continue to be the case? I feel uncomfortable when political scientists are asked to prophesy. Lipset and Raab are surely right to emphasize that American Jews "are more disposed than others to identify as liberals." But in a crisp gem of a contribution, David M. Pollock, assistant executive director of the Jewish Community Relations Council of New York, exposes a number of myths about the voting habits of New York Jews: They do not, for instance, vote as a bloc; they will vote Republican if they feel it is in their interest so to do, but they are not a "single-issue constituency."

In particular, we should note that Israel is a special case: Support for Israel is not an issue during presidential elections and thus the Democratic leanings of a majority of American Jews do not necessarily indicate any dovish tendencies on their part regarding the Middle East. Much more important for the future political behavior of American Jewry is their general perception of the Democratic party. The party's image, I would suggest, may become less attractive if it is perceived to represent an ever-wider variety of subgroups (e.g., blacks, homosexuals, feminists, proabortionists) whose interests do not coincide with those of a majority of American Jews.

GEOFFREY ALDERMAN
Royal Holloway and Bedford New College
University of London

Carole Fink, *Marc Bloch: A Life in History*. Cambridge: Cambridge University
  Press, 1989. xix + 371 pp.

A biography of a historian who shied away from biographical portraits and whose
claim to fame was his research on the average human being is in some ways a
historical irony. But Marc Bloch, a medievalist at heart, was not a common academic historian. Together with Lucien Febvre, he founded in 1929 the journal
Annales d'histoire Economique et sociale, in which the two boldly declared the
breakdown of former boundaries between disciplines, challenged the received divisions between "primitive" and "civilized" societies and sought to merge the analysis of contemporary issues in historical studies. The school of history that bears the
journal's name and orientation has emerged as one of the mainstays of the historical
profession, confirming Bloch's own description of it as a "minor intellectual revolution." Yet even such professional success would not have warranted a full-length
biography were it not for other dimensions of Bloch's life—his steadfast allegiance
to France, his active involvement in the French Resistance during the Second World
War and his tragic death at the hands of the German gestapo in June 1944. Bloch,
who wore his Jewish origin with no particular pride, was forced to accede recur-
rently to the insurmountable fences of antisemitism—a phenomenon he was reluctant to acknowledge. *A Life in History* seeks both to penetrate and to merge all these
strains in Bloch's life.

   In researching and writing this biography, Carole Fink has been true to Bloch's
"total" approach to history, that which he wrote and that which he advocated in *The
Historian's Craft:* "The variety of historical evidence is nearly infinite. Everything
that man says or writes, everything that he makes, everything he touches can and
ought to teach us about him."[1] In her quest for a complete portrayal, Fink has
mastered his writings, has fettered out of archives and family records all possible
evidence relating to Bloch's intellectual pursuit and his private and public persona,
and has pursued particular issues through interviews with surviving family and
associates. Her treatment is always empathetic, coherent and attentive to the different layers of his being.

   Born in Lyon in 1886, a scion of Alsatian Jews who were well entrenched in
French society, Bloch inherited a love of France and liberalism; like many assimilated French Jews, he viewed the Dreyfusard victory as a substantiation of his trust
in France. Bloch was reared and educated during intellectually turbulent years in
which the historical discipline in France and elsewhere was undergoing a thorough
revision that challenged the former supremacy of political history. Two premises lay
at the basis of this reorientation: History should expand its perspective by appropri-
ating methods and topics from other fields (in particular the social sciences) and yet
strive to be a comprehensive discipline. As a student at the Ecole Normale Supérieure, a forerunner in this reevaluation, Bloch received full exposure to the historical
controversy—temporarily avoiding total commitment to one position or another.
Yet his first historical study, *L'Ile-de-France* (1913), already showed a preference
for sociology over geography and revealed his particular fascination with the problem of serfdom.

Bloch's life was not one of an academic iconoclast. His historical development was twice interrupted by the havoc of war. With the outbreak of the First World War he enlisted out of conviction, sensing the danger to France's future. Wounded and decorated four times for his active combat duty, Bloch never lost sight of the human element in war. In *Memoirs of War, 1914–1915* (Cambridge: 1988), which Fink has also carefully edited and translated, Bloch appears as a concerned patriot who clearly differentiates between the exigencies of war and the kind of militant nationalism that tramples the individual's expression. Released as a captain, Bloch would return voluntarily to service in 1939.

The interwar period was the prime of Bloch's intellectual career. Fink devotes several engaging chapters to his emergence as a central figure in the French historical scene, from his appointment to the University of Strasbourg in medieval history (1919) to a chair in economic history (1936) at the Sorbonne, and shows how Strasbourg proved to be an ideal setting for Bloch's growth. Surrounded by a group of eminent scholars—Edward Vermeil, Charles Blondel, Maurice Halbwachs and Lucien Febvre—who were all interested in furthering interdisciplinary research, Bloch's historical perspective crystallized. His magisterial study *The Royal Touch: Sacred Monarchy and Scrofula in England and France* (1924) brought together Bloch's interest in comparative history while illuminating his ability to incorporate and synthesize wide-ranging factors, from economics to psychology, in the reconstruction of the past. This was a path-breaking foray into the study of "mentalities" or what Durkheim had called "collective representations." In Strasbourg, Bloch also came under the influence of Henri Pirenne (a pioneer in his own right) who labored to maintain an internationalist spirit in the study of history and who strongly supported the efforts of Bloch and Febvre to launch a new international historical journal. *Annales d'Histoire Economique et sociale* emerged in 1929 after a concerted effort on the part of its editors to engage professionals of various disciplines to cooperate: It pronounced unabashedly their desire to assume in the areas of social and economic history "le rôle de direction." For the University of Strasbourg the production of such a journal had tremendous significance, but as Fink points out, its continuation hinged on the relationship between the two editors.

Bloch's and Febvre's intellectual interaction brought the *Annales* to the center of historical interest, and their friendship withstood many trying moments that went beyond the normal sphere of academic tensions. Fink deals sensitively with their more than twenty years of dialogue, addressing herself to issues of personality, historical interpretations and emphases as well as to the frictions engendered by the course of political events during the next decade. All in all, Fink recognizes the unique relationship that bonded these historians together ("the manifesto of another generation and the embodiment of an entirely different spirit")[2] even in the face of the growing disparity in their personal situations. The 1930s were crowned with major achievements for Bloch in his historical research of medieval society—from *French Rural History* (1931) to *Feudal Society* (1939–1940), but these years were also haunted by the specter of antisemitism. Bloch could no longer bask in the political passivity of the 1920s; his candidacy for the Collège de France—the plateau of French academic life already reached by Febvre—was denied, owning in part to his Jewish origin. For similar reasons, Febvre later advised Bloch to refrain from submitting his candidacy for the directorship of the Ecole Normale Supérieure. Bloch showed no signs of acceding to his colleague's advice when war broke out. At this point, at the age of fifty-three, Captain and historian Bloch returned to active duty, motivated by his unswerving love for France and his sense of personal responsibility ("the feeling that one is serving no useful purpose in a nation at war is intolerable").[3]

Bloch's courageous and tragic involvement in the Second World War receives detailed treatment from his biographer. Fink describes Bloch's activity in and his appraisal of the "phony war" and unravels his determined but ambivalent attempts to leave France for the United States. His dilemma was shared by many native French Jews who wavered between gloom and optimism, their sense of outrage against France's antisemitic laws conflicting with their equally powerful commitment to the mother country. After resolving to remain in France and seeing employment possibilities dwindle, Bloch joined the Resistance and quickly became a dominant figure in its operations in the south of France, a position he held for more than a year until his capture in March 1944. Two months later he was shot by German officers.

Carol Fink's *A Life in History* provides an intimate and persuasive portrayal of Bloch's life and thought, although it in some ways falls short of integrating all the strands together. It would appear that more needs to be done both to penetrate Bloch's resilient residue of Jewish identification—evoked so movingly in his testament of 1941—and to assimilate it with other aspects of his life and thought. Was there, for instance, any relationship between his particular internationalist and a-political approach to history and his minority background? Was there not more in his persistent affirmation that he was "a good Frenchman" than outright patriotism, possibly an offshoot of the strategy of apologetics that often characterized Jews in Western and Central Europe in the twentieth century? Did the antisemitism he encountered at several significant conjunctures of his life leave no mark whatsoever on his personal life or historical work? Moreover, it seems hard to reconcile the fact that no tangible internal connections are found by Fink between his major oeuvres, produced during the turbulent 1930s, and the surrounding political chaos.

Nonetheless, anyone willing to pursue any of these or other avenues of interpretation will have as their guide and source this absorbing and all-encompassing biography.

RICHARD I. COHEN
The Hebrew University

Notes

1. March Bloch, *The Historian's Craft,* trans. Peter Putnam (Manchester: 1954), 66.
2. Lucien Febvre, "A Note on the Manuscripts of the Present Book," in *ibid.,* xiii.
3. March Bloch, *Strange Defeat: A Statement of Evidence Written in 1940,* trans. Gerard Hopkins (New York and London: 1968), 7.

Ruth Kozodoy, David Sidorsky and Kalman Sultanik (eds.), *Vision Confronts Reality: Historical Perspectives on the Contemporary Jewish Agenda/Herzl Yearbook Number 9*. New York: Herzl Press, 1989.

This ninth volume of the resurrected Herzl Yearbook series promises much. In the introduction, David Sidorsky announces a bold new theme, "to examine the recent research on Zionism in its historical, political, and literary contexts." While the thirteen separate contributions (excluding the introduction) are all excellent and stimulating, each in its own way, it cannot be said that more than a fraction actually rise to this challenge.

Some authors recapitulate and synthesize earlier work. This is the case with Jacob Katz, who writes on the transformation of Jewish life in the eighteenth century (a subject he has previously dealt with at length) and Jehuda Reinharz, who contributes a sizable fragment of what may once have been work-in-progress on Weizmann but which has in the meantime seen the light of day in its full glory. Michael Stanislawski's title juxtaposes Zionism and Haskalah, and in his sparkling preface he touches provocatively on the debate between the secular, humanist strain in Zionism and religious nationalism in Israel today. However, in the end, his examination of this complex relationship focuses narrowly on J. L. Gordon's thoughts and, while absorbing, fails to fully meet its own agenda.

The two pieces on Soviet Jewry, by the redoubtable Martin Gilbert and by Yoram Dinstein, whose forensic skills cut through Soviet hypocrisy, touch only tangentially on issues related to Zionism. Nor have they weathered *glasnost* at all well, though *perestroika* does not invalidate these studies to the extent that they analyze a particular phase in the struggle of the Soviet Jewish minority.

Addressing another rapidly developing world phenomenon, the essays on Islam by Hillel Fradkin and Bernard Lewis alight upon a possible new threat to Israel and Jews throughout the world. In chilling polemics, both writers make pessimistic forecasts concerning the vitality of Islam as a political force and the profundity of its animosity toward an independent Jewish entity on the Mediterranean littoral. It is nevertheless disappointing that the broader implications for the Jews, Zionism and Israel are left unstated as Fradkin and Lewis remain—perhaps understandably— within the limits of their own discipline.

Steven Spiegel's review of the strategic relationship between the United States and Israel does stress the impact on the two countries of their respective encounters with militant Islam and the effect in drawing them closer together after a period of discord and mutual disenchantment. Fate has many tricks in her pocket, however. In this case, the Pollard affair has overtaken many of the assumptions underpinning Spiegel's conclusions. It might also be noted that America's interest in Israel should ideally not be confined to the latter's role as ally or proxy in the Middle East. It is a sad fact—perhaps a symptom of the "growth of political corruption and the widely noted decline of liberal principles in Israel" remarked upon by Wasserstein (p. 173)—that Israeli Jews have recently appeared in large numbers as advisers to unsavory regimes in Central America and that Israeli arms have been shipped to armed forces in the region.

Only a handful of the contributors cross academic boundaries to take up the challenge formulated by Sidorsky. Of these, Bernard Wasserstein is the most dynamic. In the space of a few pages he surveys the recent historiography of the Italian risorgimento, compares the fate of Italian unification with the course of the Jewish national movement and crystallizes the issues in a concise account of Chaim Weizmann's career as diplomat and Jewish leader. Ezra Mendelsohn adopts the approach of comparative history to elucidate the vexed question of Zionism's success or failure in a lucid inquiry that traverses the geography and historiography of Zionist movements in the West and throughout Eastern Europe. Mendelsohn suggests that the well-known "apathy" of Jews in the West may not be an aberration or a dereliction of Zionist duty but rather the perpetuation of an enduring attachment to the diaspora, as a result of which Zionism served quite different ends than those of aliyah and the upbuilding of Eretz Israel.

The past and present politics of Israel are taken up in the contributions of Anita Shapira, Dan Miron and Yael Feldman, who all examine aspects of the interaction between Middle Eastern realities and ideology (including creative culture). Anita Shapira has achieved such an intimate knowledge of the thinkers and activists of the Yishuv that she writes as if she had been discussing matters with them just the night before. For an introspective Israeli readership such detail is fascinating and essential. For the outsider it sometimes clutters the argument. This is a pity, since the core of her thesis is very important. According to Shapira, experience radicalized the Jews of Eretz Israel. Conflict with the Palestinian Arabs pushed physical self-defense to the top of the agenda and gradually reworked the popular image of the Palestinian/Israeli Jew. Yet one ingredient is missing in her account of this metamorphosis—the impact of the ghetto fighters and partisans on the development of the idea of the "fighter" that supplanted that of the farmer and worker after the 1940s.

Because literature reflects social realities, the agonies traced by Shapira recur in a different form in the world of belle lettres. Dan Miron shows how cultural heterogeneity defied the powerful Zionist impulse to create a unified Jewish national culture. Yael Feldman suggests that, since 1967, Israeli writers have tended toward subjects suitable for psychological treatment and the exploration of their own identities although, inevitably, the "true" subject has been Israel. This process was largely unexpected and marked a departure from the detachment that characterized earlier writers. The recent fiction of Amos Oz, A. B. Yehoshua and Joshua Sobol, to name a few, has proven enormously fertile, and Feldman's admirable essay constitutes a subtle and exciting introduction.

Only a polymath could do justice to this volume. Each essay merits attention, and one of the most laudable features of the current yearbook is the conscious effort made by the editors to publish the work of evergreen veterans such as Jacob Katz alongside that of newer writers. However, as noted, the editors did not fully carry out their own stated mandate. While possessing a fine eye for quality, they were not critical and adventurous enough in their final selection.

DAVID CESARANI
Institute of Contemporary History
and Wiener Library, London

David Kraemer (ed.), *The Jewish Family: Metaphor and Memory*. New York and Oxford: Oxford University Press, 1989. 248 pp.

This volume is a collection of papers originally delivered at the Jewish Theological Seminary in 1985 that deal with marriage, childhood and the family among the Jews in a wide variety of locations, from ancient times until the modern period. Two papers deal with the talmudic period (none consider the biblical period), four examine the Middle Ages, and six treat topics from the modern period.

Within this last group, Gershon Hundert writes on children and childhood in early modern Poland. He provides a brief but very suggestive survey of the field, tracing as well the life course of the child. Anne Lerner surveys the image of childhood in the works of Isaac Dov Berkowitz and Devorah Baron. Harvey Goldberg writes on family and community in Morocco and Libya, convincingly demonstrating the utility of anthropological approaches in historical studies. Immanuel Etkes's analysis of marriage and Torah study among the elite *mitnagdim* of Eastern Europe deals with the tension between vocation and family. Paula Hyman's thought-provoking paper focuses on the changing role of the Jewish family in the modern period. Robert Alter's article, "Literary Refractions for the Jewish Family," which rounds out the volume, is an interesting study of Kafka, Agnon and Bellow.

The general level of the papers is quite high, and among the participants are some of the most original scholars working in the field. The collection as a whole gives a reasonably accurate picture of the state of research, and since some of the participants publish mainly in Hebrew, this volume is especially useful for the English reader. Most of the papers relate to specific topics and many are excellent case studies. As such they provide a useful introduction to the history of the Jewish family. However, as to be expected from a collection of conference papers, this volume does not provide a synthetic history. Some central topics and themes, such as the place of old people in Jewish family life, are missing from the table of contents and some of the titles promise a bit more than they deliver. An annotated bibliography on the history of the Jewish family would have been useful in eliminating some of these deficiencies. Oddly enough, perhaps the most valuable study on the Jewish family in the past, Leopold Loew's *Die Lebensalter in der juedischen Literatur* (1875), is not cited by any of the authors, which indicates the need for such a bibliography.

Finally, given the nature of the sources, there is a tendency to concentrate on family patterns among members of the elite, and the titles of some of the papers explicitly reflect this concern. The result is therefore somewhat misleading for the reader who does not take this bias into consideration. Future researchers who make broader use of quantitative data, comparative approaches and newer methodologies may well provide a more balanced picture of the Jewish family in the past and present.

SHAUL STAMPFER
The Hebrew University

Eli Lederhendler, *The Road to Modern Jewish Politics: Political Tradition and Political Reconstruction in the Jewish Community of Tsarist Russia*. Oxford and New York: Oxford University Press, 1989. 240 pp.

Modern Jewish historiography has long depicted the south Russian pogroms of 1881–1882 as a watershed in Jewish political development. The pogroms (runs the conventional wisdom) inspired various radical solutions to the plight of East European Jewry—some nationalist, others populist—thus initiating processes that eventually transformed the entire landscape of Jewish political expression and organization.

Cogently argued and elegantly articulated, Eli Lederhendler's book does not quibble with individual segments of that assessment. Its purpose is far more comprehensive and challenging. Acknowledging that a Jewish political "big bang" did take place in 1881–1882, he sets out to analyze the elements existing prior to the explosion that helped condition the resulting responses. To that end, Lederhendler investigates three central issues. First, which precedents existed for prescriptions advocating that Jewish behavior be secular and politically activistic rather than religious and politically quiescent? Second, which channels had already been forged for the communication of such notions? Finally, and perhaps most intriguing of all, on what basis could the handful of intellectuals (generically identified as *maskilim*) who articulated these responses claim to speak on behalf of "the Jewish people," thereby supplanting as political leaders the rabbis and wealthy laymen in whom such authority had traditionally been vested?

Lederhendler finds answers to these questions in the literature of Jewish political polemics of late nineteenth-century Russia. His meticulous review and analysis of that literature enable him to reconstruct the manner in which the *maskilim*, who were still on the periphery of Jewish public life in tsarist Russia in the 1830s and 1840s, managed to project themselves into its very center by the eve of the 1881 pogroms. Adapting and transmuting the roles of "informer," "*shtadlan*" and "social critic," the *maskilim* had already succeeded in shifting the focus of public Jewish attention to the political and material (as opposed to the exclusively spiritual) aspects of the Jewish malaise. During the same period, they likewise developed new institutional channels for the dissemination of their ideas, making particularly adept use of the press (*Hamagid, Hamelitz* and *Hacarmel*), which, in Lederhendler's phrase, provided an embryonic "scaffolding" for the new Jewish politics. Finally, they adopted positions that were to become hallmarks of advanced thinking after 1881: positing the vox populi as the ultimate repository of Jewish authority, and abandoning (certainly by 1879) the emancipatory rhetoric previously in vogue.

In recent years, some of these arguments have already been suggested (albeit in a different fashion and with less emphasis on their institutional and instrumental aspects) by such students of the period as Israel Bartal and Jonathan Frankel, whose works are rightfully acknowledged in Lederhendler's footnotes.[1] Even so, had he rested his case there, Lederhendler's book would have constituted a notable work of scholarship. Let us hope that it will bury once and for all the proposition (already diversely disputed by Daniel Elazar and David Biale) that pre-1881 Jewry lacked an explicitly political culture and strategy. But here, too, the author has a wider setting in mind. Noting recent academic sensitivity to the specifically political dimension of Jewish development, Lederhendler aims to contribute toward that field of inquiry by tracing the precise steps whereby Jewish self-government moved from a medieval to a modern mold.

This concern explains the chronological sweep of Lederhendler's book. He begins with a broad thematic map of the principal pivots of the premodern East European structure of communal politics, emphasizing the reciprocity forged during the late Middle Ages between Jewry's gentile rulers and native network of governors, as exemplified in the "derivative power" enjoyed by the *kahal*. His second chapter then shows how, during the 120 years before 1880, that structure disintegrated under the twin assaults of external pressure (culminating in the abolition of the *kahal* in 1844) and internal fragmentation (typified by the spread of Hasidism and the emergence of a new, urban Jewish intelligentsia). Lederhendler argues that these challenges had two main consequences. First, they provoked massive changes in Jewish political attitudes, which he illustrates by reviewing early nineteenth-century Jewish reactions to smuggling and to conscription. Second, and in his view even more portentously, they created a structural vacuum at the very crux of Jewish public life. This was filled when new leadership roles were formulated by (self-appointed) political leaders of a new type—the aforementioned *maskilim*.

Lederhendler is far too sophisticated a historian to exaggerate the suddenness of these shifts, even during the century of crisis that preceded the trauma of 1881. Indeed, he explicitly rejects the dichotomous perspective that clearly distinguishes periods of stasis from those of change. Jewish "modernity," he stresses, was characterized by accelerated development, not revolution; it permitted traditional structures to linger on (certainly in memory). That being the case, the challenge to analysts boils down to one of measurement: How much of the new ideological and institutional wine came out of, or was poured into, old structural bottles?

Lederhendler's self-proclaimed wariness of "pure theory" seems to have impeded his search for frameworks that might provide the appropriate gauge. This is a pity, since the information that he has himself amassed does lend itself to wider projections clamoring for at least some recognition. One longitudinal example is provided by East European reactions before 1881 to the significant advances made by Western Jewry in decidedly "modern" forms of political organization and expression. As Lederhendler notes (pp. 108, 127), the *maskilim* with whom he is concerned were aware that Moses Montefiore and Adolphe Crémieux (as well as the institutions they headed) had set new standards of Jewish political behavior. However, he does not examine how closely the programs of the *maskilim* approximated these earlier precedents.

In view of his own interest in the resilience of traditional patterns, Lederhendler's reluctance to draw latitudinal inferences from his materials is more regrettable. The *maskilim*, he notes, portrayed themselves as a third force in Jewish public life, separate from—and sometimes opposed to—the rabbis and the notables. Perceptively, he also points out that in so doing they were following paths already trodden by such earlier social critics as the *maggidim* inspired by the *musar* movement (pp. 120–122). Could it not be suggested, however, that the roots went even deeper, reaching back, even if only symbolically and subliminally, to a far more ancient tradition already established by the speculative thinkers of the High Middle Ages (e.g., the *Hasidei Ashkenaz*) and even the biblical prophets?[2]

To make such points is in no way to criticize Lederhendler's enterprise. On the contrary, not the least of the merits of his admirable book is that, notwithstanding its concentrated focus, it stimulates inquiries of a digressive nature. Thus, quite apart from making a substantial contribution to modern Jewish history, *The Road to Modern Jewish Politics* also deserves recognition as a thought-provoking essay on the broader canvas of Jewish political traditions and their adaptation.

STUART A. COHEN
Bar-Ilan University

Notes

1. The symbiosis between literati and the political public is also discussed in D. Miron, "Miyoẓrim uvonim lebanim beli bayit" in his *Im lo tihyeh Yerushalayim* (Tel-Aviv: 1987). Particularly relevant for our period are pp. 17–24.

2. For an analysis of the self-conscious adoption of the prophetic role in *Haskalah* poetry, see T. Cohen, "Mishaliaḥ ẓibur lenavi: gilgulei tefilot unevuot beshirat hahaskalah," *Bar-Ilan Annual*, 24–25 (Ramat-Gan: 1989), 61–82.

Yaakov Oved, *Two Hundred Years of American Communes*. New Brunswick, N.J.: Transaction Books, 1988. 500 pp.

It has been said that as a subject of social research only the American Indian reservations attract more attention than the kibbutz. Indeed, not only the kibbutz but communes in general have been studied extensively, as is apparent from a glance at the detailed bibliography included in Yaakov Oved's book. Somewhat surprisingly, however, in Israel itself the research on communes per se is little developed, which makes this work particularly welcome.

Oved follows the lead of others who have studied communes in the United States from the eighteenth century onward, presenting both firsthand impressions and historical research. This combination is admirable: As a historian, Oved's research is sound, and his scholarly grasp of the subject allowed him to make perceptive choices about what to look for and with whom to speak in his travels throughout the United States. Oved identifies 270 communes and deals with some 70 of them in the framework of a comprehensive historical analysis. His book is divided into various sections, one of which focuses on "the significance and implications of communal life for kibbutzim in Israel." This format permits a comparative analysis of the lifestyle of these communes, their struggle for existence and (in many cases) their dissolution.

The definition of a commune is a matter of weighty scholarly controversy. We may begin by saying that a commune is the voluntary association of a group of people interested in a life of sharing and mutual responsibility. It follows that we are not dealing with a "community of convicts" or a teachers' committee, or with such phenomena as the *kolkhozy* in the Soviet Union or the popular communes in China. Second, we must assume that such people decide to live together out of some affinity or belief, practicing the principles of equality, solidarity and cooperative conflict resolution in a setting apart from, and in contrast with, the surrounding society that is based on private property and competition.

Most of the communes discussed in this book are notable for their isolation and adherence to the Christian communal tradition. The decision to implement "ideology and beliefs through a communal lifestyle" is both the raison d'être of the communes and their greatest difficulty. A voluntary and egalitarian way of life at odds with the capitalistic society around it must be constantly reinforced; if not, the commune's disintegration and dissolution are inevitable. Communes cannot thrive on halfway solutions: Remove their very essence, and they fall apart. The accounts of various American communes, told here in a polished style and from a fund of great knowledge, offer incisive evidence for this thesis, and the lessons are clearly relevant for Israeli kibbutzim as well.

Oved deals at length with the problem of the seclusionist tendencies manifest in the history of the communes, showing that this was partly a result of the historical realities of the American frontier. At the same time, however, commune members who belonged to persecuted religious or political (e.g., socialist) sects turned their seclusion into a blessing by developing an elitist approach to their social surroundings. This approach held the group together at the outset when it was faced with the tremendous difficulties of settling unknown country—a phase that similarly characterized the early stage of kibbutz settlements although, as Martin Buber once noted, the kibbutz movement became an "experiment that did not fail" precisely because of its involvement in the problems of the Yishuv as a whole.

The "millenarian doctrine" and notions of "perfectability" as characteristics of model societies are also discussed here, although Oved might have given greater emphasis to commune members' perceptions of the alienation and degeneration caused by modern bourgeois society. It was the resulting desire to overcome these phenomena that impelled many good people to attempt a different communal lifestyle (see, for example, A. Barzel's *Midot hayaḥad* [1984] and Benjamin Zablocki's *Alienation and Charisma* [1980]).

A central problem in communes is that of continuity. Unlike the surrounding society, the communal life-style is not spontaneous and cannot be taken for granted. Precisely for this reason, the kibbutz can learn much from the account of daily life in the communes described here. How, for example, did the wish for shared family sleeping quarters influence the relationship between the family and the commune? And what parallels can be drawn, on the one hand, between the relationship of the kibbutz and the surrounding society and, on the other hand, the attitudes of the U.S. judicial system toward cooperative groups?

Finally, Oved's book offers insights concerning the development of pluralism within the kibbutz movement—a trend that has resulted not only in greater scope for differing political beliefs but also in an emergent competition between trends within this social microcosm. Oved's book is a masterly survey of the "world of communes" that includes the kibbutzim and that has a historical lesson for every actual experiment in collective life.

AVRAHAM YASSOUR
University of Haifa
Kibbutz Merhavia

Yoav Peled, *Class and Ethnicity in the Pale: The Political Economy of Jewish Workers' Nationalism in Late Imperial Russia.* Houndmills and London: Macmillan, 1989. xii + 171 pp.

The core of this very dense and compact book is a fresh evaluation of what is by now a fairly old scholarly and a very old political debate. The topic of that debate is the retreat of leaders of the Jewish Bund (the General Union of Jewish Workers in Lithuania, Poland and Russia) from their original self-identification as members of a militantly secular, class-based, internationalist movement with little use for Jewish national consciousness and their adoption by the early 1900s of a political identity that, while still both secular and anti-Zionist, placed a positive value on Jewish ethnicity and Yiddish culture, as illustrated by the Bund's adoption of the Austrian socialist notion of national-cultural autonomy. Although the issue is too complex and difficult to confine to merely two positions, scholarly sides may be roughly divided into a camp that has favored social or (Peled's preference) sociological explanation and a much smaller camp, almost reducible to one prodigious scholar (Jonathan Frankel), that has favored a political-ideological, almost antisociological approach. Or to put it somewhat differently, the sides consist of those who (like the Bundists themselves) see the Bund's attitudinal shift as determined by the party's growing involvement with the mass of Yiddish-speaking workers in the Pale and those who see it as essentially an episode in the internal history of a partially Russified Jewish socialist intelligentsia (especially those intellectuals who lived, studied and were influenced by events from abroad).

In addition to being intrinsically interesting to historians, whether specialists in Russian/East European history or specialists in Jewish history, both the debate and the book have contemporary resonance, if only for the obvious reason that the issue of national consciousness and assertiveness is now so alive and well (or sometimes alive and unwell). The debate also echoes the ongoing controversy over whether or not the gnarly history of the Soviet Union is better comprehended in the context of social history—Bolshevik leaders, at least in the early years of the Soviet Union, in some sense representing the sentiments of large segments of the urban working class, for example—or, alternatively, as a story of the political ideology of an intellectual elite in power. As someone who believes that neither alternative is satisfactory in isolation from the other, I read Peled's book with sympathy for his heroic effort, partially successful, to break with the binary mode of conceptualization that has characterized the discussion of Bund history and develop a fresh approach to the problem.

Peled's preferred solution is not so much to synthesize the best parts of the sociological and the political-intellectual explanations as to introduce analytical tools from the outside, mainly from the field of political economy, or, to be more precise, from an imaginative blend of Marxist political economy, contemporary labor economics and political sociology. (The reader is referred to Peled's book for the esoteric language in which the concepts of these disciplines are often couched.) After explaining politely and respectfully (but with some oversimplification of their positions) what he sees as the fatal flaws in the competing schools that have dominated the discussion—often using their mutual criticism to good effect—Peled offers his own explanatory model for the Bund's change of direction and the willingness of so many Jewish workers to adhere to it.

Before getting to his argument, I should point out that, despite its brevity, Peled's book also includes an excellent summary of the historical setting in which the Jewish labor movement functioned, a close analysis of the evolution of the Bund's program in all its various tergiversations, a condensed comparison with the Jewish labor movements of England and America, and an opening chapter that presents in advance the conceptual framework that Peled will later use in offering his alternative to the conventional wisdom(s). The chapters on background and program are highly derivative; though Peled has clearly mastered the primary sources himself, he probably could not have written them without the work of other fine historians, American and Israeli, to build on (Henry Tobias, Ezra Mendelsohn, and of course Frankel). To his credit, Peled is generous in his acknowledgements of their important contributions, even while seeing serious defects in all their interpretive schemes.

What, then, is the gist of Peled's argument? It hinges on a modified version of what he refers to as split labor market theory and the model of internal colonialism. For want of space I will sidestep the colonialism part, which in any case I found quite strained, and focus instead on what I take to be the key to his analysis, the split labor market. According to his application of this model, Christian (i.e., Russian, Polish, Ukrainian, etc.—Peled barely distinguishes among them) and Jewish workers entered the labor market with differential assets and liabilities. Most of the Jews were handicraft workers, whose traditional work habits (artisanal) and way of life (religious, e.g., keeping the Sabbath, a workday for other workers) made them less appealing as workers to the owners of modern, mechanized enterprises than were their Christian, mainly semipeasant rivals. Similarly, the Jewish workers' relative independence and generally higher cultural level turned them into less pliant, more rebellious employees, frequently causing even Jewish employers to opt for less "costly" non-Jewish labor. Under these circumstances, class struggle alone was proving inadequate to the Jewish workers' collective needs.

Some of this has been said already by Mendelsohn and others (though in a less social scientific idiom), but Peled has a fresh and convincing way of using the argument to explain the resurgence of ethnicity, of national sentiment and resentment, among the Jewish masses (though not among the smaller group of organized, educated, "conscious" socialist workers that began by resisting the nationalist trend). To some extent, then, he ends up fairly close to the social explanation school (hence the subtitle of Chapter 5: "Bringing Sociology Back In"), but *his* social explanation is different. It rejects what he calls, borrowing from Clifford Geertz, "primordialism" (both Bundist and Zionist variants) as a basic explanation of national consciousness wherein ethnic attachments are said to be posited as a given, a natural aspect of the Jewish (perhaps the human) condition that forced its way upward into the consciousness of Bund leaders after they had shifted to mass agitation. Instead, Peled gives that consciousness what some would still call a *material* base (the term is no longer fashionable, but Peled's notion of a material base is sophisticated, in tune with contemporary social science, less Marxist than *marxisant*). This makes it possible for him to redefine the Jewish workers of the Pale as neither purely a class nor purely an ethnos but as an "ethnic class fraction" with "ethno-class consciousness." The Bund, if I read him correctly, became an expression of the hyphenated being of its own constituency.

Has Peled made a plausible case? I found most of his argument quite convincing, and certainly plausible enough to encourage the inclusion of his book on the shelves of specialized scholars in several fields (Russian history, Jewish history, labor history, political sociology); given its important subject matter and its brevity, it may even earn the attention of nonspecialists and lay readers. If the book has a serious shortcoming, an aspect that requires and that should provoke further discussion, it is its failure to probe in depth such questions as how it is that in the modern world (many examples may also be found outside the Pale), when objective conditions such as a split labor market are present, the elective affinity between market position and preexisting religious, racial and ethnic divisions arose in the first place; why so many people seem so ready so quickly to accept ethnically based explanations of their place in those markets; why it is that ethnic identification so often has the strength and staying power to prevail even when the kind of socioeconomic constraints Peled describes so well have ceased to obtain. I suspect that the quest for answers to such questions will be aided at least as much by social psychology and cultural anthropology as by labor economics.

REGINALD E. ZELNIK
University of California at Berkeley

Moshe Shokeid, *Children of Circumstances: Israeli Emigrants in New York.* Ithaca: Cornell University Press, 1988. 226 pp.

This book explores the unique character of the emerging ethnicity of expatriate Israelis living in the New York City borough of Queens. In a thought-provoking study written in an elegantly readable style, the author describes the uniqueness of the Israeli migrants whose motives for emigration were not predominantly economic yet who now find themselves suffering from homesickness, loneliness and alienation—stigmatized both by their compatriots at home and by their potential coethnics, the New York Jewish community. Shokeid offers us some illuminating insights into how they cope with this dual stigmatization and its consequences for the structure and content of their lives. No less importantly, he also points to the disparity in modern Jewish identity between native Israelis and diaspora Jews.

This book is based on data collected by participant observation while the author was living in Queens between 1982 and 1984. Shokeid's sample consists of 116 family research units (a total of 174 individuals, when spouses are included). Such a sample is certainly small; Shokeid himself acknowledges that it is clearly not representative of some of the broad strata of Israeli emigration, especially the large number of young, unmarried migrants who have settled in New York. The study's limitations, however, are more than made up for by its in-depth analysis of this particular stratum of middle-class emigrants.

Although Shokeid does not deal at length with his respondents' motives for emigrating, his sample does tend to validate other data found in the literature on Israeli emigration. Ashkenazim in his sample are generally employed in the free professions, whereas Sephardim are concentrated in business and small industries. Moreover, most of the respondents seem to have come to America in pursuit of professional, economic or educational advancement.

According to Shokeid, the Israeli subculture in his sample is characterized by its "submerged" or, at later stages, "affective" ethnicity. In other words, the group has a common cultural language but a minimum of organizational structure even for the expression of this very commonality. Most surprisingly, perhaps, Shokeid reports the existence of no additional characteristics of ethnic affiliation of the type that studies of American Jewry—or ethnicity for that matter—often refer to. On the one hand, Israelis neither affiliate nor integrate with American Jews, even though many of them share not only a common religion but also a shared ethnic ancestry, usually in Eastern Europe. On the other hand, they do not establish a community organization of their own. Why is this so? Shokeid's answer to this question constitutes the strongest section of his book as he goes beyond his direct subject matter to a more general analysis of American Jewish ethnicity.

Before presenting Shokeid's own answer, it may be useful to spell out the implicit comparison between Jewish identity in Israel and in North America. In Israel, almost all major aspects of Jewish culture and discourse take place in the national public domain. The synagogue, at best, is designated for worship and personal rites of passage; at worst, it becomes the agency for the political secular fight in the Israeli polis, where the rabbinic courtyard often becomes an interest group seeking its own material and ideological gain, often in confrontation with nonreligious Jews. In American Jewish society, in contrast, the synagogue is the major place where identified Jews engage in Jewish discourse and where Jewish values are developed. There is thus a significant disparity between the subjective secular, quasi-national Jewish identity of many Israelis—especially the Ashkenazim—and the synagogue-based ethnoreligious identity of American Jews.

Israelis in America, Shokeid argues, cannot transfer their identification with the Jewish state to an identification with the religious basis of American Judaism. Moreover, beyond the religious question, their own Israeliness is based on a denial of the diaspora. They are alienated from diaspora Jews both ideologically and socially, and the feeling appears to be mutual. As Shokeid notes, "Each reminds the other of what they would wish to be and of the fact that they cannot reconcile themselves to the price involved in the attainment of these goals" (p. 50). For Israelis to join Jewish diaspora institutions is both to reject the basis of their national

Jewish identity and an admission of guilt concerning their departure from Israel. All this, in addition to their perceived rejection by American Jews, leads Israelis to refrain from affiliating—not with American Jews, and not even among themselves. From the standpoint of collective survival they appear to be living in a most disastrous situation of alienation. One cannot be a believing Israeli in the diaspora—only a believing Jew. The Israelis therefore respond by downgrading both other *yordim* and other Jews while continuing to maintain an anonymous affective/sentimental attachment to Israel—rootless in practice, as it is based on Hebrew culture even though their own children are mostly being raised with English as a mother tongue.

Following his presentation of the "stigma paradigm" as the basis for the Israeli diaspora condition, Shokeid outlines a series of relatively weak and unstable responses that Israelis offer to this condition. Some opt for what Herbert Gans has called symbolic ethnicity, expressed through song and anonymous voluntary and usually discontinuous participation in poorly organized "Israeli" social clubs. Many adults continue to read Hebrew newspapers. And some, usually Sephardic Israelis, choose a more "Jewish" option and seek quasi-conversion opportunities in the synagogue community, especially those offered by Chabad.

Shokeid also succeeds in showing how the Israelis differ not only from their American Jewish hosts but also from other Jewish migrant groups such as Soviet and South African Jews—and, indeed, from other non-Jewish migrant groups in the contemporary American migrant stream. The conjunction of phenomenological and deviance theory with migration theory provided by Shokeid in this regard is both fruitful and insightful.

However, while the author himself actually acknowledges the discontinuity of his own analysis of Israelis in Queens with that of the society of origin, it seems that this caveat is itself too abrupt for comfort. Shokeid's discussion might have been enhanced by a more comprehensive discussion of the nature of Israeli Jewish identity, informed by the same sensitive phenomenological perspective he brings to the examination of Israelis in New York and their American Jewish counterparts. One is left wondering to what extent the range of diversity of Israeli Jewishness influences the Jewishness of Israelis in America. In addition, his rather blunt analysis that Israel has categorically transformed traditional Judaism (p. 135)—not incorrect as far as it goes—is not given a theoretical base and thus appears to be more in the nature of an ideological assertion.

These small flaws notwithstanding, the work under review is to be highly recommended for students of ethnicity and of Israeli and American Jewish identity. The richness of Shokeid's anthropological investigation is a model for all students of contemporary Israeli and American Jewish life.

DAVID MITTELBERG
University of Haifa

Zionism, Israel and the Middle East

Michel Abitbol, *Les Deux Terres promises: les juifs de France et le sionisme*. Paris: Olivier Orban, 1989. 298 pp.

Though a few recent studies have attempted to examine the attitudes of the French government and French Jewry toward the state of Israel, Michel Abitbol's book is the first work to investigate the impact of Zionism in France in the period before the emergence of the Jewish state. His is not an easy task. Given the contemporary French Jewish community's strong attachment to Israel, it may come as a surprise to many to learn that for much of its history Zionism had only limited appeal to French Jewry. As Abitbol demonstrates, from the inception of the Zionist movement at the end of the nineteenth century to the outbreak of war in 1939, most French Jews were convinced that the ideology and activity of Jewish nationalists undermined their community's assimilationist ideals and sabotaged its efforts to defend Jewish interests through quiet diplomacy. As a result, Zionist movements in France before the Second World War tended to find their greatest support among elements such as East European immigrants, disgruntled youth and radicals, all of whom rejected the attitudes and policies of the established Jewish community.

Nor did Zionist ideals occasion much interest among the French public in the period covered by Abitbol's book. The absence of a religious biblicist tradition in French society and the popular association of Zionism with German Jewry and Germany in general meant that France never developed a strong movement of Christian Palestinophilism such as those that existed in England and Germany in the nineteenth century. In turn, French political leaders were generally unreceptive to the demands of Zionist activists in the period preceding the Second World War. Highly sensitive to Arab nationalist interests and to the concerns of the Catholic Church over the fate of the holy places in Jerusalem, government officials tended to view the idea of a Jewish homeland as a "Communist" intervention of radical East European Jews that was championed by the British to further their own Middle East policy. Indeed, the only consistently enthusiastic supporters within French society of Jewish settlement in Palestine were antisemites such as Charles Drumont, who envisioned the mass exodus of Jews as signaling the end of the latter's "stranglehold" on the nation's political and economic life.

While recognizing that French society remained generally unresponsive to Zionism before 1948, Abitbol suggests that its significance in French international policy in the period after the First World War has been overlooked by historians. In particular, the author reveals how during the first decade after the war French government leaders were convinced that Zionists had a major influence upon diplomatic negotiations over the fate of the Middle East. Of special interest are Abitbol's discussions of the activity of Sylvain Lévi, who acted as a quasi-official government representative responsible for assessing the impact of Zionism upon other Jewish communities, and of the so-called "Special Section on Religious Affairs" created at the Quai d'Orsay in 1925 to monitor the activities of the Zionist movement.

At the same time, Abitbol convincingly argues that—largely as a result of the Arab riots of 1929, the rise of Nazism and the proclamation of the British White Paper in 1939—Zionists began to show more interest in France. As events in Europe and Palestine worsened, Zionist leaders increasingly looked to France as an important counter both to Arab nationalism and British obstructionism. In the end, however, little came of such efforts since France refused to restrict the activity of Arab nationalists in Lebanon and Syria and proved unwilling to alienate its British ally as the danger of war became more imminent.

Following closely the works of Paula Hyman, Richard Cohen and David Weinberg, Abitbol also argues that events in Europe and Palestine in the 1930s made French Jews more sympathetic to Jewish settlement in Palestine. Though never pro-Zionist, French Jewish leaders such as Rabbi Jacob Kaplan began to realize in the late 1930s that the Yishuv could play an important role as an asylum for refugees. Such attitudes were reinforced by the general questioning of assimilationist assumptions that marked French Jewish discussion in the waning days of peace.

If there is a major gap in the work, it is the author's failure to examine the Zionist movement in France and its largely Yiddish press in the 1930s. Though Abitbol is correct in pointing out that membership in Zionist organizations in France was largely restricted to East European Jews and that much of their activity was characterized by bitter ideological and personality squabbles, he understates the impact of Zionist movements upon French society in the decade before the outbreak of the Second World War. Zionist-led immigrant groups such as the *Fédération des sociétés juives de France* and Zionist-oriented newspapers such as *Pariser Haint* created an ideological framework that responded to the growing despair felt by the immigrant Jewish majority in the community, while at the same time bringing the plight of Jewish refugees to the attention of both French Jewry and the French government. Zionist youth movements in the 1920s and 1930s were also instrumental in the growing accommodation between native and immigrant sons and daughters, a development that paved the way for coordinated activity among young Jews during Vichy and after the war. Indeed, Abitbol seems to accept the significance of this development in his disappointingly brief concluding chapter of the book, which discusses the central role played by Zionist activists in the French Jewish resistance during the Second World War.

Despite these shortcomings, Abitbol is to be commended for tackling a difficult subject. Though only mildly influential at the time, the rhetoric and activity of Franco-Zionism before the Second World War played no small role in the revitalization of the French Jewish community after the Holocaust, as well as the growing involvement of France in the fate of Israel in the postwar era.

DAVID WEINBERG
Bowling Green State University

Shlomo Avineri, *Arlosoroff.* London: Weidenfeld & Nicolson, 1989. 126 pp.

Shlomo Avineri's study of Hayim Arlosoroff is part of a new series on *Jewish Thinkers* (ranging from Rashi to David Ben-Gurion) edited by Arthur Hertzberg. If Avineri's concise and provocative introduction to Arlosoroff's political thought and practice is any indication, we shall soon have a number of up-to-date, highly readable and stimulating studies of seminal Jewish figures.

Avineri opens the story of Arlosoroff's life with its tragic climax in 1933, when he was murdered at the age of thirty-four. The rising labor Zionist star then headed the Political Department of the Jewish Agency and had just returned from Europe with plans to negotiate a "transfer agreement" with Nazi authorities to facilitate the immigration of German Jews to Palestine with part of their capital. Because the arrangement promoted trade between Germany and Palestine, Zionist Revisionists considered it an act of treason and launched inflammatory verbal diatribes against Arlosoroff. For this reason, suspicion for the murder fell on them. *L'Affaire Arlosoroff,* as Avineri calls it, widened the emotional rift between Revisionists and Labor Zionists, with accusations and counteraccusations continuing well into the present. Labor Zionists have long considered Arlosoroff a martyr to Jewish nationalist extremism. For Avineri as well, the murder of Arlosoroff has symbolic resonance; in his view, Israel—now led by Revisionism's successors— has abandoned Arlosoroff's pragmatism and moderation for a reckless chauvinism.

Avineri considers Arlosoroff an original social thinker of major stature, and early in the book he states his intention of concentrating on Arlosoroff's social theory over his political practice. Arlosoroff's originality as a thinker, Avineri believes, stems from his ability to combine formative intellectual influences—Marxism, Russian populism, Peter Kropotkin's communitarian anarchism, German *völkisch* thought— with a profound understanding of the special needs and circumstances of Jewry. In Arlosoroff's view, Jews fit nowhere in the conventional Marxist strategy since they lacked both a proletariat and a ruling capitalist class, were alienated from primary production, were culturally dominated in the diaspora and were victimized and hated mainly as Jews rather than as workers or as capitalists. Jews could participate in building socialism only by reconstructing their society and national culture in the land of Israel. Arlosoroff advocated the gradual development of an autonomous Jewish economy and society through socialist means: a strong public sector, cooperative economic forms and egalitarian standards of consumption. Shrewdly assessing the limits of Jewish power, he believed in the gradual development of an autonomous Jewish infrastructure, with Jewish labor anchored to the soil, and he was critical of the Revisionists' resort to the empty show of force and to aggressive demands for British favor.

Such views were mainstream Labor Zionist positions, and it is hard to see why Avineri presses the claim for Arlosoroff's originality. More fascinating and provocative is Avineri's discussion of Arlosoroff's pragmatic *raison d'état.* Undeniably, credit for the founding of a Jewish state is due to Labor Zionism's socialist humanism and pragmatic moderation, of which Arlosoroff was an exemplary practitioner.

For Avineri, what is striking about Arlosoroff is his supple pragmatism in the service of national ends. This was evident in his opposition to the Revisionist "politics of bravura" and "bloated programme of gestures" exemplified in such actions as Betar's attempt to enlarge Jewish rights of access to the Western Wall, which Arlosoroff believed had sparked the riots of 1929 and had needlessly united the entire Arab world against Zionism. All this could only interfere with the incremental creation of a strategic base for Jewish power through socialist "constructivism."

Arlosoroff's pragmatism did not always dictate nonconfrontational strategies. In a letter to Chaim Weizmann in 1932 (made public only in 1949), Arlosoroff seriously considered the option of a Jewish seizure of power and minority dictatorship in Palestine. He apparently feared that British concessions to Palestinian nationalism would abort Jewish efforts to gradually alter the demographic balance in the country and establish contiguous settlements on the land. In spite of Arlosoroff's openness to minority dictatorship, Avineri is doubtless correct in arguing that he would have favored partition in 1938, more feasible by then with the doubling of the Jewish population from that of 1932. Arlosoroff was after all unconstrained by the inflexible and grandiose Revisionist dream of a Greater Israel. As another example of his pragmatism, although an advocate of A. D. Gordon and Kropotkin's communitarian anarchism, Arlosoroff in 1933 advised Zionists to enter the increasingly powerful British state structure in Palestine, lest Jews find themselves possessed of an autonomous society and economy without any experience in wielding the levers of state power. Even Ben-Gurion criticized Arlosoroff at this time for such "statist heresy."

Avineri argues that contemporary Israel has gone astray by abandoning the pragmatic ideology of founders such as Arlosoroff. As additional evidence, he points to Arlosoroff's criticism of those who make fetishes of holy places, his early recognition of Palestinian nationalism as an authentic national liberation movement, his sobriety and moderation, and his distrust of the overreliance on force.

The case for recalling Israel to the Arlosoroff heritage, and similarly for blaming right-wing Zionist ideologies for Israel's current situation, is highly debatable. Avineri mitigates Arlosoroff's tough realism by amiably characterizing it as a social idealist's lack of naivete. Israel's problems are an outgrowth of a series of harsh choices, and Arlosoroff, from what Avineri tells us of his record, probably would have endorsed most of them.

Surely Arlosoroff would have abandoned his pastoral anarchistic social visions and supported—if only as a harsh necessity—Ben-Gurion's postindependence policy of statism and the elimination of socialism's vanguard role in the economy and in public education. This too was pragmatic *raison d'état,* no less than the socialist "constructivism" of the 1920s and 1930s. In view of Israel's heterogeneous population with the influx of Jews from Arab lands after 1948, Ben-Gurion correctly recognized that only statism and a Judaic revival could create the Israeli nation. It was thus Labor Zionism that dismantled Israel's socialist heritage. It was Ben-Gurion, not the heirs of Revisionism, who attacked the kibbutzim as a "socialist aristocracy" for refusing to take on Sephardic hired labor (Mitchell Cohen, *Zion and State* [1987]).

Similarly, we now know from Benny Morris's research that Ben-Gurion favored the compulsory "transfer" of the Palestinian population from a partitioned Jewish state at the time of the Peel Commission proposals in 1937 (*The Birth of the Palestinian Refugee Problem, 1947–1949* [1987]). Arlosoroff might well have shared this view. If he seriously considered a minority Zionist dictatorship in 1932, Arlosoroff probably would have supported the expulsion of Palestinian populations during the War of Independence as a dire necessity of national survival. One cannot blame Zionist Revisionists for the future consequences of these many decisions, necessary as they may have been.

Avineri recalls Israelis to the Arlosoroff legacy, but even by the late 1930s, with the nonsocialist bourgeois German emigration that had doubled the Yishuv's population, that legacy could no longer serve as a unifying basis for nation-building. On the other hand, Arlosoroff's heritage of idealism and unflinching pragmatism remains alive among some Israelis today, and Avineri is right in insisting on its vital importance to the future of the country.

JACQUES KORNBERG
University of Toronto

Uriel Dann (ed.), *The Great Powers in the Middle East 1919–1939*. Dayan Center for Middle Eastern and African Studies. New York and London: Holmes & Meier, 1988. viii + 434 pp.

This is a collection of twenty-eight papers delivered at a symposium convened by the late Uriel Dann, professor of history, held at Tel-Aviv University in May 1982.

Proceedings of conferences are frequently diffuse—more in the nature of collected rather than collective papers—and highlight certain aspects of the selected subject to the detriment of others. However, it is a reviewer's duty to inspect rather than expect the results. In the present case, the outcome seems better than in many others, probably as a result of Dann's able editing, in addition to the merits of the actual participants who came from Israel, the United Kingdom, France, the United States, Canada, West Germany and Egypt.

The main subjects discussed are Britain and the Arabian sphere; British policies in Egypt and Palestine; French involvement; Great Powers on the sidelines; the Italian, American, German and Soviet involvement; and regional responses from the northern tier and the Arab world, respectively. A brilliantly written conclusion by Bernard Lewis is followed by an index of persons (an index of subjects, not provided, would also have been useful). Although such volumes cannot be all-inclusive, the absence of any paper dealing with the Jewish Yishuv is noteworthy— although perhaps not surprising. Many scholars researching the twentieth-century Middle East avoid dealing with the Yishuv (and, sometimes, the state it established) in their discussion of the region, though such an omission is less understandable in the case of a conference convened at an Israeli university.

While several other works on the topic of this symposium are available, its attempt at an overall reappraisal of ideologies, policies, decision-making and responses yields some refreshing new insights. Elie Kedourie and several other participants persuasively argue that in the United Kingdom a diminishing collective will to govern was a significant factor in undermining the British position. This contrasts with the assertiveness demonstrated both by France throughout the interwar period and by Italy during the 1930s. The reasons for the limited involvement of Nazi Germany and the Soviet Union are less easy to grasp from this volume. In the case of the Soviet Union, such lack of involvement is particularly hard to understand, given both its tangible interests in the region and the resolve necessary to promote them.

Responses in the Middle East to foreign involvement are dealt with somewhat unevenly. A. Shmuelevitz's article on Ataturk's policy toward the Great Powers is all too brief (pp. 311–316, including the footnotes) and fails to discuss adequately the important switch in Turkey's foreign policy in the 1930s that resulted from its suspicion of Italy's intentions. In contrast, Israel Gershoni provides a much more comprehensive treatment of the image of the West and its rejection by the Muslim Brotherhood in Egypt, which militantly interpreted Western ideology as a counter-image of Islam that was therefore to be condemned. Ami Ayalon's examination of the attitudes of Egyptian intellectuals to fascism and Nazism, expressed in various writings of the period, yields some interesting material on the intelligentsia's widely divergent views. Ayalon's conclusion that "the voices of democracy's champions were louder than its critics" (p. 402) is heartening; one might consider his words a tribute of sorts—perhaps an unintended one—to the British and French impact in the Middle East during the interwar era.

JACOB M. LANDAU
The Hebrew University

Abraham Diskin, *Elections and Voters in Israel*. New York: Praeger, 1991. xiv+213 pp.

It is a regrettable fact that too many people, including quite a few social scientists and politicians, argue about elections, voters' behavior, survey research and electoral reforms without understanding either the issues or the rudiments of voting theory. This book is therefore a welcome addition to the literature because it discusses in depth some of the pertinent issues relating to elections and voters in Israel, thereby exposing as well some myths and fallacies.

The book is empirically oriented and very informative, with many references to voting research both in Israel and abroad. It is clearly written and accessible to readers within and outside political science, although some of the constructs of voting theory and survey research are described inaccurately.

Apart from the introduction, which introduces the reader to some basic concepts in voting theory and to Arrow's impossibility theorem (often labeled in the literature as "the paradox of voting"), the book consists of nine chapters. Chapter 1 is a presentation of the main results of all twelve general elections held to date in Israel, with the author outlining the main political events and background issues in each of these elections. In Chapter 2, the author describes the current Israeli electoral system and its practical and legal aspects, as well as associated social-choice problems and some alternatives to the system that have been proposed during the years. Despite the wealth of detail supplied in this chapter, the author does not explain why the political parties of the Yishuv chose the (pure) proportional list system of electing representatives (which continues to be the current electoral system), despite the fact that almost all other aspects of the Israeli parliamentary system parallel those existing in England. Moreover, the theoretical presentation and discussion of proportional voting in this chapter is partial; although the author presents the various techniques that are currently used in proportional voting, he fails to discuss the basic normative standard underlying the theory of proportional representation.

It is true that the principle of proportionality means that "groups with the same size of voters should be represented in the elected body by an identical number of representatives" (p. 55). However, it does not follow that proportionality is achieved either by dividing the valid votes by a quota (e.g., Droop's quota) or by dividing the valid votes that each list of candidates receives by some set of values determined in advance (e.g., d'Hondt's method [pp. 55–57]). The reason for this is simple: The number of votes a list of candidates receives is not independent of the balloting rule under which voters operate—it is quite possible that the proportion of votes a party receives will be quite different when voters can vote for only one party as opposed to being able to support more than one party (e.g., under approval voting, where voters may vote for as many parties as they approve of, provided they cast only one vote for each of these parties). Proportionality therefore implies that each party should receive a number of seats in a representative assembly that reflects, as closely as possible, the ratios of the number of voters preferring that party over each of its rivals. Serious difficulties are encountered in attempting to determine the desired proportions, but the reader of this chapter is not made aware of these difficulties or the possible ways of resolving them.

The remaining seven chapters deal with voters' behavior. Chapter 3 exemplifies the use of aggregate data in analyzing voting patterns in defined geographical units. It is shown that Israeli urban voters are very unlikely to change the party they support from one election to the next, that different parties are supported by different types of voters—some by voters who have similar socioeconomic attributes and others by voters who have dissimilar attributes—and that the main social attribute that determines how voters are going to vote is their ethnic background. Chapters 4–7 are based on sample data. In Chapter 4 (the Arab vote) and Chapter 5 (the Jewish ethnic vote), the connection between voting and country of origin/social-ethnic background is emphasized, whereas Chapter 6 (party stands, polarization and volatility) and Chapter 7 (accuracy in polls and timing the decision for whom to vote) contain discussions of the processes that shape voting on both the individual and national levels. Chapter 7 is especially interesting. As the author was the Labor party pollster during the 1984 election campaign, he is able here to provide unique and revealing "behind-the-scenes" testimony concerning the ways in which polls are used by political decision makers during election campaigns. Chapters 8 and 9 present an analysis of two main aspects of elections—how parties nominate their candidates for election, and various characteristics of the resultant Israeli coali-

tions—thereby broadening and summarizing the general historical survey introduced in Chapter 1.

A key feature of Israeli politics is the continuing phenomenon of coalition governments that in several cases have lacked a pivotal party. Despite the danger of
instability that may be associated with such coalitions and despite the incessant calls
for changing the Israeli electoral system, Diskin's book provides hard evidence that
this system has been very stable. Overall, the book is highly recommended.

DAN S. FELSENTHAL
University of Haifa

Binyamin Eliav, *Zikhronot min hayamin (Memories of the Right)*. Ed. Danny
Rubinstein. Tel-Aviv: Am Oved, 1990. 208 pp.

Over the past few years, various aspects of the Revisionist movement have become
popular subjects for historical research, as attested to by numerous books, both
memoirs and research. Several such works have been published, among them Yossi
Heller's multifaceted volume on the Lehi, Yonatan Shapiro's book on the Herut (the
first to deal with this movement), Natan Yellin-Mor's memoirs and the riveting and
exhaustive biography of Yonatan Ratosh by Yehoshua Porat. This book of memoirs
by Binyamin Eliav (Lubotzki) (1909–1974) offers a portrait of a close aide of Zev
Jabotinsky and a rising star in the Revisionist movement who was later shunted
aside, and who eventually joined the ranks of the labor movement.

According to Danny Rubinstein, the book's editor, "Eliav could have been in the
first rank of Israeli political leaders. He possessed a wealth of qualities needed by a
leader: a sharp analytical mind, a profound and extensive education, rhetorical and
decision-making ability . . . and a profound social involvement" (p. 9). Why, then,
did he not reach the top? Rubinstein claims only that he lacked "the necessary
ambition and political manipulative talents, for better or for worse" and that "he
retreated in the face of intrigues and leadership rivalries"—an explanation that only
partially accounts for the "sieve" that so often operates in Israeli society and
politics.

Eliav's memoirs are an adaptation of interviews recorded in 1965 at the Institute
of Contemporary Jewry's Oral History Division. The interviews begin with Eliav's
childhood in Riga and conclude in 1948, the year he joined Mapai and the editorial
board of its journal *Hador*. The most crucial years, in terms of his political shift to
the left, began in the 1940s, when he left the Revisionist movement following the
death of Zev Jabotinsky and the movement's failure to secure an agreement with the
Haganah. During the next few years, Eliav attempted several pathetic political
moves, among them a feeble attempt to reunite the underground factions, before
finally joining Mapai. This shift in parties apparently accounts for his need to
explain his life in retrospect. The crux of Eliav's explanation is that he never lost his
personal integrity. He didn't abandon the Revisionist movement—the movement
itself strayed from its original path. Eliav in a sense provides us with his own

version of Benedetto Croce's famous saying that "every historian is a product of his own times."

According to Eliav, the Revisionist movement was never a movement of the Right. Rather, it was one in which "two spirits"—one left-wing and the other right-wing—battled. Eliav also belittles the differences between the Revisionist movement and the Labor party in general, especially its activist faction. Eliav, a veteran member of Betar, recounts that he and his friends were convinced that as founding members of the movement named for Yosef Trumpeldor they were an integral part of the pioneering movement, not political opponents.

Eliav's concept of "two battling spirits" led him to conclude that Revisionism's antisocialist stance was "a tragic incident" rather than an inevitable outcome of the movement's political development. Such a conclusion, of course, must be viewed in the light of his attempt to probe and understand himself rather than the Revisionist movement. Today it is clear that the attempt to posit the difference between the labor and Revisionist movements as a "chasm" is a polemic, not a scientific finding. Nonetheless, there *were* several sharply defined differences between the two camps. A prominent difference centered around the degree to which it was possible to implement both socialist as well as Zionist ideals. Labor claimed that it was impossible to realize Zionism without implementing socialist ideals; for the Revisionists, the conflict between the two ideals was an inherent one, with no apparent solution. For this reason, the Revisionists' eventual antisocialist line was not a tragedy but rather a necessary outgrowth of their basic ideological outlook.

The fact that Eliav was an integral and senior member of the Revisionist movement who subsequently left it gave him the unique analytical viewpoint of an insider and an outsider: simultaneously a partner and an observer. This double perspective—to which one must add his intellectual capacity and integrity—enabled him, back in 1965, to offer analyses that were quite innovative and radical. A striking example is his discussion of Jabotinsky's role in the Revisionist movement toward the end of Jabotinsky's life. Despite his being a disciple of Jabotinsky during the 1930s, Eliav does not gloss over his mentor's deterioration during these years. He cites, for example, a letter sent in 1939 by a member of the Etzel to a representative in Paris in which Jabotinsky was "mocked, and labeled 'Hindenburg.'" It is clear that this was most insulting; it designated him as a senile, worthless person, an anachronistic historical figure bereft of real leadership" (p. 129).

Today, following Yossi Heller's analysis on Jabotinsky's attitude toward the policy of acquiescence and Yaacov Shavit's study of whether Jabotinsky was in fact "the father of the revolution," we are more fully aware of the significance of the "continuation and tradition" question in the Revisionist movement. We also know of the efforts made by the Etzel, and later Herut, to set themselves up as the "spiritual heirs of the immortal leader." We are aware to what extent they tried to conceal the fact that the dividing line between his policies and their own was no less significant than the line of continuity. However, in the mid-1960s, when research on this movement was virtually nonexistent, Eliav's attempt to see the tragic and pathetic element in Jabotinsky's character is marked by courage and considerable intellectual merit.

This review cannot survey the entire wealth of subjects concealed in this short book. It is a vibrant volume, honest and riveting, that draws a most interesting and complex picture of the Revisionist movement.

YEHIAM WEITZ
The Hebrew University

Yosef Katz, *Hayozmah haperatit bevinyan erez yisrael bitkufat ha'aliyah hasheniyah* (*Zionist Private Enterprise in the Building of Eretz Israel during the Second Aliyah, 1904–1914*). Ramat-Gan: Bar-Ilan University Press, 1989. 217 pp.

Although the book's title is a bit lengthy, it does not describe its contents accurately. This volume, together with its companion *Geulah Titnu Laarez* (on the "Geulah" Co., 1902–1914) (1987) deals with the role of private enterprise in organized Zionist settlement during the Second Aliyah period, in contrast to settlement agencies such as the Jewish Colonization Association (known as the ICA), Hovevei Zion and the World Zionist Organization that acted as patrons to individual, atomistic settlers.

The author has already established himself as an historian of the Yishuv in the late Ottoman period. Katz himself ascribes the relative neglect of his topic to the difficulties in gaining access to source material, to the fact that most private settlement organizations were liquidated during the First World War and, more important, to the prevailing conception—which he criticizes—that all ventures funded by private capital were motivated by profit only, lacking any element of ideological commitment (p. 10). Katz himself adopts the approach of people such as Arthur Ruppin and Otto Warburg, who believed in a combined set of motives for "national-capitalist settlement" (p. 177). This and similar expressions referred to people of private (usually small or medium) means who, while intending to conduct their affairs in Eretz Israel according to capitalist, profit-oriented business rules, were at the same time content to accept a smaller rate of return for reasons of Zionist ideology. As Ruppin put it, the "emotional profit was to make up the difference" (p. 13).

The issue of "Zionist capitalism" is, of course, not limited to the period of this book. The reevaluation of the role of private capital and enterprise in the upbuilding of the Yishuv and in the Israeli economy is of interest not only for historians but also in discussions of current issues; the more so in view of recent developments both in Europe and in Israel. It is therefore to Katz's particular credit that he presents his case prudently and with a sense of proportion. He describes and praises private settlement enterprises and their achievements within a comparative framework while not ignoring their weaknesses, failures and reliance on assistance from public Zionist funds.

The achievements of private settlement enterprises were mainly in the field of urban settlement: New Jewish quarters were founded and existing ones enlarged in

Tel-Aviv/Jaffa and in Haifa, and land was purchased for such purposes in other towns. Private organized groups also made their mark in the purchase of agricultural land and additions to Jewish plantations. Among the more controversial issues they dealt with were Jewish vs. mixed labor; single vs. multicrop agriculture; absentee ownership; and how to attract additional *olim* or at least investment funds from people who already owned land or a share in a settlement company in Eretz Israel. Katz finds that not only were organizations such as Hovevei Zion and the World Zionist Organization unable to mobilize enough money to carry out all—or even most—of their settlement projects but that the private enterprise agencies faced similar constraints. In this connection, though Katz does not pursue the issue, there seems to have been a certain conflict of interests between veteran local entrepreneurs, on the one hand, and their partners (whether abroad or newly arrived), on the other.

On the whole this is a thorough and comprehensive treatment of an important and interesting chapter in the history of the Yishuv. It is based on rich material from a variety of sources, analyzed according to historical and social science methodologies. The attractive format and copious additional material (index, bibliography, biographical notes) are to the publisher's credit. The book deserves a place of honor in the library of all who are interested in the history of the land of Israel in the last hundred years.

NACHUM T. GROSS
The Hebrew University

Michael Keren, *The Pen and the Sword: Israeli Intellectuals and the Making of the Nation-State*. Boulder: Westview Press, 1989. 98 pp.

This short book by Michael Keren is an interesting and concise review of the role played by Israeli intellectuals during the first generation or so of Israeli statehood. He opens with a survey of the general debate among Jewish intellectuals about their role in society—itself part of a wider one on the role of the intellectual in society. Does such involvement impair or inspire critical thinking? Is political involvement conducive to or destructive of "scholarly, literary, and artistic work," and "does life in the ivory tower produce critical humanists or . . . authoritarians frustrated over their lack of access to power?" (p. 5).

In the Jewish world Keren cites, on the one hand, diaspora Jews such as the French intellectual Julian Benda, who castigated the commitment of intellectuals to their national movement as "a return to the ghetto and betrayal of the intellectual's mission," which in Benda's view could be carried out only by those intellectuals who retained their cosmopolitanism (p. 3). On the other hand, there are the Zionist historiographers and their counterargument that "intellectual work produced in separation from any social or national context is intellectually futile and politically disastrous" (p. 4).

Keren describes and analyzes the initial mobilization of Israeli intellectuals to the service of their new state during its early years. He is concerned primarily with three groups—writers, teachers and scholars. He claims that the intellectuals' commitment to the state never led to their subordination to the Israeli establishment. Rather, they "were the first to sense the inevitable gap between the goals of the national movement and the reality of the new state" (p. 6). And though they initially basked in the personal attention paid them by Prime Minister David Ben-Gurion, Israeli intellectuals soon criticized the gap between his "messianic rhetoric and political action" (p. 36).

In the 1950s, the State Education Law attempted to unify and mobilize education in the cause of the state. But Israeli educators were disillusioned when Israel's first generation of youth followed Western culture rather than the new Israeli values they were trying to instill.

In the 1960s, younger writers rebelled against "mobilized literature," preferring to reflect "social and ethnic trends rather than predetermined ideals" (p. 37). National collective themes were abandoned in favor of the individual. Members of the older generation were enraged by what they regarded as the "disoriented imitators of modernist and existentialist fashions" prevailing in the West, accusing these writers of a lack of national responsibility. Yet in 1967, they were puzzled by the young soldiers' "willingness to sacrifice their lives in the name of national values they allegedly lacked" (p. 80). Keren himself concedes that during national crises intellectuals "abandon critical humanism and tend to rationalize their state's policy" (p. 6). Such was the case in 1967, when Israeli intellectuals were clearly intoxicated by the euphoria that followed the Six-Day War, and thus failed initially to appreciate the price it would exact of Israeli society—though Keren overloads his argument here by attributing "the lack of critical discourse after the victory" to Moshe Dayan's political dominance between 1967 and 1973 (p. 76).

In the 1970s, militant national-religious movements stepped into the vacuum that was left by the secular intellectuals. Key manifestations of the new millenarian trend were the rise of Gush Emunim in 1974 and the political triumph of Menahem Begin in 1977. Secular intellectuals who had grown up in the state of Israel rejected Begin's diaspora, ghetto mentality, which appeared to view all attacks on Israel through the prism of the Holocaust. For them, in contrast, "Jewish nationalism was not only an escape from anti-semitism but also a political movement developing as part of nineteenth-century European nationalism" (p. 93).

During the 1980s, Israeli intellectuals began to reassert their role. The 1982 War in Lebanon, the first fought without a national consensus, spawned a series of works on the limits to military power and attempts "to define moral rules and constraints for the state" (p. 94). Many wrote on "the need to return from messianic fantasies to reality," arguing for "a resumption of the lost perspective of critical humanism" (pp. 95, 97).

Israeli intellectuals have never doubted their own personal commitment to Israel (though a few have spent terms of self-imposed exile abroad). However, they have drawn the line at conformity with public sentiment, and their role as critical humanists has been as indispensable to Israel as it is to all democratic societies.

Keren's book, in sum, is a most useful review full of incisive analysis, although it could have benefited from a conclusion tying together the various issues raised.

MICHAEL J. COHEN
Bar-Ilan University

Baruch Kimmerling (ed.), *The Israeli State and Society: Boundaries and Frontiers.* Albany: State University of New York Press, 1989. x + 301 pp.

Anyone familiar with the Israeli scene during the last twenty to twenty-five years doesn't need a sociologist to learn that this country has undergone very substantial changes since the Six-Day War. But a sociologist—or, at any rate, a social scientist—may well be required to determine the significance of these changes. Have they been changes *in* the Israeli system or do they, as a whole, constitute changes *of* that system? In Baruch Kimmerling's words,

> Can the Jewish nation-state, founded in 1948 as a civil and democratic state . . . still be said to exist? . . . Is the Israeli state of the 1980s the same entity that existed in the 1960s or even the 1970s, or has it become something else? The question does not concern the pace and scope of social change alone, nor is it merely a reformulation of Heraclitus' . . . statement that "it is not possible to step twice in the same river," Rather, the question is whether that river exists at all (p. 265).

Put more prosaically, is contemporary Israel still a "democracy"? a "free country"? a "pluralistic society"? a "Jewish state"? a "welfare society"? a country "under the rule of law"?

Significantly, Kimmerling is alone among all the contributors he gathered together in this volume to take a clear stand on this issue. For him, post-1967 Israel has indeed turned into "something else" from what it once had been, hence it needs to be rethought and retheorized. Most notably, he suggests that Israel has ceased being an ordinary state, and has turned into a *control system,* that is,

> a territorial entity comprising several subcollectivities, held together by military and police forces and their civil extensions (e.g., bureaucracies and settlers). The central [difference] . . . between . . . internal colonialism, deeply-divided societies, the Soviet satellite system, slave-based societies, etc. and the control system is the ruling sector's virtually total lack of interest and ability in creating a common identity or basic value system to legitimize its use of violence to maintain the system (p. 266).

Put plainly, for Kimmerling, Israel has become an apartheid state. Other concepts Kimmerling proposes to describe contemporary Israel are *boundaries,* delimiting the various domains of the control system; *frontiers* (in Frederick Jackson Turner's sense), where the occupied territories to one side, and North America to the other, constitute the main "frontiers" for young Israelis today; a *polycentered* model of the Jewish world, with Israel proper constituting only one such center, moved by its own interests (not necessarily compatible with those of the others), engaging in various exchanges (commercial, financial, cultural, demographic, etc.) with the other centers and being affected by them as much as it affects them, if not more.

Judging from what they have to say about Israeli society and even more from the language they use to say it, Kimmerling's colleagues do not subscribe to his discontinuity thesis. All agree that significant changes have taken place in Israel, but, at least implicitly, these are still perceived as changes in the system, not of the system. Thus, for Erik Cohen, Israeli Arabs have not been drawn to irredentist separatism principally because they were granted citizen status in 1948, yet were allowed to maintain their separate religious identity. But he warns that recent regressive trends may push Israeli Arabs down the irredentist path in the wake of the Palestinians. Judith Shuval, likewise, still upholds the image of a pluralist Israel, warning, however, that it is in the danger of losing this character, mainly because of insufficient commitment by Israelis to the cultural value of tolerance. Greenbaum et al. follow suit by proposing that all children in this country be socialized into recognizing the legitimacy of minority rights. As for Nachman Ben-Yehuda, he contends that the proliferation of "alternative systems" in education, medicine, personal safety, and so on, constitutes evidence that Israel has lost much of its capacity to meet the "basic needs" of its members.

These four contributions, then, are still couched in a language and theoretical mold much like those in which Israel was analyzed in the 1950s by S. N. Eisenstadt and his associates. True, they express concern—as does Eisenstadt himself—lest the Israeli system be stretched to the point of turning into the (unnamable?) "something else" Kimmerling alludes to in the passage quoted earlier. But the very fact that they see this as a danger, not as an actuality, indicates that they feel Israel has not yet changed enough to warrant a major overhaul of their theoretical perspectives and conceptual apparatus.

Dan Horowitz differs from his colleagues in that he, at least, recognizes the need to somehow bridge the chasm between his own value-functional conception of Israeli society and more recent conflictual approaches (such as the elite-centered approach of Yonatan Shapira and the neo-Marxist approaches of Michael Shalev, Shlomo Swirski and others). In "Before the State," he seeks to join these opposites into a single explanatory framework by advancing a model of Israel—including in the era before the establishment of the state—as a "deeply-divided society" (as in South Africa, Northern Ireland and prepartition Cyprus). Viewed in this way, part of the Yishuv's history can still be accounted for in value-functional terms, while other aspects of it become amenable to conflict-theoretical explanations.

Michael Shalev, though coming at the subject from just such a conflict-theoretical perspective, also supports the continuity thesis. For him, Israel today has not *become* a labor-segregated regime, simply because it has been such a regime virtually from the start. The question that occupies him in this paper is the failure by the Histadrut labor federation, on its face a universalistic and egalitarian labor organization, to promote the class interests of *all* the working people in this country, Arabs as well as Jews. In a nutshell, his answer is that from the start the Histadrut was deliberately used—indeed, was set up—by Israel's ruling elite in order to produce and to perpetuate a split labor market, so as to ensure that the better-paying jobs always go to Jews, never to local Arabs. True, the Histadrut's strategies to achieve this objective changed over time—Shalev's contribution is to have identified three distinct phases. But the underlying logic has remained the same all along: to maintain Jewish and Arab workers apart and unequal.

Two contributions have not yet been mentioned: those by Menachem Friedman and Joel Migdal, because they are neither inscribed in the continuity-discontinuity debate nor oriented for or against Eisenstadt. Friedman's "Israel as a Theological Dilemma" relates in detail the changing stances of the ultra-Orthodox toward the state of Israel, especially Agudat Israel, up until recently a marginal and little-known component of the Israeli polity. As for Migdal, he focuses on the extraordinary degree of "stateness" of Israeli society, especially its effectiveness in enforcing its rules over all those under its jurisdiction. (Barely one hundred soldiers, for example, refused to serve in the territories during three years of the *intifada*.)

On second thought, these two papers don't fit in well because they are the only ones not written by members of The Hebrew University's Department of Sociology. Which brings me to the first of my four criticisms of this collection, namely, that the editor did not look beyond the walls of his own department for contributions on the subject of state and society in Israel. There is not a single reference, for example, to Emmanuel Marx's work, despite his pioneering research on the social anthropology of the state in Israel. Second, even more puzzling—especially in view of the editor's image of Israel as a "control system"—is the absence of contributions by Arab sociologists, whether Palestinian Israeli or Palestinian *tout court*. A third problem is the uneven quality of the contributions, as well as the tenuous link of some to the themes of the book. (What, for example, was the rationale for including the paper by Greenbaum et al.?) Finally, the book would have benefited greatly from more conscientious copyediting: Neither the numerous typos, nor the turgid style of one of the chapters, nor the exotic English of another, should have been allowed to pass muster.

Still, despite these shortcomings, students of Israeli society will find in this collection much valuable material. The articles I found outstanding were the opening and closing pieces by Migdal and Kimmerling, respectively, because of their theoretical contributions, and Shalev's and Friedman's, because of the informativeness and keenness of their analyses.

Sasha Weitman
Tel-Aviv University

Ernst Pawel, *The Labyrinth of Exile: A Life of Theodor Herzl.* New York: Farrar, Straus & Giroux, 1989. 539 pp.

Theodor Herzl, writes Ernst Pawel in *The Labyrinth of Exile,* is the greatest Jewish leader of modern times. How fitting, then, that he has been the subject of some of the more interesting biographical studies in modern Jewish history. Alex Bein's Herzl biography remains a classic; Amos Elon has contributed a lively reappraisal; the work of Carl Schorske, Peter Loewenberg, Jacques Kornberg, Chaya Harel,

Avner Falk and others have added to our now-intimate knowledge of the founder of political Zionism. Pawel, however, has provided the most incisive and comprehensive treatment of the life and times of Herzl. His book is for the most part copiously researched and beautifully written. Pawel not only captures the European world of which Herzl was a part but convincingly shows how much of Herzl's appeal and dynamism derived from the fact that he was not simply a product of the times— almost alarmingly, he was both visionary and throwback.

The questions Pawel asks are broad-ranging, if not new:

> What turned this Budapest-born German patriot into a Jewish nationalist? How, within a scant two years and without the benefit of modern mass media, was he able to impose himself as the spokesman for the Jewish people? To what extent did his spirit shape the state he helped to found, and how much of it survives today, for better and for worse? What, ultimately, is his place in history? (p. 3).

Although it remains unclear what Pawel thinks of as "modern" in reference to mass media—Herzl certainly used the popular press to his great advantage, as the author himself amply demonstrates—his agenda overall is brilliantly fulfilled. Pawel has delicately synthesized an impressive range of factors—from the new social and women's history, previously considered aspects of Central European nationalisms, and psychological and medical considerations that help account for Herzl's meteoric rise as well as the limits of his achievement. Theodor Herzl lived a life, Pawel concludes,

> of tragic grandeur that left much wreckage in its wake. In the end, though, his spirit prevailed, and in ways far more substantial than the pious myth, or the ubiquitous icon of the bearded prophet with the burning eyes. . . . Over and above all else, Herzl, by being who he was—a Jew who had stopped apologizing for being Jewish—inspired pride and hope (pp. 538–539).

One of the strengths of this book is its graceful style, which makes reading it a pleasure. *The Labyrinth of Exile* is largely unencumbered by numerous notes, historiographical comments or self-conscious revising of previous judgments. Pawel does not overtly quibble with "dead-end arguments inspired not so much by the need to know as by the compulsion to place blame and assign guilt" (p. 537). Yet this aspect of the book also has its underside. While the work is undoubtedly of interest to scholars, tracking down the background of some of Pawel's claims is likely to be difficult. Pawel notes, for instance, that "Freud dreamed about Herzl twice"—a fact that has been brought to light by Avner Falk, Peter Loewenberg and William J. McGrath, none of whom he mentions. In paying more attention to the work of such scholars, Pawel might also have averted what is possibly his most glaring error, a misreading of the only known letter from Sigmund Freud to Herzl (regarding Freud's desire to have his book *Die Traumdeutung* reviewed in the *Neue Freie Presse* in 1902). According to Pawel, the suggestion to contact Herzl originated with Herzl's "editorial colleague, Mr. Max Nordau" (p. 456)—a statement that, if true, would merit a good deal of scholarly interest. And yet Pawel notes (and rightly discredits) Freud's dismissal of Nordau as "stupid" in 1886; it is unlikely that Freud and Nordau were in touch sixteen years later. Avner Falk's deciphering of the colleague's name as "Max Neuda," who was also an editor for the *Neue Freie Presse,* seems eminently more plausible.

In addition to his judiciousness on the subject of Max Nordau (as opposed to Freud's biographer, Ernest Jones, who does not question his mentor's lead), Pawel also shows astuteness in numerous other cultural and Zionist-historical references. For example, he is careful not to lavish praise on the Viennese satirist Karl Kraus, providing instead a sound critique of Kraus's relationship to the fin-de-siècle. Pawel also demonstrates a keen awareness of the plight of women in Herzl's time, an issue Herzl himself seemed uninterested in. Pawel relates the ways in which convention frustrated both Herzl's wife and mother, who were perpetually locked in battle—a situation that fueled Herzl's tumultuous home environment. Regarding Zionism in particular, Pawel succeeds in putting the much-maligned "Uganda Plan" in its rightful context as a measure envisioned by Herzl primarily as a stopgap on the way to the promised land (p. 493ff.). And in discussing Herzl's role in the conflict with the "Democratic Faction" concerning the creation of a Hebrew culture (the so-called *Kulturdebatte*), Pawel states that Herzl "had no real quarrel" with the faction's ideas—a view opposed to that of Jehuda Reinharz and Maurice Friedman in their respective biographies of Chaim Weizmann and Martin Buber but one that seems quite balanced and sensible.

Perhaps the greatest talent Pawel has brought to bear on the Herzl story is his creative yet antideterministic use of medical data. (Pawel has a good deal of expertise in this field; in addition to being a novelist and historical writer, he has worked for an insurance company.) In June 1990, he writes, "Herzl may have been suffering from hemolytic anemia, a not uncommon complication of both malaria and lupus erythematosus and a possible cause of the blackouts he experienced with increasing frequency. . . . For months, for years now, he had been living with a sense of doom" (p. 423). Similar to his use of such material in his splendid biography of Franz Kafka (*The Nightmare of Reason* [1984]), Pawel intertwines and thoughtfully explores such issues as Herzl's unrelenting desire to be a successful playwright, office and Zionist politics, home life, and the state of his health. We are left with the most vivid, troubled, driven and believable Herzl yet described— though Pawel makes it clear as well that Herzl's hold on the Jewish world resulted from the confluence of his genuine devotion to the Zionist cause and the need of the masses for a compassionate and effective leader.

It is fitting that Herzl, who in so many ways was an outsider to the Jewish world, has Pawel as his admirer and premier biographer. For Pawel is an outsider both to academia and to the journalistic and quasi-academic circles that maintain a persistent interest in Herzl. This helps explain Pawel's dedication: "To the Spiritual Heirs of Ahad Ha-Am," which is intended as well for those who represent a critical, ethical voice within the realm of Zionist thought and Israel. While Pawel has magnificently served his immensely significant subject, Theodor Herzl, he serves as well the spirit of the movement's unmatched inner voice, Ahad Ha'am. The author's status as outsider, it is to be hoped, will not hamper the reception of this eloquent, important work.

MICHAEL BERKOWITZ
Ohio State University

Gershon Shafir, *Land, Labor and the Origins of the Israeli-Palestinian Conflict 1882–1914*. Cambridge: Cambridge University Press, 1989. xv + 288 pp.

The political upheaval of 1977 ruptured the close ties between Israel's political and intellectual establishments, creating new space for critical scholarly reflections on Israeli society. The disillusioning wars of 1973 and 1982, the discomfort felt by many intellectuals at Israel's role as an occupying power, and the accumulation of painful evidence (revolt from below and corruption from above) of the flaws and contradictions of the Israeli success story provided Jewish social scientists in Israel with compelling reasons for reinterpreting their society and wondering "where did we go wrong?" Some of the attempts to address this question have laid the blame at the door of ideological changes attendant upon statehood (for example, an overall loss of revolutionary élan, or an alleged substitution of statist and militarist values for socialist ones). Other interpretations focus on developments on the material rather than the ideal plane, arguing, for example, that the mass immigration of Middle Eastern Jews, or Israel's occupation of the West Bank and Gaza, proved to be incompatible with cultural and political standards established in happier times.

What unites these explanations is their assumption that the roots of what one recent volume describes as "trouble in utopia"[1] are to be found in the *postutopian* era—that is, after 1948. The alternative view has been largely a monopoly of Israel's most radical critics, who present its latter-day troubles as reflections of the selfsame Jewish nationalism (and denial of Palestinian national claims) that took root in the pre-1948 era. In other words, from this perspective it is Zionism that is responsible for both Israel's past glories (if that is what they were) and its present agonies. It is the special merit of Gershon Shafir's new book that it offers a fresh alternative to all three of the views noted so far. While refusing to absolve even the pre–First World War period from responsibility for the contemporary shape of Israeli society, Shafir's analysis is rooted not in the "logic" of Zionism as an abstract ideological project but in the political economy of the national conflict.

It is Shafir's contention that, in many crucial respects, Israeli society was formed in struggles between the Arabs of Palestine and Jewish settlers of the Second Aliyah to establish control over land (settlement) and labor (employment). It was in this early period, prior even to the British Mandate, that Zionist labor leaders and settlement officials fashioned methods of nation- and state-building that, responding to the peculiar circumstances of Jewish colonialization, accounted for many of the most striking continuities between pre- and postsovereign Israel. These include the political dominance of a workers' movement wedded to Jewish national interests, and both the economic and political subordination of Mizrachi (Sephardic) to Ashkenazic Jews. At the same time, Shafir argues that continuity and change have interacted historically to produce unanticipated consequences. The Zionism of the labor movement, he shows, evolved toward a readiness for territorial compromise under the unique conditions of the prestate period: the necessity of purchasing land in order to lay claim to it, the attraction of Jewish exclusivism as a means of meeting the threat of cheaper Arab labor, and the profound constraint on Jewish national aspirations imposed by the limited military and state power with which Zionism confronted Arab opposition. Given the very different conditions under which the parameters of Jewish nationalism became reopened after 1967, the political decline of the labor movement and the rise of "maximalist" Zionism can be readily understood. Indeed, many will find this analysis so persuasive as to lend Shafir's call at the close of the book for greater "realism and moderation" sadly incompatible with the thrust of his own analysis.

Both the motivation for undertaking this study and the conclusions its author draws derive quite explicitly from the contemporary angst of the Zionist Left. Yet despite its clear political message, this book is far from constituting a political tract. It is instead a richly detailed, tightly argued and scrupulously documented study of a series of concrete historical puzzles of the late Ottoman period. In each one of these case studies, Shafir combines primary historical research with interpretive frameworks drawn from social-scientific theories of settlement and ethnic conflict. While showing great sensitivity to context, he refuses to bow to the temptation of advocating a particularistic interpretation of the Zionist experience. Perhaps the most telling evidence of this commitment is the book's preoccupation with the material origins of political action and institutional innovation in the Zionist labor movement. This is one of the most important respects in which Shafir parts company with conventional sociological understandings of the Jewish Yishuv in Palestine. According to the dominant interpretation, the Yishuv is best understood as a pioneering enterprise constituted by the dedicated efforts of extraordinary leaders, and its history can best be told as the unfolding of their visionary intentions. Another equally weighty challenge to mainstream Israeli sociology is posed by this volume's insistence that both the initial formation and the subsequent evolution of Israeli society have been inextricably connected to the Jewish-Palestinian conflict. Specifically, the development of the labor movement on the basis of exclusion of both Arabs and Mizrachi Jews, its prioritizing of Zionist over socialist aspirations and its inclination toward economic collectivism can all be plausibly interpreted in realist terms as strategic responses to the exigencies of the formative years of the national conflict. These exigencies, in turn, are shown to have originated not in national rivalry or ethnic prejudice per se but rather in the clashing economic interests of Jewish settlers vis-à-vis Arab workers and peasants.

Many sacred cows are slaughtered in these pages. One of them is the well-known political contrast between the pioneers of the First and Second Aliyot, usually understood as having resulted from differences in both the character and the intensity of their beliefs. Shafir's account implies, however, that if the members of the Second Aliyah had acquired the means to become private smallholders, or alternatively, if Baron Rothschild had been willing to resume the practice of subsidizing Jewish workers' wages, their fate would probably have been similar to that of their predecessors (and to settlers on other frontiers). It was the experience of being thrown into competition with cheaper Arab labor that propelled the propertyless immigrants of the Second Aliyah to organize, to adopt interlinked demands for exclusively Jewish labor and Jewish national separatism, and to ally themselves with the only force capable of ameliorating their economic plight—the World Zionist organization (WZO).

This was the context in which cooperative settlement emerged as a method by which Jewish workers could make a living without being thrown into the labor market, while in return furnishing the WZO with the only agents willing to advance its settlement aims. It was also the context in which organized Ashkenazic labor was ready to comply with a plan launched by leading Jewish planters to replace Arab workers in unskilled agricultural work with Yemenite Jews. When the Yemenites proved to be less pliant than expected and sought to participate in the training farms and new settlements that the WZO was sponsoring for Ashkenazic workers, the latter successfully resisted having to share these privileges. It was the outcome of this struggle, rather than Ashkenazic cultural alienation from or moral indifference toward the Yemenites, that consigned the latter to the margins of Zionist history and Yishuv society. And it was in playing out this struggle that, repeating a pattern already forged in their relations with Arab labor, the Ashkenazim developed a self-serving theory of cultural superiority to explain to themselves and others why they alone deserved access to contested economic opportunities.

The book under review is not merely a poignant exposure of prevailing myths but a scholarly undertaking that belongs in the front ranks of historical sociology. Because its argumentation and evidence have been crafted with such care, neither historians nor sociologists of Israeli society, irrespective of their predilections, will be able to ignore this powerful and innovative work.

MICHAEL SHALEV
The Hebrew University

Note

1. Dan Horowitz and Moshe Lissak, *Trouble in Utopia* (Albany, N.Y.: 1989).

Margalit Shilo, *Nisyonot behityashvut: hamisrad haerez yisraeli 1908–1914 (Experiments in Settlement: The Palestine Office 1908–1914)*. Jerusalem: Yad Yitzhak Ben-Zvi, 1988. 225 pp.

An alternative title for this book could well have been "Arthur Ruppin and His Activity in the Years 1908–1914," since no history of the Palestine Office during the period under discussion is complete without relating to the forceful leadership of its founder and director—whose name was almost synonymous with that of the institution from its very inception. Margalit Shilo's admiration for Ruppin comes through time and again in this book, although she also rightly stresses the help he received from his assistant, Yaakov Thon (who, like Ruppin, was brought up in the German cultural sphere and was a lawyer trained at the University of Berlin). The author has an impressive grasp of the material, and she is thus well-placed to describe the various stages of the Palestine Office's development as the central agency in charge of settlement activities in the Yishuv from its founding in 1908 until the outbreak of the First World War.

The decision of the World Zionist Organization to adopt a program of "practical Zionism," based in the main on immigration to and land acquisition in Palestine was not a unanimous one, despite a generally held view to the contrary. Shilo demonstrates that the office did not initially enjoy total support from the Zionist leadership; opponents included the second president of the Zionist Organization, David Wolfson, and other prominent figures such as banker Jacobus Kahn and Max Bodenheimer, the chairman of the Keren Kayemet. These leaders feared what they saw as carelessness and even adventurism on the part of Ruppin. Ruppin did receive the enthusiastic support of Otto Warburg, who succeeded Wolfson in 1911. Warburg's support, however, was not translated into an adequate funding for the office, since the Zionist Organization itself, as Shilo points out, experienced great difficulties in its fund-raising efforts.

One of the most interesting sections in Shilo's book is its discussion of the Palestine Office's readiness to support any agricultural settlement that had some chance of success:

> Over a period of six years, more than ten forms of settlement were tried, funded or instigated by the Palestine Office: training farms, mixed farms, collective settlements, cooperative group settlements, private cooperatives, worker colonies, Yemenite colonies, industrial villages and private farms, as well as other experiments that did not come to fruition. Such a large number is especially surprising in light of the fact that during the years 1908–1914, fewer than 20 new settlements were established, with a total population numbering only in the hundreds (p. 123).

In this regard, the idea of collective settlement proved to be most successful. The chemistry created between Ruppin, the educated, meticulous and pedantic German Jew, and the idealistic young people from Eastern Europe—who were unconventional not only in their appearance but also in their way of life—was of historic significance. Ruppin was convinced that agricultural settlement was intrinsically tied to the spiritual revival of the nation, and that pioneering enthusiasm was an essential ingredient in this process. Disputes between the workers and the agronomist-managers of the "National Farms" brought him to the conclusion that in order to ensure the success of a settlement the needs and views of the settlers also had to be taken into account. It was the rapport between Ruppin and the fiery, questioning younger generation, together with his readiness to make available to them the resources of the Palestine Office (meager as they were), that allowed for creation of the collective settlements—which became the main form of settlement in Palestine after the First World War.

Shilo amply documents the ways in which activity of the Palestine Office can be measured not only in quantitative terms but in its daring and its pioneering of new directions of action. Ruppin's great talent, she shows, lay in his ability to recognize those initiatives that had the potential for future success and to support them, even in the face of opposition or hesitation on the part of his colleagues in the Zionist leadership.

Based on a rich variety of sources from archives, modern research literature, and contemporary newspapers and journals, the work presents a clear, accurate and in-depth picture of the way in which Ruppin and the Palestine Office operated.

DAN GILADI
Tel-Aviv

Ned Temko, *To Win or to Die: A Personal Portrait of Menachem Begin*. New York: William Morrow, 1987. 460 pp.

Menahem Begin's election as prime minister heralded a series of biographies designed to satisfy popular curiosity. Although he was a well-known public and political figure who aroused varied and conflicting reactions, Begin's personal biography was largely unknown. The first biographies are based chiefly on pre-1977 newspapers and personal memoirs. Those that followed did not necessarily add to what was already known. True, they filled in certain gaps—largely through interviews that sometimes supplied unreliable or highly subjective information—but such information did not constitute a "new biography" of the man.[1] The reason seems to lie in the subject's personality, or at least in the nature of the source material. There is almost no such material likely to give the biographer a clue to Begin's "inner life." Unlike other historical personalities, Menahem Begin revealed very few of his innermost thoughts and gave his biographers access to almost none of the personal letters that could have revealed an added dimension to his personality, one that may have differed from his public image. The biographer in each case was thus forced to rely on the impressions of various persons who may have been close to the subject, but who lacked the vital testimony of the subject himself. Begin's biographers naturally addressed the political man and the ideologue, attracted by the mystery of his metamorphosis from perpetual opposition leader to prime minister, the dramatic transition from the world of rhetoric to the arena of practical politics, from the underground to center stage. And the manner of Begin's exit from this stage, unparalleled in Israeli political life, only served to intensify the riddle and the desire to solve it.

Also noteworthy is the fact that many of the post-1977 biographies of Begin were rooted in the belief that the Herut movement was a one-man show: that Begin embodied the movement and that its survival depended on his leadership. Just as the Revisionist movement was personified by Zev Jabotinsky, Herut was personified by Begin. But as powerful as Begin's hand was in molding Herut as a "collective personality," as valid as the personification myth was in its time, it was not Begin alone who transformed the opposition into a government, and the exclusive focus on him—with the constant return to his biography as some kind of key— bespeaks a narrow view of history.

This biography of Begin written by Ned Temko, a journalist for the *Christian Science Monitor,* is one of the newer ones. While it adds numerous details supplied by interviews with sources from Begin's former hometown and others close to him, it provides little fresh information. No new written sources were discovered, as a glance at Temko's introduction to the source material indicates. He lists as one of his sources "Begin's two volumes of autobiography," possibly leading the unsuspecting reader to believe that Begin actually wrote two autobiographies, while the books in question are in fact *White Nights* and *The Revolt,* which are far from auto-biographical. Temko "discovered" the 1944 Etzel protocols, which had in fact been published in 1975 in the journal *Zionism;* similar examples abound.

This biography is designed for readers of English. For at least some of them, the tale will be new and to a great extent, perhaps, foreign. For that reason, Temko chooses to survey the various periods of Begin's life briefly and even superficially. As noted, there is little new here in the way of biography; as political biography, this is journalism rather than history. There is little basis for predicting that future source material would facilitate the writing of a more complete biography, for such material may simply not exist. Temko did not exhaust what material is available—but perhaps this is one of those stories that must be told again and again in order to be believed.

YAACOV SHAVIT
Tel-Aviv University

Note

1. The first biographies of Begin are those of Eitan Haber, *Menachem Begin, The Legend and the Man* (New York: 1978); Harry Hurwitz, *Menachem Begin* (New York: 1978); Richard Greenfeld and A. Irving, *The Life Story of Menachem Begin* (New York: 1977); Gertrude Hirschler and S. Eckman, *Menachem Begin* (New York: 1979); and Aviezer Golan and Shlomo Nakdimon, *Begin* (Jerusalem: 1978).

More recent biographies are the work of Eric Silver, *Begin: A Biography* (London: 1984); Amos Perlmutter, *The Life and Times of Menachem Begin* (New York: 1987); and Sasson Sofer, *Begin: An Anatomy of Leadership* (Oxford: 1988). Yonatan Shapiro's *Lashilton bahar-tanu* (Tel-Aviv: 1989) deals rather extensively with Begin's leadership. There are also a number of works of a polemic nature on Begin and his period of office as prime minister: e.g., Teddy Preuss, *Begin bashilton* (Jerusalem: 1984); Dov-Nir, *MiZhabotinsky 'ad Begin: biografiyah shel tenu'ah* (Tel-Aviv: 1982); and Ronald Robert, *The Rhetoric of Menachem Begin: The Myth of Redemption Through Return* (Lanham, Md.: 1985).

David Vital, *The Future of the Jews.* Cambridge: Harvard University Press, 1990. 148 pp.

David Vital is the author of three fine books on international relations and three volumes on the development and early history of Zionism and the Zionist movement that established his reputation as the preeminent authority in the field. Nevertheless, I find the thesis he proposes in his recent essay on contemporary Jewry and its national question unconvincing.

Vital is convinced that it is only through the instrument of the state that world politics can be usefully or properly pursued. Recent studies in international relations challenge this assumption. Diasporas of all kinds have become a focus for study. Jews serve as the prime but by no means sole representatives of the major role played by nongovernmental collectivities in the international arena. The Persian Gulf War, among other events, has demonstrated the power as well as the limitations of supranational loyalties and the consideration that must be given them.

The exclusive role that Vital accords the state in the formation of public policy is related to his central theme. That theme, as I understand it, is as follows. As a result of the success of political Zionism, Jews have refashioned themselves into a national political entity, but this has only taken place in the state of Israel. Those who live in Israel are now part of a more or less normal political collectivity; those who do not are not part of that entity. As a result:

> The interests and therefore, the underlying tendencies and viewpoints, of American and other Jewries, cannot fail to differ crucially from those of Israeli Jewry. And that is one key reason, quite conceivably the chief reason, why willy-nilly the Jewish world— beaten by assimilation on the one hand and by destruction and threats of further punishment on the other—is now coming apart. Where there was once a single, if certainly a scattered and far from monolithic people—indeed, a nation—there is now a sort of archipelago of discrete islands composed of rather shaky communities of all qualities, shapes and sizes, in which the Island of Israel, as it were, is fated increasingly to be in a class by itself (p. 147).

Vital assumes that Jews ought to reconstitute themselves as a national as well as a political collectivity. At some points, he suggests that this is the only way in which Jewry will survive; at others, he confesses that the capacity of Jewry to survive as a nonpolitical entity is not his concern. The insistence that Jews must refashion themselves into a national political entity (not only as an instrument to pursue their welfare but as an ultimate value) is the classic response of political Zionists to their personal predicament. Many of them feel a strong attachment to the Jewish people but possess only attenuated ties to Jewish culture and religion. They seek what they call the "normalization" of Jewish life, that is, a national-political focus of loyalty, which will presumably allow them to act on behalf of the Jewish people just as any other national collectivity acts on its own behalf. Jewish interests under these conditions can be interpreted as "interests of state," and one thus acquires an ostensibly convenient mechanism for choosing appropriate Jewish policies.

But the establishment of a Jewish state has done little to "normalize" Jewish life in the sense that Vital accords to the term. If one takes the modern European state as one's norm, Israel's policies seem to be increasingly abnormal. Its Jewish nature receives growing emphasis, religious symbols are more pervasive than ever before, increasing attention is paid to Israel's links to diaspora Jewry, and public policy reflects a conception of Israel as a Jewish shtetl, that is, with the emphasis on the interests of the Jewish community rather than "interests of state." Vital, like Boaz Evron, author of the brilliant study of Israeli nationalism *Haheshbon Haleumi* (*The National Reckoning*) might agree that Israel doesn't behave as a "normal" state ought to behave. But, he would add, this only demonstrates the unfortunate lag in Israeli thinking, the unwillingness of Israeli authorities and the Israeli public to free itself from diaspora-like responses. Perhaps. But one might also argue that Israel's present behavior is normal by the standards of other multiethnic states with a dominant majority.

As long as Israeli Jews seek to retain an identifiably Jewish state, given the environment in which they live and the responses of the Arab world, they are likely to continue to adopt policies that emphasize the Jewish nature of the state and its associations with diaspora Jewry, even when this association serves only to mask the interests of the Jewish community of Israel. The alternative is to adopt less coercive policies toward the Arab minority and seek to assimilate them into Israel's social and political structure by depoliticizing Judaism—a step that would necessarily dilute the Jewish character of the state and suggest that the Zionist vision was ultimately self-defeating.

I would argue that a "Jewish" state will never be a "normal" state according to Vital's somewhat dated terms of reference. But it *is* normal by the standards of other multiethnic societies in which each ethnic group exhibits high levels of political consciousness.

Vital's central theme is buried within a series of unconnected generalizations. Some of them strike me as acute but others are arguable, and a number of them, those which pertain to American Jews in particular, seem to me to be simply wrong. Vital dismisses, for example, the sum total of the activities of the organized Jewish community in the United States and refuses to acknowledge its status as a political community even though American politicians and policymakers accept it as such. He is particularly unfair concerning the measure of political discipline the organized Jewish community has successfully imposed on American Jews, especially with regard to support for Israel. He is far too sensitive to the statements of individual Jews who have been critical of Israeli policy; many of these individuals are marginal to the community, and none of their statements have either influenced the vast majority of Jews, diminished community support for Israel or impressed American policymakers. Vital suggests that American Jewish dissent from Israeli policies is an indication of the weak obligations felt by American Jews toward Israel, which is symptomatic of their status as an extranational community. But on the one issue concerning which American Jewry forcefully dissented from Israeli policy—that of "Who Is a Jew?"—there was a groundswell of opposition from below that suggests just how seriously American Jews take Israel and the impact of Israeli policies on their lives.

Like Vital, I'm not very happy with the behavior of American Jewry, not very confident about its capacity to survive, nor am I sanguine about the future of diaspora-Israel relations. But my feelings are based on different values and different assumptions about the nature of Jewish life and politics.

CHARLES S. LIEBMAN
Bar-Ilan University

Chaim I. Waxman, *American Aliya: Portrait of an Innovative Migration Movement.*
Detroit: Wayne State University Press, 1989. 240 pp.

With the lowest rate of aliyah per thousand Jews living in any Western country,
American Jewry has hardly been at the forefront of the "ingathering of the exiles" in
Israel. However, the relevance of Jewish migration from the United States to Israel
transcends its rather small quantitative dimensions. Aliyah constitutes a sensitive
indicator of wider demographic, social and cultural trends shaping North America's
large and dynamic Jewries; it also represents a special and intriguing case study in
the more general typology and theory of international migrations.

Perhaps more than other contemporary Jewish migrations, American aliyah can
be generally described as the product of a delicate balancing act between a "zero
option" (why move at all from the United States to a country whose economic
opportunities are vastly inferior?) and a "maximum option" (why stay at all in the
United States, where the chances for Jewish survival are being eroded?). Two
obviously distinct and unequal levels of thought are involved here, conventional
economic calculus vs. a particular version of Jewish normative idealism or, put
somewhat differently, as asymmetry between the more widely applicable frame of
general, material well-being and the much narrower idea of aliyah as the guarantee
of group solidarity and continuity. In any event, these conflicting intellectual and
emotional stimuli determine the varying attitudes of American Jewry toward aliyah,
the actual numbers of American Jews moving to Israel and their propensity to settle
there permanently.

Put more generally, the study of American aliyah offers an opportunity both to
reexamine some fundamental assumptions of the sociological theory of international
migration and to place it in the context of a systematic vision of the sociohistorical
experience of modern and contemporary Jewry, which would view Jewish life in the
United States (including Jewish *immigration*) as a dependent variable of no lesser
significance than migration from America to Israel.

In his study of American aliyah, Chaim Waxman touches upon such diverse
disciplinary and thematic perspectives. In the initial chapters of his book, he pres-
ents the wide-ranging spiritual, ideological and social forces underlying the idea of
Return to Zion and addresses relevant background themes such as Zion in Jewish
culture; messianism and the forerunners of Zionism in the nineteenth century; and
American Jewry and the land of Israel in the eighteenth and nineteenth centuries.
Later in his analysis he proceeds to discuss the centrality of Israel in American
Jewish life and Orthodox Judaism in modern American society.

To provide the necessary context to his own original empirical work on American
olim, Waxman often refers to earlier research dealing with U.S. immigration to
Israel. He also offers a brief but intensive survey of Jewish life in contemporary
America. Of special relevance in assessing the major cultural and structural variables and processes at work are the issues of the compatibility of Jewish group
consciousness with the norms of American society, and the challenge of
assimilation.

The social structure of the *olim* is discussed in relation to the main characteristics of the Jewish community in the United States. This sociodemographic analysis of American aliyah might have been helpfully assisted by use of harder data about the *olim* as provided by Israel's several population censuses. The exceptionalism, if any, of U.S. aliyah might have been further illuminated by comparison between migration to Israel from America and that from other free, affluent Western countries. At first glance, there appear to be no major differences between *olim* and the known sociodemographic profile of U.S. Jewry—a generally well-educated, predominantly professional and politically liberal group—apart from the fact that *olim* tend to be younger, are more religiously observant and have a higher proportion of singles. Waxman's study does confirm other available evidence in indicating that American *olim* experience less loss of socioeconomic status than do other groups in the early stages of immigrant absorption. For quite a few, indeed, aliyah fits in smoothly with upward occupational mobility—perhaps the more so in cases where the immigrants eventually return to the United States.

By the 1980s, U.S. immigrants displayed a rather skewed regional distribution in Israel, with a strong preference for Jerusalem. Moreover, they had one of the highest propensities—in comparison with other immigrant groups—to settle in the administered territories in Judea, Samaria, the Gaza Strip and the Golan Heights. As to personal characteristics of the settlers, Waxman's analysis provides a sobering profile of a small group whose broad variety of Jewish motivations does not always correspond with its stereotyped image of ideological extremism. In any event, these geographical preferences testify to the clear dominance of Jewish religious and ethnic identification as the main motivating force behind aliyah. This perhaps puts into question the subtitle of the book, drawn from Petersen's classic typology of migration: Is American aliyah in the cultural sense really *innovative* (in the sense of breaking with the social and cultural patterns of the country of origin), or rather *conservative?* Waxman's portrait seems to be that of a group of people whose essential concern is the preservation in Israel of a valued Jewish identity and group solidarity, whose continuity is perceived to be at risk in the United States.

American *olim* do not lack such problems as emotional adjustment, language acquisition, family adaptation or maintenance of standard of living. One main cause of stress as discussed by Waxman is the contact with the absorption authorities and the wider Israeli bureaucracy. Interestingly, in confronting similar housing or employment problems in the United States, most *olim* would probably rely more on their own judgment and family resources, whereas in Israel they become more dependent on public authorities. Such basic changes possibly reflect a typical immigrant's lack of some of the economic means commonly available in the United States, other sociodemographic traits being equal.

The opposite face of aliyah, return migration, has been comparatively more frequent among American *olim*. Common explanations for return migration, mentioned by Waxman, include family reasons and a persisting sense of foreignness in Israel. One wonders, though, to what extent the real motives may be tied to the personal and household consequences of career and economic opportunity downscaling in Israel in comparison with the (real or perceived) situation in the United States.

The final chapter of this book deals with an evaluation of the prospectives for future aliyah from the United States, and the ways and means to make it more feasible and fruitful from the point of view of the American Jewish community. All in all, it seems not too farfetched to project that, under the present circumstances, American aliyah is bound to continue to be a preciously rare social phenomenon. Waxman's valuable study offers a terse but intense picture of its many manifestations.

SERGIO DELLAPERGOLA
The Hebrew University

Eugene Weiner and Anita Weiner, *Israel, A Precarious Sanctuary: War, Death and the Jewish People*. Lanham, Md.: University Press of America, 1990. 122 pp.

This book, published in the *Studies in Judaism* series, consists of several essays written over the past twenty years that attempt to present the history of Israel at war and to provide an analysis of war's effects on the sociological and psychological reality in that country. Among the specific subjects of the book are the implications of nonviolent defense against aggression, reactions to bereavement, dynamics of heroization and the struggle to overcome fear of death. Perhaps the most gripping aspect of this book, however, is the personal revelation of the authors—Jewish academics themselves—as they weave the topics of death, war and the Jewish people together with their own physical transition in 1969 from New York to Haifa. This work portrays the ways in which the authors' Israeli identities gradually emerge and become more pronounced while their previous identities as Jewish diaspora scholars recede into the background.

Chapter 1 of the book is written from the perspective of a Conservative rabbi in the United States, whose assumption is that Israelis have doubts about their existence and normal reality as a state. It is an unlikely reality, he claims, of "being and yet not quite being" (p. 1). Eugene Weiner here theorizes that, following long centuries of exile and ultimately the Holocaust, the reality of Israel as an independent state, with the normal problems of a collective and of individual citizens, does not seem to have fully sunk in.

The image of the Jew in the diaspora, as conveyed by the authors in a number of historical-philosophical quotations, is that of the "living dead." The Jew who has survived for centuries carries, at the same time, a "death taint"; concerning Israel, "it has always appeared safer to die in the Promised Land, or to be buried there, than to live there" (p. 7). (The biblical narratives as well, they say, portray a close link between death and the land.) While these observations may seem plausible from the perspective of Jews who do not permanently reside in Israel, it seems to me that the ideas about death taint are foreign to the awareness of Israelis. Both in my long years of working in group psychotherapy and in my in-depth interviews with local men and women,[1] I have never encountered the theme of death or the nonpermanence of our existence on the land expressed in quite this way: While fear of death has been frequently expressed, it does not seem to differ from the war-related experiences described in other Western countries.

In the course of the Weiners' absorption into Israeli society, their writing begins to reflect ideas that are more in the mainstream of the Israeli local experience. A transition in their thought patterns emerges in Chapter 2, "Retaining Identity Against the Fear of Death," which is, from my point of view, the best in the book. In a letter to a friend in the United States, they start with the familiar sentence: "Seeing things up close is very different from seeing them in a newspaper or on the TV screen" (p. 27). Fully functioning in Israel, with a husband in the reserves and children in the regular army, the Weiners become privy to more intimate details about the deeper layers of Israeli existence. Only a "native" during the Yom Kippur War was close enough to observe men in the tanks riding off to battle or during artillery attack—and to notice that the men were singing. It seems macabre, but the impulse to dance is strongest when death is closest, and this is what happened.

In the same vein, we find as the book unfolds a realization of the complexity of Israeli reality. The writers seem to be more humble than they were as newcomers; they stammer a bit, and they no longer build logical, conceptual systems. Their involvements in Selma, Alabama, with Martin Luther King, their anti–Vietnam War work and their experiences in the Israeli army during the Yom Kippur War, the Lebanon War, and the more recent Israeli-Palestinian conflict are presented side by side—they know it makes some sense together but admit that there is no philosophical framework easily available to make the synthesis. This lack of a clear way out of various political and moral dilemmas is forcefully portrayed in the chapter on resisting violence, where the case of Danny Timerman—the son of Jacobo Timerman, who refused on grounds of conscience to serve in Lebanon—is presented. Here, too, the authors give up trying to offer a solution and instead divert our attention from the public to the private sphere by sensitively focusing on a jail visit, a loving moment of father and son, while avoiding taking any stand on the issues of obeying orders, justice and morality. This honest picture, to me, is the best aspect of this original piece of work.

AMIA LIEBLICH
The Hebrew University

Note

1. See Amia Lieblich, *Tin Soldiers on Jerusalem Beach* (New York: 1978), and *idem, Transition to Adulthood During Military Service—The Israeli Case* (New York: 1989).

Gadi Wolfsfeld, *The Politics of Provocation: Participation and Protest in Israel.* Albany: State University of New York Press, 1988. 210 pp.

Since the early 1970s, public protest has become an increasingly significant phenomenon in Israeli politics. On several occasions it has indirectly led to the fall of prime ministers (e.g., Golda Meir's resignation in the wake of Motti Ashkenazi's solitary protest against the government's handling of the Yom Kippur War) or the reorganization of the cabinet (e.g., the massive demonstration following the Sabra and Shatilla massacre that eventually cost Ariel Sharon his job as defense minister). To be sure, extraparliamentary behavior has become an almost normal part of politics in the postwar period, with some three thousand scholarly articles and several hundred books that have been written in an attempt to illuminate its whys and wherefores. Wolfsfeld's study, which comes out of that academic tradition, seeks to apply several of the methodologies and theories found elsewhere toward understanding the phenomenon in Israel.

Although his style is by no means overly jargonistic, Wolfsfeld's discussion proceeds on a relatively sophisticated and theoretical level. The target audience, therefore, seems to be specialists in Israeli politics and/or domestic conflict. This is not to say that the general reader cannot learn from the work—quite the contrary—but that it is more geared toward academics and students, who will find a number of specific insights into Israeli extraparliamentarism in addition to a measured methodological approach to the area as a whole.

The two central questions addressed here are "who are Israel's protesters?" and "what are the factors underlying the widespread use of this non-formal political activity?" Wolfsfeld's research project entailed a large, comprehensive and in-depth survey poll that enabled him to home in on the specific typology of the Israeli protester. Both his approach and his conclusions are too complex to be easily summarized here; suffice it to say that "psychological variables provided a more direct and powerful explanation of political action than did the social determinants" (p. 71). In other words, social background is not nearly as important as how the potential protester generally thinks and acts in determining whether he or she will in fact take to the streets for any specific issue.

Beyond the specific personal characteristics of the individual, the factors behind the large collective use of protest still need to be explained. Here, too, Wolfsfeld devotes much attention to different types of groups as well as to examining the systemic problem underlying Israeli politics as a whole: a seriously "blocked political communication" between the public and Israel's elected representatives, which leads to feelings of political inefficacy on the part of an otherwise highly interested and motivated citizenry. In order to get their political messages across, argues Wolfsfeld (continuing the line pursued earlier by Eva Etzioni-Halevy and myself), there are few avenues left open to Israelis other than the extraparliamentary one.

Wolfsfeld offers several case studies from the mid-1980s to elucidate and expand upon his theoretical conclusions: Yamit, the Lebanon War, *haredi* activism, and so on. These are especially welcome in a book of rather "heavy" theoretical analysis, as they humanize in addition to fleshing out the previous academic discussion. One comes away with a feel for Israeli politics, and not just a dry dissection of its many convulsions.

Are there any deficiencies in this book? Yes, although in the final analysis they do not detract from the overall importance of Wolfsfeld's contribution to the general as well as the Israeli literature.

First, there is no description or survey of Israeli protest as a historically developmental phenomenon. Wolfsfeld makes no attempt to describe the salient protest events or political situation in the 1950s or 1960s and devotes only scant attention to the 1970s. As a result, *The Politics of Provocation* provides a clear snapshot of the 1980s but not a running film of Israeli protest over the years.

Second, his chapter on the success of Israeli protest is highly problematic. Based on the responses of protest leaders and participants, he comes to the conclusion that "the general level of success for Israeli protests is very high" (p. 155). However, these are not exactly the most unbiased of groups to ask. My own research findings, which are based on a comprehensive survey of actual protest campaigns (not attitudinal responses) and assessed by Israeli political scientists, are quite the opposite of Wolfsfeld's. Obviously, more work has to be done here on all sides.

Finally, while I believe that Wolfsfeld's general conclusion regarding the central factor of "blocked communication" is absolutely correct as far as it goes, it does not go far enough. There is no suggestion here that other objective factors may be at play—whether economic (e.g., inflation, unemployment, high taxation) or social (population increase, inequality, etc.)—that might also explain the ups and downs in the frequency of Israeli protests. This is an especially obvious lacuna given the myriad theories found in the general theoretical literature, with which Wolfsfeld is very conversant. The reason that they are missing in this study is that the brunt of his raw data is attitudinal and related to protest events between 1979 and 1984, which is not nearly a long enough period to statistically test empirical factors such as these.

Notwithstanding these limitations, *The Politics of Provocation* is a welcome and major contribution to our understanding of a previously neglected aspect of Israeli politics. It also constitutes a modest, but by no means inconsiderable, addition to the general conflict-studies literature. That it is far from the final, or even the completely correct, word on the subject regarding Israel is less a criticism of his efforts than an admission of how complex the subject really is.

Sam Lehman-Wilzig
Bar-Ilan University

Recently Completed
Doctoral Dissertations

Niza Abarbanelli   Bar-Ilan University, 1989
"Dualiyut bidmut haishah basifrut ha'ivrit hahadasha bameot ha-19 veha-20" ("Dualism in the Image of Women in Modern Hebrew Literature in the Nineteenth and Twentieth Centuries")

Margaret Abraham   Syracuse University, 1989
"Ethnic Identity and Marginality: A Study of the Jews of India"

Ibrahim Alsaeed   University of Houston, 1988
"The Origins and Meaning of America's Special Relationship with Israel"

Ora Ambar   Tel-Aviv University, 1990
"Derakhim lehava'at hamodaliyut be'ivrit shel yameinu: 'iyun tahbiri, semanti, peragmati" ("Modality in Contemporary Hebrew: Syntax, Semantics, Pragmatics")

Liora Broide Amir   Saint Louis University, 1989
"Marital Intimacy Within Jewish-non Jewish and Jewish-Jewish Couples"

Raziel Amitai   City University of New York, 1989
"From Theater of Children to Theater for Children: The Development of Children's Theater in Israel"

Norman Allan Amsel   Yeshiva University, 1988
"A High School Judaic Values Curriculum Using Media as Motivation"

Naim Araidy   Bar-Ilan University, 1990
"Poetikah vehagut beshirat U.Ẓ. Grinberg meahar Rehovot hanahar (5710–5735)" ("Poetics and Theory in Uri Zvi Greenberg's Poetry After *Rehovot hanahar* [1950–1975]")

Yigal Arica   Bar-Ilan University, 1990
"Nesiei beit hamishpat ha'elyon: kabalat hahlatot ve'iẓuv mediniyut. Diyukan hashvaati—shelosha minisiei beit hamishpat ha'elyon—Agranat, Zusman veLandoi" ("Chief Justices of the Supreme Court: Decision and Policy-making. Three Chief Justices of the Supreme Court—Agranat, Sussman and Landau—Comparative Portraits")

Yosef Avneri   Bar-Ilan University, 1990
"Harav A. Y. Kuk kerabah harashi shel ereẓ yisrael (5671–5685): haish ufo'alo" ("Rabbi A. Y. Kook as Chief Rabbi of Eretz Israel [1921–1935]: The Man and His Deeds")

Chaim Ilous Ayalon   Yeshiva University, 1987
"Citizen Participation in Israel's Project Renewal and the Impact of Diaspora Involvement"

Michael Nathan Barnett   University of Minnesota, 1989
"War Preparation and the Restructuring of State-Society Relations: Israel and Egypt in Comparative Perspective"

Outi Bat-el   University of California, Los Angeles, 1989
"Phonology and Word Structure in Modern Hebrew"

Janet Sera Belcove-Shalin   Cornell University, 1989
"A Quest for Wholeness: The Hasidim of Boro Park"

Moshe Ben-David   The Hebrew University, 1990
"Roman milḥemet ha'aẓmaut 1949–1958" ("War Novels of the War of Independence, 1949–1958")

Yitzchak Ben-David   The Hebrew University, 1990
"Haeizor hakibuẓi ve'ir hapituaḥ—dinamikah shel rihuk ḥevrati veshituf pe'ulah: sederot-sha'ar hanegev" ("The Kibbutz Region and the Development Town—Dynamics of Social Distance and Cooperation: Sderot-Shaar Hanegev")

Eliahu Ben-Moshe   The Hebrew University, 1990
"Tahalikhei hagirah penimit beyisrael: heibetim demografiyim, etniyim veḥevratiyim" ("Internal Migration Processes in Israel: Demographic, Ethnic and Social Aspects")

Michael Berkowitz   University of Wisconsin-Madison, 1989
" 'Mind, Muscle and Men': The Imagination of a Zionist National Culture for the Jews of Central and Western Europe, 1897–1914"

Judith Bernstein   Cornell University, 1989
"The Quality of Intergenerational Relationships Between the Elderly and Their Adult Children in Rural Communities in Israel"

Carolyn S. Blackwell   Purdue University, 1988
"German Jewish Identity and German Jewish Response to National Socialism, 1933–1939"

Yigal Bonnie   Bar-Ilan University, 1990
"Dimuyah shel yisrael ba'itonut hayomit hamiẓrit" ("The Image of Israel in the Egyptian Daily Press")

David Avram Brauer   University of California, Berkeley, 1988
"Histadrut in the Israeli Economy: Centralized Collective Bargaining and Wage Restraint"

Erella Brown   Cornell University, 1989
"Allegory and Irony in the Satirical Work of Hanoch Levin"

Zaha B. Bustami   Georgetown University, 1989
"American Foreign Policy and the Question of Palestine, 1856–1939"

Richard Chess   University of Florida, 1988
"Still a Small Voice: Toward an American-Jewish Poetry"

Steven Robert Chicural   University of Kentucky, 1989
" 'George Gershwin's Songbook': Influences of Jewish Music, Ragtime and Jazz"

Judith R. Cohen   University of Montreal, 1989
"Judeo-Spanish Songs in the Sephardic Communities of Montreal and Toronto: Survival, Function and Change"

Zafrira Dean   Tel-Aviv University, 1990
" *'Yahadut mufshetet' ve 'yehudim befo'al' behagut Mikha Yosef Berdechevski: mish-*

nat 'shinui ha'arkhin' shel M"YB" (" 'Abstract Judaism' and 'Living Jews' in Micha Josef Berdyczewski's Theory of Transvaluation")

Tamar El-Or   Bar-Ilan University, 1991
"Maskilot uvurot: oryanut nashim behasidut Gur—huliyah besharsheret paradoksim" ("Educated and Ignorant Women's Literacy Among the Hassidic Sect of 'Gur'—A Link in a Chain of Paradoxes")

Ido Embar   Bar-Ilan University, 1991
"Gar'in le'ozmah avirit: hakamato vehitpathuto shel heyil haavir hayisraeli bemilhemet ha'azmaut" ("The Origins of the Israeli Air Force: Its Establishment and Development During the War of Independence")

Hava Eshkoli   Bar-Ilan University, 1989
"Mifleget po'alei erez yisrael mul shoah vehazalah, 1939–1942") ("Mapai and the Holocaust, 1939–1942")

David Joseph Evearitt   Drew University, 1988
"Jewish-Christian Missions to Jews, 1820–1935"

Bruce Joel Evensen   University of Wisconsin-Madison, 1989
"Truman, Zionists and the Press: Framing a Palestine Policy at the Coming of the Cold War"

Michael Fischer   State University of New York at Albany, 1989
"Reform Through Community: Resocializing Offenders in the Kibbutz"

Daniel Fraenkel   The Hebrew University, 1990
"Hamediniyut haziyonit usheelat yehudei germaniyah, 1933–1938" ("Zionist Policy and the Question of the Jews of Germany, 1933–1938")

Elhanan Friedlander   Tel-Aviv University, 1990
"Rupin vehamediniyut haziyonit bevinyan haarez, 1919–1926" ("Arthur Ruppin and the Zionist Policy of Building the National Home in the Years 1919–1926")

Yosef Fund   Bar-Ilan University, 1991
"Agudat yisrael mul haziyonut: ideologiyah umediniyut" ("Agudat Israel Confronting Zionism and the State of Israel: Ideology and Policy")

Martin J. Garfinkle   Adelphi University, 1989
"The Relationship Between Reported Alcohol Abuse and Self-perceived Jewishness Among Adolescents"

Shmuel Gilboa   Tel-Aviv University, 1990
"Tenu'at ze'irei-ziyon berusiyah: mimahapeikhat februar 1917 ve'ad lefilug hatenu'ah be-1920" ("The *Young Zion* Movement in Russia: From the February 1917 Revolution Until Its Schism in 1920")

Dov Goldflam   University of Miami, 1989
"Survey of Current Practices and Attitudes of Jewish History Teachers in the High Jewish Day Schools in the United States"

Helene Golencer-Schroeter   University of Utah, 1989
"Albert Cohen, Albert Memmi and Elie Wiesel and the Dilemma of Jewish Identity in French Literature and Culture"

Kenneth Hart Green   Brandeis University, 1989
"The Return to Maimonides in the Jewish Thought of Leo Strauss"

Judith Greiner Bar-Ilan University, 1990
"Hitbolilut hayehudim basifrut zorfat bameah ha-20" ("L'Assimilation des juifs dans la litterature francaise du vingtième siècle")

Nancy Jean Haggard-Gilson University of California, Berkeley, 1988
"Wounded in the House of Friends: Black and Jewish Ethnic Identity in the 1930's and 1940's"

Nina Hanan City University of New York, 1989
"The Political Education of the Israeli Society"

Hassan Bakr Hassan University of Maryland College Park, 1988
"Conflict Management in the Middle East: The American Role in the Egyptian-Israeli Peace Treaty (1973–1979)"

Sara Hauptman Bar-Ilan University, 1990
"Darkhei ha'izuv hafigurativi shel hagibor hamoderni bizirot A. A. Kabak" ("Figurative Representations of the Modern Hero in A. A. Kabak's Novels")

Stephen Ronald Haynes Emory University, 1989
"Prospects for Post-Holocaust Theology: 'Israel' in the Theologies of Karl Barth, Jurgen Moltmann and Paul van Buren"

Tamar Herman Tel-Aviv University, 1990
"MiBrit Shalom leShalom akhshav: hapazifizm haperagmati shel mahaneh hashalom beyisrael beheibet hashvaati" ("From *Brit Shalom* to *Peace Now:* The Pragmatic Pacifism of the Israeli Peace Movement in Comparative Perspective")

Jack Jacob Hirschberg McGill University, 1989
"Secular and Parochial Education of Ashkenazi and Sephardi Jewish Children in Montreal: A Study in Ethnicity"

Severin Adam Hochberg New York University, 1989
"The Jewish Community and the Aliens Question in Great Britain, 1881–1917"

Jennifer Leigh Holt-Bodner University of Houston, 1989
"Music Education in Elementary (K–6) Jewish Day Schools in the United States: Survey, Analysis, and Implications"

Avner Holzman Tel-Aviv University, 1990
"Mimaskil torani lemahapekhan sifruti; hamesh 'esrei hashanim harishonot (5647–5662) bizirato shel Mikha Yosef Berdechevski" ("Anatomy of a Literary Revolution: The First Fifteen Years [1887–1902] in the Work of M. J. Berdyczewski")

Talia Horowitz Bar-Ilan University, 1991
"Hakinah beshirat Uri Zvi Grinberg" ("The Lamentations in Uri Zvi Greenberg's Poetry")

Gregg David Ivers Emory University, 1989
"Should God Bless America? American Jewish Groups in Supreme Court Religion Cases"

Ava Fran Kahn University of California, Santa Barbara, 1989
"Pragmatists in the Promised Land: American Immigrant Voluntary Associations in Israel, 1948–1978"

Alvan Howard Kaunfer Jewish Theological Seminary of America, 1989
"Teaching Midrash in the Conservative Day School: A Rationale and Curriculum Proposal"

Ilana Kofman   University of California, Los Angeles, 1989
"The Bases of Electoral Support for the Communist Party of Israel Among the Arabs in Israel, 1948-1984"

Felicja Koray   Tel-Aviv University, 1990
"Maḥaneh skazhisko-kamyenna: maḥanot 'avodah bemishtar hanaẓiyonal-soẓiyalisti bitkufat milḥemet ha'olam hasheniyah" ("Skarzysko-Kamienna Slave Labor Camp: Labor Camps Under the National Socialist Regime During the Second World War")

Lori Ellen Krafte-Jacobs   Claremont Graduate School, 1989
"Feminism and Modern Jewish Theological Method"

Mitchell Lerner   York University, 1989
"Themes in the Life World of Children of Survivors of the Holocaust"

Jeffrey Howard Lesser   New York University, 1989
"Pawns of the Powerful: Jewish Immigration to Brazil, 1904–1945"

Abraham Levi   Fordham University, 1988
"Attitudes and Stereotypes of Eastern and Western Students in Integrated and Nonintegrated Classes in High Schools in Israel"

Gabriel Levy   Tel-Aviv University, 1990
"Hakehilah hayehudit bemaknes 'erev haprotektorat" ("The Jewish Community of Meknes on the Eve of the Protectorate")

B. Ruth Linden   Brandeis University, 1989
"Making Stories, Making Selves: The Holocaust, Identity and Memory"

Philip J. Lyons   University of Bristol, 1988
"Literary and Theological Responses to the Holocaust"

Chris McNickle   University of Chicago, 1989
"To Be Mayor of New York: The Transfer of Political Power from the Irish to the Jews and the Decline of the Political Machine in New York City, 1881–1977"

Aviva Mahalo   Bar-Ilan University, 1989
"Bein shenei nofim: temurot teimatiyot veẓuraniyot basiporet dor hama'avar bein nofei hagolah lenofei ereẓ yisrael bein shetei milḥamot 'olam" ("Between Two Horizons: Thematic and Structural Changes in the Fiction of a Generation in Transition Between the Diaspora and Eretz Israel Between Two World Wars")

Yaakov Markovici   Tel-Aviv University, 1990
"Hagaḥal: po'alo uterumato bemilḥemet ha'aẓmaut" ("Gahal's Activities and Contribution During the War of Independence")

Pnina Meislish   Bar-Ilan University, 1989
"Harav Yiẓḥak Nisenbaum veYizḥak Leibush Pereẓ: shenei maafyanim merkaziyim bapubliẓistikah hasifrutit bemizraḥ eiropah bereishit hameah ha'esrim" ("Rabbi Yitzhak Nissenbaum and Yitzhak Leibush Peretz: Two Central Figures in the Development of Literary Journalism in Eastern Europe at the Beginning of the Twentieth Century")

Janet Catherine Menard   University of Western Ontario, 1989
"Regeneration and Politics: Buber's Idea of Nationhood"

Rachel Meshorer   Bar-Ilan University, 1990
"Motivim 'amamiyim, yehudiyim veuniversaliyim biẓirato shel Y. L. Pereẓ 'mipi ha'am' shenikhtevu beyidish uve'ivrit 'al yedei hameḥaber" ("Popular, Jewish and Universal Folk Motifs in the Yiddish and Hebrew *Mipi ha'am* Tales by Y. L. Peretz")

Bennett F. Miller   Princeton Theological Seminary, 1988
"Reform Jewish Identity: Developing a Program of Ministry to Guide the New Member of a Reform Synagogue to Mature Jewish Living"

Subithra Moodley Moore   University of Washington, 1989
"The Politics of Beleaguered Ethnic States: 'Herrenvolk' Democracy in Israel and South Africa"

Bonnie Jean Morris   State University of New York at Binghamton, 1990
"Women of Valor: Female Religious Activism and Identity in the Lubavitcher Community of Brooklyn, 1955–1987"

Shai Shmu'el Nechushtai   University of California, Los Angeles, 1988
"Between Hebraism, the Melting Pot and Ethnicity: The American-Hebrew-Language Press, 1871–1914"

Naomi Barbara Nim   University of San Francisco, 1988
"Discourse of an Emerging Culture, Inter-group Community Among Young Adult Friends: Israeli Jews and Palestinian Israeli Arabs"

Dorit Orgad   Bar-Ilan University, 1988
"Zikato shel Franz Rozenzveig lerabi Yehudah Halevi" ("Franz Rosenzweig in Relation to Rabbi Yehudah Halevi")

Marvin Ray Paseur   University of Mississippi, 1988
"A History of Religious, Political and Social Influences on the Development of the Israeli School System, 1948–1987"

Yael Peled-Margolin   The Hebrew University, 1990
"Tenu'at hahitnagdut hayehudit bekrakov bitkufat hakibush hanazi 'al rek'a hahayim bekihilah uvageto" ("The Jewish Resistance Movement in Cracow During the German Occupation Against the Background of Jewish Community Life in the Ghetto")

Rakhmiel Peltz   Columbia University, 1988
"Speaking Yiddish in South Philadelphia: Changes in Language and Identity"

Max Andrew Pensky   Boston College, 1989
"The Politics of Melancholia: Studies in the Work of Walter Benjamin"

Hanina Porat   The Hebrew University, 1990
"Hamediniyut vehape'ilut haziyonit lerekhishat karka'ot vehityashvut badarom uvanegev, 1929–1946" ("Zionist Policy on Land Settlement in the Negev, 1929–1946")

Jonathan Rabinowitz   Yeshiva University, 1988
"Correlates of Social Participation in American Jewish Communities"

William Robert Reyer   Bowling Green State University, 1988
"Biblical Figures in Selected Short Fiction of Isaac Bashevis Singer"

Faith Rogow   State University of New York at Binghamton, 1989
" 'Gone to Another Meeting': A History of the National Council of Jewish Women"

Avihu Ronen   Tel-Aviv University, 1990
"Yehudei zaglembiye bitkufat hashoah, 1939–1943" ("The Jews of Zaglembie During the Holocaust, 1939–1943")

Mira Rosenthal   Fordham University, 1989
"Assimilation of Israeli Immigrants in the United States: Social Work Policy Implications"

Shaul Sapir   The Hebrew University, 1990
"Gishatah veofi terumatah shel hakehilah hayehudit bebritaniyah lehitpathut hay-
ishuv hayehudi beerez yisrael bameah ha-19" ("The Attitude of the Jewish Community in Britain and the Characteristics of Its Contribution to the Yishuv in Eretz Israel
in the 19th Century")

Lea Sarig   Bar-Ilan University, 1988
"Ba'ayot lashon betirgum prozah ma'aravit mi'aravit le'ivrit" ("Linguistic Problems
of Modern Arabic-Hebrew Prose Translation")

Harry Dean Schoenburg   University of California, Los Angeles, 1989
"The Practical Knowledge of Jewish Day School Teachers"

Bella Schonfeld   Columbia University Teachers College, 1989
"Orthodox Jewish Women Who Return to School for Graduate Degrees During Their
Middle Life Years"

Lubel Shabtai   Bar-Ilan University, 1988
"Tefisat hitnahagut tokpanit umarkiveihah bekerev yozei 'eidot mizrah ve'eidot
ma'arav: mehkar hashvaati beyisrael" ("The Perception of Aggression and Its Components Among Oriental and European Jews in Israel: A Comparative Study")

Natan Shahar   The Hebrew University, 1990
"Hashir haerez-yisraeli, 1920–1950: heibetim soziomuzikaliyim umuzikaliyim"
("The Eretz-Israeli Song, 1920–1950: Sociomusical and Musical Aspects")

Zvi Shapiro   New York University, 1988
"From Generation to Generation: Does Jewish Schooling Affect Jewish
Identification?"

Peter W. Shaw   The Hebrew University, 1990
"Hakehilah hayehudit beodesa, 1885–1900: historiyah mosadit" ("The Odessa Jewish Community, 1855–1900: An Institutional History")

Igal Shwartz   The Hebrew University, 1990
"Omanut hasipur shel Aharon Reuveni" ("The Narrative Art of Aaron Reuveni")

Elbert Siegel   Columbia University, 1988
"The Use of Mutual Aid by Russian-Jewish Immigrants in Two Connecticut Communities: An Analysis of an Informal Helping System"

Sohrab C. Sobhani   Georgetown University, 1989
"The Pragmatic Entente: Israel-Iranian Relations, 1948–1988"

Diana Lynn Staples   East Texas State University, 1988
"Post-resettlement Reflections on Life in the United States: A Naturalistic Study of
Soviet Jewish Refugees"

Deborah Steinhardt   University of California, Berkeley, 1989
"The Modernist Enterprise of Uri Nissan Gnessin: Gnessin's Narrative Technique in
the Context of Hebrew Fiction of the Late-Nineteenth and Early Twentieth Centuries"

Frank Stern   Tel-Aviv University, 1990
" 'Limhok et hatelai hazahov': philoshemiyut veantishemiyut begermaniyah
hama'aravit, 1945–1952" ("The Whitewashing of the Yellow Badge: Philosemitism
and Antisemitism in West Germany, 1945–1952")

Raymond Stern   Yeshiva University, 1988
"Israelis Teaching in American Jewish Schools: Job-Related Variables"

Marshall Field Stevenson, Jr. University of Michigan, 1988
"Points of Dispute, Acts of Resolve: Black-Jewish Relations in Detroit, 1937–1962"

Renee Taft George Washington University, 1989
"Attitudes of the Oriental Jewish Elite in Israel Toward the Arab-Israeli Conflict"

Sarah Taieb-Carlen York University, 1989
"Assessment of a Small Group Ethnic Identity: The Jews in North Africa and the North African Jews in Toronto"

Johannes Gerrit Cornelis van Aggelen McGill University, 1989
"Conflicting Claims to Sovereignty over the West-Bank: An In-Depth Analysis of the Historical Roots and Feasible Options in the Framework of a Future Settlement of the Dispute"

Miriam Weinberg Bar-Ilan University, 1988
"Tashtiyot min hamasoret biẓirot Devorah Baron (kegormim shel tokhen, 'iẓuv, 'alilah, signon, afyon vehashkafat ha'olam") ("Traditional Substrata as Factors in Designing of Plot, Characterization, Language and Description in Devora Baron's Novels")

Bella K. Weisfogel University of Massachusetts, 1988
"The Use of Structured Jewish Mourning Rituals in Aiding the Bereaved"

Benjamin Zvi Weiss Hofstra University, 1988
"Achievement, Motivation and Religiosity in Jewish and Catholic College Students"

Rachel Weissbrod Tel-Aviv University, 1990
"Megamot betirgum siporet meanglit le'ivrit, 1958–1980" ("Trends in the Translation of Prose Fiction from English to Hebrew, 1958–1980")

Hanna Yablonka-Torok The Hebrew University, 1990
"Kelitatah uva'ayot hishtalvutah shel sheerit hapeleitah baḥevrah hayisraelit hamithavah (29 lenovember 1947 'ad shalhei 1949)" ("The Absorption of Holocaust Survivors in the Emerging State of Israel and the Problems of Their Integration in Israeli Society")

Mordechai Yerushalmi University of Illinois at Chicago, 1989
"The War over Israel: Palestinian Terrorism and Israeli Counterterrorism"

Ruth Zielenziger Jewish Theological Seminary of America, 1989
"A History of the Bible Program of the Melton Research Center with Special References to the Curricular Principles on Which It Is Based"

Dorit Zilberman Bar-Ilan University, 1991
"Hayehudi hehaẓui biẓiroteihem shel A. B. Yehoshua uPhilip Roth" ("The Divided Jewish Self in the Works of A. B. Yehoshua and Philip Roth")

Zvi M. Zohar The Hebrew University, 1990
"Pesikat halakha be'idan shel temurah" ("Halakhic Decision-making in an Era of Change")

STUDIES IN
CONTEMPORARY JEWRY

IX

Edited by Ezra Mendelsohn

Eliezer Don-Yehiya, Memory and Political Culture: Israeli Society and The Holocaust

Doron Nederland, Back into the Lion's Jaws: Jewish Return Migration to Nazi Germany, 1933–1938

Review Essays

John D. Klier on new research on Soviet Jewry

Stephen Sharot on Jewish religion and identity

. . . Plus reviews and a listing of recent doctoral dissertations

Note on Editorial Policy

Studies in Contemporary Jewry is pleased to accept manuscripts for possible publication. Authors of essays on subjects generally within the contemporary Jewish sphere (from the turn of the century to the present) should send three copies to:

The Editor, Studies in Contemporary Jewry
Institute of Contemporary Jewry
The Hebrew University
Mt. Scopus, Jerusalem, Israel

Essays must not exceed thirty-five pages in length and must be double-spaced throughout (including intended quotations and footnotes). Reviews must not exceed one thousand words per book.